THIRD TO NONE

The Saga Of Savannah Jewry 1733-1983

By Rabbi Saul Jacob Rubin

From the Minutes of the Annual Meeting
January 12, 1880

"Mr. Epstein moved that the thanks of the
Congregation be and are hereby tendered to
the retiring Board for the able manner in
which they have accomplished their arduous
duties in bringing the Congregation to its
present condition—

THIRD TO NONE IN THE UNITED STATES"

CONTENTS

LIST OF ILLUSTRATIONS
(after page 176)

1733 Torah

Leaf from Sheftall "Diary"

Earliest Hebrew burial grounds on south commons, granted by General Oglethorpe in 1734

View of Levi Sheftall Burial Grounds

Old Jewish Community Cemetery given by Mordecai Sheftall used from 1770 to 1860

Historic marker at entrance to old Jewish Community Cemetery erected under authority of State of Georgia

October 28, 1761, *ketubah* (marriage contract) of Mordecai Sheftall and Francis Hart. It is believed to be the second oldest in America.

1790 Charter of Congregation "Mickva" Israel

Page of 1790 *Minute Book*

1838 edifice of K.K.M.I. from enlargement of 1871 lithograph of Savannah

1854 Judah Touro memorial

1868 letter from Robert E. Lee to Abram Minis

R. D. C. Lewin's 1868 sermon entitled "Orthodoxy vs. Reform"

Page from 1869 hymn book

1877 letter from Harry Haym, summarizing the history of B'nai B'rith Jacob Congregation

1872 proposal to combine K.K.M.I. and K.K. B'nai B'rith Jacob

Temple "Mickva" Israel in 1878.

Consecration service, April 11, 1878

Octavus Cohen window, installed in Temple "Mickva" Israel in 1878

Confirmation class, 1885

Sunday school medals, c. 1880

1893 confirmation certificate

Rabbis of Mickve Israel since 1873
   Abraham Harris (1873-1877)
   Isaac P. Mendes (1877-1904)
   George Joseph Solomon (1903-1945)
   Louis Youngerman (1944-1948)
   Solomon E. Starrels (1948-1965, emeritus 1965-)
   Joseph M. Buchler (1965-67)
   Richard A. Zionts (1969-72)
   Saul J. Rubin (1972-)

Exterior view of present Temple Mickve Israel

Interior view of present Temple Mickve Israel

Bicentennial Letter to President Ford

APPRECIATION IS HEREBY EXPRESSED TO THOSE WHO VALUED THIS ENDEAVOR AND SUSTAINED IT WITH GENEROUS CONTRIBUTIONS

BENEFACTOR

DR. AND MRS. LARRY ACKERMAN
IN HONOR OF THEIR SON, DAVID JOEL ACKERMAN'S BAR MITZVAH

PATRONS

IN MEMORY OF SAM G. ADLER
BY ELINOR ADLER DILLARD

IN MEMORY OF HENRY AND TILLIE ALEXANDER
BY RUTH ALEXANDER BECK

MR. AND MRS. B. B. BACKSTON

IN HONOR OF MR. AND MRS. D. A. BYCK, JR.
FOR THEIR 55TH ANNIVERSARY

MR. AND MRS. DAVID A. BYCK, III

JUDGE AND MRS. H. SOL CLARK

MR. AND MRS. RONALD H. COHEN
RODNEY, REBECCA, MATT

IN MEMORY OF DR. SOLOMON H. COHEN
BY MRS. SOLOMON H. COHEN

MR. AND MRS. JACK COLEMAN

IN MEMERY OF MY HUSBAND, WARNER DANZIGER
BY HERTA DANZIGER

MR. AND MRS. JULIUS EDEL

DR. AND MRS. RONALD FAGIN

JANE AND EDWIN FEILER, JR.
ANDREW, BRUCE AND CARI FEILER

DR. AND MRS L. M. FREEDMAN

viii

In Honor of Barny and Eulalia Gilmore
by Jean and Alex Gilmore

Dr. and Mrs. Samuel Goodrich

Doctors Doris and Martin Greenberg

In Memory of Jean and Walter Guthman
by Jane and Buddy Kahn

In Honor of Michelle Lise and Rachelle Klise Haysman
by Melvin L. and Roberta Haysman

In Memory of Mina W. and Hugo H. Hecht
by Rabbi and Mrs. Saul J. Rubin

Mr. and Mrs. Rupert S. Heller

Dr. and Mrs. Frank Hoffman

Mr. and Mrs. Alvin F. Kahan

Dr. and Mrs. Walter Kanter

Dr. and Mrs. Fred Kazlow

Mr. and Mrs. Martin S. Leffler

Mr. and Mrs. B. H. Levy, Sr.

In Memory of Rachel Brown Longwater
by Abraham B. Longwater

Mr. and Mrs. William Longwater

In Honor of Erika and Aaron March
by Dr. and Mrs. Lewis E. March

In Memory of Albert R. Marks, Jr.
by his Family

David and Polly Meddin

In Memory of Betty H. Michels
by Florine and Lester Michels

Mrs. Matilda Morgenstern

In Memory of Dudley G. Parsons
by Rabbi and Mrs. Saul J. Rubin

In Memory of Pearl S. and Hyman Rubin
by Rabbi and Mrs. Saul J. Rubin

In Honor of Rabbi Saul J. Rubin
by Rabbi and Mrs Edward L. Cohn

Henry H. Schaul

FOREWORD

Savannah Jewry's history, Georgia Jewish history, is different. The Savannah Jewish community was the only one in all North America in the eighteenth century that sprang full blown from the brow of Jupiter. In 1733 a band of Jewish argonauts—financed by London's Sephardic notables—debarked on the site of Georgia's first settlement. They landed but a few months after the coming of Oglethorpe himself. The Jewish adventurers, setting out to build a new life for themselves, carried with them all the cult and ritual objects needed to establish and maintain a religious community. They were determined to remain Jews. English Jewry helped them, outfitted them, never dreaming that two hundred years later American Jewry would pour millions of dollars into Europe, Asia, and Africa to succor fellow Jews in lands of suffering and oppression.

The Christian trustees who dispatched the first boatload of frontiersmen to Georgia were idealists. The new yeomen were to be taught the sanctity of labor; slavery was ruled out, but when these social goals could not be reached the colony had to start all over again. A new economic base was imperative. An Italian Jew—a convert to Christianity—was brought in to help the settlers build a viable industry, the manufacture of silk. It was a gallant but unsuccessful attempt. All the heartaches of survival in the pine barrens of Georgia were experienced by the early Jewish settlers. They farmed their plots, branded their cattle, opened shops, and when they could, held services. The leaders never forgot that they were Jews. The congregation struggled, not always successfully, to maintain some vestige of worship. It called itself Mickve Israel, the Hope of Israel. It did survive and today flourishes proudly after 250 years.

The early Jewish settlers who persevered despite initial hardships were proud of their achievements; individualistic, they were lovers of liberty and freedom. It is not surprising therefore that a scion of one of the first families to set foot on Georgia soil, a Sheftall, became the leader of the Revolt of the 1770's at a time when many of the elite refused to raise their hands against king and crown. Mordecai Sheftall was the chairman of the Parochial Committee, and when after eight years the war was over and the land was freed he wrote exultantly to his young son: "We have the world to begin againe."

Savannah Jewry was always an integral part of the city and the state. The Masons helped dedicate their first synagogue building; Christians lent them an organ. It was a descendant of one of the eighteenth-century settlers who helped finance the building of the first ship, the *Savannah*,

xi

which crossed the Atlantic with the help of steam. Savannah Jewry fought in the Civil War, survived, and then set out manfully to help rebuild the South. Their brethren in the North helped them generously. Sephardic Mickve Israel gradually turned to the left. Ashkenazic settlers drifted into the city throughout the nineteenth century. The religious leaders and their followers slowly turned away from Orthodoxy initiating reforms in liturgy and observance. This they did with dignity and responsibility. They had little choice; the accultural impact of the environment was overwhelming.

American Jewry is proud of Savannah and its century-old traditions. For many decades Mickve Israel was Georgia Jewry. We are all grateful to Rabbi Saul Rubin for having written this history of a congregation and a community that was established only a year or two after the first synagogue in all North America was dedicated in New York City. It is certainly time that the story of this pioneering congregation be presented to the world. We can have no complete history of American Jewry till the romance of this eighteenth-century community is recounted. Thank you Rabbi Rubin; future generations will rise up and call you blessed.

Jacob R. Marcus

American Jewish Archives

PREFACE

I begin this volume with the traditional *Shechechiyanu* prayer:

"PRAISED ART THOU, O LORD OUR GOD, SOVEREIGN
OF CREATION, WHO HAS SUSTAINED, QUICKENED, AND
PRESERVED US THAT WE MIGHT REACH THIS MOMENT
OF FULFILLMENT IN LIFE."

As the task of writing the history of a unique Georgia Jewish community
is undertaken, I sense the presence of many generations of Savannahians
levitating at my shoulders. America numbers six Hebrew congregations established in the Colonial period. Proper histories have been published for
all, save Mickve Israel of Savannah. It is the purpose of this book to end
that lacuna. A tale, begging to be told for a half century, is about to unfold.
A *Shechechiyanu* is indeed meet.

How to write a virgin history! Should the scholar's appetite for minutiae
be indulged? Or rather should the need for a *popular* text be the major
consideration? Balance in all things is a good motto to follow, and the
conscious decision was made to pursue that course. A perceptive eye will
detect occasional deviations, reflecting the author's taste and interest. For
Savannahians, primarily, I have included information that will have
parochial appeal. Students of architectural history will find data included
that standard Jewish histories tend to underplay. Less attention has been
given to Jewish residential patterns and commercial activities than in the
newer community histories, although the latter has not been ignored. This
author perceived the real need for a documentation of the *religious* and
cultural developments of this 250 year old Jewish settlement, with other
facets to be treated in future writings.

There are two limitations in the manuscript that require clarification.
The requirements of rabbinic service to a congregation restricted visits to
academic centers and archives, where Savannah Jewish treasures repose.
The quantity of material here is so overwhelming, and, as yet, unknown to
scholars, that to exhaust it seemed sufficient for the undertaking. The
records that left Savannah either exist in duplicate form here, or supple-
ment what is already known about Savannah Jewish personages. Also where
others have examined the documents profoundly, as in the Colonial period,
summaries are presented and the sources cited for those who seek greater
knowledge. Among those who have written perceptively and comprehensively on the earliest stage of Savannah Jewish development are Dr.
Jacob Rader Marcus and Dr. Malcolm Stern, honored teachers and friends.

Dr. Stern was consulted in an editorial capacity and chapters one through four reflect many of his suggestions. This book is enriched by his essay in chapter two which provides new information about the Colonial period.

Ample footnotes accompany each chapter. This is a defensive technique to ward off the assaults of those who heard it told differently by their forebearers. In Savannah, the power of oral history is ever with us. The accuracy of said history does not necessarily hold when the written sources are examined. Where truth ultimately rests, I cannot say. *Third to None* is rooted in first hand documents, as they are available. Remembrances have been tested against the primary records, and have been found wanting, even in broad detail. Accounting skillful oral historians as associates and friends, I had hoped for a different result.

Credit assignments run the risk of overlooking some who may merit public recognition. With the hope that corrections may be wrought in a future volume, I list the following for special thanks:

Congregation Mickve Israel, its Board of Adjunta, and its 250th Anniversary Committee. This board offered resources and encouragement, knowing that history writing isn't always compatible with rabbinic responsibilities.

Insufficient are the words chosen to praise my research assistant, Mrs. Karen Clark. Expertly trained in historical method at Armstrong State College, Karen has examined every source with an eye to error. Praise is comely for her! Patience and skill marked her labors. Assisting her in the task of indexing were Mrs. Jane Owens, Stephanie Lynn Rubin (my daughter), Gordon Schuchardt and Herbert Victor.

Mrs. Diane Neeb has been more than diligent in typing the text. The highest professionalism marked her endeavors. We are grateful to the firm of Bouhan Williams & Levy for permitting the use of advanced computers in preparing the manuscript.

To Anthony Dees, director of the Georgia Historical Society, and his accommodating staff go special accolades for responding helpfully to each request. Likewise, to Dr. Abraham Peck of the American Jewish Archives and his assistants I express appreciation for aid rendered promptly.

This work has been enhanced by the talents of three fine artists. Alex Gilmore's photographs transform ordinary documents, plaques, and scenes into gripping visual images. How fitting that he should serve as Temple president during the Semiquincentenary! Jane Abeshouse Feiler was the artistic director in charge of designing the dust jacket and cover seal. Following her conception, Deborah Ansell crafted the handsome art work you see on the binding. In all ways, Jane and husband Edwin furthered this and all progressive undertakings in the synagogue during my tenure.

Proofreaders have a tedious assignment. Mine have been enthusiastic and faithful. I salute Judge H. Sol Clark, Edwin J. Feiler, Jr., Dr. Martin Greenberg, Mrs. Jane G. Kahn, Mrs. Marsha Lebos, Philip Solomons, Jr. and cousin David Sawilowsky. Good fortune attended me the day when Mrs. Alice Crain agreed to assume some editorial responsibilities. Technical knowledge and linguistic precision are her strengths.

Indulgence is asked of the reader as homage is rendered to the memory of those whose being and values gave seed to mine. They are copartners in this project. May the blessed memory of my parents, Hyman and Pearl S. Rubin, be honored by this volume. I mention also the formative influence of my beloved grandmother, Rosa Sawilowsky, a proud and pious Jewess.

Finally, this book I dedicate to my beloved wife, Elsie. Twenty-three years ago, a covenant united us in holy wedlock. From that day to this, her *joie de vivre* has been the beam with which I balance; her loyalty, my fortress against the storm. My son and daughter, Lance Hays and Stephanie Lynn, I especially include in this dedication, because the ultimate goal of my creative endeavor is to make them proud of their dad.

We live in time; moments are precious. Research and writing remove one from responsibilities that one is obliged *not* to shirk. My family has understood my dedication to this project and has given me the opportunity to shirk without feeling guilty. History will not tolerate slouchers. It is a harsh and unrelenting taskmaster. Much time—much life—has been invested in this tome. A better use of time and life I know not, particularly if it brings into focus two and a half centuries of Jewish progress in and contribution to America's thirteenth colony.

Saul Jacob Rubin

Savannah, Georgia
September 1, 1982

CHAPTER ONE

IN THE BEGINNING

ↀↀↀↀↀↀↀↀↀↀↀↀↀↀↀↀↀↀↀↀↀↀↀↀↀↀↀ

J ews were residing in New Amsterdam (New York) before Jews were permitted to settle in London. In 1654, twenty-four entered the Hudson River basin and began a permanent community. From 1290 to 1655 Jews were barred by royal edict from residency in England.[1] Oliver Cromwell removed this prohibition.[2]

Three quarters of a century later, the Georgia colony was founded when the *Ann* sailed from Gravesend with James Edwards Oglethorpe and approximately 120 settlers on board.[3] Oglethorpe had been elected to Parliament in 1722 and had served as chairman of the Committee to Investigate the Status of English Prisons. A national scandal of mistreatment was revealed. Suddenly, prisoners were released with no place to go. Oglethorpe was among those who recommended sending them to the New World. Helping the downtrodden in England was only one motive for the creation of the Georgia settlement. B. H. Levy, Savannah attorney and historian, has summarized the other motives at play:

"Imperialistic" . . . rivalry grew between France, Spain and England for control of the Gulf of Mexico. Spain and France had strong settlements in the region. Entry to the Gulf or to the Mississippi Valley from the Atlantic seaboard led through lands south of the Savannah River. A settlement on that river would be the first step toward extending British influence southward and westward.

"Mercantile" . . . silk and wine, major English imports, might be cultivated in Georgia soil.

"Evangelical" . . . Dr. Bray's London Society for the Propagation of the Gospel in Foreign Parts had as its purpose converting Indians and slaves to the Anglican faith. Georgia was ripe for proselytizing efforts.[4]

In 1730 a score of prominent men requested a Royal Charter for Georgia, granted two years later to twenty-one individuals who constituted the Trustees for colonization. The Trustees were to be allowed sovereignty for twenty-one years; thereafter, title would revert to the Crown.

A fund-raising campaign was initiated. The response from England's middle class and wealthy elements was generous. London's Jewish community volunteered to participate in the subscriptions. Three fund-raisers

[1]

were appointed from the wealthy Sephardic congregation located in Bevis Marks: Moses da Costa, Joseph Rodrigues Sequeira, and Jacob Israel Suasso.[5] Francis Salvador (uncle of South Carolina's Jewish hero of the same name) eventually replaced Sequeira.

The subscriptions raised by the Jewish community were used to underwrite the passage of the first Jews to sail for Georgia.

In 1730 the Jewish population of London was estimated at six thousand, many of whom were in poor circumstance.[6] Both Sephardic and Askenazic Jews were accounted among the indigent. A decade earlier almost one hundred refugee couples who had escaped from Portugal (where the forces of the Inquisition still unleashed terror) were remarried as Jews in London's Sephardic synagogue. The penniless state of many of them threatened the security of the upwardly mobile London Jewish community. The opening of the Georgia colony for the "industrious" poor as well as the "industrious" skillful offered a safety valve. A ship, the *William and Sarah*, was hired to sail for Georgia under the direction of Captain Hanson.[7] It left London in January of 1733 with forty-two Hebrews aboard. The journey was arduous. Gales blew; the ship was wrecked off the coast of North Carolina; but finally on July 11, 1733, the vessel arrived in the port of Savannah to begin the largest Jewish settlement in the New World. The Trustees were furious at the turn of events. They wrote Oglethorpe urging him to

> use your best endeavor that the said Jews may be allowed no kind of settlement with any of the grantees, the Trustees being apprehensive, they will be of prejudice to the trade and welfare of the Colony.[8]

The instrument bearing the stern dictum was dated October 18, 1733, but no instructions were received by July 11th (when the Jews arrived), so Oglethorpe was free to act on his own. He wanted assurance that he was on solid ground. So he consulted legal authorities in Charleston. Since the Georgia Charter excluded only "papists" and "slaves", the lawyers affirmed the propriety of the Jewish settlement in Savannah.[9] Later, Captain Hanson, on his return to England, sought to exonerate himself in the eyes of the Trustees by claiming that he had been cheated

> by these Hebrews about three or four hundred pounds.[10]

In the original company of Georgia colonists that arrived five months earlier was a physician, William Cox. A sudden epidemic in the spring robbed the community of its sole healer. About the time that the ship bearing Jews reached the Savannah River, a new plague, probably yellow fever, threatened. Aboard the *William and Sarah* was Dr. Samuel Nunes Ribeiro, a Jewish physician who had served in Lisbon as chief physician to the Grand Inquisitor.[11] Infectious diseases were his specialty. Oglethorpe was in need of his expertise. Oglethorpe later informed the Trustees that the epidemic had killed twenty (more than ten percent), but a ship of forty Jews arriving with a physician, ... entirely put a stop to it, so that no one died afterwards.[12]

Dr. Nunes may be considered Georgia's first public hero, saving the colony from catastrophe.

Who were these forty-two ... these progenitors of Georgia Jewry?

Their names proceed to us from two primary sources. Benjamin Sheftall, one of the company, kept a chronicle in which entries were made as the occasion required. The Sheftall "diary" covers the opening period (from 1733) to 1765, the year of his demise. His son, Levi, carried on the journal until the latter's death in 1809. The manuscript that Benjamin wrote was probably *Juelisch-Deutsch* (though Levi described the language as Hebrew). Levi filled one notebook with an English translation, then rewrote it with minor changes. His manuscripts were discovered by David A. Byck, Jr. in the Keith Reid Collection at the University of Georgia. No Jewish congregation in America has such a rich source to document its "birth" moment and early development.

The second primary source is the manuscript list of settlers written by the First Earl of Egmont, President of the Georgia Company and head of the Trustees. It is divided into two lists: persons who went to Georgia at the Trustees' charge and persons who went on their own account. The Jewish colonists are enumerated on the second list.

Dr. Malcolm Stern in "New Lights on the Savannah Settlement" (hereafter called "New Lights") has worked the two sources together and proposed that the following were the pioneers who came to the Georgia wilderness. For the purposes of comparison, his list has been divided into categories: German or Portuguese; adult male or adult female or child; permanent or temporary resident; land holder or not.[13]

GERMAN JEWS NUMBERING 8 INCLUDE:

Name	Male	Female	Child	Residency	Given Lots
Benjamin Sheftall	X			Permanent	X
Perla Sheftall, his wife		X		Permanent	
Jacob Yowel (Joel?)	X			Permanent	X
Abraham Minis	X			Permanent	X
Abigail Minis		X		Permanent	
Leah Minis (daughter)			X	Permanent	
Esther Minis (daughter)			X	Permanent	
Simon Minis (Abraham's brother)	X			Permanent	X

SEPHARDIC JEWS NUMBERING 34 INCLUDE:

Name	Male	Female	Child	Residency	Given Lots
Dr. Samuel Nunes Ribeiro	X			Temporary	X
Zipporah Nunes (his mother)		X		Temporary	
Moses Nunes (son)	X			Permanent	X

SEPHARDIC JEWS NUMBERING 34 INCLUDE:

Name	Male	Female	Child	Residency	Given Lots
Daniel Nunes (son)	X			Permanent	X
Sipra (Zipporah) Nunes (daughter)			X	Temporary	
Abraham De Lyon			X	Temporary	X
Shem Noah (servant)	X			Temporary	
Isaac Nunes Henriques	X			Temporary	X
Abigail Sequiera Henriques, his wife		X		Temporary	
Henriques child . . . died at sea			X		
Shem Henriques (probably Samuel Sequeira)			X	Temporary	
Raphael Nunes Bernal	X			Temporary	X
Rachel Bernal, his wife		X		Temporary	
David (Lopez) Olivera	X			Temporary	
Jacob Lopez Olivera	X			Temporary	X
Judith Velha Olivera, (his wife)		X		Temporary	
David Olivera (son)	X			Temporary	
Isaac Olivera (son)	X			Temporary	
Leah Olivera (daughter)			X	Temporary	
Aaron DePivia (DePaiba?)	X			Temporary	
Benjamin Gideon	X			Temporary	X
Jacob Lopez Decrasto	X			Temporary	X
David Lopez DePass	X			Temporary	X
Zipporah DePass, his wife		X		Temporary	
Isaac DeCosta Villareal	X			Temporary	X
Abraham DeMolina	X			Temporary	X
David (Rodrigues) Miranda	X			Temporary	
Jacob (Rodrigues) Miranda	X			Temporary	
David Cohen Delmonte	X			Temporary	X
Rachel Delmonte (wife)		X		Temporary	
Isaac Delmonte (son)			X	Temporary	
Abigail Delmonte (daughter)			X	Temporary	
Hannah Delmonte (daughter)			X	Temporary	
Grace Delmonte (daughter)			X	Temporary	

ESTABLISHING A CONGREGATION

The intent of the Georgia Jewish settlers from the outset was to establish a congregation. The Sheftall "diary" underscored that point:

"[The first settlers] brought with them a Safertora [*Sefer Torah*] with two cloaks[14] and a Circumcision Box given by Mr. Lindo, a merchant in London, for the use of the congregation *that they intended to establish.*"[15] (Italics added.)

The *minyan* (quorum of ten adult males) was available, the religious accoutrements were on the scene, and the clear intent was to found a worshipping community. Jewish worship undoubtedly began in Savannah on day one of the settlement of Jews (July 11, 1733).

Two years later almost to the day (July 12, 1735), Sheftall recorded a *second* stage in the development of the congregation:

> The Jews meet together and agreed to open a synagogue, which was done immediately, named K.K. "Mickva" Israel.[16] *We opened the synagogue and made the proper officers.*[17] (Italics added.)

"Mickva" Israel Congregation is in fact the third founded Jewish congregation in America (following Shearith Israel, New York, with roots in 1654,[18] and the congregation of Newport, Rhode Island that dates its origins a bit later[19]). Savannah's congregation was the *first* Jewish community in the South.

It is widely acknowledged that the standard pattern of Jewish community development followed a discernible sequence: first, communal burial grounds were consecrated; second, a *mikvah* (a bath house where male and female may fulfill the *mitzvah* of ritual purification) was created; third, a synagogue was erected or rented; fourth, a *cheder* or school was instituted. Other agencies and structures, such as Hebrew orphanages, hospitals and the like, came later.

The Savannah pattern differed. The Jewish community founded a congregation as its *primary* act. The cemetery came soon thereafter as a gift from Colonel Oglethorpe.[20] B. H. Levy, in his carefully researched monograph, "Savannah's Oldest Jewish Community Cemetery," points out that the deeding of the cemetery was probably in response to the death of Benjamin and Perla Sheftall's infant son in 1735 and her subsequent death. This plot of ground at what was originally Savannah's southern boundary continued in use until 1762, when the Commons House of Assembly was asked permission to expand it, which was denied. By the 1770's the plot was outgrown and no more burial space was available. This first Jewish burial ground constitutes the median strip of present Oglethorpe Avenue west of Bull Street (directly opposite the north wall of Independent Presbyterian Church).

Savannah's third Jewish institution, a *mikvah*, was opened for the use of the congregation on April 2, 1738.[21] Where it was located is not addressed in the Sheftall manuscripts.

One further institution is mentioned in the Sheftall papers: a burial society called the *Mishivat Nefesh* (name taken from the 23rd Psalm "He restoreth my soul"). It is first referred to in 1787 in the context of the construction of a wall around the second cemetery site.[22] The society was well established by then, though nowhere else is its early history described. Clearly its function was the preparation of deceased members of the community for proper Jewish burial, maintaining and improving the Jewish cemetery, and providing comfort and consolation for the mourners.

The Sheftall "diary" gives indications of other traditional Jewish practices. The author refers to *Rosh Hodesh* (the New Moon), *Succot* (Festival of Tabernacles), and cites the names of the Hebrew months.[23] Circumcision was practiced by the Sheftalls, and each father was responsible for bringing his son into the Abrahamic Covenant.[24] The Askenazim or German-Polish Jews (the Sheftall manuscript is the record of an Askenazic Jew) retained strong connection to the ways of their forebearers, and practiced devoutly even on the Georgia frontier.

The differences between the religious practices of Askenazic (German) and Sephardic Jews (in this instance, of Portuguese origin) led to a struggle over erecting a synagogue building.

Among the forty-two who came to Savannah, only eight were of Germanic background. The majority were of Iberian birth where they had lived as Catholics, converting to Judaism on arrival in London.[25] A history of non-Jewish living was not easily reversed. Survival came first, and on the frontier, where life was raw and harsh, Jewish practice tended to suffer. Former marranos could not be expected to become pious Jews.

Tension developed between the two groups. Non-Jews saw it and wrote about it. It is this author's contention that the tension resulted in the creation of a second congregation by late 1737/early 1738. (Solomon Breibart of Charleston, South Carolina, documents a similar situation in Charleston though somewhat later in time.[26])

Here is the evidence:

1. The Reverend Samuel Quincy who served as the Anglican "chaplain" of the colony from 1733 to 1735 detected the divisions between Askenazim and Sephardim:

> We have here two sorts of Jews, Portuguese and German. The first having professed Christianity in Portugal or the Brazils are more lax in their ways . . . the German Jews . . . are a great deal more strict in their way and rigid observers of the law.[27]

2. The Reverend Martin Bolzius, pastor of the Lutheran Salzbergers, observed the identical tensions:

> The Spanish and Portuguese Jews are not so strict insofar as eating is concerned as the others are . . . The German Jews on the other hand would rather starve than eat meat they do not slaughter themselves.[28]

3. The German Jews were anxious to build a synagogue. The Sephardim were doing all in their power to quash the project. As Bolzius tells it:

> They [the Ashkenazic] do not know if they will ever get permission from the Trustees to build a synagogue. It will be quite some time; as I mentioned before, the Spanish and Portuguese Jews are *against* the

German Jews, and they are going to protest the petition by the
German Jews to build a synagogue. . . . The German Jews think
themselves entitled to have a synagogue built and are willing to have
the Spanish ones share its use. The latter, however, do not consent
but want the priority.[29] (Italics added.)

That an Askenazic congregation was actually functioning in Savannah
in 1738 is beyond debate. The Reverend Bolzius was present as the Germanic
rites were intoned. He made the point in a letter to his superior, Rev.
Callenberg, in the document mentioned above, written February 21, 1738:

The Jews use at their service, which they are holding in an old and
miserable hut, men and women separated, *the same ceremonies which
I have seen in Berlin.* A boy speaking several languages and especially
good in Hebrew is their reader and he is paid for his services. There
are not more than two families who can speak Jewish-German.[30]
(Italics added.)

The surprise is that the Sheftall "diary" made no mention of this
German congregation. It, however, does strengthen the argumentation that
such a congregation could have been established. Sheftall noted a shipment of Jewish ritual objects from London, arriving July 12, 1737, a full
seven months before Bolzius worshipped with the German Jews.[31] July 12th
was the date that Sheftall claimed the Jews first landed in Savannah in
1733 (not July 11).[32] Hence this second shipment may have been an "anniversary" gift. Benjamin Mendes da Costa of London was the generous
donor of three religious objects: a Torah (the second in the community), a
hanukkiah (Chanukkah *menorah*), and a quantity of books (which Dr.
Jacob Marcus identifies as prayerbooks).[33] *Siddurim* (prayerbooks) were
needed for congregational worship. A Chanukkah *menorah* would have
better served German Jews than Sephardim, not only because of a greater
ritualistic inclination, but because Chanukkah is so rich in Germanic em-
bellishments (*latkes, dreidle,* etc.). Two Torahs in a community would
have allowed each worshipping body to have one.

Eventually the two streams blended together and the two Torahs were
finally housed under one roof. But in the mid-to-late 1730's, two Jewish
prayer communities were *probably* functioning.

By 1740, the threat from Spanish Florida ended the Sephardic influence
in terms of numbers and prestige, terminating the divisiveness as well.

The two Torahs brought to Savannah, one by the first Jewish colonists
and the second in 1737, remain the treasured possessions of Temple Mickve
Israel. Documentary evidence indicates that these two are the oldest Torahs
continuously on American soil. An earlier scroll brought to New Amsterdam
was returned to Amsterdam by 1657.[34]

SALZBURGERS AND JEWS

Just prior to the opening up of the Georgia colony, the Catholic
Diocese of Salzburg was the scene of an expulsion of non-Jews. German

Lutheran peasants were cast forth from their native land by the Archbishop of the area and given orders to march forth. By 1734, a contingent
of these Salzburgers, as they were called, entered the Savannah River,
settling approximately twenty miles above Oglethorpe's colony. Under the
guidance of their pastors, John Martin Bolzius and Israel Christian
Gronau, they later founded a colony—Ebenezer. To this day, the stately
church they built remains intact, one of the oldest religious edifices in the
Coastal Empire.[35] An adjacent graveyard and remnants of primitive cabins
serve as reminders of what was once a bustling community.

Elements of this settlement began to trickle into Savannah, here to
carve out a new life. A meeting house was constructed by 1741 on Wright
Square; it was replaced at a later era by what is today the Lutheran Church
of the Ascension. Jew and Salzburger then began pleasant associations, leading to the aforementioned visit by Pastor Bolzius to the crude hut where
the German Jews worshipped in the manner he had witnessed earlier in
Berlin. One may ask, why should such pleasant connections develop? Why
should a Lutheran pastor attend a Jewish prayer service in 1738? The
modern tenor of interfaith relations may allow for such liberalism, but in
the 18th century, strictest separation was the common practice.

Explanation proceeds from the valuable collection of essays prepared by
Rudolph Glanz. Entitled *Studies in Judaica Americana,* Glanz's work details
the development of associations between Salzburgers and Jews.

When the German Lutherans were forced to abandon their native
territory, they wandered from community to community through much of
central and western Europe seeking a place of refuge. In every instance,
wherever they went, they were met by Hebrews bearing gifts, both in
Germany and Holland.[36] The Jews could identify with a history of persecution and homelessness, engendering bonds of compassion. Glanz cites as
source *Ausführliche Historie der Emigranten oder Vertriebenen Lutheraner
aus dem Ertz-Bissthum Salzburg,* published in Leipzig in 1732.[37] In Klein-
Noerdlingen, the Catholic population was forbidden to provide even a
drink of water to the "heretics,"

> But the Jews proved to be more compassionate than the Christians.
> They led the emigrants to their wells and handed them vessels to draw
> water for themselves and their horses. They also presented them with
> bread, beer, and a little money, as far as their meager means would
> permit.[38]

In the Hasse Cassel area, four thousand thalers were provided by the local
Jewish populace and with the gift went the words:

> The situation in which we behold you reminds us of the exodus of
> our fathers from Egypt. We are full of admiration for the reasons
> which impelled you to leave your native land. We beg you to accept
> the money as token of our sympathy for you in your present plight.[39]

Evidence of the same level of generosity proceeds from episodes in Frankfurt Am Main, Coburg, Wuerzburg and Bamberg.[40]

Strikingly, in Berlin (where Bolzius attested that he had witnessed a Jewish service in accordance with Askenazic rites), the collection for the Salzburgers was taken up by the synagogue. More than thirty-three thalers were collected and almost 205 yards of linen supplied to provide shirts for the old and needy.[41] It is likely that Rev. Martin Bolzius was in Berlin then and recalled the worship he had witnessed when in 1738 he visited the "crude hut" that served as sanctuary for Savannah's German Jews.

This background explains the cordiality that developed between the Salzburger community in Savannah and its Jewish counterpart. Not only did the two share a common language, habits, and folkways learned in childhood, but there was also a recent history of benign support. The Salzburgers commented that the local Jews engaged in industrious trade, bore arms, participated in military training, and stood guard with weapons just like any other citizen. That the Jews refused to accept the central Christian mystery was a grave concern, and for the alteration of that, the Salzburgers pressured and prayed in vain.[42]

SEMITISM . . . PHILO AND ANTI

Dr. Jacob Marcus in *The Colonial American Jew* devotes a chapter of text to instances of anti-Semitism in Colonial America and 17th and 18th century England.[43] He states:

> the good Christian of seventeenth and eighteenth century America was committed to a theology which represented the Jew as the villain in the drama and mystery of salvation. . .[44]

Increase Mather in 1669 cried out to his people,

> The guilt of the bloud [sic] of the Lord of Heaven and Earth lyeth upon that Jewish nation.[45]

The noun *Jew* was used as a verb of approbation or as an adjective of derision. *Jew merchant* is found in texts and its purpose is not to identify the faith of the individual as to signal his "villainous" character. A map of the riverfront of Savannah in 1786 shows a series of Colonial cottages each with the surname of the resident inscribed, save the instance of Jewish homeowners, which are simply designated as "Jew."[46] The image of the Jew as the invincible man of business was so strong at the time that it was believed no Christian could compete. Governor Peter Stuyvesant, a bigot, advanced this argument to try to limit Jewish participation in New Amsterdam's commerce.

Judeophobia affects Jews when the powers that be impose limitations upon them not levied upon others. It will help to understand the uniqueness of the Georgia experience to list restrictions in other colonies, including evidence of anti-Semitism; all are found in Dr. Marcus' book.

NEW AMSTERDAM

Peter Stuyvesant tried to impose these restrictions on the Jews in New Amsterdam: They were not permitted to be burghers, were restricted in commerce and excluded from military service. They were not given the right to worship publicly, own their own homes, or receive onerous appointments. Trade with Indians was specifically excluded. The West India Company urged the Jewish settlers to segregate themselves into a form of ghetto. Every limitation had to be overcome by appeal to authorities in Amsterdam.[47]

VIRGINIA

In 1730 and 1731, Jews sought to create a colony in the Shenandoah Valley and the authorities, catering to the locals, denied the prospective group political rights.[48]

RHODE ISLAND

Naphtali Hart was almost killed by an irate Rhode Islander, not an uncommon happening in the New England area. Merchant shipper John Bannister referred to Moses Lopez as

a Jew, the offscouring of the human species.[49]

Jews in Rhode Island were sometimes subject to courts which refused to naturalize them. The legislature clearly had one standard for Christians, another for Jews. Vandalism against the Newport synagogue and the historic cemetery was known as late as 1773.[50]

PENNSYLVANIA

In the period of the Revolution, a vigorous Christian minority was bent on depriving all non-Protestants of civil and religious equality. The Lutheran pastor Muhlenberg was one of the leaders of this effort.[51] The September 1776 Constitution denied public office to Jews. Vandalism against cemeteries and tombstones was publicly acknowledged in the 1750's in Philadelphia.[52]

This incomplete listing of the limitations and attempts to restrict Jewish rights and opportunities, including efforts to intimidate our people, gives some idea of real conditions north of the Carolinas.

THE GEORGIA EXPERIENCE

The saga of Georgia Jewry began under adverse conditions. The London authorities, the Trustees, were clearly opposed to any Jewish settlement. Once Jews were admitted by Oglethorpe, the Trustees did not change their minds overnight. The letter of October 18, 1733, contains this caveat:

They [the Trustees] hope that they [the Jews] will meet with no sort of encouragement and desire, sir, that the said Jews may be allowed no kind of settlement with any of the grantees; the Trustees being apprehensive they will be of prejudice to the trade and welfare of the colony.[53]

Captain Hanson reported to the Earl of Egmont, et al. that the Jews he transported were miscreants who cheated him and refused to honor their debts.[54]

On December 29, 1733, the Trustees' Common Council again let their desire be officially recorded

... as they [the Trustees] conceive the settling of Jews in Georgia will be prejudicial to the colony ... the Trustees do likewise require the said messrs ... Suasso, Salvador ... and ... Decosta ... [the subscription takers in London who diverted the funds to underwrite the passage of the Jews] ... do use their endeavors that the said Jews be removed from the colony of Georgia ...[55]

No doubt about it, the Trustees wanted the colony devoid of Jews. Attitudes altered once the Jews demonstrated their capacity to be contributors to the experiment. Indeed, Jews proved to be among the honored citizens.

By December, 1733, Jews, along with everyone else, were given grants of land by Oglethorpe. Note the list of first settlers to determine how extensive land ownership was. Once obtaining property, Jews were treated like the other settlers.

David A. Byck, Jr. has plotted the lot assignment (see Appendix A). While the majority of Jewish town lots were located near what is today Ellis Square (in Decker Ward), the only section of town without Jews was Derby Ward where Christ Church Parish was centered. Jews owned land as far away as Hampstead, a German settlement between four and five miles southwest of Savannah.

Following the distribution of lots, the question of whether Jews could expand land holdings by purchasing or leasing lands belonging to Gentiles arose. Oglethorpe's bailiff, Thomas Causton, no lover of Israelites, wrote the Trustees an inquiry asking two basic questions: (1) May land owners lease to Jews if the lease results in an improvement? (2) May a Jew lease land to a fellow Jew so that he can have a place of residence?[56] As Stern points out, before answer came back, Dr. Nunes acquired six farms; Mr. Henriques, seven; Mr. d'Olivera, seven; and Mr. Delmonte, thirty.[57]

The evolution of the Trustees' attitude from negative to positive is reflected best in Egmont's comments on individual Jewish settlers, found in his *List of Early Settlers in Georgia*:

Minas, Abrm—In 1736, four acres of his garden lot and 1 of his farm were cultivated and produced 36 bushels of Indian corn.[58]
Delyon, Abrm.—An *industrious* man in 1736, he *thoroughly* culti-

vated four acres, which produced 50 bushells [*sic*] of Indian corn, 50 of
pease [*sic*] and 24 of rice. In 1738 The Trustees lent him 200 £
upon security and on certain beneficial conditions for the province
to cultivate vines.[59] (Italics added.)

Considering how infuriated Egmont was over the initial Jewish colonization,
his charitable evaluation was remarkable. Note that the Trustees extended
credit to DeLyon, a testimony to his skill as a vintner.

Jews in New Amsterdam had to appeal for the right to bear arms, but
not the Jews of Savannah. In the February 21, 1738, letter from Bolzius to
Callenberg, evidence is cited;

> The German Jews have in Savannah the same liberties as any English-
> man. They drill with a rifle, as all the soldiers do. They have no
> other profession besides farming or dealing in small trade. . . . They
> even have a doctor who has the permission of the Trustees to cure
> them when they are sick.[60]

Worship rights were always granted. Even though Georgia was an
Anglican settlement with a state church in place, no evidence exists of any
attempt to frustrate public prayer.

Appointments to office also were open to qualified Jews. Daniel Nunes
was appointed a custom official of the Savannah port in 1784. This began a
process of involvement in public service that distinguishes Georgia. After
the Revolution, Jews were chosen by the Georgia electorate for positions
of power.

There is limited evidence of anti-Jewish sentiment once settlement
occurred: the map of the riverfront with Jewish residences designated as
"Jew," the cemetery controversy (which will be discussed anon), and a few
minor incidences constitute the known manifestations of religious intolerance in eighteenth century Savannah.

One additional event in this time frame has been characterized as an
anti-Semitic incident of consequence. The Georgia colony was not prospering as the Trustees had hoped, and William Stephens was sent in 1737 to
investigate conditions. Complaints were flowing from the colonists about
restrictions that hindered progress. Some thought the prohibition against
slave ownership was responsible; others cited the land laws which limited
the amount any single individual could own. Major Thomas Coram, a
former Trustee living in England, pointed out, in a letter dated March 9,
1934, that the presence of Jews was to blame, causing Christians to desert.
Petitions (asking for changes in governing policies) were circulated. One
hundred seventeen Savannah Christians signed it, but Jews who asked to
append their names were denied that privilege.[61] Egmont's response was
incredulity:

> This I do not believe, for why should they [the Jews] be refused, being
> Freeholders?

And then he added,

In a subsequent application they gladly admitted them to sign.[62]

The petitioners wanted to have their requests accepted. Aware of the Trustees' initial views, they judged it sagacious to disallow Jewish signatures which might turn the Trustees against them. The tact was taken not as an act of prejudice, but rather to prevent European prejudices from blocking their legitimate request.

To sum up, initially there were signs of anti-Jewish sentiment from the London leadership. Alterations in attitude occurred rather quickly as the Jewish community in Savannah assumed a constructive and vital role in the development of the colony. The Earl of Egmont shifted from enemy to advocate. Georgia Jews were accorded all rights and privileges of Englishmen of Anglican faith. The letters of Rev. Bolzius, Rev. Quincy and others testified to the friendship and esteem in which Christians held Israelites. Ultimately, the leaders of the colony, particularly Oglethorpe, must be credited with setting the tone for Jewish acceptance and integration.

FROM THESE FORTY-TWO

The descendants of the original forty-two Jewish colonists read like a "Who's Who" of American Jewry. A ponderous volume could be devoted to such a genealogical study. For the purposes of this limited history, the material will be confined to one branch of the Samuel Nunes Ribeiro family. From his seed derived the following influential American Jews:

FIRST GENERATION

— Daniel Nunes: Custom official, Port of Savannah. A Mason, 1734. In 1736 served as government interpreter.[63]
— Moses Nunes: Prominent Mason, 1734. Custom officer for the Port, 1760. Indian interpreter on the Georgia frontier.[64]
(A) Esther Nunes: Married Abraham DeLyon, famed vintner of Savannah.
(B) Zipporah Nunes: First marriage to David Mendes Machado, *hazzan* of the Shearith Israel Congregation, New York, first founded synagogue in America.[65] Second marriage to Israel Jacobs of Philadelphia.

SECOND GENERATION

(A) Esther's children:
Nine children of Esther and Abraham DeLyon and their subsequent descendants married heirs of some of America's best known Jewish families, including those of Moise and Moses of South Carolina, Brandon, Seixas and Hendricks of New York, and Nones of Philadelphia.[66]
(B) Zipporah's children

By marriage 1:

(*B1a*) Rebecca Machado: Married Jonas Phillips of Philadelphia, fur trader, *shochet* (ritual slaughterer) of Shearith Israel in New York, Revolutionary militiaman, and first president of Congregation Mikveh Israel of Philadelphia. Achieved fame for his fight against the "Test Oath" in Pennsylvania which prevented Jews from holding office.[67]

(*B1b*) Sarah Machado: Married Phillip Moses, business associate of Aaron Lopez of Newport. Merchant and fur trader in Savannah. Later in Charleston.[68]

By marriage 2:

(*B2a*) Rachel Jacobs: Married Jacob I. Cohen (his second wife), one of the first Jews to settle in Richmond, Virginia. A Revolutionary War soldier, he fought with the "Jew Company" of Charleston. Served as president of Congregation Mikveh Israel (Philadelphia). A prominent merchant and banker, he had business dealings with Daniel Boone.[69]

THIRD GENERATION

Among the twenty-one children of Rebecca Machado Phillips (*B1a*) and Jonas Phillips were:

(*C1a*) Daughter Rachel Phillips married Michael Levy, Revolutionary War soldier. She is buried on the grounds of Thomas Jefferson's estate at Monticello.[70]

(*C2a*) Daughter Zipporah Phillips married Manuel Noah, who served in the Pennsylvania Militia during the Revolutionary War, and was a New York and Charleston merchant.[71]

FOURTH GENERATION

Two of American Jewry's most prominent heroes are direct descendants of Dr. and Mrs. Samuel Nunes Ribeiro, *the two being first cousins.* Rachel Phillips Levy (*C1a*) and Michael Levy's son, Uriah Phillips Levy, became the first Jewish Commodore in the U. S. Navy. He was an extensive landholder in New York City, owner and restorer of Monticello, Jefferson's home, and the only individual to present the U. S. government with a statue of a President, Thomas Jefferson, now in the Rotunda of the Capitol Building.[72] Zipporah Phillips Noah (*C2a*) and Manual Noah begat Mordecai Manuel Noah, journalist, novelist, Tammany Hall leader, president of New York's Shearith Israel, and friend of Presidents. In 1813, he was appointed by President Monroe as Consul to Tunis. Considered America's first "Zionist," he sought in 1825 to establish a Jewish colony "Ararat" on Grand Island, in the Niagara River.[73]

AND ON AND ON

For Georgians, the most famous descendant of Dr. and Mrs. Samuel Nunes Ribeiro was Raphael Moses of Columbus, Georgia. Buried at

Esquilline Hill (near Columbus), Raphael was a great-grandchild of Dr. Nunes through granddaughter, Sarah (*B1b*) (married to Phillip Moses). A Civil War hero, he is said to have been involved in the final act of the Confederacy, when he brought cachets of gold to Augusta for distribution to needy veterans. His claim to fame as a Georgian was his development of peach orchards, and the cultivation of techniques for shipping the fruit to northern markets. Moses may be considered the father of Georgia's peach industry.[74]

CHAPTER TWO

FROM JENKINS EAR TO
SPRING HILL REDOUBT

The optimistic expectations of the Trustees and Oglethorpe that the little settlement on the Savannah River would flourish with bustling mercantilism and bountiful production of silk and wine turned into a hollow dream. By 1736, rumblings of discontent were heard. Georgia was to be without burgeoning plantations. For defense and other reasons, the land was held in limited acreage by individual yeoman farmers, the theory being that people will fight and die for their own property (the "Kibbutz" system in Israel is predicated on a similar concept). The Trustees forebade slavery in Georgia, preventing the plantation system from evolving. They believed that in a buffer colony slaves might prove discontented and eager to take up arms with the enemy.

Oglethorpe was anxious to build up the defenses of the colony, claiming land all the way to the St. Johns River (which flows through Jacksonville, Florida, today). He set up a series of frontier forts, including one at the mouth of the St. Johns, that was viewed as a threat to the Spanish. In 1736, the government of Spain tried to force England to negate claim to this southernmost region. There was tension in the area. Oglethorpe went back to England to recruit soldiers to bolster the southern flank. By May, 1738, some were in position, alarming the Spanish. At the same time, the Creek Nation's reliability was not assured, so Oglethorpe tried to smoke the peace pipe with them. Few assurances came to him of their intent, should war break out. This is the background needed to evaluate why large numbers of Jews in Savannah decided to relocate to safer terrain. Some have suggested economic limitations were the cause. One suspects that the threat of general hostilities in the area, involving the people who had spawned an Inquisition in Europe, was the primary cause. Egmont, in recording the departure of Dr. Nunes and company, verified the conviction:

> fear of the Spaniards drove to Charles Town . . . Dr. Nunes and his son Daniel . . .[1]

This was in August of 1740, the very year that Oglethorpe attacked St. Augustine and failed. That futile attempt convinced Jews that the British might not prevail in a confrontation with the Spanish. So between August and April, 1741, the majority of Sephardic Jews abandoned the colony.[2] In 1742, the Spanish did attack near Fort Frederica (on St. Simon's Island) and posed a threat to the Savannah settlement. The Battle of Jenkins Ear ended the danger. Nonetheless, Oglethorpe's letter to the Trustees of April 23, 1741, indicated

that all of the Jews except one had left the colony . . .[3]

Oglethorpe's conclusion was not quite accurate. According to the Sheftall "diary", between 1742 and 1748 Mrs. Minis was "being brot to bed" with a series of children, proving the presence in Savannah of the Minis family. Benjamin Sheftall and his *mishpacha* (family) also must have remained since Sheftall wrote the entry in the "diary."

Congregation Without a *Minyan* 1750-1773*

Savannah in 1750 was only beginning to recover from the difficulties which had aroused so much complaint on the part of the settlers. The Trustees of the Georgia colony, absentee landlords in England, had gradually yielded their utopian schemes to popular demand. Rum, slavery, the private ownership of land—all originally prohibited—now became the rule, and with these rights granted to the settlers, the colony resumed some measure of growth. Some of those who had fled in the 1740's returned. The year 1752 saw the Trustees preparing to turn over their charter to the King, and as a last gesture toward strengthening the colony they handed out land grants broadside, attracting further colonists and rewarding those who had stayed.[4]

The picture of Savannah in the late 1740's, given by Levi Sheftall in an autobiography he wrote many years later,[5] contrasts strongly with the neat appearance of the town in 1734 as drawn by Peter Gordon:[6]

At 5 years old [i.e. 1745] I was sent to school to a Mr. John Dobe, a very humain [sic] man to children.[7] In the course of a few years our school diminished, the country being with few in inhabitants, the town nothing but logs in the streets, not having a sufficient number of people in town to clear the trees away. Every kind of ferocious beasts used to come into town, take away what ever was left unsecured. With the depredations committed by the above beasts and the Indians, the inhabitants were continually on there [sic] guard, as the woods were standing from Mrs. Edward Telfair's house, Southerly on a line to Mrs. Eppinger's new house and continuing. On several of the trees were nailed pieces of board painted red. This was to show the inhabitants that they could not go over that mark to cut wood as that land was the Indians' . . .

*This section was prepared by Dr. Malcolm H. Stern from an unpublished manuscript entitled "New Light On Savannah Jewry, Part II: 1750-1773." Appreciation is expressed for permission to include it herein.

All through the eighteenth century and well into the nineteenth, the Indian settlements remained close to Savannah, although the Indian's territory was gradually purchased from them by the growing colony of whites.[8] This closeness is further reflected in Levi Sheftall's autobiography:

> I am now going to relate a transaction that took place near the bluff where my wharves were. This must have been about the year 1750, to the best of my recollection. There was a large Shead (*sic*) built for to dry bricks under; as they were made there. And five Creek Indians came to town and camped under that place. In the night a Cherokee Indian (who was at war with the Creeks) came undiscovered and fired on (--?) them. Afterwards he ran in with his land Thocnieef (?) and (scalped?) the one that had shoted (*sic*). On this, one of the Creeks (fired) at the Cherokee. This made him run of (*sic*). Next morning (my f)ather with sever more of the towns people went out (. . .) for blood and found w(h)ere the fellow had bleed (*sic*). They (. . .) it and found the fellow consealed (*sic*) in a thicket near (-birch's ?) still. He was brought to town and the doctors (stayed) with him till he was cured and he was sent home to his (people), but the man died of his wounds (his name was Ben). Anot(her) of such circumstances occurred here which is not (worthw)hile to put down . . .

One more vignette demonstrates how much of a frontier the Georgia colony was:

> About 10 or 11 years past a she (wolf?) with 3 or 4 young ones came into my brother's (place). There they stole a parcel of fouls (*sic*) out of a coop (and made) of (*sic*) with them. They came there 2 times and were shot at (. . .) ded but got away . . .

The total population of Georgia in 1750, aside from Indians, numbered less than two thousand whites and half as many Blacks.[9] The Jewish community numbered precisely sixteen souls divided among three families. Listed by name and age, they were:

MINIS: Abraham 56; Abigail, his wife, 49; and their children: Leah 24; Esther 19; Philip 16; Minis 14; Joseph 12; Judith 8; Hannah (Anna) 6; Sarah (Sally) 2.

NUNES (NUNEZ); Daniel 40; Moses 50.[10]

SHEFTALL: Benjamin 58; Hannah, nee Solomons, his second wife[11] 51; and their sons, Mordecai 15; Levi 11.

On June 23, 1752, the Trustees, having recognized their inability to continue the maintenance of Georgia as a corporate enterprise, turned their rights over to King George II and his Parliament. In the months prior to the turnover, the Trustees granted away nearly 75,000 acres to those colonists who were apparently believed to be their supporters.[12] So far as we can ascertain, no Jews were among the grantees, which may indicate one of two factors: either the Trustees continued to retain their anti-Jewish prejudice,[13] or the Jews were among those who objected to the Trustees' management.

The King's government did not assume control until 1754, and the beginnings of a legislative assembly met in January of 1755, passing badly needed legislation for the government of the colony.[14] The growth of law and order made Georgia a more desirable place in which to live, and a race for land grants began that was to involve most of Savannah's Jews. Between March of 1756 and the Revolution, Benjamin Sheftall and his two sons, Mordecai and Levi, between them acquired 3755 acres in addition to a town lot and wharf lot in Savannah and a farm lot outside; Abigail Minis, widowed in 1757, obtained 2329 acres in addition to two town lots in Savannah; her daughter Esther got a town lot and fifty acres in Savannah; and her sons Joseph and Minis got similar grants in the town of Hardwicke.[15] Abigail Minis's eagerness to acquire ever more property for the support of her large family found her several times petitioning for an extension of the required six months during which newly-acquired property was expected to be surveyed.[16] Her shrewdness as a businesswoman may account for the fact that a survey of her Savannah property which, at first, showed thirty-seven excess acres belonging to her, later proved to contain "74 acres and 3 rods."[17] Moses Nunes obtained five hundred acres, and Abraham Sarzedas, who appeared in Georgia by 1757,[18] was granted a town lot in Hardwicke.

The Nunes brothers were active in Savannah's Masonic Lodge. In a 24-page fragment of minutes of the Lodge for 1756-57 which turned up in the Library of Congress in 1926, Daniel Nunes is mentioned as being present at seventeen meetings, often when only one or two others were the only ones in attendance. His name usually appears second, directly under that of Noble Jones, indicating, probably, that both were high officials of the Lodge. Moses Nunes is marked present only twice, but absent eleven times, in one place with the notation:

in Indian nation.

Abraham Sarzedas joined the Lodge on March 1, 1757, in time to be paired off with a fellow-mason, as was Daniel Nunes, in the procession which greeted the arrival in the colony of Royal Governor Henry Ellis. Sarzedas was present on only one other occasion.[19] Daniel Nunes' home served as the Lodge's meeting-place for at least one session. His house is mentioned as having been on the north side of Congress Street, sixty-feet east of Barnard Street. Both Moses and Daniel are stated to have been among the founders of the Lodge when it was organized by Oglethorpe in 1734.[20]

Moses Nunes' absences can readily be explained by the fact that he was a trader among the Indians. In an official letter from Savannah to the Trustees, dated July 29, 1750, reporting on the suspicious activities of Mrs. Mary Bosomworth, the Indian widow of a recreant minister, the officials wrote:

. . . This account, Moses Nunes, a Trader in the Tuckabachees,[21] related to Us about ten days ago . . .[22]

Six years later, on August 30, 1756, he was in Augusta, joining in a petition of its inhabitants to the royal governor, Reynolds, recounting their fear of the Indians and the defenseless condition of the town.[23] Nunes' trading gave him sufficient knowledge of Indian tongues to become an interpreter, at first on a volunteer basis and later as professional appointee of the last royal governor, the able James Wright, who served from 1760 to 1771, and resumed from 1773 until the Revolution deposed him in February 1776.[24] In a letter to the Lords of Trade in London, dated at Savannah, July 5, 1769, Wright wrote:

> The Certificate in favour of Mr. Nunes for £50, as Indian Interpreter My Lords stands thus, Such an officer always was, now is, & will be as Long as we have any Connection with Indians absolutely Necessary, and Mr. Nunes acted as Such when I came to the Government & has continued to do so ever since, but never had any Salary or Allowance from Government till June Say Midsummer 1767. He was appointed a Lieutenant in one of the Troops of Rangers, in consideration of which he undertook to act as Indian Interpreter, and discharged that very troublesome office & duty faithfully & to my satisfaction. The Rangers were broke the last of March 1767 and then Mr. Nunes Said he could not give up so much of his time without Some Pay for it, and it being Impossible for me to receive Indians (who frequently come to me at Savannah) and transact business with them without an Interpreter I consulted the Gentl (sic) of the Council upon it, and who unanimously advised me to Continue Mr. Nunes & give him a Certificate for £50 ann (sic) to be Paid out of the Contingent Money. and which Sume (sic) I assure your Lordships he very Clearly Ea .ns, and I Cannot therefore doubt but that your Lordships will be Pleased to allow it to be Continued & Paid out of the Contingencies, it being for the Service of the Utmost Consequence & Indispensably necessary . . .[25]

On June 9, 1768, Governor Wright appointed Moses Nunes Searcher of the Port of Savannah.[26] Nunes may have still been functioning in that capacity seven years later, when he made the following deposition:

> MOSES NUNEZ being duly Sworn on the Holy Evangelist (sic) of Almighty God, maketh Oath and saith That on Wednesday the fifteenth Day of this Instant this Dep.t went to the Office (which is held at Mr. Thompsons House in Savannah) in the morning, that the said Mr. Thompson who is Collector of the Customs in the Province aforesaid, told this Dep.t that he had received an Information, that some Molasses, were going to be put on board of a Schooner, from Mr. Wells Warf (sic) & desired this Deponent to walk along with him which this Dep.t did, that they found no moore (sic) on board of the Schooner than what she had a Cocquet[27] for, upon which they discharged the Schooner—That this Dep.t saw lying (sic) upon the aforesaid Wharf. Eight Hogsheads of Molasses. That the Collector, told this Dep.t he had great reason to suspect, that there were more in one of the Stores & immediately sent James Edgar the Waiter, up to Mr. Wells House for the Key of the Store which was sent and the Store being open'd they there found Six Hogsheads and One Barrel of Sugar, That the Collector immediately order'd the Waiter to put the

Kings broad Arrow, upon the Eights Hogshead of Molasses on the Wharf & the Six Hogsheads and one Barrel of Sugar in the Store which he accordingly did, and Order'd the Waiter to Stay upon the Wharf and take care of the aforesaid Molasses & Sugar, That this Dep.[t] and the Collector came away and went in search of the Cap.[t] of a Man of War who happen'd to be in Savannah at the same Time, that they soon found him, & asked his Assistance in securing the aforesaid Goods, that he said he would, & if it was afloat, he would take care of it himself, that this Dep.[t] went in search of a Boat to put them on board, but did not succeed, That the Cap.[t] of the Man of War sent two Men from on board to Assist the Waiter in taking Charge of the aforesaid Goods the whole of the succeeding Evening.

Moses Nunez

Sworn to the 17th Day)
)
of February 1775.   ) Anthony Stokes.[28]

The 1760's brought some additions to the tiny Savannah Jewish community. Isaac DeLyon, a nephew of the Nunes brothers, who had been residing in Charleston where he had married Rinah, daughter of Joseph Tobias (the founder of Congregation Beth Elohim), brought his wife to Savannah and became a merchant. We hear of him first in September, 1760, when he was transacting business with Barnard Gratz of Philadelphia.[29]

Mordecai Sheftall also found a Charleston girl for his wife, when, on October 28, 1761, he married in that city Frances, or Fanny, Hart, sister of Charleston merchant, Joshua Hart. On her behalf, Sheftall established a trust fund.[30]

Daniel Nunes, at the age of 57, found himself a wife, on January 21, 1767, of 29-year-old Phila Hays, sister of Boston merchant, Moses Michael Hays.[31]

During all this period, Levi Sheftall had been establishing himself in various enterprises as well as in matrimony. He records the tale in his autobiography:

> From my early years to the age of 12 or 13 years old I had taken a resolution to try and endeavour to do something or other to earn a little money as my turn was for Industry or Mecanicle (sic). I thought of dressing deer skins, from the hair into what is called Indian dressed I mite (sic!) make something by it. I made a purchase. My father lent me the money to pay for them. I dressed them and afterwards sold them and repaid the money borrowed and cleared five shillings. I found the work very hard and disagreeable, but the money I thought was a full compensation for the hard labour, as I was a strong stripling and cared for no hardships. I still continued the same labour for two years and I did clear in that time twenty pounds sterling (Judge how hard I must have worked.) I thought myself as right as the greatest man.
>
> On or about the year 1758, my good friend, Capt. John Milledge, who was always fond of me from a child, was Capt. of a company of rangers that were here raised by the order of the King, on account of the Indians' behaviour. He advised me to follow the butching

business as he thought I mite make money by it. My father was agreeable to it. I then entered into copartnership with Stephen Mellin for
one year. We carreyed it on to advantage and as we were to finde
eagered (*sic*) hands to work. I, on my part, did double work to save
all the money I could. During that year, I never spent one half
penny either for fruit or otherwise, and the end of the year we parted.
I cleared £150 Sterling cash. I then entered into another copartnership. Still myself and my man* London (*London and myself worked
together) doing double work in order to save money. This we did for
3 years, I never spending one penny, which few people can say as
much. I then found myself possessed of some property. Still I caryed
(*sic*) on the same business a lone (*sic*), as the copartnership was fully
ended. I then turned my thoughts to build me a house, which I accomplished on the 1st day of January 1762—the house I now live in—
being framed and boarded. I made the purchase and had it removed
on my lott (*sic*). I was still making money very fast, having 6 or 8
good slaves. I compleatly (*sic*) furnished my house. I had an inclination to settle myself with a companion for life which I well knew
would be pleasing to my good parents. I fixed my thoughts on a
young lady. She rejected my desire. Her reason was best known to
herself. She shall be nameless here, but this much I will say: She has
paid severely since in her choice.[32] I will confess that my sufferings
on her account nearly cost me my life (a foolish thing for a young
man to give way to). Still I continued working hard, making a
fortune rapidly and not spending in six years any more than one
shilling, and that was by a mear (*sic*) accident. It was, by my
calling on a gentleman for money at a tavern, w(h)ere he paid me and
w^d insist on my calling for a bowl of punch. After hard work, I was
persuaded to go into trade in it. I (. . .) £1500, therefore I shall let
that rest and say nothing more about it. In 1765, I was engaged to be
maryed (*sic*) in Charleston to a lady. Through the imprudence of
her (tyrant) Aunt it was broken of (*sic*) by me. I omitted to mention
a circumstance which is worth noting, that I was 20 years old before
I drank any spirituous (*sic*) Liquers (*sic*) of any sort, though continuously working hard and to this very day I never drank a dram of
any kinde of Liquer in the morning. Many circumstances happened
to me in the course of these times that cannot be divulged but must
die with me (so far will, I say) that it is not of any consequence to
impeach my reputation—in any shape.
With all my losses, I still accumulated a handsome property. My
good father died 2rd October 1765, aged 73 years. I still remained
with my good aged mother whose darling and only child I was.
Business called me to the West Indias (*sic*), and while there I
maryed (*sic*) my wife in St. Croix, 25th May 1768, and in the Sept.^r
following returned home.[33]

Levi's bride was Sarah de la Motta. In his Vital Record, Levi writes:

Mrs. Sheftalls age at the time of the marriage was 14 years 4 months
and 10 dayes (*sic*).

The groom was 29.[34]

THE 1773 CEMETERY

Located on Cohen Street, a block east of Highway 17 (formerly the major artery connecting the northeast to Florida) are two of American Jewry's historic landmarks. The smaller is a family burial ground that belonged to Levi Sheftall, wherein are interred those who could claim kinship. Benjamin Sheftall, the original "diary" keeper, reposes in this piquant burial place, as do others bearing early Savannah names: DeLyon, De la Motta, and Cardozo. A number of the tombstones have been "borrowed" by neighbors for use as steps. The few that remain have been ravaged by the elements and the passage of time. The only legible tombstones are:

> Mordecai Sheftall DeLyon died February 26, 1856
> Abraham I. DeLyon died March 27, 1840
> Colonel Isaac DeLyon died February 16, 1856
> Cordelia Russell died July 5, 1823

The second (and larger) burial site reposes on a grassy knoll, protected on all sides by a stucco wall of early origins (the Sheftall diaries indicated the cornerstone was set in place on the 14th of September, 1774).[35] *It is a location of major historic significance for all Georgians, as it is the only identifiable man-made site where the Battle of Savannah occurred in October, 1779.* For the story of the fighting near this hallowed spot, the reader is referred to the section in this chapter entitled "The Jewish Role in the Revolution." B. H. Levy has examined all sources and written a definitive article on this Jewish Community Cemetery.[36] The material that follows derives from his research.

Before 1773 the Jewish burial sites were two. The earliest plat given by Oglethorpe lay at the southern edge of town (on what is today West Oglethorpe Avenue). A 1762 petition by Savannah Jews to the Commons House of Assembly for permission to enclose the cemetery indicates that it remained in use as a *public* place of interment at least until that date. Three years later, on the death of his father, Levi Sheftall's burial ground became the final resting place for those Jews who were related to him and were given permission to repose in his *private* cemetery. In 1770, a controversy that required dramatic response developed around the first burial plat.[37]

By 1770, the limited burial space on West Oglethorpe was outgrown. The town had leapfrogged that area and was growing in a southerly direction. Residential neighborhoods were constructed overlooking the burial site. A petition was submitted by Savannah Jews to the Commons House of Assembly requesting the right to enlarge the cemetery. That request triggered opposition from a number of non-Jews in the form of a counter-petition. The Commons House of Assembly passed the bill despite the protest and sent it to the Upper House. The opposition was not without logic, claiming that the burial site would be

so contiguous to many of the Houses on the South part of the Town
that it would become a Nuisance and in some measure prevent the
extending of the Town that way, and would also be a means of
lessening the Value of many of the Lots . . .[38]

In Savannah, where swamps abound, rivers limit, and water tables are so
close to the surface that solid land space is precious, the argument made
sense. But, for the first time in Savannah's official records, the petitioners
tried to appeal to bigotry:

". . . no Person would choose to buy or rent an House whose
Windows looked into a Burial Ground of any kind *particularly one
belonging to a People who might be presumed, from Prejudice of
Education to have imbibed Principles entirely repugnant to those
of our most holy religion.*[39] (Italics added.)

The matter was tabled by the Upper House. The expansion never took
place.

B. H. Levy has demonstrated that the underlying motivation for killing
the bill was the great debate taking place in Georgia at the time regarding
"state" religion. The established Church of England did not look with
favor upon any development that favored any other faith or denomination
and it did not hesitate to use its power to restrict dissenters. Coincidentally
in 1770, the Presbyterians came before the Commons House of Assembly
seeking additional burial grounds, and Episcopal Priest Samuel Frink appeared before that body to argue against. This time the parliamentary procedure of tabling was not employed. The body outrightly rejected the
petition of the Presbyterians.

Savannah Jewry was left without ample space to inter the dead. The
commandment to provide proper burial could no longer be fulfilled. Into
the breech stepped Mordecai Sheftall and provided choice land for a graveyard. To dwell on personalities is not the purpose of this history. Mordecai
Sheftall, however, was the major hero of Georgia Jewry in its formative
stage. He furthered the cause of the Revolution in Georgia passionately; he
provided leadership and philanthropy for Jewish institutional and communal life; and he taught his children to build upon the Jewish foundations which he established for them.

A tract of land had been given to Mordecai Sheftall by King George
III on September 7, 1762. Approximately one acre of this land was officially
bequeathed by him as a trust indenture to a Board of Trustees

as and for a place of Burial for persons professing the Jewish Religion.

Mordecai selected as the Trustees representatives of American and European
Jewry:

Philip Minis and Levi Sheftall, Savannah
Isaac D'Acosta and Joshua Hart [Sheftall's brother-in-law], Charleston

Abraham Hart and Joseph Gomperts, London
Sampson Simpson and Solomon Simpson, New York
Isaac Hart and Jacob Rivera, Newport, Rhode Island[40]

Tradition has it that the act that prompted the decision to give this land was a sudden death in Savannah of a Jew with no place of interment. It is clear from the constituency of the Trustees that Sheftall intended this cemetery to be open to all Jews lacking proper burial space, anywhere in the Nation and abroad.

The significance of Mordecai's deed is realized when the second aspect of the gift is detailed. In addition to the cemetery, the trust indenture added that the land also be used

> for the purpose of erecting a Synagogue or building for the worship of those of the said profession [Jews] . . .[41]

The Colonial pattern of a sanctuary side by side with a burial plot was his intention. While no synagogue ever stood on his land, the monies received from the sale of a portion of it did assist in the building of the Mordecai Sheftall Memorial (social hall and educational building of the present Temple Mickve Israel).

RECONSTITUTING THE SYNAGOGUE

The opposition to the expansion of the original burial grounds engendered a renewed commitment to Jewish communal life. Mordecai Sheftall's deed of land in 1773 started the process. On September 14, 1774, the "diary" reported:

> having a sufficient number of Jews here to make a Congregation we came to a resolution to meet at the house of Mordecai Sheftall, which was done.[42]

It is clear from another extant version of the manuscripts (as Stern explains there were two copies, one in a more expanded form) that the congregation not only formed at Mordecai's house, but continued to meet there.[43] "Mickva" Israel was again a functioning institution. The suspension of the congregation for more than three decades (1740-1774) cannot be interpreted as limiting its continuity. As soon as the population returned, the congregation revived, only to undergo a second hiatus caused by the outbreak of the American Revolution.

RUMBLINGS OF WAR

Hardly a year had passed since "Mickva" Israel was again functioning, when the Sheftall "diary" signaled impending chaos:

> 1775, December the 6th . . . The American Revolution at this time throughout America did ocation [sic] many Jews to be continually

coming and going . . . there was nothing but warr *(sic)* talked of and
Everybody had there *(sic)* hands and herts *(sic)* full.[44]

Now a war was about to break loose, and Savannah, the toe of the
thirteen colonies, was to serve as refuge for those fleeing more dangerous
terrain.

Georgia was in its fourth decade of existence when the struggle for
independence began. Loyal Tories were found here, because of close ties to
the Anglican church. For many first generation Georgians, England remained the land of their nativity. The radical group that took up arms
were, on the whole, non-Anglican and/or those born and reared on Georgia
soil. Into both categories, the overwhelming majority of Jews fell. Therefore, they were predominantly wed to the struggle for independence.
Mordecai Sheftall was at the helm of leadership in the liberation movement.

Why Jews in general were caught up in the independence effort is not
difficult to understand. The Jeffersonian ideal—including a love of religious
liberty, the recognition of the right of all to equal status under law, and
the general view that, on this soil, a new democracy would be initiated, one
totally different from European models—motivated American Jews to respond to the separatist movement. Of the heroes that America produced,
Jefferson was the one whose teachings sparked Jewish passion. The name
Thomas, the name Jefferson, even combinations of the two, dot the family
trees of many American Jews.

REVOLUTIONARY ACTIVITIES IN GEORGIA

It is beyond the purview of this book to detail the course of the war in
Georgia. Only the major events that assist in understanding the Jewish role
will be described.

Tondee's Tavern in Savannah was the meeting place for two gatherings
of rebels in the summer of 1774. The first established a Provincial Congress
that ended trade with England. Delegates were dispatched to the Second
Continental Congress in Philadelphia. Temporary governments were
ordered in the various parishes into which Georgia had been divided since
Oglethorpe's time. Called Parochial Committees of Safety, they were responsible for governing and protecting the local citizens. The British
Colonial government was, in effect, reduced to powerlessness.

The head of the local Savannah Parochial Committee of Safety (of the
parish of Christ Church as it was called) *was Mordecai Sheftall.* Only forty
years after Jews migrated to this city, trust was invested in one of our co-
religionists by the leaders of the Revolutionary effort in Georgia. Francis
Salvador's election to the Provincial Congress of South Carolina in 1774 is
taken to be a signal achievement in American Jewish history. Salvador is
lauded as the first Jew elected to a Parliament since the beginning of the
Diaspora. Historians have ignored what ranks as an equal, if not superior,
achievement by Mordecai Sheftall at the same time. Christ Church was
the most prominent, influential, and populous parish in Georgia, the seat

of British government. Sheftall was not the only Jew receiving a role of responsibility on the Committee of Safety. Philip Minis, served on the same body. Governor James Wright, the Crown's representative, documented that these two served as leaders and hinted at other Jews in leadership roles, in his September 26, 1775, instrument to the Earl of Dartmouth:

> Particularly disagreeable were the proceedings of another body in Savannah since formed under the name of a Parochial Committee, headed by one Mordecai Sheftall of Savannah, a person professing the Jewish religion, and having one or *more* members of the same persuasion, particularly Philip Minis . . .[45] (Italics added.)

Judaism influenced the course of the war for liberation in Georgia on two levels. First, some non-Jews who felt the yearnings of freedom found kindling for the soul's fire in the teachings of Torah. Providence, they asserted, would once again favor a people oppressed by assisting them in their struggle against another Pharoah, George, in another Egypt, England. During the great debate in July, 1775, in the Georgia Provincial Congress (over what should be Georgia's stance vis-a-vis the call for independence), the opening sermon, preached by the Rev. John J. Zubly, of Independent Presbyterian Church, contained this appeal, rooted in Jewish values:

> As to the Jewish religion it cannot be charged with favoring despotism. The whole system of that religion is so replete with laws against injustice and oppression; and by one of its express rites it proclaimed liberty throughout the land to all the inhabitants thereof.[46]

Second, the adherents of Judaism were involved in the Georgia Revolution by bearing arms, by assisting the Revolutionary forces through service and gifts, and by fighting on the field of battle during the 1779 Siege of Savannah. In addition, some Savannah Jews were assigned to military units elsewhere.

SIGNIFICANT EVENTS OF 1774-1775

In August, 1774, a general meeting was held in Savannah to protest the blockade of Boston Harbor and taxation without representation. A few did not like the way that protest was arranged in Tondee's Tavern and wanted to express publicly their dissatisfaction. Among the group who took issue with the smoke-filled room approach were Moses Nunes (who held office as Searcher of the Port) and one-time Jew (later Christian evangelist in Georgia) Joseph Ottolenghe.[47] On the list of 80 petitioners were such dignitaries as James Habersham and Noble Jones.

A second instance in which a Jewish name appeared on a petition is in a different category. During the First Provincial Congress meeting in Savannah in July of 1775, at which Rev. Zubly spoke so eloquently, Levi

Sheftall and thirty-five others (non-Jews) presented a resolution, stating in effect that Georgia ought to be joining other American colonies in finding

> just and legal measure to secure and restore the liberty of all America . . .

without a final rupture from England.[48] Levi's problems after the war, to be examined anon, may be related to this attempt at compromise.

Isaac DeLyon (son of Savannah's pioneer vintner, and grandson of Dr. Samuel Nunes) and Levi Sheftall, president of "Mickva" Israel in 1790, were both accused of Tory tendencies, and after the war were singled out for punishment.

These limited few constituted the only "accused" loyalists, and the suggestion that they really took exception to the revolutionary effort is less truth than accusation. *The overwhelming majority of Savannah Jews supported the Revolutionary forces with their strength and substance.* Indeed, the level of support for the rebel cause in the South exceeded the pro-independence activity in the northern sections of the Nation. Dr. Samuel Rezneck, an authority on Jews in the Revolution, states:

> Both in terms of relative numbers and degree of involvement in the Revolution, the Jews of the South particularly distinguished themselves. Perhaps it was chiefly because they had deep roots in two communities, Charleston and Savannah. Both towns were greatly affected by the war after 1778; they were captured and long occupied by the British. Thus many Jews enrolled in the military forces of both places, fought in their defense, and were taken prisoner.[49]

Contrast and compare Savannah Jewry with their brethren in the established cities of the northeast. While a contingent of Jews followed Rev. Gershom Mendes Seixas of Shearith Israel Congregation in abandoning British-occupied New York, approximately thirty families remained behind.[50] In Newport, in 1776, the Committee of Safety, which attempted to block any aid to the Revolutionary forces, included four prominent Jews among the seventy-seven committee members.[51] In Savannah, only one Jew remained after the British occupation, and none is known to have engaged in an act which could be interpreted as anti-revolutionary, once the war was engaged.

THE WAR YEARS

From 1775 to 1778, Georgia was not the focus of the military conflict. The British troops were engaging rebels in the northern colonies. On November 4, 1775, the first Revolutionary troops were authorized in the South by the Continental Congress. Up to four thousand men constituted the fighting machine. In February of 1776, the Continental Congress formed the Continental Southern Military Department including Georgia, the Carolinas, and Virginia, under Major General Charles Lee, later under

General Robert Howe. Howe came to rely on Mordecai Sheftall, whom he admired.

Geographically, Georgia was a vulnerable colony, sitting on the southern-most flank of the new Nation, close to British forts in St. Augustine and containing settlements of loyalists who fled after the colony embraced inde-pendence. Three times troops of Georgia patriots attacked St. Augustine, returning without a single victory (1776-1778). Indians of the Creek Nation added to the colony's troubles. They continually shifted sides and did their best to manipulate white against white.

The year 1778 brought a major change in British war strategy. Reversals at Saratoga in 1777 convinced the military commanders that the soft underbelly was in the South, and a victory there could change the momentum of the war. Sir Henry Clinton, new Chief Commander of the British forces, made the decision to move against Savannah in the winter of 1778. From New York and St. Augustine troops were to proceed and capture the city. The St. Augustine expeditionary force did not arrive on time and had to return. The New York contingent arrived the day before Christmas, 1778, and, led by local loyalists, moved against the city un-opposed. Two days before the year 1779 dawned, Savannah was in British hands, and the Whigs were badly routed. Seven British were killed, and nineteen wounded. The Americans, captured or slain, numbered nearly five hundred. It was a disastrous defeat. The Revolutionaries were still in control of the surrounding territory, though for a forty-mile circumference the red-coats claimed sovereignty.

The interesting tale of Widow Minis (Mrs. Abigail) and her daughter, Sally, underscores the desire of Savannah Jews to remove themselves from Georgia, so long as the British were in control. The Minis women were known Whigs and, as such, complained to Governor Wright, the Royalist Governor, that they were experiencing hard times. Permission to leave for Charleston was requested and granted. A seventy-seven year old matriarch at the time, Mrs. Minis settled down in her temporary "new found" home and began carrying on the life of commerce with as much enthusiasm as in her younger years.[52]

JEWISH ASPECTS OF THE SIEGE OF SAVANNAH

The strategic import of Savannah was realized by the American and "allied" forces. If Georgia could be persuaded to negotiate a separate peace with the British, the Carolinas would be vulnerable to invasion.[53] In September of 1779, the French naval commander Count Charles Henry D'Estaing arrived at the port with twenty-two ships and four thousand troops. The American general, Benjamin Lincoln, gathered all the forces he could muster, fifteen thousand all told, and marched upon the city. D'Estaing learned first hand that "he who hesitates is lost." His call for surrender was responded to by British General Prevost with a request for twenty-four hours to think it over. By then, the British defense lines were

fully fortified. The co-ordination between French and "allied" troops was
inadequate, and the October 9th attack on the city was unsuccessful. Some
historians have suggested that the failed attack prolonged the war several
additional years. Victory at Savannah would have demoralized a British
army that had not achieved many successes before then.

The European Military Archives house a document detailing the
contributions to the military campaign by Levi Sheftall and Philip Minis.
The two had a thorough knowledge of the area near Savannah where the
French landing party would disembark and begin the march. The house of
a Mr. Morel at "Bioulay" (Beaulieu) was to be the landing site. Sheftall proposed a second landing at "Tonder Bolt" (Thunderbolt, now a charming
fishing community on the intracoastal waterway where yachts ply, shrimp
boats sail, and draw-bridges go up and down, irritating impatient drivers
who are wending their way to Tybee Island). The landing site today seems
an unlikely spot for the beginning of an invasion assault. Minis and Sheftall
supplied the maps and descriptions which D'Estaing's forces followed.[54]

During the October, 1779, siege, General Pulaski and his Polish forces
bore the brunt of the enemy fire. Pulaski himself was slain (a monument
to him faces the present Temple Mickve Israel, approximately twenty-five
yards from its front door). Among the troops fighting with him was
Benjamin Nones. Of him, a member of Pulaski's staff wrote:

> Benjamin Nones has served as a volunteer in my Company during
> the campaign of this year, at the siege of Savannah . . . His behaviour
> under fire in all the bloody actions we fought have [sic] been marked
> by bravery and courage which a military man is expected to show . . .
> and which acts of said Nones gained in his favor the esteem of
> General Pulaski. . . .[55]

THE "JEW COMPANY"

Historians who have recounted the details of the Siege of Savannah
elaborate on the contribution of the French, the Poles, the Irish, the
Haitians, et al. Only in a few isolated Jewish histories is the tale told of
an interesting fighting force, the so-called "Jew Company" under the
command of Captain Richard Lushington.[56] Jacob I. Cohen, one of the
founders of the Richmond (Virginia) Jewish community, listed fifteen
Jewish individuals who fought together at Beaufort, Savannah, and later at
Charleston. Other historians have counted 26 to 28 Jewish members of a
Charleston militia regiment, known as the "Free Citizens."[57] They were
from all parts of America, coming from as far north as New York. Recruited
along King Street in Charleston, the company represented the only known
instance in the Revolutionary War of a group mobilization of Jews. Lushington's Jewish fighters were part of General Lincoln's invasion army.

THE JEWISH BURIAL GROUNDS

The only man-made site surviving intact from the time of the Siege of Savannah unto this day is Mordecai Sheftall's Cohen Street cemetery. General Lincoln's orders of October 8, 1779, stated:

> The second place of rallying, or the first if the redoubt should not be carried, will be at the *Jew's burying ground*, where the reserve will be placed.[58] (Italics added.)

An eyewitness serving with the French forces documented the fact that, on October 9, 1779,

> The reserve corps, commanded by M. le vicomte de Noailles, advanced as far as an old Jewish cemetery, and we placed on its right and a little to the rear the four 4-pounders.[59]

Dr. Preston Russell, creator of a diorama reconstructing the battle, has verified the significance of the Hebrew Community Cemetery (Sheftall's deeded acre) as the place where the French Reserves, in particular the Haitians, were stationed. The assault on the Spring Hill Redoubt (near the present Savannah Visitors Center) by the allied forces was to be supported by the armies gathered at the cemetery. Apparently skirmishes took place close to the Jewish landmark, and military hardware (4-pounders, shells, and the like) has been found nearby.

SHEFTALL, FATHER AND SON

The account of the Siege must leave the perceptive historian with a gnawing question: where were the leaders of the Savannah Jewish community, Mordecai Sheftall and his son, Sheftall Sheftall, at this time? Answer: in the capture of Savannah in 1778, they had been taken as prisoners-of-war and put on board a prison ship. From December to the spring of 1779, Mordecai remained captive, subsequently being paroled to Sunbury, Georgia, approximately thirty miles south of Savannah. Concern for his son prompted him to contact friends who, in turn, urged General Lincoln to persuade the British to release the teen-aged lad. In June, young Sheftall was freed from the ship and united with his father. Peaceful Sunbury soon became a center for terror as irregular Tory troops converged on the Whig parolees interred there. The Sheftalls had to flee on board a ship headed for Charleston, only to be intercepted by a British frigate which took them instead to the Island of Antigua. Mordecai Sheftall's account of life in captivity has been preserved in an aged document now the possession of his descendant.[60] A tender letter was sent to Mordecai in July, 1780, at his West Indies "compound" by his wife, telling of her privations and struggles in the city of Charleston, where she had fled. The British were then besieging the town, and this moving document details the hardships of war. By December of the same year, father and son were released and relocated to Philadelphia. Philadelphia, having been relinquished by the British in 1778, was the gathering place for many patriot Jews. There Mordecai continued to serve as Commissary for the Southern Department. Son Sheftall was commissioned by the War Board to go to Charleston on a "flag-of-truce" ship to deliver provisions to General Moultrie and his beleaguered army. Not yet of the Biblical age of majority, Sheftall carried out the dangerous assignment with skill. One suspects that his objective was to connect with his mother, whom neither husband nor son had seen since 1778.

OTHER SAVANNAH JEWS WHO SERVED IN WAR

The following list is by no means complete, but these are some of the individuals who made a noteworthy contribution on the battlefield:

David Nunes Cardozo: Cardozo was one of three brothers to fight in the war. Wounded during the 1779 siege, he was attached to the "Jew Company." Cardozo participated with Mordecai Sheftall in an attack on a British vessel in the summer of 1776 and seized a load of powder. It was an illegal and daring act. The powder made its way to Salem, Massachusetts, for use during the first phase of the Revolutionary War. In 1777, Cardozo enlisted in the Savannah Grenandiers and became a sergeant-major. Given a pension for wounds sustained and service rendered, David Nunes Cardozo settled in Charleston where he is buried. His brother Isaac was the progenitor of Benjamin, who later served as a Supreme Court Justice.[61]

Philip Minis: First Caucasian child conceived and born in Georgia (July 11, 1734, one year after the landing of the first Jewish settlers), Minis served from 1776 on as acting paymaster and a Commissary of Georgia's forces. He advanced great sums to the Revolutionary Army. Together with Levi Sheftall, he provided information and guide services for the French attack upon Savannah in 1779. During the siege of Charleston, Minis was captured while serving in the Charleston Regiment Militia.

Cushman Polock: Listed on the 1790 Charter of "Mickva" Israel, he was also a founder of Mikveh Israel Congregation in Philadelphia. In 1780, he was commended by the Georgia delegation to the Continental Congress:

> for many years past; that he gave early demonstrations of his attachment to the American cause . . . has been in several engagements against the enemy.[62]

Polock contributed of his resources to the war effort, receiving payment by authorization of Congress for the goods he supplied.[63]

David Sarzedas: A lieutenant in the Light Dragoon of Georgia, he fought at the battle of Savannah, and was later taken prisoner when Charleston fell.[64]

Abraham Seixas: He was a New Yorker by birth, and brother of Rev. Gershom Mendes Seixas, *hazzan* of Shearith Israel Congregation in New

York. (Rev. Seixas also was a patriot and attended the inauguration of President George Washington.) Abraham resided in Savannah in 1782.[65] An officer in the Revolution, he served in both South Carolina and Georgia as part of the "Jew Company."[66]

Sheftall Sheftall: In addition to the exploits referred to earlier, Sheftall served as Assistant Commissary of Issues. For his heroism in the war, he was exempted from all local taxation for the duration of his life by act of Savannah's Board of Aldermen, a gratuity which no subsequent Council has awarded to another local citizen. His "cocked hat" (which Sheftall wore routinely until his death) remains the possession of an heir. Cerveau's famous painting of Savannah depicts this Revolutionary hero, bedecked with his famed head covering, in the doorway of the Gazette Building on Bay Street.

NOTEWORTHIES OF A SECOND KIND

David Emanuel: While not a Savannahian, and perhaps not even a Jew, he was a frontier war hero and early Georgia Governor (1801). His sister's great-grandson, Judge H. D. D. Twiggs, has cited for the public record a family tradition that his ancestor was Jewish.[67] Attempts to trace this in Waynesboro, Georgia, Emanuel's hometown, have proven unsuccessful. In any instance, he did not live overtly as a Jew. Emanuel County, Georgia, honors the family name. Other (affirming) Jews settled in Waynesboro in this period.[68]

Abraham Simons: Also a non- Savannahian, he served as captain of a Georgia regiment and fought in tough campaigns against Tories and Indians. His home was in the vicinity of Augusta, where he engaged in trade and earned a considerable fortune. Of doubtful Jewish lineage, he was identified by his fellow townsfolk as a Jew. Elected to the Georgia legislature in 1804, he served the state in a formative period. After his demise, his widow married the Rev. Jesse Mercer who, with the fortune earned by Mr. Simons, endowed one of Georgia's Southern Baptist colleges, Mercer University. Simons' grave, near the old Augusta Road in Thomson, Georgia, is a unique site. Simons is buried in a standing position with his musket at his side, prepared to shoot the devil, if the "Evil One" should demonstrate an intention to seize him. The coffin was literally placed vertically, requiring extra effort on the part of the gravediggers.[69]

ECONOMIC SUPPORT FOR THE WAR EFFORT

Warfare consumes men and resources. The Continental Congress was in no position to funnel the funds to carry on the enterprise of war. Individual citizens had to take up the slack. The Georgia record of Jewish contributors to the war effort is a remarkable one, involving sacrifice and some degree of foolhardiness. Some never recouped what they had given and endured deprivation afterwards. The Jewish contribution on this level is worthy of examination.

_id is documented in a certificate jointly signed by Colonel
_ssary General, and General Howe in 1777.[70] He provided
_8.50 to cover the salaries of the North Carolina regiment, the
_egiment, and provisions for the whole of the Continental
_n South Carolina. The amount was eventually repaid, but the
_ _oan (with no guarantee) testifies to Minis' dedication to the
Revo__ _ary cause.

Cushman Polock advanced financial aid (as mentioned earlier), and
was fortunate also to have Congress' repayment.

Mordecai Sheftall served as Commissary General of Issues for the
Southern Department and, as such, had to provide for the needs of the
fighting men of Georgia and South Carolina.[71] The failure of the
Continental Congress to fund adequately the costs of supplies put him in
the unenviable position of making up the short-fall or failing in his duty.
Sheftall supplied capital and credit in great measure, though the loss of
receipts in the confusion of war made it impossible for him to be compensated. His plea to Congress after the war was not an overstatement, but
simply a yearning for right to be done:

> I must entreat the Honorable Congress to have some consideration
> for a man who has sacrificed everything in the cause of his country.
> I want nothing but justice.[72]

Sheftall was so desperate after his relocation to Philadelphia that he
borrowed heavily to purchase the schooner _Hetty_ in which he sold shares.
The _Hetty_, a privateer in quest of booty, sailed forth seeking to intercept
and capture British vessels.

Levi Sheftall also was called upon to provide arms and provisions for
several companies of soldiers on duty in the Savannah area.[73]

The story cannot be elaborated upon because the details in the sources
are rather sketchy. Nonetheless, it can be concluded from the evidence that
the commitment by some Jewish citizens of Savannah was total—their
lives, their fortunes and their sacred honor.

JEWISH LOYALISTS

Only two members of the Savannah Jewish community were singled
out for accusation and punishment at war's end. Of the two, Levi Sheftall
and Isaac DeLyon, Levi's record is a confusing series of pro- and anti-
Revolutionary acts.[74] The Resolution of 1775 signed by Levi and thirty-
four other Savannahians may have been motivated by a desire to solve the
problems separating the colonies from England without a bloody contest.
Levi may have seen himself in the role of peacemaker. Concrete action that
had negative connotations occurred in 1780, during the long siege of Charleston. A petition was signed and delivered to General Lincoln calling further
resistance "foolhardy" and urging surrender. Levi Sheftall was one of the
signatories to the document.[75] Finally, Sheftall had remained in Savannah

after its capture, and only in 1779 escaped to Charleston. His failure to vacate may have added to the impression of misplaced loyalties.

Among Levi's patriotic acts, to counterbalance the negatives, he provided arms and provisions for the Georgia troops and led the French forces from Thunderbolt to the Spring Hill Redoubt. Further, he was disqualified by the British in 1780 from holding office because of his anti-Loyalist behavior. His name, however, appears on the list of Tory sympathizers. Under the Attainder Act of 1782, passed in the fervor of newly attained power by the Georgia Assembly, Levi was denied the right to vote or hold office for fourteen years and his property was fined twelve percent. Thanks to the influence of his half-brother, Mordecai, a special act was passed by the General Assembly in 1785 which restored Levi to citizenship.[76] Two years later, a second act provided further relief.

Isaac DeLyon was also accused and punished, but under the provisions of the 1785 Act, his basic rights were restored.

A SECOND "MIKVEH ISRAEL"

The last years of the war found many of Savannah's Jewish patriots residing in Philadelphia. A strange coincidence it is that the congregation they established in Georgia, the third in the land, bears the same nomenclature as the fourth founded in the "City of Brotherly Love." In all probability, "Mickva" Israel, Savannah, influenced the choice of appellation for Mikveh Israel, Philadelphia. In March of 1782, the acting board (the *adjunta*) issued a public document announcing the formation of

a Congregation to be known and distinguished by the name of Mikve Israel in the City of Philadelphia.[77]

Thirty-six names appeared on the founding document, the following having connections to Savannah:

Mordecai Sheftall and *Cushman Polock*.[78]

Mordecai M. Mordecai, a man of Jewish learning, often referred to as "Reverend," whose wife Zipporah was a native Savannahian, the daughter of Abraham deLyon.[79] The Mordecais' son, Samuel, settled in Savannah in 1804 to live out his days.

Jonas Phillips, whose wife was a direct descendant of Dr. Nunes' daughter, Zipporah. The family's connection to Georgia's Port City never diminished, as relatives Moses and Daniel Nunes continued to reside here. Jonas Phillips was one of the leaders of the Philadelphia congregation.

WAR'S END

July 11th remains a significant day in the history of Georgia. In 1733, forty-two Jews disembarked and entered the colony. In 1782, on the identical day, the British evacuated, foresaking forevermore claim to the land. The Sheftall "manuscripts" add this note:

Their [*sic*] was no Jews at that time in the state.[80]

Within a half year (December 11, 1782), the natives returned—first, Mordecai Sheftall and his family from Philadelphia; then Cushman Polock, Barnard Spitzer, and Abraham Seixas (brother of Rev. Gershom Mendes Seixas). Lyon Henry, his wife, and son Jacob came from Rhode Island. The latter three soon became four, with the addition of a baby, Barnard. In that same period, more than a *minyan* (ten) arrived: David Cardozo, Isaac Polock, David Leion, Samuel Mordecai and family (he was a Revolutionary veteran from Charleston), Levy Abrahams, Abraham da Costa, Abraham Isaacs, Moses Simons, and Emanuel de la Motta. Add to this number a contingent of ten who arrived in February, 1784, all connected to the Ralph DePass family.[81] From 1785 to 1787, the Sheftall "diary" included the following statistics: three marriages occurred, ten infants were brought into the world, and sixteen adults with their families took up residency.

The immediate effect of the war's conclusion on the Jewish community of Savannah was to increase "the comings and the goings" and to swell the population. After peace treaties are signed in every generation, a baby boom is expected, and deferred marriages take place. As the Revolution concluded, a new era was to dawn for Savannah Jewry, an era of expansion. The time of building a congregation and a permanent community were at hand.

CHAPTER THREE
HALCYON DAYS

~~~~~~

T he successful conclusion of the Revolutionary War unleashed an optimism in the nascent Nation that was to blossom into a religious revival. America was to be a unique experiment on earth, and its birthing akin to the creation of the world. Mordecai Sheftall, in a letter to his son, Sheftall, dated April 13, 1783, put it so well:

> Every real well wisher to his country must feel himself happy to have lived to see this long and bloody contest brot [sic] to so happy an issue. Now we have independence. . . . An entier [sic] new scene will open itself, and we have the world to begin againe [sic] . . . .[1]

Yet the transition from war to peace was not without struggle. Signing the peace treaty in Paris turned attention from repelling enemies to building nationhood. For six additional years, the Georgia government reposed in a weak executive and powerful legislature.[2] Local government evolved slowly. In less than a fifteen year time span, the capital shifted from Savannah to Augusta to Louisville. Finances were at a low ebb. Boundary disputes between Georgia and South Carolina complicated the routines of daily life. The Creek Indians were not always peaceful. The opening phase of that "entier new scene" was problem-ridden.

The enthusiasm of victory and independence would not be stifled by the pressures of reality. Since the Jews of Savannah had aligned with the Whig cause, they participated broadly in the benefits that victors enjoy. Mordecai Sheftall was able to acquire several hundred acres of confiscated land formerly in the hands of vanquished Tories.[3] Yet a far greater benefit eventually accrued to him and the other members of the Savannah Jewish community. Their loyalty during the war engendered new levels of respect in the civic domain. This is demonstrated by elections and appointments to positions of public trust. Precedences were set which obtain to this day. In uncommon measure since then, Savannah Jews have been given votes of confidence by the local populace. Several anti-Semitic incidences will be noted in the post-Revolutionary period; but unlike the 1773 cemetery incident, any Judeophobic activity after 1776 was countered with vigorous

[37]

opposition. Jewish self-confidence was blooming, and, with it, a will to further Jewish institutional life.

REBUILDING

The flood of itinerants to Savannah and the new permanent Jewish residents at war's end, which the Sheftall records document, encouraged renewal. By July 7, 1786, the Sheftall "diary" notes:

> The congregation of Mickva Yisrael [sic] was again established . . . and we opened the Snogo [synagogue]. . . .[4]

Officers were chosen, including Philip Minis, *parnass* (president); David Nunes Cardozo, *gabay* (treasurer); Levi Sheftall, Cushman Polock, and Joseph Abrahams, *adjuntas* (board members). Levy Abrahams was elected secretary, while Emanuel De la Motta acted as *hazzan* (the equivalent of rabbi). This same Emanuel De la Motta played an important role in the development of K.K. Beth Elohim in Charleston a few years later. Each one of the above-named leaders was a war veteran, most having participated in the Siege of Savannah, an indication that status in the Jewish community required demonstrated loyalty to the new Nation.

Community building continued in 1787 when attention focused (again in July—the 31st) on the burial society, the "Mishe'bet [sic] Nefesh."[5] It provided funds for walling in the community (Mordecai Sheftall) burial ground. Further, Jewish rituals were scrupulously observed. In 1788, a Jewish child, Jacob Henry, born in Waynesboro, perished without benefit of circumcision. The ancient rite was performed post-mortem.[6] The circumcision kit, included in the items brought over by the first colonists, was kept in use.

Broughton Street Lane was the site of a house belonging to the Morgan family.[7] This house was the first post-war prayer space rented by the local Jews for purposes of community worship. Occasionally, the funds were not avaliable for meeting the rental and Miss Morgan did press for payment due her. Mordecai Sheftall came to the rescue, covering the debt by securing it with his own holdings. This is proved by an IOU that survives from this period, now preserved in the Temple Mickve Israel Museum.

CHARTERING A CONGREGATION

The Provisional Congress of Georgia adopted a new constitution on February 5, 1777, in the midst of war. It contained a provision for the free exercise of religion and the disestablishment of the Church of England. Furthermore, no taxes could be raised to sustain any particular religious denomination. The government could neither prevent nor interpose obstacles to the formation of a Jewish congregation in Georgia. After the Revolution, the climate for creating institutions necessary for civilized life led inevitably to institutionalizing religious associations. The day of the Charter was at hand.

The General Assembly, on the day before Christmas Eve, 1789, passed an act which incorporated Christ Episcopal Church in Savannah and Independent Congregational Church at Midway, in Liberty County. Thereafter, any religious body or society could apply for a legal charter and receive the right to be incorporated for purposes of holding land, suing and being sued, raising monies, and other customary privileges attendant to such chartering procedures. The following August, Mordecai Sheftall made a motion that "Mickva" Israel be incorporated under this provision. The Trustees of the congregation at that point included Levi Sheftall, then president, Sheftall Sheftall, treasurer, Cushman Polock, Joseph Abrahams, Mordecai Sheftall, Abraham DePass, and Emanuel De la Motta. Mordecai Sheftall was assigned the privilege of making direct application to Governor Edward Telfair, a native Savannahian, at the state capital in Augusta. On the 25th day of November, authority came to him from half-brother Levi, on behalf of the board, to proceed with the filing process.[8] Five days later, the Charter was issued.

> under my hand and the great seal of the said state at the State House in Augusta, this thirtieth day of November in the year of our Lord one thousand seven hundred and ninety, and in the fifteenth year of the Independence of the United States of America. By His Excellency's command. Signed, John Milton, Secretary. (Edward Telfair, Governor).

A photostat of the original document is displayed in the congregational museum.

The significance of the event was recognized by the *adjunta* which voted to have the document read aloud in the synagogue on *Shabbat* in the third week of December, just before the Torah was removed from the ark. Our forefathers sensed the importance of this historical moment.

"Mickva" Israel's Charter was the third issued in the city of Savannah.[9]

The issuance of the Charter triggered other legalisms. What is a congregation without rules and regulations? It is not possible in the confines of this limited history to analyze in detail the code of laws that the congregation adopted six weeks after incorporation. Dr. Jacob Rader Marcus' description summarizes its high points best: "The administrative structure was simple, a board, a president (Parnoss), a treasurer (Gabay) and a secretary."[10] Three members could appeal board action and force the congregation as a whole to deal with the issue. All charity allocations were handled by the president and the *adjunta*. Monies were raised by distributing honors. Since Savannah was a port city, all monies from non-Savannahians were to be collected immediately and not allowed to pend. (Strangers in the gate might be called to the Torah and then set sail forthwith, ignoring the obligation to present a free-will offering for the survival of the institution.) Mixed marriage, possible outside the synagogue, was forbidden in a congregational setting. Those who did not keep the Sabbath were subject to denial of synagogue honors. Dr. Marcus has pointed out the lighter side of the rules and regulations. Rule fifteen stated:

> That every person shall appear in synagogue in as decent apparel as his abilities will admit, and that no person shall be called to [the] Seipher [Torah] in boots.[11]

Elements of the laws of "Mickva" Israel were clearly adapted from the rules and regulations of Mikveh Israel in Philadelphia and Shearith Israel in New York.[12] Unique regulations reflect the Savannah frontier turn of mind.

A MALIGNED LETTER TO WASHINGTON

Adelaide Wilson has underscored the importance of the letter from the Hebrew congregation of Savannah to the first elected President of these United States:

> Of the various creeds represented in Savannah, to the Hebrew Congregation alone belongs the honor of a letter of congratulations by Levi Sheftall to George Washington upon his accession to the presidency.[13]

From a Jewish point of view, the document is a milestone in the documentary history of America. Although Washington's response to the letter of the Newport, Rhode Island, congregation (with its famed "to bigotry no sanction") is more widely known, the letter of Levi Sheftall of Savannah was the *first* official declaration of fealty by American Jews to an American President.

In addition, it signaled to the President that the cause for fealty was his espousal of religious freedom and rejection of religious bigotry. Sheftall wrote:

> Your unexampled liberality and extensive philanthropy have dispelled the cloud of bigotry and superstition which has long as a veil shaded religion-unriveted the fetters of enthusiasm-enfanchised us with all the privileges and immunities of free citizens, and initiated us into the grand mass of legislative mechanism.

The structure of the letter which Levi Sheftall composed consisted of congratulations to Washington on assuming the Presidency; praise for his conduct in office thus far; excuse for the delay in not writing sooner; appreciation of his example as President that augured well for citizens of the Jewish faith; and a prayer for the blessings of the "great Author of the world."

The phraseology was kept in mind by those who, months later, addressed congratulatory remarks to Washington in Newport and New York. Three letters reached the President: the Savannah letter dated in the majority of sources as *May 6, 1789*; the Newport letter dated August 17, 1790;

and the New York, Philadelphia, Charleston and Richmond letter dated December 13, 1790. The Sheftall letter actually provoked the other communities to act.[14] It deserves far more consideration than scholars have assigned to it.

It has been noted that the common date assigned to Levi Sheftall's letter is *May 6, 1789*. Schappes, in citing this date, refers to the existence of the *dated* manuscript from President Washington to the Hebrew congregation in Savannah as being part of the Washington Papers contained in his *Letter Book* at the Library of Congress, pages 129-130. That documentation is questionable on two counts. First, neither the Sheftall letter nor the Washington response are dated according to the versions on display in the Mickve Israel Temple Museum. Second, Levi Sheftall in his correspondence with the President apologizes for failing to offer congratulations *more promptly*:

> Our eccentric situation added to a diffidence founded on the most profound respect has thus *long prevented our address,* yet the *delay* has realized anticipation, given us an opportunity of presenting our grateful acknowledgment for the benedictions of Heaven through the energy of your federal influence . . .[15] (Italics added.)

The inauguration took place on April 30th, and if the Sheftall congratulations arrived on May 6th, the apology would hardly make sense.

A newly discovered item in the *Georgia Gazette,* dated *August 12, 1790,* solves the mystery. It reads:

> The following ADDRESS from the HEBREW CONGREGATION of the City of Savannah was, on Monday the *14th of June* last, presented to the PRESIDENT of the United States by Mr. Jackson, one of the Representatives of the State of Georgia.[16] (Italics added.)

This is followed by Sheftall's text and the President's response.

To deliver the letter to the President, one of Georgia's Revolutionary heroes was chosen, U.S. House member James Jackson. Jackson later served as Governor of Georgia in 1798-1801. His name is enshrined at Fort James Jackson on the Savannah River.[17]

The President's response deserves a full reprinting (see Appendix C). The Savannah copy has been lost (probably destroyed by the fire of 1796) and the surviving copy is in the *Letter Book* of the Washington papers. The letter displayed in the temple museum is clearly not in Washington's own hand, though the text is accurate.

Washington's reliance on Sheftall's words and sentiments is demonstrated through the italics in the following excerpt:

> I rejoice that a spirit of *liberality* and *philanthropy* is much more prevalent than it formerly was among the enlightened nations of the earth.

Happily the people of the United States have in many instances exhibited *examples worthy of imitation*, the salutary influence of which will doubtless extend much farther. . .

. . . with *reverence to the Diety and charity toward their fellow creatures.*

May the same wonder-working Diety who long since delivered the Hebrews from their Egyptian oppressors, planted them in a promised land . . . Whose Providential agency has been conspicuous in establishing these United States as an independent nation, still continue to water them with the dews of heaven . . . and make the inhabitants of every denomination participate in the temporal spiritual blessings of that people whose God is Jehovah.

Two powerful ideas in this letter have not been given sufficient attention. First, Washington believed that America came into being as an act of Providence. It was too much to believe that the rag-tag armies of disparate colonies could put to flight the mighty host of the British Empire. The cause of independence triumphed because it was the will of the God of history. Washington's understanding of the events of his time that later became the heritage of the Nation is first clearly enunciated in this letter.

Second, Washington believed that the people of Israel were bearers of Abrahamic blessing. Where Jews abide, temporal and spiritual benediction will follow. How remarkable that in a period when Judeophobia labelled Jews the scourge of the earth, the first and most popular President of the United States affirmed, in a public document, his positive view of the people whose "God is Jehovah."

It was the opinion of the leadership of Congregation Shearith Israel in New York that a single letter should be addressed to the President. Washington was sworn into office in ceremonies on Wall Street on April 30, 1789. It was not until a full year and more had passed (June 14, 1790) that the Savannah letter was dispatched to him, with Levi Sheftall's profuse apology for the embarrassing delay. Marcus describes the reaction of the five sister congregations in these terms:

Savannah Jewry had already taken the bull by the horns, much to the chagrin of the Jewish leaders in New York, who resented such individualism.[18]

The resentment had the effect of diminishing the pioneering quality of the Sheftall document. Further, the judgment of the New York Jewish leaders was, on the face of it, an attempt to cover up an obvious embarrassment caused by their own dilatory behavior on a vital project. A year and a half passed before *they* managed to congratulate the President on his inauguration. In this instance, Savannah Jewry demonstrated leadership, acted with "deliberate" punctuality, and saved the day. Manuel Josephson, president of Philadelphia's Mikveh Israel, in a letter dated June 28, 1790, gave the matter appropriate perspective when he wrote Shearith Israel in New York,

The conduct of the Georgians seems to be displeasing and hurtful to your feelings. Amongst us it is not considered in that light, for they certainly had reason to expect your congregation would long since have seen the propriety of addressing the President and inviting others to join . . . but finding your inactivity, they stept [*sic*] forward to show the exemple [*sic*] . . . . It is confessed it gave us a little disgust, *not what they had done,* but that we . . . should be left in the rear through a neglect on your part . . .[19] (Italics added.)

A SYNAGOGUE BUILDING THAT ALMOST WAS

The rhythm of community building was clearly underway by the early 1790's. A Charter was in hand, rules were enacted, a house was rented for worship, and a letter was addressed to the President. What remained undone was erecting a structure that would be the permanent house of prayer for Savannah's Jews. Rosenswaike estimates one hundred Jews lived in the town.[20] That figure is based on the number of Jews present at the annual meeting of the congregation in July, 1791. That number could afford to erect a suitable structure. On October 9, 1791, a proposal was presented to the *adjunta* for the construction of the *first synagogue building in Georgia.*[21] Abraham da Costa, wealthy local merchant, urged the congregation to erect an edifice forty-five feet by thirty-five feet with a wall of sufficient height to permit a women's gallery. The synagogue would be established on the south commons (West Oglethorpe Avenue), on ground belonging to the congregation. There are no city records to indicate where the site was, though logic compels one to assume it was in the vicinity of the plot given by Oglethorpe for Jewish burials. Da Costa's proposal included an offer to purchase all materials and pay the rent on the Morgan house until the project was completed. The congregation accepted the proposal with the provision that the *gabay* (treasurer) receive one fourth the rent in advance, and a building committee composed of da Costa, Mordecai Sheftall, Levi Sheftall, Sheftall Sheftall, and Emanuel De la Motta accept the responsibility for completing the task.

On February 12, 1792, the project collapsed. A heated letter of protest came to the officers and board from da Costa claiming that the bricks purchased were inferior and that his contribution of thirty-two pounds was being withdrawn. Six days later, a general congregational meeting passed a resolution that the *parnass* and *adjunta* form themselves into a committee of the whole and undertake the building project, determining size and cost. The stone sitting on the south commons could be disposed of as the leaders desired (the stone was claimed as the congregation's property).

That ended the project. One month later, a request was received from sister congregation, K. K. Beth Elohim in Charleston, soliciting financial assistance for the purchase of land and the construction of Charleston's first synagogue. The *parnass* and *adjunta* appointed Emanuel De la Motta (later a leading figure at K. K. Beth Elohim) and Levy Abrahams to investigate and make a recommendation.[22] Eventually they proposed taking a general subscription from Savannah Jewry and to forward the proceeds to Charleston, which was done. The gentle rivalry that exists between the two southernmost Colonial congregations in more recent years violates the close relationship of the formative years. Savannah Jewish money helped to build the first synagogue of K.K. Beth Elohim. At a later period, when Savannah's synagogue was to be consecrated, the leaders turned to Charleston authorities for counsel. The interconnections in the past were so extensive that a good case could be presented for writing a single history encompassing both communities, at least until the War Between the States.

Who was this Abraham da Costa, this dreamer and aborter of dreams? The Sheftall "diary" informs us that he was among the earliest to settle in Savannah after the Revolution in 1783.[23] He was one of the founders of K.K. Beth Elohim in Charleston in 1749, and may have been a brother of its first *hazzan*, Isaac da Costa. He subsequently opened a store in Georgetown that burned in 1778, when he returned to Charleston as a retailer.[24] During the British occupation, he was the owner of the *Irish Coffee House*.[25] Apparently he left Savannah in 1785 and returned by 1791 when the *Temple Minute Books* indicate he became a member of the congregation. A man of exceptional mercantile skill, he accumulated substance sufficient to be considered a leading Savannah entrepreneur.

The assumption may be made that his genius for business was matched by mental instability. The Sheftall "diary" (July 16, 1786) documents his suicide in colorful language:

> Abraham de Costa came to live here and he went away and returned and cut his throat.

Dreams once dreamed are not readily dislodged. The congregation, frustrated by the da Costa dispute, empowered another da Costa, Joseph, to engage in fund-raising during a trip to the West Indies. Too many other Colonial synagogues had been to that till, and it was now dry.[26]

Economic realities forced the leadership to defer the quest for a "snogo" of their own.[27] Attention shifted to maintaining the rented building and protecting the lots that were the property of the congregation. Several are identified in the minutes: one on the west commons where the "stones" paid for by Mr. da Costa were dumped; the other was Lot 23 in Franklin Ward, close to Ellis or Market Square. In *A History of the City Government of Savannah, Georgia From 1790-1901*, Mayor Thomas Gamble, Jr., documents that a lot valued at seventy pounds was presented to the Hebrew Congregation in the east commons (date unknown), and that it was exchanged in 1795 for the Franklin Ward lot (23), the difference in value being eighty pounds.[28] The *parnass* and *adjunta* were crushed by this additional debt, and a petition to City Council was presented by Mordecai Sheftall to secure said lot from default. Fortunately, the "Baptist Society" (now First Baptist Church) had received from city government a parcel of land in Franklin Ward prior to this time, in exchange for a parcel on the east commons that was valued at fifty pounds. Citing this as precedent, the board asked for equity. An eighty pound debt on land worth fifty pounds required correction.[29] (The *Temple Minute Books* confirm the existence of the First Baptist Church as a functioning institution in 1795, several years before the church's existing records document its founding.)

President Sheftall acquired 132 signatures of "respectable citizens of Savannah," and on August 4, 1795, the petition was disposed of in a manner favorable to Savannah Jewry.[30] The Franklin Ward property turned out to be critical in the congregation's effort to survive during hard times and to build the first synagogue in Georgia in more prosperous times.

A souring of the local economy stalled attempts to erect an edifice. The *parnass* and *adjunta* used every technique available to increase resources. Gifts were solicited for religious honors.[31] Often those whose names were drawn for "honors" found an excuse for not responding in the positive, though fines could be levied.[32] Minimum contributions were established in August of 1793. *Yehidim* (male members) were asked for no less than three pounds, and for the first time the category of "none [sic] yehid" was introduced, with a requirement of thirty shillings payment at the least. Mordecai and Levi Sheftall were called upon to serve as a committee to visit subscribers and "all such persons who are in any wise indebted to this congregation," because the debt was mounting and the synagogue landlord was making threats.[33] What subscription-taking could not achieve, an act of fate might. The August 17, 1795, minutes record,

> that the Gabay [treasurer] do purchase three *lottery tickets* in the poor house and seamen's hospital lottery of this city for this congregation. (Italics added.)

The November 26, 1796, fire that swept Savannah and "burnt the greater part of it" spelled disaster for the congregation's finances.[34] The rhythm of frequent meetings by the *adjunta* was interrupted and none occurred between October 9, 1796, and August 6, 1797. Losses were substantial and the majority of citizens had to rebuild from scratch. That monstrous conflagration charred the dream of a Jewish House of Worship in Savannah for nearly a quarter century.

A congregation without the wherewithal to survive relies on whatever assets are left to it to safeguard the future. The lot in Franklin Ward made the difference between being and non-being. The rented structure that had served as "snogo" was owned by the Morgan family, and relationships had not always been cordial prior to the fire. The lease commitment was for a limited period—in 1792, one year certain, two years optional. Two years later, demands were coming from the lessors, the leadership having

> received threats from Mr. Morgan, the landlord, that if he was not paid he would take such steps as would procure him his money immediately.[35]

Unfortunately, when the 1796 disaster burned down much of the town, the house belonging to the treasurer was totally destroyed, and with it all the account books of the congregation.[36] Samuel Mordecai and Levy Abrahams were chosen a committee of two "to ascertain as best they could what back rent is due to the owner of the synagogue." All former treasurers were to provide information and draw up affidavits, acceptable under law, to protect the interests of the membership. After exhaustive examination of all available information, the amount owing to "Miss Morgan" was established as "between sixty and seventy pounds back rent."[37] How to meet such a debt? The *parnass* and *adjunta* formally capitulated the dream of a building and took to leasing Lot 23 as the only way out. There is a sadness reflected in the unembellished statement of the minutes of August, 1797: the dream was formally punctured. After acknowledging the debt to the Morgan family, the text continued:

> Wheras the congregation has a lott [sic] given them by the Corporation of Savannah in Franklin Ward in this City, *and it not being in their power to build at the present,* resolved that the said Lott [sic] of land be leased for the term of Seven Years . . . . (Italics added.)

A further reflection of the desperate plight at this low moment in the congregation's history is recorded in the minutes of the same meeting. The burial society was petitioned for a loan of one hundred dollars on the best terms of interest. The fourteenth rule of the Charter, relating to admission as a *yehid* to the congregation, was repealed. That rule required a complex procedure for joining, including a letter of introduction, a majority vote by the general congregation, dues of one guinea, and a six months' residency clause. The residency requirement was changed to the expectation of remaining in the state a total of six months; no voting procedure was required; one only had to affirm one was a Jew and keep the Sabbath and Holy Days; and most importantly, one had to be prepared to pay twelve dollars per annum. As the ultimate sign of the congregation's plight, the notorious perpetrators of "violence" against Jewish law, Samuel Benedix and Moses Simons, were excused from the penalties imposed upon them, and restored to full status. (Story below.)

Astute action on all fronts enabled the situation to be redeemed. The burial society provided the funds and received the ground rent on Lot 23 until all interest and principal were recouped, at which time the lease was turned back to the board. A seven year lease was all that was initially contemplated for the lot, but Mr. Isaac Fell made an offer of one hundred dollars per annum for *ten* years.[38] It was seized, gratefully.

In Jewish life, little proceeds without unforeseen obstacles. *Parnass* Mordecai Sheftall, during whose administration the negotiations for the lease with Mr. Fell began, was summoned to his higher reward, and no *parnass* could be found to replace him. Who then could sign the Fell contract officially? Mordecai's son, attorney Sheftall Sheftall, questioned the legalities.

The board sought the legal opinion of the distinguished lawyer, Joseph Clay, Jr., who confirmed Sheftall Sheftall's reasoning.[39] The deal finally went through after some legal maneuvering, ending K. K. "Mickva" Israel's greatest challenge since the day of its chartering. For ten years minimum, the possibility of erecting a synagogue was in abeyance, and the task of restoring fiscal health became the overriding challenge.

THE RELIGIOUS LIFE

Savannah in the post-Revolutionary period was the southernmost urban settlement in the American Nation. Here President Washington journeyed on his famed tour in 1795. It was the equivalent to a coast to coast Presidential junket today. He never proceeded south of Savannah. This town abutted the frontier, an outpost of civilization surrounded by forest, native-Americans, and adventurers. In such a milieu one would hardly expect a Jewish congregation to function in manner sophisticated. Yet, complex and diverse were the religious routines that marked the spiritual life of K.K. "Mickva" Israel.

RELIGIOUS FUNCTIONARIES

A modern congregation, following the Sephardic Orthodox (Portuguese) mode, would require a variety of functionaries to carry forth worship routines: a rabbi or *hazzan* to lead the service; a *shammash* to administrate and handle the accoutrements necessary for prayer and religious observance, and to be responsible for the building and properties; and a *mohel/ shochet* to circumcise male children, as well as to arrange for kosher meat. Other religious "offices" could be delegated to the laity: the *baal tekiah* [the individual who sounds the *shofar* (ram's horn) at *Rosh Hashanah* and *Yom Kippur* services]; the *hatanim* (those who read the blessings over the Torah at the *Simchat Torah* Festival)—both the *hatan Torah* and the *hatan Biray-sheet* (the first recites the prayers over the Deuteronomy passage, and the second, the prayers preceding the Genesis passage); and the *gabay* (the individual who assigns honors to congregational members who pledge free-will offerings in return). The minutes of "Mickva" Israel as well as the Sheftall "manuscripts" indicate that every one of these functionaries was playing his part in the "snogo" (synagogue) of K. K. "Mickva" Israel.

In 1798, Emanuel De la Motta was mentioned as the *hazzan* and in 1806, Levy Abraham.[40] Without referring by name to any individual, the Temple *Minute Books* record lay *hazzanim* carrying forth responsibilities as volunteers.[41] The *hazzan* conducted worship, performed weddings and sometimes circumcisions (entry, June 21, 1807, in the Sheftall "diary" indicates Emanuel De la Motta did so, though he was not *hazzan* at this time), offered *escavot* (memorial prayers on Yom Kippur) for those who requested same and *hasimon tov* ("goodly signs" or petitions of Divine favor) for those who extended themselves through acts of generosity or service to the congregation.[42] Under Dr. Jacob De la Motta (Emanuel's son), the dignity and power of the spiritual office advanced, preparatory to the election of the first professional "rabbi" of the congregation. The minute books do not identify any of the elected leaders who acted as *hazzanim*, though one can be assured that "readers" were found in their number (both Levy Abraham and Emanuel De la Motta served as *adjuntamen*).

The *shammash* has occasionally been viewed in Jewish literature as a quasi-comical figure, more victim than mover or shaker. Being the only paid functionary of K.K.M.I. in the 1790's, he at least could take comfort in the monetary rewards of the post, though lavish they were not. (The October 15, 1797, minutes stipulate the grand sum of twenty-two dollars per year was to be reserved for the *shammash*).[43] The misadventures of one sexton, Isaac Attais, provide humorous diversion in the midst of heavy history.[44] It happened that on the second day of *Rosh Hashanah*, 1792, young Levi Sheftall, Jr., son of the famed author of the letter to President Washington, did "offend Mr. Attais . . . and do him insult and injury." All this happened in the yard of the synagogue, implying the lad should have been making penance inside. Two other boys were witnesses to the scene: Isaac Minis, son of Philip, first president of "Mickva" Israel, and A. Canter. Apparently, after a summons was issued to appear before the *adjunta*, Father (Levi) Sheftall promised to "correct" his son. The *adjunta*, in effect believing that boys will be boys, accepted the parental promise as sufficient "compensation." Three months later, "Shaumaz" Attais was on the carpet, on complaint that "[he] has not heretofore done his duty." Uncle of Levi, Jr., Mordecai Sheftall, was given power to discharge him if the negligence continued.

This same Attais figured prominently in a *halachic* (legal) struggle of the congregation, when his child by his non-Jewish wife perished, and the question of burial in the Jewish cemetery was raised. (Story below.)

The shift from Jewish *shammash* to black caretaker, which was completed by the War Between the States, was presaged when Levi Sheftall offered to provide "a negro to attend during the Holidays. . . ."[45]

The *hatan Torah* functioned once a year at *Simchat Torah* ("Rejoicing over the Torah"). The *hatan Torah* was called to the Scroll to read the blessing before the last section of Deuteronomy was chanted. His co-partner in the enterprise of blessing, the *hatan B'raysheet*, said the required prayer before Genesis Chapter One was duly read from the Sacred Parchment. The technique for choosing these lay functionaries was to draw names by lot. For the religious privilege one was expected to swell the congregation's coffers. One could decline the honor, but the rules of the synagogue required that a fine be paid. Year after year the minute books record the identical procedure, with many instances of nay-saying. A future historian might chart the economic conditions among Savannah Jews by plotting the yeas and nays, by year. The year 1801 was a particularly bad one for assigning honors. When the *hatanim Torah* were drawn, Abraham DeLyon and the *parnass* himself, Levi Sheftall, were the "winners," and both refused and were fined. A second drawing turned up David Leion and Dr. Moses

Sheftall. Leion refused, even though that left no voting members (*yehidim*) to do the honors. Gallantly, Levi Sheftall who had turned it down once, was "agreeable to serve."[46] In 1803, the story was repeated. Goodman Mordecai, "the chosen," declined, and Mr. John Jones was given the opportunity. John Jones, a mysterious figure whose Jewish origins remain suspect, declined on grounds it would be out of his power to serve.[47] Sheftall Sheftall saved the day. But from that time on, the assignment by lots to the Torah functionaries ceased. One assumes the president simply made the selection of fit candidates and no gifts were expected in return.

The saga of a *hatan Torah*, who became the founding father of one of America's most influential Jewish communities, needs to be told at this juncture. Isaac Polock was his name. The Sheftall "diary" mentions his arrival in Savannah in 1783, as one of the first Jews to take up residency after the war.[48] In 1793, Mr. Polock received a sharp letter from the *parnass*, Mordecai Sheftall, telling him that he had violated the "laws of God and the rules of this congregation" by having his business open on the Sabbath.[49] Within two days, Mr. Polock responded in writing with this explanation: a consignment of goods was shipped to him from Charleston, and the captain of the ship had them delivered to his home on the Sabbath without his permission and "he ordered his clark [sic] to store them." To the *adjunta* this seemed a legitimate excuse, so no penalty was imposed. That very year at the September 1st meeting, Isaac Polock was chosen one of the *hatanim*. A second time, the honor of being *hatan Torah* was accorded him by lot (on August 18, 1794). According to the October 3, 1794, minutes,

> the Parnass informed the Adjuncta that he was yesterday informed that Mr. Isaac Polock who was drawn hotton [sic] Torah would not be in town, for that he was going northward . . . .

In that comment is hidden a significant historical event. This self-same Isaac Polock wended his way to Washington, D.C., and was the founder of the Jewish community of our Nation's capital. Quoting Postal and Koppman,

> Polock was well-known in the city's business and social life. On a large land parcel on Pennsylvania Avenue he built six large brick houses, one of which still stands.[50]

Among the distinguished citizens to rent from him was the first Secretary of the Navy. A second building was occupied by the Department of State. Dolly and James Madison were tenants in the third building, while Madison was serving as Secretary of State. Real estate and building were Polock's game, and apparently the success denied him in the Port City pursued him to his new place of settlement on the Potomac.

THE *Baal Tekiah*

The distinguished few who served the congregation in the high and holy work of trumpeting the *shofar* during the Solemn Days of Awe were listed in the records of the congregation. To perform this *mitzvah,* all were eager, no refusals being recorded. A gift offering was not asked of the *"shofar* blowers," which may account for the unblemished record.

In 1790, David Cardozo, the veteran of the American Revolution was "appointed battakea [*sic*]."[51] His successor, Abraham Jacobs, was selected on September 12, 1795, reconfirmed the following September, and replaced by David Leion on August 26, 1798. From that day to this, there have emerged from the congregation individuals in each generation who have accepted the *mitzvah* of sounding blasts on the ram's horn on *Rosh Hashanah.* This tradition of Colonial derivation still retains power.

THE *Shochet*

It is clear from Rev. Bolzius' description of Jewish life among the German Jews in the late 1730's (see Chapter One) that kosher meat was consumed exclusively. No ritual slaughterer being present, one assumes that some lay people knew the technique. The only mention of a *shochet* prior to the third decade of the 1800's appeared in the accounting of the annual meeting of 1817, during which $150 was appropriated for hiring a "chochet" [*sic*]. The job did not have tenure. At the following annual meeting the congregants rescinded the motion.

LAY GOVERNANCE

The Charter of K. K. "Mickva" Israel called for a governing board made up of a *parnass* (president) and six *adjuntamen* (board members) all duly elected by the voting members (*yehidim*) at the annual meeting. Of the six *adjuntamen,* all of whom had to be over the age of twenty-one years, one was elected by the *yehidim* as *gabay* (treasurer). In time a third governing official, a secretary, emerged to play a major role in preserving the historical records.

The president could convene regular and special meetings, distribute charity monies to the limit of twenty shillings, was to be notified of life cycle events so that he might instruct the *hazzan* as to his responsibility, fine an individual who behaved in an unruly manner in the synagogue, deny honors to those who had refused them in the past, and in general was to function as the executive officer of the congregation. The minute books offer clear testimony to the power of the *parnass* to define priorities and influence the decisions of the congregation. Both Mordecai Sheftall and Dr. Moses Sheftall, his son, were particularly adroit at moving the congregation forward, both in terms of internal organization and external building programs.

The *gabay* was second to the president, responsible for keeping the books, collecting the offerings, and rendering accounts annually to the members. Fines were established for failure to handle the task correctly. In time, other responsibilities accrued to the treasurer's office.[52] In October,

1796, the preparation of the *sukkah* (booth for the Festival of Tabernacles) was reposed in him, in consideration of the fact that he controlled the purse. By 1798 (October 10th), the *gabay*'s duties included calling upon each member individually and seeking the payment of debts owing to the congregation. The August 15, 1814, annual meeting was distinguished by heated competition for the treasurer's job, pitting the incumbent Samuel Mordecai against hopeful Isaac Russell. By the actual count of "ones" in the minute book, Russell prevailed, nine votes to six votes. At the 1815 annual meeting, Samuel Mordecai was instructed to present "a gen'l [general] statement of his accounts during the time of being in office." By August of 1816, when the accounts were presented before the *yehidim*, a committee of two was appointed to scrutinize them and report back. The fiscal health of K.K. "Mickva" Israel was then sound, and the treasury had to be safeguarded. Along with dues, rentals from property were coming in, and the hope of constructing a building was once again embraced.

The secretary's office was mentioned in rule 11 of the Charter, but the manner of selection was not defined. Through a process of evolution, the secretary came to be chosen in the same manner as the *gabay*. The minute books bear witness to the refined penmanship of those who functioned in this essential role, and to their skill in distilling complex arguments into concise summations. For some spelling was a lost art, but considering the debt historians owe to these laymen, that flaw seems a trifle. In 1818, an annual stipend was awarded to Secretary A. I. DeLyon, and for four years he drew a salary.[53] What the congregation giveth, it can also take away. Future secretaries found no bonuses awaiting them for a job well done. As a consequence, it should not surprise us to read that some scribes did not handle their duties with diligence. The August 15, 1817, minutes inform us that a motion was passed

> that the secretary elect be allowed twenty five dollars *for bringing up the back minutes* of the congregation. (Italics added.)

Structurally, the synagogue government consisted of three executive officers and the *adjuntamen*. The rest of the people were *yehidim* (congregants). A *yehid* had a fiscal responsibility to sustain the congregation and, by so doing, he could vote and, if elected, hold office. Originally, the Charter did not conceive of any role for Jews who chose not to be members. Economic necessity soon led to a different vision. In the May 9, 1793, minutes, a minimum fee of thirty shillings was set for "non yehids." In addition, they were expected to make yearly offerings (one assumes for the High Holy Days). *Yehidim* were required to sign the rule book of the congregation. The most impressive section of the *Mickva Israel Minute Book, Volume One,* is that list of signatures.

The attempt to provide a system by which the rules of the congregation could operate occupied the energies of the *parnass* and *adjunta* through the last decade of the eighteenth century and the opening period of the 1800's. Congregation building paralleled Nation building. K. K. "Mickva" Israel was a microcosm of the processes at work in the formation of democratic government under an untested constitution.

The detailed nature of that process is reflected in the careful attention given to institutional arrangements, especially the assignment of pews. The September 1, 1793, minutes list the subscribers with prescribed pew seats. Of the twenty-nine benches, twenty-five were occupied by males. The last four rows on one side were unlisted, the assumption being that the women sat in them. Here is a copy of the first pew chart in the history of the congregation, establishing a tradition:

1. Mordecai Sheftall	15.	Levi Sheftall, Jr.
2. Ralph Depass	16.	David Polock
3. Samuel Mordecai	17.	Abraham Canter
4. Israel Delieben	18.	Isaac Minis
5. Abraham Jacobs	19.	Isaac Abraham
6. Isaac Polock	20.	Benjamin Sheftall, Jr.
7. Abraham D. Abraham	21.	Moses Sheftall
8. David Brandon	22.	Sheftall Sheftall
9. Benjamin Joel (Jewel)	23.	Levy Abrahams
10. Isaac Attais	24.	David Leon (Leion)
11. No Listing	25.	Abraham DeLyon
12. No Listing	26.	E. De la Motta
13. No Listing	27.	David Cardozo
14. No Listing	28.	Joseph Abrahams
	29.	Levi Sheftall

The listing is followed by a motion assigning Mrs. Abigail Polock to the seat of the late Mrs. Henry, and Mrs. Delieben to the seat formerly belonging to Mrs. Cardozo. One imagines a *mechitza* (partition separating men from women) being part of this rented building. Clearly, fathers and sons did not sit together (notice Mordecai in seat 1, Moses in seat 21, and Sheftall in seat 22). The possibility exists that seats 1 and 29 were opposite each other, putting the two Sheftall half brothers side by side, and the mothers closer to the children.

Tendencies in contemporary Jewish life have antecedents in Colonial times. At the first annual meeting of the congregation in August of 1791, there arose the question of who was entitled to a particular pew. Mrs. Polock, it was claimed, had the one due by right to Mrs. Cardozo. The latter had priority by virtue of being the eldest married woman among the congregants. The issue was resolved temporarily by assigning Mrs. Polock to Mrs. Cardozo's seat and letting Mrs. Cardozo reign over the "senior" pew. The festering wounds of that confrontation surfaced in August of 1793, when Cushman Polock refused to be a contributor until

this Adjuncta will do away their former Minutes with respect of Mrs.
Polock's seat and restore her to her seat which is her right . . .

Constitutions and rules of governance were applied easily to most human
situations. Occasionally, circumstances necessitated interpretation to insure
equity. The leadership of K.K. "Mickva" Israel was blessed with sagacity.
Three instances are singled out for examination. Unreported in published
Jewish histories, they provide insight into the skillful application of charter
law to life experience.

On August 17, 1795, Abraham DeLyon Abrahams found himself
designated the *hatan Torah* by lot. Testing the resolve of the *adjunta*, he
accepted the honor but regretted to inform the body that he was not a
contributor. How could a non-*yehid* be given such an honor? And how
could he be fined for rejecting the honor when he was ready to accept it?
A letter was dispatched to Mr. Abrahams informing him that he was indeed
a *yehid* of the congregation and therefore had to be a contributor. To convince him that he had best comply, the resolution passed in August of 1793
by the *adjunta* stated:

> resolved that the secretary do give notice in writing that such of
> yehidim who hitherto have refused to subscribe to the support of the
> synagogue, that if they do not subscribe to the same . . . that they shall
> not be eligible to hold any honors in the synagogue, be deprived of
> a permanent seat in the same and that the right of voting be suspend-
> ed until they comply.

A new situation was met with an old answer. Precedence was found, and
the threat of the resolution was understood.

The second incident is of consequence because it deals with an issue of
Jewish law and provides background for an unusual ritual act. According
to the Torah, if a man dies without male issue, a surviving brother is expected to marry the widow. She must not marry another, unless a ritual by
which he repudiates his claim is performed. (This ritual of repudiation is
called *chalitza*.) On May 9, 1793, the *adjunta* of "Mickva" Israel was given
a thorny problem to resolve. Mr. Israel Delieben made application to the
parnass requesting the attendance of the *hazzan* at his marriage to Mrs.
Hart, a widow. Mordecai Sheftall as president had reservations about the
situation. No children had blessed the Hart home. A brother was known
to survive, but he had refused to give *chalitza*. The lack of ceremonial did
not abort the marriage, because it was confirmed that the brother of the
deceased Mr. Hart had already married the sister of the prospective Mrs.
Delieben, making null and void the requirement for *chalitza*. Unanimously, the *adjunta* gave permission that "the intended bride be intitled
[*sic*] to the usual honors on such occasions."

A year earlier, a *chalitza* ceremony involving Savannah Jews had occurred in Philadelphia. In 1792, Elkaleh (Nelly) Bush was preparing to

marry the famed son of Mordecai and Francis Hart Sheftall, Dr. Moses. The
young man was a student of the eminent Dr. Benjamin Rush, signatory to
the Declaration of Independence and close associate of Thomas Jefferson.
To forestall any possibility of a claim upon her by Sheftall Sheftall, Moses'
brother, the ceremony of *chalitzah* was performed prior to the wedding,
rather than after her husband's demise. The leviration consisted of removing
the ceremonial shoe from Sheftall's foot, after which he declared that he
would provide formal *chalitza* three months after his brother's passing.[54]
The shoe remains a treasured artifact of the Philadelphia congregation,
K. K. Mikveh Israel. Mordecai Sheftall valued this ritual, hence was aware
of its implications when Mr. Delieben and Mrs. Hart made application.

The third incident tested the capacities of the leaders and congregation
by pitting an issue of consequence under Jewish law against the natural
compassion that flows to one's fellow Jew in an hour of anguish. The former
shammash, Isaac Attais, came to Mordecai Sheftall to seek his help in a
tragic circumstance. His son had just passed away, and Attais requested a
Jewish burial. Although the lad was circumcised, his mother was not of the
faith. Question—Should the child's religious identity depend upon his
mother's affiliation or had he been ushered into the Jewish fold through
the "Covenant of the Flesh?" The aforementioned Mr. Delieben was well-
versed in Jewish law, and the *parnass* consulted him. Before the *adjunta* he
voiced his view:

> Altho the child was circumcised on the 8th day yet having been
> borne of a Christian woman and not undergoing the ceremony of
> *tabelah* (ritual immersion) before its death, it could not be con-
> sidered a Jew . . .[55]

The *adjunta* proceeded to vote: Mordecai Sheftall, Emanuel De la Motta
and Sheftall Sheftall for burial; Levi Sheftall, David Cardozo and Benjamin
Sheftall, Jr., against. The full congregation had to be assembled to make
the ultimate decision. Nine to four, it voted against.

Two Who Rebelled

The American Revolution was fought for fundamental freedoms, among
them the freedom of religious association. The earliest activity of the
congregation was to create an institution with rules and regulations. Each
could *not* do what was right in his own eyes, if a unified community was to
evolve. But there were some in the congregation who cherished individual
liberty and sought to engage in the observance of the faith in a manner that
displeased the leadership of K.K. (*Kahal Kadosh*, the Holy Congregation)
"Mickva Israel. The central actors are Samuel Benedix and Moses Simons.

On October 2, 1791, Samuel Benedix was cited for acting contrary to
the law of God and the rules of the congregation by engaging in commerce
both days of *Rosh Hashanah* and on the Sabbath. The secretary delivered
the message to him, requiring him to report to the president on a given day.

On said day, the president waited an hour and a half for the offender, but to no avail. So the twelfth rule, suspending all honors, was invoked against him.[56] This was but the beginning of his religious rebellion.

The zenith was reached in 1795. On September 20th, it was reported to the *parnass* that Samuel Benedix and Moses Simons had spent the second day of *Rosh Hashanah* in the Benedix home. It was further reported that before breakfast, a conch shell was produced, and the traditional tunes normally sounded on the ram's horn were blown on the *terafah* (non-kosher) shell. Having performed the essential requirement of the day, the rebels "repaired to their morning meal." The board's shock over this incident is reflected in Sheftall's request

> that it is incumbant [*sic*] on this adjunctas, to take some notice of these (?) behaviors, so that others may be deterred from behaving in so irreligious a manner in future.[57]

The next evening a meeting was called, and the two offenders were ordered to appear along with Mr. Reuben Rainor, Mr. Abraham Hart, and Master Jonathan Canter. Both Benedix and Simons attended. Simons confessed to evrything, and asserted his independence by stating that he

> would do it again and that this Adjuncta had no jurisdiction over him that he was no congregator.

Benedix took a different tact. He would not say a word until he knew who had informed on him. To that Master Jonathan Canter declared that Benedix had called him into his home and that he had heard Mr. Benedix say *tekiah* (the word declared before sounding the *shofar*) and had seen Mr. Simons blow the conch. After which Benedix told Simons to go home and have breakfast since he had listened to the *shofar* blast. Abraham Hart refused to betray a gentleman's honor by telling what happened in the house, but apparently he had confided in Levi Sheftall who furthered the story by adding a few details. The conch shell, according to Levi, had feathers in it, and was covered over with a clean handkerchief, with two Hebrew books either on the conch or under it. In elaborate detail, Levi related how the required prayers were read, and all sounds customarily trumpeted on the *shofar* were blown, and then off to breakfast the two went. In a bold move, Sheftall called on Hart to deny the truth of his story, which he did not. Samuel Benedix finally spoke up and declared that he was already under penalty of the congregation, that he was not a congregator, and that "they might do what they pleased."

Such defiance required a harsh decree:

> that neither of said persons shall be allowed to be buried within the walls of the beshayom [*Bet Hayyim*, cemetery] of this congregation untill [*sic*] they make such concessions as the parnass and adjunta shall think proper.

Events have a way of altering what seems to be a final resolution of the
issue. The later "delicacy" of the financial condition of K. K. "Mickva"
Israel resulted in the following resolution by its *adjuntamen* on August 21,
1799:

> That all pains and penalties inflicted on Samuel Benedix and Moses
> Simons heretofore be repealed.

Savannah has known other expressions of the quest for diversity in religious expression. The famed "tolling of the bells" incident at Independent
Presbyterian Church is of a similar genre.[59]

CYCLES AND CIRCLES

From the minutes and from the Sheftall "manuscripts," it is possible to
reconstruct the character of Jewish religious observance in the initial phase
of congregation building. The details are sketchy but a general picture
emerges.

The Jewish calendar year was marked by the same heightened activity at
the Season of Penitence that is characteristic of Jewish life today. *"Ros-
hanah"* (*Rosh Hashanah*) was observed for two days, and *"Kipur"* (*Yom Kippur*) commanded a place of supreme reverence. Two practices characteristic
of the Portuguese *Minhag* (rite) were central to the Atonement worship. A
"basimontob" (a petition beseeching Divine favor upon an individual or
group) was characteristically pronounced by the *hazzan*. The beneficiaries
were: (a) always the president and members of the *Meshivat Nefesh*
(the Burial Society), and (b) those who bestowed valuable gifts upon
the congregation. Abraham Moses of Charleston presented a beautiful
shofar to K.K. "Mickva" Israel, and on *"Kipur"* eve he was mentioned in
the community's prayers.[60] Similarly, Joseph Davis donated "two grandoles"
(ornamental branched candelabra, one assumes seven-branched *menorahs*)
in 1803, and Heavenly Grace was fervently beseeched for him.[61] On only one
occasion was a *"basimontob"* made for a living congregational president,
Mordecai Sheftall.[62]

A second prayer that distinguished the *"Kipur"* liturgy was the *escava*,
the Sephardic (Mediterranean) equivalent of *yizkor* (the memorial prayer).
The first president of the congregation, Philip Minis, was to be eternally
remembered, and after his death, Mordecai Sheftall.[63] On *"Kipur"* 1791,
for the first and only time, the name Moses Cohen was included in the *escava*.
The practice evolved that any who wished their departed to be mentioned
during the Memorial Service might present the *hazzan* with a list of names.[64]

Succot (the Festival of Tabernacles) did not always receive the attention
that its harvest-thanksgiving theme merited. In 1791, a good year for religious fervor, the *gabay* who had the responsibility for erecting the booth
was instructed to cooperate with Levi Sheftall "to build a tabernacle out of
board and scantling" (small pieces of lumber).[65] There were only a few in-

stances thereafter when any effort was made to observe the ancient custom of *sukkah* building. Evidence indicates that limited resources and the struggle for economic survival in a city plagued by fire, storms, and epidemics diverted energies.

Shabbat, the weekly holy day, was routinely observed and examples of citations to those who violated it have already been mentioned. *Shabbat "Biraysheet"* (the Sabbath when Genesis I is read in the synagogue) was cited in the minutes of October 7, 1798, and *Shabbat "Nachamu"* (the Sabbath after the ninth day of *Ab*) was likewise mentioned.[66]

Interestingly, there is no hint of Chanukkah, *Purim,* or even Passover. These festivals were far removed from the High Holy Day season when the synagogue functioned at a vigorous pace. Passover and Chanukkah especially were oriented to home and dining room table rather than to the House of Prayer.

The Sheftall "manuscripts" mention other holidays in the instance of a marriage, death, or birth occurring thereon, even demonstrating awareness of *"holamode"* (*chol hamoed*—the common days of the Festival, the first and last two days being sacred).[67] Passover is called *"pasco,"* a Sephardic name for the Paschal celebration. *Rosh Hodesh* (the New Moon) was known to Sheftall who was clearly sophisticated in matters of Hebrew calendaring.[68]

Jewish life flourished around the cycles of growth and change that mark the human pilgrimage. Thus far we have noted instances of circumcisions by lay functionaries, even by parents (Mordecai Sheftall circumcised his son Benjamin).[69] Marriages occurred with the blessings of a lay *hazzan.* The minute books reflected awareness of such an obscure ceremony as leviration (*chalitza*). Funeral ceremonies were likewise performed by the *hazzan,* permission of the *parnass* being a requirement, to be certain that the deceased was entitled to burial in the congregation's cemetery.

The fullness of Jewish life today existed in Colonial times, though the evidence indicates that observances of bar mitzvah, Passover, *Purim,* and Chanukkah were rarer than in 20th century Savannah.

CHAPTER FOUR

YEARS OF HARVEST

F rom the late 1790's into the first two decades of the 1800's, the attention of the leaders of K.K. "Mickva" Israel focused on the hope of possessing their own edifice. To accomplish the dream they required the funding that could come from a stable body of worshippers with stable leaders. The impact of events in the general community cannot be underestimated. Within a year after a Jewish contingent witnessed the dedication of Independent Presbyterian Church, the first synagogue in Georgia was erected.

ACHIEVING FISCAL SOUNDNESS

Before the leadership could concentrate energy and resources on returning to the first item on their agenda—building a synagogue—they had to relieve themselves of the financial burdens of the past. That included the cumulative debt to the Morgan family, a sum reported in the August 25, 1798, minutes as $244. The committee also owed $80 rental for the coming year. To meet this obligation every resource was tapped. The *gabay* was to visit each individual in arrears personally.[1] Another technique was to raise a separate subscription "independent of any offerings that may have been made in the synagogue."[2] To collect the subscription, others were involved besides the treasurer. A separate committee chosen by the *parnass* was to go knocking at the doors. By the annual meeting of 1804, announcement was made that at the next election all people must come "prepared to settle in some way their account." The year 1806 brought a new collections policy:

> All persons who may be indebted to this congregation not having paid at least ten percent on the amount of his account during the year and settle up the balance by note or otherwise at least ten days before the annual election shall not be entitled to a vote on that day, sickness or absence from the city excepted.[3]

Considering the purpose for all these maneuvers (increasing the treasury so a synagogue might be raised), one is astonished by the tightening of the membership rules in 1818.[4] This was two years before the building program commenced and every dollar counted. Nonetheless, the residency requirement was increased to two years; a period of six months was required between the time of application and the annual meeting; and a majority of the congregation had to vote favorably on the candidate at said meeting. Because Savannah was a port of entry, transients came and departed with great frequency. If the destiny of the congregation was not determined by those who were intending to stay, problems would result. The reality of the "gypsy" Jews was addressed in the Sheftall "diary."[5] In 1806, so many people were appearing and disappearing that the author was moved to write

> there is [sic] now 2 or 3 people which I have not put there [sic] names down as they are no residencers but are only birds of passage.

One year after the stringent clause was passed, it was repealed, and the original rule was reinstated.

Despite these efforts, the diverse fund-raising schemes were insufficient to underwrite a building program. The ways of Providence, in this instance, worked favorably for the Israelites of Savannah. Gilbert Fell, who had rented the Franklin Ward property for ten years, was prepared to give up the lease after three years had passed. Fell had constructed buildings on the leased property which he was willing to sell to the congregation for seven hundred dollars. On September 24, 1800, the board convened and invited those with keen business acumen, including Abraham and Isaac Minis, Isaac Benedix, Saul Simons, Abraham DeLyon, David Leion, and David Suares to join the deliberations and give counsel. The Fell proposal was manna from heaven, and action was quickly taken. A committee was to examine the buildings, and, if all was well, to seal the deal. Expecting a favorable outcome, the *parnass* was instructed to make application to the *Mishivat Nefesh* (burial society) for a loan of two hundred dollars. Again, that body saved the day. Two other measures were quickly instituted. First, the treasurer was to make an accounting that evening and collect the monies owing. The second action was that Dr. Moses Sheftall received authority to borrow whatever money was needed "from any person," using the future rents of the buildings as collateral. On October 2, 1800, the president informed the *adjuntamen* that, according to instructions, Levi Sheftall had purchased the buildings from Mr. Fell, and that the following individuals made contributions: the two Minis men—$25 each; Isaac Benedix—$20; Benjamin Sheftall and David Suares—$15; Jonas Elkin and Levi Sheftall—$10; and Mordecai Sheftall, Jr.—$5. That $125 total, added to the $200 borrowed and the $300.30 in the *gabay*'s account, with an extra $43.20 which he advanced (discounting $37.50 rents due from the building), made enough to cover the $700 purchase price, plus the $4 owing to Mr. Stites for drawing up the title. Within the month, the transaction was accomplished. This was the turning point that enabled the dreamers to get their synagogue erected. As the story unfolds, the buildings in Franklin Ward provided payment for the master builder and the materials required for constructing Georgia's first Jewish House of Prayer.

From 1800 to 1820, the congregation's fiscal concerns were collecting rents, paying off obligations, safeguarding the money during some very hard times, electing trustworthy *gabayyim*, and appointing committees to examine accounts.[6] As of August 19, 1816, the rents from the buildings were bringing in almost $289 per year, and the congregation was in the black by almost $230. The future looked secure.

LEADERSHIP

The power of a single individual to shape the destiny of a community is attested to in this period—by Dr. Moses Sheftall above all others. His skill was in defining priorities, involving the best people to carry forth the work, and establishing firm leadership. The *Temple Minute Books* document his performance as the visionary who inspired the building program. It was he who called the investors together when Mr. Fell was ready to sell the buildings in Franklin Ward. Cleverly, he involved those sophisticated in finance in the *adjunta's* deliberation (for the first time on record). They became the most generous givers. No one was more highly respected in Savannah than his uncle, Levi, so he turned to him for direct negotiations with Mr. Fell. The master stroke that demonstrated his role as a leader was executed at the annual meeting of 1816.[7] Before the meeting began, the doctor informed the *yehidim* present that he had to decline being a candidate for the high office of *parnass* (which he had held, off and on, for many years). An election took place and Doctor Sheftall was duly elected. Once again he affirmed his wish not to serve. Another ballot was counted, and again the same results. This time, seeing the respect and trust reposed in him, "he consented to serve." His stature in the congregation was then manifest to all, and he was in a position to make history.

Twelve years earlier, Dr. Sheftall had offended his people by an act of impatience and self-righteousness.[8] He had tendered his resignation as *parnass* of "Mickva" Israel. The strong language he used in his resignation letter has been preserved:

> Dr. Sir
> By my son you will receive the key of the synagogue and from this day forward I take this method of communicating to you and the Adjuncto my Resignation as Parnoss of this Congregation. I would observe that I do not decline being a yehid[;] to the contrary, I will do everything in my power to keep up the congregation. It will ever be my desire to attend public worship[.] [T]he motive that induces me to resign are [*sic*] that some members of the congregation think [it] proper to carry private resentment into the house of God[,] and as I deem such person[s] not worthy to be governed by any person of Respectability, I think it best to decline the appointment I hold in order that they may govern themselves.

With my best wishes for your personal prosperity as well as that of the congregation[,] beleave [*sic*] me [I remain] with sincere esteem and respect. Your Friend, [signed] Moses Sheftall.
[P.S.] You will plese [sic] lay this before the adjunto.

Doctor Sheftall was capable of writing powerful letters, as will be attested to in his letter to the Dancing Society. (See the section on anti-Semitic incidents.)

The "adjunto" ignored his communication, pretending it had never been written. At the next election, his name was not submitted for leadership. Four years had to pass before the congregation turned to him again. By 1816 the past was buried, and a strong president was ready to govern K.K. "Mickva" Israel.

THE BUILDING SYNDROME

When a congregation is preparing to invest resources in a permanent structure, a building fever surfaces that cannot be disguised. The *parnass* and *adjunta*, throughout the period of stabilizing finances, diverted dollars into repairing and restoring whatever property they had: namely, the cemetery, the rented synagogue, and the buildings on Lot 23 of Franklin Ward. A brief synopsis of these fixing up projects will document the energy that their dreams unleashed.

In 1800, Levi Sheftall and Levy Abrahams constituted a committee of two "to have the immediate repairs done to the synagogue that may be necessary."[9] Whatever amount was required was to be reimbursed by the treasurer. Three years later (September 4, 1803), the rented synagogue was reshingled and the front coated with fresh paint. Normally, the Morgan family would have had to bear the financial burden of fixing up a structure belonging to them, but not when a rhythm of building was in progress. Attention turned to the Hebrew Community Cemetery a year later. The gates of the burial grounds were totally "rotton," and its walls in need of repairs.[10] Unanimously, the *adjunta* voted to have a new gate "sheathed with iron" erected, and the walls "properly repaired." The *Mishivat Nefesh* (burial society) was not sent a bill as in the past. The funds were allocated from the congregation's treasury.

In 1804, attention turned to the five buildings then located on Lot 23, Franklin Ward. Rudimentary repairs were made including the sinking of a "privy."[11] Further rehabilitations, later authorized for this property, were of sufficient size to merit the appointment of a special committee, including the *gabay*, Isaac Russell, plus A. DeLyon and Isaac Cohen.[12] They were essential for the pivotal role which these structures played in building the first synagogue.

THE FINAL IMPETUS

At the annual meeting in 1817, the *yehidim* were informed that "the building now occupied by them as a synagogue was sold." K. K. "Mickva" Israel was without a place to gather for worship. The first plan was to put into order one of the buildings in Franklin Ward. At the least, the religious properties belonging to the congregation had to be protected from damage and loss. The *Sepher Torahs* (of ancient vintage), the *menorahs*, the books, the benches, and the *shofar*—all needed a home. The residence of a member was not acceptable, as memory of the fire of 1796 that destroyed records and documents in the possession of the *gabay,* was yet vivid. The buildings on Lot 23 were more substantial. The intent was *not* to conduct worship in these buildings, for the committee was instructed to "fix upon some place for the congregation to meet and for other purposes."[13] Where they "fixed upon" records do not tell. The following two annual meetings (1818 and 1819) occurred at "there [sic] place of meeting," with no other description. One might deduce that where the Building Committee met, David Leion's home, was "there [sic] place."[14] The argument is advanced that since Leion was neither president or officer but only a member of the *adjunta* and Building Committee, his home would be selected for assembling by the committee, only if it was of good size and hospitable to guests. Such a setting would make a worthy, *temporary* House of Prayer.

There was no question about whether or not to build. The only unresolved issue was when.

THE COMMITMENT TO BUILD

No minutes in the early record books of the congregation are more important than the minutes of August 17, 1819, and August 21, 1820. All the details of the building program and the consecration procedures for the cornerstone-laying and the building itself are succinctly recorded. The secretaries of both the Building Committee and the *adjunta* were aware that they were spokesmen for history and that an epochal event was about to unfold for the Jews of Georgia. Almost a century had passed since Jews claimed Savannah as their home; and the dream of many generations, a Jewish sanctuary, a symbol of the God of Israel on this sandy soil, was about to be fulfilled. The procrastination of the past gave way to an accelerated construction effort that went from nothing in August, 1819, to a proud edifice, ready for elaborate dedication rites on July 21, 1820 (note the significance of July, the month of great happenings for Savannah Jews, since the initial landing on July 11, 1733).

THE DAY OF DECISION

The Jewish community of Savannah must have been geared up for the 7th day of August, 1819. Annual meetings at the beginning of the decade attracted five *yehidim* (1812, 1813), seven (1810), and eight (1811). By

1814, fifteen were in attendance; the high being reached in 1817 when the rented synagogue was sold. The annual meeting of 1819 was among the largest, with fifteen members present for decision-making.

The dynamic at play at that annual meeting was fed by the dynamic taking place in the city. Savannah was booming. From 1810 to 1819, the population increased almost fifty percent.[15] In 1810, 5,215 individuals inhabited the Forest City; in 1820, 7,523 persons. There was excitement in the air because three months earlier (May 9, 1819), Independent Presbyterian Church was formally dedicated in impressive ceremonies, to which the Jewish community more than likely sent representatives. Dr. Henry Kollock, Independent's spiritual leader, cultivated friendship with Jewish people, attested to by the reserved space given them at his funeral cortege.[16] An incumbent President of the United States, James Monroe, was in the congregation, as the Presbyterian consecration rites were read.

The event must have impressed the Jewish leadership and helped to generate the new commitment to a building program. This is evident in the service for the dedication of the synagogue; there was some reliance upon what had happened at Independent Presbyterian Church, *resulting in the earliest Jewish ritual "reform" on the American continent.* That story will soon unfold.

Resolutions were presented to the fifteen who gathered for the annual meeting that fateful August day, 1819:

> Whereas it is deemed expedient in order to secure the possession of the lot granted by the Corporation of the City to the Hebrew Congregation and in conformity with the will of *some* of the congregators to have a suitable building erected on the said Lot as a place of public worship to which they may have *occasional resort* to offer up there [sic] prayers to the God of Israel[:] be it therefore *Resolved,* that a committee of four be appointed and invested with full power to contract with some *master builder* to erect as soon as practicable on the lot granted by the corporation, a Synagogue[,] and the *expence* [sic] *necessarily accruing be defrayed by a lease of the Houses[,] the property of the congregation[,]* for such term of years as shall by the committee be deemed sufficient to liquidate the demands made for such a building. (Italics added.)

The appointed Building Committee included A. DeLyon, D. Leion, Moses Sheftall, and Sheftall Sheftall. Later Dr. Jacob De la Motta, a man who was to attain immortality for his dedicatory address, was added to the committee as its secretary.

The lot on which the sanctuary was to be constructed was not previously owned by K. K. "Mickva" Israel. By grant of the City Corporation, sixteen days after the annual meeting, Council awarded Lot 55 (northwest corner of Drayton Street and Liberty Street), south commons, Brown Ward.[17] It was decided against building on *that land,* and on March 27, 1820, the City Corporation exchanged said lot for Lot 64, Brown Ward (corner of Whitaker Street and Perry Lane, one half block north of Liberty Street). Two half

blocks north was the lot on which First Baptist Church was later constructed (in 1833). The original synagogue was to have been situated in
Franklin Ward (Lot 23), in close proximity to the *first* First Baptist Church
structure. (Southern Baptists and Jews in Savannah had neighboring
sanctuaries until the last quarter of the nineteenth century.)

The awarding of the lot on March 27th permits us to estimate the time
required for the construction effort. The master builder had it completed in
107 days (the dedication was on July 21). Less than four months elapsed
between receiving the lot and nailing up the *mezuzah* (religious object
attached to the doorpost). Considering that the cornerstone was laid in place
on April 19th, the actual construction effort lasted ninety-five days.[18]

THE BUILDING COMMITTEE

The minutes of August 21, 1820, detail the committee's work, from over-
seeing the construction effort and negotiating with the master builder, to
planning the cornerstone consecration ritual and the synagogue dedication.
The Building Committee's minutes were faithfully kept and read to the
full congregation after the building had been solemnized to God's glory.

The first Building Committee meeting convened on March 15, at Mr.
David Leion's "dwelling." The action taken was two-fold. Dr. Jacob De la
Motta was appointed secretary. Several proposals were put to the body, the
one of Mr. Evans, "master builder being accepted." This Mr. Evans was
most probably John C. Evans, ship's carpenter, who was rescued at sea after
his ship sank.[19] The record of the transference of the buildings on Lot 23
in Franklin Ward, for the term of his contract, listed his full name. No other
John C. Evans with building skills can be found in the 1820 census or local
newspapers. Since two doctors, in joint practice, sat in on the committee
(Moses Sheftall and Jacob De la Motta), it is entirely possible that the water-
logged victim of a capsized vessel was brought to a Jewish physician's office,
thus making the initial contact. As far as existing records document, Mr.
Evans' career as a Savannah builder is limited to this one structure.

One month later (April 14th), plans were being readied for the laying
of the cornerstone (on the northeast corner), according to Masonic tradition.
The stone with the names of the Building Committee etched thereon and
the Hebrew month and year of dedication was commissioned. Emanuel
De la Motta of Charleston, one of the founders of the Supreme Council
of the Scottish Rite and father of Dr. Jacob, provided the form of
ceremony. The *Temple Minute Books* describe, in elaborate verbiage, everything that transpired at the "stone-laying." The members of the congregation who were Masons met at the Masonic Hall of the Grand Lodge.[20]
Non-Masons gathered nearby. After a ritual involving the cornerstone,
the procession formed. The Tyler led, followed by two deacons with
wands, and then the stone on a cushion, carried by the members of the
Building Committee. Next paraded two deacons, members of the Junior
Lodge in pairs, the treasurer, the secretary, the wardens, the past master,

the worship master, more deacons, the members of the other lodges besides
the Grand Lodge, and the members of the Mother Lodge in the rear.
Behind them marched the mayor, aldermen, and members of the congregation, two-by-two. The Masons, upon arriving at the hallowed spot, formed
a corridor through which dignitaries passed, after which they formed a
large circle. The required Masonic cornerstone examination was conducted,
and the Building Committee of five deposited the quoin in its ordained
position. A prayer in Hebrew and English was offered, an address followed,
and the Masonic sign terminated the ritual. With the stone in place, the
procession reversed, and returned whence it had come.[21]

It is assumed that, somewhere in the brief ceremony, the advice of
Emanuel De la Motta was heeded, and the local officials were introduced
and paid a compliment for so liberally donating the land.[22] According to
the text of the letter of appreciation sent to De la Motta from a member of
the Building Committee, Abraham DeLyon,

> The Masonic procession was very grand and it was attended by a
> large Concourse of Spectators of both sexes[.] [T]he day was fine and
> fair which added to the splendor of our heavenly undertaking.[23]

The event was so well received that the Charleston expert was invited to
attend the dedicatory rites in July. Any recommendations he had to suggest for that historic moment would be gratefully received.

Four days later, the Building Committee assembled again at Mr. Leion's
domicile. The business was three-fold: first, the *parnass* was requested to
send a letter of thanks to Mr. De la Motta of Charleston (the letter referred
to above); second, Mr. Isaac Russell, the treasurer, was to provide the
twenty-five dollar honorarium for the music that accompanied the processional and cornerstone-laying; and third, Dr. Jacob De la Motta was "requested to prepare suitable prayers and a discourse for the occasion of the
Consecration" of the building.[24]

The third meeting of the committee occured almost two months later.
The thrust of that session was to sketch out the details of the dedication. The
date agreed upon for the event was Friday afternoon, 10 *Av* 5580 (one day
after *Tisha B'av*, a fast day marking the destruction of the Jerusalem Temple
in 70 CE)—corresponding with the 21st day of July, 1820.[25] Appropriately,
it was *Shabbat Nachamu*, the Sabbath when the fortieth chapter
of Isaiah is the lesson from the Prophets. The words of comfort to the exiles
in Babylonia whose time of testing was at an end must have resonated in the
hearts of Savannah Jews who had waited so long for this time of hope and
elevation in their lives. The committee decided to extend invitations to "the
citizens" of Savannah, the mayor and aldermen, and the distinguished clergy
who would be favored with reserved seating. All these details parallel the
dedication of Independent Presbyterian Church. Whatever other details had
to be arranged, the committee empowered itself to accomplish, assigning to
David Leion and Dr. Moses Sheftall two vital responsibilities—negotiating

a room in the Free School for purposes of assembling the procession and procuring an *organ* for the occasion.

The final committee meeting occurred two days after the consecration ceremony, on July 23rd. Two motivations dictated the meeting—the preparation of a written record of the event for posterity in the *Temple Minute Books,* and the extension of thanks to all who merited recognition. Here is a reconstruction of what is recorded regarding the consecration on that Friday afternoon, close to sunset.

The entire congregation assembled in the lower room of the Free School. This institution, founded in 1816 to provide private instruction, gratis, to Savannah's children, was located on West Perry Street and Whitaker Street, across the lane from the north wall of the 1820 synagogue.[26] At exactly 5:00 p.m., the acting *hazzan,* Dr. Jacob De la Motta, led the processional, followed by David Leion and Dr. Moses Sheftall, carrying the two Torahs under a *chuppah* (canopy). Behind them marched the *parnass,* the *gabay,* and the congregation. When they arrived at the door, it was "thrown open" by Sheftall Sheftall. The service began; prayers were spoken; and Psalms carefully selected for the occasion were sung, accompanied by the *organ.*

Seven times the Torahs were carried around the central altar (the *tabah*), followed by a rousing address by Dr. Jacob De la Motta. A dedication is a time for reviewing the past. With these words, De la Motta summarized the essence of his address:

> . . . assembled as we are, to re-establish by commemoration, the Congregation of this remnant . . ., your expectation of a brief sketch of our History, and particularly as connection with a primeval residence in this City . . . shall be realized; and may I trust, it will not be un-interesting, as it will include the well known fact, that many Jews struggled, and sacrificed their dearest interest, for the independence of this country.

De la Motta rehearsed the facts for the first time in a public setting, stating that approximately twenty "respectable" families constituted the first Jews to come to Savannah on July 11, 1733, "corresponding with the 16th Tamus . . . that German Jews were among them"; that lots were assigned to them; "and certain tracts are still retained by the descendents [*sic*] of those who possessed the original grants."

The speaker noted their civil entitlements:

> The Jews stood on the same eminence with other sects, and by the privileges extended to them . . . they were bound by no common tie, save for the general weal. Thanks to the protectors of our liberties, here we still continue to dwell, and enjoy the same rights.

The community's periods of waxing and waning were defined, including specific mention of 1757 when the Jewish residents were

> gradually diminished to three or four families, branches of those posterity are within the sound of my voice.

Highlighted in the speech was the creation of the Union Society, whose founders were

> an Episcopalian, a Catholic and a Jew. From such a union of opposites in mode of worship, hence the name [Union Society][,] not uniformity evolved, but rather service to others, and devotion "to the best interest of humanity."

The concluding section of the speech reflected on the virtues of religious life, so that the Jewish inhabitants of Savannah might be worthy of "Divine Favor." Especially emphasized was the virtue of engaging in regular worship of God:

> Were we not influenced by religious zeal, a decent respect to the *custom of the community in which we live* should activate us to observe public worship [meaning, in Savannah, the tradition is to be pew occupiers, and Jews must not be the exception]. (Italics added.)

De la Motta called for fealty to worship on a higher level: "No stronger inducement" is there "than the imperious mandate . . . in our sacred Decalogue" to remember the Sabbath day, the day of rest. "Who can expect his soul to rest, who will not rest with his God?" The sermon ended with a hortatory flourish:

> May it [the Sabbath] hereafter be perpetually observed: and may it be among this remnant of Israel, as a holy convocation.[27]

It was a powerful speech. De la Motta's skill as an orator was well established as far north as New York City. Among those who preached eulogies at the final rites for Rev. Gershom Mendes Seixas, America's most honored Colonial rabbi, was this Savannah physician.[28]

The Building Committee requested of the eloquent preacher "the manuscript of the discourse for publication." The printed version was disseminated widely; copies were sent to two former Presidents, Thomas Jefferson and James Madison. Impressed by the tenor and the contents of the speech, they each returned a letter of thanks to the author in which each commented on the principle of religious freedom and the uniqueness of the form of governance which they played fundamental roles in shaping. These letters are noteworthy examples of the felicitous style and crystalline thought of both Jefferson and Madison. The texts are reproduced here without further comment. Only one other Jewish congregation can pride itself on having Presidential letters from three of the first four elected Chief Executives of the Nation—Shearith Israel of New York City.

THOMAS JEFFERSON'S LETTER

Th. Jefferson returns his thanks to Doct. DelaMotta for the eloquent discourse on the Consecration of the Synagogue of Savannah which he has been so kind as to send him. It excites in him the

gratifying reflection that his own country has been the first to prove
to the world two truths, the most salutary to human society, that man
can govern himself, and that religious freedom is the most effectual
anodyne against religious dissension, the maxim of civil government
being reversed in that of religion, where it's [sic] true form is "divided
we stand, united we fall." He is happy in the restoration, of the Jews
particularly, to their social rights, and hopes they will be seen taking
their seats on the benches of science, as preparatory to their doing
the same at the board of government. He salutes Dr. DelaMotta with
sentiments of great respect.

JAMES MADISON'S LETTER

Sir—I have received your letter of the 7th, inst. with the Discourse
delivered at the Consecration of the Hebrew Synagogue at Savannah,
for which you will please to accept my thanks.

The history of the Jews must for ever be interesting. The modern
part of it is at the same time so little generally known, that every
ray of light on the subject has its value.

Among the features peculiar to the political system of the U.
States is the perfect equality of rights which it secures to every religious sect. And it is particularly pleasing to observe in the good
citizenship of such as have been most distrusted and oppressed elsewhere, a happy illustration of the safety & success of this experiment
of a just & benignant policy. Equal laws protecting equal rights are
found as they ought to be presumed, the best guarantee of loyalty &
love of country; as well as best calculated to cherish that mutual
respect & good will among Citizens of every religious denomination,
which are necessary to social harmony and most favorable to the
advancement of truth. The account you give of the Jews of your
Congregation brings them fully within the scope of these observations.

I tender, Sir, my respects & good wishes

James Madison

AN ACT OF REFORM

The 1820 dedication ceremony marked the *first time in American
history that an organ was played in a Jewish House of Prayer*. The minutes
state,

Psalms where [sic] selected for [the] Occasion [and] sung accompanied
by an *organ*, during the seven times that the Sapharim where [sic]
carried around the Taba.[29] (Italics added.)

After the discourse by Dr. De la Motta, "the Evening Sabath [sic] Service
concluded." The organ was in the sanctuary on a *Shabbat*; that is clear. The
owner of the organ was Dr. Henry Kollock, minister of Independent Presbyterian Church and friend of many Jews. The organist and choir director
(Psalms were sung) was Mr. Mason, who received thanks from the congregation for "his polite services on the organ in aid of the dedication." Lowell
Mason served as music director of Independent Presbyterian Church from
1815 to 1817. He is well represented in modern church hymnals, and is
acknowledged as the father of modern hymnology.[30] "From Greenland's Icy
Mountains" is one of his better know compositions.

The beginning date of Reform Judaism in America is taken as 1824, when the Reformed Society of Israelites broke away from the mother congregation, K.K. Beth Elohim in Charleston. The introduction of the organ was one of the demands of the reformers. In 1840, after they had reunited with the mother congregation and a new synagogue was under construction, the inclusion of an organ became the center of a court battle and a new separation from the Charleston synagogue. And yet in 1820, this *temporary* reform occurred in Savannah, demonstrating that a distaste for the organ was not that strong in the Sephardic mode of worship, not strong enough, at least, to preclude instrumental music on or near *Shabbat.*

Unfathomable was the response of Dr. Jacob De la Motta to the use of the organ in the sanctuary. This distinguished physician, *hazzan,* and man of eloquence offered no resistance to Mr. Mason's playing during the dedication rites in Savannah in 1820. But after relocating to Charleston and attaching himself to K.K. Beth Elohim, he was a most vocal opponent of the reformers who requested that an organ be installed in the Hassell Street building. It was he who provided the leadership for the group that pulled out over this issue to form a new congregation, Sherith Israel.[31]

The *Temple Minute Books* clearly document the *central role of Dr. Moses Sheftall* in the building program. Dr. De la Motta's participation as secretary of the Building Committee, as *hazzan* and orator, and, perhaps, as the individual who made contact with the master builder assures him a prominent place in Savannah Jewish history. Isaac Leeser, reader of Philadelphia's K.K. Mikveh Israel and editor of *The Occident* (the first significant Jewish journal circulated among American Jews), in the October, 1843, issue of his publication wrote revisionary history. Leeser (who was no friend of the "reformers") in his account ignored Dr. Sheftall and credited De la Motta as the prime mover of Georgia's first synagogue. No doubt he was influenced by De la Motta's role in organizing the splinter congregation in Charleston to preserve Leeser's brand of Orthodoxy.

REDUCED TO ASHES

Dr. Moses Sheftall's call to the congregation to build a structure on August 17, 1819, embodied prophetic truth. The will of *some* of the congregants was to have "a suitable building erected . . . as a place of public worship." But the truth was manifest in the words that followed: "to which they may have *occasional* resort." (Italics added.) Indeed the resort was so occasional that the 1823 minutes record that the annual dues were reduced by half "as the synagogue is so seldom opened."[32] The simple wooden structure (of which no reproduction, plan, or artist renderings survive) stood all but deserted, save for the High Holy Days.

The decade of the 1820's that opened with such fervor closed with a tragic fire. Once the dedication was over, the congregation seemed to lose interest.[33] The managers of the institution carried on with sound fiscal policies and proper upkeep of the structures (the synagogue, the cemetery, and the buildings on Lot 23). In 1825, a fund-raising effort was announced (for the month of November) to underwrite the construction of a brick wall around the sanctuary.[34] No record exists of whether the intention was matched by action.

Four years later, the *parnass* reported an expense required to build steps up to the front door of the synagogue, an expense equal to the funds coming into the treasury annually (deducting yearly expenses).[35] The cost was five dollars, *hard* cash.

The most massive construction project of the latter part of the decade (1820-1830), and the most noteworthy, from the perspective of the history of the Hebrew Burial Grounds, was initiated in 1829. A new gate made of cast iron and *imported* by Amos Scudder was "erected in a workmanlike manner," and other repairs were made to the walls themselves (completed by the 1830 annual meeting).[36] The total cost was a substantial one hundred fifty dollars. Savannahians have a particular affinity for the Scudder name and tradition. Some of the fine historic buildings in town bear the Scudder impress, including "Scudder Row." Amos Scudder was the least famous of the Scudder master builders, but there are surviving examples of his handiwork, including 24-26 East Bryan Street, built in 1824 for Mrs. Ann Hamilton. The heavy iron gate that presently protects the Burial Grounds dates from 1829-1830.

The financial situation of the congregation was not sound during the early part of the decade, and the leaders did the best they could. To protect their investment in the synagogue, the *adjunta* did insure the building for three thousand dollars with a Charleston firm, which was reduced to fifteen hundred dollars in 1829.[37] The insuring company was "Etna" [*sic*] of Hartford, Connecticut, a company not unknown to contemporary Americans.

Once again, as in the past, Providence smiled benignly upon the *parnass* and *adjunta*. After six years of a ten year lease to Mr. Evans, the master builder of the synagogue, the buildings were returned to the congregation through his agent, Mr. Hopkins. Mr. Evans apparently was compelled to leave the community to settle elsewhere, and his attention passed from leasing the property on Lot 23 of Franklin Ward and receiving that income as payment for his materials and services in erecting the synagogue.[38] By the next year, rents were coming in at a noteworthy pace, and in 1828, the congregation had no debt and a little left over in the till. In 1829, enough was available again for the congregation to engage in games of chance. Ten to twelve dollars was sanctioned for the purchase of lottery tickets. Then fate struck a cruel blow.

THE FIRE

Congregation Mickve Israel has had three sanctuaries of its own in its 250 year history. Two were victims of major and disastrous fires, the 1820 building being totally lost in a conflagration.[39] It happened on December

4, 1829. The minutes report the event succinctly, reflecting little sense of loss:

> This day between the hours of 12 & 1 o'clock the new synagogue erected and dedicated in July 1820 was, unfortunately, consumed by fire by accident. The *Sepharim* and *Ark* was [sic] saved without injury together with the benches—tamid & etc.

The local newspaper offered little elaboration, save to add that the building was not frequented:

> The Hebrew Synagogue, on the south common was destroyed by fire yesterday morning. From the situation of the building and the state of the wind, which was fresh from the NE[,] no injury was sustained by neighboring houses. We understand that the building was insured. It had not been open for two months and the fire is supposed to have originated from a spark communicated accidentally to the roof. The books and robes were saved.[40]

It took almost a century to build that first building, and in an hour or so it was all gone. But the congregation was not left without blessings, midst the curse. The valuable ritual objects—the Torahs, the eternal light, the benches, etc.—were all rescued. The insurance payments provided a handsome nest egg for any future building endeavors, and the rents from the property in Franklin Ward offered encouragement for fiscal integrity. The future was not bleak at all.

THE PHOENIX RISES

The 1829 fire returned the congregation to its former homeless estate. Nine years had to pass before another—this time a more noteworthy—structure stood on the ruins of the mother synagogue. A painful lesson was learned. No more frame buildings would be constructed. Savannah was too prone to catastrophic fires. The next "Mickva" Israel would be protected with brick and mortar.

The issues that earlier dominated synagogue life again came into focus—safeguarding and raising monies for the building, protecting the valuables (the Torahs, the benches, the *tamid*, the ark, etc.), attending to the lot and buildings in Franklin Ward which provided operating income, and making repairs to whatever needed repairing. The old leadership continued to lead wisely, Dr. Moses Sheftall primarily. Young and vigorous personalities emerged, ready to assume responsibility when death claimed the honored doctor. Among them were men who shall be heard of again and again—Solomon Cohen, Octavus Cohen (Solomon's brother), Dr. Abraham Sheftall, Benjamin Sheftall, Jr., Jacob De la Motta, Jr. (the attorney, also called Esquire), Levi Hart, and Isaac Cohen.

A MATTER OF MONEY

The July 1, 1830, meeting opened with a letter from the *parnass*, Dr. Moses Sheftall, informing the gentlemen that he was in receipt of fourteen hundred dollars insurance money from the fire, courtesy of "Etna [*sic*] Insurance Company of Hartford."[41] He wanted their instructions as to how it should best be invested. The money had been deposited in the Marine Fire Insurance Bank at four percent interest, temporarily, awaiting the body's decision. Isaac Minis, a man of demonstrated ability in financial matters, advised the loan of the money to some trustworthy individual on eight percent interest for a three year term. Flexibility was advised in the contract, contingent on whether it was advisable to build a building or not. If not, the money could be lent out again, provided that the security was sound.

The year 1819 had been marred by a panic and depression, but Georgia's banking system was relatively stable.[42] In hard times, the demand for credit expands, and the timing was perfect. When Mr. Bancroft Penney came, hat in hand, the money was loaned to him on bond and mortgage of his property, with insurance sufficient to cover same transferred to K.K. "Mickva" Israel.[43] The negotiations with Mr. Penney were often difficult. In 1831, he asked to sell the mortgaged property and substitute another in his possession. The *adjunta* refused.[44] The interest due in 1831 was paid by a note co-signed by William Williams.[45] A year later, it was a repeat performance with Mr. and Mrs. P. Bowen.[46] In July, 1832, when the bond came due, there was an agreement to extend it for a six month period, until January, 1833.[47] In January, the bond and interest were fully paid and the congregation had a substantial nest egg in the bank. By the special meeting, called in April, it amounted to $2,112.50.[48]

A second source of income, in this period of temporary homelessness, was the rent received from the buildings on Lot 23 in Franklin Ward. The president reported at the July 1, 1830, special meeting that approximately fifty dollars a year was being realized from them, sufficient to rent quarters for worship and storage. From 1831 to 1832, more than double that amount was collected (accounting given at the annual meeting of August 20, 1832). That figure was maintained in the following year's report, but those August 19, 1833, minutes signalled trouble ahead. Fly-by-nights were accepted as tenants, evidenced by the fact that

> some of the occupants of the buildings belonging to the congregation have removed owing $14.50 which will not be recovered.[49]

The property was not what it once was, and the residents abused the structures. Less than a decade later (as we shall see in a later section), the deterioration was so drastic that once solid buildings had to be put on public auction and torn down. But in the 1830's, "Baptist Square" was a good place for Jewish property, and the flow of income encouraged the leadership to think in expansive terms.

So expansive was the thinking, that the old gambling instincts returned (September 13, 1831, minutes, for example). Lottery tickets were sanctioned to the tune of twenty dollars in 1833.[50] The congregation had enough to risk on games of chance.

THE PROPERTIES

The fire of 1829 did not totally obliterate the possessions of the congregation. The Torahs, the *tamid,* the benches, the ark, all were saved. The president reported at the meeting after the fire (July 1, 1830) that the shutters, the lashes, and the pews were redeemed and were gathering dust in his cellar. The ark and the Torahs fell into the hands of Dr. Abraham Sheftall for safekeeping.[51]

As the *adjunta* planned to rebuild, attention turned to the most precious and sacred properties of K. K. "Mickva" Israel, the two Torahs brought to Savannah in 1733 and 1737. They had to be restored and to be put in proper repair. Hence, the leadership sought help in Charleston. The record of the aid and assistance provided by K.K. "Bet" Elohim is documented in the record books. In 1830, the *parnass* was instructed at the annual meeting to write:

> to the parnas of the K.K. Bet Elohim of Charleston, S.C., requesting them [*sic*] to keep for this congregation their suphurem [*sic*] until wanted by them and that they have done on them any necessary repairs . . . and that so soon as he should receive an affirmative answer, he be authorized to ship them and pay all necessary expences [*sic*] . . .

In his letter to K.K. Beth Elohim, Dr. Moses Sheftall described the ancient scrolls as being in poor condition

> . . . from the length of time they have been out of use and the want of proper persons to overhaul them. . . .

Not knowing if there was adequate space to house them in the synagogue's ark, Dr. Moses stated that both the *"Ahul [hechal,* i.e. ark] and the stand on which it is fixed" could be sent.[52] One year later, S. Valentine, secretary of Beth Elohim, responded with a resolution spelled out in these hospitable terms:

> *Unanimously* resolved:
>
> That the Board of Trustees will comply with pleasure with the request of the congregation in Savannah and take charge of the Sepharim and have them rectified and retain them until called for, and their being room enough in our *Ahul* (Italics added) [ark] neither Ahul nor stand from Savannah will be necessary.

S. Valentine wanted them shipped to his attention as soon as possible, as the Board of Trustees was about to change. Though he was assured of the new board's interest in the project, it was still best to expedite the matter.[53]

Two weeks later, Mr. Valentine received notice that the Torahs were to be shipped to him via a trusted seaman, Captain Sisson, being prepared for their journey "in the best possible manner." The thanks of Dr. Moses was expressed to the Charleston trustees, with heartfelt appreciation. For the first and only time in 250 years the historic scrolls were removed from their resting place in Savannah and sent elsewhere.* Internal evidence suggests that Charleston was a center where Torah scribes with sufficient expertise to repair and restore scrolls could be found.[54] Eleven months were needed to make one scroll "kosher" again, at a cost of ten dollars (a pittance by today's standards). Jacob De la Motta, Jr., who had visited Charleston and checked the workmanship, reported that "the situation" of one of the Torahs "was such that it could only be repaired by sending it to Europe."[58] This the *yehidim* did not think advisable. S. Valentine's response of June 6, 1832, indicated that payment was made and both Torahs were returned. Once again the congregation was in possession of that treasure which served as a constant reminder of the opening moment of Georgia Jewish history. The 1733 Torah remains to this day the *oldest ritual object on Georgia soil,* surviving from the year of the colony's founding. It is a venerable symbol for inhabitants of this state, whatever their faith orientation.

A SECOND SYNAGOGUE IS BUILT

Preliminary to recounting the story of the rebuilding of K. K. "Mickva" Israel, it is essential to point out the uniqueness of the second building and its 1820 precursor. In the annals of American Jewish history, nowhere is the construction of two synagogues recorded without substantial contributions from the Jewish community. In Savannah, the first two structures were erected with the generous help of non-Jews. The 1820 building was made possible by the grant of land from the Corporation of the City of Savannah and a lease thereof to Mr. Fell, who built buildings on the site. These buildings were leased to the master builder, John C. Evans, who, in turn, provided the materials and the labor for the 1820 structure, without

---

*Dr. Jacob Rader Marcus has suggested that one of the ancient Scrolls of Law was removed from Georgia in the 1740's. His argument was that when the Sephardic Jews abandoned Savannah because of the Spanish incursions at Fort Frederica, they carried with them this treasured ritual object to New York. This suggestion was made prior to the discovery of the Sheftall "diary" which offers no evidence of the removal of either the 1733 or 1737 Torah in this period. See *Early American Jewry The Jews of Pennsylvania and the South 1655-1790* (Philadelphia: The Jewish Publication Society of America, 1953), Vol. II, p. 290.

additional payment. The second building was made possible by the investment of monies paid by the "Etna" [sic] Insurance Company of Hartford (from the 1829 fire) and rentals on the Franklin Ward structures, supplemented by a general subscription of the Gentile inhabitants of Savannah.

At the August 15, 1831, meeting, President Moses Sheftall recounted all the monies in the treasury of the congregation, the amount received from rentals, and the bond from Mr. Penney with appropriate interest. Sheftall hoped the revenues would be sufficient to "enable us to commense [sic] the rebuilding and of brick another synagogue." Two years were to pass before the authority was forthcoming. A resolution was passed:

> that the Parnass be requested to assertain [sic] the cost for the construction of Synagogue of Brick of the same dimensions of the former one and on the same foundation, the contractor to furnish all materials.[56]

This Sheftall did, reporting at a special convocation that public notice has been given "through the medium of the Gazetts [sic] of the City." Several plans were submitted "by different mechanicks [sic]," including two detailed drawings.[57] Dr. Sheftall requested two committees to function, a Building Committee to make determinations relative to the structure, and a Subscription Committee to solicit the goodly tokens of the citizens of Savannah for this worthy project. Four served on the Building Committee: Dr. Moses Sheftall, Mordecai Myers, Isaac Minis, and Isaac Cohen. On June 14, 1834, another special meeting was called, at which the good news was heard that the *parnass* had raised from "different citizens" $1130, with $103 of that total yet to be collected. The word *citizens* in other contexts in the minutes translates as residents of the city, non-Jews, who wanted to further a worthy local project. Note that the congregational members were *not* asked to provide funds for the building campaign.

With such substance in hand, Mr. Levi Hart made the following resolution, which passed easily:

> Wheras [sic] it is desirous and proper that a suitable building should be erected in lieu of the one burnt down where the Congregation can have resort to offer up their devotions to the God of Israel and wheras [sic] from the success the Parnass has met with in making collections there is no doubt but that a sufficient amount with which is now on hand will be before long collected to enable the building of a Synagogue in this City . . .[59]

It was resolved that full authority be vested in Dr. Moses Sheftall and Jacob De la Motta, Jr., "to make contracts with some master builder or builders," including the right to purchase all necessary materials and furnishings. The two men had the power to begin as soon as they deemed appropriate. The only stipulations which limited the committee's freedom were (1) the building had to be brick, and (2) the building had to be raised on the Perry Lane and Whitaker Street lot.

By October, 1834, the workmen were supposed to begin.[59] The problems
that were to plague the building of the third structure in 1876 to 1878
affected this second sanctuary also. Just as the "mechanicks" were about to
be hired, the key figure in the process, Dr. Moses Sheftall, was summoned
from this earth.[60] Jacob De la Motta, Jr., was unwilling to act on his own.
In his report of the committee's work, he related that a plan was chosen, a
plan that was referred to builders for estimates. But the builders were
slow to make estimates, and Mr. De la Motta's business compelled him to
journey out of town (he frequently went to New York as we shall see). Not
until the following November did the committee actually meet. Then
death intervened and everything ceased.

The congregation unanimously appointed Isaac Cohen to replace the
lamented *parnass,* and Isaac DeLyon became an additional Building Committee member.

He who was a powerhouse of energy and a major leader of K. K.
"Mickva" Israel for a multitude of years, like his namesake at Mount Nebo,
never beheld the dream that he envisioned for his people. A brick structure
was to rise, but this latter day Moses was not to set eyes upon it. With
saddened hearts, the *yehidim* expressed their sense of loss in these words,
permanently inscribed in the *Temple Minute Books*:

> This meeting deeply deplores the loss which the congregation of this
> city has sustained in the death of Doctor Moses Sheftall whose zeal for
> its welfare has always been exercised particularly during the number
> of years he has been its head principal officer.

On *"Kipur"* his name, along with Philip Minis and Mordecai Sheftall,
was to be read during the *"escava"* (memorial prayer). Permanently and
forever, this was to be the practice as the minutes stated:

> Either in the synagogue to be built or *other* place appointed for
> public worship . . . on each and every recurrence of that sacred
> day.[61] (Italics added.)

Strangely, no mention of the building program is included in the 1835
and 1836 minutes. In the accounting of the new *parnass,* Isaac Cohen, dated
August, 1837, two items document that the structure was being raised.
Gilbert Butler was given $450 as first payment for the woodwork contracted
for the new synagogue, and E. Jones was compensated $781 for his work
as the brick mason.[62] On July 13, 1838, six years after the congregation
voted to commence a building project, the second sanctuary of K. K.
"Mickva" Israel (hereafter referred to as K.K.M.I.) stood ready to be dedicated to the glory of the Almighty One.[63] Unfortunately, more was expended
than anticipated, inflation then being rampant. The total cost was almost
$3800 for what the Building Committee members described as a "neat and
substantial edifice."[64] Proudly, J. De la Motta, Jr. and Isaac Cohen stated:

Not a dollar has been received from any one of the congregation[.] [I]ndeed the liberal subscription of the citizens of Savannah added to the amount received from the insurance company for the burning of the old building, together with the interest that accrued from the whole amount and the rents of the small delapidated buildings belonging to the congregation have rendered it unnecessary to ask aid from the congregation individually . . .[65]

Combined with the payments made to E. Jones and G. Butler in the 1836-1837 fiscal year, the additional sums paid out in the 1838 budget confirm that these two master builders received a total of $2343 for the stonemasonry and $1350 for the woodwork, making a total of $3693. Add a few extras—$10.87 additional to Mr. Jones, $25 additional to Mr. Butler, plus the cost of the cornerstone which was imported from New York by Mr. De la Motta—and the full cost of the building, excepting furnishings, was $3753.87, almost half again the amount anticipated.

The timing of the building project was perfect. In August, 1832, the first resolution to build a synagogue was passed. It was during a period of growth and prosperity in the Nation, state, and city.[66] Later we will describe the expansionism in which Jews participated, ranging from steamboats and cotton to railroads and agricultural products. This was followed by a depression, lasting from 1837 to the early 1840's.[67] Savannah was particularly hard hit. To add to the disaster, 1839 was remembered as one of the sickliest in the history of the city.[68] Heat and drought plagued the area. In between the outbreak of disease and the collapse of the economy, K.K.M.I.'s building program was sandwiched. Remarkably, the synagogue was constructed close to the time of the one hundredth birthday of Georgia. Coincidentally, the *third* sanctuary of K.K. "Mickva" Israel was begun during America's Centenary.

THE BUILDERS

Two master builders and carpenters were responsible for the second Jewish House of God to stand in the State of Georgia—Gilbert Butler and Edward Shepherd Jones. Butler was born in Hudson, Columbia County, New York, in 1797. At age 18, he relocated to Savannah, remaining for sixty years in this Forest City. His most notable achievements were the Christ Episcopal Church in 1838 (assisting in its construction) and the City Market.[69] Savannah's first chartered church and Savannah's first chartered synagogue were erected in the exact same time-frame, with the identical woodworker providing the interior design.[70]

Edward Jones is less well known, though his later work has special interest to native Savannahians.[71] In 1853, his firm (Lufborrow and Jones) laid the foundation for the famous Pulaski Monument which faces the present Mickve Israel Synagogue on Monterey Square. The 1850 home of George Wimberly Jones DeRenne on Broughton Street, west of Lincoln, was also erected by this same contractor. G. W. J. DeRenne played a role in the building of the *third* K.K.M.I. sanctuary.

FURNISHINGS

From the bills and other records, certain details of the interior of the building can be reconstructed. Handsome molding and woodwork dominated the sanctuary, the trademark of Gilbert Butler's craft. A huge chandelier was positioned to provide central light, while fifteen side lamps illuminated the women's gallery and the side sections. These were purchased in New York by Isaac Cohen and Jacob De la Motta, Jr., from D. E. Delavan & Brothers in 1838 for $57.50. The benches from the 1820 building, the ark, and the Torahs of 1733 and 1737 vintage found a prominent place in the new structure.[72] The accounts for 1839 document the restoration of all the wooden furniture, for which Mr. D. Ferguson received $21.50.[73]

The story of the "candlesticks" (menorahs) for the new building merits recounting. In 1839, President Isaac Cohen issued a draft to N. Phillips of New York for the astonishing amount of $43.50 (considering the cost of the huge chandelier and fifteen side lamps totalled $57.50) to cover the cost of the menorahs. Delivery, he was told, would be in "ten or fifteen" days. That was in March, and five months passed with no word from Mr. Phillips. Jacob De la Motta, Jr., who frequented New York, tried to communicate with him "but cannot obtain an answer."[74] The congregation was told,

> Mr. Phillips['] conduct has been so strange in that business, that I advise a resolution being passed by this congregation as to the course to be pursued towards him for the recovery back of [the] sum of $43.50.[75]

A resolution was passed instituting proceedings against Mr. Phillips, and

> that the parnass place the same immediately in [the] hands of some responsible person for collection.

A year later, "the candle stands, etc." from "Mr. N. Phillips of New York" stood in the new synagogue.[76]

This N. Phillips is, most likely Naphtali Phillips, son of Jonas Phillips (who married a descendant of Dr. Samuel Nunes of Savannah).[77] He was an uncle of Uriah Phillips Levy, famed commodore and owner of Monticello, and M. M. Noah, commonly identified as the first American Zionist. His brother, Manuel Phillips, had been a student of Dr. Benjamin Rush of Philadelphia at about the same time as Dr. Moses Sheftall. Naphtali was appointed to the New York Customs Office in the 1820's as an appraiser.[78] Jacob De la Motta, Jr., who negotiated with him, most likely knew him through his cousin, Dr. Jacob De la Motta. Both Naphtali Phillips and Dr. Jacob De la Motta preached orations at the funeral of Rev. Gershom Mendes Seixas.[79]

The heat for the building came from a "firing stove" purchased in New York by J. De la Motta, Jr., at a cost to the congregation of twenty-five dollars.[80] One assumes it was placed in the main sanctuary, as was the custom in that day.

The account ledgers, presented by the *parnass* at the annual meeting in 1841, list other items that bedecked the impressive sanctuary. A payment to C. Chanone for silk and other materials permits speculation that the Torah covers and the altar cloths were of the finest materials. Lamp oil is mentioned in the purchase record, assuring us that, by wick, the chandelier and side lamps offered illumination. The sanctuary was carpeted with eleven yards of carpeting, priced at one dollar per yard. It is possible that the carpet was laid from entrance to ark, making the building thirty-three feet long. The old *tamid* (eternal light) from the 1820 structure was set in place above the ark, where its light radiated day and night.

Consecrating a New Synagogue

The new Jewish House of Prayer awaited the dedication ritual that would mark its formal opening as an institution. At the August 30, 1838, annual meeting, the congregation heard from the Building Committee that it "fondly hope that they will succeed in obtaining the services of the Rev. Mr. Posnaski [sic] of Charleston." November, 1838, was the projected date for the ceremony. A letter was sent to the trustees of K. K. Beth Elohim requesting Rev. Poznanski's services, at the same time that a similar instrument was sent to him. Whatever time and date he chose would be suitable. The Charleston trustees immediately granted date-setting authority to the honored leader of their congregation. A few days later, the rabbi begged off, "saying sickness in his family preventing his accepting of the favour." No offer to visit at some other time in the future was tendered. The best light was put on the rejection:

> Possibly he feared the sickness had in his family would continue for several months after and that it would not answer for him to fix a distant period . . .[81]

After a year had passed, it was evident that there was no point in asking "Mr. P" a second time, "after his former treatment." Two years following the exchange with Charleston, the sanctuary remained "unblessed," though it was in use.[82] Jacob De la Motta, Jr., suggested another "gentlemen" [sic] in Charleston, a Mr. Surinam or Simmons (the text is unclear), who would require compensation since his pockets were empty. The plan did not materialize.

Not until February 24, 1841, a Wednesday, was the consecration rite performed. A man, who later emerged as a powerful figure on the American Jewish scene, the Rev. Isaac Leeser, "hazan of the Congregation Mickva [sic] Israel at Philadelphia," conducted the services and preached the dedicatory address.[83] As mentioned earlier, Leeser edited and published *The Occident*, the first Jewish periodical to have subscribers in almost every Jewish community. One can surmise why he was in the Port City. As *hazzan* of Philadelphia's Mikveh Israel, he was well acquainted with the Gratz family, particularly Rebecca, with whom he labored to establish the first Jewish Sunday school. Her beloved niece, Miriam Gratz Moses (whom she raised after the death of her sister, Rachel), married Solomon Cohen in 1836, and the couple had settled in Savannah. Leeser had a connection in Savannah with a family which was prominent in *his* congregation and friendly to *him*. He was to visit the Cohens on this and subsequent occasions.

The February dedication ceremony itself is described in glowing terms in the August 16, 1841, minutes. The Hebrew date was 3 Adar, 5607, nearly two weeks before *Purim*. A large number of people "of both sexes and of different denominations and also of our own congregation" were present. Clearly, it was a community event. Again, a room in the Free School was rented, and a procession involving the *yehidim* proceeded at one o'clock in the afternoon to the new synagogue. Rev. Leeser led, followed by Levi Hart and Isaac DeLyon carrying, "under a white silk canopy" (*chuppah*), the old Torahs. Then followed the *parnass,* Isaac Cohen, the secretary, J. De la Motta, Jr., and the remaining members of the congregation. The door was thrown open by Mordecai Sheftall, Sr. Appropriate prayers were said, and Psalms of David were chanted (no hint of an organ or instrumental music this time). Solomon Cohen had the unique honor of lighting the *tamid* (eternal light, the one rescued from the 1820 building). Jacob De la Motta, Jr., like his cousin at the first dedication, conducted the liturgy. Leeser's discourse was praised as being "impressive and well written."

A touching letter was addressed to him one day after the event:

Dear Sir:

We beg leave in behalf of our congregation and for ourselves to return you thanks for your ready compliance with our request in consecrating our Synagogue and the able address you delivered on that interesting occasion[.] [T]he advice you gave we hope will be duly appreciated and that it may be in our power at a day not far distant to advise you of its beneficial effects. This we know would be pleasing to you. [W]ill you favour us with a copy of your address for publication . . .

A check was enclosed, and the instrument was duly signed by the three members of the Building Committee.

Ever attentive to duty, Leeser promptly responded:

Gentlemen:

Your kind communication of this morning has this moment been handed to me, and having but a few minutes to spare before departing, I have not sufficient leisure to answer in detail, but this I will say that it is a source of high gratification that it was in [my] power to serve you. You may take a copy of my address, but be good enough to send me the original at your earliest convenience.

Wishing you long life and prosperity, and the increase of goodness and piety among the body you represent. I remain gentlemen your friend.

Leeser's graciousness resulted in the lament by the president that more than fifty dollars was not forthcoming to him for his benignity, since the state of the accounts would not permit a higher sum (reckon it in 1983 dollars, and it was a princely perquisite).

The address was printed at a cost of twenty-three dollars for one hundred copies.[84]

The era of building came to an end with this dedication in 1841. Amidst all the positive signs of renewal and rededication to faith and piety, rumblings of financial problems provided unpleasant background noise. The buildings on Lot 23 of Franklin Ward, source of economic provender for the congregation from the turn of the 19th century, were condemned by the Board of Health and "pulled down."[85] The lot was, however, leased to I. E. Walker & Brothers, for five years, at $150 per year.[86] Deterioration was occurring in the neighborhood, and this temporary arrangement signaled fiscal problems would again surface, as this period of construction, catastrophe, and rebuilding came to a close.

PATTERNS OF LIFE

The flow of history-telling is temporarily interrupted, and even turned backward, as attention shifts to the ways in which Jews integrated into the community. The saga is of the people—how they prospered in commerce and in the professions; the positions of political influence that came to them; incidences of acceptance and disaffection; and the way they related to their fellows in faith. Life among the Jews of Savannah will be fleshed in. The time-frame will be, *primarily*, from the American Revolution until after the War Between the States.

JEWS IN COMMERCE AND THE PROFESSIONS

The temperate clime of coastal Georgia and the natural lushness of forest and field made land-ownership the base for wealth-building. The Sheftall family understood this well. By 1755, Mordecai petitioned for a land grant, which came to him in 1756—a fifty acre parcel.[87] Father Benjamin followed suit, and, because he claimed a wife, two sons, and two negroes, he was granted two hundred acres of the 359 he was seeking. Undaunted in 1763, claiming five negroes, he requested more, and received 250 additional acres.[88]

Levi, Benjamin's other son, not to be bested, accumulated 750 acres by 1766 and numbered nine negroes in his household.[89]

Mordecai, during the identical time frame, had also come into possession of a wharf lot of one hundred feet on the river, where merchandise could be stored or collected for shipping.[90] The second great asset of the Savannah

locus was discerned by him. A river wends its way from this protected port
to the Atlantic and ocean trade routes.

Abraham Minis and wife, Abigail, prospered in the merchandising
business, and wife more than husband gathered land in large quantities (a
land grant from King George III in St. Mary's parish, where the Trident
submarine base is now located, was deeded to her). The Minises, like the
Sheftalls, were involved in ranching on an extensive scale.[91] Exporting and
importing were pursuits of Abraham and Abigail and their descendants.
The progenitor of the family used his small boat to provide supplies for
General Oglethorpe during his expeditions against the Spanish, plying frequently between Savannah and Fort Fredrica, near Brunswick.[92] Isaac
DeLyon and the Sheftalls also were involved in coastal trade.[93] Among
American Jewish women, Abigail Minis stands out as business woman *par
excellence*. Left a widow with eight mouths to feed, she took over the
operation of her husband's ranches, farms, store, and even a tavern.[94] On the
King's birthday in 1772, Mrs. Minis served a company of seventy distinguished celebrants.[95]

The Revolution impoverished Mordecai Sheftall more than the others,
the result of his benignity to the American forces. Son Sheftall's efforts in
the 1790's to press the U.S. Treasury for repayment of loans were fruitless.[96]
The Mordecai Sheftall branch had to begin again, almost from scratch. By
1783 he was functioning as an exporter and was again gathering land in
quantity.[97]

From an almost desolate and impoverished city of the post-Revolutionary
War years, Savannah grew in size from a mere twenty-five hundred citizens
in 1794 to more than double that figure by the turn of the century.[98] The
growth was not constant. The 1796 fire destroyed more than two hundred
buildings and reduced multitudes to pauperism. Listed as sufferers in the
Columbian Museum and Savannah Advertiser were Messers. da Costa,
Sarzedas, Wolf, Isaacs, Moses, Cohen, and DeLyon.[99] The local newspaper
implied that others, not identified, had witnessed their life savings go up in
smoke.

In the last decade of the 18th century, Jewish merchants were plying
their wares in significant establishments, if one may judge by the advertisements in the press. Isaac Polock, celebrated as the first Jew to settle in the
Nation's capital, began in this area with "a grocery and liquor store." His
1790 business offered such diverse products as

> green and bohea teas: old Jamaica spirits, Philadelphia beer, gin
> and brandy, loaf and brown sugar, Spanish olives, basket salt, tur-
> pentine soap, spermacetti and tallow candles . . .[100]

Dry goods were found on the shelves including Irish linen, Philadelphia-
made shoes, Dutch toweling, plated buckles, buttons, et al. Within
three years, I. Polock opened a brick building on the bay where im-
porters and exporters could store their produce until their ships came

in.[101] A year later, Polock continued diversifying by investing in land in Washington County.[102] Philip Jacob Cohen made his mark on the world in real estate. The bay property belonging to Captain Horatio Marbury was put on lease through his office.[103] Factoring must have been a sideline as well. A State of Georgia advertisement in the *Georgia Gazette*, in 1787, contained a request to unknown persons to pick up their copper kettles, shipped in via the Savannah packet, but still occupying space in Cohen's warehouse.[104]

Samuel Mordecai, in contrast to the above-mentioned success stories, showed a lack of business acumen. Notice of his suit in Inferior Court appeared in the local press in 1790. It was equivalent to a bankruptcy case.[105] Samuel Mordecai was elected treasurer (*gabay*) of the congregation, and, was replaced through a determined effort of the *yehidim*. A younger namesake must also have had financial problems for a gift of charity was presented to him in 1829 by the president of "Mickva" Israel, in consideration of his plight.[106]

David Cardozo had the ill fortune of entering into partnership with David Leion, as did Isaac Benedix. Both ended in separation, one in 1786, and the other, three years later.[107] In 1799, Leion terminated another partnership, his marriage to Hannah Minis, daughter of Abraham and Abigail. This constituted the first and only case of Jewish *divorce* in the Colonial period. The marriage lasted just a little over a year.[108]

Excluding the Sheftalls and Minises, Isaac Benedix tasted the sweetness of success beyond all others. As postmaster of the community, he was in a powerful position.[109] Where the mail is gathered, there information is exchanged, and knowledge of wheeling-and-dealing is garnered. (A political history of the U.S. would be incomplete without examining the critical role of the postmaster in urban and rural settings.)

Benedix was not the only Jew to hold this coveted position. At a later date, Solomon Cohen received President Pierce's appointment to serve as postmaster of Savannah. Upon that base, he also established political power.

Benedix & Company was a complex operation. It purchased indentures of the State of South Carolina and other certificates for speculation.[110] Next to Mr. Polock's store on Market Square, Mr. Benedix operated his dry goods establishment which proudly advertised in 1795

> oznabrigs, hessians, cotton bagging, roll linen, humhums, platillas, royal, brown holland, holland and Russian sail duck, bed ticking . . . black peper, brimstone, a few quarter casks Madera, wine of an excellent quality, Northward rum.[111]

By 1797, the company was on the wharf, conducting a factorage and commission business, with building materials for sale.[112] A year later, real estate was added. Bay lots were on lease.[113] Successful entrepreneurs make good executors of estates. So thought Lyon Norden when he chose Isaac Benedix to handle his will.[114] Benedix & Co. may have been the first Jewish firm to sell weapons. A 1798 advertisement mentioned "air guns, broad swords, pistols double and single barrel" for sale.[115] Clearly, no item was too strange to merchandise. Benedix & Co. let the public know that "a likely horse" was available which could carry either chair or saddle.[116] Taking advantage of local produce, Benedix made rice a major staple of his thriving general store.[117] Like Isaac Polock, Isaac Benedix had left Georgia in 1793, but reconsidered and became one of the respected leaders of Savannah upon his return.[118] When President Washington (in 1798) called upon the American people to conduct prayer services for the safety of the Nation, Isaac Benedix was the man chosen to deliver the discourse for Savannah Jewry.

In addition to his land holdings, ranches, and shipping interests, Levi Sheftall dabbled in rice and cotton and had a brickyard on the side.[119] In the late 1790's, he was negotiating in choice real estate, advertising, *for sale,* a commodious home belonging to Colonel Tatnall, and, *for rent,* a house in St. James Square near Major Habersham's.[120]

Non-commercial vocations also appealed to Savannah Jews. Among the barristers in town were Sheftall Sheftall and his cousin, Benjamin Sheftall.[121] In 1797, the former stopped practicing law, but retained his notary public function and added the conveying and real estate business, as well.[122] He also developed a firewood operation.[123] Jewish physicians were functioning here as well. The Sheftall family counted two: Dr. Abraham Sheftall, son of Levi, and the better known Dr. Moses Sheftall, son of Mordecai. In practice with Dr. Moses was Dr. Jacob De la Motta. Upon the Savannah scene, young Moses burst with an announcement in the *Georgia Gazette* that "he means to practice physic and surgury," literally in his father's house on Broughton Street.[124] Physicians of the time were accustomed to dispense medicine to those who preferred drugs without checkup. Hence in the same ad, the public was informed that he had in his possession a small assortment of French medicines, part of which he sold "low for cash." A year later, he occupied a mid-town location at Broughton and Barnard, close to Market Square.[125] The 1796 fire destroyed this building, so back to Father Mordecai's house he proceeded.[126] The pattern of moving about was continued for several years. Apparently, by 1799, the doctor had achieved a position of prominence, advertising in the *Columbian Museum and Savannah Advertiser* that his choice horse, branded with an "M", had strayed or was stolen, and a handsome reward of four dollars was available to him who returned it.[127] Then as now, a skillful physicician was not lacking in life's little luxuries.

Jewish educators were found in the community. The Sheftall "diary" mentions "Rapheal DaCosta Musqueta" who taught Levi Sheftall's children and even performed marriages on the side.[128] Emanuel De la Motta opened a school for the instruction of young people in English, French, composition, and arithmetic. He rented a lovely cottage on the south commons as his school house.[129]

Savannah's unique environment resulted in an unusual choice of professions by native Jews. The proximity of ocean breezes lured some to ply the seas as ship's captains. Moses Cohen was captain of the schooner *Eagle*.[130] Master Canter found a home aboard the schooner *Polly*.[131] The *Clarrisa*, the *Brig Newton*, and the *Harriot* were guided over much of the Caribbean and western Atlantic by Captain Joseph da Costa.[132]

In addition to Abigail Minis, the ladies were represented in the commercial world by Esther Sheftall, who

> respectfully informed the ladies of Savannah that she has for some time past carried on the mantua-making business. . . .[133]

In addition to designing and hand preparing lavish garments, Miss Sheftall had in stock such appealing outfits (imported from Baltimore), as

> Morning Robe, Derby Morning Dress, Rutland Habit, Derby Robe, Whin Breast Habit, Beaufort Habit and the Wirtemberg Jacket.[134]

Her advertisements are second in number to Isaac Benedix in this period. Mordecai and Frances' daughter was quite an entrepreneur!

In the 1790's, earning a livelihood was a struggle, even for the swiftest. Such is attested to by the list of tax defaulters, including David Cardozo, Isaac and Abraham Abraham, Jacob Phillip Cohen, Isaac Polock, Daniel Nunes, Samuel Mordecai, even Dr. Moses Sheftall, Mordecai Sheftall, Sheftall Sheftall, and Levi Sheftall.[135] (Add Israel Delieben, Abraham DeLyon, Abraham Jacobs, and David Leion, as well.)[136] A full listing of defaulters on taxes included almost every Jew in town. Life was arduous in the last decade of the 18th century, and financial reverses were almost universal.

Prosperity was possible, however, in the first two decades of the nineteenth century, Jewish businessmen were among the most successful leaders of the community. Isaac Cohen (whose achievements as Building Committee chairman have been previously noted in this chapter) was representative of the fast-rising, young business man. Between 1817 and 1822, he was involved in general merchandising, with an eye to imports and exports. Initially, he was connected with I.K. Tefft, a prosperous merchant in the hardware and commission business.[137] Once on his own, he proceeded to handle general merchandise, everything from liquors and intoxicating spirits to iron bricks, corn, tobacco, sugar, and even bacon and ham.[138] On one occasion, he acted as agent for the sale of the fast sailing sloop, *Manhattan*.[139] Whether he had training in the law or not is unrecorded, but it is known that he functioned as the attorney for his brother-in-law, Dr. Moses Sheftall, during his absence from the community.[140] Real estate transactions were in his domain as well.[141] Reflecting the growth and development of business life in Savannah, Isaac Cohen moved from behind-the-counter merchandising to the board rooms of industries, banks, and commercial enterprises. In 1837, he took a seat as a director of the Central Railroad and Banking Company, in which he owned seven hundred dollars stock.[142] There he served with bank president and famed railroad magnate, W. W. Gordon. After several years, he moved on to the Planters Bank as a board member, serving throughout the 1850's into the early 1860's.[143] Charitable endeavors merited his help, as in 1838 when he collected donations for the fire sufferers in Charleston.[144] Interested in all expansions that benefitted this city, he was elected a director of the Savannah Ogeechee Canal Company in 1850.[145] The Chamber of Commerce recognized his booster spirit and appointed him to its Committee of Appeals in 1853.[146] With these connections, where else to move but into the political arena; and that he did in 1852 when he ran for alderman of the city.[147] His career continued into the era of the War Between the States. In 1861, he was representing Savannah's interests at the Commercial Convention in Macon. In 1865, he was given a critical responsibility as member of a committee to develop a plan for restoring Georgia to her original condition as part of the United States of America.[148]

Another Isaac, of the Minis family, followed a similar route, though, as inheritor of property and means from his father, Philip, his path to the top was more easily gained. William Harden's *History of Savannah and South Georgia* provides little detail about his life, other than that he served in the War of 1812 as a private in Captain William Bulloch's company of artillery and was married to Divinah Cohen of Georgetown, South Carolina, oldest sister of Solomon and Octavus. In the import-export business, he had a wharf on Hutchinson Island where lumber and lime were stored, and a lower wharf on the Savannah side of the river.[150] Ships journeying up and down the coast had cargo consigned to him.[151] In addition, he handled passenger service on luxurious fleet ships headed for Liverpool.[152] Stephen Birmingham mentions the prominent role played by Isaac Minis in commissioning the steamship *Savannah* (the first of its kind to sail from these shores to a European destination).[153] By the 1830's-1840's, he was owner of a corps of skilled slaves whom he leased out or sold, including seamstresses, masons, and plasterers.[154] At the same time, he served as Commissioner of the Central Railroad and Banking Company of Georgia.[155] As a sign that he was valued by the top leadership of the city, he was chosen by City Council (together with Octavus Cohen) to serve on an Investment Committee, charged with handling public funds.[156] His connection with a private boys' school in West Chester, Pennsylvania, A. Bolmar's Institution for Boys, indicated broad acceptance in the higher echelons of society.[157] He served as a local reference for the school. His death, in 1856, was noted in the *Daily Morning News* with the comment, "Mr. Minis was one of our oldest and most respected fellow citizens."[158]

Levy Hart never reached the heights of the aforementioned Isaacs (Cohen and Minis). Married to Levi Sheftall's daughter, Abigail Minis Sheftall, he had the associations needed to function effectively in town. In 1811, his general merchandise firm with Joseph Davis, known as Levy Hart & Co., was dissolved.[159] He expanded on his own into an import-export business, handling all manner of goods, from prime beef to whiskey.[160] The offices of the *Daily Georgian* (local newspaper) became the center of his export operation.[161] Lucky in games of chance, he won the gold lottery in 1832. Unlucky in "chattel," he was exasperated by a very valuable slave, Sandy, who functioned as a butcher, and was prone to "take off" now and again.[162]

Colonel Mordecai I. Myers will be treated more comprehensively for his political acuity, but let it be noted here that his commercial skill provided him with sufficient finances to function at the "benches of government." Hutchinson Island, directly opposite the Savannah riverfront, has been the scene of wharves and shipping enterprises from almost the beginning of the port development. Colonel Myers was a landowner on the island.[163] He served also as a director of the Bank of the State of Georgia in 1833 and represented the interests of Planters Bank and the Darien Bank at a bank convention in Charleston in 1838.[164] His prominence locally is attested to by his election as president of the Ogeechee and Altamaha Canal Co. in 1833.[156]

Abraham Minis, son of Isaac, become associated with the commission firm of Paddleford and Fay, as a clerk. Later he joined James H. Johnston in a similar venture. After the death of Johnston, he created the firm of A. Minis & Sons (with his two boys), a shipping business. In addition to successes in local politics, he took his place on the boards of several local banks and railroad firms, including the Southern Bank and the Central Railroad and Banking Company of Georgia. Devoted to the South, he invested heavily in Confederate bonds at the outbreak of the Civil War. The failure of the Confederacy undid him, and, following the conflict, he had to commence anew, proving himself, once again, a high achiever.[166]

Physicians and attorneys of Jewish origins have found a place of prominence in Savannah from the earliest time (doctors, that is, as lawyers were initially banned from the colony). Dr. Moses Sheftall and Dr. Jacob De la Motta were not only builders of the first Temple "Mickva" Israel, they were also co-partners in practice. Moses' cousin, Dr. Abraham Sheftall, practiced the healing arts in his private office and in the local prison as jail physician, an elected post.[167] Philip Minis (a descendant of the original Philip) married out of the Jewish faith (in New York City to Miss Sarah Augusta, daughter of John Swift Livingston, Esq.—a minister, Rev. A. Verren, performing the rite), then entered the military (31st regiment of the U.S. Artillery), served as assistant surgeon in 1836, and that same year was elevated to full surgeon.[168] Three years later, he was back in Savannah healing the sick and running a brick yard on the side.[169]

In addition to Sheftall Sheftall, Esq. and others mentioned earlier, the 1830's and 1840's brought two distinguished barristers to the city, Jacob De la Motta, Jr., and Solomon Cohen, both of whom became *parnassim* of "Mickva" Israel. Whether by coincidence or not, both were most adroit in the political arena, as attested to by elections and appointments to high public office. Colonel De la Motta, as he was commonly known (serving as an aide-de-camp to the Governor), was an "enterprising and successful lawyer" with interests in real estate and banks, both in Darien and Savannah.[170] In 1837, he was elected Secretary-Treasurer of the Savannah, Ogeechee & Altamaha Canal Company (notice how many Jews functioned in this enterprise and in the Central Railroad of Georgia as well).[171] He was admitted to practice before the Supreme Court of Georgia.[172] Solomon Cohen, whose career is the subject of the next chapter, was associated in law with M.H. McAllister and argued cases before the U.S. Courts at Milledgeville and Savannah, as well as the Superior Courts of the Eastern Circuit.[173]

Surprisingly, Savannah has also produced and/or hosted its share of Jewish newspaper editors. Jacob Nunez Cardozo, whose roots were in this city, became editor of the *Southern Patriot* in Charleston.[174] He had served on the editorial staff of the *Savannah Morning News*.[175] Emanuel De la Motta, the brother of Dr. Jacob and cousin of lawyer Jacob, joined with Mr. Fell in 1830 to co-own and edit a newspaper called *The Savannah Republican*.[176] The first free circulating journal in the South, *The Daily Advertiser*, enlarged its format in January of 1868 and became a subscription newspaper under its editor, S. Yates Levy (also a prominent attorney). Levy was not prone to moderation (nor were his sisters Eugenia Levy Phillips and Phoebe Pember), and his editorials during the time of Union occupation resulted in pressure from General Meade to either tone down or get out. Levy was compelled to resign.[177]

JEWS IN POLITICS

The record of the participation by Savannah Jews in the political life of the city, state and Nation may be unrivalled on the American continent. Once the Revolutionary War was ended, local Jews viewed themselves as full citizens, with all privileges attendant thereto. Therefore, fearlessly, they entered public service. Lists make for poor reading, but when the record is so extensive, limitations of space allow for no other procedure. The following material is taken from Thomas Gamble, Jr.'s *History of the City Government,* and enumerates only elected and appointed officials in Chatham County:

Aldermen (an alphabetical listing)[178]

Name	Term
Jacob J. Abrams	1881-83
Henry Blun	1879-81
Simon E. Byck	1881-83
Solomon Cohen	1842-43, 48-51, 53-57, 60-61
Emanuel De la Motta	1835-36
Levi DeLyon	1815-17, 19-22, 27-29
Isaac DeLyon	1835-36
S. H. Eckman	1874-77
A. S. Guckenheimer	1897-99
Isaac G. Haas	1899-1901

Samuel P. Hamilton	1877-79, 81-87, 97-98
C. S. Henry*	1834-35
Jacob P. Henry	1816-17, 19-22, 27-28
Herbert Moses*	1818-24
Jacob Hersman*	1813-16
S. Krouskoff	1897-99
Adolph Leffler	1896-97
Joseph Lippman	1849-51, 62-65
Mathias H. Meyer*	1866-69, 70-77[179]
Abraham Minis	1859-60; acting Mayor, 1860
Isaac Minis	1810-13, 15-16, 24-28, 30-32
J. Florence Minis	1883-85
Herman Myers	1885-95; Mayor afterwards
Mordecai Myers	1818
Samuel Russell	1815-16
Levi Sheftall	1799-1801,1802-03, 04-05
Mordecai Sheftall, Sr.	1818-22
Moses Sheftall	1821-24, 26-27, 28-30
A. A. Solomons	1861-62
Moses J. Solomons	1869-71
Samuel Solomons	1851-52, 53-54
A. L. Weil	1897-1900
Elias Weil	1879-81

CLERK OF CITY COUNCIL[180]

Mordecai Myers	1819-41

CLERK OF MAYOR'S COURT[181]

Abraham Minis	1798-1801
Benjamin Sheftall	1815-1820

SHERIFF OF MAYOR'S COURT[182]

Isaac DeLyon	1813-19
Abraham I. DeLyon	1820

PORT WARDENS[183]

Isaac Russell	1816
Joseph David*	1819, 1821-22, 1826-27
Levi Hart	1835-41, 43, 45
Levi S. Russell	1859, 61, 65
Alexander Abrams	1870-72, 82-84

CLERKS OF THE MARKET[184]

Isaac DeLyon	1829-30
Waring Russell	1853-54
Mathias H. Meyer*	1856-59
Emanuel Sheftall	1864-65
Henry L. Davis	1870-81
Aleck Mendel	1901

POLICE CHIEFS[185]

Mordecai Sheftall, Jr.	1849-51

[In the 20th century, Charles Garfunkel (1903-1906) and David Epstein (1975-1980) have served as Chiefs of the Savannah Police Department.]

DEPUTY SUPERINTENDENT (OF THE POLICE)

Isaac Russell	1812, 19, 22
Mordecai Sheftall, Jr.	1843
Waring Russell	1851
Mordecai DeLyon	1852

Thomas J. Sheftall served as second in command in 1880 and 1883.

FIRE CHIEF[186]

Levi Sheftall	1801-02 (called fire master), 1805-06
Isaac Minis	1804-05, 09-10
Moses Sheftall	1808-09
Jacob Hershman*	1810-11
S. Barnett	1812-13
Benjamin Sheftall	1813-14
Philip M. Russell	1874-75

CITY HEALTH OFFICER[187]

Dr. Moses Sheftall	1800-02

JAILORS

Isaac DeLyon	1850-53
Waring Russell	1859 (removed then reinstated by Superior Court)

COMMISSIONER OF THE MARKET (3 SERVED TOGETHER)

Levi Sheftall	1801-02
Levy Abraham	1802-03, 04, 07-09
Moses Sheftall	1802-04, 10-11, 18-19
Samuel Simons*	1808-10
Samuel Barnett	1812-13
Benjamin Sheftall	1820-23

MASSIE SCHOOL COMMISSIONERS

Samuel P. Hamilton	1881, 83-84
Lee Roy Myers	1888-90
Herman Myers	1895-96, 1889-1901 (as Mayor)

KEEPERS OF THE POWDER MAGAZINE

Joseph Lippman	1852
H. L. Davis*	1866-69

* Jewish identity not certain.

Participation on such a broad scale in the governmental institutions of the community was the external manifestation of a deeper involvement in the political process. Jews were party workers, as attested to in the record. Jacob De la Motta, Jr., for example, participated in the Washington Ward machine, and was active in the Democratic-Republican Association.[188] In 1838, he was a delegate to the Union and States Rights Convention.[189] No wonder that he was appointed, in 1852, an aide-de-camp to the Governor of Georgia, with rank of Colonel.[190] Abraham Minis followed a similar path, as did Jacob's cousin, Emanuel De la Motta.[191] In 1840, Levi S. Hart convinced the United German Society to join the South Oglethorpe Ward Association in backing Martin Van Buren as Democratic candidate for President.[162] Savannah Jewry produced one of the deftest politicians of the pre-Civil War period, Colonel Mordecai Myers. He fashioned alliances with all the ethnic political factions in town: the Irish, the Germans, the Poles— even with the Democrats-Republicans, and plain Democrats, it mattered not.[193] So well accepted was he that he became chairman of the meeting of Democrats in Chatham County in 1840.[194] Political plums came his way, including appointments as Judge of Inferior Court and as a member of the Public Roads Commission of Chatham County.[195] He was given official support to run for the U.S. House of Representatives and for the Senate.[196]

On a state level, a few items of interest need to be cited. Levi S. Hart was appointed by Governor Brown to the sensitive post of military storekeeper at Savannah just prior to the War Between the States.[197] In a previous chapter, the appointment of Daniel Nunes, in 1784, as Harbor Master for the port of Savannah (an appointment by the House of Assembly of Georgia) was mentioned as the first state-wide appointment that any local Israelite received.[198] Savannah Jews who have been chosen Chatham County representatives to the State Legislature include:

Asa Emanuel*	1787-89
Dr. Moses Sheftall	1808, 1818-19
Isaac Minis	1815
Levi S. DeLyon	1820-21
Mordecai Sheftall	1821
(a descendant of the original Mordecai Sheftall)	
Colonel Mordecai Myers	1824-26, 1828-29, 1831, 1837
Solomon Cohen	1842
Philip M. Russell	1863-66, 1877-79, 1886-87

* Jewish identity not certain.

[In this century, Girard M. Cohen (1937-38) served in the Georgia House, as have Alan S. Gaynor (1969-72) and Ronald E. Ginsberg (1981 to present). The above information (excepting Ginsberg) is to be found in the *State of Georgia Official and Statistical Register,* 1971-72, compiled and edited by Edna Lackey, HML&P Printers, Atlanta, Georgia, pp. 1416-1418.]

Prior to Solomon Cohen's elevation by President Pierce to postmaster of Savannah (see next chapter), only Isaac Benedix could claim to hold a Federal office by act of the United States Government. In 1799, he was declared the official postmaster of Savannah, probably appointed to that position through the influence of his good friend, Joseph Habersham, Washington's Postmaster-General.[199] In 1792, Habersham had chosen Benedix to supervise a lottery for the benefit of the city of Savannah.[200] Habersham served in Washington's administration from 1795-1801.[201]

JEWISH NON-JEWISH INTERACTION

Attention turns to the communal connections of Jews, and the manner in which they entered into associations with others for the vitality and weal of the city. Two areas of special contribution, the Union Society and Freemasonry, will receive more elaborate treatment at the end of this section.

Savannah Jews were counted among the great patriots of Georgia. Patriotism can bind together people of disparate beliefs. It should not surprise the reader to find such personages as Col. Mordecai Myers officiating at the National Anniversary Dinner in 1836, or, four years later, Jacob De la Motta, Jr., making local arrangements for the Fourth of July celebration.[202] References have been or will be cited relative to the participation of Port City Israelites in the various Savannah Home Guard units in peace time and war.[203]

Few cities have a stronger tradition of ethnic festival observances than Savannah. The local St. Patrick's Day festivities are legendary. The Hibernian Society, now an Irish fellowship, accounted among its charter members Isaac Minis.[204] In 1836, another Jew, Emanuel De la Motta, proposed a toast at the 1836 annual Hiberian dinner.[205] This author was the first rabbi to invoke Divine favor upon the assembled revelers at their annual banquet in 1977. Railroads and horse flesh are reverenced in coastal Georgia, accounting for both Colonel Myers and Abraham Minis involving themselves with celebrations for the former—while S. Yates Levy evidenced equestrian interests as secretary-treasurer of the Savannah Jockey Club.[206] It was Colonel Myers' view that if Jews and Gentiles could rejoice and have fun together, prejudice would be less likely to surface. At least one suspects that was his view in light of his *promotion* of balloonist, Professor Frigert, from the College of Bayeau in France, who, under Myers' aegis, ascended in a balloon from the "Oglethorpe cantonement" in 1836![207]

Mutualism can result from engaging in common labor for worthy causes. In 1857, Solomon Cohen was active in raising funds for the Massie School.[208] In the midst of the Civil War, the three Bycks (S.E., C.E., and Lehman) joined the aforementioned Mr. Cohen in providing resources for the Soldier Relief Fund.[209] Mrs. Solomon Cohen and Mrs. H. Minis were active in agencies in the community, the former with the Savannah Female Asylum and the latter with the Free School.[210]

Respect for Jews is enhanced when Jews advance the educational level of a community. Levi Hart, III, excelled at the Chatham Academy and received public recognition.[211] He was the first Jew mentioned in the sources to attend the University of Georgia (in 1834), being admitted to the sophomore class.[212] Among the most notable and respected orators and educators in Savannah were adherents of the Jewish faith. S. Yates Levy's lecture on English history made the second page of the *Savannah Daily Herald* in 1865.[213] Throughout his sojourn in Savannah, Dr. Jacob De la Motta enthralled audiences with his eloquence.[214] At the Georgia Hotel, on July 4,

1820, this *Portuguese* Jew gave the toast to *Spain* at the Georgia Hussar's Dinner.[215] An *Iberian* is an *Iberian*—at least on the banks of the Ogeechee! The first known Greek lecturer to come to the city, Mr. Perdicaries, came with the recommendation of Emanuel De la Motta in 1836.[216] Some of America's fine private schools solicited local Jews to act as public relations figures. Isaac Minis had an interest in a young men's academy in West Chester, Pennsylvania, and Col. M. Myers was the reference for the school of James L. Rossignol and John P. Knox.[217]

It was a Jew in the healing profession, Dr. Nunes, who paved the way for the first Jewish settlement in Savannah. Thereafter, Jewish doctors have enhanced the image of Jewry in this region, none more than Dr. Moses Sheftall. He was credited with helping to found the Georgia Medical Society. Of the eighteen charter members, he was the only Jew.[218] Dr. Jacob De la Motta, his partner, carved out an honored name among his fellow professionals.[219] The Chatham Dispensary, in 1819, listed him as one of its attending physicians. As evidence of his stature, invitations came to him, year after year, to present the anniversary address for the Georgia Medical Society.[220] When, in 1820, Dr. De la Motta's remarks at the consecration of the first "Mickva" Israel led two former U.S. Presidents to send letters of congratulations, the local press reponded by carrying the Presidential documents, with these attendant words:

> The enlightened and liberal sentiments entertained by these venerable sages—their mild and discriminating charity for the religious principles of those who may differ from our own, is well worthy of general observance, and forms a happy contrast with the blind and enduring animosity still displayed by too many in our community.[221]

THE *Union Society*

Believed to be one of the oldest charitable organizations in America, the Society was an offshoot of a social and benevolent club founded in 1750. Its purpose was to provide assistance for orphan children in the colony, whose plight touched the hearts of its five charter members. Only three are yet remembered by name: Benjamin Sheftall, Richard Milledge, and Peter Tondee. As its membership grew, it became known as the *St. George's Society* and evolved into the *Union Society* prior to 1765. Tradition has it that, because the founders were of diverse faiths, their coming together represented unity midst diversity, hence the name *Union Society*. The Society almost went out of existence during the Revolution because of the occupation of Savannah in 1778. It was Mordecai Sheftall's suggestion that the prisoners at Sunbury, of whom *four* were members, convene an annual meeting each year to insure compliance with the charter. The first such meeting took place on April 23, 1779. Mordecai Sheftall was elected vice-president, and Levi Sheftall, constable.[222] In 1833, the part played by this quartet was publicly recognized at the anniversary dinner, when they were toasted for their saving act.

On April 23, 1830, Mrs. Perla Sheftall Solomons, a direct descendant of Benjamin, Mordecai, and the 1815 *Union Society* president, Dr. Moses Sheftall (her father), presented a wooden box made from the live oak at Sunbury, under whose branches the four prisoners-of-war gathered to keep the Society going.[223] Bethesda Orphanage, the handiwork of Rev. George Whitfield, became the chief concern of the organization, which incorporated in 1786. Its enterprise expanded as it sought to assist widows as well as orphans, an increasing body in the post-Revolutionary War era.[224] In 1854, the Board of Managers bought 125 acres of the Bethesda estate, and erected buildings for the accommodation of orphans (the buildings yet stand).[225] Participation in the *Union Society* was accounted a symbol of prestige, and Savannah's noteworthy attached to it.[226] The Jewish presence from the beginning not only created a tradition of close association among Jewish and non-Jewish leaders in the city, but allowed for the basic ethical commandments of the Jewish and Christian faiths to be carried forth. Other Jews rose to high positions in the *Union Society,* including Abraham Minis (vice-president in 1854 and president in 1869). Solomon Cohen, preceded him in this high office by several years.[227]

FREE-MASONRY

Dr. Samuel Reznick has pointed out that Masonry in America served the purpose of bridging differences between Jews and Gentiles.[228] In Europe, Jewry lived apart, removed from the political and social concerns of the broader society. Here, the Masonic orders enabled those from separate heritages to develop bonds of amity and to learn how to relate. The emphasis on King Solomon and the Temple cult, plus a strong "Old Testament" base, enabled Jews to feel comfortable with Masonic lore and ritual, and increased their awareness of the Scriptural heritage they shared with non-Jews. Masonry provided the environment for growing trust between faith groups, essential for enabling them to take up arms together and fight as comrades for American independence.

A popular Masonic history (distributed locally) states that Solomon's Lodge No. 1 F & A.M. derived from the premier Grand Lodge in London. On February 21, 1734, Colonel Oglethorpe and a group of English Freemasons met and formally organized a lodge in Savannah, warranted in December of 1735.[229] It was the second duly constituted Masonic Lodge in North America. According to an article in the author's possession (from an undated Masonic publication) entitled "The Synagogue and George Washington," both Moses and Daniel Nunes appeared on the oldest roster of members (February 21, 1734). Benjamin Sheftall was a Past Master, as were all those who saved the Union Society at Sunbury, including Mordecai Sheftall. Among the notable heroes of the American Revolution were men

attached to this lodge. Included in the select possessions of Solomon's Lodge
is a gavel made from the Sunbury oak where the first Masonic meeting was
held in 1734—the gift of the Sheftall family.

The Jewish participation in Solomon's Lodge and the others that later
formed was substantial. In the late 1860's, as recorded by Agnew and Lee,
Georgia Chapter No. 3 elected S. P. Hamilton as chaplain; and Zerubbabel
Lodge No. 15 included Rev. Brother R. D. C. Lewin (the rabbi of "Mickva"
Israel), Simon Hexter, Jacob Belsinger, J. Vetsburg, Levy S. Byck, and Lewis
Kayton as members.[230] Zerubbabel Lodge consistently attracted the largest
contingent of Hebrews. The role of the lodges in the cornerstone-laying
ceremonies of the 1820 synagogue has already been noted. Their participation in the consecration of the chief stone for the 1876-78 K.K.M.I. will be
described in a later chapter. All the rabbis of "Mickva" Israel, from Lewin
through Solomon, were staunch supporters of Masonic activity, and in most
instances proceeded through the degrees with determination.

The Supreme Council of Scottish Rite Masonry was founded in nearby
Charleston by nine patriarchs, four of whom were Jews (three having lived
some portion of their lives in this city)—Emanuel De la Motta, treasurer-
general; Abraham Alexander, secretary-general; Israel Delieben, and Moses
C. Levy, inspector-general.[231] Dr. Jacob De la Motta in 1844 (after leaving
Savannah) rose to become Grand Commander of the Supreme Council of
the Scottish Rite.[232]

The Scottish Rite Temple on Bull and Charlton Streets in Savannah,
described in Masonic literature as "the most symbollic building in the
South," was erected in 1912 by "Mickva" Israel member, Hyman Wallace
Witcover, a 33° Sovereign Grand Inspector General of Georgia.[233] The
building remains one of the admired tourist sites in town.

THE ABRAHAMS HOME

The one benevolent institution in Savannah which owes its existence
to the wife of an adherent of the Jewish faith is the Abrahams Home on
Broughton and East Broad Streets. Built in 1858 (by John Norris) as a place
where aged and indigent females might find shelter from life's storms, it expanded as a consequence of a philanthropic act by Mrs. Dorothea Abrahams.
The governing board has frequently included Jewish members, and while
its role has changed over the past century and a half (it now serves as a
nursing home), it continues to be a haven for widows and a refuge for
the destitute.[234]

INSTANCES OF PHILO AND ANTI-SEMITISM

Prior to the American Revolution, the only major incident demonstrating Judeophobia (apart from the opening episode of settlement) involved
the denial of expanded Jewish burial space on the south commons by the
Commons House of Assembly in 1770. Whatever moved this body to deny

same is unknown, but what moved the petitioners *against* to put pressure on the legislators is a matter of record. They had no wish to live in the vicinity of a graveyard where reposed those who "by prejudice of education . . . imbibed principles entirely repugnant to those of our most holy religion."[235] There is no evidence of a Jewish response to this instance of bigotry. Following the War for Independence, the slightest incidence revealing anti-Jewish sentiment elicited decisive action. Three episodes are here singled out.

In 1800, a desecration took place at the Hebrew Community Cemetery. The gate was damaged, and the walls injured in a "shameful" manner. A fifty dollar reward was posted for any information leading to the conviction of the guilty one(s). Sheftall Sheftall, then *parnass* of the congregation, placed the following notice in the *Columbian Museum and Savannah Advertiser:*

> Whereas some evil minded person or persons have destroyed the gate belonging to the burial ground of the Hebrew congregation of Savannah, and have injured the walls of said burying ground, in a shameful manner, I do therefore in the name and on behalf of the said congregation hearby [*sic*] offer a reward of fifty dollars, to any person or persons who will give information against said offender or offenders so that they may be prosecuted agreeable to law.[236]

In 1812, the burial grounds were the locale of another unpleasant happening. More vandalism was perpetrated against the sacred site. Whether anti-Semitism was at play or not is unspecified, but, regardless of the motivation, President Moses Sheftall wanted it stopped. Again the newspaper was the medium for making known the congregation's displeasure:

> Caution! Those persons who make a practice of setting up TARGETS against the gates of the burial ground of the Hebrew congregation, of this city, to shoot at, are informed that a strict lookout is kept for them and if caught at it they may rely on being prosecuted as far as the law will go. A reward of ten dollars will be paid for prosecution, to conviction by   Moses Sheftall
> President Hebrew Congregation[237]

The final and most distressing of all instances of anti-Jewish activity in the antebellum period is the first known incident of *social* anti-Semitism in Georgia. In 1807, a dancing assembly was operating in Savannah, and Dr. Moses Sheftall's name was proposed for membership. It came as a shock to him, considering how highly respected he and his forebearers were in the city, to be blackballed. On the day after Christmas, 1807, he had the following letter, addressed to the managers of the cotillion, published in the *Republican and Savannah Evening Ledger*. The names of the guilty were there to read in black and white— John M. Berrien, George **Glen**, A. S. Roe, George Scott, Joseph Caruthers, Robert Habersham, Thomas **Bourns**, and Hazen Kimball. Below are exerpts from the text:

Doubtless you will be surprised at finding yourselves this publically [*sic*] called on to answer for your ungentlemenlike conduct, exercised toward me, under cover of night of Wednesday last; but when you have taken upon yourselves to determine by ballot, whether I was, what you deem worthy of becoming a subscriber to the dancing assemblies, of which you are the managers, and that on your presuming to a ballot on my name, I was rejected; you can have no objection, to answer a public call to assign your reasons for such a singular proceedings [*sic*], particularly when I dare to make such, and to tell you, one and all, that I bid defiance to your malignity . . . It cannot be unknown to most of you, that I have for years past, had the honor of holding public appointments of trust and honor; and that to such whom I am bound to account for my conduct it has been approved of. I do not know that I should have deemed it worth my while to have called on you to exhibit any charge that you may have or pretend to have against me, but sirs, the report has got general circulation, and I am well aware that such report is designed by you to injure my reputation, as far as in such men's power lays; and being solicited by a number of my friends to demand of you why you have acted thus, I shall expect an immediate reply.

I would ask what motives could have influenced your proceedings —did it proceed from any personal opposition? If so why thus dastardly make the attack? Why not step forward and declare the same to me; and not, at one of your nightly meetings, by balloting. . .

I am not a mushroom, of a night's growth, nor a bird of passage; nor yet am I an exotic of another clime, lately transplanted to this soil. No sirs; I am a native, and the descendant of a native; and one who has been reared within the small circle of this city.

Can you . . . say that my political sentiments had no influence on your decision? Should this have been the case, I must rejoice to think I was refused admittance, although I might say, I should not have considered myself highly honored had I been admitted.

But sirs, I believe the *true* reason for your conduct has not yet been touched upon by me. *I would therefore ask you, whether your conduct has not been influenced on account of my religion? If this has been the course, pray tell me what has a religion to do with ballrooms.* If this is a crime, take a look amongst yourselves and see whether there's none of you whose moral conduct has been more liable to censure than mine; if so, then why bring *religious persuasion* to justify your base conduct towards[238] (Italics added.) Moses Sheftall

Savannah, December 23, 1807

These local incidences gave way to one that generated concern on an international scale. Known in the sources as the *Damascus Affair*, it centered on a blood libel case involving a Father Thomas, in the year 1840. It has been claimed that a latent "national consciousness sprang into overt existence" for the first time, as a consequence of this case, providing the humus out of which modern Zionism sprang.[239]

For background, in 1840 Syria had been wrested from Turkish control by the Viceroy of Egypt. The disappearance of Father Thomas, at a time when the European nations had eyes turned to the Middle East, gave heightened meaning to the case. A Jewish barber, Negrim, "confessed" after

torture that the killing of the priest was accomplished by the richest Jews in
Damascus and that the priest's blood was removed for "ritual purposes."
The Jews of western Europe felt threatened by this revival of medievalism,
and sought ways to act in concert to counter the surge of anti-Semitism.
Complicating the problem were the territorial ambitions of the European
states. *France* backed Egypt; *England* supported Russia, Prussia and
Austria (which were attached to the Turkish Sultan).[240] English Jews, led
by Sir Moses Montefiore, could exercise little leverage in the situation, so
it was necessary to ally with French Jews under the leadership of M.
Crémieux. The two aforementioned philanthropists journeyed together
to Egypt, seeking release and exoneration for the Damascus Jewish
leaders.[241]

News of what was transpiring appeared in the American press and led
to rallies in New York City (with J.B. Kursheet as chairman) on August 17,
1840, and in Philadelphia on August 27 at the Mikveh Israel Synagogue
(Hyman Gratz may have convened the latter). Representatives of the clergy
were present (in Philadelphia) to hear Rev. Isaac Leeser repudiate the
blood-accusation charge as abhorrent to the tenets of "our holy religion."
Resolutions were passed in both cities, although the U.S. Government had
already dispatched messages to diplomats on the scene to redress the wrongs
of the Damascus Jews.[242] Reference was made at the Philadelphia meeting
to action taken by the Jews of Richmond, Virginia. In no source, discovered
by this writer, was the Savannah response to the *Damascus Affair* mentioned,
so that the following adds a new chapter to what is known by American
Jewish historians.

On September 4, 1840 (only a few weeks after the mass meetings in New
York and Philadelphia), it was reported in the *Daily Georgian* that the
Mayor of Savannah, Robert M. Charlton, had called a public meeting
"to take into consideration the persecution of the Jews at Damascus." Multi-
tudes of Christians were present to express their concern, leading Solomon
Cohen to address the assembled body and

> return his and their [the Jewish citizens of Savannah] thanks to the
> Christians of this community for their generous sympathy . . .[243]

In 1841, interest in the *Affair* continued, as the *Daily Georgian* reported in
detail what was transpiring with the persecuted Jews of far-off Syria.[214] In
Savannah, action on the highest level of local government occurred in sym-
pathy with the plight of the Jews. *The Damascus Affair* was a precursor of
of the famed *Mortara Incident* (to be considered in Chapter Six).

The *Damascus Affair* provides a perfect transition from an examination
of the record on anti-Semitism to its flip side, philo-Semitism. The occur-
rence that follows also depended on the positive attitude of another mayor—
John Y. Noel. On December 6, 1806, the *Columbian Museum and Savannah Advertiser* publicized the motion of Council—that Wednesday, December 10th, be set aside as a day of supplication and prayer to Almighty
God

imploring his [*sic*] blessing on this city in [the] future, and an exemption from such misfortunes and calamities as it has heretofore been visited with.

All were called upon to cease commercial activity, and

> the several ministers of the gospel be requested to perform divine services [with] discourses appropriate to the occasion.[245]

Two days earlier, the *parnass* of "Mickva" Israel, Levy Abrahams, convened the *adjunta* to inform them that he had received correspondence from the mayor of the city with the above resolution. The letter read:

Dear Sirs

> Enclosed is a copy of the Resolution passed by the City Council to which I beg leaf [*sic*] to call the attention of the Religious Society with which you are connected. Tho' you differ with other Societies in many important points yet with them *you worship the only true God* and with them you acknowledge his [*sic*] supreme power as well as his [*sic*] providential dispensation. I therefore flatter myself [by assuming that] your Congregation will unite with us in the solemn duty required by the Resolution. I am Respectfully (Italics added.)

> > Sir Your Obt. Servt.
> > John Y. Noel
> > Mayor
> > Dec.ʳ 2, 1806[246]

Not only did the mayor acknowledge the validity of Judaism by affirming that Jews worship the "only true God," but he solicited the Jewish community's prayers as efficacious. The particular event that triggered this "day of supplication" is unknown. There is no record of fire or disease that ravaged that year.[247] The great storm of September, 1804, was long remembered for its destructive ferocity, but the hurricane season historically ended thirty days before December.[248] Thomas Gamble, Jr., attributes the prayer to the fear of devastating fire, though evidence is not cited in the text.[249]

By 1806, Savannah Jewry had already established patterns of worship in harmony with the traditions of the city and Nation. In 1795 (in February), the board invited Dr. Moses Sheftall to prepare a discourse for the observance of a day of "prayer and thanksgiving" ordained by a Presidential Proclamation throughout the United States.[250] The invitation was accepted, and presumably local Jews congregated for Thanksgiving prayer. In 1798, President Washington again enjoined upon the American people to set aside May 9th, a Wednesday, as "a day of prayer and fasting." In consequence thereof, the *adjunta* ordered that the "synagogue be opened on that day at ten o'clock," and invited Isaac Benedix, leading merchant, citizen, and politician (local postmaster), to select "a few prayers adopted to the above occasion . . ."[251]

BETWEEN JEW AND JEW

Concern for the destiny of Jews everywhere has been a distinguishing feature of the local Jewish populace from an early day. Suffering among Jews in Palestine particularly excited generosity. Indeed this community was one of the more philanthropic in America.[252] The Charter of "Mickva" Israel included a rule that sanctioned gifts to those deemed in need by the *parnass*, without recourse to the *adjunta*.

An interesting example of benignity to Jews far removed from this Forest City is found in the minutes of November 5, 1816. Revolutionary War hero Marks (Markes or Marcus) Lazarus was a prominent member of K.K. Beth Elohim in Charleston, serving on its general *adjunta* in 1820.[253] Dr. Moses Sheftall, *parnass*, received a letter from him, via a Mr. Natabi "who reports himself to be from Tunis." From community to community he was travelling to raise funds for the oppressed "brethren in that quarter of the globe." Under the congregational rules, only twenty shillings could be given without board action (an inadequate sum), so that body was convened. Dr. Sheftall attested that Mr. Natabi appeared "sincere in his pursuits," based on certain papers in his possession. Thirty dollars was voted as a donation.

Instances of direct assistance to local Jews, who had need of fraternal aid, are to be found. The most pitiful plea to be brought to the attention of the *adjunta* occurred in 1816. The petitioner was a man of distinguished Jewish lineage, Isaac DeLyon, Sr. (probably the first of the family with the name *Isaac* who was married to Rinah Tobias, although his age seems problematical—he would be seventy-seven at the time of this letter).[254] He was a direct descendant of Dr. and Mrs. Samuel Nunes, and Abraham DeLyon, local vintner. The petition came in the following instrument.

> Dr. Sir [written to Moses Sheftall]
>   As parnoss of this congregation I am obliged to address you[.] I am in a most distressed situation without house or home[.] I am obliged to leave the place where I have stayed[.] I have no other resource but under the market where I expect to perish with the cold[.] I am unable to pay for my board where I stay any longer which forced me away from it and you are the ruling officer of the congregation[.] I have thought proper to state my situation[.] I have no doubt as a gentleman of humanity you will give me some releaf [sic] out of the funds of the congregation[.] You will excuse the deficiency of my address.[255]

Whereupon the vote was taken, and the sum of fifty dollars was allocated. It has been a tradition in Savannah, over the course of the centuries, to respond both to the international needs of our people and to the plight of locals. The pattern commenced in this era.

CHAPTER FIVE

THE PREACHER FROM POSEN

B etween 1840 and 1861 was a time of expansion in Georgia. The largest city in the state by 1860, Savannah (population 22,292), thrived as an industrial and commercial center, producing goods valued at nearly $2 million, and burgeoning as a major seaport with foreign exports upwards of $19 million.[1]

Sustaining the growth was a well developed system of railroads connecting southwest and central Georgia to the Savannah matrix. By the end of this twenty-year time frame cotton was king; rice and corn were finding vast markets; and lumber products were peaking at the $2 million level.[2] The year 1857 brought a "panic," but Georgia bankers were conservative managers, minimizing the damage.[3] On the whole, the two decades preceding the great Internecine Conflict were bullish times for the thirteenth state.

The Jewish community of Savannah participated fully in this commercial harvest. K. K. "Mickva" Israel blossomed in terms of financial strength, membership count, and institutional health. In this twenty year span, a "professional" *hazzan* (reader and teacher) was "called;" other functionaries were hired to carry on the requirements of Jewish life; the synagogue was renovated and improved; the cemetery expanded; and a new leadership emerged from among men of prestige and wealth, who were attuned to structuring the institution on "modern" principles of governance and fiscal integrity. When change occurs, expect friction to follow. Reflecting a contentious epoch, some of the most exciting battles royal in the temple's history were waged.

THE PERMANENT FUND

The perceived role of Jewish women was that home and family were their special domains, and the destiny of synagogues reposed in the hands of the men. At K.K.M.I., however, the ladies were responsible for initiating a project that enabled the congregation to move forward in a direction not seriously entertained before—finding the means to sustain a rabbi.

In 1843, Mesdames Solomon Cohen and Octavus Cohen initiated a Community Fair involving "the ladies of the congregation" on March 17th (St.

[101]

Patrick's Day). For several days the event lasted at the Exchange, resulting in $1522.33 profit.[4] In transmitting same to the *adjunta*, it was requested that the monies form

> a permanent fund, the interest of which is to be appropriated to the maintenance of a suitable reader for the congregation . . . until sufficient is received for that purpose, the interest that accrues in secure bonds . . . be invested in such a manner as the parnass may deem best to effect the object in view.[5]

Each of the participating matrons ran "tables" or booths; a total of six were "manned" by the two Cohen sisters-in-law, Miss Rebecca DeLyon and Miss R. Cohen, sisters, Mrs. Perla Sheftall, Mrs. Isaac Cohen and Misses G. and S. Russell and Miss Francis Sheftall. Jewesses were not the only "hawkers of wares," for the *Congregational Minute Books* relate "many of the other persuasions [*sic*] graciously participated."[6] The initiators of the project, the Mesdames Cohens, were women of proud lineage, molded by the strong women who reared them. Mrs. Solomon Cohen was Rachel Gratz Moses' daughter. Aunt Rebecca Gratz of *Ivanhoe* fame parented her after Rachel's untimely death. Mrs. Octavus Cohen was the former Henrietta Yates Levy. Her two sisters were Phoebe Pember (matron of Chimborazo Hospital in Richmond) and Eugenia Levy Phillips (wife of Congressman Philip Phillips and Civil War spy).

A second fair resulted in $101.12 accruing to the kitty.[7] The $1600 total was invested in bonds of the Central Railroad and Banking Company. So rapidly did these bonds advance in value that by the end of 1843 the Permanent Fund investments escalated to $4418.30.[8] News of the fund and its success reached other areas, for the minutes of August 21, 1843, related the application of Reverend B. C. Carillon for the "office of hazzan." (In 1842, Rabbi Carillon served as rabbi of Montego Bay, Jamaica, where controversy swirled about him for attempting "violent and unauthorized changes in the usual form of worship as currently amongst Portuguese Jews.")[9] K.K.M.I. regretted turning him down, but the synagogue's resources were not sufficient.

The Fund continued to grow at a substantial pace ($4,400 in 1843, more than $5,600 in 1846, and $6,900 in 1849), so that by the time advertisements for a *hazzan* were carried in the Jewish press, here and in England, its capital assets approached $8,000. Ironically, the major beneficiary of the fund for a substantial period of time was the husband of its progenitor—the Honorable Solomon Cohen. At the May 2, 1847, meeting, the *parnass*, Isaac Cohen (a second cousin), recommended that a major portion of the Permanent Fund be given out on loan to him with security in the form of a mortgage on real estate, underwritten by proper insurance. This technique had proven valuable in the period of building the second sanctuary. The maturing railroad bonds no longer seemed the best way to invest, so this became the viable alternative. The 1846-47 cash accounts recorded $6,000 advanced to Solomon Cohen. A safer debtor could nowhere be found. Year after year, promptly and punctiliously, the congregation received the amount owing from the man who would become its foremost leader in years to come. The property which Cohen provided for security was Lot 3, Wilmington Tything, Derby Ward, a lot on the south side of Bay Street, between Bull and Whitaker Streets.[10]

Considering the high and holy purpose to which the Permanent Fund was dedicated, one would hardly imagine dissension over it. Rule 17 of the new rules and by-laws, adopted August 21, 1848, declared the trust

> for the support of a reader or Hazzan . . . shall never be diverted from said purpose and shall be vested in three trustees elected by the congregation . . . and they shall make a report at the annual meeting.

In November of the following year, the *adjunta* was up in arms because a bill had been introduced into the Georgia Legislature by Senator Purse of Chatham County. President Mordecai Sheftall, Sr. (son of Levi) was at odds with the bill and induced the other board members to pass the following motion:

> Whereas the officers and vestry . . . in whom full power and authority are vested by the Charter of Incorporation dated in the year 1790 and the Constitution bye laws . . . passed in pursuance thereof[,] have received information from the public gazette of said city that the Honorable Thomas Purse . . . has introduced a bill into the Legislature to be entitled an act to Incorporate the Trustees of the Permanent Fund of the Hebrew congregation of Savannah[,] and whereas the person or persons who has or have transmitted the same for purpose aforesaid has or have acted *officiously unauthorized* and without assent or consent of the officers and members generally of the said Hebrew congregation . . .,

and

> whereas there is ample security afforded for the protection and safety of the said Permanent Fund . . . invested in trustees . . . [who have] acted and made loans[,] and whereas the officers of said Hebrew Congregation for themselves and the members thereof perceive no necessity for incorporating . . . when the Hebrew congregation as a body in church is already incorporated[,] therefore do enter into solemn protest against the passage of the bill . . .[11]

Clearly a member or members of the congregation, untrustful of the stewardship of the acting leadership, wanted the monies secured by creating an independent trust fund incorporated under separate auspices. This was a direct affront to the integrity of the *adjunta*, and was greeted with opposition. The Georgia Legislature, meeting in Milledgeville, was soon "invaded" by Mordecai Sheftall, Sr. and Levy Hart, lobbyists for K.K.M.I.,

> for the purpose of using their efforts to defeat the passage of a bill by the Senate of Georgia . . . and that the sum of sixty dollars be . . . appropriated . . . to defray their necessary expenses.[12]

If one had to pick the antagonist in the tale, one would be tempted to focus on Isaac Cohen. Immediately after the resolution to protest the bill was passed, the honored ex-*parnass* submitted his resignation.[13] A punitive urge prompted Sheftall, Sr., (Cohen's distant cousin) to press for the passage of a rule allowing no graves to be dug without permission of the *parnass* and requiring a separate key to be made for the Community Burial Grounds. Isaac Cohen, who married Dr. Moses Sheftall's daughter, must have had ready access to the cemetery his wife's grandfather bequeathed, and the intent of the resolution was to subvert his control.

IN QUEST OF A READER/TEACHER

Evidence could sustain the view that K.K.M.I. had the services of a *hazzan* long before the first "professional" was paid for his ministrations. Dr. Jacob De la Motta, whose sermon at the 1820 dedication of the first synagogue building gained the attention of national leaders, was a man of broad Jewish learning. During his residency in Savannah, he was "spiritual" leader of the Jewish community. In previous chapters, we have referred to others who functioned in this role. Special mention must be made of Levy Hart, the first recompensed lay reader. In May of 1842, he received the commendation of the *adjuntamen,*

> for his services in performing divine service in the synagogue for some months past [a twelve to fifteen month span].

Apparently what was given with one hand was taken away with the other. In the same record, the point is made that

> it was . . . contrary to the principals [sic] of our holy faith to extend thanks to any individual for being permited [sic] to do that which conferred an honor on him . . .

Thanks, but no thanks, Mr. Hart!

In the May, 1842, minutes, a motion was made by Isaac Russell to induce Levy Hart to perform the duties of "minister" and to pay him for his services. As each member was assessed a five dollar fee to sustain the new synagogue staff member, Levy Hart can be considered the first paid "rabbi" in the congregation's history.

On January 16, 1844, a letter from Mordecai Sheftall, Sr., to the *adjunta* was read, announcing that in Savannah there was an individual who had the qualifications to serve as *hazzan.* His instrument called for a

> meeting of the congregation speedily for the purpose of taking into consideration the propriety of engaging a competent person and of appropriate character to perform service[s] in the synagogue,

and further, "that it was highly probable that there is now in Savannah a gentlemen who will answer for the station." The request was denied, on the grounds that there was no way to pay such a "gentlemen." In addition, the synagogue was in foul shape and could not be used for public worship. The board immediately ordered that the building be repaired. The repair motion added that once the building was decent again the *parnass* was

> authorized to permit the use of it for the performance of Divine Service to any competent reader in the Minhag Sephardim [Mediterranean-style ritual] who may be desireous [*sic*] of officiating *gratuitously*.[14] (Italics added.)

Two years later, no change in the status of the *hazzan* could be reported. The August 17th board meeting put the responsibility to Mr. "Barnard" (probably Mr. Barnett) "to procure a suitable person to read for the congregation during the approaching holy days." To him also fell the burden of raising, "through private subscription," monies to provide compensation.

Two additional years were to pass before the issue of the paid spiritual leader was advanced with serious intent. At the August 21, 1848, meeting (important in the congregation's history because a new set of by-laws was voted upon), Solomon Cohen placed before the assembled body the following resolution:

> *Resolved* that the parnoss be requested to advertise in *The Occident*, a periodical published in the city of Philadelphia, and *Voice of Jacob* in London for a hazan. *Resolved* that the salary shall be eight hundred dollars per annum and the applicant shall be able to perform the service according to the Portuguese minhag and deliver at least two English discourses each month.

To meet the sudden expense, the congregation sought a mentor. Who better to address with hands outstretched than philanthropist *Judah Touro* of New Orleans. A letter to "our co-religionist" was rushed via the mails asking of him "his aid in the raising of funds for a hazan."[15] At a later time, Mr. Touro provided generously to K.K.M.I., but not on this occasion.

The ad met with no success as the September 20, 1849, meeting proved. An offer of two hundred dollars was tendered Levy Hart in payment of his expected yearly service as *hazzan*. In the letter addressed to him, there was clear reference to the congregation's "present difficulties." This was the period of the "hoopla" over the legislature incorporating the Permanent Fund. The congregation was divided. In the hope of reconciling the warring factions, Mr. Hart agreed to serve in whatever way he could, proffering this letter to communicate his sentiments:

> September 20, 1849
> Mordecai Sheftall, Sen.
> Parnoss K.K.M.I.
> Sir your note of this date wherein you are desirous to obtain my services as reader for the congregation for the term of 12 months at a salary of $200.00 I have received, and respond to the call with a degree of anxiety, as the issues involved are weighty, and important.

Should I decline to respond to the call, our place of worship will be forever closed, and our children grope in darkness; should I accept, it may be the means of permanently opening the building, and in that way allay all feeling, unite all interest, and bring together our *divided* people[.] [W]ith the *ardent hope* that I may be the *instrument* of *uniting* all interests, and *classes* into one brotherhood, induced me to accept the call made. Allow me to state the compensation offered is no inducement. I would that my services be considered '*gratuitous*' as an *offering* on the 'altar of peace' . . . (Italics added.)

A streak of messianism is known to surface among Jewish functionaries from time to time. The above document is of importance because it reflects the real fears of the time. The congregation was divided (note that Levy Hart perceived class distinctions at play); the building was rarely open for worship; and the children were receiving no Jewish exposure. After receiving his letter, the board confirmed him as "temporary" reader, until a recognized authority could be found.

Despite *"Hazzan"* Hart's benign gesture, bickering in K.K.M.I. was not stilled. During the August 19, 1850, meeting, controversy abounded. The seeds of contention, scattered throughout the land, took root in this temperate clime. Two factions drew up sides and used the meeting as battling ground. On one side was *Parnass* Mordecai Sheftall, Sr., on the other, Solomon Cohen. So rough was the election of officers that the individual who opposed Levi J. Hart, Sheftall's candidate for secretary, was recorded in the minutes as "blank . . . rec'd 5 votes."

The moment of high drama came when Waring Russell proposed that the congregation *"proceed forthwith to elect a hazan to perform the services of the synagogue for a term of two years . . ."* (Italics added for emphasis.) No trained *hazzan* had made application, so this could only be an attempt to forego the search and empower Levy Hart to function more than temporarily. The opposing lines were again sharply drawn. To Levy Hart's candidacy, an opposing rabbi's name was advanced, the Rev. Isaac Leeser, editor of *The Occident* and *hazzan* of K.K. Mikveh Israel in Philadelphia. Hart received fourteen votes and *Leeser only five*. Knowing that he had received a vote of confidence in preference to one of America's greatest rabbinic leaders ought to have surfeited Hart's ego. In less than a year's time (July 1, 1851), Hart's resignation was formally submitted to the *parnass* and *adjunta*.

One cannot end the tale of congregational in-fighting without recording Philip M. Russell's plea to the 1850 congregational meeting:

Whereas there is at present existing among the members of the congregation a feeling calculated to injure the standing of this congregation in the eyes of the public and for the purpose of reconciling matters and bringing about a friendly feeling[,] resolved that a committee be appointed by the parnas with a view to arrange [resolve?] if possible the existing difficulty or misunderstanding . . .[16]

To this petition for some act of reconciliation, a motion to adjourn was offered, and lost. Solomon Cohen and Jacob De la Motta spoke on one side, and Judge Mordecai Sheftall, Sr., *parnass*, and P. M. Russell spoke on the other side. Isaac Cohen of the Solomon Cohen faction and Solomon Sheftall of the *parnass'* faction asked for a vote to adjourn, putting to an end the first "Civil War," K.K.M.I. style.

A week later, Philip M. Russell tendered his resignation in writing, not only as one of the *adjunta*, but also as a member of the congregation.

HIRING A HAZZAN; ALMOST, BUT NOT QUITE

Dr. Morris Raphall, rabbi of New York's B'nai Jeshurun Congregation (the first body of worshippers to break away from historic Shearith Israel in 1825), was the city's leading Jewish clergyman in the 1850's.[17] Of English birth and rearing, he had attained considerable fame in his native land as a lecturer on the Bible. In America, he was given the high honor of being the first Jewish "reverend" to open the U. S. Congress with prayer in 1860.[18] Jewish merchants of Savannah regularly visited New York and were connected enough to the Rev. Doctor to approach him about a *hazzan*.[19] Raphall recommended the Rev. A. de Sola, reader of the Sephardic congregation in Montreal, and communication with him was initiated. Despite the urgings of the *parnass*, at the November 6, 1851, meeting, no motion was passed to pursue the matter.

Money was the issue. By the December 4th meeting, President De la Motta "brought to the attention of the adjunta the necessity of some action as regards engaging a reader" and suggested as

> preparatory step that a list be opened for each congregator to subscribe the sum he is willing to pay towards the support of a reader for five years . . .

By the following meeting, $550 had been pledged by eight gentlemen.[20]

By a legislative decree of the Georgia Senate and House, the annual meeting in August was changed to the first Monday in January and the January 4, 1852, convocation was the time for all major business of the congregation to be conducted. Jacob De la Motta expedited the procurement of a *hazzan* by pushing the following resolution:

> That the adjunta be authorized to elect a Hazzan and fix his salary—that he shall hold his office as long as it is agreeable to the congregation, to be decided by a majority of two thirds of the members present at the time, but, that the congregation must give him six months notice before he can be dismissed . . . the same being required of him should he choose to leave.

By this time the Permanent Fund had accumulated $8,208, and could expect several hundred dollars interest annually. Not one to waste time, De la Motta convened the *adjunta* on January 25, 1852 and advocated the

election of the Rev. Abraham de Sola as *"preacher* to the congregation"
at a salary of one thousand dollars per annum, payable quarterly "in
advance." The resolution was forwarded to Rev. de Sola, requesting acceptance and offering a salary advance of $250.

After eleven members came forward to pledge an additional $1,075 for
the support of the *hazzan,* there was no cause to fear that the congregation
was in over its head.[21]

A word about the Rev. Abraham de Sola: a direct descendant of the
ninth century Ibn Daud family, the rabbi could count among his ancestors some of Jewry's foremost leaders, rabbis, sages, and scholars.[22]
His father, David, was a renowned London rabbi; his son, Aaron Meldola
de Sola, followed in the path of his father and grandfather in New York
City. Rabbi David de Sola Pool of New York's Shearith Israel was the
grandchild of his eldest sister, Sarah.

To the initial call, the Rev. de Sola responded with this letter of February 15, 1852:

Respected Sir:

I have recd . . . your valued favor dated 6th shebat enclosing
'a copy of the resolution passed by the congregation K.K.M. Israel' . . .

Permit me sir to request you to convey to your colleagues . . .
the assurance of my warmest respect and gratitude for the very
flattering distinction they have pleased to confer on me[,] a distinction of which I indeed feel my unworthiness; for the postion your
kind preference has called me to assume is one requiring ability and
zeal infinitely greater than I could in even arrogance pretend to
possess . . . yet I am constrained to inform you that it is out of my
power now to accept the kind offer of your congregation, since you
require your minister to commense [*sic*] his labors on Passover
next . . . for even by giving six months notice to my congregation of
my desire to remove south, I could not leave Montreal before the
first of September next. And I should here remark that I have no
warrant for supposing that my congregation here would be at all
desirous for, or pleased with, an abrupt severance of our present
connection which I am pleased to be enabled to state is an agreeable
one for all parties. And as I once had the honor of writing a respected member of your Adjunta [Is this an indication that de
Sola had made an earlier contact or that a 'secret' overture had
come to him?] I could not for any consideration . . . abandon my flock
without seeking for them . . . spiritual guidance for the future. But
though the arrangement above . . . may the present prevent my
laboring in so interesting a field as Savannah, yet shall my best
wishes and warmest interest be centered in your congregation. And
if it meets the views of your constituents, I will . . . communicate
with my father, the Rev. Dct. de Sola of London that he may seek for
you a competent person of tried, stable principles and character.

Faced with this inconclusive resolution of the issue, the *adjunta* could
not

but highly approve of the motives [as stated in the letter] which actuated him in not wishing to leave his congregation without first affording them an opportunity of filling his place and giving them timely notice . . .[23]

The invitation was again extended to the rabbi, asking that he commence his duties sometime in October and answer as soon as practicable. By February 27, 1852, De la Motta had another instrument in the mail conveying the board's sentiment and adding,

> thanking you for your offer to write to your rev'd. father at London for a competent person to act as hazan, *we hope that you will not make that necessary* . . . (Italics added.)

By March 16th, a reply was returned from de Sola. He stated that he needed five or six weeks to give a decisive answer, not anticipating the second call. He cited Dr. Raphall who knew no one in America who could suit the Montreal congregation, so he had to turn to his father in England to find a successor. He promised to meet with his president and urge him to write London, or he would do so. He touched upon a sore issue when he wrote that in the letter to his father, he would

> ascertain whether there be one in his congregation to suit . . . for here [in Montreal] as much as with you they require their hazzan to be not a mere reader, but a minister and instructor of both old and young.

A definite reply to the call would be given in May, de Sola promised, requesting another letter from De la Motta to indicate whether this was acceptable or not.

A week after his letter was received, Dr. Raphall addressed a note to De la Motta with the intent to bolster de Sola's candidacy.

> I sincerely congratulate your congregation in having thus secured the ministration of a talented and honorable young man whose piety is genuine and whose zeal is free from bigotry, while his character is of the highest and his family one of the most eminent in the annals of Hebrew learning. As you were kind enough to say that it was entirely on the strength of my opinion as expressed to you that the Savannah congregation felt induced to give him the preference, permit me to assure you that while I duly appreciate the importance assigned to my opinion, I am by no means disposed to shrink from the responsibility which is thus made to rest upon me, as I am quite convinced you could not make a better choice . . .[24]

Did Raphall believe the pulpit had been filled, or was he merely trying to keep the congregation in abeyance by implying that de Sola would be theirs, he assuming it already?

On May 19, 1852, the final word came from de Sola, and it was disheartening: *"It is with unaffected regret that I find myself obliged to decline their flattering call."* (Italics added for emphasis.) The reasons: no one suitable for Montreal could be found in London; furthermore,

> my congregation all but perfected arrangements which would render my stay among them even more desirable than I have always found it, the arrangements have tended to show me the warm attachment of my flock . . .

The six years of his service had engendered deep ties which resulted in tangible expression. An additional and favorable result of de Sola's decision not to leave was the determination to begin family, leading to the birth of his eldest son, Aaron, on November 22, 1853 (eighteen months later), ultimately multiplying rabbinic leadership in the world.[25]

THE SEARCH BROADENS

Following de Sola's rejection, it was back to *The Occident, Asmonean,* and *London Jewish Chronicle* with advertisements for a spiritual leader

> competent to perform the duties of Hazzan and Preacher, the term of service probationary will be one year but if on or before the expiration of the time, mutual satisfaction should be given, the incumbent [*sic*] will be elected for life . . .

provided two-thirds of the congregation did not vote to invalidate the tenure.[26] The application for the post was to be accompanied by "the best testimonials of capacity."

November 5, 1852, was the day mentioned in the Jewish newspapers as the day of decision. Three candidates, Rev. M. A. Henry of Syracuse, New York, Rev. I. H. Buriah of Louisville, Kentucky, and Rev. I. H. Salky of Buffalo, New York, had applied, but lacking "testimonials of qualifications" they were *ipso facto* eliminated from the competition. The *parnass* reported that he had heard of the resignation of the Rev. M. N. Nathan as *hazzan* of a New Orleans congregation, and had made contact, but to no avail. Retirement from the ministry was his preference. The Rev. "Mendez" [*sic*] of Birmingham, England, was solicited, but because he was well situated there and not impressed by the sufficiency of the salary, he declared reluctance. That was enough to induce the *adjunta* to vote an additional two hundred dollars per annum. This eminent rabbi was the uncle of Isaac P. Mendes, who later served K.K. "Mickva" Israel as its honored rabbi for twenty-seven years (Rev. Abraham de Sola of Montreal was also Mendes' nephew by marriage.[27]) Rev. Abraham Pereira Mendes would eventually forsake English and West Indian pulpits to serve the Jews of Newport, Rhode Island, at the same time nephew Isaac was serving the Jews of Savannah.

The day would not pass before a *hazzan* was called. K.K.M.I. was about to experience rabbinic leadership of the professional kind.

Hazzan AND PREACHER—JACOB ROSENFELD

Searching American Jewish history books, one will discover limited mention of this peripatetic religious leader. Yet he had a significant effect on several Jewish communities in their formative periods. When K.K. Beth Elohim in Charleston fell upon controversy in 1840 with the installation of the organ in the new synagogue building, Dr. Jacob De la Motta (who dedicated the first building of K.K.M.I.) pulled away and organized a new congregation, Sherith Israel. Who was the first rabbi of Sherith Israel? An 1842 immigrant from Lissa, Posen, the Rev. Jacob Rosenfeld.[28] Who should he take to wife? Lenora Moses of the South Carolina Moses family. A. A. Solomons of Savannah, at whose home Rosenfeld was introduced to the leadership of "Mickva" Israel, was a brother-in-law. The Ottolenguis, the Alexanders, the Jonases, and others were *mishpacha* (family).[29] Indeed, Annie Jonas, wife of Abraham Moses, the brother of Rosenfeld's wife, was the daughter of Joseph Jonas, the first Jew to settle in Cincinnati. Abraham Jonas (Abraham Lincoln's Jewish confidant), the postmaster of Quincy, Illinois, was Annie's uncle.[30] From Charleston, Rev. Rosenfeld proceeded to Cincinnati where he served as minister of K.K. Bene Jeshurun. Who was his successor? The architect of Reform Judaism in America, Isaac Mayer Wise. In Cincinnati, Rosenfeld's connection to the Jonas family strengthened his ministry and gave him access to the leadership of this budding Jewish community on the shores of the Ohio River. While in Savannah, Jacob Rosenfeld not only molded K.K.M.I. as its rabbi for nine years, but was the founding rabbi of Savannah's second congregation, B'nai B'rith Jacob.

At the November 5, 1852, *adjunta* meeting, Rev. Rosenfeld was officially invited to become *hazzan* of the congregation. The historic resolution read:

> Resolved that the Rev. Jacob Rosenfeld now of Cincinnati be and he is elected Hazzan and preacher to the congregation on the terms and conditions as stated in the advertizement [*sic*] in the American Occident and London Jewish Chronicle viz for a probating term of one year for the expiration of which, should mutual satisfaction prevail[,] for life, with the understanding that should he become objectionable to two thirds of the congregation, he will on six months notice vacate his place and the like notice be given by him if he wishes to retire.

Brother-in-law A. A. Solomons was pleased to record this election in the *Temple Minute Books*.[31]

By December 10th, President De la Motta reported that Rev. Rosenfeld was informed of his call and accepted. He requested time to relocate his family from Cincinnati and for his congregation to "supply his place." He also asked that the expense of packing and moving be honored by K.K.M.I. One week before the Passover season, he could be expected. The April 10, 1853, minutes included the sad news of a death and sickness in the Rosenfeld family, delaying the move to Savannah beyond the spring festival. The *adjunta* expressed regrets, but understood. In late May, a communication was received from a committee of the *hazzan's* former congregation, K.K. Bene Jeshurun, which was complimentary of his ministry. By June 5th, the Rosenfelds were in the South, visiting nearby Charleston, home of his wife. The next board meeting was called two days later at brother-in-law A. A. Solomon's home, where the new *hazzan* was introduced by the *parnass* and welcomed by all.

ROSENFELD'S "MICKVA" ISRAEL YEARS

Nowhere in the minutes is mention made of the new *hazzan's* skill as an educator of youth. Yet, this was the area in which he made an enduring contribution. Leeser's periodical, *The Occident,* is the primary source for the information.

During his service in Charleston, Rosenfeld's pedagogical career began. Annual examinations were given to students of the "School Of Instruction Of Jewish Youth" to see how well they understood creedal matters. The first class of the school was proctored by Rev. Rosenfeld.[32] That humble beginning was to lead to three major educative responsibilities during his tenure in Cincinnati. In 1852, he served as Superintendent of the Talmud Yelodim Institute, as Superintendent of the Lodge Street Synagogue School, and as Superintendent of the Bene Jeshurun Congregation Sunday School.[33] As wife and co-partner, Mrs. Rosenfeld worked side by side with her husband (during the Charleston years) as a Sunday school teacher in 1845.[34] Though the *K.K.M.I. Minute Books* are silent, one has to surmise that the *adjunta* valued Rosenfeld's talent in this realm, boosting his candidacy for the position of *hazzan.*

Prior to the coming of the new reader, religious school education at K.K.M.I. was non-existent. Up to then, the only recorded instance of youth indoctrination was in the Levi Sheftall family. A private tutor was hired for his children. Rev. Rosenfeld inspired the formation of a Sunday school within a few weeks of his arrival. The following information proceeds from an article in an 1856 issue of *The Occident,* entitled "Sunday School in Savannah."[35] The 250 Israelites of the city had produced forty students. The school, established in 1853, had been on shaky ground for two years, but was about to flourish. Public examinations before Passover had gratified parents, teachers, and the young people involved. As reward, Joseph Lippman suggested that a "Pic Nic" be provided, gratuitously, for the children, educators, and officers of the school. The officers of the Sunday school in 1856 were Mrs. Solomon Cohen, president (whose Aunt Rebecca Gratz founded the first Sunday school in Philadelphia); Miss Anna DeLyon, vice-president; and Mrs. M. S. Cohen, secretary/treasurer. The six teachers included Miss Fanny Minis, Mrs. Frances Meyer, Miss Eugenia Hart, Miss Rachel Cohen, Mr. Solomon Cohen, and Rev. J. Rosenfeld. Founders of the K.K.M.I. Sunday school included Perla Sheftall, Fanny Minis, and Frances Meyer.

The opening phase of Rosenfeld's rabbinate in Savannah could be described as a "honeymoon." Trouble with the *shochet*, a perennial predicament, was solved easily when Mr. Herchberg agreed to abide by the board's rulings.[36] Perhaps Rosenfeld's training as a *shochet* gave him credibility in negotiating with his fellow professional.[37] His first service on *Shavuot* must have awed the folks in the pews.[38] The *parnass* happily reported that the congregation "was regularly and in successful operation."[39] That *Shavuot* service made history. *The Occident* reported the elaborately decorated sanctuary was filled with worshippers awaiting the first appearance of the new *hazzan*.[40] Unfortunately, illness overtook him and he was incapacitated over the Sabbath. Determined to begin his ministry on "Pentecost" Sunday, he proceeded forthwith to the Whitaker Street building and addressed a full sanctuary. All were impressed by his beautiful discourse. That night and the next morning, he preached again. His messages

> drew tears from some of his hearers, when he . . . exhorted all to a strict observance of the Sabbath . . .[41]

By mid-week, every seat in the women's gallery was sold, and downstairs there were but few pews that were not snatched up. In one day, $1,625 was raised. That amount with the interest of the Permanent Fund made the treasury sufficient to sustain the *hazzan* for quite a while. The June 19, 1853, minutes noted that ninety seats were paid for and chairs were set up in the gallery between benches. With such over-crowding, a motion was made directing the president to ventilate the balcony immediately.[42]

If only such a high and holy beginning could have been sustained! However, the *hazzan* was ensnared in the affairs of the *shochet* again and again. On September 2, 1853, the board asked that he recommend a suitable slaughterer. On November 6, 1853, the board wanted him to examine the new *shochet* to make sure he was adept at his art.

Checking after kosher butchers was a step down from eloquent preaching that set the ladies a-sobbing, but it was more to be desired than public insult and injury. Mr. Blumensing, a congregator, offended Rev. Rosenfeld with an "insult offered him in the synagogue on the 29th October," 1853, only six months after his inaugural sermon.[43] The board unanimously suspended all honors to one who had abused their minister. Blumensing delayed until April of the next year before "apologizing for his rudeness to the Rev. Jacob Rosenfeld which was accepted."[44]

In February of 1854, the election of Rev. Rosenfeld was reconfirmed, with an increment of three hundred dollars. The price exacted for the increase was submission to a whole series of rules and regulations.

In summary they were:

1. He was to attend the synagogue on every Sabbath eve and morrow, on all Holy Days and Festivals; read the prayers in the original Hebrew according to the Portuguese *Minhag* save the

prayer for the government; deliver English discourses on *Shabbat* and first day of Holy Days. (The board allowed sickness and good cause to cover absenteeism.)

2. He was to conduct all funerals of Jews buried in Savannah and to be available to the family through the *shivah* (seven days of mourning).

3. He was to keep records of births, deaths, and marriages. (Where is this valuable document?)

4. He was to perform no marriage in the synagogue without the consent of the president or *adjunta*.

5. He was to superintend the Sunday school and advise regarding religious instruction.

6. "He shall obey all lawful orders of the Parnass for the time being so far as they may be consistent with the Jewish law and usage."

7. "He shall abide by and support the charter and by laws as they apply to him."[45]

The sixth rule was more than Rosenfeld could tolerate. He asked for clarification, and the board gave it: *"By the sixth rule nothing was meant inconsistent with the usual duties of an Hazzan."*[46] (Italics added for emphasis.)

Rule 1 also implied that the board could dictate the character of the service. Again clarification was sought, leading to this answer, "that he [the *hazzan*] was not prevented from giving the usual English prayer," meaning he was to keep doing what he was presently doing.[47]

By May 14, 1854, Rev. Rosenfeld met with the board to seek an alteration of that sixth rule. He managed to shape it so that it did not undermine his religious authority:

> . . . the sixth rule was altered to read as follows: 'He shall comply with all wishes of the Parnas provided he deems them consistent with the Jewish law and usages.'

Apparently, the friction that had earlier divided the Israelites of Savannah into two camps did not end with the appointment of the *hazzan*. It remained to Abraham Einstein to attempt a unifying act. Everyone loves a *simcha* (a time of rejoicing); every Jew reverences the Torah. Einstein put the two together. On May 22, 1855, he arranged a celebration around the gift of a Scroll of Law which he had ordered from his uncle, Rabbi Loeb Saenger of Buttenwiesen, Bavaria.[48] Yellow fever lessened attendance at the party; though after lavish food, gracious hospitality, and toasts galore, the mood must have been mellow. Rev. Rosenfeld used his toast to underscore what brought Jews together.

> Union in Israel! As a nation among nations, the chosen people of God; the most ancient family in existence, associated by the most in-

dissoluble ties of race and religion, cemented together by common suffering . . . and maintained by common hopes, expectations and destiny. May we never forget that Judaism is our common cause . . .

Before the evening was over, all were saluting one another with complimentary toasts, including this one by Solomon Cohen to his rabbi:

> The Rev. Mr. Rosenfeld, our minister: may he always have full benches, up stairs and downstairs.

One suspects that underlying the effort at promoting unity was awareness that a divisive issue was about to surface, *reform*. President Jacob De la Motta, Esquire, alluded to it in his toast:

> The sacred scroll of the law, now before us, the emblem of our faith; may it never be polluted by the misconstruction of innovations . . .

The souring of the *shitach* (union) between Rosenfeld and the board occurred in 1855. On April 12th, the reverend's salary was not paid in advance as he had contracted, and that led to an exchange of letters. The board acknowledged its obligation but pleaded temporary insolvency. More than nine thousand dollars was sitting in the Permanent Fund at the time, so Rev. Rosenfeld placed little reliance upon the plea.

In the middle and last phase of his initial ministry at K.K.M.I., Rosenfeld moved about more freely, journeying to other communities. Perhaps he was the first rabbi to visit Atlanta, the occasion being recorded in *The Occident* in 1854.[49] By 1859, he was reported in Macon.[50] (In 1872, he revisited Macon to deliver the oration at the laying of the cornerstone of the new Hebrew synagogue.[51]) That November, he ventured to Cincinnati for the marriage of his wife's kinswoman, Anna Jonas, daughter of Joseph Jonas.[52] The minutes lead us to conclude that the *adjunta* was not as forthcoming to him as his needs required, often a sign of discontent. *The Occident* reported a surprise party given in his honor in 1859, the opposite signal.[53] One of the crushing events visited upon the Rosenfeld family that year was the unexpected death of their one-year old son, Jacob M. Rosenfeld, of water-on-the-brain.[54]

The only record of Rev. Rosenfeld's involvement in the general community was the prayer he delivered before the Georgia State Convention in March of 1861.[55]

Rosenfeld's nine-year tenure ended abruptly. Ill feeling was generated when Mr. S. Berz brought forth the issue of a Hebrew school for Savannah's Jewish children.[56] Berz and A. Einstein were appointed a committee of two to compile two lists, one of parents who could afford tuition, and a second of those who would require scholarships. When Mr. Rosenfeld, in August of 1862, requested a salary increase, the board declined his entreaty, informing him that he could earn a substantial amount by instituting a Hebrew school. Hidden in the board's action was the implication that there was a dereliction of duty.

Add to this the discontent that the reverend expressed in a letter addressed to the *adjunta*, protesting the absence of the *shochet*, Mr. Zechariah, from the city, leaving the Jewish population with "a scarcity of cosher [*sic*] meat."[57] The substitute, Mr. Amram (ancestor of David Amram, contemporary composer), was, in Rosenfeld's sight, unsuitable.

The board backed the *shochet* on this issue, stating that he was only out of town to perform a circumcision and it was better

> that the congregation should suffer an occasional temporary inconvenience than that any child of Israel should fail to receive the holy rite . . .[58]

Further, didn't Mr. Rosenfeld realize that a Civil War was raging? Food, generally, was scarce in the city. To demolish the *hazzan's* authority, the board recognized Mr. Amram as a worthy substitute.[59]

Mr. Rosenfeld then made a daring move to determine how the cards were stacked. He petitioned the *parnass* for the right to circumcise a Jewish infant out of the city. When the *parnass* denied the request, the only honorable course left was to resign. The board accepted the resignation, informing Mr. Rosenfeld of his contractual obligations (wherein he had to give six months' notice), but at the same time stating, "his resignation be accepted unconditionally."[60]

In what may have been the first "lock-out" in American Jewish history, the *parnass* ordered that the synagogue be immediately shut tight. On *Shabbat*, when Rev. Rosenfeld came to the door of the synagogue, he found it sealed. Sunday morning he prepared the following letter which was delivered forthwith to Mr. Cohen:

> Savannah 14 Sept. 1862
> Solomon Cohen Esq.
> Parnoss Cong. M.I.
> Dear Sir,
>   When I went on last Friday evening to the Synagogue to begin Sabbath Service as usual I found, to my astonishment, the Synagogue closed and on inquiry I learned that it was done by your orders because you as well as the other members of the adjunta are under the impression that I meant my resignation to go into effect immediately —this is a misapprehension which I deeply regret and hasten to correct, assuring you that though I found myself forced to resign . . . I had not the remotest intention of violating my obligation to serve six months after my resignation . . .
>   I should have replied to your second note of the 9th instant in which you informed me that such was my duty in accordance with my election, but I felt too indignant to believe that you considered me so mean and degraded as to be capable of violating an obligation which I have always considered sacred. It is still more a matter of regret to me that the adjunta should believe me capable of intentionally placing the congregation in such a dilemma at this time when another minister cannot so easily be found to fill the vacancy . . .

In the remainder of the document, Rev. Rosenfeld informed the board that, in accordance with his contract, he was still the minister of the congregation "Mikveh" Israel and intended to "fulfill the duties of my office until the expiration of six months."[61]

That night, the board met to hear the letter read and decided to reconvene three days later. At the meeting, a resolution was drawn to the effect that (a) whereas in a note dated September 9, 1862, Rev. Rosenfeld declared "he would not submit to his [the president's] authority and that said note may be considered as his resignation;" (b) whereas he violated his duty by leaving the city without presidential permission, and (c) whereas the adjunta unanimously accepted his resignation unconditionally; therefore it was resolved that "the Revd. J. Rosenfeld is not the minister of our congregation and shall not officiate as such under existing circumstances."

A rider was attached to the resolution, namely, that if he would "ask leave" to withdraw his resignation, that would be considered six month notice, provided he pledged never to leave the city without permission from the president.

That rider was unanimously rejected, so that, from the synagogue's standpoint, Mr. Rosenfeld was the "late" minister. His temporary replacement was the *shochet*, Mr. Amram.[62] (How ironic that Rosenfeld's daughter Rosa married Mr. Amram's relative Emile![63])

The resignation did not end Rosenfeld's attachment to Savannah. Here he remained to found B'nai "Berith" Jacob Congregation, serving as its first *president and rabbi* and later returning to K.K.M.I. as acting rabbi in 1870.[64] In 1874 Jacob Rosenfeld was elected *hazzan* of the Rampart St. Synagogue in New Orleans, where he died on December 5, 1876.[65] In Laurel Grove (cemetery) he rests, ironically, in a plot adjacent to the final resting place of the president who negotiated his dismissal, Solomon Cohen.

Of *Shammashim* AND *Shoch'tim*

The pressure to "professionalize" the operation of the synagogue led to the employment of other Jewish functionaries. When the congregation was yet meeting in rented quarters, there were individuals, occasionally non-Jews, who cared for the building and its accoutrements. The ritual slaughter of meat in manner prescribed by tradition was arranged for by individuals in the community who knew the technique (Benjamin Sheftall being one). The same was true for the performance of circumcision. By 1840-1860, the quality of life required such necessities to be rendered by others.

The case of the *Shammash* Henry requires highlighting. In the May 4, 1842, minutes, Henry was identified as a slave who was compensated five dollars "for his attention in cleaning and lighting the lamps, etc. of the synagogue." By 1855, his salary had increased to $12.50. Note that he is described in this text as "sexton." At the August 17, 1854, meeting, Isaac Cohen made the resolution that

Twenty-five dollars be paid to Henry a slave for his gratuitous lighting and cleaning the synagogue . . . and that the sum of fifty dollars
be paid him annually to perform the same duty . . . Mr. Cohen stated
that he had offered these two last resolutions without the knowledge
or consent of the owner of Henry, but as an act of gratuity to the boy
Henry and for his benefit alone.

Henry probably functioned as *Shabbos goy/shammash* (kindling of
lights on *Shabbat* is forbidden to Orthodox Jews, so that a non-Jew is required to handle the "work-related" chores of the synagogue). Anyway, he
was not dismissed when a Jewish *shammash* was hired. The finances of the
congregation were such that while the board had authority to appoint one
individual to serve as *shammash* and another as *shochet,* it also had the
power to arrange for the "two offices to be blended in one."[66] It was not until
June 25, 1855, that the office of *shammash* was clearly defined. The individual was required to

attend the synagogue whenever open for divine worship and summon
the adjunta when required and shall attend to the perpetual lamp.

The *shammash* also had responsibility for supervising the burial procedure and maintaining the cemetery. Fifty dollars per annum was the
salary in 1855, with the advantage of having

a man to light and extinguish the gas whenever the synagogue is open
at night and sweep out, dust and scour the building . . . to be superintended by the shamas.[67]

Whatever the minutes stipulated, modest means insured that Henry
functioned alone, save when the *shochet* assumed the *shammash* tasks. The
only exception occured in 1853, when Jeremiah Herch was elected *shammash
only,* at a compensation of four hundred dollars per annum.[68]
    The record of "ritual slaughterers" during 1840 to 1860 has already been
alluded to in passing. In this period, Mr. A. Simpson was elected *shochet.*[69]
There is no record of payment to him, but he may have levied fees for his
services. By August of 1852, Mr. Bendane (Bendheim?) of Richmond and Mr.
Lewis Herchberg of New York applied for the position, and the latter was
employed. The April 16, 1853, *adjunta* meeting enacted rules and regulations
so elaborate that Herchberg resigned. After Rev. Rosenfeld came on the
scene, Herchberg reconsidered, but that decision did not endure. Solomon
Cohen made an inquiry of Rosenfeld as to the availability of someone
else to function in Herchberg's place, which prompted the incumbent *shochet*
to disengage from duty.[70] His successor was Mr. L. Sternheimer, elected December 18, 1853. Two years later, June 25, 1855, new controls were placed on
him. A member of the *adjunta* was to serve as an "authority" over him for a
month's time, on a rotating basis. Mr. Berz was the first given that privilege,
including the right to

direct the Schochet where he shall kill and generally to establish rules for his government; he may fine the Shochet in a sum not exceeding one dollar, but the Shochet shall at all times have the power of appeal to the Adjunta.[71]

By February of 1856, discontent toward Sternheimer was such that his salary was reduced from $400 to $350 and five percent of any collections he made was treated as his income. Apparently the *shochet/shammash* was given the responsibility of going from place to place, making collections of dues. That very year, Mr. Sternheimer vacated his office. A less expensive replacement (*shochet* only) was found in Mr. Zachariah, whose remuneration was but $250.[72] Mr. Milhauser was appointed *shammash* at $150 per annum, plus five percent commission. The records of the accounts collected indicated that Mr. Milhauser was an expert at the subscription game, and added to his purse many bonuses.[73]

Restrictions were placed upon this new functionary, including the stipulation that no journey outside the city for any religious ritual was allowed without the expressed permission of the *adjunta*.[74]

The episode involving Rosenfeld, Zachariah, and President Solomon Cohen has been discussed in a preceding section. Following the resignation of Rev. Rosenfeld, Zachariah pressed for a raise in salary, else he would resign.[75] The response of the *parnass* was to hold him in abeyance by asking him to remain in office until a collection of monies could be made from the "Israelites" in the city who were *not* members of the congregation.[76] This casual reference in the minutes is significant. As we shall learn in the next chapter, Rev. Rosenfeld turned to these "non-synagogued" Jews to create a new congregation in Savannah.

IMPROVING THE BUILDING

It was not uncommon in those days for congregations to renovate and refurbish their structures in preparation for the coming of a new rabbi to the community. In anticipation of its first *hazzan*, the Perry Lane Synagogue received all manner of improvements from the 1850's to the 1860's. It began in 1843 with the recognition that the five-year-old building was in a state of disrepair:

> *Resolved*, that the synagogue for want of some necessary repairs is not at present in a passable condition to be used for public worship.[77]

Not until August 18, 1851, when Solomon Cohen made the resolution that the "adjuncta just elected shall forthwith take measures to put the synagogue in proper order . . .," was the foot-dragging ended. Note that the action was taken immediately prior to the "vestry's" first contact with Dr. Raphall in New York, seeking a "minister".[78] At the same meeting, it was reported that a bank account had been opened since *non-Jews* had contributed five hundred to six hundred dollars for this purpose. With that sum in hand, the project was begun in the expectation that "it will be necessary to ask of our own people the balance required . . ." In Temple "Mickva" Israel's history, the cost of structures was underwritten, directly or indirectly, by "other denominations," and here is another instance of generosity by non-Israelites.

The nature of the repairs to be undertaken included a new *hechal* (ark) and *tabah* (central altar), both to be "of a modern style"; the synagogue itself was to be totally repaired; the exterior was to be rough cast; the ladies' gallery and downstairs were to be fitted with new seating; and any other improvements that the committee, comprised of Jacob De la Motta and Lizer Solomons, determined were to be accomplished. To the committee, David Lopez Cohen was later added. Both Mr. Cohen and Mr. Solomons were master builders. To protect the property from encroachment the same committee was empowered to act, implying that the front lot facing Liberty Street was about to be developed.

In January, 1852, the president informed the board that the repairs to the synagogue were progressing rapidly and that an iron railing was to be installed. He received authority to sell the old benches, lamps, and other accoutrements.

The ladies of the congregation sustained the men by special fund-raising projects. The "daughters of Israel" collected $113 for "the internal improvement of our place of worship."[79] President De la Motta's acknowledgment of their contribution bears quoting, as it reflects the political rhetoric of the times.

> In tendering to you my sincere acknowledgement and that of the congregation over which I have the honor to preside, for this munificence[,] be assured of the high estimation in which your pious efforts as well as those you represent are held by us[.] [I]t is another evidence of the untiring zeal of our sisters in Israel in this place to accomplish all have so much at heart, *a perfect organization of our congregation*[,] to secure regular and permanent worship in our synagogue and to be instructed in the tenets of our holy faith which will secure eternal happiness.[80] (Italics added.)

In the middle of 1852, the carpentry was completed, the iron railing installed, and the plastering alone remained undone. Mr. Isaac Brunno was in charge of the latter, which he was willing to complete for two hundred dollars, excluding the fluting of the columns. Mr. Brunno was also responsible for rough-casting the building.[81] The first mention of heating by gas appears in the minutes of this period. Solomon Cohen offered to install the pipes at his own expense.[82]

One of the relatives of an early Jewish settler in Savannah, Grace Abendanone (daughter-in-law of Hyam Abendanone), presented to the congregation a *tamid* (eternal light) made of silverplate and stained glass. In appreciation for the generous gift, the congregation extended to her a front seat in the gallery whenever she chose to visit Savannah and worship.[83] That *tamid* was later given to a Jacksonville congregation.

One gift occasioned a second. *Parnass* De la Motta presented a silver pointer (*yad*) for use on a new Torah (yet to be discussed). The congregation was so pleased that it had his name engraved upon it. The museum of K.K.M.I. displays this artifact, given at the June 13, 1852, meeting.

By August of 1852, the building was complete, save for painting which would be done in time for the *hazzan*'s arrival. Two new Torahs were to be placed in the holy building, as well as the necessary carpeting, altar cloths, etc. The funds raised by the congregation and the community were insufficient, so twelve hundred dollars had to be taken on loan, by mortgaging Lot 23 in Franklin Ward.[84]

Once Mr. Rosenfeld was on the scene, an additional amount was needed to pay Mr. Falligant to ventilate the women's gallery and to purchase a chandelier and shutters for the building. Mr. Brunno contributed to the building fund fifty dollars, a gesture of friendship.[85] The records for March 12, April 19, and December 31, 1852, give an accounting of the final expenses, including $648.72 for the services of David Lopez Cohen, a member of the Building Committee.

Improvements continued, as is evidenced by the minutes of April 10, 1853, when the treasurer was ordered to pay Mr. Bogardus fifteen dollars for varnishing the new ark and an additional thirty dollars for installing a "sofa" on the *tabah* (central pulpit).

When the renovation project was completed at a cost approaching the initial construction, the synagogue was acknowledged to be a gem. Isaac Leeser carried a description of it in *The Occident* which verified that Gilbert Butler and E. S. Jones had constructed the original building, and that it was architecturally noteworthy.[86] Leeser reported the restoration exceeded three thousand dollars, the designer being "Charles Shole [*sic*], an English architect," and the work was executed by two Jewish master mechanics,

> Mr. Lizer Solomons and Mr. D. Lopez Cohen . . . the gallery front is of iron and presents quite a neat and light appearance.[87]

Mr. Charles "Shole" is the famed architect Charles Sholl who frequently joined efforts with Calvin Fay in designing some of Savannah's impressive structures along Bay Street (commonly known as Factors Walk). These include 112-130 West Bay Street, 102-110 East Bay Street (abutting the Savannah Cotton Exchange), and 112-130 East Bay Street, a structure built for G. Wimberly Jones of the Noble Jones family.

There is every reason to conclude that by 1853, when Rev. Rosenfeld appeared on the scene, the Perry Lane Synagogue presented a chaste facade to the citizens of Savannah.[88]

THE NEW TORAHS

K.K.M.I. is the possessor of two venerated Scrolls, brought to Savannah in 1733 and 1737. Repaired in the third decade of the 1800's, they were more in the category of valuable symbols than readable Torahs for weekly use. In

August of 1850, Solomon Cohen and Lizer Solomons offered a motion, directing the president to purchase two *Sepharim* (Torahs). Two years later, the *parnass* reported that an order had been placed with Mr. Asher Kursheedt.[89] An elite member of New York's Jewish society and active in Jewish philanthropic and religious causes, Kursheedt was associated with B'nai Jeshurun and its rabbi, Dr. Raphall.[90] The *parnass'* association with Raphall in seeking a *hazzan* was recorded earlier, so that one suspects Raphall put De la Motta in contact with Kursheedt. By June, the Torahs were still not in hand, and a rumor was reported to the *adjunta* that the purchaser had died. But the November meeting brought information that one of the Scrolls had arrived from Germany and was received by a still living Mr. Kursheedt. The second was expected shortly. In February of 1853, the two Scrolls arrived in New York, and by April were in Savannah. The *parnass* found errors in them and returned them to Mr. Kursheedt, who was prevailed upon to order two others.[91] By May of 1853, the Scrolls were returned "in a perfect state."[92] (The two Scrolls remain the treasured possession of the congregation to this day. K.K.M.I. has Torahs whose history can be traced to the 18th, 19th, and 20th centuries.)

Two other ritual objects were mentioned in the minutes. In the cash accounts of 1855, President De la Motta purchased a "citron box" for four dollars for use on *Succot* (Feast of Booths). Also, Mr. Morrell was paid $7.50 for his work on a "Hooparr" [*sic*], a wedding canopy.[93]

THE CEMETERY

The Hebrew Burial Grounds on Cohen Street served the needs of the Jewish community for a full century. The original walled-in area became insufficient as the congregation expanded. By the end of the 1840-1860 era, the Mordecai Sheftall gift reached its capacity, and as the next period unfolded, a new Jewish cemetery site (Laurel Grove) had to be located.

In August of 1844, a committee of two was appointed to obtain estimates of costs for expanding the Cohen Street cemetery wall to include as much available space as possible. The exact dimensions of the plat were sought, and mention was made of a record in the clerk's office of Chatham County, dated August 3, 1803. By August 18, 1845, the committee reported the dimensions as "one acre, six chains and thirty five ducks." There being several options for expanding, the committee wanted the congregation to make a choice, but to no avail. Two hundred-fifty dollars was the estimate for one option, and the manner of fund-raising recommended was private subscriptions of all Israelites in the city. The committee decided that the expansion should be made from the northwest and southeast, doubling the space. Raising subscriptions was rigorous labor, and the committee members reported that monies were lacking.[94] They were urged to continue the solicitation, with the understanding that the funds of the congregation would meet the deficit. But the cemetery had to be enlarged forthwith.

In 1847 a new problem arose *vis-a-vis* the cemetery. Mr. H. Roberts' land prevented public access to it. Solomon Cohen, Levy Hart, and Dr. Solomon Sheftall were delegated to apply to Mr. Roberts and ask for the right to a public thoroughfare. Failing to obtain his assent, the committee was to negotiate with the mayor and aldermen. By August of 1847, the cemetery expansion was completed. Again, Amos Scudder, famed Savannah builder and architect, was responsible for the work.[95] Eighty feet were added to the east and seventy-five feet to the north and south, thus doubling the space. Of the $260 expended, $152 was raised by the local Jewish population, and the congregation footed the rest of the bill. By 1853, the land around the cemetery was growing in value, and Lizer Solomons had developed a scheme to mark it off into "building lots" for the congregation's benefit.[96]

The expansion was a noble effort to meet a growing need. It sufficed for the moment, but provided no permanent solution. The Cohen Street burial site would soon be by-passed as the only available spot for Jewish interments.

GIANTS PASS AWAY

When some individuals die, the community is irrevocably altered. They may be symbols or provide leadership uncommon for an age. Three were mourned in the 1840's-1860's, two members of the congregation, and the third, a nationally known Jewish personality.

At the August 16, 1847, regular meeting, the secretary announced the death of Sheftall Sheftall. At eighty-six, his life was prolonged, though prosperity eluded him. In announcing his demise, the minutes described him as

the venerable Sheftall Sheftall, Esq., a soldier of the Revolution, a pious Israelite and an honest man, one who for many years and to the period of his death has been a member of the Adjunta and besides had held many stations in this congregation.

Unanimous resolutions were passed, including:
1. That an *escava* (memorial prayer) be made for him each *Yom Kippur* perpetually.
2. That the congregation attend his funeral that afternoon (August 16) at five o'clock.

The minutes documented the date of his death as August 15, 1847, at 6:30 p.m. at his residence.

Jacob De la Motta, Esquire, was another whose leadership was relied on. He had served as president during the period when the building was refurbished, the cemetery expanded, the Torahs purchased, and the *hazzan* hired. In the 1840's-1860's, his name appeared on more committees and charitable endeavors than any other.

On January 16, 1857, a resolution was passed, noting the death of

our good and pious Brother in faith, Jacob De la Motta of this city [to distinguish him from Dr. Jacob De la Motta of Charleston] who for many years served as Trustee and Parnass of this Congregation and was indefatigable in his exertions for its welfare . . .

To his memory, "a Tablet of Marble [was to] be placed in the Synagogue, on the southern side of the achol (ark) . . ." That tablet was installed and, after the dedication of the third K.K.M.I., was relocated to the present sanctuary. It is affixed to the eastern wall, adjacent to the *bima* (pulpit).

When Savannahians grieve the loss of one not native to this city, it is because the individual has attained uncommon status in Jewish life. Judah Touro's death in 1854 led to the following resolution:

> . . . In the death of the late Judah Touro of New Orleans we mourn the loss of a philanthropist whose charity was boundless and whose virtues have cast a halo around the name of Jew . . . that a tablet of marble with proper inscription be placed in the synagogue as a memorial of his worth and a memento of our gratitude . . . that on the eve of the day of atonement of each year the hazan shall offer an escobah to the memory of the deceased . . . that a committee be appointed to attend the remains of Mr. Touro when they shall be conveyed to New Port.[97]

Notice of the above was published in *The Occident* and *Asmonean* and sent to the executor of the Touro estate.

The following words were chosen for the marble tablet:

> In memory of Judah Touro, the pious Jew . . . the virtuous citizen, a memento of this congregation for his liberality.[98]

The plaque was attached to the wall of the second synagogue, and later affixed to the eastern wall in the 1876-78 building where it remains to this day. The wording has been slightly changed. "The pious Israelite" appears instead of "the pious Jew."

A five thousand dollar legacy from the Touro estate was bequeathed to the congregation, received as a "bill on a Boston bank."[99] The congregation then had a debt of twelve hundred dollars so that the Touro money was manna from heaven. Manna may be too rich for the blood, and, in this instance, it proved a divisive blessing. *Parnass* De la Motta made a motion to use a portion to retire the debt and to refer the remainder to the congregation for a decision regarding its disposition. A dissenting group argued if the *adjunta* could determine how to use any part thereof, it had the power to decide the use of the whole. The vote was recorded and the *parnass'* motion lost. Solomon Cohen offered an alternative: one thousand dollars be used to pay off all loans, and the rest be invested for two years on loan to an individual on mortgage of real estate, creating thereby a new fund, "the Touro Fund." As the treasurer received monies he was to deposit them in the fund until it built up to its original amount. To that proposal, the *parnass* objected. (Every line in the minutes is capped with quotation marks to underscore the intensity of his comment.) He insisted that the congregation, not the board, received the legacy, and only at a general meeting could it be dispersed in any manner, except to retire debts. When brought to the next board meeting, M. S. Cohen moved that the monies be used to retire the debt, and the residue be invested in city bonds, banks, or stock. That motion succeeded.[100] Mr. R. D. Walker was paid one hundred dollars for the marble Touro memorial tablet, and the division was laid to rest.[101]

The August 17, 1854, meeting included a report of the final interment of Judah Touro on June 5, 1854.[102] No Savannahian could be present, so Mr. Asher "Kurschedt" [sic] (purchasing agent for the two Torahs) was designated the official delegate of the congregation. Wrote Mr. Kursheedt, "the ceremony was imposing and solemn." Kursheedt was impressed that K.K.M.I. ranked in the procession next to Charleston, then the largest community of Jews in America. Joseph Soria of New York was also chosen a substitute delegate, but due to indisposition, could not attend.[103]

The news of the congregation's good fortune spread to other areas. By June 18, 1854, a letter was received from the Hebrew Congregation in Augusta, Georgia, soliciting aid to enable them to build "a new synagogue." (The Augusta congregation is the second oldest in the state.) No action was taken on the request. In 1858, "the congregation of the House of Israel of Baltimore" petitioned for aid "to enable them to pay their debts."[104] Baltimore's Beth Israel, a Sephardic congregation organized in the 1850's, did not survive.[105]

BY-LAW CHANGES AND OTHER ALTERATIONS

The generation preceeding the Internecine Conflict was caught up in the fervor of expansion and change. The synagogue building enjoyed massive improvements. The ladies and men extended themselves in an effort to attract and pay for the functionaries essential to a full Jewish life: a *hazzan*, a *shammash*, a *shochet/mohel*. The cemetery was enlarged and its boundaries secured by law. Parents began to feel the need for an educational system that would introduce their young to the rudiments of our "Holy Faith." A momentum was gathering that manifested itself in updating the congregational rules and regulations.

A major revision of the by-laws was accomplished at the August 21, 1848, annual meeting. The changes included:

1. Money offerings during public worship were prohibited. All contributions were to be sent directly to the *gabay* (treasurer). (Rule 2)

2. Instead of the congregation electing the *gabay* and secretary, the *adjunta* would do so. (Rule 4)

3. The amount the *parnass* could allocate for charitable purposes was increased to five dollars per individual. (Rule 6)

4. "The gabay shall keep proper books in the *English* language" (a surprise considering all the records of the congregation were kept in the vernacular from 1790 on). (Rule 7)

5. Same for the secretary. (Rule 9)

6. Any officer of the congregation, neglecting his responsibilities, could be fined twenty dollars and by a two-thirds vote of the *adjunta* be expelled from the congregation. (Rule 11)

7. Rule 14 defined proper synagogue etiquette:

> *A decent deportment and dress* shall be observed during the divine services, and any violation of the rule either in letter or spirit may be reported by any member of the congregation to the parnas . . . (Italics added.)

The punishment consisted of a summons by the president to appear before him, and, if guilty, expulsion, a fine of up to twenty dollars, or a reprimand, depending upon the severity of the act.

8. Any male twenty-one years or older

> professing the Jewish religion living 6 months in Chatham County, can apply for membership to the President.

Said application was to be put to the *adjunta* at the next meeting, and, if it pleased the majority, the individual paid five dollars and signed the rules. (Rule 15)

9. Rule 17 established the *Permanent Fund,* intended solely to sustain the *hazzan.* No funds could be diverted for any other purpose. The trustees, numbering three, had to be elected from the congregation.

10. Rule 18 dealt with vacancies in the trustees, which were to be filled by surviving members.

On August 18, 1851, Rule 15 was altered as follows:

> All persons professing the Jewish religion ["male" is not specified] may become seatholders by paying the annual rent for the same and all other annual dues or assessments.

Solomon Cohen introduced this alteration to put the congregation on a paying basis by charging for seats and creating a mechanism for raising monies through special assessments.

Further, Cohen suggested a new requirement for becoming a "corporator" or member.

> No person shall . . . become a corporator until he has been a seat holder for five years and has regularly paid his dues . . .

The process then was the same as in Rule 15, save the fee was increased to ten dollars.

An addendum was also included in Rule 15:

> No person who is not a seat holder shall be entitled to vote at any election on any subject . . . and membership shall be lost by failing to pay all dues for one year.

These changes were to be submitted to the legislature of Georgia, inasmuch as they required an amendment to the Charter. On December 4, 1851, another change was included in the bill which Solomon Cohen introduced at the state capital in Milledgeville, namely, the annual meeting was moved from August to the first Monday in January. The bill passed, and, on January 5, 1852, the full text was read to the congregation at its annual meeting, held for the first time in the first month of the secular year. The bill was dated December 19, 1851, and signed by Governor Howell Cobb.

The January 1, 1855, meeting agreed to alter the 16th rule by abolishing the annual contribution of three dollars. An additional by-law was put on the table, ordaining

> that no money from the fund of the congregation should be appropriated to any other than congregational purposes.

This was not to the president's liking, because funds were regularly disbursed by him for charitable purposes, as Rule 3 sanctioned. The rules change passed, though *Parnass* De la Motta requested his vote to be recorded in the negative.[106]

Despite the shift of the annual meeting date from midsummer (when many Savannahians were on vacation) to the first Monday in January, attendance was still a problem. A legal fiction was concocted by Solomon Cohen:

> resolved that the annual meeting shall remain as is but we hereby agree, simply to meet and always adjourn over to the next Sunday at 12 o'clock.

That passed unanimously.[107]

The January 6, 1862, meeting brought forth a defensive resolution that indicated fear of a take-over by new elements in the community. It read,

> that the bye laws be so ammended [*sic*] as not to allow any person to be a member of the Adjuncta until he has been a member of the congregation for *10 years*. (Italics added.)

While the change was not enacted at the next annual meeting (possibly because of the turmoil created by the resignation of *Hazzan* Rosenfeld and the founding of a Polish congregation, "B'nai Berith Jacob"), the proposal confirmed the tension and suspicion then at play at K.K.M.I.

For those who believe that fees for use of facilities and personnel are modern inventions, consider the following schedule of 1859 vintage:

> . . . All persons using the synagogue for marriage purposes shall be charged five dollars for the use of same[,] the said sum to be equally divided between the shamos and the congregation[,] and that the shamos be allowed to charge two dollars for his services when required for funerals.[108]

MAIN SANCTUARY

Name	Pew #	Rental/per Annum
A. Backer**		$13
Jacob De la Motta	2, 10	13 and 10
S. Solomons	3	10
I. M. Solomons	4	12
M. I. Solomons	5	15
H. Silber**	6	14
G. Brown**	7	15
S. Mayer**	8	17
C. E. Byck**	9	11
S. H. Eckman**	12	
W. Russell	14	16
N. Mayer**	17	
M. Lillienthal**	18	
L. Lillienthal**	20	
S. Morris**	23	
J. Sickle**	47	
Blume[n]sing**	48	
L. Hart	52	10
S. S. Hart	54	
M. S. Cohen**	55	
Abram Minis	57	
Isaac Minis	59	
A. A. Solomons	63, 65	
A. Einstein**	66	
Isaac Cohen	67, 69	
S. E. Byck**	70	
M. Boley**		
D. Rosenblatt**	11	
A. Nathans	13	18
D. L. Cohen	15	
P. M. Russell	14	18
F. J. Rosenberg**	19	
A. H. Mass [Moss?]**	21	10
W. Barnett	24	12
A. Abrahams	50	13
Solomon Cohen	58, 60	
Octavus Cohen	56	
S. Berz**	62	
A. Mode**	64	
D. Abrahams	68	
Misses H. & P. (?) Minis		
Mrs. Solomon Sheftall		
Miss DeLyon		
Mrs. E. E. Hertz**		
Mrs. E. S. Solomons		

WOMEN'S GALLERY

Name	Pew #	Rental/per Annum
Mrs. Backer	62	$22
Mrs. De la Motta	26	15
Mrs. Solomon	58, 65	58
Mrs. Solomons	43, 44	33
Mrs. Solomons	60	22
Mrs. Silber	57	20
Mrs. Brown	54	22
Mrs. Mayer	52	22
Mrs. Eckman	50	47†
Mrs. Mayer	25	25
Mrs. Lillienthal	23	41†
Mrs. Lillienthal	48	45†
Mrs. Morris	21	23†
Family	28, 33, 37, 39	44†
Mrs. Blume[n]sing	23	16†
Family	20, 22	40†
Family	49, 51	56†
Family	53, 55	51†
Family	1, 3, 59, 61, 65	116†
Mrs. Solomons	6	44†
Family	14, 24	55†
Family	30, 32, 34, 36, 38, 40	123†
Mrs. Byck	18	32†
	27	12†
Mrs. Rosenblatt	47	20†
Mrs. Cohen	56	52†
Mrs. Rosenberg	22	20†
Family	5, 7, 9, 11, 13	90†
Family	15, 17, 19	51†
Mrs. Berz	10	45†
Mrs. Mode	12	47†
Mrs. Abrahams	16, 35	41†
	2, 4	25
	29	8
	31	15
	41	10
	42, 45	36

** [Of the forty-five listings, thirty were probably first generation Americans, of Germanic extraction, arriving from the 1840's on. These names are represented by a double asterick.]   † Total.

SEATING ARRANGEMENTS

The anticipated arrival of Jacob Rosenfeld occasioned a return to the synagogue. A listing of the seats from the minutes of June 19, 1853, provides an interesting picture of the humans who populated the sanctuary 130 years ago. (See page 128.)

The names reflect changes in the Jewish population. Only the Minises, the Sheftalls, and the DeLyons, a small number on the list, were of Savannah ancestry, dating back to the eighteenth century. The rest were imports, some connected to Colonial families, as the Solomons, the Abrahams, the Cohens, the Barnetts, the Russells, the De la Mottas and the Harts.

The names of other newcomers to Savannah that appear in the records of this period include: Jacob Clavius Levy (whose offspring included Phoebe Pember, Eugenia Levy Phillips, Samuel Yates Levy, and Henrietta [Mrs. Octavus] Cohen), H. Rothschild, J. Wineburg (a Charleston name), R. Berlin, Levy Nathans, J. Rosenband, R. Sanger, S. Wolf, L. Wolf, D. Abrams, Mr. Hersh, J. Zachariah, S. Zachariah, V. A. Mack, Davis(d ?) Abrahams, Elias Einstein, E. Kahnwallar, Isachar Zachaire, A. L. Hines, B. Goldburg, E. Levy, S. Goldsmith, Judah M. Isaacks, Joseph Lippman, Herman Silber, Emanuel Mehling, L. J. Myers, R. Einstein, Simon Hirschfield, Joseph Mode, and David Morris.[109] Savannah Jewry burgeoned as economic opportunities attracted native-born American Jews from adjacent states, and German-Jewish immigrants found Savannah a host city of some potential.

DIVERSE AND SUNDRY ITEMS

In the ante-bellum period, other Jewish organizations began to form, probably as a consequence of the needs of the immigrant population. In the minutes of June 18, 1854, two ladies' organizations were mentioned as charitable enterprises, the German Hebrew Ladies Society and the Hebrew Ladies Benevolent Society. In response to the distressed condition of Jews in Palestine, both groups contributed a total of forty-five dollars. In *The Occident*, a men's organization, the Hebrew Benevolent Society, was singled out.[110] Leeser records the chartering of this benign body at the 1852-53 state legislative session. Solomon Cohen was then its president. The minutes of October 10, 1849, documented the existence of the Society three years earlier. Its contribution of five dollars for meeting at K.K.M.I. was refunded. At a later date, the petition of the Society to use the Perry Lane building was refused.[111] More information about these service organizations will be presented elsewhere in the text.

In 1841, the congregation was invited to attend a significant convocation in Philadelphia. The Jews of that city were pressing for a union of congregations "for the purpose of concert of action in sustaining our holy faith." To this, the board responded by stating,

The congregation approve the plan *generally* and will be happy to lend their aid. The congregation however object to the time of the (?) meeting as it would be inconvenient for Southern delegates to attend, and propose the first Sunday in August as the day of the Meeting.[112]

This passage refers to Isaac Leeser's first attempt to create an alliance of all Jewish congregations in America for a three-fold purpose: (1) to raise the standards of the rabbinate and the manner of ritual slaughter; (2) to organize a system of Jewish schools; and (3) to provide a structure for unified action when needed. Leeser and another Philadelphian *hazzan* convinced five laymen to sign an appeal which was relayed to all existing congregations.[113] This was the first known effort to bring forth a union of congregations in the New World.

In the formative period of K.K.M.I., religious issues gained attention: i.e., *chalitza* for Mrs. Hart of Charleston (to wed Mr. Delieben); the burial of the son of Isaac Attais, whose wife was a non-Jew, and similar afore-mentioned items. Following the turn of the century, few *shaalot* (responsa—questions dealing with religious practice) were asked. In 1850, Theodore Minis passed away, but Theodore Minis was an uncircumcised Jew. Solomon Cohen requested that permission be granted for burial in the Hebrew cemetery.[114] When the votes were taken, only Judge Mordecai Sheftall, Sr. and P. M. Russell (his brother-in-law) voted "aye," while Waring Russell, W. Barnett, and Levi J. Hart turned thumbs down. A three to two vote of rejection was insufficient, so the issue was brought to the full congregation that very evening after Divine worship (an indication that daily services were the tradition). By a nine-to-three vote, the aforementioned Mr. Minis was given the privilege of final repose in the Cohen Street cemetery. Shortly thereafter, Solomon Cohen introduced the resolution to secure a *shochet/mohel* (circumcision expert) for the congregation.

Theodore Minis was the son of Isaac Minis, prosperous Savannah merchant, and grandson of Philip Minis, first Caucasian child conceived and born in Georgia (also the first president of Congregation "Mickva" Israel). Emily Tobias of Charleston was Theodore's wife.[115]

Tzedakah (CHARITABLE ACTS)

By this era, the tradition of sustaining the needy was well established. On two levels, the poor were not allowed to languish, locally and internationally. When Mr. Simpson, the *shochet* lost everything in a fire, *Parnass* De la Motta designated it "an act of charity to pay him his salary to the end of his term . . ."[116] The first money to come into the treasury was to be disbursed for this purpose.

Under the leadership of Jacob De la Motta, subscriptions were taken routinely for the

poor of our brethren in the Holy Land who were poor and in great distress for the want of the means of support.[117]

What prompted the request was a petition from the Reverend S. M. Isaacs of New York, who ranked with Dr. Raphall as a leading figure in the New York Jewish community.[118] Working with Sir Moses Montefiore, Isaacs raised funds for Palestine, all duly noted in *The Occident*.[119]

In 1852, two donations were recorded, one for twenty-five dollars from Rev. Rice of Baltimore, and an equal amount collected by Jacob De la Motta "from a portion of the Cong. Mikveh Yisrael [*sic*]." In the June 18, 1854, minutes, De la Motta again "drew the attention of the meeting to the destitute condition of our brethren in Palestine . . ." and called for a campaign. By June 26th, one hundred dollars was appropriated from congregational funds, and by August 17th, a total of $160 was raised from all but a few Israelites in the city. That, combined with twenty-five dollars from the German Hebrew Ladies Society, and twenty dollars from the Hebrew Ladies Benevolent Society, added up to a grand total of $305. A check was forwarded to Rev. Isaacs to be sent on to Sir Moses Montefiore "for the benevolent purposes intended."[120] A private circular was returned from the Rev. Doctor Adler, chief "rabi" [*sic*] of London, and Sir Montefiore documenting the amount subscribed in America and Europe and how it reached the needy in Jerusalem.[121]

The Occident of 1854 featured expressions of appreciation for contributions made to the Palestine Relief Fund with a full listing of gifts.[122] Savannah's charity was the most sizeable, save for Wheeling, West Virginia, and Steubenville, Ohio, whose collections were added together. On the list was a gift of twenty-five dollars from S. Wolf of Ridgeland, South Carolina, a nearby town, never known to be populated by more than a sprinkling of Jews.

Another charitable request that received official response in the minutes came from the Board of Officers of the Association for the Relief of "Jewish widows and orphans" at New Orleans.[123]

THE MORTARA AFFAIR

A pivotal event in American Jewish history is the Mortara case. One is emboldened to claim that this strange episode in Bologna, Italy, crystallized the need for interconnection among the Jewish communities of this country. No longer was it defensible for each enclave of Jews to function in isolation. The Rev. Isaac Leeser's campaign for unity of action and a confederation of institutions was substantially advanced.

The event was bizarre. In June of 1858, in the city of Bologna, a Papal State, the forces of the Inquisition seized Edgardo Mortara, the youngest son of an humble Jewish lace merchant, and took him away. Why? Because seven years before Edgardo had been close to death and the family servant, Anna Morisi, a Catholic, was fearful the child might die without the benefit of baptism. From a neighboring grocer, she learned the technique of immersion. One day when the Mortara family was absent, she performed the holy rite. Years later the story became known; and when the Archbishop of Bologna was told, he acted on Pope Benedict XIV's principle that if a Hebrew infant was baptized, even illegally, he must be separated from his family and raised in the Catholic faith. A world-wide storm of protest was unleashed. Sir Moses Montefiore journeyed to Rome in 1859 to obtain the release of the child from the Pope, who, he claimed, would grant him an audience.

The response in America was tremendous. Outrage was expressed in the press and from the pulpit. The Know-Nothing movement enjoyed a sudden revival on the wave of anti-Catholic sentiment. On November 27, 1859, delegates from twenty-nine congregations in thirteen cities met in New York to create the *first national Jewish organization, the Board of Delegates of American Israelites.* Henceforth, it would provide a forum for identifying Jewish problems and a mechanism for responding on a national level.[134]

Savannah's participation in the *Mortara Affair* is documented in the minutes and in other sources. At the June 9, 1858, meeting, President Solomon Cohen read a letter

> from Sir Moses Montefiore on the subject of the abduction of a Jewish child at Bologna, Italy addressed to our parnass and a copy of his letter to the President of the United States . . .

In November of 1858, Solomon Cohen wrote to President Buchanan, enclosing a copy of the Montefiore instrument. The leader of K.K.M.I., a powerful local and state politician, appealed on behalf of the Jews of Savannah. Referring to the *Damascus Affair* (an earlier kidnapping), he urged a formal protest to the American Minister in Rome, or a special mission to the Pope himself. Wrote Cohen,

> I am well aware that our government has no right to interfere by coercion, but it has a right to interpose its moral influence in favor of [the] oppressed . . . and that is all I ask.[125]

As Savannah Jews had been invited to participate in the Philadelphia Conference for Jewish Union earlier in the period, so would they be asked to join with other Israelites in cooperative endeavors, to vouchsafe Jewish rights and to foster spiritual networking. Ironically, at the very time that forces were in motion to dissolve the American "Union," efforts to promote Jewish confraternity were gaining momentum.

CHAPTER SIX

HOSTILITY TO "HARMONIE"

F ew eras in Savannah Jewish history shaped the future as definitively as the 1860's to 1880's. The hostilities that pitted North against South resulted in little physical damage to Savannah. The city was spared Sherman's arsonistic "March to the Sea," falling in mid-December and being presented to President Lincoln as a "Christmas gift."[1] Georgia was in ruin; three-fourths of its wealth vanished.[2] A social and economic revolution resulted. A way of life disappeared; the plantation system was ended. Forty thousand citizens had perished in the name of sectionalism. The spirit of a very proud state was crushed.[3]

Monumental Jewish events transpired: the introduction of "reforms" in ritual and thought; the spawning of a second congregation; a passing parade of preachers; surmounting obstacles to build a sanctuary described by the local press as "one of the handsomest in the south . . . excelled in architectural beauty by none."[4]

PATTERNS OF JEWISH INTEGRATION

Savannah Jews had a long tradition of "being at home" in this town. As Bertram Korn has pointed out,

> Nowhere else in America—certainly not in the ante-bellum North —had Jews been accorded such an opportunity to be complete equals as in the old South.[5]

Integration within the community, including intermingling and inter-marrying with its elite, was broad. Josephine Clay Habersham, a local socialite, befriended Octavus Cohen, Jr., Mamie Cohen (Solomon Cohen's daughter), and others.[6] Phoebe Levy, daughter of Jacob Clavius Levy, wedded Dr. Thomas Noyes Pember of Boston, a Swiss Gentile. Upon his death she ventured to the Confederate capital (Richmond, Virginia) and connected to Mrs. Georgia Randolph, wife of the Secretary of War, who arranged to have her appointed as matron of Chimborazo Hospital. Phoebe once proposed to her niece, Fanny Phillips of Savannah, that she pursue (with matrimonial intent) Shirley Carter (of Carter Plantation fame).[7]

[133]

Phoebe's diary, *A Southern Woman's Story*, is considered a source book of Confederate society in Richmond during the war years.

Sister Eugenia Levy married Philip Phillips, one of the first Jews elected to Congress. Elected to the Alabama legislature before a stint in Washington, Phillips was a leader of the state Democratic party, attended the 1852 National Party Convention in Baltimore which nominated Pierce for President, and served in the 33rd Congress (the House of Representatives) from 1853 to 1855. He negotiated the Kansas-Nebraska Act (which negated the Missouri Compromise, eventually led to the birth of the Republican Party, and advanced the outbreak of the Civil War).[8]

Phillips played a role at the very conclusion of the war that is not generally known. When the end came, his family was residing in LaGrange, Georgia. As attested to in his diary, he accompanied Confederate cabinet member, C. C. Clay, to the Macon depot as his attorney. There, the captured Jefferson Davis was put on board a train, along with Clay. That was the beginning of a grim pilgrimage that ended in imprisonment at Fort Monroe, Virginia. As the final curtain descended upon the Confederacy, Philip Phillips was witness.[9] After the War, he returned to Washington, arguing fifty cases before the Supreme Court. He was honored by the members of that Court at a memorial service in the Supreme Court Building.[10]

Octavus Cohen, Philip Phillips' brother-in-law (wives Henrietta Cohen and Eugenia Phillips were sisters), was a man of substantial means, gained through investment in the Central Railroad and Banking Co. (which he later served as director) and as a trustee of the Chatham Mutual Loan Association.[11] In addition to investments, he ran a thriving business, dabbled in management of The Black Star Line, a steamship company, and advanced by 1860 to chairman of the Executive Committee of the Democratic party.[12] A leader in the commercial and public life of the city, with strong Confederate loyalties, he was responsible for raising funds for Mrs. Jefferson Davis while her husband was in prison.[13] A letter from her to the "Honorable Octavus Cohen" expressing appreciation for his generous spirit reposes in the Confederate Museum in Richmond, Virginia.

Octavus' brother, Solomon Cohen, moved about the upper strata of Savannah society with ease and finesse. His bride, Miriam, was of Gratz descent. Her famous Philadelphia aunt, Rebecca Gratz, attended to her rearing upon her mother's demise. Husband Solomon was appointed a District Attorney of the United States for the Georgia District in 1840 by President Van Buren. In 1850, this promising attorney became cashier of the Central of Georgia Railroad. Like Philip Phillips, he was appointed delegate to the Baltimore Convention in 1852 (which nominated Pierce).[14] Reward came to him in the appointment by the newly-elected President as postmaster for the City of Savannah. A more efficacious post to build a political base upon did not exist. By 1854, Cohen was an alderman and functioned as mayor pro-tem. The war years brought tragedy to the Cohen family. Never an advocate of secession, Cohen suffered the loss of his only son,

Gratz, who perished at the Battle of Bentonville.[15] It was his strong Orthodox faith and his connection to the synagogue which sustained him.

Seeking public office at war's end, Solomon Cohen entered the race for Congress from Georgia's First Congressional District and won, the only Jew in Savannah history to be elected to the U. S. House of Representatives.[16] In 1865, the Provisional Governor of Georgia declared him duly elected, but the Reconstructionist Congress would not accept his credentials. From this humiliation, he bounced back, devoting himself to the office of president of the Georgia Historical Society, a position entrusted to the most socially acceptable in the city.[17] His children married out of the faith: Belle betrothed Francis O'Driscoll, whose father was a Belgian consul and a prominent merchant; Mamie (Miriam) wedded James Troup Dent, scion of a family which owned the rice plantation, Hofwyl, outside of Darien and which produced a governor of Georgia, George H. Troup (whose name is attached to streets, counties and public buildings in all sections of the state).

Mrs. Solomon Cohen followed the "Gratz" tradition of public service, officiating as an officer of the Female Orphan Society in 1839 and in 1851 as president of the Needle Woman's Friend Society.[18] The famous Community Fair that initiated the Permanent Fund of Congregation M.I. was the result of her imagination. The Cohens, husband and wife and children, were fully accepted into local society. (Their lovely home on Barnard and Liberty Streets survives as the "Liberty Inn.")

The Jacob Clavius Levy family produced two other socially prominent Savannahians, Emma Levy Hamilton and Samuel Yates Levy.[19] Most Savannahians admire the three story edifice on Lafayette Square built for Samuel P. Hamilton in 1873.[20] According to an unverified tradition, the house inspired the Adams' family mansion depicted by Charles Adams for his *New Yorker Magazine* cartoons. Samuel Prioleau Hamilton was a naval officer assigned to the port of Savannah during the War Between the States. A South Carolinian of Hugenot and English descent, he embraced Judaism sufficiently to be buried as an Israelite. During his Savannah sojourn, he was proprietor of the jewelry store "S. P. Hamilton—Watches, Jewelry and Silver Ware."[21] He was chosen president of the Arkwright Cotton Factory, a manufacturer of cotton yarn, and later became a real estate magnate.[22] Emma Levy Hamilton, his wife, was a community leader in her own right.

Samuel Yates Levy, the sole male of the Jacob Clavius Levy family, was a lawyer and editor of considerable talent. His military service during the War Between the States is documented in Agnew and Lee's book. Holding the rank of major, the highest ranking Jewish officer from this city, he was included in Savannah's "Roll of Honor."[23] After the war, he was appointed editor of *The Daily Advertiser*, the first free circulating journal in the South. When it enlarged and attempted to rival other newspapers in January of 1868, Levy rose to editor-in-chief. His editorials were so pungent that Union General Meade issued orders either to suppress or moderate them, occasioning Levy's resignation.[24] S. Yates Levy retreated to the discipline of law, serving as the congregation's attorney when called upon and carving out an honored name before the Chatham County Bar.

JEWISH PARTICIPATION IN THE WAR

Savannah's Jewish citizens distinguished themselves in the Civil War. Phoebe Levy Pember served as matron of Chimborazo Hospital, the largest military infirmary of the Confederacy. Her sister, Eugenia Levy Phillips, has been widely noted for her work as spy for the South.[25] Brother Samuel Yates Levy served as the highest ranking local Jewish military officer. Others listed in Agnew and Lee's book include: Lieutenants Henry Herman (killed in action), M. Molina* and W. A. Russell; Privates J. M. Abrahams, J. J. Abrams, J. A. Brown, Samuel Brown, B. Brady, J. Brady, J. A. Bessinger (Belsinger), S. S. Bessinger (Belsinger), Isaac Cohen (wounded in action), Isaac S. Cohen, M. Cohen, M. S. Cohen, Morris Cohen, A. Goodman, M. Henry, F. E. Hertz, Samuel P. Hamilton, Lewis Lippman, P. H. Minis (wounded in action), Daniel Moses, Clavius Phillips (killed in action), Aaron Rice, David Roos, A. M. Smith, J. L. Solomons, W. G. Solomon, G. W. Strous, M. Schine,* H. B. Trist (Triest), and L. H. Zachary.[26] (*Jewish identity uncertain)

Clearly the above list is incomplete, excluding, for example, Gratz Cohen who was mortally wounded at the Battle of Bentonville.

Fort Pulaski near Tybee Island served as a military outpost during the war. There David Levy (Yulee), of Florida, the first Jew elected to the U. S. Senate, was imprisoned.[27] General Joe Johnston interceded for him, resulting in his release more than a year after the conflict ended. Only Jefferson Davis and C. C. Clay remained incarcerated for a more protracted term.

THE WAR AND CONGREGATIONAL LIFE

One would hardly know there was a war raging if one consulted the *Congregational Minute Books.* The leadership resolved to continue worship life uninterrupted while the foundations of the Republic were being shaken.[28] Only two entries confirm the ravages: Rev. Rosenfeld's complaint against the *shochet* for providing too little kosher beef. Also, at war's end, the comment was made in the minutes that a resolution from 1864 was not recorded because of

> the much deranged state of affairs (politically) that existed in our city and the consequent distress of mind therefrom . . .[29]

In 1865, the Jews of Savannah were in need of support from their brethren in the Nation. It was *Pesach,* and *matzah* (unleavened bread) was unavailable. A plea proceeded to Rev. Isaac Leeser and S. M. Isaacs (a fundraiser previously mentioned), that many of the inhabitants, formerly wealthy, are now in extremely straightened circumstances; and besides we have entirely lost the means of baking for the ensuing Passover.[30]

New York Jews shipped three thousand pounds of Passover food and Philadelphia sent two thousand pounds.[31] Reading the minutes, one is unaware that conditions were so desperate. Remarkably, within a few years, an impressive synagogue was erected by the members of Savannah's second Jewish congregation, at a cost of seventen thousand dollars.

AN ANTI-SEMITIC SKIRMISH

Judeophobia tends to accentuate during times of deterioration. The North's strategy was to blockade southern ports to prevent the flow of necessities. City merchants sent agents to rural communities to stock up on critical supplies leaving the interior with reduced stock.[32] Because merchants in the rural communities tended to be Jewish, in the popular mind the shortages were viewed as an attempt to milk the populace and to multiply personal fortunes, heedless of human suffering. The forces of the free market were functioning, but people preferred scapegoating. In January of 1863, Confederate Congressman Henry S. Foote of Tennessee made a public proclamation identifying the Jewish businessmen as controlling nine-tenths of the Nation's commerce. Under the protection of those in high places (an indirect attack on Judah P. Benjamin), he claimed that northern Jews were able to infiltrate the South and gain control of all the property of the Confederate States. Representatives Chilton of Alabama, Miles of South Carolina, and Hilton of Florida added their voices to the accusation that Jews were consuming the resources of the South and "monopolizing its trade." This led to the belief that Jews were profiteering and were not involved in the war effort. Earlier (August 1862) a public meeting had been called in Thomasville, Georgia. Resolutions were passed in which

> German Jews were denounced in unmeasured terms . . . prohibited from visiting the village, and banishing all those now resident in that place.

In Talbotton, a Grand Jury returned a presentment which in effect denounced the unpatriotic ways of the Jewish merchants.[33] Lazarus Strauss (later the purchaser of the New York department store R. H. Macy & Co.) was the only Jew in the county, and his response was to move his family and business to Columbus, Georgia, and then eventually on to the North.[34] Milledgeville, Georgia, was also the scene of a similar anti-Jewish proclamation by public officials.[35]

The response of the Savannah Jewish community was sharp and determined. Because the Thomasville "incident" had singled out "German" Jews, their counterparts in the Port City convened a meeting on September 13, 1862. Magnus Loewenthal, a local official associated with the city administration and a close friend of Solomon Cohen, chaired a gathering with A. L. Grabfelder acting as secretary. A "Committee of Five," including Jews from both congregations, was appointed to draft a response—J. Rosenthal, S. Gardner, M. Selig, H. Meinhard, and M. Brown. The proclamation read as follows:

> Whereas, we have read [in the *Savannah Republican*] with amazement and contempt the proceedings of the meeting at Thomasville held on the 30th of August last [1862], in which German Jews are denounced in unmeasured terms—are prohibited from visiting that village, and banishing all those [Jews] now resident in that place.
> This wholesale slander, persecution, and denunciation of a people, many of whom are pouring out their blood on the battle fields of their country in defence of civil and religious liberty, is at war with the spirit of the age—the letter of the constitution—and the principles of religion and can find no parallel except in the barbarities of the inquisition and the persecution of the dark ages. We feel that we have no remedy but in an appeal to an enlightened public opinion, and to that we do appeal . . .[36]

There followed statements about the honesty and integrity of the Jewish people, assuring the public that Jews had more merit than those who slandered them. Further, all who participated in the act of denouncing Jews were condemned as enemies of human liberty and freedom of conscience; and any newspaper which published the slander connected with the Thomasville meeting was to be denied Jewish patronage and support. The *Savannah Republican* which "supported civil and religious liberty . . ." was requested to print the full text of the resolution.[37]

The tradition of Savannah Jews has been to meet prejudice directly and expose its anti-American visage. The response to the Thomasville "expulsion" was forthright and effective. Anti-Semitism did not erupt locally, though communities 150 miles away (such as Milledgeville) experienced trauma.

IN THE NAME OF REFORM

The reformation of K.K.M.I. can be attributed to its second *hazzan* and minister, Raphael de Castro Lewin. His tenure was brief (1867-1869), but his impact powerful.

In earlier history, three incidents signalled some non-Orthodox tendencies in the congregation: (1) at the 1820 dedication of the first synagogue building, the organ was played on *Shabbat*.[38] (2) By a vote of the congregation, Theodore Minis was permitted to be buried in the Hebrew Cemetery, even though he had never been circumcised.[39] (3) In 1857, by action of the board, the ladies of the synagogue received permission to leave the balcony "and . . . be permitted to come downstairs" to hear Rev. Rosenfeld's sermon.[40] The legal fiction was created that the lecture was delivered after the service, so that the presence of women did not violate the law. The separation of women from men is a principle staunchly defended in strict Orthodoxy, so this alteration can be considered a "reform."

The rhythm of change accelerated with the election of Rev. Raphael de Castro Lewin. On November 25, 1867, the president requested *Hazzan* Lewin and Mr. Meinhard to form a congregational choir. The choir was mixed (females included). A choir book (dated 1869) belonging to Zipporah Solomons (Mrs. Joseph M. Solomons) is on display in the Temple Museum. The choir book featured a number of hymns in English, as well as "Ayn Kelohaynoo," "Yigdal," and other favorites. The mixed choir was the first *enduring* "reform" sanctioned in the congregation's history.

At that same meeting, the practice of naming children was altered. Rev. Lewin was asked by the board to assign names for newborns from the *tabah* (the central pulpit) rather than the "yahal" (*hechal*—i.e., the ark).

In a far-reaching sermon, delivered on *Shabbat* morning, February 1, 1868, Lewin defined the elements of dissimilarity between Reform Judaism and Orthodox Judaism. The text, which was printed and circulated as a monograph, has been preserved (a photostatic copy is housed in the K.K.M.I. Archives). Lewin did not conceal his preference for a liberal approach to the ancestral faith. Basing his sermon on the text of Isaiah 6, he quoted Holy Scripture:

> Ye hear indeed, but ye understand not . . . obdurate is the heart of this people . . . would that they would only see with their eyes, and hear with their ears, and understand with their hearts,

Then he asserted,

> throughout the length and breadth of the land . . . is heard a noise in Israel's camp . . . discussion resounds and wherever we turn we find division and dissensions. Congregations are quarreling . . . even the pulpit is not free from angry effusions and bitter invectives. Whence arise these manifold evils . . . "Oh," says Orthodoxy, "Reform is the cause . . ."

Lewin then defined Orthodoxy:

> Orthodoxy implies not only a belief in the genuine doctrines taught in the Scriptures but also a belief in doctrines not taught in the Scriptures [meaning, the Oral Law is given equal weight to the Divine Revelation of the Torah].

Calling the Oral Law fallacious

> since the Divine Being could never have placed the salvation of man to be dependent on a tradition or any law . . . orally transmitted from generation to generation,

Lewin affirmed that the very premise of Orthodoxy was erroneous. The Oral Tradition cannot be viewed as equal to Scripture.

Assailing the Orthodox in the congregation, who paid lip service to the Law, the minister asked rhetorically, who of you keep these laws . . . who of you will even believe that these laws are to be found in rabbinical writings? Ye scoff and ye mock at them, and ignore them altogether.

And what was Reform? The preacher gave his definition.

> Reform is an amendment of what is defective . . . corrupt, or depraved. A restoration to a former good state . . .
> Whatever is defective or corrupt in our present observance of religious forms, whatever abuses may exist in our worship . . . these are to be Reformed . . . Reform, my brethren, is to restore the Mosaic religion to its original beauty; Reform, my brethren, is to tear down the cloak of rabbinism . . . Reform, my brethren, is to uproot the belief in two laws, and to declare . . . that God is one, and that his law is one. . . . your first duty is to dismiss anger and passion from your minds, so that your reason may come . . . to your aid.
> Go now to your homes, and may the spirit of truth follow you thither, and reign triumphant in your meditations, so that peace and *harmony* may prevail among you and so that our pure and lovable faith may soon shine forth in all its pristine brilliance . . . (Italics added.)

The sermon triggered a general meeting of the congregation on February 4, 1868. Thirty-one members occupied the benches that day. Barnett Phillips, secretary, requested that the by-laws be put aside so that all seat-holders members could speak their minds. Parliamentary rules however were adhered to. A. Minis requested that the meeting be deferred until the Charter and Constitution of the congregation could be printed and circulated. The request was carried by a vote of sixteen-to-fifteen. Rev. Lewin, invited for this emotion-fraught occasion, rose, claiming embarrassment for not being given an opportunity to explain the nature of Reform he was proposing, and asked for the privilege of addressing the assembled body. S. H. Eckman and Octavus Cohen engaged in parliamentary procedures that won for Rev. Lewin his right to speak.

After defining what he considered to be the duties of the "minister of the congregation," he outlined the changes he was after: a choir with music, the abrogation of the second days of Festivals, and some minor dimunition of the ritual, including certain repetitions irrelevant to Divine worship.

A committee of five was appointed to consult with Mr. Lewin for the purpose of drawing up proposals to be submitted to the entire congregation. Octavus Cohen, L. E. Byck, M. Lillienthal, J. Hausman and M. Selig were given that assignment.

The role of Octavus Cohen in the effort to further the reformation process came as a surprise. The Orthodox opposition was led by his brother, Solomon Cohen, friend of Isaac Leeser. Seeking victory, Octavus tried to swell the membership. His father-in-law (Jacob Clavius Levy) applied for membership and was duly elected prior to the February 11, 1869, general meeting.

Another large turn-out greeted the leadership on that fateful February 11th night. The "Committee of Five" delivered its recommendations, which, with minor amendment, were unanimously accepted. K.K.M.I. at the moment could be properly called a Reform congregation.

Here are the alterations:

1. Second days of all Festivals and Holy Days were declared non-essential "to true Biblical Judaism as expounded by Moses." In the spirit of early Reform Judaism, this represented a shift to a Scriptural-based expression of the faith.
2. Music and a choir were to be introduced during the worship hour. The organ, as such, was not recommended in Rev. Lewin's proposal.
3. Ritual matters were altered. The *kabbalat Shabbat* section (the opening portion of the Sabbath Eve Service) was reduced.
4. On *Shabbat* morning, the portion from the Prophets (the *haftarah*) was "to be left out." The English prayer for the welfare of the congregation, already in vogue during Rev. Rosenfeld's day, was retained.
5. On Passover Eve, the traditional *hallel* was cut, and the format established for *Shabbat* eve and morn was carried over to the Festival liturgy. This proposal was amended by Isaac Cohen, restoring Psalms 95-100 into the Passover service. Cohen's traditionalism prompted a few other minor amendments which were deemed acceptable to the assemblage.

The "Committee of Five" made known the "considerations" that prompted their proposals:

First, the principles of true Biblical teaching, and, second, the improvement of our mode of divine service and, third, the preservation of peace and harmony in our congregation.

Their resort to the word "harmony" revealed the undercurrent of divisiveness that was pitting brother against brother.

The creation of the choir was *the* priority. At the March meeting, it was decided to place the choir in the ladies gallery, and for the congregation to purchase the seats of those who occupied the required space.[41] By 1869, Professor Lessing functioned as choir master and probably organist, though no mention is made in the minutes of the purchase of an organ.[42] The first definite indication that an organ provided instrumental music during worship is to be found in the February 1, 1870, minutes, when J. M. Solomons and S. H. Eckman, music committee members, reported conversations "with several organists in the city . . ." all of whom "recommended the election of Mr. Isidor Rosenfeld" as music director and organist.

The tide of innovation that manifested itself in major reforms was soon spent. The traditionalists were waiting for a moment when an open attack was possible. (Be assured that Solomon Cohen was in the forefront of this movement, with Isaac Leeser possibly providing the intellectual fuel for the foray. Leeser, a frequent visitor to Savannah, was opposed to all manifestations of Reform Judaism.)[43]

The circumstance that provided the opposition its "cause celebre" was the refusal by Rev. Lewin to read the Hebrew service. Rev. E. Fisher, a Hebrew teacher, hired for the staff of his school (The Savannah Hebrew Collegiate Institute), rendered the liturgy and Lewin preached and recited only a few, limited prayers.[44] In defining his duties as "minister" at the February 4, 1868, special congregational meeting, he differentiated the role of *hazzan* from the role of minister. Minister Lewin had earlier informed the leadership of his position, but they assumed the Rev. R. C. Lewin "was suffering in health . . ." and therefore declined to be *hazzan,* due to a physical incapacity.[45] Instead of resolving the matter, the *adjunta* "in order to promote good will and *harmony* in the congregation" (Italics added) settled on a general meeting of the congregators which convened on November 19, 1868.[46] Thirty-three filed into the Perry Lane Synagogue. The president, Abraham Einstein, did not consider himself non-partisan on the issue, for

> in consideration of reasons of a private character, he requested that some member of the congregation take his place as chairman of the meeting.

Einstein's second daughter, Adeline, was Rev. Lewin's bride, the two having been united by the aforementioned Rev. E. Fisher (then rabbi of Augusta) on July 20, 1867.[47] The body that November 19, 1868, night decided on a five man committee to meet with Lewin and Fisher, and to call a general meeting on Thursday, November 26 (seven days later). Solomon Cohen, H. Meinhard, I. Cohen, L. H. Eckman, and A. Epstein constituted the committee. A complicating factor was that the contract of Rev. Lewin had expired and his status was unresolved.

The November 26, 1868, meeting was told that Rev. Lewin was prepared to continue as "minister" indefinitely, for the same salary, the engagement to be terminated by either side with three months notice. Rev. Fisher would function gratuitously as *hazzan* until Passover. Thereafter, he would expect appropriate compensation. A bitter debate ensued when Mr. Lewin denied that it was by his summons that Mr. Fisher read the service. Rather his father-in-law, President Einstein and Mr. Isaac Cohen had invited Fisher to read "in the hope of giving . . . an opportunity of showing his capability." This was kept from the *adjunta.* The committee made it clear that legally Mr. Lewin was required to perform the duties of minister and *hazzan* according to his contract. Had he wished to relocate, he could have terminated his position as of September, 1868, but he continued to function, receiving salary until December; so, "legally and morally," the committee considered him bound to honor his initial contract which required the dual role. Rev. Lewin was engaged in so many non-congregational endeavors that the committee did not want to "tax his physical powers beyond what is reasonable," so that when he was sick or unable to read the prayers, Mr. Fisher could substitute.[48] Mr. Fisher was granted the position of reader, save in his absence, Lewin would substitute for him.

A letter to that effect was directed to Rev. Lewin, and it resulted in this reply:

> . . . Upon mature consideration and as I am most desirous that peace and *harmony* shall prevail in the congregation, I have determined to accept the engagement as under the resolution . . . with ardent hope that good feeling may soon return on all sides, to ensure which will be my study . . .[49] (Italics added.)

Mr. Fisher wrote an instrument affirming that "his services" were "gratuitously" offered "as Mr. Lewin's health was not good . . ."[50]

The result of the *hazzan*/minister controversy was a weakening of R.D.C. Lewin's authority. The reforms which he had instituted on a ritual and philosophical level were challenged by Solomon Cohen. His election as *parnass* at the 1869 annual meeting was the beginning of the end for unbridled "reform" and its rabbinic spokesman.[51]

Cohen's unanimously accepted 1869 resolution began the assault.

> Resolved that although this congregation . . . has assented to a change in synagogue worship, yet it faithfully adheres to all the fundamental principles of our ancient faith. Synagogue worship involves no moral, or religious principle, and may be altered to suit the taste of the congregation, but the principles on which Judaism rests are from God, and are eternal, and unchangeable;
>
> Resolved, that the congregation recognizes among these fundamental principles a belief in the ultimate restoration of Israel to the law of their Fathers and that the Redeemer will come to Zion;
>
> Resolved that though many of us may violate the law of God regulating the diet of Israelites and prohibiting the eating of certain articles of food—for there is no man that sinneth not—yet we recognize those 'commandments and statutes' as binding, and a part of the code of laws, which God in His wisdom, has established for the government of His people.

The statement concluded

> Resolved that the President serve a copy of these resolutions to the Rev. Mr. Lewin, as the sentiments, opinions, and beliefs of this congregation.[52]

Ironically, at the same meeting in which the traditionalists triumphed, a resolution was passed to hire Mr. Lessing, the organist, for one month's time at fifty dollars.[53]

Two years earlier, Solomon Cohen's daughter, Belle, married one of another faith orientation, Francis C. O'Driscoll, with Judge William B. Fleming presiding.[54] Daughter Miriam later betrothed James Troup Dent, nephew of Governor Troup of Georgia.[55] Son Gratz died at the Battle of Bentonville in 1865, mateless. This great defender of Orthodoxy produced no grandchild to follow in the ways of his ancestors.

The resolutions of January 10, 1869, were followed by the resignation of
Rev. Lewin, the next day. It was expected, so no special meeting was called,
and the resignation letter was the third agenda item of the next regular
meeting. Mr. Lewin stated that he would vacate his office on April 11th, three
months' notice being tendered. The resignation was unanimously accepted. The text of the letter he sent to Mr. Cohen was read to the board
but not copied in the minutes as "the Adjuncta disapproved the letter of
Mr. Lewin, but decided to take no notice of the same." Advertisements
for a

> Reader *and* Lecturer in English, or for a Lecturer *alone* for the Portu-
> guese Congregation Mickva Israel of Savannah Georgia (Italics
> added.)

were to be placed in the Jewish newspapers, including the statement

> for particulars as to salary—which will be *large* and as to worship,
> etc., address the undersigned. (Italics added.)

Abraham Einstein who had something personal at stake in the Lewin
situation immediately resigned from the congregation, and his return was
earnestly entreated.[56]

Two weeks later, Mr. Lewin asked for a leave of absence for three or
four weeks, and it was granted. Rev. Fisher, in response to the resignation,
withdrew his gratuitous offer to act as reader. By February, Mr. Fisher was a
candidate for the post of reader and minister, and a term of six months at a
salary of $150 was offered. In addition, $125 was paid to him for services
during Rev. Lewin's leave.[57]

Two months after Lewin's resignation, a circular from the founder of
Reform Judaism in America, Isaac Mayer Wise, was reported to the April
8th board meeting. A representative of the congregation was requested to
attend a "convention to be held in Cincinnati on the 15th day of June
next" (1869). To Wise, Solomon Cohen wrote a letter stating that,
lacking a minister, the *adjunta*

> respectfully decline to send a delegate, but that if our affairs are
> satisfactorily settled in time, we may cooperate.[58]

The conference failed from a lack of interest and was pre-empted by the
Philadelphia conference (1869), at which Rabbi David Einhorn carried the
day. The Philadelphia Platform, the first creedal statement of Reform, was
adopted. It rejected both a personal Messiah and a return to Zion, central
affirmations in Solomon Cohen's resolution of January 10, 1869.[59]

The re-emergence of the Orthodox faction at K.K.M.I. was challenged
at the April 8, 1869, meeting. A petition, bearing the names of eighteen
persons in the congregation "claiming to be members," demanded a meeting of the full membership for the purpose of finding "the means of retain-

ing the services of the Rev. R.D.C. Lewin." At that convocation, a letter from Joseph Lippman to the same end was read. At 10:00 a.m. the following day, the board reconvened. Four new members were proposed, Lewis and Jacob Lippman, Zachariah Falk and Nathan Gazan; all save Jacob Lippman were accepted on the spot. The *adjunta* voted that since Mr. Lewin had resigned (the resignation was to go into effect on April 11, three days later), and the board had accepted it, it was up to Lewin to withdraw the resignation before any consideration of the petition could be allowed. Affirming its authority, the board resolved that even

> though under the charter, the adjuncta have the sole control of the matter, as a courtesy to the petitioners a meeting would be held.[60]

Among those receiving a copy of the resolution were the four advocates of Rev. Lewin—Isaac Epstein, L. Lillienthal, S. Yates Levy, and Octavus Cohen. The pro-Lewin forces were picking up steam and the congregation was adding new members ready to exercise their right of franchise, Jacob Lippman and L. Mohr having been accepted at the April 11th session.

The day of confrontation was April 13, 1869. Thirty-five congregants, a record number, were in their seats when the call to order was proclaimed. First up was Octavus Cohen to present a resolution:

> Resolved that the resolutions, passed on the 10th day of January 1869 declaratory of the convictions of this congregation as to questions of religious observance be reconsidered.

The younger Cohen stated that the purpose of the meeting was to find the means of keeping Lewin on staff, declaring his resignation "in consequence of the above resolutions."

S. Yates Levy rose to offer a new set of creedal statements.[61] To effect compromise, the first statement of Solomon Cohen's resolution was reaffirmed (that K.K.M.I. allowed ritual changes, but held the principles of Judaism to be immutable).

The second emphasized the centrality of Biblical teaching, affirming

> that the creed and principles of Judaism are plainly set forth, and prescribed in the laws of Moses, and the teachings of scripture, and that such creed and principle are to be construed by the letter of scripture, aided by the teachings of the minister of the congregation, sustained by the conscience of each adherent of Judaism, acting for himself.[62]

The Talmud and Codes were denied primal authority. Only Scripture was binding. The rabbi was allowed freedom to interpret and the people freedom of conscience.

The third and final resolution was

> . . . if the teachings of the minister . . . are foreign to the ideals and conscience of his congregation, he shall, after a meeting, and vote

of the congregation [note the *adjunta's* dominion is denied] be so informed, but that in no case is the congregation clothed with the power to declare what is true Judaism, and what is not, the law and scriptures being the sole criterion of that question.[63] (Italics added.)

Only the first motion carried, and a divided membership voted thirteen *aye* and sixteen *nay* on resolution two, eleven *aye* and fifteen *nay* on resolution three. The traditionalists triumphed again, but the rupture was in the open. No one called for blessed *harmony*. Rev. Lewin's ministry in Savannah was permanently ended.

At the March 19, 1871, meeting, the three resolutions were reconsidered, and this time carried. Mr. Lewin was no longer in the pulpit but his teachings prevailed. Even after the repudiation of the reforms initiated by Lewin, the process continued. At decade's end, the *adjunta* banned *aliyahs* (summoning people to the pulpit to recite the benedictions over the Torah) save in the instance of a bar mitzvah.[64] That "coming of age" rite (here mentioned for the first time in nineteenth century records) involved giving the boy an *aliyah* on his special day.

A SECOND CONGREGATION

"B'nai Berith Jacob" (hereafter referred to as B.B. Jacob, B.B.J., or K.K.B.B.J.) claims to be the South's oldest congregation continually affiliated with Orthodox Judaism. From humble beginnings, it has become a major religious institution in the city. Unfortunately, its records and minutes have not survived into the twentieth century, except for a letter that came (by accident) into this writer's hands. Newspaper articles and secondary sources constitute the only other research material.

The argument is herein advanced that the name "B'nai Berith Jacob" hints at the way the congregation was created. Members of the local chapter of the B'nai B'rith, who were people of more modest resources or uncomfortable with the Portuguese *Minhag*, formed a coalition with a group of former members of "Mickva" Israel who separated from the mother congregation when Rev. Jacob Rosenfeld resigned. The unusual nomenclature—B'nai B'rith Jacob—is a fusion of the fraternal order B'nai B'rith with "Jacob," the first name of one of the founding fathers. The following data is cited to sustain the theory.

F. D. Lee and J. L. Agnew published a history of Savannah in 1869.[65] Wrongly, the authors affirmed the founding date of B.B.J. as September, 1860, but rightly stated it was established

after the departure of the Rev. J. Rosenfeld from the "Mickva Israel" congregation.[66]

On September 10, 1862, *Hazzan* Rosenfeld's resignation was accepted by the *adjuntamen*.[67] Lee and Agnew continued:

It owes its origin to a society bearing the name of B'nai Berith, which existed prior to the formation of the congregation, but which resolved itself into the congregation, retaining the original name with the addition of the title "Jacob."[68]

A document exists that provides information about the circumstance and date of the founding of B.B. Jacob. It is a letter of resignation dated January 9, 1877, written to the president and Board of Trustees of the synagogue by Harry Haym, a former president and charter member.[69] Mr. Haym outlined the major historical developments within the congregation from its opening moments until 1877. Here are selected passages from the text, interspersed with comments:

> In retiring from the honorable office as president, I take the liberty to submit the following report for your attention, viz:
> In the early part of the year *1861*, the late deceased Rev. Jacob Rosenfeld called on me for consultation to organize a second Congregation in this City, when immediately upon consultation with G. Brown.[70] we called a meeting of Israelites and founded the present named Congregation, of which I had the honor to be elected as the first Vice President and Treasurer, and Rev. J. Rosenfeld as first President who also officiated as Minister at the rented 'Armory Hall'. (Italics added.)

The year 1861 is the most probable for the formation of K.K.B.B.J. There is a lag in the M.I. *Minute Books* which recorded Rosenfeld's departure at the meeting of September 10, 1862. Lee and Agnew's 1860 was probably too early.

Rev. Rosenfeld was not a silent partner in the enterprise. He called upon leaders and activated them to form a second synagogue. To solve the "authority" problem he had with the president of K.K.M.I., he effectively combined the two offices, president and rabbi. Henceforth, he could absent himself from the city without beseeching presidential permission.

The first meeting place of the synagogue, "Armory Hall," was located at Bull and State Streets, in the northeast portion of Wright Square (across from the Post Office in present day Savannah).[71]

When the Civil War was raging, Haym's letter reported

> ... Still we continued all during that struggle increasing in membership and it is mostly due to the energy of G. Brown, that by the end of the war through his good financial management, the congregation was possessed of the amount valued at $7000.00 U.S. currency.

G. Brown was Haym's brother-in-law according to the family tree in the possession of a descendant.[72]

In 1865, Mr. Rosenfeld decided to go into business and abandoned Savannah, settling, temporarily, in Tallahassee.[73] Simon Gertsman agreed to function as lay reader, at the urging of H. Haym, the new president.[74] In 1867, controversy erupted. H. Haym described it thusly:

Looking to the interest of the congregation's assets, with the prospect of increasing the same until sufficient to be enabled for erecting a synagogue, but alas I regret that just at the time the difficulties commenced, as the party strife in the year 1867 elected Simon Gertsman as president, who at once . . . has undertaken at once without taking into consideration, wether [sic] the assets of the congregation is [sic] sufficient for contracting to build a synagogue, but in spite of my objection, and also of the previous financial manager G. Brown and many other prominent members the contract was concluded, and the result was that the present *little* synagogue was built at the cost of $15,000 which if properly managed would hardly have cost half that amount. (Italics added.)

A fifteen thousand dollar building in the 1860's ought to have been an elaborate structure. Thirty years earlier K.K.M.I. erected a synagogue of stone for four thousand dollars. Judging by the architects employed, Muller and Bruyn, it must have been a more distinguished building than Haym stated.[75] The Kehoe House, (later Goette's Funeral Home), close to the Davenport House on Columbia Square, and the improvements to John Norris' Mercer House (opposite the present K.K.M.I.) are but two of the notable works of Bruyn (and, in one instance, Muller).[76]

The synagogue stood on the corner of Montgomery and State Streets on Liberty Square, Lot 18 (between Broughton and Oglethorpe).[77] On this site, the second building was constructed, the 1908 Hyman Witcover structure now owned by St. Andrews Independent Episcopal Church. In 1820 a Catholic chapel had occupied Lot 19, the space directly opposite this site, but by the 1850's, it was vacant.[78] The Chatham County Courthouse presently occupies Lot 19, and Liberty Square has been realigned, permitting heavy traffic, but obliterating the beauty of a green oasis.

How the land came into the possession of B.B.J. cannot be determined. Gamble records Lot 36, Franklin Ward as belonging to the congregation (the northwest corner of Broughton and Montgomery Streets).[79] If an exchange occurred, it was not recorded in the city registry.

The Cornerstone Consecration Ceremony of the first building was an elaborate event. The congregation assembled at Armory Hall for worship early on July 16, 1867. Following the prayers, a large contingent began the march to the Liberty Square site, assembling on State Street. At the head was a band of music. Behind the B.B.J. members and families marched the three lodges of Odd Fellows (Oglethorpe, Live Oak and DeKalb) and Joseph Lodge #76 of the International Order of the B'nai B'rith. The mayor and aldermen were next in the processional, the architect behind, followed by the trustees of the congregation, then the *adjunta* of K.K.M.I. The ceremonies were impressive. *Yigdal* was sung; Psalm 127 recited. Rev. Lewin offered an English prayer for the government. Psalm 29 was chanted, and a prayer for the congregation was offered. President Haym presented the trowel and spoke briefly, after which the cornerstone was laid. A scholarly address by Rev. R. D. C. Lewin was the high point of the ceremonies. The eloquence of Samuel Yates Levy silenced his Honor, Mayor Anderson, who "excused himself upon the plea of being poor of ready speech." Mr. S. E. Byck, president of the B'nai B'rith, challenged the members to "assist in completing the temple. . . ." *Adon Olam* and the benediction concluded the celebration. Special marshals, Phillip Dzialynski, Elias Brown, S. W. Silverberg, and Lewis Levy, directed the crowd on a return march to Armory Hall, where all were dismissed. In the cornerstone was sealed a metal box containing

> a Bible, a Hebrew prayer book, the Constitution and by-laws of the Congregation . . . programmes of the order of service and order of procession, two scrolls of parchment with the name of the layer of the stone, the names of officers and members of the congregation Bnai Brith Jacob, the names of the founders . . . the names of the Building Committee, names of ex-officers, the names of the architects and builders . . . of the President of the United States, Governor of the State, and Mayor and Aldermen of the city; also various old coins . . . the Jewish periodicals in the United States and the daily papers of the city.[80]

Rev. R. D. C. Lewin's address was printed in the *Daily News and Herald* (July 18, 1867). It was a theological exposition of Judaism, the flavor of which is captured in this brief selection:

> Regarding then, the multitude before me assembled as the children of One Parent, united together by those indissoluble ties of humanity which no differences of creed or belief should separate, it becomes my duty to set before you a synopsis of Israel's faith, in order that when the principles by which we are bound are better understood, we may be the better appreciated.

Justifying taking such an unusual tact at a Cornerstone Consecration Service, Lewin pointed out

> no subject may be selected as more appropriate to the occasion, for inasmuch as the true dignity of the building to be reared on this spot will consist, not in its architectural skill, nor in the elaborate workmanship of the designer, but in the fervor and zeal of the worshippers who will therein congregate. . . .[81]

In the third month after the cornerstone was placed, the synagogue was solemnly dedicated by Rev. Lewin (September 27, 1867). In 1868, Simon Gertsman resigned as president and functioned no longer as lay reader. A. B. Weslow of the Wessolowsky clan replaced him about the time Rev. Jacob Rosenfeld returned to the city from Florida.[82] He was immediately elected paid minister of B.B. Jacob. An estimated thirty members constituted the worshipping community which followed the Polish *Minhag*.[83]

Harry Haym's letter reflects the internal dissension that marked the opening period of the new synagogue. Those who pushed for the building, claimed Haym, "are now scattered all over the broad land . . .", a heavy burden of eight thousand dollars in debts having to be dealt with. At one point the sheriff advertised "synagogue for sale" in the local newspaper and the membership was diminishing as a consequence. Then Haym was re-elected for a period of time to restore health and order.

> I was called again to the office of president, but could not possibly succeed altogether, in having the entire debts cleared, still we managed the affairs of the congregation until I retired in the year 1872 . . .

The retirement was forced upon him "on account of various obstacles and misunderstanding among the members."[84]

For the next four years, Jacob Cohen, W. Barnett and L. Fried served as presidents, all of whom exerted themselves to get the synagogue in the black; but instead of decreasing the debts, they increased.[85]

Haym credited three with saving the synagogue from bankruptcy: the Honorable P. M. Russell, Colonel Waring Russell and Mrs. Virginia Nathan, former members of K.K.M.I. (The males even served on the *adjunta*.) Borrowing the fund-raising techniques introduced by the ladies who initiated the K.K.M.I. Permanent Fund, these three spearheaded a "Hebrew Fair" which netted eighteen hundred dollars, saving the congregation from ruination.

In 1876, Haym was again elected president and admitted that some resigned or expressed pain over that turn of events. He accepted, only to be sure the funds would be administered frugally. One surmises that Mr. Haym was concerned that no charge of mismanagement would be levied against him as he stated in his letter:

> . . . but I hope that after my retiring from office, no present or previous Fellow [*sic*] members can bring any charges against me for misappropriation—all my doings as President I considered myself as "Right" . . .

What concerned Mr. Haym was that Levy S. Hart had been secretary of the congregation and for the year 1876 had

> neglected entirely the books . . . that I myself entered in the Treasury account as the best I could . . .

In 1870, after Rev. Rosenfeld returned to K.K.M.I. to function as "minister," J. "Walewski" (possibly Wessolowsky) replaced him as B.B.J.'s paid spiritual leader. It was not an appointment "Walewski" sought, as payment for the year 1876 was not as contracted. Despite these adversities, K.K.B.J. made it through the opening phase, and came to prosper as new waves of settlers situated in Savannah from the 1880's on.

SPIRITUAL LEADER WANTED

The departure of Rev. Rosenfeld in 1862 as *hazzan* of M.I. led to the following resolution: "We will keep the synagogue open and have the service regularly performed . . ." Mr. Amram, the *shochet*, was requested to read the services on Sabbath eve, morn and Holy Days. The salary proferred him for his religious ministrations was $87.50 per quarter.[86] A year later, Mr. Milhauser was requested to act as reader for two hundred dollars per quarter, in addition to his pay as *shammash*, on condition that he find someone to do the sexton's chores and reimburse the gentleman out of his own pocket. This was to be a temporary arrangement ". . . until we [K.K.M.I. board] can obtain a regular minister . . ."[87] In 1864, Mr. Milhauser was complimented for

> the reverent and dignified manner in which he . . . performed the services for our synagogue . . .

A prayer (for a restoration of Milhauser's health), appended to the resolution, signalled trouble. In the breech, Mr. A. Epstein showed forth "that noble Jewish feeling" and offered his services gratuitously for Sabbaths and Holy Days.[8f] Within two years desperation was setting in. A search committee that had been appointed to get a "suitable hazzan" reported no luck, and a salary of four thousand dollars was made available to the chosen one. Advertisements in Jewish newspapers here and abroad were submitted.[89] On January 12, 1867, Isaac Leeser was back in Savannah preaching a "very pious and instructive lecture" at the synagogue.[90] The same year, connection was initiated with R. D. C. Lewin. The secretary corresponded with him, offering three thousand dollars (a reduction by one-quarter from the original high offer made in 1866). Lewin had officiated in both New Orleans and Shreveport, where Secretary Barnett Phillips' letters proceeded.[91]

Lewin accepted, and the congregation was no longer on hold. Little did it realize the appointment of the new *hazzan* and minister would lead to veering in the direction of Reform Judaism, and the *shitach* (union of rabbi and congregation) would be for only two years. By January 17, 1869, the resignation letter of Lewin was in hand, and subsequent efforts to reinstate him did not reap success. Hebrew teacher, E. Fisher, read the services as the acting *hazzan* for six months, at a reduced salary of $150 per month.[92] Once again, it was back to the drawing board to design advertisements for a suitable minister and *hazzan*.

By December of 1869, applications were reaching the search committee, and a sense of the importance of the congregation was developing. The Reverends Fleugel and A. Laser asked to be considered. So did Jacob Rosenfeld, first minister of M.I. and first minister of "B'nai Berith Jacob." While not looking with favor on any of these, the *adjunta* offered everyone an opportunity to "officiate at his own expense."[93]

One applicant, Rev. "Mr. Wecksler," was invited to visit Savannah at the congregation's expense. "Mr. Wecksler" was Rev. S. Wechsler, former "rabbi" of Nashville, Tennessee. The *Savannah Morning News* declared that he had accepted the call to serve M.I.[94] In this instance, the local press had information, unknown to the *adjunta* and congregation. Rev. E. M. Myers of New York had also come to Savannah and lectured without compensation. Some negotiation had taken place but he was put off with a fifty dollar check and a statement "that there being applications for the office from other persons the *adjunta* declined making a selection at present."[95]

As the decade of the 1870's commenced, a committee of three, A. Epstein, L. Elsinger and S. Guckenheimer, was appointed to confer with Rev. Rosenfeld.[96] Officially, they were to notify him of a one year appointment as rabbi at a diminished $1800 stipend with the following stipulation:

> That Mr. Rosenfeld shall marry and also perform the funeral services for all persons professing the Jewish religion in the city . . . when so called upon *but he shall not leave the city at any time without the permission of the parnas. . .*[97] (Italics added.)

The past was not forgotten, and a weaker but wiser Rosenfeld did not dissent this time.

During his second term of office, *Hazzan* Rosenfeld was given a special honor. A new synagogue was to be consecrated in the sister city of Augusta, Georgia, and the services of K.K.M.I's spiritual leader were earnestly sought by Mr. A. Mendelson, its president. Without hesitation the request was allowed.[98] A letter dated November 25, 1870, to Mr. A. Mendelson was sent by Solomon Cohen, inquiring whether the reverend had given a positive response to the invitation.

In the meantime, applicants for the post of *hazzan* of the congregation were still being received. Revs. Baar and Nathan were invited to give test lectures.[99] Solomon Cohen wrote a letter on November 25, 1870, to Rev. N. Baar in New Orleans, stating that the board received his instrument, and

> are pleased with its tone, but instructed me to say, that they could not make a persuant engagement without a further and better acquaintance.

Inquiry was made as to the end of Rev. Baar's present engagement, and the invitation extended to visit Savannah at an early day. Cohen requested that kind regards to Mr. Jacobs be tendered.[100] A letter to Rev. Henry S. Jacobs of New Orleans, dated January 7, 1871, complained

> Now nearly two months since I addressed a letter to Dr. Baar and which I enclose you a copy, and up to this time have had no reply. Will you do me the favor to ascertain if it was received . . .[101]

Cohen confessed that the congregation was

> badly in want of a lecturer and I fear if we are much longer without one that our congregation will be broken up and our place of worship closed.

Rev. Jacobs had a brother, George, and there was a notion to approach him.[102]

I think your brother would suit us, but know not how to approach him. Our people are generally opposed to engaging a minister without first seeing and hearing him . . .[103]

Cohen wanted Rev. Jacobs to find out his brother's inclination toward "Mickva" Israel, and if he was available, Cohen would "use all my influence to have a tender made to him."[104] In a remarkable statement of candor, the normally "steely" Solomon Cohen asked,

Can you help me in any way. I am almost worn down in my great anxiety about our congregational affairs.[105]

To the second applicant, Rev. M. Nathan of St. Thomas, an abrupt letter was addressed stating in effect that another candidate was being considered. It was dated November 25, 1870, the same date as the letter to Rev. Baar.[106]

In 1871 at the January 23rd annual meeting, Rev. Rosenfeld was again elected for a one year term. The Rosenfeld family was very musical; the children and extended kin constituted the choir, while I. M. Rosenfeld (no kin) was appointed organist. The reverend's election was made contingent upon the continuance of the musical program. Mr. Moses pointed out the inequity of the situation and the *hazzan* was voted in on his own merit. However, he declined the post because only one month's notice on either side could end the relationship. The *hazzan* was aware that he was not the congregation's first choice and that the leadership was sending out "feelers," as attested to by the letters of Solomon Cohen. More severance time was demanded.[107] A special meeting was called; the full congregation approved a change to three months' notice, and elected the "reader" for a second year's term.[108] The minutes do not mention the termination of Rev. Rosenfeld's ministry at "Mickva" Israel, but, by the High Holy Days of 1871, he was not conducting worship. His replacement was S. Hexter, a gentleman endowed with a voice of sufficient beauty to remain a M.I. choir member for a prolonged term.

As the *first former hazzan* was functioning in the pulpit, the congregation was negotiating with the *second former hazzan*, R. D. C. Lewin.[109] An effort was made to rescind Solomon Cohen's resolutions (which reaffirmed the "Orthodox" orientation of the congregation) to open the way for Mr. Lewin to send his letter of application for the position of "minister." Samuel Yates Levy's defeated resolutions were, this time, victorious. By June 18, 1871, the effort to recall R. D. C. Lewin was full blown. The *Ashkenazic* members of the *adjunta*, Eckman, Weil, Ferst, Guckenheimer, Lillienthal, and Moses (Solomon Cohen was the sole Sephardic Jew on the board) had the votes to issue the call. Only Moses dissented. Surprisingly, Solomon Cohen had shifted from anti to pro. Apparently the dismay he expressed in his letter to Rev. Jacobs was real and the future of the synagogue was more important to him than the preservation of pure Orthodoxy.

Solomon Cohen's letter to R. D. C. Lewin (then residing in New York) reflects an attitudinal change:

As the presiding officer I am instructed by the Adjuncta . . . to open correspondence with you on the subject of supplying our congregation with a reader or hazan and a lecturer united in one person. The Adjuncta desires me to say that they wish to engage the services of one capable to perform the duty of the above named offices. They desire he should read the prayers and deliver an English discourse every Sabbath and Holy day, perform the marriages and burial services for all members of the congregation or seat holders and their families when requested so to do and perform all other duties incident to the holy vocation of hazan and lecturer. *The form of prayer for the present will be that selected and read by you when formerly filling said offices for our congregation.* It is however very probable that the 'Minhag America' will be introduced at an early day, nor is it supposed that there would be any serious objection to divide the Five Books of Moses into smaller lessons so as to read them through in three years instead of one . . .[110] (Italics added.)

This is followed by the request from Rev. Lewin to submit an application for the job and a statement that salary was negotiable but by High Holy Day time the *hazzan* would have to be in Savannah.

Minhag America was Isaac Mayer Wise's chief instrument for "reforming" Jewish liturgy. Dividing the Torah readings into a triennial cycle was also a major Reform innovation. The once staunch champion of the Leeser brand of Judaism capitulated to the realities of the times.

In follow-up correspondence dated July 5, 1871, from Cohen to Lewin (at 67-69 Williams Street, New York), the *parnass* thanked him for

the very kind offer of your services in obtaining a minister and reader for our congregation, and should they fail in securing *your* services, they will ask leave to avail themselves of your offer . . .[111] (Italics added.)

In his communication, Rev. Lewin underscored the difference between "*hazzan*" and "reader." Cohen acknowledged that the *adjunta* approved of that view though

As I am acting merely as amanuensis for the Adjuncta *I* express no opinion on the subject.

The central issue was the term of the election which Cohen defined as "one year-no longer *now* . . ." to see whether both parties would suit one another (as if R. D. C. Lewin was an unknown quantity with undefined views). Concerning the prayer book, Cohen wrote,

but if the "Minhag America" is rejected, the Adjuncta would prefer the prayers selected and read by you when you acted as minister and reader of the congregation. They have no objection to your leaving off the taleth [prayer shawl].

This was the first indication of a further ritual alteration.

Cohen thanked the former *hazzan* for including copies of his published materials, including five newsletters and a pamphlet. Lewin had embarked on journalistic endeavors, which he did not want to abandon should he return to Savannah. Cohen assured him,

> Nor do they [the *adjunta*] see any difficulty in your continuing the publication of your periodical . . .

As Cohen's letter did not specify salary and seemed to imply a limited engagement, Lewin made inquiry on the 8th of July, to which answer was forthcoming on the 14th.

> They will not elect you for a longer period than one year. . . . They will not adopt your prayer book as the ritual of the congregation, and this I expressed as delicately as possible in my letter of the 5th inst.—using the word 'prefer' instead of the absolute refusal I am now forced to use. Such are the views of the Adjuncta as I understood them—the clear expression of their opinions being adverse to electing you for over one year for the present, and to the adoption of your prayerbook.

The hope of a restoration of Lewin's ministry was fast dimming.[112]

The Cohen letter of the 14th of July was in response to a board meeting held on Independence Day, 1871. A resolution was adopted unanimously expressing preference for the *Minhag America*, Wise's prayerbook, but allowing Lewin to select passages from the Leeser prayerbook.

The *adjunta* was not prepared for a final break-down in negotiations. On April 9, 1872, (almost a year later) in the absence of President Cohen, Mr. Lillienthal (the first to be called vice-president) responded to several members of the board who requested a hearing to seek a way to bring Lewin back. On motion of Mr. Weil, seconded by Mr. Elsinger, a committee of three headed by Mr. Lillienthal was to invite *Hazzan* Lewin to deliver a lecture on the following Sabbath, and to see whether he would at the same time be willing to receive a call.

Three days later, Rev. Lewin was in Savannah to officiate at the marriage of Abraham Einstein's daughter Carrie (Lewin's sister-in-law) to A. Friedenberg.[113] Questions: Was father-in-law Abraham Einstein responsible for dovetailing the Lewin visit (for the wedding) with the trial sermon? Was Solomon Cohen's absence from the April 9th board meeting an essential element in the plot?

Sometime that week, Rev. Lewin addressed "the Israelites of Savannah" (both congregations) on the subject of "Jewish Ministry." His effort was received with much appreciation as an "able literary treat" which was enjoyed. So determined was the board to win Lewin back that a salary of five thousand dollars per year was tendered, provided "he will read the services as formerly declared by him, when officiating in this congregation."[114] In this instance, a second connection was not possible and silence in the minutes signalled all negotiations collapsed. No further board meetings were held between April and October, 1872.

While the negotiations were proceeding with Lewin, President Cohen was seeking out others who might serve as "readers" and "ministers." A letter dated February 20, 1871, proceeded to Henry W. Schneeberger, later the esteemed "Orthodox" rabbi of Congregation "Poel Zedek" in New York City (and still later of Congregation Chizek Amuno in Baltimore).[115] Dr. Schneeberger's wife, Sarah, the daughter of Charles and Fanny Nussbaum of New York City, had a sister, Miriam, the wife of Jonathan Stern (born in Hirschaid, Bavaria). The Jonathan Sterns resided in Savannah most of their adult lives. (Daughter Ruth was the beloved secretary of K.K.M.I. during the tenure of Rabbis George Solomon, Louis Youngerman, and Solomon Starrels. Another Nussbaum sister, Jeanette, married Dr. Simon Tuska, rabbi of Rochester, New York, and Memphis, Tennessee, the first graduate of an American university to serve as rabbi.[116])

The letter was written prior to Schneeberger's decision to enter the rabbinate:

> Having recently learned that you were about to enter upon the holy and honorable career of a Minister of our Faith I ask leave to open a correspondence with you on the subject of our synagogue. We are in want of a Minister whom we are able and willing to pay liberally.

After describing the delicacies of entering such negotiations so that the two parties "may become known to each other . . .," Cohen characterized the congregation in Savannah thusly:

> This is a fine field for a man of zeal and energy—the society is good and the congregation may be enlarged greatly.[117]

No board action was taken on the subject, so one assumes Cohen was acting on his own. Answer from Schneeberger is not to be found in the congregational records. At a later period, Schneeberger was consulted by the body, indicating close ties existed, presumably as a consequence of the Stern family connection.[118]

Rev. Joseph H. M. Chumaceiro of Charleston was in contact with Mr. Cohen, seeking the pulpit during the time of negotiations with R. D. C. Lewin. In an instrument dated June 20, 1871, the president informed him that the letter Chumaceiro addressed to the congregation was placed before the board but "they had other views, previously entertained." Cohen's advice to him was "for the present at least, you will be forced to retain your present position."[119] As minister of K.K. Beth Elohim, Chumaceiro served from 1868 to 1874, a period marked by tension. The congregation's finances were problematic, resulting in criticism of the rabbi and his taking offense at the "negativism" of the temple leadership.[120]

The Reverend Mr. Fleugel again applied for the office of rabbi (first mention of this term in the minutes) and English lecturer. The board on

March 3, 1872, requested President Cohen to contact Rev. "Gertheim" (Gutheim) of New Orleans about him.[121] That letter has been preserved, revealing that concerns of a century ago remain central today:

> Permit me to put in the form of interrogatories [Cohen was a lawyer] the information I desire. Do you think he will suit a congregation who desires a lecturer in English and a Reader, or Cantor [first time this term is used also] united in one person. Is he a married man, and what size family has he.[122]

Whether this information was received or not, Fleugel was not to be a "bird" in hand. By October 8, 1872, the Rev. Mr. Jacobs (Henry or George, we know not) was being paid two hundred dollars for officiating at the synagogue during the High Holy Days. On October 27, 1872, a letter from Mr. Philip Wineman of Charleston recommending the Rev. Mr. Harris of London as *hazzan* seized the attention of the *adjunta*. When adequate data on the "honorable" gentleman was received a week later (November 3), a fixed offer was sent to the minister destined to become the third "professional" spiritual leader of K.K.M.I.[123]

As this pivotal decision was being made, the congregation was negotiating with B. B. Jacob about combining the two institutions, and the dream of building a third sanctuary was nearing realization. An effort to buy land on Monterey Square was seriously entertained.

R. D. C. LEWIN—A FINAL WORD

A two year rabbinate seems insufficient to make a permanent impress upon a community. That, however, R. D. C. Lewin achieved. He was the progenitor of Reform Judaism in Savannah. "Mickva" Israel altered ritual practices. A mixed choir and organ were accepted, *aliyahs* were permissible only at a bar mitzvah, the *tallit* was no longer mandatory for the minister, a three year Torah reading cycle was allowed, the Portuguese *Minhag* was not the only permissible form, and Wise's *Minhag America* was allowed. Underlying the alteration of forms was a change in theology. Scripturalism became the focus, not rabbinism. The freedom of the rabbi to interpret text and the freedom of the people to reject the interpretation on the basis of conscience were affirmed. Affiliation with the Union of American Hebrew Congregations and Isaac Mayer Wise's other institutional creations would be postponed until the twentieth century, but the notion that K.K.M.I. retained *Sephardic* Orthodox rites after R. D. C. Lewin must be viewed as errant.

In two other areas, interfaith relations and education, Rev. Lewin affected arrangements in the community. The *Savannah Morning News* of January 16, 1869, documented the respect he gained among the people of the city:

> ... Rev. R. D. C. Lewin, pastor of the "Mickvo [sic] Israel" Congregation has tendered his resignation, to take effect on the 11th of April ...

[He has] a host of friends in this city who will deeply *deplore* his departure.[124] (Italics added.)

The congregational minutes do not relate his accomplishments among the citizens of Savannah. Newspaper accounts and Lee and Agnew's book provide the source material for reconstructing them. A preacher of note, he was chosen to address the graduating class of the Savannah Medical College at its annual commencement in 1868.[125] His sermons were read by the general populace, being advertised in the "New Book" columns of the local newspapers. "Orthodoxy vs. Reform" was advertised by Cooper, Olcott & Co. in the *Savannah Daily News*. A second sermon, "What is Judaism," was offered by Herman L. Schreiner.[126] The Masons elected him to Zerubbabel Lodge No. 15, calling him Rev. Brother.[127] Joseph Lodge of the I.O.B.B. (Independent Order of B'nai B'rith) elevated him as its lecturer in 1868.[128] So popular were his sermons that a public announcement that he would repeat a *Yom Kippur* address, "A Call to Repentence," was given coverage in the press.[129] Commenting on Lewin's leadership, Agnew and Lee wrote,

> If the government of the congregation continues to be conducted in the same spirit as it is at present, it must undoubtedly be among the most prosperous in the country.[130]

Among the Jewish inhabitants of the Forest City, Lewin was esteemed. He was chosen to dedicate the new edifice of K.K.B.B. Jacob in 1869, as well as to deliver the address at the Cornerstone Consecration Ceremony earlier that year. Evidence of his leadership ability was the Jewish educational institution that he founded, *The Savannah Hebrew Collegiate Institute*. Supported by both congregations and lauded by the Jewish and Christian leadership of the city, it functioned smoothly under Lewin's aegis. While bearing a title that would seem to limit students to those of Jewish origins, the school attracted representatives of every denomination and creed. Religious instruction was provided, but in a manner that did not exclude non-Jews. The education was the best available in the city according to Agnew and Lee, who praised the institution thusly:

> Of all the educational establishments which grace our 'Forest City' none stands higher or claims more admiration . . .[131]

Organized in 1867 at a meeting convened by Lewin and presided over by Octavus Cohen, the Institute was governed by a provisional council made up of representatives of the total Jewish community: Barnett Phillips, A. J. Brady, Simon Gertsman (president of B. B. Jacob), A. Epstein, P. Dzialynski, W. Barnett, and the founding rabbi, Lewin, who also was chairman. The intent was to create a European-style high school staffed by an array of scholars. The *hazzan* undertook the extensive fundraising effort to which the Jewish community as a whole responded. On November 1, 1867, the school opened. A permanent council, consisting of Octavus Cohen, B. Phillips, A. B. Weslow (of B.B. Jacob), H. Meinhard, M. Selig, P. Dzialynski (of B.B. Jacob) and S. H. Eckman, was elected. Cohen served as president, Weslow as treasurer, and Phillips as secretary.

In addition to a superior education, the Institute offered public lectures. Among the guest speakers were the Honorable Henry Root Jackson and the Honorable Henry S. Fitch.[132]

The following year, Solomon Cohen was elected president, and others elected to serve on the board included Henry Meinhard, Marcus Selig and S. H. Eckman. The Institute increased in number, added more advanced education, and was thriving. At its hey-day, it included a high school for boys and a high school for girls. The subject matter taught included geometry, algebra, bookkeeping, natural philosophy, French, German, Hebrew, and Latin. R. D. C. Lewin was superintendent and principal of the theology department; Charles N. West was instructor in *belles-lettres* and mathematics; Professor Albert Eiswald was instructor in languages; Rev. Fisher was instructor in Hebrew and theology; and Edwin Knapp taught bookkeeping.[133]

Among the individuals who served on the Savannah Hebrew Collegiate Institute faculty was Edward Benjamin Morris Browne (known as "Alphabet" Browne). He later enrolled at the Hebrew Union College in Cincinnati, receiving ordination from Isaac Mayer Wise. His quicksilver temperament led to short ministries in many communities. He officiated at The Temple (Hebrew Benevolent Society) of Atlanta from 1877 to 1881, where he became known as a spellbinder. Following Lewin's model, he combined the duties of *hazzan*/minister and editor, publishing the Jewish journal, the *Jewish South,* from 1877 to 1880.[134]

The Savannah Hebrew Collegiate Institute was an expression of a broader movement in Jewish life. In an 1847 issue of *The Occident,* Leeser reacted to the inadequacies of the American rabbinate and the insufficient loyalties of American Jews to their ancestral faith. As remedy he proposed

> to establish a high school for general education . . . whence may issue men of ample religious and literary endowment . . . men in whose hand the future destinies of their respective congregations could be placed with safety . . .[135]

Lewin was responding to a movement of some moment in America. That he managed to unite Savannah Jewry for such an endeavor is an indication of his charisma.

The destiny of the school is unknown. No record exists verifying why or when its doors were sealed.

THIRD IN A GENERATION

On November 5, 1872, Solomon Cohen wrote the following communication to Rev. A. Harris, St. Mary Ave-Bena Viste, London:

My Dear Sir:
    I take great pleasure in informing you that the Board of Trustees
or Adjuncta of the congregation 'Mickva Israel of Savannah, Georgia'
have unanimously directed me to invite you to become our minister
and lecturer, we would wish you to come to us as early as compatible
with your convenience, but would like an answer to this call, in
person if possible . . .[136]

Twelve hundred and fifty dollars was the amount offered for the initial
six-month term of service, to be followed by a five year contract, if all
worked out as anticipated. The letter intimated that the two men
had earlier discussed terms, the implication being that the *hazzan* wanted
more and the president could not persuade the congregation to exceed the
promised amount.

    Abraham Harris was born in Edinburgh, Scotland, in 1836.[137] He was a
mature man of thirty-six when he arrived in the Port City. Educated in
London and Berlin, he had served as English tutor to Crown Prince
Frederick of Prussia and was associated also with Bismarck and Field Marshal
Von Moltke.[138] His nature was conservative so that the radical reforms experienced under Lewin were destined to taper off. To understand the level
of his scholarship, one needs to be aware that he proceeded from the
K.K.M.I. pulpit to the Hebrew Union College faculty at the invitation of
its founder and president, Isaac Mayer Wise. Rev. Henry Jacobs, Solomon
Cohen's rabbinical counselor, was a friend of the Scottish rabbi, preaching
his funeral oration in 1891.[139] While Phillip Wineman of Charleston was
responsible for the first introduction, Henry Jacobs' approval must have
sealed the covenant.[140]

    At the January 6, 1873, annual meeting, the president informed the
body that Rev. Harris was engaged and would arrive that very month.[141]
The synagogue was to be refurbished in anticipation.

    Clarification of Harris' duties was necessary, and part of the board meet-
ing of February 16, 1873, was devoted thereto. In addition to the standard
responsibilities, the leveling of perquisites by the rabbi was permitted. For
burials and marriages, a fee of no less than ten dollars, no more than twenty
was established. On Friday, February 21, Rev. Harris was in the
pulpit delivering his "consecration" sermon. For the occasion, the president
had a "gown" made, the first mention of this religious garb.[142]

    The congregational minutes do not provide the details to flesh out
Harris' career. The notable achievement was the formation of a first-rate
choir. Rev. Lewin in his famed sermon on "Orthodoxy and Reform" had
proposed that a choir and music be added to enrich the service. Alterations
were made in the choir loft to accommodate the mixed group and the
melodian (pump organ).[143] Two organists were recorded in the minutes:
Professor Lessing, a musician of high standards, and I. M. Rosenfeld.[144] In
addition to concertizing, Lessing managed a music store on the corner of
Whitaker and Broughton Lane.[145] One choir was made up of kinsmen and
relatives of Rev. Rosenfeld.[146] S. H. Eckman and J. M. Solomon (whose wife

Zipporah was in an early choir) were responsible for finding and preserving a permanent "corps" of singers.[147] A new committee (Solomon Cohen, S. H. Eckman, S. Elsinger and B. Kohn) was created at the very time the new *hazzan* arrived for the purpose of organizing a "quire." [*sic*][148] Simon Hexter, member of the congregation and leading tenor, had led the chanting of the services in the period following Lewin's departure and it deferred to him to choose the members. At the June 25, 1873, meeting, he announced his choir and organist. While Professor Lessing isn't mentioned specifically, it is assumed that he was the chief musician after I. M. Rosenfeld resigned. To him a yearly stipend of six hundred dollars was given, and in descending order of reward: Mr. Hexter, tenor (five hundred dollars per annum), Mrs. Pearlman, soprano (four hundred dollars), Miss Gross, contralto ($240.00), and Mr. Blois, basso ($240.00). The choir was not only mixed by gender but non-Jews participated. In August of 1874, the choir members wanted an increase (Professor Lessing's name is mentioned in this text). Mr. Hexter who acted as "manager" recommended that Mrs. Pearlman's demand for a sum exceeding his not be honored.[149] Mr. Blois was replaced by Mr. Mallette, who later advanced to the position of choirmaster (in this period he functioned as basso). The "Mickva" Israel choir flourished during Dr. Harris' tenure.

The process of reform did not diminish during his term. No longer was the rabbi pushing it; the impetus proceeded from the laity. Joseph Rosenheim and Samuel Herman recommended that

> our minister [Mr. Harris] be requested to abolish the reading in *Hebrew* as heretofore read, of *ashras* [Psalm 145, David's Psalm of Praise] and hereafter to read the same alone in English.[150] (Italics added.)

This was unanimously adopted along with a petition that the minister "shorten his prayers." Pressure for dignity during the worship process resulted in a request to the *shammash*, Mr. Boley, to see that

> every person . . . rise and be seated when the president does so that uniformity will exist . . .[151]

If Harris' rabbinate lacked success, it would be in the area of religious education. In 1872 an independent Sunday school for the instruction of the Jewish children of Savannah "irrespective of congregation" was proposed and a first meeting was held at K.K.M.I. for all interested parents, children and concerned others.[152] In 1873 (March 30) the board allowed the officers of the Sunday school to use the facilities of the synagogue. A community Sunday school was functioning at least for a period of time. In 1877 (April 2) when the final chapter in the Savannah career of Abraham Harris was being recorded, Mr. N. E. Solomon called to the attention of the congregation the growing necessity of having a school, for the benefit of the rising generation, who he was sorry to say were sadly neglected and were deprived of the opportunity of learning the tenets of our religion . . ."

Dr. Harris was responsible for one innovation for which his successors bear him a debt of gratitude. On June 28, 1874, he requested of the board a leave of absence from July 4th to the end of August.[153] The result was a respite "for three or four weeks." Presidential authority was such that Mr. Cohen did not hesitate to tell the rabbi where to vacation, allowing him leave to "go to Sullivan's Island," a spa close to Charleston. The next May, the rabbi was back, beseeching sufficient time after July 1 to return to England, having business to attend to there. Negotiations proceeded with the president and vice-president in a cordial spirit, so that the leadership was pleased to grant him four weeks.[154]

The ladies of the congregation reposed affection in Dr. Harris. When they assembled in planning session to arrange another "bazaar," the board requested the rabbi to attend.[155] At the moment when it counted most, the daughters of "Mickva" Israel rallied to the rabbi's support.

No signs of dissatisfaction between rabbi and congregation were detectable in the minutes of 1873 through 1876. Destiny intervened in the form of a yellow fever plague described in the December 11, 1876, minutes as a

terrible epidemic . . . which had been raging in the city for the past two months.

The disease periodically visited Savannah, invariably at those times when "Mickva" Israel was engaged in major building programs—1820, 1854 (in the time of the restoration of the second K.K.M.I.), and in 1876 (when the third and present structure was being raised). The 1876 epidemic began in August of the Nation's Centenary and peaked on October 15th. More than fifty-five hundred people were afflicted within a month and a half. With only thirty thousand people in the community that summer, more than one in six were victimized. Ten days later, a census of the city showed a total population of less than nineteen thousand; eleven thousand had fled. Mayor Anderson reported,

. . . almost the entire population whose circumstance permitted withdrew from our limits, leaving only those who, whether citizens or strangers, gave their personal service in any capacity.[156]

Among those who did not remain in the city to be struck down by the affliction was K.K.M.I's minister, Abraham Harris. Criticism came from Zachariah Falk, who addressed a letter to the *adjunta* "protest[ing] against his [Mr. Harris] again entering the pulpit" on account of deserting his post during the late epidemic.[157] That was followed by a letter from Rev. Harris, "resigning his position of minister of the congregation to take effect at once . . ."[158] Harris' letter was addressed to Treasurer Henry Meinhard.

My dear Sir,

In the absence of the Pres. I herewith beg to send you my resignation as Minister of the Congregation Mickvah Israel to take effect at once.

I shall always look back with pleasure to the time I have spent in your midst and I shall ever pray the Almighty to shower his blessings on you all. I shall be most happy to officiate for you gratuitously, until you can succeed in obtaining the services of a competent minister. . . .

The document is dated November 30, 1876.

A general meeting was called for the 14th of December to deal with the issue. The secretary recorded, "considerable discussion followed the reading of this resignation, participated in by many members." Falk and J. A. Einstein wanted the letter of resignation returned as the rabbi had not resumed his ministrations at the end of his one month vacation and therefore he should be suspended, with no claim to wages for any work since. N. E. Solomon offered a counter proposal, namely that the resignation be accepted as of September 10th, when his leave of absence ended. This was carried. Lee Roy Myers recommended that the offer of gratuitous service not be accepted but that a committee meet with Harris to make arrangements with him to serve temporarily until a new minister could be procured. The proposal was accepted by the body.

The matter lay dormant until the board meeting of March 26, 1877, when a petition from Mrs. M. G. Cohen, signed by every lady of note in the congregation (forty-eight signatures in toto) was received by President Simon Guckenheimer. It read as follows:

We the undersigned attendants at the synagogue, being fully impressed with the advantage and comfort derived from the spiritual teachings of Rev. Mr. Harris and dreading the fearful loss that would be sustained by the rising generation, as well as ourselves, should we be deprived of listening to his fervid exposition of pure Biblical Judaism, we would earnestly petition your honorable body to take measures to retain the Rev. Mr. Harris for our minister.

When such a bevy of formidable females petitions, wise boards act. A special meeting was called, and taking advantage of the passion of the moment, those in arrears were informed that to vote one had to be in good standing.[159]

The synagogue was again packed for the April 2, 1877, called meeting. Forty-one were in attendance, including ten females. Lizer Solomons moved that a committee of five be appointed to confer with Mr. Harris on the subject of his remaining. Abraham Minis spoke out in praise of Harris, stating that while

he did not think Mr. Harris had acted right in not returning to his post of duty, during the late epidemic, he was convinced that for other weighty and justifiable reasons, which Mr. Harris had given, it would not be charitable to judge him harshly.

Minis described the minister as "a good and conscientious man." Amending Lizer Solomons' resolution, he proposed that the petition of the ladies be granted and that the sense of the meeting be conveyed to the board and rabbi. Thirty favored it; six did not; two abstained. Every effort to re-instate Rev. Harris was pursued.

After the vote was taken, Z. Falk submitted his resignation in writing, declaring:

> I was very glad to hear that Mr. Harris regrets his action, which has been the cause of so much dissatisfaction of many members of the congregation. Had I been informed before of this fact, I certainly would have cooperated in bringing permanent peace so essential to the welfare of all organizations governed by the vote of majorities.[160]

In defeat, Mr. Falk was gracious enough to state:

> Mr. Harris' generous offer, as communicated last evening, certainly deserves consideration and the thanks of every member.[161]

The trustees appointed a committee to "wait upon him" (Mr. Falk) and request a reconsideration.

Rev. Harris, disturbed by the notion that he was in the wrong for failing to serve his people in a time of danger, withdrew his offer to remain and instead wrote:

> After mature reflection, I have come to the conclusion not to accept an engagement if offered. I shall be most happy to serve the congregation, as I have done, until you can secure the services of a competent minister.

His instrument was dated April 8, 1877.

Angered by Mr. Harris' proclamation from the pulpit on the Sabbath "that he had done nothing to regret on his actions, during the last epidemic . . .," the board passed a unanimous resolution calling the statement "uncalled for, in bad taste, and unbecoming to his station." Further, since he had

> made a verbal arrangement with a member of the Adjuncta, prior to the last meeting of the congregation to accept an engagement as minister for 12 months, and now declines to serve, the Board recommends that the congregation decline the further services of its late preacher.[162]

Other applicants had petitioned for the office of *hazzan* and minister; therefore, the relationship with Mr. Harris was concluded. All that remained was the formality of the April 9, 1877, special meeting attended by thirty-five members. President Guckenheimer read the board's recommendation and Mr. Kayton moved that it be accepted, "as the voice of the congregation." N. E. Solomon moved that the vote be reconsidered after it carried, stating that he was not in favor of Mr. Harris, but thought the congregation should not adopt a condemnatory resolution which would appear in the minutes. Mr. Guckenheimer retorted that the board had handled the issue so well that not a single member resigned but that the action of Mr. Harris in speaking out on the subject had inflamed the situation. Mrs. M. G. Cohen expressed her joy in the reconsideration of the vote because

> she had been a constant attendant at the synagogue for many years and had never heard any sermons by which she had been so much benefitted as those of Mr. Harris. He was a good, a truthful man, and she feared if we lost him, we could not replace him. It was his truthfulness which prompted him to say what he did and she hoped the congregation would not condemn him.[163]

This led to a slight modification. Mr. Rosenheim explained that the body had voted only to accept Mr. Harris' resignation, which *he* (the rabbi) wanted, and that the congregation needed to understand that the *adjunta* would endeavor to provide

> some one to read the prayers until we could procure another minister, so as not to have the synagogue closed.

Mr. Harris was not vindicated, but his worth as preacher, teacher and spokesman of Judaism was underscored in the official record.

Following his brief stint at the Hebrew Union College in Cincinnati, Dr. Harris was elected to the pulpit of Congregation Beth Ahabah in Richmond, Virginia, serving from 1879 until his death in 1891.[164] The congregation flourished under his aegis, resulting in a building program that produced a sanctuary by 1880. Renowned as author, speaker and scholar, he was embraced by the Richmond community, and as his obituary stated:

> He went in all direction doing good . . . no man was more beloved by the Hebrews of the city.[165]

J. Cleveland Hall, Rector of Zion Church, Fairfax Courthouse, Virginia, was moved to write "a minister's tribute to Dr. Harris" which appeared in the *Richmond Times Dispatch*:

> I mourn his loss to the world; I mourn his loss to Judaism; I mourn his loss to his people and I have lost a friend.[166]

Beth Ahabah congregants are told today of his sudden death on the pulpit in 1891 after preaching a Sabbath message. That pulpit was removed and preserved. Harris' memory is also enshrined in a stained glass window in the present Beth Ahabah sanctuary.

CHAPTER SEVEN

ON MONTEREY SQUARE A GOTHIC TEMPLE STANDS

The decade, 1870 to 1880, was an unlikely time for renewal to occur. The Age of Reconstruction still plagued Georgians. Impoverished at war's end, hosts of southerners became yeoman farmers, realizing but a subsistence living from the soil. Without capital or the means of borrowing capital, there was no way to buy equipment, fertilizer, and seed. What was produced could not be readily sold, as the marketing system deteriorated during the Internecine Conflict, and no replacement was instantaneously substituted. The factorage system also collapsed. Buyers could no longer count on sellers to supply them with the materials needed at a given time. A vacuum existed which choked off the agricultural-based economy. Wholesale merchant houses, many Jewish-owned or operated, eventually filled the breach, providing a mechanism for capitalization and distribution. The peddler played a vital role by going into the hinterlands and organizing small general stores wherever people congregated for trade. By 1880, the system was fully operative.[1] Savannah Jewry, settled in an area of the state rich in farmland and timber, waxed prosperous whenever these resources were in demand. In 1860, the total value of exports from Savannah was $17,798,922. During the war years, the port was blockaded excising all profit. By 1866, trade escalated to almost $42 million.[2]

The year 1876 will long be remembered in Chatham County as the year of pestilence. One-sixth of the population perished from yellow fever. Twelve thousand out of the city's summer black population of fourteen thousand were out of work and dependent on charity.[3] The loss to the city was estimated at $6,000,000, a crushing blow.[4]

That very year the American economy was in the throes of a reversal. The Panic of 1873 resulted from an overexpansion of the railroads and the accompanying profiteering; over extended loans to meet the industrial expansion; tragic fires in Chicago and Boston in 1871 and 1872 which blighted insurance companies (by almost $300,000,000); and the souring of conditions in Europe which led to a crash on the Vienna Bourse in May of 1873. When European investers dumped American securities, depressing the stock market that summer, a crash was inevitable. It took five years for the American economy to rebound.[5]

Nevertheless, on March 1, 1876, the "chief stone" of the Monterey Square Sanctuary was set in place midst joyous and impressive ceremonies.

RAISING A THIRD SHRINE

Major developments are not "mushrooms of a night's growth." Careful preparation, often over a number of years, precedes the commitment to act. In 1867, there was a proposal to submit to the mayor and alder-men of the city a petition requesting the right to sell the present lot occupied by the congregation,

> the proceeds [to] be diverted to the purchase of another lot for a new and larger synagogue.[6]

In 1868, it was noted that the flooring of the synagogue was giving away, and that, without immediate attention, an accident would occur.[7] The congrega-tion was being alerted to the deteriorating structure that functioned as their "House of Assembly."

The uncertainties of *Reconstruction* interrupted the rhythm of *con-struction*. Of equal import was the experience of the B'nai B'rith Jacob Congregation which was struggling against debt. Another tact could be taken. Why not combine institutions and resources, and come up with one financially secure synagogue?

EFFORTS AT UNION

It all began with the *shochet* (ritual slaughterer).[8] Mr. M. P. Levy as secretary of B. B. Jacob wrote to the president of M.I. stating that his con-gregation

> agreed to unite in defraying the expenses of a schoket [sic] by paying the sum of two hundred dollars per annum.[9]

In 1867, a committee of three (Epstein, Lillienthal, and Phillips) conferred with a comparable committee from B.B.J. to recruit a "slaughterer," since both congregations were faced with a resignation from the incumbent.[10] Difficulties with the new *shochet* led to the formation of a second committee made up of Messrs. Eckman and Epstein from M.I., and G. Brown and S. Gertsman from B.B.J. Their function was to determine which butchers would be agreeable to the visitations of the chosen functionary. By June 26, 1867, a new committee was in charge. In addition to cooperation on this level, the Savannah Hebrew Collegiate Institute required harmony from the lead-ers of both institutions. Major events at B. B. Jacob were celebrated with officers and representatives of the rabbinate of M.I. Mother and daughter were in amiable relationship.

In February of 1872, the question was raised: under what conditions could the two congregations become one? Harry Haym, president of B.B.

Jacob, on behalf of its trustees, forwarded the following proposal (original in the K.K.M.I. Museum) containing seven provisions.[11] In summary they included: (1) consideration of a new name; (2) all property of both congregations to be transferred to the new congregation; (3) the present officers resign; (4) all services to be in Hebrew and the Torah readings to follow the "Schulchan Arooch" (Joseph Karo's Orthodox Code of Laws); (5) in order to change (4), a unanimous vote was required; (6) only members may purchase pews; (7) no new members may be added by either congregation until the new one was formed.

Following the R. D. C. Lewin ministry, the ideological issue reflected in (4) was unacceptable. The final reply was not long in coming: (1) the M.I. board could not change its chartered name; (2) it would assume the liabilities of B.B. Jacob if the transfer of its property to "Mickva" Israel occurred; (3) regarding the resignation of officers, the M.I. Charter must be followed: (4) the form of service could only be determined by the members; (5) the board could not bind future generations as this would require; (6) totally agreeable; (7) we could not refuse membership to a worthy Israelite who chose to apply.

At the next K.K.M.I. board meeting, the subject of purchasing a lot for a new building was introduced.[12]

LOTS 25 AND 26 MONTEREY WARD

Among the benefactions that James Edward Oglethorpe bestowed upon Georgia's Port City were the twenty-odd squares. Monterey Square is thought by some to be the most aesthetically appealing. Located at the farthest point south on the Bull Street strand of squares before the "big park" (Forsyth Park), its residences vary from Grammercy Park structures to Italianate and Victorian-styled homes of vintage 1850-1880, all facing the impressive Pulaski Monument. They represent creations of such noteworthy builders and architects as John Norris, Henrik Wallin, Augustus Schwaab, and brothers, Ephraim and John Scudder.[13]

In the 1870's, the trust lots (originally intended by Oglethorpe for public buildings) were occupied by three structures, two of which are yet standing: to the southwest, the Hugh Mercer House, built in 1860 by John Norris; and to the northwest, the twin Grammercy Park houses, built for Rev. Charles H. Rogers in 1858. To the northeast, First Presbyterian Church rose in chaste beauty (now replaced by the United Way Building). The southeast trust lot was unoccupied.

The history of the southeast parcel solicits attention. Ownership was vested in some of Savannah's wealthiest citizens.[14] Charles F. Hamilton was the first to purchase Lot 26 from the city (at auction) in 1847 for $1,206. By 1852 he had increased the value twofold by adding the 60 x 90 foot Lot 25. For $1,855 Hamilton conferred title upon Alexander A. Smets, Vice-Consul for France in Savannah.[15] Smets sold the two properties a year later to Edward A. Soullard for $2,348. Soullard attained prominence as a cotton factor and merchant.[16] In 1853, the choice lots again changed hands, this time coming into the possession of Savannah architect, John S. Norris. (Monterey Square and vicinity have two fine examples of his handiwork: the Hugh Mercer House and the William Brantly Home at 20 West Gaston Street.)[17] Norris intended this beautiful site as the setting for his personal residence, but the Sectional War ended the plan. He relocated to the North in 1861, selling Lots 25 and 26 to John Stoddard, a planter from Massachusetts, whose fortune is attested to by the purchase price of $5,000. In 1868, for $7,500, they came into the hands of "Mickva" Israelite, Henry Meinhard, who negotiated the eastern portion of Lot 25 in 1868 to Frederic Grosclaude, a Swiss jeweler and watch-maker for $3,000.[18] Grosclaude's widow, Martha, sold the land for $2,500 in 1870 to Alexander R. Lawton, attorney-at-law. In 1869, Lawton purchased Lot 26 and the western portion of Lot 25 from Henry Meinhard for the sum of $6,000. Lawton presented the deed to William Hunter, president of the Planters Bank, in exchange for $10,000. Hunter had purchased the land for Miller Ketchum, who used it as collateral in 1872, transferring title temporarily to his banker. In 1874, the debt was paid and Miller Ketchum was again full owner.

On March 3, 1872, President Solomon Cohen reported to the board that the lots on Monterey Square were for sale. Ten thousand dollars was the asking price. The board directed Cohen to confer with the owner, William Hunter, about a possible purchase. One week later, the board was told that the funds would have to be raised in a month's time, and it was deemed inexpedient to negotiate further. A copy of Cohen's letter to William Hunter, Esquire, survives, describing the terms as possible only "at a ruinous sacrifice," and declaring that the idea has been "abandoned altogether" by the congregation.[19]

But abandonment of such an ideal locus was not to be. By March 30, 1873, the board was again convened to consider

> a certain lot, facing Pulasky [sic] Square, suitable for building a synagogue and which can be purchased very reasonable.

A committee of five, including President Cohen, B. Kohn, S. Guckenheimer, J. M. Solomon, and one time owner of the lots, Henry Meinhard, was to investigate the costs and the means of meeting same. On April 5th of the following year, the firm of Blun and Demere contacted Solomon Cohen and offered the land for sale. Samuel Herman moved that a committee of two negotiate forthwith. He and Joseph Lippman were entrusted with authority to act. On May 7, 1874, they reported that "the choice trust lots" were now owned by K.K.M.I., and the 60 x 180 feet parcels cost $7,250. The actual deed was dated June 18, 1874. Miller Ketchum went into bankruptcy with his co-partner, Alfred Hartridge. Acting on behalf of the court, Robert N. Gaudin and Louis S. Young, assignees, handled the negotiations, with Henry Blun serving as notary.

All the deeds herein mentioned are filed in the Temple Archives.

STAGE TWO—HIRING AN ARCHITECT

Temple "Mickva" Israel is the *only* synagogue building of un-
compromised Gothic design on this continent. Tourists and visitors respond
to the graceful upward sweep of the structure and appreciate its cathedral-
like atmosphere. Stereotyped images of what a synagogue ought to look
like (meaning a structure of Romanesque or Moorish design) do not match
the appearance of K.K.M.I., and so some visitors express surprise—occasionally dismay. One who approaches synagogue architecture with an open
mind learns that there is no distinctive Jewish architecture, and that stylistic
borrowings are commonplace throughout history. Jewish sanctuaries have
been constructed in the form of pagan Greek temples, Polish fortresses, and
Japanese pagodas.

The question "whence came this unique Gothic Temple" has been
answered heretofore in a variety of ways, not all rooted in facts. A myth-
ology has developed over a protracted period of time, which claims that
the Monterey Square Temple is an imitation of the Cathedral of St. John
the Baptist, the seat of Savannah's Roman Catholic diocese. The cathedral
plans by Baldwin and Price of Baltimore were supposedly purchased at a
reduced price, and the sanctuary was likewise reduced by one-third. For
this oft-told tale there is no evidence in the minutes.

The June 28, 1874, *adjunta* meeting resulted in the formation of a
Building Committee. The entire board with the addition of Abraham
Einstein and Henry Meinhard was to obtain plans and estimates for a
great edifice, with the details to be accomplished by a subcommittee of
three (Simon Guckenheimer, Joseph Lippman, and the aforesaid Mr.
Einstein). Two weeks later (July 13), the board assembled with invited
guests, Mr. Foley, an architect, and Mr. David Lopez Cohen, a contractor
and congregator, whose work on the second synagogue was detailed in a
previous chapter. Mr. Foley's role in the construction of the building is
critical.

At the July 13th meeting, Foley submitted a ground sketch of *a*
structure. Mr. Cohen offered comments, although those comments have not
been preserved. After hearing and seeing, the committee had reservations
about Foley's proposal, indicated by a request for "references" in regard
to his credentials, and a further request "in company with him, [to] . . .
visit several churches in the city for inspection." *Obviously Foley's first plans
were not distinguished, else they would have been accepted.* The tour of the
city's main religious institutions resulted in no decision-making, ruling out
the argument that the plans of the cathedral were appropriated. At this
time the seat of Savannah's Catholic diocese was well under construction.[20]
Indeed the walking tour opened up the search for a new and different style
of structure. At the September 27, 1874, meeting of the committee, Mr.
Einstein laid before it plans and specifications from *"different architects."*
(Italics added.) The decision was to show these plans to builders in Savannah
to get some ideas as to which would be the most practical and least expensive.

Among those who submitted proposals was T. H. Abrahams of the firm of Abrahams and Seyle of Charleston. Harmon Hendricks DeLeon[21] wrote a letter to Solomon Cohen commending Abrahams in these terms:

> Should he be selected to draw plans and superintend the work, I am satisfied he will give satisfaction and do justice to your congregation, he is willing to furnish plans until you are suited.[22]

How many others submitted renderings is unknown.

A second architect, Henry G. Harrison, originally from London, then newly settled in New York, also submitted plans. It is this author's contention (based upon internal evidence) that Harrison's designs were appealing to the Building Committee, and, even when cost factors precluded their adoption, *Mr. Foley used them as the basis for the final architectural renderings of the Monterey Square Synagogue.*

Before examining the records, the question is posed, "How would a non-Jewish, London-born, New York architect be aware that a Jewish congregation, hundreds of miles away, was seeking architectural plans for a religious building?" Posing that question and searching for an answer has clarified, in part, why the people of K.K.M.I. would accept an architectural style so closely identified with the Christian faith.

Two documents in the Temple Archives offer the key to solution. One is a letter from Solomon Cohen to the second rabbi of the temple, Raphael de Castro Lewin. (It has been noted earlier that the leadership pursued him, offering a salary of five thousand dollars if he would only return from New York and again lead Savannah Jewry.) The letter is dated July 5, 1871, and is addressed to 'No. *67-69 William Street*, New York."[23] (Italics added.) The second document is a note dated February 1, 1975, from Mrs. Howard Morrison, Savannah architectural historian. Citing the 1876 *New York City Directory*, she noted the address of Henry G. Harrison

Henry G. Harrison, architect off. *67 William Street*, New York, res. Dobbs Ferry, New York. (Italics added.)

Rev. Lewin and Henry Harrison had offices in the same building and were neighbors. Conclusion: Harrison was recommended to the Building Committee through Lewin, whose popularity in Savannah was at its peak. The individual who promoted Harrison's plans was Abraham Einstein. Lewin was married to Einstein's second daughter, Adelaide.

Return now to the unfolding drama. At the September 27, 1874, meeting, Mr. Einstein laid some plans for the committee to inspect, and then he was told to see some of

> the best builders in the city, to give us their views, as to which would be the most practicable and the cheapest to build . . .

Two months were to elapse before the Building Committee was again convened. As the board instructed, the various plans had been submitted to the best master-mechanics, but nothing definite as to costs could be determined. However, a strange passage was inserted in the minutes of December 6, 1874. Mr. Foley stated

> that the plan submitted by the architect . . . [name missing] in New York could be put up for $35,000 whereupon on motion it was resolved that the committee write to . . . [name missing] instructing *them,* that as the cost for a building on the plan submitted would be more than we could afford, they should submit another plan on the same style of architecture. . . . (Italics added.)

What follows is clear evidence that the style of the plan was Gothic.

> . . . curtailing expenses in the height of the *spires* and that the dimensions of the building should be 60 feet front by 130 feet in depth. (Italics added.)

That R. D. C. Lewin was involved is documented in the January 10, 1875, minutes where it is stated

> . . . the thanks of the congregation was [*sic*] due to the Rev. R. D. C. Lewin, for the interest manifested by him for the welfare of the congregation, *in procuring plans for a building.* (Italics added.)

His neighbor, Harrison, it is assumed, drew up the plans.

The next Building Committee meeting was called for March of 1875 because

> the plans for the erection of a temple [were] just received from the architect in New York, *Mr. Harrison.*" (Italics added.)

Who exhibited and explained them? Lewin's father-in-law, Abraham Einstein. After listening to the specifications, a letter from Mr. Harrison was read, giving estimates of the cost. On unanimous vote, the secretary and Mr. Einstein were to write to the "New York architect," informing him

> that plan numbered 1 and 2 are *very much admired* by the committee. . . .[24] (Italics added.)

Such language constituted the first statement of *approval* for a structural design. The cost, however, required containment. The estimates, they wrote him,

> . . . aggregate an amount beyond our means. We think however as labor and materials are very cheap here at present [a reference to the 1873-1878 depression] and everything very dull that we could even get the building erected on this plan at $35,000 which is the extent of our ability. . . .

Harrison was requested to submit ". . . working plans forthwith." The committee would then advertise for bids, and if it failed to obtain contracts for the work, it would be compelled to fall back "upon the other plan." What other plan is not explained in the text.

Less than a month later, Harrison's advocate, Abraham Einstein, was removed from the realm of the living.[25] The momentum of the Building Committee was interrupted. To replace Einstein, Lizer Solomons, master builder of the second temple restoration project, was chosen.

At this point in the proceedings, Mr. Foley had an opportunity to voice his opinion. The bids were not issued as the March 28th meeting enjoined. Foley had examined the plans and specifications for the projected edifice and returned them, *claiming no estimate could be made, because of "faults and imperfections"* (Italics added) *in the proposals.* He agreed to put his explanation in writing in a letter to the president, identifying all the "serious" flaws. Once the letter was in hand, the secretary was instructed to write New York and explain,

> that as the plans and specifications submitted . . . were faulty and inaccurate and [blurred word] the strength and stability which our temple would require, and . . . in consequence of these facts, we could get no bids upon them, and the only approximate cost of the building was $52,500 which as we assured him before was much beyond our limit, *we are therefore compelled to reject the plans and specifications and will hold them subject to his order.* (Italics added.)

In the next breath, a motion was adopted to request Mr. Foley to draw up a plan and to present it for consideration "at as early a date as possible."[26]

No further mention of Henry G. Harrison appears in the minutes. Whether his plans were returned or not is unknowable. Questions remain, and value judgments are called for. Was Foley accurate in his criticism of Harrison's plans? Harrison's expertise outstripped Foley's. Did the Savannah architect sense that the committee's enthusiasm for Harrison's plans 1 and 2 was about to cost him a commission, and, by any means, a halt had to be called to the momentum building up? Why were bids not submitted to other contractors? Why only to Foley? The mysteries remain. It is a belief held in this corner that the specifications Foley later submitted were based upon Harrison's model, with slight variation.

To bolster the argument that Foley's plans were adaptations of Henry G. Harrison's originals is the design of the only other known religious edifice attributed to Foley. In the *Savannah Morning News* of December 8, 1875, a description of the Monterey Temple plan appeared with this accompanying statement:

> This nave roof will be the second of its kind in the United States, the Catholic Church in Huntsville, Alabama, having one somewhat similar; they were both, however, designed by the architect of the present temple.[27]

Foley's St. Mary's of the Visitation Church of Huntsville survives on Jefferson Street North. Now included on the *National Register of Historic Places,* it is a monument of the "Rocket City." Father Robert A. Wagner, incumbent pastor of the Huntsville church, supplied this writer with photographs of the interior and exterior, as well as an architectural exposition written by Harvie P. Jones of the Huntsville Historical Commission. In the exposition, the following description of the church appears:

> Romanesque-revival of steep gabled wood frame roof and regular cornered coursed limestone bearing walls. Two hexagonal stone towers at front corners, originally with tall hexagonal wooden spires. . . . Large main central entry of double paneled doors topped by a round arch with wood panel infill over the doors. . . . All windows are round arched in the Romanesque manner.

This 1870 building (predating the Temple by six years) differs in all significant details from the present Mickve Israel with its dominant English *Gothic* elements.

By May 12th, Foley submitted a pencil sketch of the side elevation of a proposed Temple, and by July *his* plan was ready. The building was to be 60 x 140 feet, costing $39,000 (Harrison's original plan was 60 x 130 feet).[28] Mr. Guckenheimer, Mr. Eckman, and Octavus Cohen were appointed a committee to encourage Foley

> to draw a plan . . . *to assimilate in style of architecture to the one proposed, to be reduced in size* so that it will seat four hundred and fifty persons comfortably, not to cost . . . over $33,000 including the school or meeting room in the rear. (Italics added.)

Fall was the season when work was to commence, so Foley was asked to come up with all drawings and detailed specifications "definitely and plainly set forth."[29]

On October 11, 1875, the Building Committee met for the hour of decision-making. Mr. Foley's father was invited to be present, an indication that "mature" support was needed. The committee voted to submit the plans to a

> competent person who understands building to ascertain if there are any objections or errors in them . . .[30]

Ten days later, the committee reconvened with master mechanic David Lopez Cohen present by invitation. It was reported that the builders who examined the specifications found them correct and suitable. A few alterations and additions were made, whereupon the committee gave its unanimous approval. On October 24th, the full congregation was called into session. Octavus Cohen, having replaced deceased brother Solomon as Building Committee chairman, invited all in attendance to come forward and carefully examine the plans, Lizer Solomons being available to provide explanation and answer questions. After this process, A. Epstein recommended that the matter be entrusted entirely to the Building Committee. The full congregation approved a Gothic sanctuary, without a dissenting voice heard.[31]

Henry G. Harrison's plan was not accepted officially, but his influence was stamped all over the design. He was the first to suggest a building with spires, with the approximate proportions (60' x 130') of the actual building (48' x 140'). The structure had English Gothic elements rather than the French Gothic that distinguishes the Cathedral of St. John the Baptist in Savannah.[32] The rejection of Foley's first plans and the acceptance of his post-Harrison proposal is logically explained by assuming a synthesis took place, and much "borrowing" in style and detail occurred.

Henry G. Harrison was an architect "of considerable distinction in New York."[33] Among his major buildings were the Women's Hospital in Manhattan and the Manhattan Market,

which was, at the time of its erection, one of the wonders of the town.[34]

His fame as an architect of religious edifices derived from his Cathedral of the Incarnation, the Episcopal diocesan center at Garden City, New York, begun on June 28, 1877. This ornamented 13th century English Gothic-styled structure was fashioned as a memorial to A. T. Stewart, prominent department store owner and real estate magnate.[35] The Episcopal diocese of Omaha, Nebraska, is also housed in a Harrison-designed shrine.[36]

An anecdotal reference will bring to light a linkage between Harrison, "Mickva" Israel, A. T. Stewart, Judge Henry Hilton, and the Seligman family of New York. A. T. Stewart was the owner of the Grand Union Hotel in Saratoga Springs, New York, a posh summer resort, visited annually by members of the German-Jewish "Our Crowd." The Joseph Seligman family was counted among its regular clientele. Judge Henry Hilton, political associate of "Boss" Tweed, was A. T. Stewart's confidant and attorney. When Joseph Seligman and his confreres broke the Tweed machine, Hilton exerted pressure upon Stewart. This resulted in the embarrassing "refusal of accommodations" incident, when the Seligman clan arrived at the Grand Union Hotel in the summer of 1877. From that incident, exclusionary policies spread to a number of America's "grand hotels," including the Cloisters on Sea Island, Georgia.[37] Seligman influenced the business community of New York to boycott A. T. Stewart's enterprises in the city, leading to the latter's demise as a businessman, and, perhaps, hastening his death. Ironically, the architect who designed the Stewart Memorial (Harrison) had earlier submitted plans for a synagogue in Savannah, Georgia.

CORNERSTONE DEDICATION

Wednesday, March 1, 1876, was another notable milestone in the history of the congregation. At 3:00 o'clock in the afternoon, the members and seat holders of "Mickva" Israel, members and officers of the "Joseph Lodge No. 76" and the Savannah Lodge No. 217 of the Independent Order of B'nai B'rith and of Georgia Lodge 132, K.S.B. (*Kesher Shel Barzel*) assembled at the Perry Lane Synagogue, along with the Grand Master of Georgia's Masons, David E. Butler. In attendance also were the mayor and aldermen, the judges of various courts, and the clergy "of all denominations." The Grand Lodge of Georgia escorted the jubilant crowd (which was led by a great band of music) on the march to Monterey Square. In an open carriage rode Reverend Abraham Harris. Upon arriving at the chosen site, prayers and "a very beautiful address" were offered by the rabbi.

As the cornerstone was laid with Masonic rites, the choir of the congregation intoned conformable music (Masonic odes). Professor Mallette, formerly basso Mallette, was in charge of the musical offering. To conclude the ceremonies, Samuel Yates Levy, "in a very beautiful and appropriate manner," presented the Grand Master with a "very handsome jewel." The procession formed again and returned "to the place of starting."[38]

In the newspaper account, the items placed in the cornerstone were enumerated. (All efforts to recover this box and its contents have failed, despite the advances of modern technology.)

In 1976, in commemoration of the centenary of the cornerstone-laying ceremony, a re-enactment service took place, again with the Grand Master of the Masons of Georgia, the clergy, and the mayor and aldermen participating. A second cornerstone box, laden with tokens and documents, was sunk. The Temple's Centenary and the Bicentennial anniversary of the American Nation coincided.

THE FUND-RAISING EFFORT

In 1820, and again in 1836-38, the congregation raised synagogues without seeking general subscriptions from members and seat holders. By contrast, the 1876-78 structure required sacrifice by many "Mickva" Israelites because of the 1873-78 panic. The temple was begun at an auspicious time as far as recruiting labor inexpensively was concerned, but at an adverse time for soliciting financial support. Indeed, there is evidence in the minutes that the congregation had difficulty meeting normal expenses.

By 1873, things had eroded so badly that the gas company closed the meter feeding the Perry Lane sanctuary.[39] In June of the same year, congregational treasurer L. Lillienthal sent a letter to President Solomon Cohen stating,

> Mr. Harris, having called on me for money, and being not in funds, would you not be kind enough to draw on the sinking fund for about 400 or 500 dolls [dollars].[40]

By May of 1875, the situation had not improved. The minutes state,

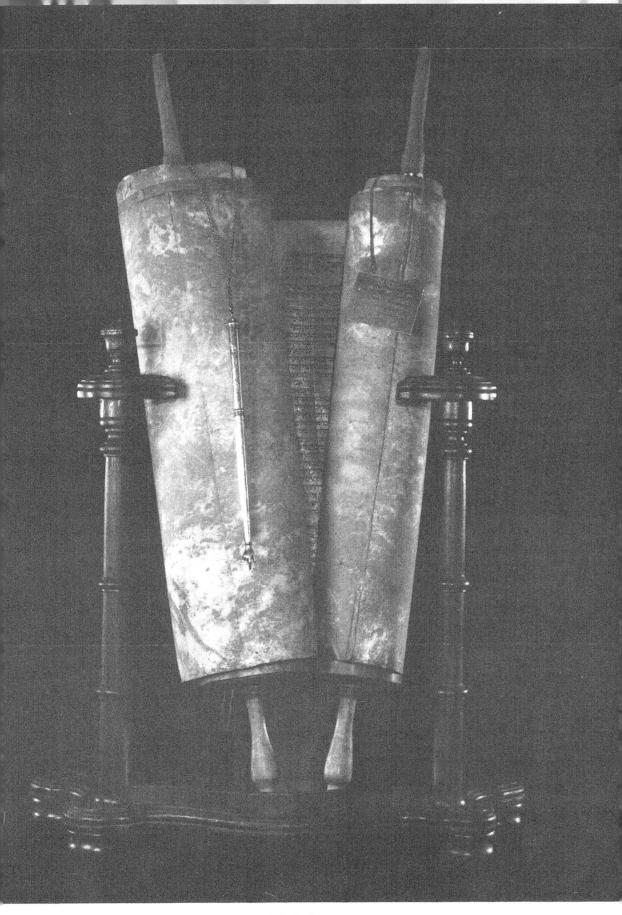

1733 Torah

1734 July 11th

Mrs. Minis was brought to bed with a Son Named Philip.

1734 August the 2

Mrs. Delyon was brought to bed with a Daughter Named Rachel

Buta   1734 August the 3d
Mrs. Sheftall was brought to bed of a Son Named Sheftall Sheftall
who died very occationed by his nurse being lett Acrous to take through ignorance.

1735 in the month of July
the Jews meet together, and agreed to open a Synagouge, which was done imediately, named K: K: Mickua Israel.

1735 July 12th
Mrs. Lessims was brought to bed of a Daughter Named Rebecka

1735 December the 2d
Mrs. Sheftall was brought to bed with a Son Named no and & she died 11 no

Leaf from Sheftall "Diary". (Original in the Keith Reid Collection, University of Georgia)

Earliest Hebrew burial grounds on south commons, granted by General Oglethorpe in 1734

View of Levi Sheftall Burial Grounds (used for interments from 1770 on)

Old Jewish Community Cemetery given by Mordecai Sheftall, used from 1770 to 1860. (Photo by Herb Pilcher)

Historic marker at entrance to old Jewish Community Cemetery, erected under authority of State of Georgia. (Photo by Herb Pilcher)

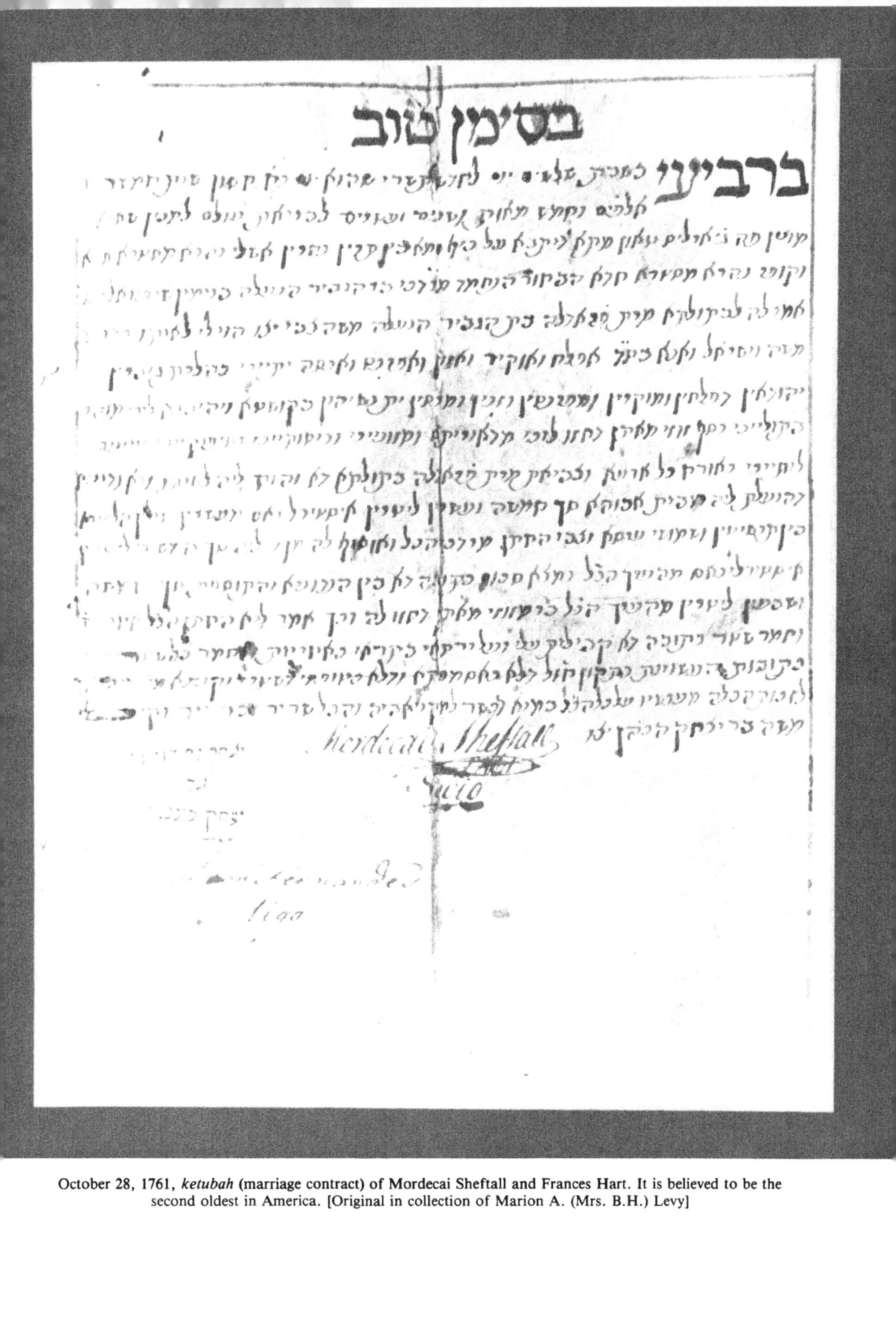

בסימן טוב

ברביעי

Mordecai Sheftall

October 28, 1761, *ketubah* (marriage contract) of Mordecai Sheftall and Frances Hart. It is believed to be the second oldest in America. [Original in collection of Marion A. (Mrs. B.H.) Levy]

1790 Charter of Congregation "Mickva" Israel

Rule 19

Lastly WE whose names are hereunto subscribed do solemnly promise upon our sacred honours each for ourselves, and not one for the other to abide by and consider ourselves as bound by the foregoing Rules, untill they shall be altered or amended by three fourths of the Jehadim Present.

Mordecai Sheftall Died 6th July 1797 —	Moses Sheftall Died 18 January 1835
Levi Sheftall Died 26th Jany 1809	D Abrahams Died 16th April 1849
Joseph Abrahams Dead	Isaac Jacob Abrahams died 18 november 1849
David Cardozo Dead	Benjn Sheftall Junr Dead
Saml Mordecai dead	Erased the 15th of February 1794 — by his desire
Cushman Polock Dead	Abraham Depass his Mark Dead
David Leion Dead	Isaac Franks dead
Levy Abrahams Died 29th Dec 1809	Jonas Elkin dead
E H Motta Dead	Abm Delyon died 10 October 1855
Sheftall Sheftall Dead Isaac Polock dead	Joseph Davis dead
Benjn Sheftall died 5th of October 1794	I M Jacobs Dead

Page of 1790 *Minute Book* (with signatures of earliest subscribers)

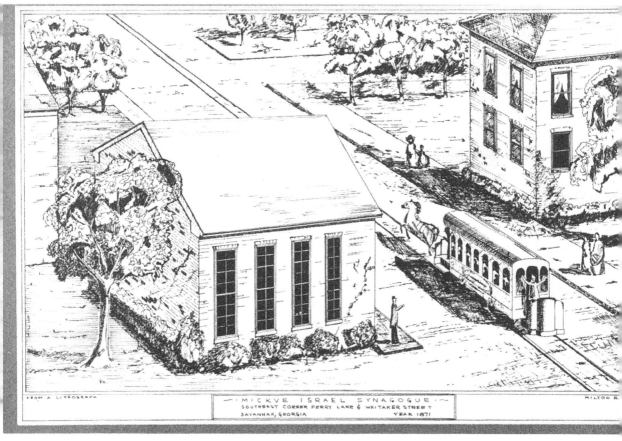

1838 edifice of K.K.M.I. from enlargement of 1871 lithograph of Savannah (of questionable accuracy)

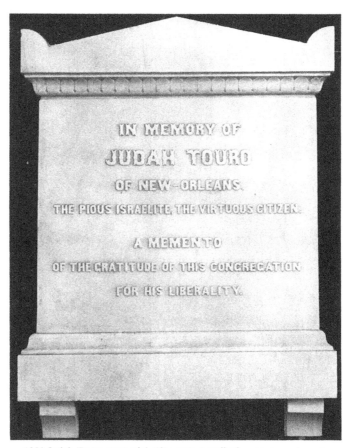

1854 Judah Touro memorial. (On eastern wall of present sanctuary)

1868 letter from Robert E. Lee to Abram Minis. (Original in possession of A. Minis, Jr.)

ORTHODOXY vs. REFORM.

A SERMON

DELIVERED ON SABBATH FEBRUARY 1ST, 1868.

BEFORE THE CONGREGATION

"MICKVA ISRAEL,"

OF SAVANNAH, GEORGIA,

BY

REV. RAPHAEL D. C. LEWIN,

(MINISTER OF THE CONGREGATION.)

SAVANNAH:
E. J. Purse, Printer,
1868.

Hyman Hess.

R.D.C. Lewin's 1868 sermon entitled "Orthodoxy vs. Reform"

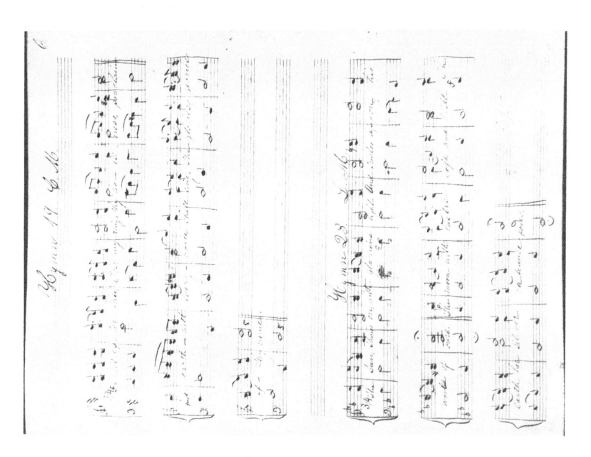

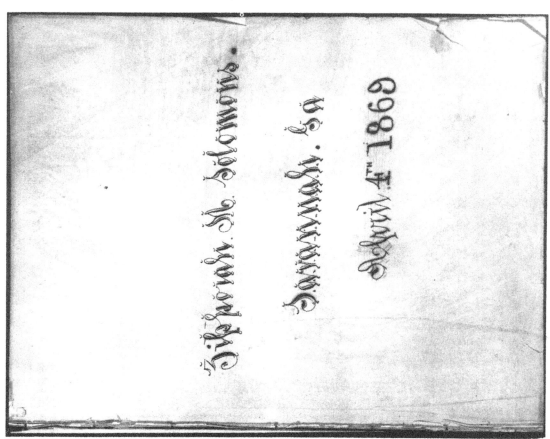

Page from 1869 hymn book (belonging to Mrs. Zipporah M. Solomons)

Savannah February 7th 1872.

At a meeting of the Board of Trustees of the Congregation Brai Brith Jacob, held this day, the following preamble and Resolution were offered and adopted

Whereas the Congregation Mikveh Israel of this City has proposed to this Congregation, of which we are the Trustees to form a union of the two Congregations, and by consolidating them, form a New Congregation, which it is hoped, may have the beneficial tendency of uniting all the resident Israelites of this City into One religious Community whereby the cause of our Holy Religion may be promoted &c &c. Therefore be it resolved,

Resolved   That the Congregation agrees to form this desired Union upon the following Conditions to be considered the Platform of the New Congregation

I   That the Name by which this Congregation is known at present or a portion thereof shall be embodied and retained in the Name which is to be given to the New Congregation, so that its identity be preserved

II   That the property now in possession and owned by both Congregations respectively be transferred to the new Congregation arising from this consolidation of the two Congregations as soon as a charter be obtained for the same, which property is to be used

1872 proposal to combine K.K.M.I. and K.K. B'nai B'rith Jacob

Temple "Mickva" Israel in 1878. (Artist unknown)

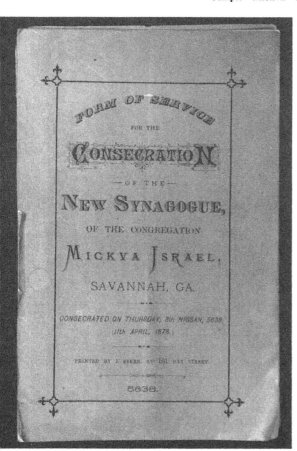

Consecration service, April 11, 1878

Octavus Cohen window, installed in
Temple "Mickva" Israel in 1878

Confirmation class, 1885

Sunday school medals, c. 1880

1893 confirmation certificate

Abraham Harris (1873-1877)   Rabbis of   Isaac P. Mendes (1877-1904)
Mickve Israel since 1873

George Joseph Solomon (1903-1945)   Louis Youngerman (1944-1948)

Solomon E. Starrels (1948-1965, emeritus, 1965-   )

Joseph M. Buchler (1965-67)

Richard A. Zionts (1969-72)

Saul J. Rubin (1972-   )

Exterior view of present Temple Mickve Israel

Interior view of present Temple Mickve Israel

A Bicentennial Letter From The Rabbis of the Six Colonial Jewish Congregations

The President
The White House
Washington, D.C.

Dear Mr. President:

We, the spiritual leaders of the six Colonial Jewish Congregations, commend to you and our Nation congratulations and divine benediction as the Bicentennial celebration climaxes.

As our forefathers tendered President Washington felicitations on the occasion of his Inauguration, expressing in those documents love of America and dedication on the part of its Jewish citizens to the majestic precepts and freedoms for which it was established, we, in this generation, would affirm their sentiments. May the blessings of liberty, justice and compassion be forthcoming unto our more than two hundred million citizens, to them and their progeny after them. May Washington's promise "to bigotry no sanction, to persecution no assistance" continue to be the bedrock of public policy.

As the founding fathers so clearly understood, love and loyalty to country increase in proportion to the freedoms secured, the privileges extended, and the egalitarian principles promoted. The commitment of the stock of Abraham is ever to vouchsafe these American values for all people, whether descendants of the first settlers, or more recently removed to these shores.

Be assured, Sir, of the steadfast loyalty of the American Jewish community to the American dream and the American territory. We will defend it against its enemies, foreign or domestic. We will give of our energies, wisdom and skill for the common weal. We will promote the cause of other democracies in this world, including the land of Israel, sacred to all generations of our people. We do so on the conviction that democratic governments need the unique strength which sister democracies can provide, especially in a world where many nations are hostile to elemental human freedoms.

May the "wonder-working Deity" Who has revealed to His children their common origin and destiny and has commanded them to be brethren one to the other, excite the will of all American races and stocks to observe this 200th Birthday in benevolent spirit. May we remember that which is most inspiring in the past. May we reclaim the conviction of Presidents Washington, Jefferson and Madison that in this nation men will forever govern themselves.

Your humble and obedient servants,

Rabbi,	Rabbi,	Rabbi,	Rabbi,	Rabbi,	Rabbi,
The Congregation	Congregation	Congregation	The Congregation	Kahal Kadosh	Congregation
Shearith Israel	Jeshuat Israel	Mickve Israel	Mikveh Israel	Beth Elohim	Beth Ahabah-
New York,	[Touro Synagogue]	Savannah, Georgia	Philadelphia,	Charleston,	Beth Shalome
New York	Newport, Rhode Island		Pennsylvania	South Carolina	Richmond,
					Virginia

Bicentennial Letter to President Ford

As many parties were in arrears for seat hire and the congregation finds difficulty in meeting the current expenses, the President be requested to write out an appeal which the secty should have printed and send one to every one in arrears.[41]

As was its habit, the leadership first turned elsewhere for the fund-raising effort. This time, merchants who traded with mercantile establishments in the North were asked to approach their jobbers:

Resolved that the President appoint a committee to make collections at the North and elsewhere, when the following gentlemen were appointed [notice individuals are mentioned, along with firms] Mess. A. Friedenberg & Co.; Einstein, Eckman & Co.; H. Meinhard, Lillienthal & Kohn; S. Guckenheimer, L. Kayton, Boehm Bendheim & Co., Isaac Meinhard, Herman Myers, M. Ferst, Joseph Lippman, Jacob Triest & Octavus Cohen.[42]

What amount was collected is unreported. The obituary of Mr. Joseph Lippman credited him with being

the first of our members to lead the list, by a munificent donation of one thousand dollars, towards erecting a new and larger edifice to worship the God of Israel.[43]

Fund-raising in the best of times is exhaustive enterprise. In the midst of a national depression and a yellow fever epidemic, how much the more so! Particularly when the "grim reaper" was decimating the wealthy leadership. On April 25, 1875, Abraham Einstein, a former president, Building Committee chairman, and board member for many terms, departed this sphere. Five months later the Honorable Solomon Cohen, *parnass* for a host of years and head of the Building Committee at the time, was laid to his eternal rest.[44] Less than a month passed and another *adjuntaman,* Building Committee member, Joseph Lippman, was interred, to the dismay of the membership.[45] Finally, Solomon Cohen's brother and replacement as head of the Building Committee, Octavus, was smitten (one suspects, from the report in the minutes, by yellow fever) in December of 1876.[46] Even before the loss of Octavus Cohen, President Simon Guckenheimer commented at an annual meeting "with much feeling and deep regret" that three "irreparable losses" had been sustained by the K.K.M.I. community, all "assistants in the completion of the building." He expressed the hope that

as the duties and responsibilities of the Building Committee would be very great, that the members . . . would assist us all in their power in pushing ahead and completing the good work.[47]

On May 4, 1876, Octavus Cohen had announced a simple, yet effective, subscription-raising scheme. A committee of six, the chairman plus Meinhard, Eckman, Friedenberg, E. A. Weil, and Guckenheimer would raise monies in Savannah. A second committee of twenty-nine would be responsible for contacting contributors in the North. These included: Meinhard (again), Eckman (again), J. A. Einstein, A. Vetsberg, S. Meinhard, L. Lillienthal, J. Rosenheim, I. Epstein, G. Eckstein, A. Mohr, Z. Falk, L. Fried, A. Friedenberg (again), L. Friedenberg, L. Kayton, N. E. Solomon, A. Leffler, M. Ferst, H. Myers, Lee Roy Myers, S. Herman, S. Guckenheimer (again), Jacob Lippman, Lewis Lippman, Lawrence Lippman, and R. R. Bren. Two former Savannahians functioned on this committee, A. L. Grabfelder and Isaac Meinhard, both of New York.

Eleven days later, the organizational chart was carefully drawn up for the Subscription Committee. Louis Kayton recommended to the chair that five subcommittees be formed with a chairman for each. The five were:

> Committee on grocery, liquor and tobacco stores, Mess. A. Friedenberg, Chm; committee on boot and shoe trade, Mess. H. Meinhard, Chm; committee on dry goods trade, Mess S. H. Eckman, Chm; committee on hat trade, Mess. Z. Falk, Chm; committee on drug trade, Mess. Lippman Bros.[48]

Mr. Isaac Meinhard of New York was elected overall chairman to whom the five committee chairmen reported amounts raised. Each committee head received a blank subscription list, printed up for this task, with all committee members listed thereon as authorized fund-raisers.

Cohen's fund-raising scheme met with some success, as the president reported that over $25,000 already had been expended, leaving $9,000 owing (a figure exceeding by $1,000 what Foley had estimated) to satisfy the contract with the architect.[50] Simon Guckenheimer, who succeeded Octavus Cohen as Building Committee chairman, attributed the $9,000 debt in 1877 to

> . . . the terrible epidemic, which has raged with such fearful violence during the past few months,

as well as the

> severe loss the committee had suffered in the death of Mr. Octavus Cohen . . . upon whom the committee in a great measure depended to assist in raising subscriptions . . .

Times were tough and President Guckenheimer lamented

> Some of the members are considerably behind in the payment of their seat hire, the treasury was empty and it was impossible to pay current expenses without prompt payment of seat hire . . .

A committee was formed to call on delinquents and to urge their cooperation. Discretion was recommended in the instance "some members were not able to pay." At the 1877 annual meeting, it was reported that the synagogue was "now nearly completed."[51]

In 1875 (January 4), the assets of the Permanent Fund were $17,700. Two years later (January 7, 1877) they totalled $9,847. Octavus Cohen, chairman of the Permanent Fund, had expended $7,500 for a lot upon which the Gleason Foundry was situated.[49] This was identified in the Permanent Fund as Lot 7, Franklin Ward (the second lot east of the northeast corner of Bay and West Broad Streets). The $9,847 included Lot 23, Franklin Ward. A large investment in Southwestern Railroad stock and Central Rail Road stock accounted for the cash-poor condition of the Fund. Resources for the building effort had to be found elsewhere.

Whenever "Mickva" Israel has been in a bind, it has received support from unexpected places. In the 1790's, the burial society provided succor. In 1877, the Hebrew Benevolent Society came to the rescue with a loan of one thousand dollars for a year's time.[52] Also sixteen hundred dollars required to pay the workmen was graciously offered by five three hundred dollar loans from Messrs. Guckenheimer, Weil, Friedenberg, Eckman, and Herman, leaving one hundred dollars due from the treasury. In April of 1877, at a meeting called for the purpose of hiring a rabbi, Guckenheimer announced that to pay the contractor and to furnish the interior of the sanctuary a "considerable" sum had to be pledged. He requested that the members empower the *adjunta* to issue bonds up to a twelve thousand dollar limit, on seven percent interest, payable semiannually. Permission was granted on condition that the new lot and synagogue would serve as collateral.[53] Taking advantage of the great interest in the competition between Rev. J. L. Meyer of Houston and Isaac P. Mendes of Richmond, Virginia, for the post of *hazzan and* rabbi of M.I., the general membership was convened twenty days later, at which time they were informed, not only about the pulpit contestants, but also about the issuance of bonds in denominations of $250 and $500. Four of the latter were made payable in three years, eight of the former in the same time frame; a second grouping of the identical valuations for five years; and a third set for seven years, making a total of twelve thousand dollars.[54] To each bond was affixed the seal of the congregation which the president was instructed to buy (the same seal is used to this day). The need for further subscription-taking was ended, and an improving economy in the 1880's allowed the retirement of debt to occur on schedule.

A word needs to be added about the contribution of persons of other faiths to the building program. All of the contracts required for the project were handled by the Honorable Walter S. Chisholm. Thanks were formally conveyed to him "for his liberality" in attending to the paperwork, without wish for compensation.[55] George Wymberly Jones DeRenne, descendant of the Noble Jones family, contributed two hundred dollars to the building project, an expression of his attachment to the "Mickva" Israel community.[56]

RAISING A SANCTUARY

Attention turns from the problem of procuring an architect and mounting a fund-raising campaign to the challenge of erecting a synagogue structure. Add to the testing visited upon the leadership—plague, depression, and death—the complication of working with a temperamental architect-builder.

The contract for the building was awarded on the basis of sealed bids. January 3, 1876, was the announced date for all proposals to be submitted, and "a considerable number of sealed proposals" were in the secretary's possession by the deadline. The bidders were invited to be present to insure that propriety prevailed. J. O. Smith was prepared to contract the work for $29,863, with an additional $1,750 to construct the ark. After investigating his credentials and receiving confirmation of his skill from Mr. Foley, his bid was accepted and the contract let, with two provisions: John M. Williams had to be hired to do the masonry, and a $10,000 "satisfactory bond" was to be signed as security. Messrs. Anlem, McDonough, and J. J. Clemence were the bondsmen for the contract. The Building Committee was expanded to include L. Lillienthal, Lizer Solomons, and E. A. Weil.[57]

J. O. Smith was described in the *Savannah Morning News* as "a leading contractor and builder." Born and reared in England, a native of London, he came to America as a young man and gained fame in Savannah for two buildings, described in his obituary as "the Mickva Israel Synagogue and the Morning News building."[58] He also perfected an invention that solved the problem of canal navigation, important to the city because of the Ogeechee Canal.[59]

Brickmason John M. Williams was craftsman for such beautiful Savannah structures as the Augustus Bonard home, 313-317 East Jones Street, and the Fred Hull residence at 126 E. Gaston Street.[60] Political alliances aided him in attaining civic posts of responsibility, including city assessor for the Third District and a seat on the Board of Education. Williams had connectons with Lizar Solomons.[61]

Sixteen months after the day of decision (January 3, 1876), Temple "Mickva" Israel stood tall against the sky, ready for decorative touches. On April 16, 1877, more bidding occurred, this time for the plasterer and painter. The firm of McKenna and Hanley, interior painters, agreed to furnish labor and materials for $650. To James Russell, plasterer, went the contract for exterior stucco work. All scaffolding, molds strips, etc. were to be furnished and the work to be completed "in a substantial and workmanlike manner" for a total of $696.[62] It was later decided to erect a lightning rod on the tower. The bill from Mr. Cornell amounted to $64.[63]

The ornamentation of the interior was carefully wrought. "Mickva" Israel lays claim to being the first *public* building in Savannah with *iron* pillars for support.[64] To disguise the metallic appearance, the columns were "painted of imitation of marble."[65] A picket fence around the exterior of the building was purchased from Palmer Brothers for $185.[66] It connected to an iron railing made for the front of the building by Cook and Radley of

New York.[67] Gas light fixtures were purchased by President Guckenheimer in New York from either Messr. Fellows Hoffman and Co. or Panevast Manufacturing Co. for $400.[68] The metal fixtures were clipped to the iron pilasters, forming a circle of gaseous light. The pulpit, designed by Mr. W. G. Butler, was hand wrought in New York under Guckenheimer's supervision.[69]

Other interior refinements included pew cushions (costing $535, prepared by E. A. Schwarz) and book racks on the back of the pews ($ .75 per rack was the low bid of John O. Smith, builder).[70] The original eternal light, given by Grace Abendenone, was repaired and "arranged with pulley and weights" for the Monterey Square building.[71] Marble tablets bearing the Ten Commandments were purchased by Messrs. Weil and Guckenheimer.[72] Of less exalted status, but vital to the sanitation of the sanctuary, were the 150 "spittoons" that the Building Committee purchased for $4.50 per dozen.[73] Footracks were ordered for the pews following the dedication, as well as a marble clock and a marble "slab" with the names of the Building Committee engraved thereon.[74] The latter was either never mounted or has been removed from the present sanctuary. Also installed were three magnificent memorial windows, handwrought pulpit furniture, and a great organ. These require individual consideration.

Above the ark, in the easternmost portion of the sanctuary, three "cathedral" glass windows were installed. Mr. Rosenheim and Mr. Meinhard (of New York) had together visited the establishment of William Gibson's Sons in New York. For three elaborate stained glass windows, valued at more than $100,000 today, they were authorized to expend a total of $500 (the middle one to sell for $300, and the side panes for $100 each). Rev. Mendes, the new rabbi, submitted appropriate designs which were received by the committee and incorporated into the glass.[75] The final cost was $530, including installation.[76]

Patrons to consecrate the windows as solemn memorials were identified, because of the threefold loss the congregation had suffered. To the widows of Abraham Einstein, Octavus Cohen, and Solomon Cohen the opportunity was proffered. Henrietta Levy Cohen requested the central panel to perpetuate the remembrance of husband, Octavus, and Mrs. Abraham Einstein selected the southern window. Mrs. Solomon Cohen did not respond, and eventually the glass was consecrated in memory of Simon Guckenheimer, M.I. president and Building Committee chairman in 1877. Mrs. Joseph Lippman was afforded the opportunity prior to Mrs. Guckenheimer.[77]

When the temple was completed and dedicated, the side windows were plate glass. Shades or blinds were recommended to shield the eyes of the worshippers.[78] Eight stained glass windows were later installed. Three of the eight are unaccounted for in the *Temple Minute Books.*

No mention is made of where the "Officer's Chairs" were procured or the amount paid for them. Mr. Joseph Rosenheim simply announced that they were received at the February 24, 1878, meeting, implying that they were not purchased locally but shipped in. The 1878 Gothic-styled chairs bedeck the *bima* today.

No investment was more debated than the organ. Mr. Eckman began the process of selection, by providing for the board a catalogue which Messrs. Guckenheimer and Rosenheim used for consultation with Professor Lessing, Temple organist.[79] By the August 13th meeting, "L. Knauf & Son" of Philadelphia had written a letter offering their services, and Mr. Weil, a committee of one, conferred with Lessing as to his needs. "L. Knauf" turned out to be H. Knauff & Son of Philadelphia, which submitted a sketch with plans and specifications which could be installed for $1,850. At the same meeting, the Brooklyn firm, James M. Mandeville, Church Organ Manufacturers, made a proposal for $1,800. It was a duplicate of the synagogue organ that graced K.K. Beth Elohim in Charleston.[80] Weil and Eckman constituted the third and final Organ Committee, empowered to finalize the purchase. The Philadelphia manufacturer (H. Knauff & Son) received the contract, but, contrary to terms, did not install the instrument in time for the April 11, 1878, dedication. Not until June 9, 1878, was the organ installed by Mr. H. W. Knauff, himself. His request for immediate payment was delayed because the congregation wished to reimburse him for the cost of the organ, minus the amount required to rent a "massive pump organ from Ludden & Bates" for the dedication rites.[81] By September 15, 1878, the dispute was settled, and the instrument was unencumbered by debt.

The *Savannah Morning News* commented on the new instrument thusly:

> The organ is very handsome, and similar to the ones in the Independent Presbyterian and Christ Churches, which were made by the same firm.[82]

IT STARTED OVER AN ARK

D. S. Foley's tenure as architect/builder was tenuous. That his time of service would be abbreviated was presaged in the November 21, 1875, minutes. In submitting his final plans, he withdrew plan No. 9, the sketch of the *Aron haKodesh* (the Holy Ark, wherein the Scrolls of Law repose). Two days later, Mr. Foley acknowledged that the "vanished" plan was excluded as an oversight.[83] For more than two years, peace was restored, but controversy surfaced in May of 1877 when Mr. Foley quit. Why? Mr. Foley and Mr. Russell, the plasterer, disagreed as to how the work should be done. Seeking the opinion of a master-builder, Mr. Guckenheimer, chairman of the project, was told that the architect's responsibility included furnishing "proper plans and a pencil sketch of the work required."[84] When Guckenheimer reported this to Foley, he refused to comply without additional compensation. The congregation sought legal advice and then hired Mr. Butler, described in the May 29, 1877, minutes as the man "who superintended the building of the Cathedral." (Hence may have come the tale of the plans of the cathedral being purchased and reduced one-third for the Monterey Square Temple. Also, the original plans that

Harrison submitted were reduced one-third by Foley, as the *Savannah Morning News* reported on April 12, 1878, in its description of the dedicatory rites.) Willoughby G. Butler was known as a "skillful architect" who distinguished himself primarily in the Catholic community by his work on the Cathedral of St. John the Baptist and the construction of Our Lady of Perpetual Help.[85]

THURSDAY, APRIL 11, 1878—THE DAY OF DEDICATION

Extensive coverage was given to the "impressive consecration rites" both in the minutes, courtesy of Joseph Rosenheim, and in the *Savannah Morning News* on April 12, 1878.[86] At 3:00 p.m., the doors were opened for "all Israelites" and for "all others holding cards by invitation." Occupying the left side pews were Mayor John F. Wheaton and the Board of Aldermen. The right front pews were assigned to Rev. Mr. Harley of the First Baptist Church, Rev. Mr. Simmons of New Houston Street Methodist Church, and Rev. Mr. Dunlap of St. Matthews Episcopal Church. At 3:30 p.m., Rev. Mendes and Rev. David Levy of Charleston's K.K. Beth Elohim, along with the members of the Building Committee, entered "five carriages" at the old Temple site, the rabbis in robes, the laymen "with scarfs thrown across their shoulders." An overflowing crowd packed the new sanctuary, awaiting the arrival of the religious officiants. Three knocks were sounded on the front doors, followed by the words, "Open unto us the Gates of Righteousness," shouted by Mendes in Hebrew, with the choir responding, "This is the Gate of the Lord; the righteous shall enter therein." The eternal light from the old building was lowered and rekindled in an "imposing" manner. Immediately thereafter, the ark was opened, the Torahs were then carried on circuits around the sanctuary by members and officers who subsequently deposited them in their new home.

Rev. Mendes' sermon was "very eloquent and was listened to with marked attention." The text chosen was Genesis 28:

> And he [Jacob] was afraid, and said, 'How dreadful is this place; this is none other but the house of God, and this is the gate of Heaven,'

the latter half of the verse being accentuated. Mendes' address and the consecration prayer of Rev. Levy were reproduced the next morning in *The Savannah Recorder*. The choir for the occasion was under Professor Lessing's direction, with Simon Hexter leading the regular volunteers, supplemented by Mrs. Cleveland, soprano, Miss Gross, alto, and Professor Charles H. Mallette, basso (Mr. Hexter doing double duty as tenor). J. Rosenheim summed up the emotions of the congregation when he wrote:

> happiness and satisfaction was [*sic*] depicted upon every countenance and all seemed rejoiced at the completion and consecration of so beautiful a building. Altogether the day will be long remembered as an important epoch in the history of our time honored congregation.

The service of dedication (a copy of which is in the Temple Museum) was compiled by Rev. Mendes and Simon Hexter. Hexter's contribution was a "form of service which he had received from Baltimore."[87] However, the liturgy was most influenced by the September, 1876, consecration of the Hebrew Congregation "Dispersed of Judah (Nefutzoth Yehudah)." Mendes' relatives were members of that New Orleans synagogue (including I. O. de Castro), and the text of the dedication appears in Mendes' scrapbook.[88] The similarities, particularly in the opening section, are striking.

How that generation viewed the new building is reflected in the words of two diverse publications: *The Savannah Recorder* noted,

> The synagogue is one of the most tasty and elegant in the south, and surpasses in beauty many in larger cities.[89]

And *The Hebrew Leader* reported, from a letter dated May 5, 1878,

> We have entered at last into our new temple, which is a perfect gem of architecture . . .[90]

ARCHITECTURAL DESCRIPTION

The newspaper description of the dedication included information relating to the structure as it was in 1878.[91] The general plan was a parallelogram with narrow transcepts. Over the vestibule and occupying the area of the tower, with wings projecting slightly over the sanctuary, was the choir loft. The main auditorium terminated in a semi-octagonal niche in which the ark reposed three feet above the level of the pews. The platform itself was octagonal, occupying the entire chancel, three sides projecting into the sanctuary. The ceilings were groined with molded ribs, bosses and finials, the nave ceiling being double-vaulted and half-groined, with crested cornices dividing the two ceilings.

Externally, the main entrance had a Gothic-arched and gabled portico, with sliding main doors. Over it was placed a double-mullioned choir window. Above that rose an embattled single story tower and the third bell story tower, crowned by an octagon lantern, surmounted by a dome with a weathervane on top. The total tower height was 150 feet from the ground. The facade included external walls that acted as flying buttresses. The style of the architecture was declared 14th century Gothic.

When all costs were in, this monument to Israel's faith required an expenditure of $50,128.83.[92] The leadership reflected on how wonderful its efforts had proven, considering a depression had been overcome, and the Temple was saddled with a debt of only $8,750 (reduced to $3,250 in April of 1879).[93] The internal furnishings were partially paid for by the women of the congregation, led by Mrs. Octavus Cohen (Henrietta Levy Cohen). Another "Fair" was held, this time at the Masonic Hall, resulting in almost $6,400 profit.[94] Announcements of this "Grand Fair" appeared in the local press, and descriptions of the entertainments, booths, and auctions were also reported by the local correspondent *Confy,* a Savannah "stringer" to the *Jewish South*.[95]

The Perry Lane Synagogue was eventually purchased by Mr. Grimball, with the intent of tearing it down and building dwellings or stores thereon.[96] At the 1879 annual meeting, the congregation unanimously approved the sale of their former "prayer space" for $3,500. It was understood that the cornerstone and its contents were to be delivered to the congregation in the future.[97] What happened to the box remains a mystery.

SUCCORING SISTER SYNAGOGUES

K.K.M.I. members were numbered among the prominent and prosperous citizens of the community, whose esteem extended to neighboring communities. From the 1860's on, the congregation was solicited to provide religious assistance to Jews of the southeast.

It has been noted that Rev. Rosenfeld of K.K.M.I. was involved in the dedication of new synagogues in Augusta and Macon. A Torah was lent to the Hebrew Benevolent Society (The Temple) in Atlanta during its gestation.[98] Other communities that requested assistance, usually Scrolls of Law for the High Holy Days, included Thomasville, Georgia; Brunswick, Georgia; and Monticello, Florida.[99] In 1880, when Thomasville Jewry dedicated their first sanctuary, they requested that the "Sefer Torah" remain in their city until the time of consecration.[100]

Of special consideration is the gift that proceeded from K.K.M.I. to the Jewish community of Jacksonville, Florida, in 1879. A request to purchase the ark (*hechal*) and the pulpit of the old synagogue building was responded to by providing them gratuitously. Only the cost of shipping and disassembling was asked of the Jacksonville congregation. Henry Weiskoff, secretary of the Hebrew Benevolent Society (now Congregation Ahavath Chesed), acknowledged the donation with the assurance that "the Ark, pulpit etc" (what the etc. included is unknown) would adorn the synagogue "which I trust will soon be erected."[101] Later that year, a letter was received from Albany, Georgia, addressed to S. Guckenheimer from S. Mayer and Glauber, "dealers in general merchandise at wholesale and retail," requesting the identical ritual objects for the Albany Hebrew Congregation (letter in K.K.M.I. Archives).[102]

STRENGTHENING THE GROUP

When Jews begin to feel secure in their surroundings, they create tangible symbols—institutions, buildings, and cultural and social instrumentalities—clubs, societies and associations. These are to be considered less a turning from the company of non-Jews, and more a search for Jewish intensification.

The era of close community life lasted into the 1880's, when migrations from central and eastern Europe swelled Savannah's Jewish population with "strangers" to the New World. Their needs were for the basics—food, shelter, clothing, and acculturation. In response, most (not all) Jewish social, cultural, and charitable organizations reached out to their brethren-in-faith, offering succor. The following societies were founded in the 1860's and 1870's, but not until the 1880's and 1890's did they flourish.

THE HARMONIE CLUB

Preceding by ten years Savannah's Oglethorpe Club, the "Harmonie" was Georgia's first founded Jewish social club. Established at the boarding house of Mr. Augustus Reich, on September 28, 1865, it was instituted for purposes of social intercourse and intellectual improvement.[103] The first president, Mr. Wolf, rented St. Andrews Hall for the opening banquet, which took place on October 22, 1865. More social than its New York namesake of 1847 vintage, it placed less emphasis on establishing libraries and reading rooms and more on sponsoring Winter Balls and *Purim* Entertainments.[104] At the opening meeting, Lawrence Lippman (later vice-president of K.K.M.I.) addressed the assembled body and defined the purposes of the organization: to fashion together a "society" which would be, in effect, the building block of a better social order. It would result from

> pleasant companionship . . . upright bearing of ourselves to each other and in everything which makes this life pleasant and enjoyable.

The intent was to form an ideal enclave of humanity, where men could relate with respect, integrity, and honor. The "society" was, in Lippman's words,

> to hand down to posterity, a great 'harmonie' without a stain or blemish on her escutcheon.[105]

Membership was inclusive of both congregations. In 1869, K.K.M.I. was represented by Magnus Loewenthal, president, L. Elsinger, vice-president and J. Vetsburg, secretary, while the monies were entrusted into the safekeeping of Treasurer Simon Gertsman, a founder and president of B.B. Jacob.

On June 3, 1887, the Harmonie Club was officially chartered. Through the issuance of bonds (some of which were purchased by K.K.M.I.), funds were raised to purchase a permanent "downtown clubhouse," the ample residence of Alexander A. Smets (who formerly owned one lot now occupied by the Temple). Into the third decade of the 20th century, this meeting place (on the northeast corner of Bull and Jones) served as a recreational center for the Reform Jewish community, in particular. Its proximity to the temple made it a convenient place for the Board of *Adjunta* to assemble, as well as the Building Committee of the Temple, while the present sanctuary was under construction.[106]

Youth's Historical Society

Like their elders, the Jewish young men of the city desired Jewish companionship and intellectual exchange. To this end, on May 17, 1874, an organization was founded which functioned as a debating society, literary club, and charitable organization. The initiator and guiding spirit was Master M. Strauss, who shortly after its founding moved to Baltimore.[107] George Dzialynski was elected Strauss' successor.[108]

Not until 1879 was a charter granted in Superior Court, though the Y.H.S. functioned successfully over the course of the intervening years.[109] The annual banquet, featuring good food, a debate, and "several declamations by the members," was the major function of the year. In 1875, Nathan Platshek, "young and gifted author," delivered the lecture. Master Platshek had contributed articles to various northern newspapers. In the style of the times, he adopted a pseudonym, *Venus*, which he affixed to assorted "letters to the editor."[110] In subsequent years, debates in German, balls, and dramatic entertainments were featured.[111] In 1878, for the benefit of the yellow fever victims, a night of dramatic entertainment was presented at a local theatre.[112] By 1885, the group met every Thursday at the Masonic Temple. Included in the leadership were H. M. Boley, president, S. S. Guckenheimer, vice-president, I. Solomons and M. Lillienthal, secretary and treasurer, respectively. Y.H.S. possessed a 600-volume library.[113] In the Temple Museum, a Y.H.S. pin remains on permanent display.

Kesher Shel Barzel

The *Savannah Morning News* of January 28, 1876, announced to the Savannah community the inauguration of a new "Lodge," the ancient order of *Kesher Shel Barzel* or "the Mystic Bond of Iron." Claiming to be one of the most ancient orders in the world and having more than 150 units in the United States, it appealed to the leaders of the Jewish community, judging by its officers: J. J. Abrahams, president; Jacob Weichselbaum, vice-president; Jacob Gardner, secretary; Julius Levkoy, treasurer; and H. Haym, conductor.[114] Other leaders included Solomon Cohen, I. G. Cohen, M. Jacoby, J. Lehwald, and L. Ohlman.[115]

The Savannah chapter was the first in the state, and, on the occasion of its initiation, Dr. S. Mendelsohn, *hazzan* of Congregation Beth-el of Norfolk, Virginia, was present.[116] The Grand Lodge of Pennsylvania provided a charter which Dr. Mendelsohn entrusted to local enthusiasts. Quite numerous they were, too, according to the local press.[117] *Kesher Shel Barzel* was a national fraternal order, similar to the Free Sons of Israel. It provided sick and death benefits, and engaged in charitable activities and "secretive" rituals of the genre of the Masons. All Jews, of whatever denominational inclination, were eligible for membership. Life was then less colorful, so the dramaturgy of the order was impressive.[118] Among the members who later attained high position in the organization were J. G.

Schwarzbaum, I. Isaacs, Robert Levison, Morris Apple, J. Harrison, M. Brown, N. H. Levy, L. Michaels, and A. Robitsback.[119]

Kesher provided an alternative to synagogue membership for those of limited resources. Additionally, it offered mutual aid benefits following the 1876 panic. Whether the Lodge continued beyond the year 1880 cannot be determined. Newspaper accounts ceased at that point.[120]

THE HEBREW BENEVOLENT SOCIETIES

The Sheftall "diary" informs us of the *Mishivat Nefesh* (burial society) which functioned prior to 1800. Its role was to provide for the maintenance of the cemetery, but it may have sustained Jewish families in need. In New York City, a contingent of Jews founded a *"Meshibat Nefesh"* order in 1822, for purposes of dispensing charity.[121] It later became the Hebrew Benevolent Society. The H.B.S. may have evolved likewise in Savannah. In a previous chapter its beneficent activity was noted prior to the War Between the States. In the 1870's and beyond, its programs centered around Charity Balls, "dime readings" (a fund-raising scheme), and honoring distinguished members of the Jewish community after death.[122] As the congregations retreated from dispensing charity, H.B.S. took up the slack. Its supporters were primarily the leaders of the synagogues and the Jewish community.[123] The flow from Hebrew Benevolent Society to synagogue did not occur in Savannah, as it did in Jacksonville and Atlanta (reflected in their synagogue nomenclature). K.K.M.I. predated H.B.S.

B'NAI B'RITH

The I.O.B.B. (Independent Order of B'nai B'rith) had functioned in Savannah prior to the 1860's and formed the basis for the creation of the second synagogue, B'nai B'rith Jacob. A Jewish version of the Odd Fellows Lodges, it provided fraternal pleasures for those who preferred parochial attachments. While associating with the Odd Fellows in ceremonial ways, I.O.B.B. allowed for two goals to be fulfilled:[124] (a) mutual aid for those in need, particularly recent immigrants, and (b) a mechanism for dealing with anti-Semitism, particularly during and immediately following the War Between the States. For those unable to sustain pews or those who chose not to be a part of a synagogue, it offered an alternative way of relating fraternally to Jews.[125]

By the 1870's, the I.O.B.B. was attracting some of the leaders of K.K.M.I., including Joseph Rosenheim, Samuel Herman, S. A. Einstein, and Elias Weil.[126]

The crowning achievement of the local B'nai B'rith Lodges occurred in 1877, when a "grand picnic" was held at the Hermitage, and nearly two hundred dollars was raised for the establishment of a Hebrew orphanage.[127] The orphanage was constructed in Atlanta and was recognized as the leading Jewish benevolent institution in the southeast.[128]

The existence of organizations that appealed to Israelites only did not exclude Jewish participation in general clubs and societies. The instance of Joseph Lippman is cited as illustration. A leader of the synagogue, a participant in B'nai B'rith and the Harmonie Club, he was also active in the German Friendly Society which paid a "tribute of respect" upon his demise.[129]

CHAPTER EIGHT

THE MENDES TERM

A̲t a meeting of the Southern Rabbinical Conference, January 3, 1905, Rabbi A. G. Moses of Mobile, Alabama, was called upon to eulogize a colleague revered by the body of assembled rabbinic leaders—the Rev. Dr. Isaac P. Mendes. In the same address, note was taken of two other leaders who had been removed from earth in the course of the year. One of the two was *Theodor Herzl*. It would have pleased the venerated "Shepherd of Israel" to have been lauded with the progenitor of Zionism.[1]

Born in Kingston, Jamaica, on January 10, 1854, Dr. Mendes claimed descent from a distinguished rabbinic family.[2] His ancestors had been marranos in Spain. After escaping the Inquisition, the family went to Jamaica by way of England. Joseph, Rabbi Mendes' father, was the fourth generation to live on the island. His brother was the London rabbi, Rev. Abraham Pereira Mendes.[3] Joseph sent young Isaac to him to study for the rabbinate. Contemporaneously, Isaac received a secular education at Norwich College in London.[4] At age 19, Mendes was called to the sixth oldest congregation in America, K.K. Beth Shalome of Richmond, Virginia. It was the second largest synagogue in the city, boasting seventy families by 1877.[5] Apparently the New Orleans rabbi, Henry Jacobs (whose brother George had just vacated the pulpit), recommended the novice "minister" and that helped seal the contract.[6] While in Richmond, Isaac took to wife the aptly named Grace de Castro, daughter of Colonel and Mrs. Jacob de Castro.[7] Grace's mother, Hannah, was a de Sola, of lineage traceable to the Ibn Daud family of the 11th century.[8] Honored rabbinic figures dotted the family tree, including Rabbi Elijah de Sola of Granada (1420), Rabbi David de Sola of London (19th century), and his great grandson, Rabbi David de Sola Pool, rabbi of New York's Shearith Israel Congregation.[9] Grace's sister, Alice, married Samuel Louis Lazaron of Savannah, and among their offspring was Savannah's sole rabbinic product, the late Rabbi Morris Lazeron, senior rabbi of the Baltimore Hebrew Congregation. Dr. Mendes was his uncle.[10]

The Richmond rabbinate lasted four years and demonstrated that the fledgling spiritual leader was a man of talent. Non-Jews as well as Jews flocked to his services, and *The Richmond Dispatch* carried the text of several of his orations.[11] Swelling crowds confirmed the impression of one journalist that

his [Mendes'] diction was very chaste, his voice clear and ringing, his
enunciation distinct, his gestures easy and graceful, and his sermon on
the whole a very interesting and impressive one.[12]

His reputation spread beyond the "Old Dominion." *The Jewish Messenger*,
a New York based Jewish journal, published information about his activities, including bar mitzvahs and religious school programs.[13] *The New
Orleans Times* carried the text of a sermon preached on June 25, 1875, con-
firming his success in building a national reputation.[14] Mendes was beholden
to Sir Moses Montefiore, and that attachment was manifest even in this early
period.[15]

Were it not for the new responsibilities that came to him as husband
and father, Rabbi Mendes might have remained in Richmond for a more
prolonged term. His requests for salary increases were beyond the capacity
of a "dying" congregation.[16] In 1877 the time was ripe for a move. Beth
Shalome's leadership, particularly its president, S. A. Winstock, demonstrated affection and admiration for the departing *hazzan*. Winstock presented him with a handsome silver *kiddush* cup, (presently displayed in
the K.K.M.I. Museum) and encouraged his new ministry by a donation to
Temple "Mickva" Israel's building fund.[17] A "tribute of respect" was
tendered to Mendes on Tuesday, June 26, 1877, by Beth Shalome. The
official resolution "expressive of the feelings of this congregation at the
resignation of the Rev. Isaac P. Mendes" included the panegyrics:

> . . . he has endeared himself to his congregation by his upright, con-
> scientious and able administrations of his ministerial duties;
>
> We desire to express our sense of the great loss we sustain [by his
> resignation];
>
> [We] acknowledge the high estimation in which we hold him as a man
> and sacred minister.[18]

THE COMPETITION

The *Richmond Times Dispatch* of June 7, 1877, described the Savannah
Hebrew congregation as "one of the wealthiest in this section of the
country."[19] Prospering synagogues tend to attract able candidates, and
from the time of Rabbi Harris' departure, letters from applicants
were placed before the *adjunta*. The list included Rev. Marx Moses of New
Orleans, Louisiana; J. L. Meyer of Houston, Texas; Dr. Sarner, Memphis,
Tennessee; Isaac Stemple, Williamsport, Pennsylvania; Alexander Rosen-
spritz, Nashville, Tennessee; M. Fluegel, Erie, Pennsylvania; Dr. A. Hahn,
Cleveland, Ohio; and Nahman I. Benson, Shreveport, Louisiana.[20] Interestingly, Dr. Hahn included in his application a "catechism" which was noted
in the minutes.[21] That first contingent was considered, and only Rev. J. L.
Meyer and Rev. Marx Moses were informed that they were being "taken
into due consideration."[22] Meyer wanted questions answered and was advised that the salary would not exceed $2,500 per year, though he could

anticipate additional remuneration if he was a good "Hebrew teacher," and willing to teach children on the side.[23] Mendes was not among the early candidates.

On March 26, I. P. Mendes was heard from for the first time as were two others, the Rev. Dr. Moritz Tinter of Cincinnati, Ohio, and Rev. B. A. Bonheim of Columbus, Georgia.[24] The final candidate was Rev. S. Mendelsohn of Wilmington, North Carolina, whose application was rejected out of hand, primarily because the congregation was already leaning toward Mendes.[25] The board was so overwhelmed with all the spiritual leaders seeking to attach to M.I. that *The Jewish Messenger* ad was withdrawn after the first applications poured in.[26]

On April 9, 1877, the field was narrowed to two: Meyer of Houston and Mendes of Richmond. A trial sermon was thought best; since the *adjunta* was leaning toward Meyer, the opportunity to preach was presented to him first.[27] A telegram to that effect went to Texas on April 10th.[28] By April 29, the Houston "reverend" had come and gone, and his *Shabbat* trial sermon was judged impressive.[29] Before a final decision was made, the opportunity to hear Mendes was requested, and a telegram inviting him "at once" was dispatched.[30] A general meeting was called on May 27 attended by thirty Israelites. The unanimous vote was for Mendes. A term of one year and a salary of $2,500 were offered to him. Prior contact with the "Portuguese" preacher indicated that if elected he would be ready to start by August of 1877 and the congregation could expect that a Sunday school and a confirmation class would begin soon thereafter. Three were appointed a committee to wait upon his needs: H. Solomon, M. Ferst and Lizer Solomons.[31] The tedious process of negotiating for a "minister" was concluded. Richmond giveth and Richmond taketh away—Mendes and Harris, passing in the night.

Little is known of Rev. J. L. Meyer, save that he came to Houston from Plattsburgh, New York, in 1873 and was re-elected rabbi of Congregation Beth Israel by acclamation. The depression of the 1870's so disrupted Texas Jewish life that in 1877 the services of Rev. Meyer were dispensed with.[32]

THE MENDES MINISTRY—PHASE I

A year had passed since Rev. Harris fell into disfavor. When Mendes took charge in August of 1877, the congregation had gone through trauma. By April of the ensuing year, a new temple building was to be dedicated, and the formats of religious life had to be established. The task at hand was for Mendes to demonstrate command of the pulpit. By May 5, 1878, *ILA*, a regular correspondent to the *Hebrew Leader*, wrote the following:

> The Israelites of our city form, as it were, one large family, looking up and respecting their minister as head of same.[33]

By August 11, said stringer was commenting on the "noble minister" who, in but four months, had trained Lawrence Lippman for his bar mitzvah. The lecture he delivered on the occasion

> was so impressive and so full of truthful lessons . . . that I must conclude . . . that Rev. Mendes had added one other to his many well-earned laurels . . .[34]

RELIGIOUS EDUCATION

At the initial interview, Mendes made a commitment to establish, as soon as feasible, a religious school and a confirmation class. A year was to pass before these projects could be initiated. *ILA* in his September 19, 1878, column accounted for the delay as "owing to the poor health of Rev. Mr. Mendes."[35] This passing reference focuses attention on his frail condition which affected him at K.K.M.I., and resulted in an abbreviated span on earth. True to his word, the school began immediately after the Holy Days. The board instructed him to admit only children of members and seatholders.[36] The prospect of a first rate Sunday school in Savannah, it was believed, could attract members to the synagogue.

By September 30th, Mendes received permission to purchase books and to charge them to the congregation. Rules and regulations were drawn up by the board to systematize the educative process.[37] A Sunday School Committee was instituted with S. Guckenheimer as chairman and B. Kohn as secretary. Rev. Mendes was empowered to function as superintendent of the school. Rules were adopted by the full board, including assigning a name ("The Mickva Israel Sunday School"); forming a school board (composed of the president and members of the *adjunta*); standardizing the method of application (all students must receive vouchers of admissions, properly signed by the secretary of the school board, all vouchers to be submitted to the superintendent before admission was possible); arranging for supervision by the board (two members were to attend every Sunday); establishing rules about books (distributed on opening day by the superintendent, each student being responsible for their safety); conduct (disorderly behavior required the superintendent to record the instance in a book and report it to the school board for action); entrance requirements (child must have reading skill); and governance of school (all authority for the internal operation was entrusted to the superintendent).[38] By 1879, ninety-eight students were enrolled.[39]

Mendes established free Hebrew classes in March of 1879, the boys meeting on Monday afternoons and the girls on Thursdays.[40] In December of that year Mr. Nathan Cohen made application as Hebrew teacher, offering to teach each child individually at two dollars per month.[41] A second Hebrew instructor, Mr. B. Miller of Charleston, tendered his services as a Hebrew-German teacher, with the board seeking information from M. Triest and N. Lewin about his credentials.[42] Apparently the report of the two Charlestonians was "uncomplimentary" as B. Miller's application was rejected.[43]

Finally, Mr. Rehfeld submitted an application as Hebrew-German teacher. The board was prepared to allow him the use of the meeting room for his purposes, but offered him no salary. Information was requested as to the charges he would levy for his tutelage.[44]

In June, 1879, a motivational device was introduced—Sunday school medals and certificates. At the closing exercises of the school, the ablest students received "tangible" tokens, as evidence of their excellent performances. Following an elaborate speech in which Mendes informed the children and their parents that one hundred young people were in the school (divided into ten grades), the awards were distributed to those who had passed their examinations with top grades. The list of medal winners was as follows (note the teachers as well):

> Fifth class, three sections: Miss M.J. Solomons, Miss S.J. Solomons and Miss S.G. Nathans, teachers. Medal winners: Harry J. Solomons, Sam Oppenheimer, and Celia Stern.
> Fourth class, two sections: Miss G. Berg, Mr. J.A. Solomons, teachers. Medal winners: tie between Ida Reiser and Ophelia Stern and Adolph Wachenheimer.
> Third class, one section: Miss Alice de Castro, teacher. Medal winner: Nattie Solomon.
> Second class, three sections: Mrs. Hexter, Mrs. Mendes and Mrs. R.F. Berlin, teachers, Medal winners: Harry Oppenheimer and Sam Selig, tied, Adele Meyer, Miriam Weil and Carrie Grabfelder, tied.
> First class, one section: Mr. Lee Roy Myers, teacher. Medal winner: Henrietta Ohlman.

Rev. Mendes, in his remarks about the successful results attained during the first year of the school, made mention of the overcrowded facilities.[45] It would take two decades before his comment resulted in an enlarged facility. In addition to the local press, both the *Jewish South* and *The Jewish Messenger* carried the details of the ceremony.

Another tradition dating from an earlier time, the Sunday school picnic, was reinstituted on June 8, 1879, at Schutzen Park. Mr. Solomon Eckman and Mr. Ferst managed the entire affair which was pleasurably received by the crowd in attendance.[47] On all levels, educationally and socially, the Sunday school of M.I. was being touted as an example worthy of emulation by other congregations throughout the United States.[48]

The next step in shaping the religious school was the development of a confirmation class. On May 16, 1880, *Shavuot* morning, six fledglings in the household of Israel had the honor of receiving the blessings of confirmation: Frances Lowenthal, Sabina Guckenheimer, Adele Meyer, Blanche E. Morales, Fannie Leffler, and Master Leonard Lippman. The *Savannah Recorder* described the event in elaborate detail from the floral decorations to the white dresses with trimmings and ribbons that were chosen by the young ladies as symbolic of the "pure-heart preparation for the holy rite of Confirmation." An explanatory section preceded the service, instruction as to the purpose and value of the rite. A special feature was the religious examination of each confirmand, and demonstration that, even in such a short time, each learned the rudiments of the faith well. The emotion was so powerful that the reporter was aware of the "tears in the eyes of sturdy manhood. . . ."[49] Music directed by Professor Mallette, individual blessings of the confirmands, all but an elaborate reception, made the event comparable to a confirmation exercise in our time. To Reverend Mendes, the first class of confirmands presented a silver tilting water pitcher with goblets inscribed "to Rev. I.P. Mendes from his First Confirmation Class, 1880." Flowery tributes came from the class as a whole, and from Fannie Leffler and Sabina Guckenheimer.[50]

Mendes instituted a "rigid written examination" the following year, plus a gold "I.P. Mendes Confirmation Medal." Confirmation was taught by Dr. Mendes in the sanctuary with doors open.[51]

The Mendes' scrapbook contains newspaper accounts of the confirmation classes of 1881, 1882, 1883, 1885, and 1887.[52] Normally five were confirmed, the majority being of the fairer sex with an occasional male. Bar mitzvah was the customary rite for boys.

The dilemma of Jewish education today—exciting the young to value Jewish knowledge, while the example of their parents is otherwise—troubled Rev. Mendes as well. The *American Hebrew* in 1883 published a column by a new Savannah writer, *From Time to Time*, with the following analysis:

> A child is taught certain truths in the Sunday School, and made to believe in the existence of God who demands something from him in return for the benefits daily conferred. Here the modern parent steps in, with precept as well as example, declares the teaching of the teacher 'nonsense' and forthwith places in the hands of the child weapons with which . . . it hurts itself.

The author was moved to write these words after hearing Mendes' sermon, reproving the parents of K.K.M.I. for a lack of proper interest "in the welfare of their children."[53]

Judging from the diminished excitement about the religious school in the press and in the minutes during the mid-1880's, a new tendency had developed, alluded to in a column in the *American Hebrew*, dated September 17, 1882, (confirmed also by *From Time to Time*)—namely,

> an exodus among our young people; cause, off to New York, to boarding school to finish their education.[54]

This may explain why few confirmation accounts exist in the Mendes' scrapbook after 1887.

The emphasis on medals and awards had inherent dangers. When the children of the congregational president received the highest awards, as happened, the rabbi was exposed to charges of favoritism. By 1889 a committee of the board was chosen to examine the papers and to select the winners, freeing Mendes of responsibility.[55] Perfect attendance entitled the student to a prize at year's end, a standard which some parents objected to. In 1889 it was reduced to six perfect months; by May 2, 1890, it was further cut to five perfect months.[56] Spearheading this effort was the Teacher's Union, an independent body which reported to the board the attitudes of the teachers. Jacob Gazan was its first secretary, and he notified the board of its creation on December 5, 1889.

The Teacher's Union objected to the manner in which the prizes were awarded, but the board did not look with favor upon their objection.[57] A death knell was sounded for the system in 1893 when several ties were reported and the board recommended that the winners in each category draw lots to see who would receive "the sterling." To insure fairness, both the president and vice-president were present to "superintend the drawing."[58] The minutes make no mention of any Sunday school medals thereafter.

In 1894, the Teacher's Union instructed Mr. I. M. Frank, its secretary, to communicate to the *adjunta*

> that the conduct of three certain boys is of such a nature that the same be expelled from Sunday School . . .

The board did not wish "to act hastily" but instead notified the parents and suggested that

> unless their future conduct will be such as not to violate the discipline of the school otherwise they would be expelled.[59]

This was symptomatic of a shift occuring in the school, a lessening of interest by the board and parents alike. Not until 1899 was this erosion checked, when Mrs. Miriam S. Wolf, secretary of the Teacher's Union, wrote a letter to the president to be read at the annual meeting:

> Resolved that the teachers note with pleasure the great improvement in every respect in the children attending Sunday School . . .[60]

The resolution was premature. Three years later the same union requested a congregational committee to attend school each Sunday to "materially aid in the decorum."[61]

At "Mickva" Israel Sunday School, assemblies began through a joint effort of the Teacher's Union and the Temple Guild (forerunner of the Sisterhood). For the smaller children an authentic worship experience was sought on *Shabbat* morning, immediately preceding the 10:00 o'clock adult service. To achieve this end, it was requested that the adult prayer hour be postponed until 10:30 a.m. From this beginning developed the Children's Service or Family Service.

In the newspaper account of the first closing exercises of the Sunday school, Rev. Mendes cited the large numbers of students in the school and the need for expanded facilities.[62] This theme was picked up in 1902 when the Temple Guild requested use of the ground adjoining the Sunday school "for the purpose of enlarging the school rooms."[63] Four days later Mrs. E.M. Minis, secretary of the Guild, requested permission to move ahead with the project. It was granted. When Leopold Adler recommended that subscriptions be solicited from the full membership to aid the ladies, the project was enlarged.[64] Within months, a new Sunday school and chapel were in the planning stage. That will be the subject of a separate and later accounting.

THE MUSIC MAKERS

Considering the strong Orthodox inclination of Mr. Mendes, it seems incongruous that the musical program of the synagogue would flourish during his term of service, not that he actively encouraged it. It simply suited the tastes of his congregants to hear choral hymns and responses as they sat in the pews.

Never the metropolis, yet ever the seeker of high culture, Savannah proved a happy home for some fine musicians in the course of twenty-five decades. Foremost among them was Lowell Mason, who played the organ at the dedication of the first building of M.I. (1820). In seeking the best virtuosi to handle its program, the temple showcased the heritage of Israel's song. Some years were better than others; the musicianship ranged from first class to adequate. Stability was earnestly sought in principle, but constant "reorganization" was the reality. There were some gifted singers, organists and choirmasters who deserve attention, particularly in this period of temple history when happenings in the choir loft commanded the board's consideration routinely.

At first the loft area featured Israelites. Isidor Rosenfeld was organist in the early 1870's; the Amram/Rosenfeld females sang the traditional tunes. Others filled the sanctuary with song: Mrs. Zipporah Solomons, Mr. Simon Hexter, Mrs. Pearlman and Miss Gross. When Jewish musicians were unavailable, Gentiles were added to the quartet, including Mr. Blois and Mr. Mallette. By the time of the dedication of the Monterey Square synagogue, Professor Lessing was at the console, and "the regular choir" included Miss Gross and Mr. Hexter, Jews, Mrs. Cleveland and Mr. Mallette, Christians. In the words of the reporter covering the April 11, 1878, consecration,

> the music was superb and was a most impressive feature of the service.[65]

During the height of Mendes' ministry, Jewish voices were more frequently heard in the temple, among them Sophia Lillienthal, Rachel Ferst, Miss Gross, Isabelle Lazeron, Ellen E. de Castro and Dolly Dub.[66] Lazeron and de Castro were related to the rabbi through his wife, whose sister married S. L. Lazeron. In 1878 the congregation was caught up in the excitement of its first volunteer chorus, composed of Alice de Castro, Rachel Ferst,

Henrietta Berlin, Sallie G. Nathan, Hennie Haym and Sophia Lillienthal. In appreciation of services rendered gratuitously, the board presented each with a golden chain, eliciting effusive letters of appreciation.[67] By October 10th, *ILA* was informing her readers in the *Hebrew Reader* that, at *Rosh Hashanah* services,

> particularly noticeable were the young ladies of the choir, each resplendent in a handsome gold neck-chain . . .[68]

How proud the congregation was of its "youthful choir"![69]

The dominant musical personality from 1870-1888 was Professor F. Lessing. A concert pianist by training, he was responsible for organizing musical entertainments which received favorable comment in the local press.[70] His excellence as a musician contrasted with his insufficiency as a human being. When President Elias Weil was told of Lessing's intoxicated state, he issued a stern warning. The scandal is recorded in the January 8, 1884, minutes:

> The attention of the Board being called to the fact that Prof. F. Lessing had several times appeared too much under the influence of liquor to properly perform his duties as organist, he was notified that upon a reoccurrence of the offense, the President was authorized to immediately dismiss him.

In honor of the congregational officers, Lessing earlier composed a *Boruch* and *Shema* (responses of the Hebrew service) for the High Holy Days.[71] His success as a teacher of young people was demonstrated by the musical presentations of the "youthful choir" and the organ lessons he provided for the children of temple members.[72]

"Professor" Mallette (as he is referred to in the *Temple Minutes*) was not only the basso of the choir, but also an accomplished musician who directed the musical program for the cornerstone consecration in 1876.[73] Resident expert on Jewish music in Savannah, he opened in Armory Hall a "Hebrew School for Sacred Music," an institution whose life span was attenuated (the local press cites only a singular reference to it).[74]

The musical program of the synagogue was reorganized with the hiring of H. E. Rebarer as choirmaster.[75] In 1885 the board hired Rebarer "as leader and instructor" and also tenor soloist.[76] The following year the congregation expended almost a quarter of its budget for music ($1,523.63 out of a total of $7,047.76) while the Sunday school received less than $100 annually.[77] What happened in the loft was clearly a priority item.

By 1888, a shift took place in the religious background of the singers. The only Israelite harmonizing for the congregation was Isabel Lazeron, kinswoman of Rabbi Mendes. Julian Walker, H. E. Rebarer, and Mrs. William P. Hunter were the others in the quartet.[78] Replacing Professor Lessing at the keyboard was Mr. Stewart, whose five year musical ministry the board acknowledged as providing "valuable services."[79] Miss Colding replaced him at a much reduced price.[80]

Reorganizations of the choir were routine; one occurred in 1893 (April 18), another in 1897 (January 10). During the latter, the salaries were reduced a full third.[81] This development paralleled the Panic of 1893, which particularly affected agricultural areas.[82] Savannah endured a time of fiscal insecurity, as the price of cotton plummeted, and property values in Georgia declined by a third. Wheat prices were low, yet many Georgians sat at dining room tables, bereft of the staff of life.[83] No wonder that competition among singers for employment at the synagogue was intense; three altos applied at the same time.[84] By 1898 the recession was still virulent so that the choir's request for "full salary" was not honored.[85]

Throughout his career, Mendes avoided disputation with staff members and congregants on matters not involving principle. Within a short time of his employment, Rebarer was clashing with the rabbi prompting a letter from Mendes to the board and the appointment of a committee to meet with the two men to resolve the issue of authority over the musical program.[86]

The annual Sunday school picnic was the means by which the board furthered bonds of fellowship among teachers, administration, and students. The comparable occasion for the choir was the fish supper at Thunderbolt (as on the occasion of Dr. Mendes' Silver Anniversary).[87]

MENDES AND REFORM

In a previous chapter, the role of Raphael de Castro Lewin, the mentor of Reform in Savannah, has been carefully examined. Though removed from K.K.M.I., his influence was felt from afar, as the leadership made overtures to woo him back to the community. When they were erecting a temple, Lewin was consulted and reliance reposed in his views. The Rev. A. Harris, Lewin's successor, had no interest in returning the congregation to the Portuguese Orthodoxy that it espoused prior to 1868. From Savannah, Harris moved on to the Hebrew Union College, the Reform seminary, for a teaching appointment, and from there to the Reform congregation, Beth Ahabah, in Richmond. By the time Mendes received the "call," the forces of "liberal Judaism" were firmly entrenched.

Mendes' religious inclinations were traditional. In *tallit* (prayer shawl) and *yarmulke* (prayer cap) he was arrayed, whenever engaged in prayer.[88] It was the proud and long heritage of ancestry that bound him immutably to the Portuguese Orthodox way. His uncle, Abraham Pereira Mendes, was married to the daughter of Rev. D. A. de Sola, rabbi of New York's first founded synagogue Shearith Israel, and the couple had served at the mother congregation of Sephardic Jewry, Bevis Marks in London (whence came the 1733 and 1737 Torah Scrolls to Savannah). From this union accrued two "shepherds of Israel," I. P. Mendes' cousins, Frederick de Sola Mendes, rabbi of New York's West End Synagogue, and H. Pereira Mendes, also a rabbi of

New York's Spanish and Portuguese Synagogue (Shearith Israel).[89] The latter
served in 1904 as president of the Union of Orthodox Jewish Congregations
and was its primary spokesman. Through his wife, Grace, I. P. Mendes
could claim familial connection to Rev. Aaron David Meldola de Sola of
Montreal, Canada, another giant of Orthodoxy.[90]

Yet the people he served had long abandoned Orthodox forms and were
staunchly in favor of liberalism. It is a tribute to Mendes' approach to ministry that he endeared himself to the congregation, even as he was not in
harmony with the congregation. On basics he would not budge, risking the
anger of the opposition. On minor issues, he demonstrated flexibility, especially when the end result was a strengthening of the Jewish religion.
Only once did he enter upon a "holy crusade" in the name of *Shabbat*.
From that he learned that, once a practice is abandoned, habit steps in, and
where habit abides, there inflexibility is found. If Mendes' mission was to
hold back the dawn, he succeeded. If he intended to extract the tap root of
Reform, it was not accomplished. The rhythm of change decelerated only
temporarily to gain momentum when the descendant of marranos was no
longer at the helm.

From these general statements, we proceed to the documentary evidence. The thread is picked up with the last phase of Dr. Harris' rabbinate.

As the congregation prepared to build its new temple in 1874, Abraham
Einstein and Joseph Lippman introduced a motion that the Reform
Minhag be the sanctioned one in the new temple building. To further this,
correspondence was opened with Dr. Heubsch, requesting a copy of the
form of service in his congregation "on Lexington Avenue" in New York
City.[91]

A year later, the first documented instance of mixed seating occurred
when Mr. E.J. Moses applied for "the chair seat adjoining the one now
occupied by his wife."[92] This transpired in the Perry Lane Synagogue. The
Monterey Square Temple was built without a balcony, evidence that a
mechitza (partition to separate the sexes) was not operative. Family pews became the established practice.

The first test of Mendes' religious mettle occurred in 1879, two years
into his ministry. At issue was the *chuppah* (the marriage canopy) which
some wanted to abolish.[93] The subject, being "delicate," was deferred until
the annual meeting when the full congregation could have its say. At that
convocation (January 12, 1880), N.E. Solomon argued for the *chuppah* to
be left to the discretion of the family. This optional approach was opposed
by Joseph Rosenheim who moved that the canopy be retained. By a vote of
twelve to two the Rosenheim motion carried. Solomon protested per-
suasively enough that Rosenheim suggested a reconsideration of Solomon's
proposal. This time by a vote of sixteen to one, the *chuppah* was made
optional.

The final outcome displeased Mendes. When a second reformation was proposed making the *yarmulke* an act of individual choice, Mendes reacted vigorously. Elias Weil proposed to the 1892 annual meeting that

> the custom of wearing hats by male members of the congregation at divine services be abolished.[94]

Mr. J. A. Einstein amended the motion, asking for a meeting of the full congregation on February 7th so that this issue and the *chuppah* issue could be amply debated. Making the most of dissension, the board gathered on February 3rd, four days before the vote, to act upon a number of membership applications.

To the February 7th meeting, Rabbi Mendes was invited. The president requested all with views to speak them out fully:

> Rev. Mendes was called for and he at once rose, and expressed his opinion and in adition, [sic] sited [sic] Divine Authoritys [sic] in the custom of wearing hats, closing his argument with the distinct remark, that he was opposed to the change.[95]

Others strongly concurred and upon putting the question to a vote, Mendes triumphed by a large majority. When the motion for an optional *chuppah* was up for discussion, he again expressed his view: keep the *chuppah* with no option! This time also he succeeded. But Elias Weil did not desist. At the annual meeting of 1893 (January 8) the optional *yarmulke* again was put on the table and a full congregational convocation was called for one month hence.

On February 5th, the special meeting was convened, and again by a vote of nine in favor and fifteen opposed, the Weil faction was thrashed. Defeat did not dissuade, and at the 1894 annual meeting (January 7), the question of head coverings was put to the people, this time by Weil's kinsman by marriage, Mr. A. E. Smith, with Lawrence Lippman as seconder. The proposal was stronger—no option; simply abolish the practice of *yarmulkes*. Fair-minded Mr. Weil suggested another special meeting of the congregation to make a final determination. Cards were to be sent to everyone. On the day of the "great assembly," May 27, 1894, the board came together in the Sunday school meeting room to process membership applications from six prospectives, eager to vote on the "hot question." (This phrase is ascribed to Abram Minis, Jr., at the January 7, 1894, meeting). By forcing the issue and calling for abolishment, the proponents may have intended compromise, and that is what happened. A substitute was put on the table, making hats optional during Divine services. When the vote was to be taken, S. Elsinger and J. Cohen proposed tabling indefinitely and that carried. Whereupon Abram Minis, Jr., and Simon Hexter requested a reconsideration, and their view prevailed. When the full count was in, twenty-four voted for the option, seventeen did not. For Mendes it was a very sad day. He never mentioned the issue again. To his dying day he stood tall *with hat on head* whenever reading the prayers.

Earlier in his Savannah rabbinate, Dr. Mendes engaged in a crusade to restore the Sabbath as a day of rest. It began with his *Yom Kippur* message, reported by *Veritas* in the *Jewish South,* dateline September 21, 1879. The members were told steps to take "towards the general observance of the Sabbath day . . ." What began as a sermon was furthered by a call from Mendes to the board members regarding a strategy for the closing of all Jewish commerce on the Sabbath.[96] The *adjunta* met on September 18, 1879,

> to take into consideration the closing up of our respective places of business on the sabbath [*sic*] day.

Upon motion, the board and three members of the congregation were to constitute a committee

> to consult with all Israelites in the city and endeavor, if possible, to bring about the desired end.

Lawrence Lippman, N.E. Solomon and B.H. Levy were the three chosen from the congregation-at-large.[97] The project gained regional attention and all forms of tribute for Mendes. Examples:
Jewish South:

> Rev. Mendez [*sic*] understands his duty . . . he will thereby have gained the greatest victory of Israel's cause and also receive the approval of his heavenly master [*sic*].[98]

Veritas also had much commendation for the one engaged "in this noble work."[99] Enthusiasm gave way to "commercial necessity." By October 6, 1879, *Veritas* reported to the readers of the *Jewish South*

> the disappointment experienced thus far, at the nonconcurrence by some as well as the delay in action by all.[100]

Adonis, another columnist, perceived more than nonconcurrence. Though the committee did have some initial favorable responses when it contacted some merchants, that was insufficient to claim success.

> From the beginning I noticed a lack of interest in the matter among our people, as I regret to say the prime movers were altogether too hasty in their work.[101]

Adonis claimed that the committee was comprised of wholesale merchants for whom Sabbath transactions were of little consequence. An indication that Mendes' Sabbath-closing project elicited opposition is found in a letter to the editor of the *Jewish South* dated December 21, 1879:

> I am led to believe from what I have seen and heard that our co-religionists do not appreciate the services of the talented Rabbi, Mr. J. [*sic*] P. Mendez [*sic*].[102]

The rabbi dropped further mention of a divisive issue, and in a public statement told his people

> that this would be the last time he would request them to do so [observe the Sabbath properly].[103]

The flow of criticism did not end with this utterance. It took a new form after he condemned the interest of some of his members in Christmas observances. *Adonis* reported that he overheard some young ladies conversing; one saying:

> I'll show Mr. Mendez [*sic*] that he can't get the best of me, I shall go right to the grocery store and buy a dressed turkey for a Christmas dinner . . .

which prompted *Adonis* to plead,

> I earnestly request the members of the temple to be more careful in their criticisms and actions toward Mr. Mendez [*sic*] as they may some day repent for it. He is well fitted for the position he holds, and does everything for his people's own good.[104]

In one final area, Mendes' Orthodox inclinations surfaced openly. He expressed discomfort about participating in conversions. Unwilling to shoulder the responsibility alone, he requested a vote of the board before any "Jew-by-choice" would be accepted. The first recorded instance of a formal conversion occurred in 1892. Mrs. F. A. Ehrlich had come to him, requesting admission "to the ancient faith of Israel." Rabbi Mendes related to the *adjuntamen* the circumstance of his decision, affirming

> that it was an act of her own free will and accord, no mercenary motives, but simply a pure desire and love for our holy religion.

After reading to the board her "entreating letter," he voiced the view "that he has no faith in conversion."[105] Due to the exceptional character of Mrs. Ehrlich, he was willing, however, to convert her, whereupon the board complied with the request and granted him permission. A second instance of conversion is recorded in 1898. It involved Miss Heyman who had addressed a letter to the rabbi requesting admission to the Jewish fold. The matter was brought before the leadership,

> Rev. Mendes not wishing to perform this act of conversion without the consent of the Board . . .

Consent was granted after the president and vice-president had the opportunity to interview Miss Heyman to determine her sincerity.[106]

In practice and preaching, Mendes cleaved to Orthodox Judaism. Yet to balance the picture, his was a ministry open to the best in Reform. Innovations were not opposed automatically, and, in some cases, were actually advanced.

First, Reform was not, on principle, distasteful to him. Its emphasis on rationality, its attempt to liberate historic Judaism from superstitious excesses, and its focus on Jewish "core" principles had appeal. In his scrapbook, volume I, Mendes pasted a clipping (without references cited) containing these words:

> Reform goes on with steady stride in the new world and the old. The gems of Judaism are being slowly but surely cleansed of the accumulated dust of centuries and their brilliancy begins to shine forth again.[107]

Mendes' opposition to the "reformers" in the congregation may have been sparked by an indiscriminate tossing out of that which was sacred to him.

Second, he cultivated close associations with leaders of the Reform movement, especially Rabbi David Marx of Atlanta, whom he invited to address the congregation on his silver anniversary as rabbi of K.K.M.I.[108] The compliment was returned when Mendes participated in the dedication of "The Temple" in Atlanta on September 12-13, 1902.[109]

Among the changes which Dr. Mendes introduced were confirmation for boys and girls on *Shavuot* day (the Jewish Pentecost); the elimination of services during the heat of summer (usually from mid-June to September the rabbi and his family vacated the city, leading to a suspension of worship);[110] a Memorial service on *Yom Kippur* afternoon;[111] an annual Thanksgiving service;[112] and book reviews from the pulpit.[113] When it was suggested that Dr. Mendes abandon his procedure of addressing comments to the bar mitzvah at the Sabbath services, the rabbi complied even if the young man remained more ignored than instructed.[114]

In the area of interfaith activity, Mendes embraced the pattern of the Reform rabbis of his generation. Within the Savannah Christian community and among the ordained clergy, he was well-known and respected. His scrapbooks bear witness to the attention he received from the local press. His messages were often carried verbatim. Representative is the interview in the *Savannah Morning News* (date unrecorded) as the nineteenth century ended. Six Savannah clergymen were asked to reflect on what the future might augur. Mendes' comments were highlighted, along with those of the pastors of the Independent Presbyterian Church, St. Paul's Episcopal Church, Trinity Methodist, the Christian Church, and Wesley Monumental Church.[115] Christians flocked to hear his sermons on Passover as well as on *Yom Kippur*. The appearance of worshipful Gentiles at the Monterey Square edifice was not an anomaly. *ILA* stated that at the *Yom Kippur* services "several of our most prominent and influential Christian citizens" were in the sanctuary.[116] Also the April 17, 1879, letter from the same source to the same journal mentions a "goodly number of Christians" in attendance for the Passover liturgy.[117] Mendes' prayers were offered at many local gatherings.[118]

His concern for the welfare of the poor and helpless won him the affection of the Gentile leadership in the city.[119] In witness to the power of his interfaith connections, the clergy from the major churches of the city were present in the sanctuary for the celebrations associated with his 25th anniversary as rabbi of K.K.M.I. The program has been preserved along with the text that Dr. J. Y. Fair of Independent Presbyterian Church and Rev. Charles H. Strong, Rector of St. John's Episcopal Church spoke on behalf of the clergy. Among the testimonials that Dr. Strong voiced were these:

> As a public teacher, you belong to a larger circle than that of your own congregation. Your scholarship and learning have already been recognized by the university of your state. . . . We can and we do gladly testify to the fact that your voice has ever been lifted up in defense of the highest things in life. . . .[120]

Despite Mendes' attempt to bridle a formal connection to Reform Judaism, the leadership pressed forward. The Union of American Hebrew Congregations, the parent body of the Reform synagogues of America, considered K.K.M.I. a prospective member. In 1880 it contacted the *adjunta* regarding a memorial service for Adolphe Crémieux.[121] That is the first mention in the minutes of any linkage with a clearly identified Reform institution. A Ritual Committee was charged with revising the prayerbook, and by 1887 had begun consultations with Rev. Mendes to shape one more palatable to the tastes and beliefs of the members.[122] Jacob Gazan was added to the committee because he had suggested a particular prayer book, which was taken as a sign of interest. At the annual meeting two years later, it was reported that the Ritual Committee was deadlocked.[123] Mr. Gazan insisted a new committee of five be appointed, made up of Simon Hexter, chairman, Lee Roy Myers, S. Guckenheimer, Jacob Cohen and B. H. Levy. These five were to consult with the rabbi and advance the project quickly. Eleven months later, the revised liturgy was tested in the temple on two consecutive Friday nights.[124]

In 1890 the new *siddur* (prayerbook) was formally adopted by the congregation at its annual meeting, and the committee was authorized to begin preparation of a High Holy Day prayerbook.[125] In 1891, volume I was still not in hand, as the printers were having difficulty typesetting the Hebrew.[126] Another annual meeting came and passed, yet no results were reported.[127] Not until 1895 was Mr. Hexter able to announce that the task was completed. Sales were disappointing. More than two thousand dollars was expended for five hundred copies of each volume. One hundred seventy-two copies of volume I were sold, and only ninety-four copies of volume II. The congregation possessed more than seven hundred unsold tomes with the name "Mickva Israel" stamped in gold, and a debt of nine hundred dollars to liquidate.[128] By 1896, the president was including the cost of the unsold prayerbooks as the cause of the congregation's elevated indebtedness.[129] Eventually the Morrocco and roan-bound treasures were reduced in price from $5/$4 to $2/$1.50 for volume I and $2.50/$2 for

volume II.[130] Copies have been preserved in the Temple Museum, volume I
bearing the publishing date 1891, with printers listed as J. Stern of Savannah and Sarasohn & Sons, Publishers. It follows the back-to-front opening
of traditional Hebrew liturgy, and includes services for *Shabbat*, weekdays
(*shacharit, mincha* and *ma'ariv*—the morning, afternoon and evening
prayers), plus a burial service and lections (Scriptural readings for the
festivals), 268 pages in toto. Volume II, dated 1894, was printed by J. Stern
and the Friedenwald Company of Baltimore, a 378 page, gilt-edged text. The
Leeser prayerbook was relied on for the High Holy Day liturgy, though the
committee acknowledged "we have drawn largely from other and, to us,
most desirable sources."[131] *Avodath Yisrael* was the only other reference
book cited, and Rabbi Benjamin Szold (father of Henrietta, founder of
Hadassah) and Rev. Dr. Jastrow of Philadelphia were praised in the *Temple
Minutes* for allowing portions of their prayerbooks to be reprinted.[132] While
the Hebrew text remained intact and the service Orthodox, the English
translation was modern and felicitous.

Two years after the prayer book "sale" (January 12, 1898), Samuel
Herman and S. L. Lazaron (father of Rabbi Morris Lazaron) moved and
seconded the adoption of the Reform publication, the *Union Prayer Book*.[133]
A temporary postponement of a final decision was effected through the appointment of an Investigative Committee which made its recommendations
on June 7, 1901. The members reported

> that they unanimously recommend the adoption of the Union Prayer-
> book for Sabbaths, Festivals and daily Prayers.

They suggested the retention of the present prayer book for the High Holy
Days. K.K.M.I. had followed the Portuguese *Minhag* since its inception. That
was its chartered tradition. Samuel Herman recommended that the constitution be amended

> by striking out the words 'according to the Portuguese Minhag,
> moderately reformed [*sic*] . . . and substituting the phrase 'conserva-
> tively reformed [*sic*].'

That had to await the full approval of the congregation at its next annual
meeting. On January 12, 1902, both proposals were ratified by the congregation. The members were later notified by card of the change, with the request to place orders for the Reform prayerbooks at a cost of $ .80 per
volume, regular, or $1.20, leather bound. Twelve copies were purchased by
the congregation.[134]

HIGHLIGHTS OF A CAREER

After Mendes' initial election, every two years during the spring, the
board reaffirmed its contractual obligation, usually with sizable increases
(beginning May 16, 1878, and continuing every second April, May or June

thereafter). In 1887 and 1890 the election was for a three year term, increased to five years in June, 1893. After the last contract was negotiated in 1897 for five years, Rabbi Mendes was elevated to Emeritus-for-life (in 1902). Frequently, the vote was unanimous, an indication of the general affection that prevailed.[135] When local proprietor, K. Platshek offered a tilting pitcher with goblets to the most popular clergyman in the city, the balloting occurring in his store, Rev. Mendes polled second to Rev. Charles Strong of St. John's Episcopal Church.[136] High moments of celebration were marked during his career. It is assumed that the 100th Anniversary of the K.K.M.I. Charter was greeted with festivities on November 30, 1890, although the minutes simply tell that President Weil called attention to it in time to make adequate preparations.[137] The centenary of Sir Moses Montefiore's birth was observed in Savannah by a special service and tribute to the British philanthropist. It fell on Sunday afternoon, October 26, 1884; Jews and Christians in record numbers gathered into the Monterey Temple, taxing its facilities. The *Daily Times* called Mendes' tribute "one of the master efforts of the minister's life." An elaborate program featuring Montefiore's profile on the cover was distributed, a token that has been preserved. A cablegram was sent to the great friend of the oppressed—oppressed Jews particularly—with the following words:

> six hundred of your co-religionists send you greetings of affection and honor.[138]

One year later, when Montefiore passed away, his admirer in Savannah had the pulpit draped in black, with an elegiac portrait of the hero hung beneath.[139] A memorial service attracted multitudes to M.I. Not since the memorial service for Adolphe Crémieux, founder of the Board of Delegates of the American Israelites and Montefiore's co-worker, did Savannah Jews publicly mourn the loss of a "non-resident."[140]

For Mendes, personally, there were three instances in his career when his cup ran over. On June 21, 1899, a telegram was sent to him from Peter W. Meldrim, Trustee of the University of Georgia and former Mayor of Savannah, stating,

> [I] congratulate you on degree of Doctor [of] Divinity this day conferred.[141]

The *Atlanta Journal* of June 22, 1899, noted that

> Mendes is the only Jewish Rabbi who has received the Doctor of Divinity degree from the university.

The item was carried in the Savannah, Athens, and Atlanta newspapers, as well as in the *Jewish South* and *Jewish Sentiment* which considered it of significance "from country's end to country's end . . ."[142] Mendes had received his master's degree from the university in 1893.

Instance number two came on the occasion of his first publication, *Pure Words,* in 1884. A collection of prayers and meditations for special occasions, it was greeted with favorable reviews by the *Savannah Daily Times, The Morning News,* and *The American Israelite* of Cincinnati (which cited the cost as $1 and the distributor as "The Bloch Publishing and Printing Co., Cincinnati, Ohio").[143] The *American Hebrew* particularly recommended the volume to the mothers of Israel

> for it will do much to further that prayerful spirit which is the best guarantee of a home's purity, righteousness and happiness.[144]

Mendes may have published a second book, a Hebrew primer, cited in a recent history of Richmond Jewry, although the work is not mentioned in Mendes' scrapbooks.[145]

The final event was his 25th anniversary celebration as K.K.M.I.'s rabbi (1902). A souvenir booklet was prepared, summarizing the testimonials from adults and children, Jews and Gentiles alike. Gifts of silver bedecked the Mendes' table, offerings of appreciation from the Teacher's Union, from individual members, from Sunday school classes, and from such organizations as the Council of Jewish Women and the Junior Council. A pair of silver candlesticks was received from the Jacksonville, Florida, temple. The congregation presented to the rabbi and his family a deed to his Gwinnett Street home, making it mortgage-free.[146] It was Mendes' time of harvest.

CONGREGATIONAL EVENTS

The Mendes years were good ones for K.K.M.I. The membership roster multiplied as new families were added: Sigo Myers, B. H. Levy, Sidney Mitchell, Jacob Cohen, A. Mohr, Sigmund Friedenberg, Max Krauss, A. Leffler, Joseph Roos, L. W. Wortsman, and Jacob Gardner in 1879 alone. In 1892 (February 3) at one meeting the following were admitted into membership: L. Putzel, J. Fried, S. C. Phiscotta, M. N. Schaul, I. Collat, S. Gardner, D. J. Morrison, N. Levy, A. S. Cohen, A. S. Millius, S. L. Lazeron, J. Roos, L. W. Stern, Julius Perlinski, J. Bigler, J. Lehwald, M. Brown, Solomon Cohen, K. Platshek and N. N. Levington. Mendes could telegram Montefiore on his centenary, boasting that he represented six hundred Israelites. The congregation had reached a high point in terms of prestige and size.

Sudden growth occasions budgetary enlargements. The resources of the congregation multiplied so rapidly that the bonded indebtedness for the building was disposed of by January 7, 1883, five years after the dedication. Instead of burning the mortgage, the bonds were put to the torch.[147] Improvements to the building were continuous; the biggest expenditures were for the repair of the roof.[148] The congregation turned to the gifted architect, Alfred Eichberg, who designed structures for the Central of Georgia Railroad (the main building), Simon Guckenheimer, Harry Haym and others, and had collaborated with Calvin Fay.[149] Eichberg suggested that the roof be tiled, ending a vexation which plagued the board.[150]

Fires have historically scourged Savannah, and the temple was not immune. The first building (1820) had been levelled by flames in 1829. The Monterey Square Temple experienced two conflagrations, one very serious, and the second of lesser intensity. The great fire of 1927 remains for Chapter Nine, but the turn of the century conflagration is the purview of this one. On October 31, 1899, just a few weeks after new memorial windows were installed, the evening calm was shattered by a

slight conflagration which did internal damage to the walls.

The young men of the congregation rushed in to save the Torahs, and the people of the community expressed their concern. The congregation was moved by the action of Rev. Arthur J. Smith of the First Presbyterian Church, who offered the use of his facilities across the street, and a second offer tendered by Wesley Monumental Methodist Church.[151] A dozen years earlier (August 17, 1887) when the temple was being rerooofed and refurbished, Wesley's Board of Stewards was prepared to open their doors for their Jewish friends across Drayton Street.[152] "Mickva" Israelites have used Wesley when circumstances required, the favor being frequently returned. This 1887 letter marks the genesis of this amicable arrangement. Preserved in the minutes also is correspondence from Jacob Paulsen of the Evangelical Lutheran Church of the Ascension, dated December 2, 1899, stating

> inasmuch as your beautiful Synagogue was damaged by fire on last evening, this Board in behalf of the Pastor and Members . . . tender to you and your congregation the use of our church, for such services as may be agreeable to you to hold therein.

K.K.M.I. Board expressed deep appreciation for the

beautiful acts of kindnesses which we shall forever cherish . . .

The letter mentions that

> the fire damage was not so extensive as to prevent the use of the synagogue.[153]

A major decision, relative to the temple structure, was endorsed at a special meeting of the congregation on December 9, 1902. The people ratified a proposal allowing for the removal of the original meeting room behind the temple, and replacing it with the "Mordecai Sheftall Memorial Chapel." In effect the Board of *Adjunta* and the president entered into an agreement with the trustees of the old Hebrew Burial Ground (Mordecai Sheftall Cemetery), the full text of which is spelled out in the minutes of November 24, 1902. The land used for the structure was retained by the congregation. However, *the new building, when erected, was to be the property of the Cemetery Trustees and their successors, with management, control and upkeep the responsibility and privilege of the congregation and, under certain circumstances, the Trustees as well.* In the instance of fire or destruction, the monies gained from the insurance (required as part of the arrangement) were mandated solely to rebuild or repair the structure. For a sum of $7,250, the congregation at any time could purchase the building. A tablet of marble in memory of Mordecai Sheftall, donor, was to be erected at the time of the completion of the structure. This contract is probably unique in synagogue life. A temple addition was erected without any subscription-taking, to be governed by, but not to be the possession of, the host synagogue.[154] The land is the synagogue's, but not the fullness thereof.

How came the Cemetery Trustees into resources of this magnitude? In 1893, the city limits were expanding in the area of the cemetery, permitting a "good deal of the land" outside the walls to be developed for residential use.[155] Some litigation conducted by lawyer Lazeron resulted in $1,250 profit.[156] By June 14, 1902, the surrounding land, except one parcel for a keeper's lodge, had been sold, and the trustees realized $11,856.[157] Mordecai Sheftall's original intent had been to use the land for a synagogue and cemetery. A century and a quarter later, his deeded parcel provided the wherewithal to expand the temple's facilities.

Why build a new annex? During the first year of the Sunday school, at that famed picnic, the rabbi addressed the people on the enlarged religious school enrollment and the need for expanded facilities. So too the Teacher's Union and the Temple Guild had apprised the board of overcrowded conditions. The Guild was prepared to build a structure on the back half of Lot 25, without tampering with the existing meeting room.[158] The initial group of ninety-eight students in 1878 expanded over the years, and many non-affiliated Jews were sending their children to the school.[159] Once the panic of 1893 ran its course (the impact lasted through 1898), the momentum was right to undertake building projects. On January 11, 1902, eleven months before the Mordecai Sheftall Chapel was begun, the trustees of the Permanent Fund contracted to erect four structures (yet standing) on Lot 23 of Franklin Ward (presently housing Belford Coffee Co.) at a cost exceeding $12,000. The purpose was to augment the income of the Permanent Fund, which had been decreasing precipitously. (At that time the projected income of the Fund was in the range of $1,400 per annum.)

Back to the annex. To carry forth the building in a first rate manner, one of the ablest architects in the city, Hyman Wallace Witcover, a member of the synagogue, was chosen. His notable achievements in Savannah are City Hall, the Scottish Rite Temple (Bull and Charlton streets), and the Lewis Kayton Home, now the site of Fox and Weeks Mortuary. (The second building of the B'nai B'rith Jacob Congregation on Montgomery and State Streets, a downtown landmark, must also be included in this list.) J. R. Eason was the contractor/builder; Mr. Furrer, the painter.[160] Substantial pews were designed by Witcover, and his assistant, Mr. Smith, was responsible for making sure they were acceptable to the board.[161] A marble plaque was affixed to the wall separating the sanctuary from the chapel, and inscribed thusly:

Mordecai Sheftall Memorial—
    A good man, patriotic citizen and pious Jew
    This building erected in the year 5663 in accordance with the
    terms of the trust made by Mordecai Sheftall in the year 5533

The central assembly room of the chapel was a miniature sanctuary, boxed in by classrooms along the three walls. No mention is made in the minutes of a dedicatory service.

When the addition was completed, the congregation was experiencing trauma over the failing eyesight of its rabbinic leader and naught else mattered.

NEW MEMORIAL WINDOWS

When the Monterey Square Temple was dedicated in 1878, three stained glass windows graced the pulpit area. The remainder of the assembly room was bathed in sunlight, as plate glass (perhaps opaque) filled the Gothic-arched appertures. Rabbi Mendes envisioned the sanctuary glowing with cathedral-like colors and had in mind a series of stained glass panels. On May 6, 1899, several petitioners approached President Rosenheim, requesting the opportunity to commission memorial and honorial windows. Concerned because the congregation

had spent a good deal of money on our former windows to make them perfectly secure against all sorts of weather,

the president sought the board's advice before granting permission. *Interestingly, the petitioners did not ask the congregation to have the windows installed but rather "pledge[d] themselves that the work will be done in the best workman-like manner,"* (Italics added) meaning the families assumed responsibility for negotiating with the craftsmen to set the glass in place. Under those conditions, the following windows were accepted: the Simon E. Byck Window, opposite the family pew, a memorial from his sons; the Lehman Byck Window, adjacent to his pew, memorialized by his children, Max L. and Edward L. Byck; the Moses Ferst Window, a gift of his family; the Samuel S. Guckenheimer Window, a memorial to their son by Mr. and Mrs. Simon Guckenheimer; and the J. R. Window, a gift of President Joseph Rosenheim, "in recognition of gratitude over the recovery of his beloved wife."[162] (Mrs. Rosenheim had suffered from a debilitating illness, requiring a visit to European specialists before healing came.)

The dedicatory rites for the stained glass windows took place on October 6, 1899, and the ceremonies were reported in the *Savannah Press.*

The design was chosen by Dr. Mendes, and according to the newspaper, it was his initiative that resulted in the project's success.[163] The five windows followed a general plan: borders of stained cathedral glass; central panels divided into three parts—symbols at the top, statements in the middle, and memorial wreaths (one honorial wreath) with the name of the departed at the base; two curved palm leaves bent toward each other at the top, forming the upper part of the arch. When these five were installed, only three plate glass windows remained.

FISCAL CHALLENGES

The structural improvements of 1902 were evidence of flourishing economic life. By contrast, a few years earlier, the congregation weathered a difficult struggle. The depression of the 1890's made it imperative that the board pursue a policy of winning new members. Mr. I. Haas recommended canvassing the surrounding communities and urging the Jewish citizens to affiliate with "Mickva" Israel.[164] A committee of three was chosen to solicit non-affiliates *in town,* following a report that income had diminished.[165] The results of the campaign were not encouraging, so new techniques had to be explored.

The first was engaging Dr. Joseph Krauskopf, Reform rabbi, founder of a farm school for orphan boys near Doylestown, Pennsylvania. The renowned lecturer of Philadelphia's Keneseth Israel Congregation was on a southern tour to raise funds; hence he was available to address the people of Savannah.[166] The board schemed to derive "the benefit of the surplus," provided a large number of tickets could be sold. March 25, 1896, was the day the rabbi spoke, assisting the congregation to raise $58.00 for the Temple Fund.[167]

Not overwhelmed by the success of the Krauskopf lecture, the board proposed that a dazzling social event be undertaken by the Temple Guild.[168] The ladies arranged "a charity ball" for New Year's Eve, 1897. Held at the Guard's Hall (Armory), it was attended by 273 (the number of tickets sold); and with the proceeds from a cash bar, a coat and hat service, and the sale of Mrs. Lillienthal's roasted turkey, the temple treasury expanded by $1,431.59, after expenses.[169] Effusive were the compliments that proceeded to all involved, from the Temple Guild to Mr. Cann of the Guard's Hall (including West Co. for the loan of their dishes).[170]

CEMETERIES OLD AND NEW

During an expansive era, not only institutions for the weal of the living expand; even resting places for the deceased benefit. The "old" cemetery (the Hebrew Community Burial Grounds) absorbed the attention of the board, as crisis followed crisis. In 1878 it was a fire that damaged the wall. Four years later, Lizer Solomons, who had a special interest by virtue of his marriage to Perla Sheftall (Mordecai's direct descendant), reported to the *adjunta* that the cemetery was in very bad "order." His dwelling "on the subject for some time" led to definitive action.[171] By September 22nd, the congregation undertook the rebuilding of the wall, Lizar Solomons superintending the work. Nine years later it was the gate that had deteriorated.[172] Problems with the wall surfaced in 1893, and Lizer Solomons was again pressing for repairs.[173] After her husband's death, Perla Sheftall Solomons was the most interested party and given the responsibility of keeping the cemetery locked. Apparently cattle had been seen lolling among the hallowed graves.[174]

The final "disaster" to be visited upon that sacred spot was the storm of 1896 which blew the walls down.[175] That same storm wrought structural damage to the synagogue, requiring the board to authorize funds to return both cemetery and synagogue to their former estates. The next year another hurricane struck the temple, blowing out a 15-inch piece of the Octavus Cohen Window, centrally located above the ark. It required the return of the glass artists, William Gibson's Sons of New York.[176] Havoc was done in 1898 by another "blower."[177] The cost of the repairs was recorded in the accounts of Lawrence Lippman, treasurer, dated January 9, 1897, January 9, 1898, and January 7, 1899. The total amounted to $1,000 to undo what the tempests of nature had wrought. Elias Weil pressed the board to provide "guards" for the protection of the windows following the second storm, and he was given full power to act.[178] This was prior to the installation of the five "new" windows in the main sanctuary.

Returning to the cemeteries: As early as the 1860's, there were Jewish interments in the third cemetery site, *Laurel Grove*. There reposed Gratz Cohen, Solomon Cohen's son who died at the Battle of Bentonville. Laurel Grove, a city cemetery, "open to all creeds" (the first of its kind in Savannah) dated its founding to 1852, in the administration of Mayor R. D. Arnold. The land is alternately high and low, limiting usable space, the Jewish section being particularly limited.[179] In the general section, such illustrious figures as Juliette Gordon Low, founder of the Girl Scouts of America, and James S. Pierpont, the composer of *Jingle Bells,* sleep in the sod. In the Jewish section, among many local notables (Solomon Cohen and family, the Minises, Rev. Rosenfeld et al.), rest two whose names are well known to students of American Jewish history: Philip Phillips, among the first Jews to serve in the United States Congress, and his wife, Eugenia Levy Phillips, Civil War spy.

The *Temple Minutes Books* do not mention Laurel Grove as a Jewish burial site until the Hebrew Community Burial Grounds were almost filled. In 1881, Samuel Herman and President E. A. Weil were requested to determine if there was any ground available at Laurel Grove for additional graves and the construction of a "metah[?] house" (caretakers' building).[180] It did not prove fruitful exploration, because by 1887 twenty-nine lots were unoccupied, and only a score were available for purchase, "which for a growing community as Savannah is entirely insufficient" according to the

investigators.[181] J. Gardner wanted the board to investigate the purchase
of land in a new location and to ascertain the interest of the congregators in
investing in it. At the annual meeting of 1887, Gardner and his committee
reported that the lands north of the Jewish section constituted a "bottom"
until the

colored cemetery is reached—making it an undesirable portion . . .[182]

While investigating other land a year later, the board was still focused on
Laurel Grove, because it made contact with the city to have the low lying
areas filled in and made suitable for graves.[183]

The attempt was without success. Interest then shifted to *Bonaventure,*
listed in Agnew and Lee's history under "suburban resorts." Four miles from
Savannah, it was originally an estate, described in the late 1860's as a place
of "melancholy beauty" where "nature and the wise neglect of man" made
it a "sublime and picturesque" site.[184]

Bonaventure dates back to the 1760's when a Charlestonian, John
Mulryne, settled on that spot. Being on high ground with a choice view of the
river (now the intracoastal waterway), it suited perfectly the building of a
family home. The estate fell into the hands of the Tatnall family, when
Josiah married Mulryne's daughter, Mary. With the Revolutionary War
underway, the Tatnalls with one exception were loyal to the Crown,
and the property was confiscated by the State of Georgia. The one exception
was Josiah, Jr., who so loved Georgia that he returned from England,
joined the forces of General Greene, and fought the hero's fight. In appreciation of his service, a portion of the family property was returned to him,
including the old homestead. In 1847, it was purchased by Captain Peter
Wiltberger who had long wished to turn this site into a cemetery. He incorporated it in December, 1847, as the "Evergreen Cemetery Company of
Bonaventure." It remained inactive until 1869.[185] Limited space in Laurel
Grove made Bonaventure all the more necessary and appealing. At the aforementioned January 2, 1888, K.K.M.I. annual meeting, J. Gardner recommended that "a portion of the Wiltberger tract adjoining Bonaventure
and north of Thunderbolt" be the site of a new Jewish cemetery because it
had

the easiest of access, finest location, prettiest site and in every way best
suited for the purpose desired.

Ten and a half acres belonged to George Parsons, who initially declined to
sell any property; but an adjoining portion was the possession of Mrs.
Lovell and was available for $125.00 per acre highland and $100.00 per
acre lowland. The total of 47½ acres would last 125 years by Gardner's

reckoning. He conceived of the cemetery as meeting the needs of *all* Israelites in the community and wanted to involve B.B.J. in his project. The only action taken by the congregation was to encourage Gardner's committee to come up with information to present before the body next year. Deferral continued until 1889. By February the land under consideration was withdrawn from sale.[186] The last mention in the minutes of the project was

> an informal decision by the Board as to buying a cemetery and the Board resolved to act as a committee of the whole and report any 'desirable plots'—

meaning the purchase of land in Bonaventure ended as an abandoned adventure.[187] Eventually the City of Savannah took possession of the property, and a Jewish section was set aside for the interment of Savannah Jewry.

IN PLACES OF PROMINENCE AND POWER

The Mendes years coincided with the emergence of the "New South." Savannah Jewish life had been generally free of the contagion of anti-Semitism. From the 1870's on, when vigorous anti-Semitic incidents were eroding the fabric of American society, Port City "Hebrews" retained places of honor and distinction.

Dr. Mendes' scrapbooks are rich sources of material relating to American anti-Semitism in this period. In 1879 the American Society for the Suppression of Jews, presided over by the notorious Jew-hater and member of "Boss" Tweed's gang, Henry Hilton, gathered at the Grand Union Hotel, the very place where the Seligman family had been turned away as they were registering for their customary Saratoga Springs vacation. The purpose of the Society was to activate Christians

> to put themselves on record as utterly opposed to the toleration of Jews in American society.[188]

After calling upon Society members never to vote for any Jews for public office; never to attend plays, concerts, readings featuring either Jewish performers or the works of Jewish authors and composers; and never to engage in trade with the major insurance companies and firms owned by Jews, or having Jewish directors—the body of fanatics endorsed obscene anti-Jewish resolutions. One: That the Treaty of Berlin guaranteeing Jews equal rights to Christians in Roumania be overturned and every effort be made to limit emancipation and return Jews to ghettoes (restoring the Inquisition was also proposed). Two: That the Bible itself be excluded from Christian reading lists, and the society members pledge themselves not to accept the Ten Commandments written by the Jew, Moses. Three: The body called for the expulsion of Jews from all "first class society." In a final fit of passion, the meeting ended with three cheers for Haman and Hilton, Torquemada and Corbin, the Inquisition and the Manhattan Beach Hotel.[189]

The Dreyfus case in the 1890's provided additional evidence that the age of true enlightenment had not yet dawned, distressing Savannah's rabbi. He lashed out in sermons and comments to the local press. In his *Yom Kippur* address, he declared Dreyfus innocent; that the wrong must be punished; that the Jews were God's chosen. Pardon was not enough! Dreyfus had to be exonerated![190] To Mendes the French had engaged in a patently anti-Semitic act, on an official level, tarnishing their national honor.[191]

Anti-Semitism in another form surfaced in the mayoralty campaign of 1899. Jews were singled out from Christian pulpits as perpetrators of gambling and other vices. Mendes made known his displeasure in a letter to the editor of the *Savannah Press*, published on September 25, 1899.[192] Such accusations were of the genre levelled against Dreyfus. Senator Vance's philo-Semitic essay, "The Scattered Nation," was featured prominently in the rabbi's scrapbook.[193] It convinced Mendes and, through him, the congregators of "Mickva" Israel that there were good Christians who valued the Jewish people.

If anti-Jewish sentiment was given credence in some quarters, including slurs spoken from the pulpits of the city, it did not have a significant effect. On the contrary, when it came to political influence, Jews were chosen with regularity and in surprising numbers to serve the people. From 1870-1900, these aldermen were elected:

1869-71	Moses J. Solomons
1870-77	Mathias H. Meyer
1874-77	S.H. Eckman
1877-79, 1881-87, and 1897-98	Samuel P. Hamilton
1879-81	Elias Weil
1881-83	Jacob J. Abrams and Simon E. Byck
1883-85	J. Florance Minis
1885-95	Herman Myers
1896-97	A. Leffler
1897-99	S. Krouskoff, A.L. Weil and A.S. Guckenheimer
1899-1900	Isaac G. Haas[194]

During this time, there were twelve aldermen serving on the council, and in several instances one sixth were Jewish. In the 1897-99 term, a fourth of the aldermen affirmed Israel's faith.

The advancement of Jews as leading citizens of Savannah from the 1870's to early 1900's is symbolized best by Herman Myers, who served as Savannah's only Jewish mayor for ten years, 1895-97, 1899-1907. In the period extending roughly from 1880 to 1914, Jewish mayors served the South's major port cities from the Mason-Dixon Line to the Texas gulf.[195] Charleston was the exception. Only Martin Behrman of New Orleans dominated city politics for a longer span than Myers.[196] A Bavarian by birth, Myers began his American pilgrimage in Richmond, Virginia, arriving

in 1867 in Savannah. A progressive entrepreneur, he and his two brothers
began in the tobacco business. Later he rose to president and chief stock-
holder of the National Bank of Savannah. Myers had investments in such
enterprises as the Savannah and Tybee Railroad, the Tybee Hotel Company,
the Savannah Grocery Company, the Southbound Railway Company (as
vice-president), and participated in the syndicate that owned the Macon
(Georgia) Street Railway and Lighting System.[197] Prior to his election as
mayor, he served eleven years as alderman. Business acumen made him a
logical candidate for mayor of a city anxious to emerge into national
prominence. Among his achievements (aside from putting the community
on a sound fiscal basis without increased taxation) were the following: he
created the Chamber of Commerce; he encouraged the spirit of "boosterism";
he issued a call for a public auditorium (with B. H. Levy and J. A. Estill
in charge); he expanded the paving of streets, particularly the north-south
corridors, which conditioned the pattern of city growth; he turned Savannah into the third largest port in the South, the busiest between Baltimore
and New Orleans, the largest naval stores exporter, and the third largest
cotton export center. Under his aegis the present City Hall was constructed,
without expense to the citizens. Savannah began to emerge as a modern
American city in Mayor Myers' term, with a residential building boom of significant proportion.[198] His administration was not without problems, but in
the issues that counted, Myers was effective. His connection to politics was
stronger than to synagogue, although there are occasional references to his
service to K.K.M.I.[199]

Elias Weil deserves mention in passing, not only as a merchant and
president of the congregation, but also as political leader and involved
citizen.[200] A partner in the firm of Frank and Co., he was president of Oglethorpe Realty Co., a partner in the Savannah Construction Co. (which
built the Southbound Railroad), and advanced the DeSoto Hotel as an
original subscriber.[201] City Council designated him to wait upon President
Grant during his visit to Savannah and to act as the official Presidential
escort.[202] In the aldermanic election of 1879, he received the largest number
of votes. The home in which Weil later resided (on Bull and Gordon streets)
had been visited by President Chester A. Arthur when he sojourned in Savannah as guest of his relative, Major Henry T. Botts.[203]

Jewish merchants advanced the fiscal health of the city, and evidence of
their contribution was demonstrated every *Yom Kippur* when the cogs of
commerce slowed. Columnist *Adonis* in his letter to the *Jewish South* dated
September 28, 1879, declared,

our Hebrew citizens represent the business elements of the city . . .

In backing the Sabbath closing, *Adonis* stated that if the Jewish establishments were sealed for *Shabbat*—Fridays, Mondays, and even Saturday nights
would become substitutes for the Saturday shopping spree.[204] Evidence of
the Jewish presence in the commercial life of 1870-1910 Savannah is sealed

into the bricks of some of the city's structures. Leroy (Lee Roy) Myers Cigar Company, of 1911 vintage, now serves as Parish House for Christ Episcopal Church; on Congress Street stood Mohr Brothers Store (1881); Broughton Street housed Levy and Golden's Company and David Morrison's building (1905); 127 West Congress was the site of Benjamin Lillienthal and Jacob Kohn's operation; 225 West Bay was built for Simon Guckenheimer (adjacent to the site of Days Inn Hotel of Downtown Savannah).[205] An examination of *Historic Savannah* by Mrs. Mary Morrison identifies which Jewish merchants owned noteworthy buildings. Some were tenants, and, it is assumed, took possession of the real estate from the owners at a later date. The advertisements in Lee and Agnew's *Historical Record of the City of Savannah* verify that, in 1869, Jewish merchants were numerous in downtown Savannah.

THE RUSSIANS ARE COMING

Between 1890 and 1900, Savannah's population grew more than twenty-five percent, totalling 54,284. Twenty-seven thousand were Caucasian, and ninety-five hundred were "ethnics." By 1900, 314 recent immigrants of voting age were identified whose roots were Russian or Polish.[206] Thus ten percent of the foreign-born population were probably eastern European descendants of Abraham.

The story of the great waves of migration from 1880 to 1920, mainly from the "Pale of Settlement" in the Russias, has been told in detail in scholarly works.[207] In summation, the Alliance Israélite Universelle in Europe (under Crémieux) and its American counterpart, the Board of Delegates of American Israelites under Rev. S. M. Isaacs (triggered by the Mortara Affair in Italy) served as watchdogs for Jews everywhere on earth. In 1869-70 there had been a famine in Russia, and a few thousand Jews fled to this *goldine medina* (golden province). By 1870, the Hebrew Immigrants Aid Society was formed in New York to assist migrant Jews in self-help endeavors, lest they prove a burden to society.[208] The Union of American Hebrew Congregations touted the idea of agricultural settlements for the "new Americans" and indeed many such colonies (some in the South) did develop.[209] Czar Alexander's assasination brought to an end the hope of emancipation and ushered in the age of "pogroms." Jews were driven out of villages. The major cities cited the temporary laws of May 31, 1882, as pretext for similar expulsions.[210] Constantine Pobedonostzev wielded power in Russia, and his formula for handling the Jewish issue was to convert a third, slaughter a third, and expel a third. The Jews responded to the last alternative, and within ten years (1880-1890), two hundred thousand had emigrated. The figure doubled in the next decade.[211]

Treatises have been published, documenting the mixed sentiments toward these "tempest tossed."[212] *Mendes' Scrapbook* (Volume I) informs us that the Jews of Savannah were involved in a rally convened by the mayor on behalf of Russian Jewry in 1882.[213] Many Christians joined their fellow

Israelites to express indignation over the persecutions. Three thousand dollars was collected and was forwarded to the New York fund-raisers.

A year later, Savannah welcomed its first Russian Jews. Columnist *From Time to Time* reported to the readers of the *American Hebrew,*

> several Russian Jews have come to Savannah, for the purpose of locating in this city. In many instances they have preferred to go further on, none of our merchants being willing to surrender their entire business and time to these gentlemen. Those who really came for work were furnished it by our President, E.A. Weill [*sic*], Esq. whose efforts on their behalf will compare favorably with any New York Committee.[214]

This article dated the arrival of Russian Jewry and substantiated the claim that the temple leaders were prepared to extend themselves for those seeking honest labor. The first mention in the *Temple Minutes* of a Russian Jewish presence in Savannah is a passing statement by Mr. A. S. Solomons, dealing with the upcoming 1890 U.S. Census.[215] An anti-immigration mood had engulfed the American Nation. By March of 1891, Congress passed a comprehensive bill, including a provision that immigrants brought over with the assistance of a charitable agency would be subject to deportation if the Secretary of the Treasury deemed it proper.[216] Census figures were important because the limitations were to be based on the percentage of residents in the states who came from foreign homelands. Mr. Solomons' letter to the board had this intent.

In 1892, the board received a request from Mrs. E. A. Weil for the use of a Sunday school room

> for the purpose of instructing the Russian children in needlework.[217]

At first the board refused on grounds that the space was inappropriate. But when Miss Maria Minis insisted, the facility was given

> once a week for the purpose of teaching sewing to the poor Jewish children.[218]

Russian Jewish children were given the tools for earning a livelihood.

In the same period, an influx of tots into the religious school was noted, especially those whose parents were neither pew owners or renters.[219] One suspects immigrant children were involved.

Concern for the "poor Jewish children" motivated the Sunday school students to petition the board for use of the schoolrooms to hold a fair. Never before had the youngest generation applied to their elders for a fund-raising function. It was granted with an exclamation mark![220]

The Savannah response to the eastern-European Jew was, on the whole, positive. With the exception of the 1893 panic, the economy was burgeoning, and the term "New South" implied a turning from agriculture to manufacturing.[221] Cottage industries have flowered in this setting, and the need for blue collar workers was pressing. Georgia was the "Empire State" of the South. The era of the factory was ushered in with the International Cotton Exposition in Atlanta in 1881, the equivalent of a World's Fair.[222] Textile mills, naval store manufacturing, and fertilizer plants dotted Chatham County and environs. Cheap labor, particularly the reliable cheap labor which immigrant populations could provide, was in demand.

If antipathy between Russian and German Jews existed, it simmered beneath the surface. Herman Myers, the symbol of aristocratic German Jewry, received the full support of his eastern-European brethren in his campaigns.[223] Russian Jews clustered on the north end of the city, near the river, in neighborhoods contiguous with the Irish.[224] David Goldberg has found evidence in the early 1900's of an ambivalent attitude toward immigrants from southern and eastern Europe, though hardly a thousand lived here.[225] In 1906 there was talk of making Savannah a port of entry.[226] Division developed among those who wished to actively seek "desirables" from northern and western Europe, and those who rejected exclusivity. Myers opposed great numbers of eastern-Europeans entering the port.

The "pogroms" of 1903 triggered anger on the part of the Jewish community, and a public rally was convened at the B. B. Jacob Synagogue. An overflowing crowd heard passionate speeches by Rabbi George Solomon, newly elected to the pulpit of K.K.M.I., and Dr. Mendes, then a sightless rabbi. S. L. Lazeron advocated an appeal to the Czarina to intercede with her husband before the terrible massacre should occur. D. Epstein, an immigrant, pledged fifty dollars and pleaded for those who might escape. The emotion-charged meeting ended with the appointment of a committee of five to investigate what could be done: Chairman A. J. Garfunkel, Rabbi George Solomon, Dr. Mendes, J. Stern, M. Rauzine and B. Weitz. The announcement that President Theodore Roosevelt had contacted the Honorable Simon Wolf of Washington, declaring to him that "he would not be wanting" if action was required, calmed anxious hearts. All were invited to join the B'nai B'rith as a sign of unity. The *Savannah Morning News* article of December 31, 1903, reported the details herein described.[227]

The opening phase of the development of an eastern-European presence among Savannah Jewry was generally free of enmity on the part of the established Jewish community. There were charitable endeavors to aid the needy, attempts to provide education for the children, and a desire to join in protests against Russian anti-Semitism.

JEWISH COMMUNITY LIFE

In the absence of records, it is difficult to assess the progress of Congregation B'nai B'rith Jacob in this period. Only two references could be found. One was an 1882 letter by *From Time to Time* in the *American Hebrew*, reporting on the return of Simon Gertsman to the city. Gertsman had served as an early B.B.J. president and reader (following Jacob Rosenfeld). The letter put to rest the theory that Gertsman was preparing to fill the pulpit since *Rev. J. Beer* was handling it "with acceptability." Beer's ministrations resulted in considerable improvement according to the document.[228] The second reference was a *Savannah Morning News* report about the election of the new B.B.J. officers in 1891, including President H. Haym, Vice-President J. White, Secretary H. Gabel, board members, S. Krouskoff (later alderman), A. Samuels, M. Brown, J. Lehwald, and W. Barnett.[229]

According to the local press, two other congregations sprang up for an unknown span of time, congregations which exist no more. The one

> seceded from the synagogue on Montgomery Street and have [sic] been worshipping on Broughton Street in rented rooms.

The article pointed out that the congregation was for Russian Jews, "representing a branch of orthodox [sic] Jews."[230] What prompted the publicity was an unusual incident in which Joseph Mirsky, officiating "rabbi" of this new congregation, was confronted by Mr. Levitan, while conducting services. Mirsky was accused of building a fire on *Shabbat*. The public interruption so vexed him that he reached across the table and slapped Levitan, who had him arrested. The trial in City Court was reported by the Fourth Estate, revealing the existence of a Russian-Orthodox Jewish congregation.

A second congregation was mentioned in the *Savannah Morning News*, bearing the name "Hebra Talmud Torah Synagogue." It functioned in Turner Hall.[231] It received public notice only once, the occasion being the wedding of "Bertha Schwarz" and "Charles Collman" (Coleman). The marriage ceremony was conducted by Dr. Mendes. Among the participants were Aleck Mendel, I.L. Rich, Philip M. Russell, Justice Thomas J. Sheftall and the female attendants, Miss Kelin, Miss Hurvitz, Miss Lena Alexander and Miss Sadie Garfunkel. The presence of many who were not of Russian Jewish descent indicates that this was a congregation distinct from the above-mentioned "Broughton Street" *schul*.

The *Youth's Historical Society*, described in a previous chapter, moved beyond its traditional literary activities and entertainments. In 1886, it sponsored a *Purim* Ball Masque. The list of those in attendance reads like a "Who's Who" of Savannah Jewry.[232] A repeat performance in 1887 met with additional success.[233] In 1889, a meeting of the *Young Men's Hebrew Association* was held at "Mickva" Israel, its purpose being to draw up a constitution and by-laws. A week earlier, the Youth's Historical Society decided to merge with the Y.M.H.A. One hundred and thirty active members were claimed by the new group, with the expectation that the roster would soon swell to three hundred. Rev. Mendes, who served as president of the "Y," claimed that if the magical three hundred could be reached, the Savannah chapter would be the largest in the South.[234] By May, plans were afoot to erect a building and to organize a stock company to sell shares and raise funds.[235] Less than a year later, the monthly meeting of the Y.M.H.A. convened at its Masonic Hall headquarters, and the discussion turned to purchasing gymnasium equipment and finding an athletic instructor. A committee of fund-raisers who would put on a bazaar was sought, the group desiring to erect a substantial building. The "Y" owned a library (probably deeded from the Youth's Historical Society), intended to use the space in the Masonic building for a gym, and projected a time when a facility would be available for outdoor sports—lawn tennis and croquet.[236] *Conceptually,* the Y.M.H.A. may have been the forerunner of the present Savannah Jewish Center (Jewish Educational Alliance). The officers in 1891 were leaders of "Mickva" Israel including President S. Herman, Vice-Presidents A. P. Solomon and J. Gazan, Recording Secretary I. M. Frank, Treasurer I. G. Haas, Directors Rev. Mendes, M. S. Byck and A. S. Cohen. B'nai B'rith Jacob was represented by David Robinson, corresponding secretary, M. A. David and Max Robinson, trustees.[237] The group sponsored cultural events including a concert at the Masonic Temple featuring the "Japanese Village and Girls' Orchestra."[238]

The *Young Ladies Hebrew Benevolent Society* continued its fund-raising activities, including a ball in 1889.[239] The *Independent Order of B'nai B'rith* flourished, particularly after the Honorable Simon Wolf visited Savannah in 1887.[240] He who had negotiated with President Grant and later Theodore Roosevelt for relief of Russian Jewry was a popular figure and a huge audience came to Temple "Mickva" Israel to hear his address. He used the occasion to announce the building of a Hebrew Orphan's Home in Atlanta. Social events were arranged to assist in the philanthropic undertaking, A Hebrew Charity Ball at the Hussars' Bazaar Hall attracted 450 for a lavish supper, catered by the Ladies Hebrew Benevolent Society and the Young Ladies Hebrew Benevolent Society. Supper was followed by a bazaar and dancing.[241] The B'nai B'rith sponsored this social event which was attended by the "leading society people of the city." The Orphanage so inspired Savannah's Jews that a year later, six hundred adults gathered at the Masonic Hall for a children's carnival, which featured a youth orchestra, tableaus, and "melodies by the infant class."[242]

One of the organizations spawned by the orphanage was *The Little Helpers* whose *Minute Books* have survived (thanks to Mrs. Josephine Hirsch Cranman for the use of these documents). On April 8, presumably 1891, Rosa Roos, Clemmie Smith, Helen Milius, Bessie Krauss, Dora Mendes, Irene Putzel, Lenora Amram, Rosa Putzel and Alma Mendes met together to elect officers (Rosa Roos became the first president) and to prepare needlework projects for sale,

> the proceeds of same to be donated to the Hebrew Orphan's Home in Atlanta.[243]

Dues were set at ten cents monthly, and a fine of a nickel for any absence from the monthly meeting, "except for providential causes," was levied.[244]

The group added members and established the following rules at the February, 1892, meeting:

> No secrets during meetings. No *profound* language also. [Italics added.]

The good work of The Little Helpers resulted in thank-you letters from the Superintendent of the Hebrew Orphan's Home (R. A. Sonn) and an acknowledgement for *Purim* tokens for the children from Mr. Joseph Hirsch of Atlanta (March 1892). On December 7, 1892, the young people raised one hundred dollars from their "fair," a sizable sum. In March, 1894, the last minutes were recorded, the destiny of the organization obscure.

Like their children, the adults created a new organization to assist the Atlanta Hebrew Orphan's Home. The *Hebrew Auxiliary Aid Society* coalesced in 1889 for this purpose, with such men in leadership as Elias Weil, president, A. Minis, vice-president, S. L. Lazeron, secretary, and I. G. Haas, treasurer.[245]

The late 1880's saw the beginnings of the *Hebrah Gemiluth Hesed Society* of Savannah, Georgia (organized June 20, 1888). A mutual help association providing free loans, sick benefits, disability allowances, and burial payments, it was designed to dispense aid and comfort to its members. The loan fund of two thousand dollars could be expended only on recommendation of the executive committee.[246] The organization included a committee to visit the sick and to comfort the mourners during the *shiva* (mourning) period. Membership was limited to "Hebrews" ages 18-50 and excluded those married out of the faith.[247] Fees for admission escalated from $3 for 18-25 year olds to $50 for 45-50 year olds.[248] Dues were $8 per annum payable quarterly. Loans and relief were available to a maximum of $50, with a program for repayment.[249] A $5 sick benefit was tendered for eight weeks per year.[250] Funeral expenses were assumed by the organization, including a hearse and two carriages, but not to exceed $35. Ten months after the death of a member a tombstone was to be erected by the Society.[251] The officers and board members were required to be present for the unveiling ceremony.[252] Although in 1916 the Society counted among its members persons from both congregations, its value was primarily for new immigrants.[253] To make them comfortable, records were kept in Yiddish or English, and any member could speak in either language during meetings.[254] The Hebrah Gemiluth Hesed Society (H.G.H.) prospered through the first third of the twentieth century and survives today.

Unlike charitable and mutual aid societies that abounded during this era, the *Teacher's Union* was formed solely for an educative function at Temple "Mickva" Israel. Its first meeting was convened in the Mendes residence on October 23, 1900, for the purpose of organizing the school, arranging for teachers, setting standards, and negotiating curriculum. One record book of the organization has survived, documenting the history of the school from 1900 to 1903, the date when Rabbi Mendes was afflicted with blindness.

One hundred seventy-six pupils, ages 5 to 15, were enrolled in 1903; fourteen teachers had charge of their religious indoctrination.[255] From time to time, the T.U. acted as a lobby for the interests of the rabbi and the children.[256] The discipline problems of the early 1900's were not dissimilar from ours. Examples: Rabbi Mendes once reported

> he feared discipline of the school was on the wane. He urged teachers to remain with their classes during school hours and thereby bring back the lost ground.[257]

On March 3, 1901, Mendes lectured the teachers on

> the importance of remaining with their classes thereby improving the general order in the school room and reverence for the building.[258]

One youngster left school because the rabbi had "reproved him and another lad." His mother let it be known that her husband was "not particular if . . . he returned or not."[259]

In 1901, the T.U. corresponded with the secretary of the Sunday School Union of the United States for purposes of affiliation.[260]

Both teachers and students engaged in fund-raising for the new Mordecai Sheftall Memorial Chapel.[261] Of special interest to the Reform community of America is the documentation in the *T.U. Minutes* of Morris Lazeron's first rabbinic experience. He who later served the Baltimore Hebrew Congregation led a Sunday school assembly in February, 1902, when he was chosen by his Uncle I. P. Mendes to be "the minister."[262]

CHAPTER NINE

SOLOMON'S TEMPLE

$\blacktriangleright\!\!\sim\!\!\sim\!\!\sim\!\!\sim\!\!\sim\!\!\sim\!\!\sim\!\!\sim\!\!\sim\!\!\sim\!\!\sim\!\!\sim\!\!\sim\!\!\blacktriangleleft$

For forty-two years, George Solomon wielded spiritual authority at Temple "Mickva" Israel. His election in 1903, as successor to Mendes, began a career that spanned two world wars, the Great Depression, Prohibition, ebbs and tides in the business cycle, and ebbs and tides in moral standards. Queen Victoria's rule terminated two years before the Solomon years commenced; at mid-career the flappers were loosening things up; and by its waning, Jewry watched helplessly as the world went mad. "Uncle" George raised several generations and is remembered yet among Jews and Gentiles for his progressive and innovative ministry.

Mystery surrounds Savannah's longest-tenured rabbi. Details of his formative years are not found in any source, including obituaries. By careful examination of his written material (where on occasion a guarded secret is exposed), this much can be reconstructed.[1]

Members of the family have been told that the rabbi was of Irish-Jewish descent, and that he was born and reared in New York City.[2] His own testimony regarding his maternal ancestry confirms that his mother had been accustomed to a life of comfort.[3] His earliest memories, however, were of poverty and struggle. The family recognized his promise and considered him constituted for a business career. His choice of the rabbinate as a life-dedication was not greeted by hurrahs.[4] Whether Isaac Mayer Wise found him in an orphanage and offered him the affection of a substitute father, as he did for so many others, is a suggested scenario for which no documentation exists. Only once did he speak of the kiss which Rabbi Wise bestowed upon him at Ordination, a cherished memory recalled many years after. The words of admiration and affection that Solomon used to glorify Wise over the course of his rabbinate is evidence of an uncommon attachment.

After his Ordination on June 14, 1895 [his *semicha* (Ordination certificate) is on display in the Temple Archives], George Solomon was called to Vicksburg, Mississippi, where he served Congregation Anshe Chesed until 1902, claiming for his bride the flower of the Feist family, Julia. Though childless, husband and wife were interested in young people. In Vicksburg he functioned as the principal of a local high school, in addition to performing his ministerial duties.[5] While serving in Savannah, this interest prompted

him to gain ownership of Camp Osceola near Hendersonville, North Carolina. Many young men and women summered in the facility that George and
Julia developed with the intent of building wholesome bodies, minds, and
character. In Savannah, the rabbi's wife displayed leadership talents in
Sisterhood, Council, and, most importantly, in the religious school (which
she superintended for a host of years).

THE STRESS OF TRANSITION

On Christmas Day, 1902, President Rosenheim called a special *adjunta*
meeting to report that a detached retinal condition, which earlier had
blinded Dr. Mendes in one eye, had "spread" to the second eye, and a total
loss of sight was possible.[6] Rosenheim had to assume rabbinic duties as well
as presidential responsibilities. The *Savannah Morning News* preempted
the board meeting by announcing on the 25th of December, 1902, "Will Become Blind."[7] Dr. Julian Chisholm was called in on the case, but advised
sending for the specialist, Dr. Calhoun, from Atlanta. Evidence of the
concern of the community over the turn of events was reflected in the details
released by the *Savannah Evening Press* on December 26th, the *Savannah
Morning News* on December 27th, and the *Savannah Evening Press* on December 27th. The prayers of Mendes' friend, the pastor at St. John's Episcopal Church, made journalistic grist in the *Savannah Morning News*.[8] The
New Orleans paper and the *Jewish Spectator* covered the item as well.[9] Occasional rumors of improvement were reported in the January 19, 1903,
Savannah Morning News, and the January 6th *Savannah Evening Press* (also
January 28, 1903). Clearly what was happening was troubling to the community when Dr. Calhoun finally arrived, examined the patient, and offered
little hope. Rabbi Mendes could only distinguish light from darkness and
"considerable objects which may be before him." Reading was out of the
question.[10] Hence the board had to make plans for the future which took
the form of seeking an assistant rabbi from the Hebrew Union College
(Wise's Reform seminary). The qualities looked for included "capacity, trust
and honor." A new position was being conceived for Mendes, "minister-
emeritus *in charge*."[11] (Italics added.) Rabbi Marx of Atlanta was consulted
as Mendes' friend. The congregation was told that the rabbi

> deplored the affliction which had befallen him for the sake of the
> congregation for he feared his usefullness [*sic*] to them was at an
> end.[12]

Suggestions were made, including getting someone cheaply so that
Mendes' salary could be preserved, and recruiting from Brunswick, Georgia,
a young minister about whom good reports had been heard.[13] Rabbi
Marcuson, leader of Macon, Georgia, for a host of years, was mentioned as a
candidate at the board meeting of January 25, 1902. The President of the
Hebrew Union College, Judah L. Magnes, offered his assistance in finding a
suitable "Associate minister."[14] Mrs. Mendes was concerned about the situa-

tion and contacted a cousin, Dr. Frederick de Sola Mendes, who wrote to President Rosenheim "concerning a *temporary* minister to help." (Italics added.) The president had to notify him that Mrs. Mendes did not understand the position of the congregation, explaining "we want a permanent assistant," as Dr. Mendes would be elevated to rabbi-emeritus. It was *Rabbi David Marx of Atlanta* who first advanced the name of *Rabbi George Solomon of Vicksburg*.[15]

After Dr. Calhoun's visit, the *adjunta* understood that the history of the disease was normally progressive, and that the diminishing sight would one day end. From Cleveland, Ohio, came a letter from I.G. Haas offering help, and another from Rabbi I.J. Feuerlicht of Augusta praising George Solomon. That, combined with a second letter from Rabbi David Marx, affirming Solomon's skill and merit, led Lawrence Lippman to recommend that negotiations begin with him. To E. A. Weil, J. Rosenheim, and Samuel Herman fell the ineluctable task of explaining the congregation's need for another minister to its incumbent minister.[16] Mendes met with the leaders and was clearly distressed:

> [He] did not take kindly to the proposition offered—stating that he was in possession of all his faculties except sight

and that only an assistant who could read was needed. Fear of friction between the emeritus and his successor began to be voiced at the board meetings. A salary of $1,800 to $2,100 was to be forthcoming to Mendes, and $2,500 to the new active rabbi (assistant, associate, whatever).[17] The board convened a congregational meeting on February 10, 1903, forty-seven males being present. The board had come to the conclusion that if the leader chosen by the congregation was not viewed as *the* rabbi, "it would never do." Confidentially, the president informed the members that Mendes' condition was unstable, and that it was unfair to put the strain of being a full-time spiritual leader upon his shoulders, particularly a man who had served them so faithfully for more than twenty-five years. The new rabbi would have to be in a position to take charge and accept responsibility. Solomon seemed the right man, but a natural reserve over someone unknown led to a discussion of how to gather information about him.[18]

It was suggested that a committee of three go to Vicksburg, hear him preach, consult with his people, and get some sense of his strengths and flaws. B. H. Levy suggested a better plan: namely, invite Rabbi Solomon to Savannah—if that would not put him in jeopardy—to meet with the people and to deliver a trial sermon. One way or another, the board was given authority to investigate thoroughly and to seek his ministrations. Mendes' status was considered and the position of rabbi-emeritus was officially conferred by the congregation, with the understanding that

> no one would deny him to lecture and perform such duties as he felt able to do.[19]

On February 19, 1903, a letter was read stating that Solomon would come to Savannah. A special committee of the board (with female escorts) was appointed to look after his welfare and to entertain him suitably.[20]

During the week of March 1, 1903, George Solomon arrived in the city "at the depot," and was interviewed and greeted by many.[21] His official election took place at a special convocation on March 8th. A.E. Smith recommended that the initial election be for one year, with a six-months' notice clause, at $2,500 per annum. A.S. Guckenheimer amended the motion to eliminate the one year term and stipulated "that he be elected for no specified term."[22] The initial election was unanimous.

The election meeting also provided a forum for disposing of the Mendes' issue. There were men of high impulse who wanted a commitment to Mendes for his entire life span, in recognition of his serving the congregation

> well for 25 years and [because he] stands so well in the community and has brought the social position of the Jews of this city, to the high standard it now enjoys.[23]

Others felt the commitment was too broad. Who knew what the future would bring for the congregation, and whether the younger generation would honor their parents' wishes? Albeit A. S. Guckenheimer offered a motion to elect Mendes

> minister emeritus . . . with fixed salary never to be less than $1800 per year, increasing if the Board has the necessary wherewithal.

A slight modification (raising the limit to $1,800 *or* $2,100) was carried unanimously, and the rabbi was made emeritus "for life."[24]

SOLOMON'S RABBINATE—PHASE I

It will simplify the process of analysis to divide George Solomon's forty-two year ministry into two phases: 1903 until the end of World War I, phase I; and 1920-1945, phase II. The first period was given to establishing himself as *the* rabbi and leader and connecting the institution *officially to Reform Judaism*. The second period was devoted to nurturing new structures in the Jewish community and building up "Mickva" Israel internally. Overlap occurred, so the categories should not be considered as inflexible.

In his acceptance letter, Rabbi Solomon revealed youthful exuberance:

> It is my earnest hope that I may fill all the expectations of the members of the congregation, and I trust the unanimity of sentiment displayed on the occasion of my election, may continue as long as I am spared to fill the position . . . with the further pledge that the best of which I am capable will always be at the service of Mickva Israel, I am
>
> Sincerely yours,
> George Solomon[25]

Upon arriving in Savannah, he was to discover that the sightless Mendes was still a powerful leader in the congregation and community. Evidence that Solomon was prepared to take a back seat flows from the Jewish community rally over the Kishinev Pogrom (mentioned in the last chapter), a rally that Mendes dominated. So long as the "Emeritus-for-Life" had life there is no mention in the minutes of Solomon's energetic control. That situation was to change abruptly.

On June 28, 1904, the board met at 210 Gwinnett Street, the Mendes' residence, to make arrangements for the interment service of its deceased emeritus. The date of June 30th at 5:00 p.m. (at the temple) was chosen. Dr. David Marx of Atlanta was asked to deliver the eulogy, Rabbi Solomon being assigned the reading of the liturgy. The pallbearers included Joseph Rosenheim, Lee Roy Myers, B. H. Levy, Max L. Byck, Abe E. Smith, A. A. Solomons, Jacob Weichselbaum, and Lawrence Lippman. Honorary pallbearers were Joseph M. Solomons, Dr. T. J. Charlton, Abram Falk, Judge Samuel B. Adams, Amson Mohr, Dr. E. R. Corson, Dr. Julian Chisholm, Samuel Herman, Rev. Charles H. Strong of St. John's Church, Rev. John D. Jordon of First Baptist Church, and former *shammashim*, J. Mirsky and Henry Boley. In death as in life, Mendes retained an Orthodox inclination, requesting no flowers, and all in attendance be garbed in "hats."[26] The costs were underwritten by the congregation, and all arrangements were placed in the hands of "Messr. Hendersons undertakers."[27] The coffin was opened for a last view, one hour before the service.[28] Music was sounded in the sanctuary as the casket entered to Leybach's *Funeral March*.[29] The merchants of the temple closed their establishments for the time of the funeral, advertisements to that effect appearing in the local press.[30] En masse the people of B.B. Jacob attended to pay a final tribute.[31] Members of the family who came to the funeral included I. O. de Castro of New Orleans, Mr. H. J. Williams of New York, and Dr. H. Pereira Mendes, rabbi of New York's Shearith Israel.[32] Notice of the death was carried in this country and abroad and was reported in *The American Israelite* (July 7, 1904), the *Jewish Spectator* (July 1, 1904), the *Hebrew Standard* (no date), and the *Jewish Chronicle of London* (July 8, 1904).[33]

The congregation agreed to provide a stipend to Mendes' widow of $100 per month for the first year, $83.33 monthly for the second two years, $75 per month until June of 1909, the end of the fifth year.[34] In the instance of Mrs. Mendes' death, the remainder was to be deposited to her estate. This was in addition to the insurance policy which the congregation had underwritten since early in Mendes' ministry. Four pages of the minute books were given to an elaborately drawn resolution of the board.[35] The newspaper was given a copy which was published on July 19, 1904.[36] Finally, in 1906, a body of women petitioned the board for a marble plaque to be placed near the De la Motta tablet to honor the memory of the Portuguese rabbi. All costs they agreed to absorb, so the board willingly complied.[37] (The tablet remains on the Gordon Street side of the sanctuary.)

Sensitive to the impact all of this outpouring of affection was having on the new rabbi, the congregation, in meeting assembled on the 3rd of July, 1904, expressed

> its appreciation of the labors of its Rev. Rabbi Geo. Solomon during his incumbancy [*sic*] and particularly commends the works of benevolence and broad philanthropy he has so zealously undertaken and accomplished.

Increasing his salary by twenty percent also helped. At the same meeting, a vacation was granted to him immediately. All of which can be read as signs that the congregation wanted to show kindness to their new spiritual guide, even as proprieties and affection required paying appropriate tribute to their deceased rabbi.

AN EXPLOSION OF REFORMS

The end of the Mendes years marked the termination of gradualism. In seeking a new rabbi, the congregation turned to the Hebrew Union College and now had one of its graduates in the pulpit. Laity and spiritual leader alike pursued a rapid course of reformation.

Here in outline form is the series of changes:

1904, January 10—8:30 p.m. Friday night services were instituted (on motion of A.S. Guckenheimer and A.E. Smith).

1904, January 10—the congregation joined the Union of American Hebrew Congregations (U.A.H.C.).

1904, April 7—the congregation was urged to have representation to the Central Conference of American Rabbis at Louisville, Kentucky (on motion of A.S. Guckenheimer and J.E. Gutman that the matter be placed in the president's hands). The C.C.A.R. is composed of the Reform rabbis of this Nation and Canada.

1904, April 10—the *Union Prayer Book* for the High Holidays was adopted (on motion of A.S. Guckenheimer and S. Herman, amended slightly by A.A. Solomons, Jr.). The congregation wanted to retain some of the Portuguese "minach" [*sic*] so that its history would not be totally overturned. The rabbi was to incorporate portions of the latter into the Reform prayers.

1907, October 27—a bill from the U.A.H.C. was submitted and paid, evidence of a fiscal attachment.[38]

1907, December 24—the religious school prayerbook, originally written by Mendes, was revised by Solomon to reflect a Reform perspective.

1908, January 12—Saturday morning worship was changed from 10:30 a.m. to 10:00 a.m. to last no more than one hour (motion of B. H. Levy). The Committee on Public Worship was to take the motion under advisement. The fact that such a committee existed was also evidence of a reform, Orthodox congregations reposing all matters of ritual in the hands of the rabbi.

1908, January 30—Rabbi Solomon received board permission to institute a series of midweek lectures for both the congregation and the *community*.

1909, January 4—the congregation appointed B.J. Apple delegate to the U.A.H.C. convention in Philadelphia, scheduled for January 19. Due to sickness, Rabbi Solomon substituted.

1909, May 10—a connection was established with the Jewish Chautauqua Society, a Reform organization to disseminate information about Jews and Judaism through public lectures on college campuses and elsewhere. Rabbi Solomon was sent as a delegate to the annual meeting of the J.C.S.

1909, October 14—the congregation has its first *all* Gentile choir and organist.

1911, January 22—K.K.M.I. became a "free" synagogue for a period of one year.

1913, January 12—a leading Reform rabbi, Dr. Abram Simon of the Washington Hebrew Congregation, was the first speaker in a "scholar-in-residence" program instituted by Rabbi Solomon.

1913, January 12—Solomon proposed an exchange of pulpits among Reform rabbis in the region.

1916, November 16—the Temple Guild was officially renamed the Temple Sisterhood.

1917, January 7—the ladies of the congregation were present, for the first time, at an annual meeting and given the privilege of participating in the discussions and voting.

1918, June 18—only Friday evening services were held in the summer. Saturday services were suspended.

1919, January 9—Rabbi Solomon proposed that a Temple Brotherhood be formed, and, on motion of Judge Charles Feidelson, the resolution to create such a body was unanimously endorsed.

1919, January 9—the newly revised *Union Prayer Book* was recommended by Rabbi Solomon.

The minutes reflect not only Reform developments within the congregation, but steps in the building of the Reform Movement nationally. In addition to the above-mentioned examples (i.e., the Jewish Chautauqua Society, the Temple Brotherhood, and Temple Sisterhood) the following should be added:

(1) In 1913, a Bureau of Synagogue and School Extension was created to strengthen congregations in rural areas and to prepare at minimum expense texts for religious schools.[39] This was the forerunner of two departments presently functioning at the U.A.H.C.—the Department of Synagogue Administration and the Department of Education and Publications. In 1913 the Union invited the congregation to appoint a member to its Advisory Board.[40]

(2) The same report mentioned the dedication of new buildings at the Cincinnati campus of the Hebrew Union College (H.U.C.) at the 1913 Biennial Meeting of the Union of American Hebrew Congregations.

(3) Outreach programs by professors of the college were also mentioned, as the visit of Professor Julian Morgenstern (later H.U.C. President) to Savannah, to provide instruction for religious school teachers in the area of Jewish history.[41]

Heritage and tradition were not easily overturned. The crescendo of reforms at K.K.M.I. was opposed and, on occasion, reversed. In an age when "classical" Reform was the rage, the members of the temple defined themselves as "conservatively reformed [sic]." Mendes' relative, H. Pereira Mendes, president (and founder) of the Union of Orthodox Jewish Congregations, made overtures to K.K.M.I. that were received as information rather than acted upon (January 7, 1906). The question of the time for Shabbat worship was one that surfaced again and again. In 1904, A. A. Solomons requested a restoration of the sunset hour for Sabbath and holiday prayer.[42] Even after the 8:30 p.m. service was adopted, I. A. Solomons made a motion to change it to before dinner, rather than after.[43]

The most telling evidence of a "conservative" Reform tendency was the engagement of a cantor. In 1915, the board retained the services of Cantor Joseph Goldberger.[44] Rabbi Solomon was the one who proposed the office, and he was the one who was delighted when the decision was made to rehire Goldberger.[45] The cantor possessed a fine voice, but facility in English he did not command, making it difficult for him to manage a volunteer choir which the congregation desired (particularly in the summer months when the regular choir was on vacation).[46] His contract lasted until July 1st and with that ended the post.[47] Sol Hirsch, chairman of the Choir Committee, was not opposed to the cantor per se, but only to the incumbent. He wanted a man well versed in English, a capable musician who could substitute for the rabbi during his absence, provide direction for the volunteers, and "take over the collections of the congregation."[48] Such a combination was not easily found, and a replacement, though desired, remained in the breech. George Solomon's "cantorial find" in Wildwood, New Jersey, S. Kobisch, agreed to render the traditional melodies at $50 per month, but the board's pleasure was not forthcoming. The low estate of the finances dampened the enthusiasm.[49]

HIGH MOMENTS

The first stage of the Solomon rabbinate was marked by creativity and focused leadership. What is noticed, in particular, were his problem solving skills, an aptitude for energizing members, and managerial capacities.

In 1906, he instituted a tradition that obtains in the congregation to this day. At the annual congregational meeting, the president reported to the assembled body that the rabbi was present and that he "desired to address the members on various matters."[50] Solomon stood before his people and declared their deficiencies. Attendance at temple was poor and they bore responsibility for it; and the Sunday school children were not encouraged by their parents to value religious education or worship services properly.

The following year, he reiterated his criticism—"better attendance is needed at Sabbath services," and added a theme that would be repeated—the need to build a new Sunday school building.[51] This time the congregation wanted him to know that, despite its inaction, it still reposed confidence in his leadership.

In 1908, he escalated the challenge. To the January 12th meeting he issued a call for a *new temple building* claiming spatial constraints limited membership and commodious Sunday school facilities. The only solution was to erect a larger structure. A committee was formed to deal with the issue. It recommended postponing action until the real needs of the congregation could be ascertained.

In 1909, the issue of the religious school was brought forth by the Religious School Committee. Having purchased a series of maps as educational tools, it reported that the facility did not allow them to be displayed, robbing the children of available materials. The limited space made the task of instructing the young impossible. To dramatize the problem, the rabbi conducted all classes himself, each grade on a different day, inconveniencing the parents.[52] Again no action resulted.

Two years later, Rabbi Solomon's address was included in the *Temple Minutes.* An excerpt follows:

> The bald truth is that there is practically an utter lack of interest in all things pertaining to the synagogue on the part of the congregation. The notion seems to be getting annually more prevalent that the Rabbi and the President constitute the congregation. . . . My experience has been . . . coming home after the summer trip, after visiting some of the larger congregations in the great cities . . . that they point out to me how far we fall short of many things there seen.[53]

The rabbi cited a forty percent diminution in synagogue attendance, both on Friday evenings and Saturday mornings, and a similar statistic for the religious school, which he accounted for thusly:

> The children of the orthodox [*sic*] people who formerly came to us, now have a school of their own . . .

To combat the disinterest, he suggested later Friday night services (during the cooler season) and suspending all worship from April 2 to August 31. Also advocated was an "emergency fund" which he could use to bring Jewish orators to Savannah in hopes that the Sabbath crowd might swell.

For George Solomon, 1911 was a low point, as attested to in his forthright evaluation of his role:

> With our present arrangement, the rabbi is a sort of general utility man for the congregation, many smaller and almost menial duties falling to his lot. No man can successfully be manager, errand boy and clerk all in one. . . .

Additionally, he called for triennial meetings of the congregation, expanding the six member *adjunta* to twelve, and following the example of his
colleague, Dr. Henry Berkowitz, by raising dues and assessments for those
who could afford increase.

Of most significance for his ministry was his view of the purpose of the
synagogue. He envisioned it as

> a bringing of people nearer, not only to God, but primarily . . . to
> each other. There is unfortunately an utter lack of this feeling in our
> synagogue. It can and should be there. The stranger, Jew or non-
> Jew, should particularly be made welcome. . . .

A major development occurred between the 1911 and 1912 annual meetings. Solomon, together with his close associate, Judge Charles N. Feidelson,
organized the forerunner of the Savannah Jewish Council. It was
called the *Federated Hebrew Charities*. A call was issued to each Jewish
organization and institution in town, including the temple, to support and
cooperate.[54] Committees of three were to be chosen for a joint meeting a
month later to formulate an umbrella organization (a council). The role
of the F.H.C. was to act

> as an information bureau, as a logical instrument for the collection
> and payment of our larger charities and as an authentic weapon for
> the fighting of local evils.

George Solomon served as temporary chairman.

The temple board rejected the proposal as foreign to its purposes.[55]
While dispensing *tzedakah* (charity) had been one of its functions since
the Federal period, the temple, under Solomon Cohen, ceased to assume
responsibility for what individual Jews were mandated by Jewish law to do.

George Solomon plowed ahead with his vision, and, by 1916, was accepting plaudits for fathering the newest Jewish institution in Savannah, a
Jewish Center (the *Jewish Educational Alliance*).

In the 1912 annual report, the subject of the Federated Hebrew Charities
was glossed over. Divine services and religious school were his concern. In
the former category, another twenty-five percent drop was recorded, sixty-
five percent over a two year span. George Solomon was weary of rows of
wood, unsoiled by human flesh. Sunday school enrollment did pick up,
which gave him "some small measure of consolation." His words for his
generation appeal to children of the age of anxiety.

> I find some hope and consolation in the reflection that though we
> may long flaunt the advice of the physician, persisting in our un-
> natural method of living, we have eventually to submit to his treat-
> ment to win back shattered health and nerves. The pace [of life] has
> become so fast and furious, and the life of average men and women
> is so empty, inane, and vacuous, that a change must soon come. . . .[56]

In addition to advocating a new temple and more equitable dues, the rabbi took a new tact, not advocated by the Placement Bureau of the Central Conference of Rabbis.

> Ever since I have been the Rabbi of this Congregation, your Board of Trustees has contained some of my warmest and closest friends, yet I feel in duty bound to assert that, on the above qualifications [congregational leaders who are interested in Jewish life and eager to serve in God's house], it has never been properly representative. . . . We need and should have a truly representative Board; we can get it only if the members of the congregation attend the annual meetings and perform their full duty in the selection and election of their officers.[57]

Other items that demanded congregational attention were the choir, the conduct of funerals in the home (to which Solomon strongly objected), and the inclusion of women on the Religious School Committee.

For last, the rabbi reserved comment about three major gifts that the congregation had received in 1912: the brass *menorahs* (that grace the pulpit today), presented by Mrs. Ida Seeburger; the *ner tamid* (eternal light) which D. A. Byck donated (yet burning); and a bronze *hanukkiah* (a Chanukkah *menorah*), an anonymous thanksgiving offering. The rabbi suggested that further tokens might be presented to the sanctuary:

> A birthday, an anniversary, an engagement or a wedding might well be commemorated by a gift to the synagogue. . . .[58]

Then he recommended a "permanent improvement fund" for the combined purpose of improving the present building and for *"the erection of a new synagogue."* (Italics added.) Solomon told his people that he had been aware that "estates aggregating easily and constructively two million dollars have been left" since his ministry commenced, and, of that sum, the synagogue should have been partial beneficiary.

By 1913, temple attendance was described as "wretchedly poor," and it mattered not when the rabbi conducted services on Friday—early or late it was still a losing proposition. A record fifty percent increase in the religious school enrollment was a positive sign, save

> there is an absolute lack of interest and encouragement on the part of the congregation and of the parents.

A board member came to religious school on one occasion which the rabbi described as "mere accident."

Three items of consequence filled Solomon's 1913 report. (1) He suggested that each temple committee submit a budget so that the congregation could operate in a more business-like fashion.

> Many times during the year I have been called upon to assume

direction of business affairs of the congregation with which of right I have no right or duty.[59]

This was a revelation, which the board, at its next meeting, requested the rabbi to clarify.[60] (2) Solomon claimed that an active Membership Committee was vital because

> I know there are fully 50, of the *same class, if not directly of the same blood as our present membership*, that I could add to our roster.[61]

In Solomon's mind, the synagogue was all-embracing, and Jews of non-Germanic ancestry he welcomed, though he sensed hesitancy on the part of the leadership. The earlier separations between Sephardic and Ashkenazic Jews had a later counterpart in the divisions between Jews of German extraction and those whose origins were eastern-European. (3) The 1913 annual meeting provided Solomon with an opportunity to speak about the Union of American Hebrew Congregations and the Hebrew Union College, the central institutions of Reform. To him *Reform* and *American* were interchangeable terms. He declared:

> Every American Jewish congregation loyally and generously should support the Union, for during the past 25 years it has been the one source whence we can draw our Rabbis fitted for the American pulpit.[62]

In response to Solomon's sense of failure (due to poor attendance at worship and the disinterest of the members), the Board of Trustees tried to lift his spirits with a gift in 1913. In acknowledgement, he wrote:

> Public service, and most particularly the ministry, while it is the highest and noblest field of endeavor, has its corresponding difficulties. Though in common with all who honestly and earnestly try to do such work, I have had my heartaches and periods of despondency, I have never fallen into despair, for whatever the discouragement, there was always hope and cheer in the knowledge of the kindly friendship and encouraging sympathy of the officers of this congregation.[63]

The bound minutes of the congregation are lacking the written reports of the 1914 and 1915 annual meetings. Only the financial statements for the latter were included in the official record.[64] The mystery surrounding these vital documents awaits another investigator, for no clue is forthcoming from archival materials or conversations.[65]

OVER THERE

The years prior to America's entry into World War I were not marked by isolation. On February 4, 1915, the German government announced a "war zone" in the Atlantic, *verboten* to all ships, military and civilian. Submarines ploughed the seas and sank on sight any offending vessel. Formal protests by our government did not dissuade the Germans from sinking the *Lusitania* in May of 1915, resulting in a loss of 124 Americans. After other sinkings and a clear backing away from an illegal procedure (no "search" operations were conducted before torpedoing the vessels), a dynamic was operative that led to preparations for war. Following the Battle of Jutland in the spring of 1916, British naval superiority was questionable, and America's vital shipping links to Europe were no longer secure. The cogs of the Nation's military-industrial complex began meshing. A Council of National Defense and a U.S. Shipping Board were established to ensure preparedness on an unprecedented scale. The temporary lull of the 1916 Presidential election was shattered by submarine damage to U.S. shipping as 1917 dawned. This led to the War Resolution by Congress on April 4, 1917. America was a fully committed belligerent.[66]

The Savannah Jewish community responded to the war effort with fervor (in contrast to the populace of Georgia which, on the whole, was less caught up in jingoism). The popularist politician-turned-bigot, Tom Watson, used every forum to oppose the draft; cotton prices fell almost two-thirds and President Wilson's popularity collapsed with it.[67] Eventually, the tendency was turned around and Georgia became a full participant in the conflict, though the impact of the war upon the state was in the territory of a ripple.

To pay for the military buildup, Congress enacted four Loan Acts, known as the "Liberty Loans," in April of 1917.[68] Julia Feist Solomon, the rabbi's wife and president of the Sisterhood, informed the annual meeting of 1918 that the monies which the ladies had raised to recarpet the sanctuary would instead be invested in Liberty Bonds. (The cemetery trustees likewise reported to the congregation that their funds had been similarly disposed of.)[69] Mrs. Solomon's 1918 Sisterhood report also contained a plea for being charitable to the synagogue as well as the Red Cross and the Liberty Loan.

The irrationality of war tends to remove self-confidence in what human hands can achieve, inclining us to the Ultimate Power in command of "nations and men." Hence, Solomon's jeremiads were not required at the 1918 annual meeting. Temple attendance was improving rapidly since 1915, and the religious school was "exceptionally large."[70] In 1917, the rabbi gave no report, the consequence of an illness that required hospitalization.[71] By 1918, some carping about poor attendance was heard again, though the condemnatory rabbinic tones were wondrously restrained. In 1919, as the battle was winding down and the grief and shock over Americans killed and maimed touched home, the rabbi could report four special services which attracted the multitudes and convinced him

   that religion, and the House of God have deeper hold than we
   knew . . .[72]

Shortages are expected in a time of crisis. Herbert Hoover, as head of the Food Administration, advocated "wheatless and meatless" days as well as "war" gardens. Coal and oil supplies were under the control of a Fuel Administration because foreign trade was off and importations of these vital energy sources were curbed.[73] In Mrs. Solomon's 1918 Sisterhood annual report, she included this statement,

> With cries of a coal famine on all sides and wanting to conserve the coal as much as possible we decided to do away with the heating of the Synagogue for the Choir rehearsal.

Hence the Sisterhood bought two oil stoves "to drive away the chill."[74] The pump organ in the chapel was removed to the sanctuary, the only heated room on Sunday mornings during the winter season. All religious education classes were conducted in the Gothic assembly hall. The result was not too pleasing, eliciting these comments from the *rebbitzen* (rabbi's spouse):

> Many are the complaints that have been registered about the synagogue being cold and damp.

Rabbi Solomon asked leave of the congregation in August of 1917 to attend "food conservation classes" in Washington.[75]

It was not only on the home front that the fight was waged. Sons of K.K.M.I. entered the military, risking life and limb. In December, 1917, Leopold Adler suggested that the board keep upon the roll of membership

> without charge of dues any member of the congregation serving in the Army or Navy of the United States.[76]

After the war, a Roll of Honor was prepared and was proudly displayed in the temple vestibule.[77]

If there are pivotal points in each man's rabbinate, 1918-1919 were Rabbi Solomon's. His actions so elated the members that the only *public* congregational meeting in the history of Mickve Israel took place on October 20, 1918. It is described in the minutes thusly:

> A special *open air meeting* of the congregation was held this day on *Wayne Street* between our Temple and the First Presbyterian Church. . . . (Italics added.)

And why should the affairs of Savannah Israelites be aired on a thoroughfare in the heart of the city (for all passersby to see and hear)? Answer: A proud congregation of Jews was about to confer authority upon its spiritual leader to serve in the military of the American Nation. Chaplain George Solomon would be the symbol of Savannah Jewry's love for their land.

At the 1918 annual meeting, the rabbi forewarned his people,

as the months pass we will have painful enough evidence that it is
our very existence that is at stake.

Solomon was no warmonger:

> I need hardly waste your time or mine in repeating that I am in no
> sense a militarist. With every fibre of my being, I hate war and all it
> stands for. For this very reason I am in violent opposition to the
> pacifist doctrine.

The Prussian menace was so threatening to the ideals of western democracies
that only a conclusive victory was acceptable as a goal. Having read the war
literature of the past, Rabbi Solomon had no illusions about the evil inherent in warfare. To him it was repulsive to play on the glory of battle and
to unleash hate in men's hearts. The thunder in Europe was evidence that
the idea of individualism, without responsibility to community and nation,
was an idea out of joint. The prophetic dream (in this context he quoted
Lincoln's "of the people, for the people, and by the people") of communal
cooperation for the common weal was the only dream that had withstood the
test of time.

The rabbi had earlier taken on "welfare work" for the Jewish soldiers in
nearby camps. To serve the fifty thousand Jewish fighting men who would
safeguard the Nation was the most important task any rabbi could shoulder,
and if the congregation must suffer, so be it. The Emergency Fund, set up to
bring speakers to Mickve Israel, was diverted to the needs of the young men
in the "cantonments" he served. On October 16, 1918, Rabbi Solomon
addressed a letter to the board requesting an indefinite leave of absence and
detailing the need for Jewish chaplains. A document was appended to it
from the War Department, asking him to appear at the examining board
at Camp Wheeler and to make plans for possible induction in November.
Knowing the technicalities of his rabbinic contract (which required six
months' notice in the instance of official severance), Solomon explained the
nature of the emergency and informed the board that the Hebrew Union
College was offering students in

> the eighth and ninth year classes to fill the pulpits of such Rabbis as
> are drafted. . . .

Before signing off, he gave way to noble sentiment:

> Realizing as you must what it must mean for me to leave the wife and
> the home and friends I dearly love, I need hardly emphasize the fact
> that in taking this step I am influenced by the conviction that the
> paramount duty of the hour is the answering of our country's call.[78]

Included in the congregational record is a formal letter from the New York
headquarters of the Jewish Welfare Board, informing all congregations
that, if requested, their rabbis ought to be granted leaves of absence for the

duration of the war, and that the difference in salary, resulting from a reduced military schedule, be made up by the "mother" synagogue. Among the signatories were Jacob Schiff, Nathan Strauss, and Louis Marshall, with J. Walter Freiberg signing for the Union of American Hebrew Congregations. At the aforementioned open-air meeting of October 20, 1918, the "leave" was granted. On motion of Hugo Frank, a committee was created to take into account the best interests of K.K.M.I. and to procure suitable rabbinic ministrations. Judge Charles N. Feidelson assumed the work of minister in Solomon's absence.[79] From time to time, President Joseph Rosenheim officiated as well.[80]

For only five months Rabbi Solomon was out of the city. Military leaves were granted to him to attend to weddings and funerals. Serving thousands of Jewish boys, he suggested, prepared him to serve the young men of the local community. Four aforementioned services, held during 1918, impressed him. He commented on them at the annual meeting of 1919: the first was "a day of prayer and meditation" which the President enjoined upon Americans all; the second occurred on November 11th, when the Armistice Treaty was signed; the third was "Thanksgiving Day last;" and the fourth, the observance of New Year in the temple, January 1, 1919. Each event was marked "by solemnity" and "spontaneity," an atmosphere of "interest and devotion, worthy of note."

To begin the process of transformation from war to peace, Solomon suggested a reception for the forty-or-so veterans, all products of K.K.M.I., who would soon return.[81] Plans would have to be made, he advocated, to give them an honored place in their House of God. How? A Temple Brotherhood should be organized. A bulletin should be published by the Brotherhood at frequent intervals to stimulate synagogue attendance. In another vein, he challenged the Sisterhood to take on tasks other than housekeeping, being to the temple what the National Council of Jewish Women was to the community. Also, a "Sinking Fund" or "Extension Fund" needed to be developed, which would provide resources for meeting the basics of the budget. Then the temple could eliminate pew rents and survive on "free will offerings." K.K.M.I. needed to be a "free" synagogue in the tradition of Rabbi Stephen Wise's New York synagogue. Each of these suggestions was eventually picked up and implemented.

The people of K.K.M.I. were solidly behind the war effort and exhibited signs of patriotism. The following factors may have contributed to the gestalt:

A. *The Leo Frank Case* in 1915. Whatever the root factors that led to the trial and conviction of Leo Frank and his subsequent lynching—anti-Semitism spouted from Christian pulpits, the economic dislocations induced by recessions, or the unsettled conditions during the shift from a rural southern economy to a more urban, industrialized system—the consequence of the case was horrendous to Georgia Jews.[82] Popularist Thomas E. Watson used xenophobia for political purposes and filled *Watson's Maga-*

zine and the *Weekly Jeffersonian* with anti-Semitic slurs.[83] Southern Jewry, witnessing Jew-hatred in a century of "progress" (in a state that had been native soil for Jews for nine score years) was left reeling. Two years later, when the President and Congress set into motion the machines of war, the Jewish community may have seen this as an opportunity to demonstrate Americanism.

B. *Immigration.* From 1880 on, waves of the "tempest-tossed" took up residence in America, many in the South. They were viewed as clinging together, retaining "Old World" ways, and turning sections of American cities into "European slums."[84] The radicalism of the labor movement was attributed generally to the presence of "foreign agitators."[85] Americans began to question the loyalty of those who were strangers to these shores. The Immigration Bill put before the President in 1915 required a literacy test, and was opposed by the U.A.H.C.[86] Congressman Charles Edwards of the First District of Georgia received a telegram from President Joseph Rosenheim stating:

> The congregation Mickve Israel, representing in large part the Jewish community of Savannah, respectfully requests and urges you to work and vote against the passing of the Immigration Bill over the veto of the President.[87]

This position may have resulted in the need to demonstrate Jewish support of the American involvement in World War I.

C. *Anti-Germanic Sentiments.* Congregation Mickve Israel may have had Portuguese roots, but its membership during the war years was primarily German-Jewish. War breeds intolerance for the enemy *and* for those who, by extraction, may harbor "dual" loyalties. The German language was practically eliminated from American high schools and colleges. Citizens of foreign extraction were made to feel inferior to native Americans. Artists and musicians of German background were publicly humiliated, including Frederick Stock and Fritz Kreisler.[88] To convince others of their loyalty to the Nation, the people of K.K.M.I. dedicated substance and strength to the war effort.

Again, in citing these subliminal factors, it is speculative as to whether they were operative in decision-making processes. Rabbi George Solomon was *the* leader, and independence of thought characterized his ministry.

ZIONISM

The end of the war opened up a new chapter in the changeful career of the Jewish people. George Solomon put it this way at the annual meeting of 1919:

> Jewish history is the spiritual epitome of world history, it is but natural that the latest development of human history closely touches the life and future of the Jew.

Palestine has been officially guaranteed by the allied powers as *A* if not *THE* homeland of the Jew. The position of the Jew must now be definitely determined. Both for himself and the outer world he must decide what he is and what he wants to be. His attitude toward Jewish national[ism] or Zionism demands to be settled. (Italics added.)

Calling the question "all important and all absorbing," he directed his people to attend open forums where scrutiny could be given to every position. Prophetically, he concluded,

> . . . Yes, the very essentials of our existence and our present and future status in the world will be caught up in the issue of the Third Commonwealth.[89]

Joseph Rosenheim, in April of 1918, brought to the attention of the board the request of "Miss Leon of Palestine," who wished to have a mass meeting at Mickve Israel for the purpose of interesting all Jews in the city in the "Restoration Fund of Palestine."[90] On April 14th, the meeting was held in the Mordecai Sheftall Chapel, with Congregation B'nai B'rith Jacob and its president, Mr. Weitz, as guests. The issue of Zion restored was not as yet engaged at K.K.M.I., and Rabbi Solomon, as his predecessor, saw it as in the hands of Providence. At this stage, as throughout much of his life, Solomon *vacillated* on the issue of *a* homeland for Jews on ancestral soil.

IDEOLOGY AND ACHIEVEMENTS

In 1904 (March 12th) at the Central Conference of American Rabbis' convention in Birmingham, Alabama, Rabbi Solomon was honored by preaching the conference sermon. The text, preserved among his papers in the Temple Archives, advocated a view of Zionism opposed to that which he expressed at the end of World War I. He rejected the thesis of Max Nordau,

> that the genius of the Jew tends to politics, hence Zionism, or the establishment of a Hebrew nation in Palestine, is the only solution to the problem [of the secularity of Jews and their apathy to spiritual considerations].

He disavowed Zangwell's solution to the Jewish problem:

> disappearance (assimilation), national regeneration, i.e., Zionism, or religious regeneration . . .

This appeared to him as "epigrammatic brilliancy." Solomon remonstrated that Zionism "even if realized, would not completely solve the problem." Why?

The most superficial knowledge of Jewish history conclusively shows that the Jew as a nation was an absolute failure.

In his day, he reckoned that only

the spiritual[ly] as well as materially poorer element . . . would form the projected state

so

Zionism would be but a confession of weakness. It would be an inglorious retreat from the position won by centuries of splendid achievement. For the Jew to retire from the world and return to Palestine, would be to justify the hatred, the scorn, and contempt that have been heaped upon them.[91]

Israel would no longer be "a light unto the nations."[92]

Espousing an elitist solution, namely that "when the sublime idea . . . was revealed to Abraham," he found it "impossible to impress it on his kinsmen," (and so too Moses, the Judges, the Prophets, etc.), Solomon argued that Jewish leaders, not the people, were always the movers and shakers:

It was the unremitting labor of the Rabbis and teachers that kept Judaism alive, since all the while the masses . . . were lukewarm or indifferent to their faith. . . .[93]

Accepting this as the essential condition of the ministry, he advocated abandoning

all kinds of fads, fashions and novelties to make the synagogue attractive. The time has come to recognize that if the synagogue is to exert a lasting influence then it must assume a more strictly Jewish character.

Believing that there is a yearning in Jews for "the bread of religion," he questioned why

so many of our pulpits persist in offering the dazzling, brilliant, but no less satisfying stones of everything else but religion, and especially Judaism.

Rejecting a ministry of words, Solomon sounded his personal credo:

Nine years of experience has [sic] impressed upon me the fact that we can never expect to accomplish anything through our preaching, unless we make the most of the chances given for exerting close *personal* influence over our people.[94] (Italics added.)

Solomon held fast to this vision of the rabbi's role. In an undated sermonic outline, he concluded: "never rest satisfied—always have an ideal to attain." To this end he projected his goals: "(a) spiritualize cong. (b) Judaize com[munity]," the instrument for accomplishing the goal being "Rabbi's person. A large factor." (c) "Trying to live up to my ideal—no sensationalism—progressive but not mere novelty."[95]

On the women's issue:

> The superior strength of might over right here plays a great part [in the repression of women] . . . we maintain that not nature, but external causes have made woman so far the physical inferior of man.[96]

Further:

> it is argued that woman's intellectual faculties are inferior to man's. This again is but a hasty and doubtful statement.[97]

And finally,

> Men have been very careful that women should not be men, but they do not see that man is fast becoming what they decided woman should not be, and have fallen into the feebleness which they have cultured so long in their companions.[98]

On Evolution:

> Science and religion are at one in the declaration that life is growth. . . .[99] The conflict between religion and science arises only from the blindness to the fact that these are not different and di-vergent, but correlated and interdependent methods of interpret-ing and expressing Life. Science, as the technique, discovering the laws of living, cannot explain or produce Life. . . . Religion, the supreme Art of Life, concerned with the essence of things, illumined with the visions which give color and joy and meaning to life, needs the aid of the technique to actualize and complete the picture. . . .[100] In this whole controversy the argument has hinged on the point as to the agreement of Evolution with the Bible. . . . To begin with the Bible is not and was not regarded by the Hebrews and subsequent teachers as a manual of history or a text book of science.[101]

With the knife of reason, he cut apart William Jennings Bryan's claim that the book of *Genesis* is the *immutable revelation of God*. His question was put thusly: How can

> Mr. Bryan and his ilk . . . explain by what dialectical subtlety they can divest the balance of this and subsequent books of the Old Testa-ment of their divine character, for *certainly they make no pretense of following its commands or accepting its standards.*[102] (Italics added.)

On Religion in the Schools:

The Chatham County School Board (in 1917) ordained that Christmas carols could be sung in the public schools and those

> whom the language of the songs offended would be granted permission to leave the room.

Pointing out the danger of this deviation from American standards (i.e., the separation of church and state), Rabbi Solomon argued that the mere recognition that offense could be taken with carol singing is argument enough not to inject it

> in the regular school hours and classes. . . . Its inclusion in any case is a tyrannical exercise of majority might. . . . It is neither fair nor a privilege to permit those children to whom it does not appeal, to leave the room . . . *it always requires a high degree of moral courage to pointedly and publicly disagree with the majority. Such courage is rare in adults and is wholly unreasonable to expect of children.*[103] (Italics added.)

Solomon's conclusion was that if public schools wished to have community Christmas trees and celebrations, *before* or *after* school hours was the appropriate time. In 1907, a letter appeared in the *Savannah Press* from the rabbi commenting on the effort in New York State to exclude Christianity from the classroom. The local press called it "an infidel propaganda," a movement fostered by a "band of blatant irreligionists." Countering the attack, Solomon argued

> that Church and State in this Republic are to be and to remain separate. While we all feel that religion is the greatest force making for civilization, . . . much of the warfare, and most of the suffering and bloodshed . . . has [sic] been caused by warring religious factions, each struggling for supremacy. Every truly religious man should hail as a boon any plan whereby religion is rendered secure from being brought into the arena of strife. Peace and goodwill, not antagonisms and prejudices and persecution are the ends of religion.[104]

Further Solomon gibed,

> the public schools are purely secular institutions. *They are the property of the whole people, paid for and maintained by . . . the citizens, generally, irrespective of religious or other affiliation. In them . . . should and can be taught only what is beneficial for and satisfactory to the people as a whole.*[105] (Italics added.)

On Socialism:

While rejecting socialism as an economic system, he understood it as a protest against injustices in the world:

> If the working man, or the less favored classes generally, have in
> socialism voiced their protest and have shown a tendency to become
> anxious to destroy law . . .

it was in reaction to the inequities in the criminal justice system. As a
prophetic Jew, Solomon decried inequity under law:

> We can ill afford to sneer at the follies of the laboring man's socialism,
> when our editors can find room for the joke that a man may expect ten
> years for stealing a dollar and six months if he is lucky to steal a
> million.[106]

The *Racial Issue* is not discussed in any surviving document. Members
of the rabbi's family recall him as providing leadership in establishing
harmony between blacks and whites in Savannah in this period.[107]

On Jewish issues he was equally outspoken. Of *Reform Judaism* he said:

> Reform Judaism is . . . an unfortunate term, and is employed only
> because of popular usage. "Historical" Judaism would be the more
> satisfactory and truer to the facts. . . . Judaism is a progressive un-
> folding, and unending growth . . . there can be no break in the
> continuity . . . the only "Reform" Judaism I can admit is to be found
> in the church or mosque, not in the synagogue.

In essence, Rabbi Solomon was saying that the difference between Reform
and Orthodoxy is in the recognition of the progressive, evolving character
of Judaism; Orthodoxy affirming that the principle of immutability is
operative; Reform declaring the opposite. Identifying the flaw in each
denomination, Solomon surmised:

> Orthodoxy may be said to think only of . . . finding its warrant and
> its life only in the past . . . while reform [*sic*] equally erroneously
> thinks only of the future, careless and heedless of the past.

As he conceived it,

> Modern liberal Judaism stands for a continuation of the historical
> character of Israel's faith. It . . . recognizes its debt to the past,
> hoping to influence the future, only by fidelity to the best of that
> past. It refuses to accept any ceremonial because it is a ceremonial, but
> it recognizes that only through the ceremonial can the religious life
> find expression. It would welcome and hold fast to every form in
> which breathes the spirit of Judaism.[108]

Hence Rabbi Solomon believed in bar mitzvah, *Rosh Chodesh* (the New
Moon holiday), and circumcision.[109] He created his own circumcision ceremony:

> Blessed be thy coming, little one. With prayerful benediction we wel-
> come thee into the covenant hallowed by Father Abraham in the long
> ago. May the sign with which we now mark they [*sic*] slender body

be ever more and more a symbol of the sublime teachings of the glorious faith it is intended to represent.

He believed that conversion had to be practiced according to *halachah* (Jewish law) including a rigorous examination.[110] Immersion in a *mikvah* (ritual bath) was however not stipulated.

His views on *confirmation* appeared in *The Jewish Conservator*. He declared,

> I believe . . . that one born a Jew can never be anything else, all attempts to make him so being but mere trumpetry.[111]

But accident of birth was not enough to be a Jew, hence confirmation was necessary. His definition of confirmation was

> The strengthening and impressing more fully through the medium of the *consecrating* service upon the Jewish consciousness of the child.[112]

It was *not* an entrance into Judaism, a time of formal affiliation with the congregation, or the end of religious training.[113]

The *Mixed Marriage* controversy obtained in his day. In a letter addressed to Mr. Victor H. Kriegshaber of Atlanta, he explained why he could not perform a wedding ceremony involving his niece, a Christian Scientist:

> I am firmly of the opinion that one can not be a Jew and a Christian scientist [*sic*], they are to me mutually exclusive.

Solomon's hands were tied not because of any personal views,

> but the Central Conference of American Rabbis has very definitely and unequivocally gone on record that Christian science [*sic*] is foreign to Judaism, and neither Dr. Marx nor I could take any other stand . . . as official representatives of Judaism, our concern is with purely Jewish matters and we decline to go outside of this.[114]

On Gentile Defenders of Israel's Faith. His letter to author, Madison C. Peters (who had announced a tour of the South at a reasonable price, if the rabbi of K.K.M.I. would set up the lecture), revealed his concern:[115]

> I regret to have to say that the project does not at all appeal to me

because

> it is high time . . . that the Jew should become aware of the high dignity which is his, and that he should resent, rather than welcome the patting on the back, which has of late become the vogue. . . . I have no right to question your high motives, nor would I presume to do so. Nonetheless, I must say that I do not think your lectures on this subject are productive of good.

Why? Only Jews attend. Those who are bigots "have not sufficient interest to come and listen."[116]

On Jews in Politics:

In 1906, the Hebrew Democratic Club was formed, and the local press brought it to the public's attention.[117] The next day, a letter from Solomon reached the editor:

> I wish to say that there is and can be no such thing as a Jewish political club. The present organization is in my mind the subtle work of some designing politician, and the few who compose it [actually there were 150] do not understand enough of the language and institutions to realize the nature of the club.[118]

After demeaning the members ("the prominence of the members is ludicrous"), he continued,

> I can unhesitatingly claim that I am voicing the sentiment of at least 95 percent of the Jewish citizenship of Savannah in calling the club a desecration of the Jewish religion. There is no Jewish vote here or elsewhere. I think I may rightly claim to have as much influence among the Jewish people of Savannah, of all classes, as any other one man, and I know it would be the height of folly for me to attempt to influence my people to vote one way or the other.

To defend his attack, the rabbi resorted to a Constitutional argument—church and state in America must be "irrevocably divorced." The Jew more than any other element in American society rejoices in his religious freedom, and "resents any mingling of politics with religion." A letter of protest was filed on December 21, 1906, with the Honorable George Cann, Judge of the Superior Court of Chatham County, requesting a denial of charter on similar grounds.[119] The newspaper editors published a comment, entitled "A Merited Rebuke" pointing out

> so far as politics is concerned, we are all Americans. . . . There is nothing in the local situation . . . requiring a distinctly Jewish organization.[120]

Another clipping, undated, contains the news that the "Hebrew Democratic Club may change its name." The new one chosen, out of deference to the rabbi, was "The Independent Democratic Club."[121]

Among the activities and appointments that marked Rabbi Solomon's early rabbinate were the following:

A. *Chaired the National Coordinating Committee for Refugees (Savannah Branch).* A letter addressed to him from I. Irving Lipsitch of the United Hebrew Charities, U.S. Immigration Station on Ellis Island, singled him out as *the* person in Savannah in charge of arranging for new immigrants (Russians) to be connected to kin. The letter was dated November 2, 1906.

B. *Chaired the Mass Meeting of Jews* which, in 1905, sent messages to the President, Senators Bacon and Clay, and Congressman Lester requesting the U.S. government seek ways to end the massacre of the Jews in the land of the Czars.[122]

C. *Participated in services of Rededication, Temple B'nai Israel, Columbus, Georgia.* He preached the dedicatory oration on February 8, 1908.[123] The rabbi also was a visitor to other pulpits in the area, as an article in the *Augusta Chronicle* confirmed.[124] The reporter wrote:

> The discourse before the congregation Children of Israel at the Temple yesterday morning by Dr. Geo. Solomon of Savannah, provided one of the most eloquent and inspiring addresses heard in that sacred edifice in a number of years.

Whether the intent was to flatter Solomon or distress the incumbent rabbi is unclear from the text.

D. *Addressed the Grand Lodge of the B'nai B'rith, District 5* (Southeast) at its annual meeting in Wilmington, North Carolina, in May, 1908.[125] He served the same Grand Lodge as secretary for many years, as attested to by his annual meeting messages which were generally typed on stationery bearing the masthead of this organization.

E. *Supervised District 13, Southern Georgia and Florida, Union of American Hebrew Congregations, Department of Synagogue and School Extension* under Rabbi George Zepin.[126]

F. *Addressed the Grand Lodge of Georgia Masons,* delivering the oration to those who earned their 18th degree in the Scottish Rite.[127] Solomon was a 33rd degree Mason and was Master Emeritus of Temple Chapter Rose Croix, Ancient and Accepted Scottish Rite. He also served as Past Master of Zerubabbel Lodge no. 15, F. & A. M.[128]

G. *Presented the annual memorial address to the Elks, and spoke before other civic clubs.*[129] An active Rotarian, he charged the Savannah Rotary Club to assist the needy boys of the community. His speech was partially responsible for the creation of the Big Brother movement in Savannah. (The text survives in the Temple Archives.)

H. *Initiated the Associated Charities Organization in Savannah,* as indicated in a speech preserved without date (after 1912 because of the heading "Mickve" Israel" on the stationery). The visit of Jacob Riis convinced Solomon and others that the consolidation of existing eleemosynary institutions was necessary to meet the needs of the disadvantaged in the city. After World War I, the rabbi was elected president of the General Charities Organization, the forerunner of the Community Chest and United Way.[130]

I. *Lectured annually for the Jewish Chautauqua Society at the University of North Carolina Summer School at Chapel Hill.* The *Raleigh News and Observer* reported that his presence was a distinct feature of the school, winning "the whole school with his first address." His public sessions "drew increasingly large audiences until the end."[131] Another clipping (undated) announced his address at the State Normal College in Greensboro, remarking,

> He is a man of profound scholarship and will certainly have something of great interest to say to the people of Greensboro. . . .

These special lectures were among the earliest endeavors of the Jewish Chautauqua Society.

THE JEWISH EDUCATIONAL ALLIANCE

Exceeding every other accomplishment of Solomon's early ministry was the creation of the Jewish Educational Alliance (J.E.A.). In his annual report to the congregation in 1916, the rabbi effervesced:

> I am deeply and humbly grateful to God that I have lived to see the completion of the Jewish Educational Alliance—the Jewish community club house—and I feel it is the one real contribution I have made to the welfare of this community.[132]

In its first publication, *The Scroll*, the Council of the J.E.A. outlined the process by which the new institution became a reality. In 1913, Colonel Sigo Myers and members of his family presented a gift of $25,000 for the erection of a "community center," this in memory of his brother, the deceased Mayor of Savannah, Herman Myers. Behind this gift was the persuasive power of Rabbi Solomon. *The Scroll* acknowledged it in announcing that the project was held dear by many but "by none more dearly than Rabbi Geo. Solomon." Once the Myers' bequest was in hand, all elements in the Jewish community were solicited, resulting in "a community enterprise in the fullest sense."[133]

The J.E.A. evolved indirectly from the Y.M.H.A. which had been on the Savannah scene before 1900.[134] The creation of a Federation of Hebrew Charities has been described in an earlier section, also the handiwork of George Solomon (and Charles N. Feidelson).[135] All Jewish organizations and agencies were invited, and from the initial meeting, the promise of community cooperation was realized. Meanwhile, the Council of Jewish Women conducted a mission kindergarten project (for Russian Jewish children), and, needing more space, the ladies brought their concerns to a dozen or so Jewish leaders.[136] There was unanimity in approving the Jewish kindergarten, and that led to a proposal to build a modest structure. Colonel Sigo Myers entered the picture, confiding to Rabbi Solomon his interest in a suitable memorial to his brother. Once the gift was publicly announced (in the winter of 1912), a board was constituted, a charter procured, and a lot purchased. The first J.E.A. was to be erected on Oglethorpe Avenue, just west of Barnard, in the vicinity of the Savannah Civic Center today. The land was purchased, but being inadequate to the size building required, it had to be sold and a profit of one thousand dollars was realized. A structure was finally raised on Pulaski Square, on the trust lot located on West Charlton and Barnard (in proximity to St. John's Episcopal Church). The 1914 building remains, having served most recently as the Salvation Army headquarters.[137] In the year required for construction, the Alliance rented a house on Barnard and Harris Streets.[138] The Building Committee was comprised almost entirely of Mickve Israelites: Sigo Myers, chairman, Adolph Shulhafer, Joseph Litchenstein, D. A. Byck, and George Solomon. Ben Weitz and Max Blumenthal were representatives of B.B. Jacob.

Rabbi Solomon's role in establishing mechanisms and negotiating the finances for the project put him in a delicate situation, so far as his own congregation was concerned. How could he advocate a new communal institution which would *rival* M.I. and *absorb* young people in leisure activity? To this the rabbi responded:

> I am not willing that its province [M.I.'s] be invaded. Everything of a strictly *religious* character must be centered here. Only matters of a larger *social* nature belong in the Alliance.[139] (Italics added.)

WITHIN THE TEMPLE COMMUNITY

The years 1902-1920 were marked by struggle and adjustment. Reforms were instituted which divided the congregation between those who saw change as threatening and those who saw change as saving.

The shift taking place in the first two decades of the twentieth century was reflected in ways other than liturgical reform. As the Portuguese *Minhag* gave way, so did the Sephardic spelling of "Mickva" Israel. Oft have the questions been raised: How did 'Mickva' Israel become 'Mickve' Israel? When did it occur? While inconsistencies in spelling have been noted during the nineteenth and early twentieth centuries, the official turning point occurred in 1912. New stationery was printed by M. S. and D. A. Byck Co., and the 1913 annual message of the rabbi appeared on copies thereof.[140] The new masthead read "Congregation Mickve Israel."[141] The only printed stationery surviving from a previous period had the date 1910 typed thereon, and belonged to Rabbi Solomon.[142] Its spelling is "Mickva Israel." To recapitulate, the inconsistency in spelling prior to 1911 is altered by 1912, when new stationery with the present spelling was printed. From that point on, "Mickve Israel" was official.

The limitations of the Mordecai Sheftall Memorial Chapel were an annoying reality from the opening day of the Solomonic era. The assembly room consisted of a stage which abutted the pulpit, separated by the sanctuary's rear wall. It was dotted with cell-like rooms projecting from the three remaining walls. The only way to cope with teaching little ones in such confined space was to wring one's hand and bellow for change. The teachers did the former; Rabbi Solomon the latter. In 1904 the famed architect, Hyman Wallace Witcover, was consulted, and he suggested expanding the classroom space. The trustees of the Hebrew Community Cemetery provided the resources necessary to effect the change.[143] The thousand dollars borrowed from them was forgotten, surfacing at a later and more critical time in the congregation's history, and complicating a delicate fiscal situation (see next chapter for details).

In his 1909 annual message, the rabbi campaigned for a broader building project, erecting a *new* Temple "Mickva" Israel. At a special congregational meeting on April 18th, Solomon elaborated on his proposal, claiming it was the only way to "infuse new life into the congregation." A motion was proposed "that a new synagog [*sic*] be built." The ayes dominated, 18 to 14. The division of opinion led to a resolution by A.S. Guckenheimer that a committee of ten, five in favor and five opposed, be appointed with intent to seek either a new temple or enlarge the present one. On April 29th, the committee reported that neither was feasible, and the matter was disposed of.

In 1916, the need for remodeling the chapel and repairing the sanctuary again surfaced. A. Shulhafer was chairman of the Building Committee, and by May 9th submitted plans costing either six thousand or twelve thousand dollars.[144] Both were beyond the means of the treasury, so the matter was deferred. Almost three thousand dollars of indebtedness to the bank was on the minds of the leaders, as was the deficit in the operating budget from uncollected pew rents.[145]

In June of 1916, Morton H. Levy, architect and member of the congregation, was summoned by the board to advise on the condition of the building. His recommendation (which carried) was for structural improvements. The responsibility for renovating was entrusted to him, and the bid of Mr. McCauley to repair the chapel and synagogue for $3,400 was accepted.[146] Leopold Adler had undertaken a fund-raising project in 1915 and had collected over fifteen hundred dollars, which was tucked away in the Building Fund.[147] The balance needed was to be raised during the High Holy Days.[148] At the annual meeting in 1917, Mr. A. Schulhafer, Building Chairman, reported that $3,900 had been expended on minimal repairs, painting, and renovations. Much more remained undone—carpeting, rewiring, improving the light fixtures. etc.[149]

The struggle for fiscal integrity was ongoing in this period, and the battle to balance the budget was only occasionally won. Heroes in the battle surfaced from time to time and were rewarded with positions of honor. Leopold Adler's fund-raising venture in 1915 enabled him to aspire to the office of president, after Joseph Rosenheim retired. David Amram Byck and Hugo I. Frank were appointed at the 1918 annual meeting as a committee of two to retire the congregational debt of $2,600.[150] Exceeding that sum, they presented their report, with a list of all contributors appended thereto. Among the contributors was a leader of Reform Judaism who would later provide a sizable endowment to the temple and help to create a camp in the mountains of Georgia to serve the needs of the Southeast Federation of the Union of American Hebrew Congregations. Philip N. Coleman appeared on the list as a contributor (as did his brother, Leo C. Coleman). With such success, Frank and Byck were catapulted into positions of responsibility, the former as chairman of the Permanent Fund, the latter as vice-president of K.K.M.I.[151]

Among the physical alterations to the temple during this period was the removal of the iron picket fence that gave a park-like effect to the Bull Street entrance. At first deposited in the cellar, the fence was later installed on the Bonaventure lots purchased by the congregation.[152]

Storms spent their fury upon Savannah in this era as earlier. The Octavus Cohen Memorial window, original to the 1876-78 structure, was partially blown out by the tornado of 1907.[153] One of the side windows had to be shipped to the stained glass maker so the colors could be matched and the authenticity retained.[154] The Sisterhood underwrote the cost of the replacement.[155]

Functional improvements and changes were slow in coming, even when budgetary concerns were not the issue. Rabbi Solomon repeatedly called for the abandonment of the pew system and the institution of a "free" synagogue model (funds were to be raised by voluntary contributions from each member).[156] For one year it was tried and abandoned. Solomon also requested an expanded board (an increase from six to twelve members) so that more elements of the congregation could be represented. The increase enacted was half that number.[157] Other changes in this era prompted by rabbinic suggestion included the introduction of the voucher system, a committee system for the conduct of business, and the denial of life cycle ceremonies to non-members.[158]

EVENTS OF NOTE—ACTIONS OF CONSEQUENCE

It remains the task of the historian to highlight high moments of the past. Those living through the moments may not have had awareness that something monumental transpired. What to this generation is important, to our ancestors may have appeared a trifle. Several items belong in this category.

In 1906 an earthquake struck San Francisco (remembered yet thanks to Clark Gable and Jeanette McDonald). A hasty note in the minutes indicated that a plea for aid was received from earthquake sufferers, but since individuals were providing charity, the board could not respond.[159]

When the Jewish Publication Society announced plans to publish a new translation of the Hebrew Scriptures and requested tokens of support, not a pence proceeded from K.K.M.I. to sustain this history-making project.[160] But when the Jewish communities of Monroe and Bastrap, Louisiana, requested a donation for their first Houses of Worship, treasure was extended.[161]

The University of Georgia has been a hospitable setting for Jews, and

Mickve Israel entertained regard for the institution which had conferred upon its Rabbi Mendes the honorary degree of Doctor of Divinity. Hence in April, 1907, when M. G. Michael, president of the Chamber of Commerce of Athens, informed the board

> that 17 students were presently enrolled and that funds were needed to purchase Jewish literature for them[,]

a check for twenty-five dollars was drawn up by the treasurer.[162]

Many leaders died in the twenty-year span covered in this chapter. Two deserve special attention because they were perceived by their generation as among "Mickva" Israel's noblest sons. *Elias Weil* perished out of town in 1905, and a special board meeting was convened to determine who might best tender respect. The entire board attended his remains and ordered a special resolution to be drawn up for him. The resolution was presented at a meeting of the congregation called solely for that purpose.[163] Because he had served the temple well, his virtues were amplified in a resolution in the minutes of December 3, 1905. The congregation had sustained "an irreparable loss." For *Samuel Herman,* perpetual vice-president and occasional treasurer in Joseph Rosenheim's administration, a similar special meeting was convened in October, 1909.[164] The drafting of a resolution was never accomplished, so for this leader of the temple a full (almost empty) page in the minutes was reserved.[165]

BONAVENTURE

In a previous chapter, it was noted that the problems resulting from spatial limitations at Laurel Grove (cemetery) prompted an interest in finding a new *bet chayyim* (burial ground). Attempts to purchase sections of Bonaventure have been chronicled elsewhere; the conclusion being that the congregation would not invest in such an endeavor. However, in 1907, the City of Savannah gained control of the choice site. To A. S. Guckenheimer, a member of City Council, was given the responsibility of negotiating with the mayor and aldermen for a plot of fifteen acres for a Jewish cemetery.[166] B. B. Jacob wished to be included in the purchase agreement, as evidenced by an instrument from M. Wilensky, congregational president.[167] By January 10, 1909, the cemetery was a reality, the Jewish section fully demarcated. On motion of A. S. Guckenheimer, the trustees of the cemetery fund (Mordecai Sheftall Memorial Trust) were asked to purchase lots and donate them to the congregation. This was done, and the tract of land became a synagogue asset.[168]

In anticipation of this development, plans for building a Jewish mortuary chapel were proposed. Committees of B.B. Jacob, "Mickva" Israel and the H.G.H. (*Hebrah Gemiluth Hesed*) met together and discussed how to erect the sacred structure.[169] The initial meeting was unsuccessful, and the committee disbanded after two months' service.[170] Not until 1917 was the project picked up again, by Mrs. A.J. Garfunkel, head of the *B'noth Hesed Shel Emeth* (female burial society). She suggested that all Jewish congregations in the city "request six lots from the city park and tree commission." The purpose of the chapel was defined in her correspondence, dated May 3, 1917:

> For your information, we will state that this chapel is to be used on any occasion that it may be required by the Jewish people of this city, and no charges are to be made for its use. . . .

It required a resolution from K.K.M.I's board to get the project approved.[171]

RELATIONSHIPS WITH B.B. JACOB

Lacking the records of Savannah's historic Orthodox congregation, one can only substantiate developments as they are reported in other sources. In the period between 1902 and 1920, the surviving sources are the "Mickva" Israel *Minute Books* and limited secondary materials (the local newspapers have not been catalogued for this period, imposing an obstacle to the researcher).[172]

The spirit of cooperation between the mother and daughter congregations was cordial, on the whole. In 1907, B'nai B'rith Jacob undertook a substantial building project. On the same site (Montgomery and State Streets) where stood its first sanctuary in 1869, the congregation built a Victorian structure, fortress-like on the exterior, but with airy, Venetian details on the interior. Temple "Mickva" Israel member, Hyman Wallace Witcover, was responsible for the design.[173] The Building Committee consisted of Max Blumenthal, chairman, B. Weitz, vice-chairman, S. Blumenthal, S. Friedman, M. Blumenthal, and J. Stern. The cost of the project was $45,000. Two years elapsed before the building was completed (January, 1909). Rabbinic leadership came in the person of Rabbi Hirsch Goldberg, a graduate of the Jewish Theological Seminary (the Conservative *yeshiva*) who was a prized protege of Solomon Schecter, the seminary president. The first Sunday school of B.B.J. was instituted by Rabbi Goldberg. His sudden death led to the choice of Rabbi Charles Blumenthal of Fort Worth, Texas, in 1913. His career was marked by extending the school, improving Hebrew education, and offering instruction to young and old alike.[174] (Son, Leo Blumenthal, is now a respected member of Congregation Mickve Israel.).

In 1908, the leaders of B.B.J. requested the use of the Sheftall Chapel for fund-raising activities. Permission was granted and an "entertainment" ensued. The M.I. board proferred the use of its building for worship, while the new B.B.J. was being erected.[175] There is no indication in the text whether the offer was accepted. The only signal of any rivalry within the family of institutions was a note in George Solomon's 1911 report to the annual meeting that the religious school had been reduced by forty percent, occasioned by the fact that the children of the orthodox [sic] people who formerly came to us now have a school of their own.[176]

LOT 23, FRANKLIN WARD

In previous chapters we noted how a 1795 grant of land by the city enabled Congregation "Mickva" Israel to weather economic storms and pay for erecting temples. Deterioration set in over the course of years, and the brick buildings on the lot were in need of repair. In 1913 (January 12) the trustees of the Permanent Fund hinted at a

> strong possibility of disposing of the property at a figure which will yield considerable [sic] better income. . . .

The hint became a full-blown proposition by August when a special meeting of the congregation was held to provide authority for the sale.[177] An aggregate of $23,000 resulted from negotiations with W. T. Belford, a local entrepreneur. A visitor to Lot 23 today would happen upon the Belford Company offices, occupying that ancient site. The property is part of the northwest quadrant of the city and is expected to undergo improvements in the 1980's.

THE WOMEN

The ladies of "Mickva" Israel organized for enterprises to benefit the temple. The *Temple Guild*, created in the 1880's, developed out of concern for the deteriorating appearance of the synagogue. Its activity multiplied when there were carpets to be purchased, pew cushions to be installed, and pulpit chairs to be upholstered. Otherwise, it functioned in the breech. In 1905, the Guild was reorganized, with Mrs. I. P. Mendes serving as honorary president and Mrs. George Solomon as president. In addition to improving the temple facilities, the ladies took on new tasks—supervising the janitorial staff, providing pulpit flowers, visiting the Sunday school, and calling upon the sick. The storm of 1911 so devastated the temple that the ladies agreed to pay for major repairs. To raise the funds, they catered the various "entertainments" of the Harmonie Club. In 1913, the Guild officially became the *Temple Sisterhood*, joining the National Federation of Temple Sisterhoods.[178]

Expanding its efforts beyond "women's" work, Sisterhood urged a social event at the annual meeting, leading to the present catered banquet.[179] By 1917, the ladies were in attendance at annual meetings and were accepted as full voting members of the congregation.[180] In the effort to gain participation on all levels, the Sisterhood petitioned the board to appoint representative females to the Religious School Committee and the Music and Choir Committee.[181] The latter was expected as Sisterhood provided a volunteer choir in the summer and a 25-voice chorus for monthly "Song Services."[182]

A Growing Congregation

Temple "Mickva" Israel experienced expansion during the opening phase of the Solomonic term. From eighty-eight pew holders in 1907, the corpus of congregators multiplied almost two fold to 156 by 1910.[183]

In 1920 a membership roster was printed, and that list totals 196. For those whose forebearers were part of the congregation during the 1900-20 era, a list of 1920 membership is included in the appendices (Appendix F).

CHAPTER TEN

FIRE, DEBT, AND TEARS

The events that constitute the substance of this chapter are within memory of the living. Savannah Jews speak of them as if they happened only yesterday. Of the human capacity to remember, this much can be safely said: subsequent events modify it. Side by side with this "official" telling will endure an "unofficial" record, embedded in the minds of those who were participants. Their record constitutes the "oral" history that etches in the color of the passing parade.

The quarter century that spanned the conclusion of both World War I and World War II (1920-1945) shook the American Nation to its very root. The returning "doughboys" who served their country well were disillusioned after mustering out. For their sacrifice, they had forfeited opportunities to gain a start in the world of commerce, as had those who remained out of uniform. Congress responded with some paid up life insurance, against which borrowing was possible.[1] It was a pallative to alleviate, not balm to cure. In the early 1920's, the Emergency Immigration Act was signed, imposing quotas that favored "Nordic" populations. Several later laws were passed to the same end.[2] Scandals rocked the administration; Harding's Attorney General, the Veteran's Bureau, and the "caretakers" of the naval oil reserves at Teapot Dome and Elk Hills were all implicated in a complicated scheme of graft and payoff.[3] In addition, the war debt was substantial and burdened the economy.

As evidence of the dissension in American society, one cites the "red baiting" that climaxed in the Sacco-Venzetti trial, and the rebirth of the Klan in Atlanta, Georgia, with its anti-black, anti-Catholic, anti-Jewish and anti-foreigner agenda. The Prohibition Amendment of 1919 imposed the standards of one segment of the American religious community upon all Americans.[4] In addition to this divisiveness, there were sectional conflicts (the farmer versus the eastern/midwestern industrialist), labor-management disputations and confrontations, and the development of a left-wing radicalism.[5] The administration of Calvin Coolidge is often characterized as a time of growth and prosperity. On the contrary, his policies diverted resources into the hands of the industrialists of the north, midwest and eastern seaboard, leaving the southern tier of states languishing in poverty.[6]

Contemporary Georgia has participated so broadly in the industrialization of the sun belt states that it is surprising to realize that in 1940, sixty-five percent of its people lived on farms, and only six percent of the farmers in 1930 had access to hard surfaced roads.[7] Cotton was the dominant crop, and with low cotton prices on world markets, farm indebtedness increased. So did sharecropping. In 1930 more than sixty-eight percent of Georgia farmers were "tenants."[8] World War I brought prosperity, but it was eroded by plunging post-war agricultural prices and massive boll weevil damage.[9] It took the policies of the New Deal and the emergence of a second international conflict to bring agriculture in Georgia into the twentieth century— through diversification of crops, rural electrification, modern pesticides, and mechanized equipment.[10] The amount of land ownership in the hands of small farmers had declined significantly until the Roosevelt administration reversed the situation. This was not enough, however, to prevent smaller farmers from selling out to the landed gentry who could withhold part of their lands from growing and receive federal subsidies.[11]

Georgia and the South had advantages that attracted northern industries—proximity to raw materials, cheap electricity, non-unionized labor, abundant water, and a mild climate.[12] The textile industry was the first to expand in the state, resulting in a host of "mill villages." In 1901, Charles Herty, chemist at the University of Georgia, discovered a new method for extracting turpentine from wood products, leading to the rapid expansion of the naval stores' industry in the state (making it number one in the Nation).[13] In the 1930's, his inventiveness resulted in a new process for making newsprint from southern pine. Both of these processes stimulated major industrial growth in Savannah, particularly when Union Bag and Paper Corporation (Union Camp today) relocated on the Savannah River. (Charles Herty's daughter, Dorothy, was wed to Henry P. Minis, a direct descendant of Abraham and Abigail Minis, two of Savannah's earliest Jewish settlers.[14] The offspring of that union, Henry P. Minis, Jr., married the daughter of a Conservative rabbi.)

If any industry can be identified as uniquely Georgian, the Coca Cola Company would surely qualify. Capitalizing on the formula devised by John Styth Pemberton, small drug store owner, Asa Griggs Candler, purchased the syrup and in the early 1900's began shaping Georgia's first international corporation.[15] Georgia Jews lament that Joseph Jacobs, chain drug store owner, exchanged one-third interest in the "liquid concoction" for stock in a glass company.[16]

Tourism became an important Georgia industry by the 1920's (continuing today). Savannah, one of America's loveliest planned cities, and Georgia's principal port, had a double base on which to flourish. By the 1940's, paper, naval stores, and sugar were produced along its water artery. However, the industrial boom that enabled Atlanta to multiply five-fold in the half century (ending with 1940) did not occur anywhere else in the state. Atlanta's industrialization did not boost Georgia into one of the major industrial areas. With textiles predominant, the economic level of the masses was below the national norm. What was for other Americans a time of prosperity (the era prior to the Depression) was an era of paucity for the average citizen of the 13th state.[17]

FIRE

As an urban center, Savannah flourished during the Coolidge years, and with it, Congregation Mickve Israel. Rabbi Solomon received satisfactory compensation ($6000 in 1925), indicative of the temple's healthy economic state.[18] A budget of more than $13,500 sustained the congregational activities, and ninety-five percent of the dues pledged were collected.[19] The Permanent Fund supplemented dues by $1300, all from leases on real estate. By contrast, in 1929 the board was faced with the reality that there was no money in the treasury, salaries could not be paid, the banks had to be approached for additional loans, and a $19,300 debt proved an oppressive burden.[20] As property values plunged and poverty spread, loans could not be paid off, and the Permanent Fund foreclosed its real estate holdings.[21] That translated into reduced monies for the operation of the congregation.

In part, the financial yoke that brought headaches to the leadership was the consequence of a trifling act. The observance in 1926 of the fiftieth anniversary of the cornerstone-laying ceremony turned attention to the deterioration of the temple's interior and exterior. T. J. Dooley & Co. was employed to refurbish the sanctuary.[22] The handsome wooden cupola above the entrance and the elaborate exterior woodwork required a specialist, so Robert Taylor & Son was given the contract.[23] On the 19th day of April, 1927, (a Tuesday morning) at 11:00 o'clock, a workman who was employed by said company was using a blowtorch to remove the scaly paint on the tower and accidentally left the tool on while he descended for a break. It ignited the tower, the roof, and the upper structure of the building.[24] For several days thereafter it was impossible to determine the level of damage from smoke, water, and fire. According to the *Savannah News Press*, the scaffolding was located on the Gordon Street side when the flames began to leap into the air, twenty-five feet. Apparently, bird's nests fed the flames, accounting for the instantaneous conflagration. As the flames spread from cupola to front roof, it was necessary for firemen to break through the tile and enter the interior, throwing tons of water upon the ceiling. The initial estimate of the damage was between $35,000 and $40,000, a substantial figure, considering that the building, the furnishings, and two lots cost just over $50,000.[25]

The most treasured possessions of the congregation were the two 18th century Torahs (vintage 1733 and 1737 in Savannah), and, according to the *Savannah Morning News,* Mrs. Edmund H. Abrahams (now Mildred Abrahams Kuhr) and Mrs. Carl Triest Herman were credited with rescuing the Scrolls.[26] In 1927, the original *hechal* (ark) remained a treasure of the congregation, and that too was delivered, by whom we do not know. Rabbi

Solomon was in his study at the time of the tragedy, and he directed the small crowd that gathered into the Sheftall Memorial Chapel in rescue efforts. All the valuable ornaments and documents in the Chapel were saved. The Savannah press claimed that the Torahs, altar furniture, and *menorahs* were carried across Gordon Street to the home of Dr. Raymond Harris.[27] Other members of the congregation joined firemen in pushing the furnishings that were too cumbersome to carry toward the rear of the auditorium, in hopes of avoiding the streams of water and clouds of smoke.[28] To Willie Tyson, custodian of the temple for ten years, goes the credit for rushing into the choir loft, a place of considerable danger (the burning cupola was just above), and saving the musical manuscripts.

In addition to the damage to the cupola, roof, and interior furnishings, some of the stained glass windows shattered, one near the top of the sanctuary and a second in the rear.[29] Smaller stained glass rosettes were also broken. The organ and the choir loft were total losses.

In tragic circumstance, elements of humor may surface. The 1927 fire was in some ways a comedy of errors. Examples:

Mrs. Charles McLean, a neighbor of the temple, turned in the first alarm, a telephone call. The newspaper claimed it was misleading, inasmuch as Chemical Company No. 1 and Engine Company No. 1 raced for the wrong synagogue. Arriving at B'nai B'rith Jacob on State and Montgomery Streets (instead of the Bull and Gordon Streets temple), no fire was found and confusion temporarily reigned.[30]

Charles McLean was busy on the scene, taking photos (preserved in the *Temple Minute Books*) and supplying liquid refreshment to the firefighters. The newspaper documents that these were *soft* drinks and took the occasion to express to Mr. McLean the appreciation of the Men in Red.

After the hoses had been connected, it was discovered that the main was not powerful enough to provide the needed pressure. Pumpers were dispatched, and that helped to save the building.

As the fire trucks raced through the historic district, the children of Massie School, assuming their building was on fire, marched out in perfect fire drill order and poured onto the street, increasing congestion.[31] After witnessing the excitement, the children were returned in orderly manner to their learning centers.

Rabbi Solomon, who had been pressing for years for an expanded facility in a new location, reported to the newspaper:

> The whole structure seems to be a total loss. So much damage was done that to restore what is left . . . would cost practically as much as a *new edifice*. [32] (Italics added.)

He went so far as to claim that a "new building would probably be advisable" while noting that no decisions had as yet been made.

In a comprehensive report, Morton H. Levy confirmed that Dr. Solomon's dream was given serious consideration. Several meetings were called by the president to debate the issue. Agreement was reached to re-store and not to rebuild, for the following reasons (quoting Levy):

> 1st—The Mordecai Sheftall Chapel building was intact, though not in the best state of repair, and it was felt that the congregation had a *real house of worship that while not especially Jewish in character,* yet was one of the too few real architectural landmarks of the com-munity, a building of pure gothic design with a tower of exceptional grace, and that there would develop considerable opposition if it were not restored.[33] [Italics added. This is the first indication in the official records of the congregation that the church-like appearance of the Monterey Square structure was of any concern.]
> 2nd—It was estimated that the cost of a new structure would exceed $100,000, beyond the means of the Jewish community at that time. Hence the decision to restore.

The fire insurance companies were prepared to pay $20,000, but the congregation tendered a claim of $45,000. A Board of Arbitration was created to settle the issue, resulting in the award of $40,224.24 as final settlement.

Morton H. Levy was chosen as the synagogue architect and Artley Company was named builder. Improvements were made in the building: the tower was constructed of reinforced concrete, totally fireproof; the syna-gogue was stuccoed on the exterior, and new lighting fixtures were installed along with new wiring. The Building Committee, made up of Edwin Leffler, Edwin Epstein, and Levy, arranged for the majority of the work.

Replacing the organ was entrusted to a committee of two, Herbert S. Traub, chairman of the Organ and Choir Committee, and Leopold Adler, president of the synagogue. A contract was entered into with the Skinner Organ Company of Boston, following approval by the architects and Addie May Jackson, organist. The installation, including console, wiring, wind pipes, et al., cost $11,000.

The pews required extensive work; only the hardwood borders were preserved. New benches were ordered through M. S. & D. A. Byck and Co. Hardwood floors were added, with aisle carpeting. The Temple Sister-hood was involved in adding decorative touches.[34]

The restoration effort amounted to $61,090.96, more than the original cost of the building, thus burdening the congregation with a $20,000 debt. The struggle for solvency marked the next decade and a third (the depres-sion years). While the grasping after donations diverted the attention of the leaders from programmatic and spiritual issues, it ultimately led to the development of active affiliates, with dedicated leaders, who rose through the ranks to become officers and board members of the congregation. Once the debt ceased, the interest of the members lapsed.

The massive construction effort following the fire prompted a number of congregants to request memorials. The most notable are the following:[35]

The swinging doors in the vestibule were beautified with three stained glass panels executed by Binswanger & Co.[36] They were presented by Mrs.

Helena Weil, in memory of her husband, Ferdinand Weil; Mrs. Rebecca Levy, in memory of her husband, B. H. Levy; and by Milton Triest Herman, in memory of his wife, Lucille (Mr. and Mrs. B. H. Levy's daughter). One of the hymn boards was dedicated by Mrs. Isaac P. Mendes, in memory of the rabbi's parents and Mrs. Mendes' parents. Mrs. J. Joseph donated the ark doors, prepared by Savannah Iron & Wire Works, as a memorial to her husband and son.[37] The *mogen Daveed* light (Jewish Star) in the interior of the ark was a gift of Sylvan Byck, memorializing his parents. The ushers' book table was consecrated by Julius Gazan in memory of Walter Gazan, and the pulpit itself served as a memorial to the parents of Mr. and Mrs. Edwin Leffler. All other honorials and memorials damaged in the fire were replaced by the congregation.

From April to December, the congregation was without a spiritual home. Within hours of the blaze, offers from nearby congregations, Christian and Jewish, poured in. B. B. Jacob President, L. Weitz, extended the facilities of his Montgomery Street Synagogue, as did the Jewish Educational Alliance. From the Christian community came invitations for the use of St. John's Episcopal Church by its rector, W. A. Jonnard, and St. Paul's Lutheran Church by way of its pastor, J. M. Epting. Even the president of the Catholic Association, John G. Butler, offered the facilities of the Catholic Club.[38] A long-standing friendship, marked by sharing facilities in an emergency, motivated the leadership to accept the invitation of Wesley Monumental Methodist Church, sister congregation across Drayton Street. The *Savannah Press* of Wednesday, September 21, 1927, informed the public that *Rosh Hashanah* services would be held in the Methodist sanctuary and were open to all. The column carried details of the *Yom Kippur* (Atonement Day) worship schedule as well. In appreciation

> Rabbi Solomon paid a tribute to the splendid neighborly spirit of Wesley Monumental whose officers, pastors and membership spontaneously and independently of each other tendered the use of their splendid building.[39]

However, the undamaged Sheftall Memorial Chapel was the scene of *Sabbath* worship in the intervening eight months of repair, and Confirmation was held in Lawton Memorial, present home of the St. Paul's Orthodox Church.[40]

Other offers poured in from the general community, not all altruistic. In the 1920's, the Chatham Land and Hotel Company had an ambition to build a grand hotel in what is today the Ardsley Park section of Savannah. Where presently abides the Savannah High School, a luxurious resort was to have risen. Along bordering Victory Drive, land was purchased for resale to individuals who wished to live on choice property. (Eventually the project atrophied, and the resort was constructed instead on Wilmington Island. It is commonly referred to as the Savannah Inn and Country Club.) The fire that devastated the temple came to the attention of the Chatham

Land and Hotel Company President, Harvey Granger. Within two days, he delivered a proposal to Rabbi Solomon:

> It occurred to the writer . . . that as a great number of churches are looking to the future and moving farther south, your present location would be a wonderful site for an *apartment house.* . . . I have a number of very beautiful sites on Victory Drive or 47th Street which would be suitable for your church.[41] (Italics added.)

On Chanukkah, 1927, masses of Savannahians gathered into the restored temple for a service of rededication. The *Savannah News Press* described the restored building as

> truly not the largest church in this city but a work of art and one of the most beautiful houses of worship in Savannah today."[42]

Participating in the service (in addition to Rabbi Solomon) was Philip Weinberg of Baltimore, representing the National Federation of Temple Brotherhoods (who urged the men to become more active in synagogue life). Rabbi Louis Mendoza, a golden-voiced orator and honored rabbi of Temple Ohef Sholom of Norfolk, Virginia, delivered the dedicatory address. It so appealed to the local editor that an editorial was published entitled "Dr. Mendoza's Appeal." Recalling his eloquence during World War I, when he appeared in Savannah on behalf of the war effort (at the Municipal Auditorium), it noted:

> Dr. Mendoza is not only a scholar and an orator but he is a consecrated man.[43]

Turning to the choir as symbol, the editor commented on the mixed faiths represented, as well as the sense of pride of the entire community in the achievements of Rabbi Solomon and the esteem of the synagogue he served among peoples of all faiths and "sect" [sic].

DEBT

Less than two years after the rededication rites, the Nation was plunged into a great depression. During October 24-29, 1929, a frantic sell-off occurred. A decline of thirty-seven percent in the value of stocks was recorded.[44] For four years the stock prices plummeted, reaching a value of one-fifth the inflated figures of October 29th by March 1, 1933. At the end of 1930, six to seven million workers were unemployed, and, two years later, the number doubled.[45] Georgians had never come out of the 1920 post-war deflation. Between 1929 and 1933, farm prices fell sixty percent.[46] On all levels, a tragic constriction threw multitudes into poverty and reduced the standard of living for all but a wealthy few. The people of Mickve Israel were not immune.

From 1929 to 1937 the leadership of the temple engaged in an earnest effort to keep their House of God solvent. Attitudes were formed that obtain to this day. Survival was at stake, and extreme measures were required. They are recounted here, only to document how a congregation, then over two hundred years old, may encounter circumstances that bring it to the brink.

The era of the early twenties was not without money problems. In 1921, the board discovered that it owed a thousand dollars to the Sheftall Memorial Trust for a loan to restore the building.[47] Expenses exceeded income in 1925, requiring the board to authorize a "borrowing" from the Savannah Bank and Trust of another thousand dollars.[48] Delinquents were substantial, and almost five percent of the budget was owing by the annual meeting of 1926.[49] Everything from "discounts on dues" to a system of free will offerings on the High Holy Days were instituted.[50] When conditions were threatening, the rabbi was requested to impress the *Rosh Hashanah* crowds with the traditional *"ayn kemach ayn Torah"* (no material wherewithal, no religious life).[51]

The temple budget is a strong indicator of economic weal or woe. In 1929, before the panic, it required $14,000 to operate the temple. By 1931, the total income from all sources was $7,072.00, almost a fifty percent decrease. In 1939, when the depression had about run its course, pledges were in the category of $8000. In 1940 they had fallen to $7800, and in 1941 to less than $7600.[52] Such drastic reductions required slashing everything, salaries included. Rabbi Solomon's stipend declined from $6000 before 1929 to $5400 in 1932 (even to $4080 in 1934).[53] Other staff members were not awarded contracts, but worked from month to month, hopeful that the finances would allow their continuance.[54] Borrowing was necessary, and the congregational debt reached in excess of $29,000 (owed to the bank), including $16,500 indentures.[55] The professional choir had to be disbanded, and one year the teachers were denied compensation.[56] Spending more than was taken in was not an exceptional practice.[57] The shame of not paying the Union of American Hebrew Congregations was experienced in 1930.[58] In 1935 the full debt owing to the Savannah Bank and Trust Company was collectible in a year's time, and no plausible strategy existed to honor it.[59] Savannah is storm country, and only in desperation does one reduce tornado and hurricane insurance,[60] but it had to be done. Similar desperation was reflected in the abandoning of the sanctuary during the winter months and holding services in the Sheftall Memorial Chapel.[61] When the leadership reported that the building was rotting because there was no heat, and the organist, Addie Mae Jackson, pleaded for warmth in the sanctuary lest the delicate machinery of the Skinner organ erode, Mickve Israel reached rock bottom.[62]

While none may underestimate the role of the board of *adjunta* and the congregational presidents (particularly Morton H. Levy and Edmund H. Abrahams) in providing the leadership to deal with the crisis, the affiliate organizations of K.K.M.I. supplied the labor and innovative approaches. In 1906, the Temple Auxiliary was founded by Edwin Epstein as a mechanism for involving the younger men of the congregation in the affairs of the congregation.[63] When the transition to a "free" synagogue began, and pew rentals no longer provided the bulk of the finances, new fund-raising techniques were employed. The Auxiliary divided the temple membership list by neighborhoods and informed the people that they could expect a personal visitation on a given day (normally Sunday) to make their annual pledges. The system (with minor variation) worked effectively until the Great Depression hit.[64] In 1930, on November 7th, the Auxiliary was abolished, and the Temple Brotherhood (which George Solomon championed) was revived.[65] A new and energetic contingent of young leaders emerged. The annual fund drive was conducted by Brotherhood's Fund Drive chairman, although the board assumed the responsibility for the annual campaign in 1931.[66] Supplementary funds were gained by a variety of programs, most co-sponsored by Brotherhood and Sisterhood. In 1933, the Downey Circus was brought to town, and almost nine hundred dollars was realized from a percentage of the gate. Sims Guckenheimer (later Gaynor) and Edgar Wortsman were credited with the brilliant stroke.[67] The next year Guckenheimer was joined by Al Chaskin in arranging a second circus engagement, and a comparable sum was raised.[68] The monies represented almost fifteen percent of the annual budget.

Equally innovative, and profitable, was Brotherhood's investment in two memorial tablets. The first bronze tablet placed in the sanctuary in 1936 was quickly filled with plaques and was soon followed by a mate.[69] The profits proceeded to the congregation, redeeming it from insolvency.

Along the same lines, Mrs. Harry Raskin, in memory of her parents, Esther and William Marcus, gifted the temple with a leather-bound "Book of Life," which allowed memorials to be permanently recorded, less expensively.[70] The Brotherhood nurtured the concept and received recognition for its success.

Kudos proceeded to the Temple Brotherhood from the congregational president in 1939 when he credited it with helping to save the temple, by bringing new people into the synagogue family and acquiring additional revenues through increased pledges.[71] As a consequence, the Brotherhood president was invited into the counsels of the board until a chair was reserved for him whenever the leadership met. From the ranks of Brotherhood presidents came officers of the congregation, Joseph H. Mendes, the rabbi's son, being representative of the company. Brotherhood served as training ground for those who would eventually direct the destiny of K.K.M.I.

The *adjunta* struggled with the problem of decreasing revenues and came up with "gimmicks" to obtain resources. A partial list would include:

(1) Selling the cemetery lots in Bonaventure, given at an earlier period by the Sheftall Cemetery Trust.[72]

(2) Contacting out-of-towners with ties to Savannah and apprising them

of the congregation's needs. Among the respondents were Mr. and Mrs. Milton Dammon of New York, whose donations proved a boon.[73]

(3) Circulating questionnaires to give all a chance to express their views, on the theory that involved members would be more generous.[74] Occasionally, the board invited selected members of the congregation to discuss temple's affairs.[75]

(4) Issuing Sunday school admissions cards at a fee. Charges were levied for attending High Holy Day worship, and non-members were required to receive a permit from the president before any life cycle ceremony could be performed.[76]

(5) Using the offering technique at other holy seasons, since the *Rosh Hashanah* offering proved efficacious. In 1935, for the first and only time, a *Shavuot* (Pentecost) solicitation was made.[77]

(6) Creating a "Memoriam Fund." The congregation was notified of the concept, and the monies received were given to the Permanent Fund for investment. Gifts were reported frequently and made part of the minutes.[78]

(7) The minutes of June 5, 1936, reported that the children of the Religious School produced a play for profit and turned over the $25 earned to the board for its budgetary needs. Pride prevented the acceptance of the gift, the money proceeding to the religious school library for the purchase of children's books.

Ultimately, a three-pronged strategy lifted the temple out of its economic morass. First, a campaign was initiated soliciting the aid of the congregation's lawyers to convince congregators to include the temple in their wills. This had (and continues to have) a benign effect on Mickve Israel's resources. The project was initiated in 1940 before World War II.[79] Interest from investments supplemented the dues; that was its aim and objective.

Second, hampering financial health was the strapping debt incurred through debentures owned by the members and by local banks. Interest payments strained the budget. Devices were conceived to retire the debt a little at a time. Finally, a small body of devoted temple men initiated a vigorous campaign. In response to a High Holy Day appeal by Rabbi Solomon in 1942, Rudolph Lieberls prevailed upon his son-in-law, Benjamin K. Victor, to organize a campaign. Those who assisted him were enumerated in *Contact* (the Brotherhood bulletin).[80] They included Sidney Victor, Joseph Mendes, Joseph Perelstine, Morton H. Levy, Edgar Wortsman, Dr. William Weichselbaum, Jr., Casper Wiseman, Sylvan Byck, Louis Roos, Max Guthman, Herman Edel, I. A. Solomons, Jr., L. S. Lieberls, Wallace Brown, and Philip Bodziner. More than twelve thousand dollars was raised, and, for the first time in a quarter century, Mickve Israel was unencumbered. The committee under "Benny" Victor built upon the initial effort of a Bonds Retirement Committee composed of Abram Minis, Jr., chairman, Dr. Everette Iseman, and Herman Edel, who were appointed by the board in 1940 and succeeded in diminishing the debt by twenty percent.[81]

Third, the final strategy for ensuring fiscal soundness was the creation of the Memorial Endowment Foundation. Announced to the congregation in a special publication entitled "The Voice of Mickve Israel" (compiled by its temporary trustees, Percy H. Myers, chairman, Dr. Semon Eisenberg, and Raymond M. Kuhr, all appointees of Temple President Joseph H. Mendes), its purpose was enumerated thusly:

> (1) Ensuing [sic] the continuance of Mickve Israel for coming gener-
> ations on a standard befitting its position as one of the outstanding
> reformed [sic] Jewish congregations in the United States; (2) to be
> prepared to meet any financial crisis that might come to our congre-
> gation or in our community; (3) to reach the position where officers
> of the congregation can devote their efforts to spiritual matters rather
> than toward financial problems . . .; (4) to honor living affiliates of
> the congregation and perpetuate the memory of the departed members
> of their families.

Minimum donations of one thousand dollars ensured a plaque on the Memorial Endowment tablet in the sanctuary. Lesser gifts were gratefully received, and a listing of all benefactions was maintained in the records. According to the minutes of June 28, 1944, the Memorial Endowment Foundation was to function as an adjunct to the board of trustees, with three elected officials chosen for two, four, and six year terms. The net income of the fund of the previous calendar year was to be available to the board for its budgetary needs, but any excess could be reinvested. To ensure liquidity,

> Fifty percent of the principal of the Foundation *must be* held in cash,
> state of Georgia 'Legals' or United States Government Securities. . . .
> (Italics added.)

As of December 29, 1944, almost $7500 was received as gifts (representing five endowment plaques), and more than five thousand dollars in United States Savings Bonds was transferred to the Fund.

With Raymond Kuhr reporting to the June 9, 1943, board meeting that his committee on increasing subscriptions had received positive responses from half the congregation (amounting to almost half the depression budget), and with a certificate recording the destruction of the debentures (concluding all debt) incorporated into the official minutes, the pain of the past was expunged. By July 1st, the *adjunta* was making plans to call the temple's second assistant rabbi in a century.

The focus of the board during the depression years was on vexing internal problems. Yet there is evidence that individual members of the temple and its affiliates reached out to the needy and the distressed. Jacob G. Smith was chosen recipient of the Lucas Trophy for sustaining four thousand undernourished children in Savannah each day.[82] In her annual Sisterhood report, President Riette (Mrs. Herman) Edel reported the heroic work of the Committee on Community Cooperation, which "assisted in the welfare work for the unemployed."[83]

TEARS

What epoch in Jewish history is comparable to the years of Nazi Holocaust! In what terms can the terror unleashed be defined, or the insanity and immorality of it be communicated! In response, the civilized nations on earth unleashed the machinery of war with such fury that, after the peace treaties were signed, new symbols of human death-making emerged: Auschwitz, Dresden, and Hiroshima.

The first level of response to the disaster befalling European Jewry was to organize fund-raising efforts and to rescue "the captives." As early as 1934, the annual report of the president of the congregation included a statement that Sam G. Adler (son of former Temple President Leopold Adler) led a campaign, involving many Jewish organizations in the city, to solicit monies

for aid for the Jews in Germany.

The presence of this esteemed temple family in such an undertaking set the tone. In 1937 Morris Bernstein chaired the United Jewish Appeal campaign, and *Contact* announced ten thousand dollars was needed to be raised locally.[84] A year later, Rabbi George Solomon was spending time in Brunswick, Georgia, organizing the UJA campaign in that port city.[85] In 1942, *Contact* was strongly urging generosity for the UJA, as the campaign was chaired by the two rabbis of the community, George Solomon and Rabbi Drazin (B.B.J.).[86] Through its Community Cooperation Committee, Sisterhood furnished workers for the

yearly refugee aid and overseas needs campaign.[87] (Italics added.)

Contact proudly announced in 1940 that Herbert Kayton would lead the drive to raise $33,000 locally, as part of a national campaign of $23,000,000, chaired by Rabbi Jonah B. Wise and Rabbi Abba Hillel Silver. Thousands of destitute refugees would be helped to reach Palestine.[88] Despite the congregation's plight, the bulletin urged generous donations for overseas assistance because Jewish lives were at stake.[89] Temple President Morton H. Levy was chosen vice chairman of the local American Joint Distribution Committee (to help distressed Jews and war refugees), and in 1940 he was chosen general chairman for Georgia.[90]

As a port city, Savannah received a proportion of those fortunate enough to escape Nazi barbarism. The Israelites of the city provided for them all the necessities of life, and some luxuries too.[91] Efforts were made to place children in local homes, and *Contact* reported three such incidences (implying that these were the first, with more to come).[92] A spokesman for the Atlanta Hebrew Orphan's Home addressed the local Council of Jewish

Women on the process of placement. The C.J.W. had a "German-Jewish"
Refugee Fund to assist in such projects, sustained in part by operating a
thrift shop.[93] The new Americans were not only recipients of basic aid to
care for primary needs, but other benefactions to make them self-sufficient.
The instance of one attending Georgia Teachers' College at Milledgeville
was reported in the minutes.[84] The hearts of many Savannah Jews went out
to those who were transplanted to a new culture.

They were the lucky ones. While concern was shown for them, the
struggle was to find a haven for those in danger. Clearly this concern motivated the editor of *Contact* to inform the members of Mickve Israel that a
section of British Guiana (the Rumini) was being considered by President
Roosevelt's Advisory Committee on Political Refugees as a place of refuge
for persecuted Jews.[95] That scheme, unremembered by most historians, was
disassembled, as "the final solution" was implemented with grotesque
efficiency. Meanwhile, it comforted the local Jewish population to think that
serious efforts were underway to save European Jewry.

Community rallies have traditionally served Savannah Jews as a way of
gathering strength in times of crisis. On November 21, 1938, a joint service
was held at Mickve Israel, and all synagogue populations formally participated. Prayers for the oppressed in Europe were voiced and Orthodox, Conservative, and Reform spiritual leaders united in petition.[96] The Jewish response was picked up by the Christian churches of the city, of all denominations, Protestant and Catholic.[97] Of significance for historians of black-
Jewish relations is the record of a resolution passed by the "Negro Public
Forum" in 1939, expressing friendship and support for the Jewish people,

> in painful recognition of the ordeal through which you [the Jewish
> people] are going through.[98]

Other demonstrations of support were received and reported. P. N. Hodgins,
national president of the Federal Postal Employees Association, sent a
message to the Jewish community of Savannah which included powerful
statements about the Christians' debt to the Jews, especially in Germany.
Hodgins denounced flagwaving American groups that were anti-Jewish
societies, posing under false colors.

> All true Americans should use their utmost endeavors to wipe out
> all such truly subversive doctrines. . . .[99]

President Hodgins' speech was front page copy. Equally appealing to
Contact was Harry Newman's brochure, "An Irishman Looks at the Jews
and Hitler." This pro-Jewish, anti-Nazi essay was distributed to all Brotherhood members, with the advice to circulate it among non-Jewish friends
and associates.[100]

The assault on Jewry abroad unleashed pockets of anti-Semitism in the
United States. To combat the erosion of the Jewish position in Savannah,

efforts were made to combat bigotry. In 1938, the board allocated an appropriation for

procuring material to combat anti-semitism [sic].

At the annual meeting of 1939, President Edmund H. Abrahams commented on the cordial relations that existed in this city and

urged that all Jews present a solid front so that this condition might continue.

Rabbi Solomon was outspoken in urging his people to recognize that being Jewish meant being different:

. . . Our safety lies in proving that what makes us distinctive gives quality and worth to our lives. Before it is possible that instinctive scorn and hatred for the Jew becomes part of the American feeling, as it has for centuries been imbred into Germans, we need to build up a tradition that the Jew is a valuable and indispensible element in the national life.[102]

At that same meeting, Solomon mentioned the harmful work of an evangelist who popped up in the Savannah area and was known to fan anti-Semitic feelings in other communities. To the Christian clergy, Solomon presented his case and they disavowed support, undermining the evangelist's credibility. A lesson was drawn for his people. Because, over the years, he had been involved in positive communal work that benefitted Savannah's citizens, and he had been openly identified as a Jew and a rabbi, the image of the Jew was enhanced. Any threat that he identified would be perceived as harmful to Savannah itself. Solomon was, in effect, telling his people to be altruistic, affirmative Jews, and the community would respond to their worth.

The campaign to connect to the Christian religious community for the above-mentioned reasons resulted in new arrangements and activities. A Savannah Roundtable was created, a forum for promoting interfaith understanding. Described as an organization

comprising leaders of all faiths, professions, and trades,

it met at Temple Mickve Israel on Brotherhood Day, 1940, at the invitation of the K.K.M.I. Brotherhood. Dean Mattingly of the University of Florida spoke on "American Democracy." Andrew J. Ryan, Jr., Grand Knight of the Knights of Columbus, was in attendance, representing the Catholic community. Seated at the speaker's table were the president of Armstrong College and head of the Roundtable, Ernest A. Lowe, and one who would later rise to the rank of Bishop, the Reverend Thomas J. McNamara, priest of the Cathedral of St. John the Baptist.[103] The Roundtable evolved into a local chapter of the National Conference of Christians and Jews.

In 1940, Frank Graham, president of the University of North Carolina, was to be the featured speaker during Brotherhood Day (which the NCCJ sponsored).[104] Three years later, National Brotherhood Week was observed with a series of panels planned by a special committee, Rabbi Solomon, Dr. Leroy Cleverdon of First Baptist Church, and Msgr. McNamara.[105] This was the first interfaith endeavor, involving clergy of the three major faiths.

Another mechanism for combating anti-Semitism was the Jewish Chautauqua Society. Functioning under the auspices of the National Federation of Temple Brotherhoods, it provided lecturers for college campuses to enlighten and inform students and teachers alike.[106] *Contact* extolled its ability to dispel ignorance and defuse hate.

The World's Fair of 1939 attracted multitudes, and *Contact* announced that Brotherhood Day that year would be observed in the "temple of religion," the symbol of cooperative efforts among American religious organizations. The temple was dedicated to spiritual freedom, and served as a symbol of that which distinguished America from Nazi Germany.[107]

Along similar lines was the pilgrimage organized by the Union of American Hebrew Congregations. One hundred outstanding American Jews, including Joseph H. Mendes of Savannah, made a grand sweep of the Nation, addressing masses on the subject of Judaism and democracy.[108] The temple was proud that one of its own ranked high enough on a national scene to be chosen for this task.

In times of uncertainty, when the Jew feels less secure because of winds that blow ill-tidings, he may turn to his history for strength and assurance. The Jews of Savannah have deep roots in this locale, and through the war years they made themselves and others aware of their nativity. In 1940, the Sesquicentennial Anniversary of the chartering of the congregation was observed with elaborate ceremonies. Mayor Thomas Gamble, Jr. used the occasion to rehearse the history and the contribution of the Jew to this coastal community. A newspaper editorial was written taking note of it.[109] The editor commented on the observances at Mickve Israel (its Sesquicentenary) and St. John's Episcopal Church (its Centenary) occurring at the same time:

> The buildings [St. John's and K.K.M.I.] have been the places of worship of Savannahians, who while they might tread different theological paths, have lived together in a reverence and brotherhood that have brought this city peace, prosperity and the high joy of living. There could be no better wish than that the next hundred, one hundred and fifty and more years will see the same spirit prevailing.[110]

These words brought comfort to a community of Jews unsettled by reports of cattle cars and concentration camps abroad. As a consequence, the idea of preparing a history of the Savannah Jewish experience was advanced (to be explored anon).

For similar effect, the board (for the first and only time) decided to

publish the rabbi's annual report to the congregation in the local press.[111]
The rabbi's analysis of what was happening overseas was thus circulated for
Savannahians to read.

To spread awareness of Judaism, Rabbi Solomon met with Christian
groups that sought his wisdom. For example, a class of children from
Swainsboro, Georgia, came to Savannah to learn about Jews. After the visit,
the teacher honored Solomon with a letter:

> I feel that all the world needs a closer understanding and awakening
> to the possibility of good in all people. Then such creatures as Hitler
> will not be permitted to sway the people of their country. I have
> always been a great admirer of the people of your faith and am
> deeply grateful for the wonderful things in all the fields of progress
> they have given to mankind in all ages.[112]

Contact carried the full text.

Even the children of the synagogue were drawn into the strategy. It was
proposed that the Sunday school students engage in visitations to churches,
so that misconceptions about Jews could be dispelled.[113]

Education was the key to Jewish survival. Non-Jews were to be exposed
to Jewish beliefs, practices, and contributions, so that they might place value
on the Jewish presence. If the Jew was to be a conveyor of knowledge, he
needed information himself. To this end, adult studies were sponsored.
Brotherhood meetings featured lectures as standard operating procedure.
Sisterhood organized classes, including a study group to examine in depth
Dr. Jacob Rader Marcus' *The Rise and Destiny of the German Jew*.[114]

The name of John William Weston may not be remembered by many
of this generation. Yet Mr. Weston served a symbollic role; he was a constant
reminder that among non-Jews there were to be found philo-Semites. In
1940, the Weston family relocated to St. Louis, and *Contact* took note of his
interest in synagogue worship and the work of Brotherhood.[115] Upon his
death in 1944, a memorial vase was presented by his widow to the congregation even though he was not an adherent of the faith.[116]

Close to war's end, a tragic event provided the opportunity for bonding
Jews and Christians. Over the years, Wesley Monumental Church and
Mickve Israel have been cordial neighbors. In 1945, the Methodist sanctuary was struck by lightning and severely damaged by the fire that ensued.
Immediately, the facilities of Mickve Israel were offered, and during the
months following, the main auditorium of the temple was a gathering place
of Savannah's Methodists. Eight years later (1953), almost an identical
incident resulted in severe damage to Wesley, requiring seventy-five firemen to extinguish the blaze. Both the rabbi (Starrels) and temple president
(Raymond Kuhr) offered the use of the Monterey Square Synagogue, with
no encumbrances, for as long as needed. Rev. Albert Trulock, church
pastor, in his church bulletin, eloquently paid tribute to his Jewish
neighbors. Noting the realities of religious prejudice, he affirmed:

But the outstanding instance of neighborly kindness between people of divergent faiths is the relationship of the Congregation Mickve Israel toward the people of Wesley Monumental Church. . . . For nearly a year, we have enjoyed their gracious hospitality for worship, baptisms, weddings, etc. . . . At times they have re-adjusted their own plans to take care of us and our pressing needs. Now as we prepare to go back to our own church, we must tell the world again of this prime example of 'LOVING YOUR NEIGHBOR.' Newspapers from Corpus Christi to Miami have carried stories of this beautiful exemplification of the good neighbor policy. We have reported the gracious deed to the National Conference of Christians and Jews for their files.[117]

RESPONSE TO WAR

On December 7, 1941, America was plunged into a global war. The Nation's capacity to deal with hostile armies on two continents was severely tested. American communities marshalled the local populace to make the sacrifices that would eventuate in victory

The response of Savannah Jews was comparable to that of other Americans in every town, hamlet, and village of the land. The records verify the fervor that marked K.K.M.I's involvement in the fight "to end tyranny."

Campaigns to sell war bonds and stamps were generated through *Contact*, as the congregation itself invested its limited resources in war bonds in the amount of $5,000.[118] The Sheftall Chapel became a division of the U.S.O., a place where the military could gather for recreation and a home-like environment. Begun in 1944, the "chapel day room" was a place to relax for over two thousand servicemen.[119] A Sisterhood War Services Committee connected to the U.S.O.-J.W.B. (Jewish Welfare Board) at the Jewish Educational Alliance, which entertained service-people at the "Saturday Night Socials" (under the direction of Mrs. Edwin J. Feiler and Mrs. Meyer Utitz).[120] The Jewish community provided home hospitality; five hundred families volunteered their homes during the High Holy Days.[121] So long as no chaplain was available to the Jewish soldiers at Camp Stewart (near Hinesville, Georgia), the local Jewish Welfare Board, chaired by Morton H. Levy, supplied lay readers, Joseph H. Mendes being responsible. Rabbi David Sherman later replaced him as full-time, resident rabbi. In 1941, U.S.O.-J.W.B. professional, Martin Sherry, was appointed director of the Savannah area. As innovator of the "adopt a soldier plan" (individual fighting men were matched with Jewish families who agreed to act as surrogates during their training period), Sherry was praised by First Lady Eleanor Roosevelt, in her syndicated column, "May Day." Lilla Victor (now Mrs. Robert Myers) assisted Mr. Sherry in implementing the noteworthy program.

The temple affiliates (Sisterhood and Brotherhood) provided for the needs of local fighting men/women. At the request of the canteen division of the Red Cross, the Sheftall Chapel was the site of a luncheon, prepared by the Sisterhood ladies for all the soldiers who marched in the Armistice Day Parade in 1941. When the home guard was called to duty, the chapel was again used to nourish those about to enter the service. Under the direction of Mrs. Herman Edel, a Red Cross unit of the Sisterhood redoubled its efforts to assist in various defense duties. Mrs. Gladys Schwab, Sisterhood president, was in charge of these efforts and reported them to the 1942 annual meeting.[123] During the war, the traditional Sisterhood luncheons and teas were suspended as inappropriate.[124] Brotherhood functioned in similar ways to provide aid and comfort. The annual congregational Passover *Seder* was open to all servicemen in the area.[125] Entertainments were also arranged for the military at the Jewish Alliance under Brotherhood's sponsorship.[126] Touching was the response of the Sunday school children to the exigencies of war. At the annual meeting of 1941, it was reported that the Sunday school young people abandoned their annual Chanukkah party, and Sisterhood diverted the funds to the Red Cross.[127]

In the *Temple Minutes*, it was recorded that, as early as 1935, the base at Fort Screven, Tybee Island, was the scene of military preparations. A "citizens training camp" was held, and invitations were issued to the Jewish "citizen-soldiers" to attend worship at Mickve Israel.[128] This was six years before the United States entered World War II.

In many ways the congregation extended itself for the war effort. It was decreed that any member of the temple, serving his country, would be exempt from paying dues as long as the conflict raged.[129] If a member died in the Nation's cause, a *yahrzeit* (memorial) tablet was to be consecrated to his memory, gratuitously.[130] It was decreed also that the temple should be open every day, so that any soldier in need of prayer could find solace in God's House.[131] The temple bulletin proudly listed the names of all congregants who were prepared to make the supreme sacrifice in defense of the country. The names of service people, twenty-four all told, were published in the May, 1942, *Contact*.[132] The list multiplied as the war proceeded. Of particular interest was the first Jewish female from K.K.M.I. to don a uniform in World War II—Mary Hirsch, former chairperson for Chatham County of the Women's Division, Georgia Defense Committee.[133] In 1942, she received a first lieutenant's commission, returning to Savannah to render service after her training in Des Moines.[134] Others rendered service on the homefront, too extensive to record. In the temple records a few are enumerated for special consideration. Lawrence M. Steinheimer was chosen president of a committee appointed by President I. A. Solomons, Jr., to increase the sale of United States defense bonds in the congregation.[135] Between Mickve Israel and the Treasury Department a partnership developed for the purpose of furthering the war effort. Mrs. Louis J. Roos directed the house-to-house canvass for the sale of war savings stamps in Savannah and Chatham County.[136] Mrs. Wallace (Rosalyn) Hohenstein served for many years as chairperson of the Chatham County Junior Red Cross, instructing thousands of young women.[137] An interesting contribution to the war effort is attributed to Casper Wiseman, Brotherhood leader. The executive secretary to the general manager of the Bethlehem Steel Corporation was his kin, and Wiseman's suggestion was made by him to President Roosevelt that three merchant ships be named after American Jewish heroes. Thus, the *Judah P. Benjamin* and the *Louis D. Brandeis* were commissioned as per suggestion. *The Haym Salomon* was the third, but there is no evidence that it ever floated.[138]

War exacts its bitter toll; young men and women fall in battle. Mickve Israel's first gold star was posted for Martin Edwin Kirschbaum, Jr.[139] In his memory a plate was affixed to the Memorial Tablet by the Brotherhood, honoring one

who gave his all in defense of that, which he knew to be right.[140]

(Eventually the Savannah Jewish War Veterans would affix his name to its post number and honor his memory with a portrait.) In September, 1944, Milton Hymes and Herman Cranman were declared missing and presumed lost.[141] In 1945 the Air Medal and Oak Leaf Cluster were awarded to Mrs. Georgia Hymes, whose son (Milton) had died heroically on a mission in Europe.[142] (Herman Cranman survived and was safely returned.) The November, 1944, issue of *Contact* listed two others who perished in war, both in the Italian compaign, Pfc. Leon Lindauer and Lieutenant Simon Michael. Former Savannahian Lieutenant William S. Beck died in the North African campaign and was awarded, posthumously, three Oak Leaf Clusters and the Air Medal for bravery.[143]

The bulletin reported faithfully on the whereabouts, the advancements, and achievements of the temple's own.

Rabbi George Solomon had performed chaplaincy service in World War I, but age and infirmity prevented active participation in the Great War. Rabbi Louis Youngerman, who was chosen as his assistant and successor, volunteered for the military in 1945, ministering to the Jews at Hunter Field and Chatham Field.[144] The congregation released him from conducting Sabbath worship one Friday night a month so that a prayer service could be conducted at these military posts.

ISSUES AND EVENTS

In the two and a half decades from the beginning of World War I to the end of World War II, opposing forces were unleashed in American society (the flappers on the one hand and proponents of Prohibition on the other). When, by Constitutional amendment, the distribution and sale of alcoholic spirits were forbidden, the Jewish community was faced with a dilemma. Sacramental wine constituted an element of religious celebration. The temple minutes of 1923 reflected the need for guidance. At the April 9, 1923, board meeting, a letter was read from Julius Rosenwald of the Union of American Hebrew Congregations, stating that the Union was proposing the following resolutions for adoption:

Fermented wines and spiritous liquors are not necessary for Jewish religious observances.

The board resolved to endorse the proposal and forwarded same to the secretary of the U.A.H.C. The resolution passed at the 27th Council meeting held in New York on January 25, 1923. This was in response to the action of the Central Conference of American Rabbis, which went on record as favoring it. The contents of the resolution indicated that abuses were taking place by persons of ignoble character, who obtained permits for sacramental wines, and then distributed them commercially.[145]

In 1924, the centennial celebration of the founding of the Reformed Society of Israelites was marked with festivities in Charleston. Greetings were wired from the congregation in Savannah, without hint that any delegate participated in the ceremonies.[146]

The Georgia colony was begun on February 12, 1733, and in 1933, the Bicentenary was observed appropriately in Savannah. (President Franklin Delano Roosevelt was present for the commemoration.) President Morton H. Levy laid the foundations for a Jewish counterpart. Savannah in 1933 was to be the scene of the Union Biennial, the gathering place of hundreds of Sisterhood, Brotherhood, and Union delegates from all parts of the country. A delegation of prominent Mickve Israel leaders went to the 1932 Philadelphia convention and tendered the offer, which was accepted by the national Reform leadership. A general chairman, Jacob Gazan, was appointed. Leopold Adler, honorary chairman, Abram Minis, honorary vice chairman, and non-Savannahians, Harold Hirsch and Mrs. Irma Horowitz, were named to the Arrangements Committee.[147] By June 9, 1932, the disappointing news was revealed to the board that Union representative, Rabbi Zepin (occasionally called "Zeppelin" in the minutes), had been in Savannah and cancelled the event. President Levy at the 1933 annual meeting announced the apparent reason. World's Fair fever prompted the shift to Chicago.[148] One suspects that the subsidies required by the Union could not be raised locally.[149] An alternative celebration had to be hastily concocted. Sisterhood announced plans for a tri-state convention (Alabama-Georgia-Florida) of Temple Sisterhoods during the month of May.[150] In addition, the congregation had in mind a major event, with

an outstanding co-religionist to deliver the principal address.[151]

By the April 6th board meeting, the bicentennial of the congregation's founding had been formulated. Invitations were issued to the mayor and board of aldermen, county commissioners, the president of Georgia's Bicentennial Commission, Pleasant A. Stovall, chairman of the Savannah section of the Commission, Gordon Saussy, and representatives of the Jewish community, including Morris Slotin and Rabbi Max, president and spiritual leader, respectively, of Congregation B.B. Jacob, Jack Kline and Rabbi Labowitz, their counterparts at Congregation Yeshurun, and S. Tenenbaum, president of the Agudath Achim Congregation.[152] The program, bearing the dates July 11, 1733, to May 7, 1933, was retained in the *Temple Minute Books*. Prayers were offered by Rabbis Morris Max and

Labowitz; the Honorable Harold Hirsch, prominent Atlanta Jewish attorney, was the scheduled speaker; and George Solomon recited the liturgy he
had written for the occasion. A concise record of the major happenings in
the history of Mickve Israel was included in the program, as were the names
of the officers and trustees of the congregation and its constituent funds and
affiliates. The volunteer choir, made up of twenty-one singers, all female,
under the direction of Addie Mae Jackson, was also listed, with soloist Mrs.
A. J. Cohen (Mildred) given special attention for her solo "Hear Ye Israel"
from Mendelssohn's *Elijah*. The *Savannah Morning Press*, May 8, 1933,
noted the "impressive program" over which Rabbi Solomon presided, including the participation of the more Orthodox synagogue, B.B. Jacob, and
"the more modern congregation, Yeshurun." Edmund H. Abrahams, chairman of the celebration, had to substitute for Harold Hirsch (a death in
the family prevented his coming). Unannounced on the program was the
participation of Benjamin Sheftall and Abram Minis, descendants of first
Jewish settlers, who were given the honor of carrying the Torahs during the
ceremonies.

Six months later, a second great celebration brought the people of
Savannah, Jews and Christians alike, into K.K.M.I. George Solomon had
reached his thirtieth anniversary as rabbi of the congregation. In addition to
the participation of the Orthodox and Conservative rabbis, greetings proceeded to him from Reform colleagues, Rabbi Isaac E. Marcuson of Macon
and Rabbi David Marx of Atlanta. So too, Savannah's influential Southern
Baptist spokesman, Rev. John S. Wilder of Calvary Baptist Temple, addressed the crowd, as did Rev. David Cady Wright, rector of Christ Episcopal Church. The latter was not only a religious colleague, but a devout
golfing partner. Monsignor Joseph D. Mitchell of St. Patrick's Catholic
Church (since torn down) was unable to attend, but sent a letter that was
read aloud. Rabbi Marx characterized the mood of the service when he said:

> I come here in no official capacity, but because it is a privilege and
> an honor to see a community pour out honors to a friend.

Solomon would not let sentimentalism prevail. On this "rosy" occasion, he
chose to say:

> *I have not and will not preach what the people like to hear. I have
> preached and I'll continue to preach what they need. I have
> upheld the dignity of this pulpit whether you liked it or not.*[153]
> (Italics added.)

Further the rabbi noted:

> I am willing to be a voice crying out in the wilderness. It is some-
> thing of a compliment to have empty pews.[154]

(A compilation of the gifts, congratulatory letters and telegrams received on this occasion are found in a scrapbook in the possession of his niece, Mildred Cohen [Mrs. A. J. Cohen, Sr.].)

In 1938, Solomon's thirty-fifth anniversary was observed with less fanfare.[155] The rabbi referred to the warmth and generosity of the members.[156] A banquet in the Gold Room of the DeSoto Hotel was planned for October 27th, and on that occasion a purse was collected as token of esteem.[157]

No testimonial of the past measured up to the fortieth anniversary observance. The September, 1943, issue of *Contact* was dedicated to "George Solomon, Citizen of Savannah for Forty Years." Rabbi Morris Lazeron (who viewed himself as a disciple) elaborated on Solomon's virtue:

> To minister to one congregation and community for so long a time is a tribute both to the rabbi and his congregation. Something more than mere staying quality is necessary. Time tests men as it appraises institutions. A long ministry indicates in the minister essential integrity; in the congregation it is a mark of steady and growing appreciation of the basic worth of a man, his work and the things to which he has dedicated his life. . .
> He has seen two generations grow from childhood to maturity. He has taught them not only by word of mouth but by the example of a life of sacrifice and devotion that there are values in life that cannot be bought in the marketplace. He has spoken words of truth and justice, often to his own hurt. Quietly, day by day, year after year he has stood at his post often the victim of misunderstanding[,] walking in loneliness, frequently with no other guerdon [*sic*] than his love of God and his fellowman and his own sense of consecration of his work.

Mayor Thomas Gamble, Jr., elaborated on his community spirit, calling him, "a citizen of Savannah." Emmolation was the next step, and as indication that it was intended, *Contact* published an extract from the *Savannah Evening Press*, relative to the first Holy Day sermon that he preached from the K.K.M.I. pulpit, on September 27, 1903.[158] A substantial gift was collected for him.[159] As an additional token of "appreciation," the congregation began to actively seek an assistant rabbi.

By this time George Solomon was not a well man. In 1942 he had to be relieved of his duties for one month while he visited Mayo Clinic.[160] Sisterhood tendered him a hearty welcome home.[161] By April 15, 1943, the board wanted a committee appointed to meet with the rabbi and gain his consent in seeking an assistant. I. A. Solomons, Jr., E. H. Abrahams, M. H. Levy and Joseph H. Mendes constituted the "blue ribbon" committee. At the June meeting, Dr. Solomon's report on this matter was brought to the attention of the *adjunta*. The first name on a preferred list of candidates was Bertram W. Korn, rabbi of Mobile, Alabama, (later of Reform Congregation Keneseth Israel, Elkins Park, Pennsylvania). A signal was requested from him as to whether he would entertain such a move. Other rabbis were contacted informally, including Rabbi Barnston of Houston, Texas, and Rabbi Wolfe of Dothan, Alabama. Barnston refused and Wolfe did not officially consent to having his name placed in nomination.[162] At the same board meeting, an overture to Rabbi Sylvan Schwartzman, then rabbi of the Walton Way Temple in Augusta (later Professor of Jewish Education at the Hebrew Union College) was suggested and approved. A speaking engagement was carefully arranged.[163] Meanwhile, George Solomon attended the Union of American Hebrew Congregation's meeting in Cincinnati and used the occasion to investigate an assistant.[164] Neither approach brought success. The name of Louis Youngerman surfaced, and by November 9, 1943, a visit was scheduled under the auspices of the Brotherhood. Rabbi Youngerman worked with young adults first at the University of Florida and later at the University of Maryland as director of the Hillel Foundation. His only prior experience in a congregational setting was as student rabbi in Danville, Illinois. A single visit to Savannah convinced the board that he was a rabbi of capacity. At a special meeting of the congregation on November 30, 1943, Edmund H. Abrahams made the motion, seconded by I. A. Solomons, Jr., that

> . . . the Board of Trustees be instructed to correspond with Dr. Youngerman as to whether he would be interested in accepting a position as assistant to Dr. Solomon. . . .

The motion easily passed, and a new assistant rabbi was chosen for the Monterey Square Synagogue. At the January 9, 1944, annual meeting, his term was announced as one year, beginning July 1, 1944. Louis Youngerman was not the first to serve as Rabbi Solomon's assistant. On May 2, 1924, the board authorized the Public Worship Committee to engage a rabbi during the summer months when Rabbi Solomon was out of the city. The accounts of July 18, 1924, verify that Rabbi Joseph Utchens (name misspelled in the text) functioned in Solomon's stead.[165]

The climactic event of the twenty-five years that circumscribe this chapter was the 150th anniversary of the chartering of Mickve Israel. In October of 1940, the committee for arrangements was constituted with Morton H. Levy as chairman.[166] In his report to the president and board, dated November 30, 1940, Levy outlined the program. November 29th, the Friday nearest the Charter date, was chosen for celebration. The principal address would be delivered by His Honor, Thomas Gamble, Jr., mayor of Savannah and local historian. Two (actually three) Georgia congregations were chartered prior to Mickve Israel; hence, invitations were extended to the Rev. Middleton S. Barnwell, Episcopal Bishop of Georgia (representing Christ Church Parish), and to the Honorable A. Gordon Cassels, a lay leader of the Independent Congregational Church at Midway (commonly known as Midway Church). Mrs. Meyer Collat and Max Guthman, with Rabbi Solomon and congregational President Edmund H. Abrahams, constituted the program subcommittee. The publicity numbered eight articles, including one published in the *Atlanta Journal* and an Associated Press dispatch to all southern newspapers.[167] The *New York Times* received detailed information (copies of which have been preserved in Mr. Levy's files). The area's populace was informed that Jews settled in Georgia in 1733, received letters from Presidents Washington and Jefferson (Madison was ignored) and retained the original Torah brought over by the first Jewish colonists. An historic document was sent to the congregation from the Oval Office in Washington, D.C., in honor of the occasion. It read:

November 26, 1940

Dear Rabbi Solomon:

My hearty greetings on the happy occasion of the one hundred and fiftieth anniversary of the granting of the charter to Congregation Mickve Israel of Savannah. I trust for long years to come that this Congregation, which has been a center of religious influence for a century and a half, will continue its ministrations to the spiritual life of the city and the community.

Very sincerely yours,
/s/ Franklin D. Roosevelt

Mayor Gamble was the ideal guest speaker. Using the occasion to rehearse details of the congregation's history, he stirred the overflowing congregation with such utterances as:

The people of no other faith can look back over as long a history as you, back to an 'ancient commonwealth ordained of God.' . . . From your prophets came the concept to which we cling of a God of justice, righteousness, mercy and love. . . . Recent writers analyzing conditions that underlay the rise and temporary victories of the Hitlerian philosophy, now assert that it was mainly the 'spiritual poverty' of Germany which produced Hitler. . . . Today there is a need for unity of spirit, of accord of action, among all who cling to a faith in God. . . .[168]

Two suggestions were advanced by the mayor to document the Jewish development in Savannah. First, he recommended a plaque be placed at the first Jewish "meeting house" on Market Square which he stated was the residence of Dr. Nunes (actually it was Daniel Nunes). (He also stated that it was the site of Solomon's Lodge in the early 1730's.[169] This suggestion was never acted upon and is worthy of consideration today).

The second suggestion was instituted. Mayor Gamble recommended that a perpetual marker be installed at the Liberty Street and Perry Lane locus of the first synagogue erected in Georgia (in 1820). It took a decade and a half before Savannah Jewry negotiated the marker, which is embedded in Georgia concrete on the site.

The mayor's presentation (in 1940) again stimulated the congregation to consider publishing a history book documenting the 208-year adventure of Savannah Jewry. In 1938 Morton Levy introduced a series of articles in *Contact* entitled "Historical Facts of Jewish Life in Savannah."[170] From March until August, they continued. A surge of interest resulted. By August of 1938, it was announced that definite arrangements had been made to proceed with the publication

of a book entitled *Two Hundred Years of Jewish History*. Those involved in the project included Edgar L. Wortsman, Jacob G. Smith, Edmund H. Abrahams, A. Minis, Jr., Herbert L. Kayton, Samuel Adler, B. I. Friedman, Joseph H. Mendes, Morton H. Levy, and Casper Wiseman. "An author of prominence" was recruited for the project. With that announcement, Morton H. Levy signed off his monthly columns, assured that the work would be

... the most exhaustive of its type ever presented in this country . . .[171]

In the September/October, 1938, issue, the author of prominence was announced

... the Honorable Mayor Thomas Gamble

and the date of the publication

... late fall, 1939.[172]

By January of 1939, *Contact* informed its readers that three copies had been ordered from a publishing house and book agency in Roumania.[173] Interest was international. A month later the publishing date slipped indefinitely, due to the re-election of the popular Mayor Gamble.[174]

The momentum dissipated as promise turned into postponement. Gamble was re-elected and then died in office, the history project expiring with him (now being revived four decades later in time for the 250th anniversary).[175]

Of lesser consequence, are the following events of the same quarter century:

In 1932, Mickve Israel joined other Reform congregations in transmitting condolences to the family of a prominent Reform Jew and philanthropist, Julius Rosenwald. The minutes of January 10, 1932, contain a resolution lamenting his departure.

In 1921 Morris Lepinsky died, leaving property to the rabbi of Congregation Mickve Israel, as trustee. It depended upon the demise of his associate who was to receive the rentals until death. Eventually, the buildings on 308-312 State Street were disposed of, and from the proceeds, as shall be noted in the next chapter, a major endowment resulted, providing seed money for the new Mordecai Sheftall Memorial in the 1950's.[176]

The fortieth wedding anniversary of Rabbi and Mrs. Solomon resulted in a happy celebration, accompanied by a gift from the congregation.[177]

The Levi Sheftall Cemetery was in abysmal condition in 1934, and the board considered disposing of it by deeding it to the city and entrusting it with the restoration. The city agreed only to provide materials, and a group of men, Edmund H. Abrahams, S. Goldin, Samuel Hornstein, and Edgar L. Wortsman, with the support of the *Chevra Kadisha* (burial society) of B.B. Jacob, reconditioned the old burial site.[178]

The death of Eugenia Coleman, noted in the rabbi's report of 1936, eventuated in the creation of the Coleman Library (to be considered in Chapter 11).

Another storm struck Savannah in 1940. The damage was small, but the temple resources were still limited, and this warning of nature did not induce the board to apply for hurricane insurance.[179]

Note was taken of the influenza epidemic of 1936. The religious school children sneezed their way through two cancelled sessions of religious school.[180]

Lastly, the Brotherhood publication, *Contact*, was issued for the first time in 1937, commencing with the April issue. Sidney L. Wortsman served as editor and writer. Others, especially Edgar L. Wortsman and Dr. Harry Kandel, assisted and later edited, after Sidney's passing. *Contact* was read widely in the congregation and throughout America, receiving praise from Brotherhood leaders as a source of informative and original materials. (*Contact* is published even to this day.)

In the Family of Reform

Since January 10, 1904, Mickve Israel has been a partner in the Union of American Hebrew Congregations and the Hebrew Union College. It sustained the Union by paying the required dues per member, though when visiting representatives came calling, intent on increasing collections, they were usually deferred. Such was the fate of Jacob Schwartz and Rabbi Michael Aaronson, travelling representatives of the Union.[181] Laymen too were accorded similar treatment, including Simon Lazarus, Ohio merchant prince.[182] During the Depression, the prescribed amount was impossible to meet, and the Union had to survive as best it could.[183] Morton H. Levy appreciated the responsiveness of the Union

upon who [sic] we have learned to call for aid heartily given.

When in 1941 Union dues were raised three-fold, the congregational board notified the leadership that it would proceed with funding as usual. If that was unsatisfactory, it would present the matter

to the annual meeting to withdraw.[184]

By 1943 the pro-Union forces, determined to

further the fine work of this association,

agreed to fund the U.A.H.C. as requested.[185]

In other ways the congregation connected to the Union, the Hebrew

Union College, and the C.C.A.R. (Central Conference of American Rabbis). In 1925, the Subsistance and Subvention Fund of the C.C.A.R. was created, and, in response to a request for fifty dollars from Sol L. Kory, Conference secretary, a donation was forthcoming.[186] Aging and infirm rabbis were the beneficiaries. (The Fund continues to this day.) In 1923, Sisterhood forwarded eleven hundred dollars to the Dormitory Fund of the Hebrew Union College.[187] Year after year, the Uniongram Committee of Sisterhood used the proceeds from sales for scholarships (to underwrite the expense of training Reform rabbis).[188] Among the honors that came to Rabbi Solomon, as a consequence of his loyalty to H.U.C., was his election as president of the Alumni Association in 1926. (Few have been holders of this high office in the century-plus history of the oldest seminary in the New World.) In 1944, the United Jewish Appeal was authorized to distribute a portion of the funds raised in Savannah to further the central institutions of Reform Judaism.[189]

Mickve Israel and its rabbi were among the formulators of the Southeastern Region of the U.A.H.C. In 1924, the Hebrew Benevolent Congregation (The Temple) in Atlanta and Dr. Marx, its rabbi, requested a representative from Savannah to attend a meeting in the state capital for purposes of establishing the *Union of Georgia Hebrew Congregations.*[190] E. S. Epstein was delegated to represent K.K.M.I. He reported back to the board on April 4th that one member was needed from K.K.M.I. to serve on the Steering Committee. As the most interested party, he was chosen. In the general report of the meeting held on May 16th in Atlanta, he had already been designated for a committee of three (with Ralph Rosenbaum of Atlanta and Gates Waxelbaum of Macon). Albany, Augusta, Macon, Savannah, West Point, Atlanta, and Columbus were all represented. The Union of Georgia Hebrew Congregations was intended as a federation of Reform temples and leaders, to act in consonance on matters pertaining to Jewish interests in the state (i.e., Bible readings in the school, replies to prejudicial attacks such as Henry Ford's anti-Semitic utterances, European sufferers' relief, and congregational-rabbinic assistance when the rabbi was on leave).[191] The first action by the body was to call for cooperation by all the rabbis of the state, so that, from June through August, at least two would be available to serve the needs of Reform Jews. The M.I. Board gave its approval on December 5, 1924. By 1930, the U.A.H.C. stepped into the picture, organizing a convention in Atlanta,

> for the purpose of bringing into a closer unit the Congregations, Sisterhoods and Brotherhoods of the Southeastern States.[192]

Mickve Israel agreed to collaborate. The tentative program, scheduled for March 30th, appeared in the *Temple Minute Books.*[193] The theme was "The Obligation of the Organized Synagogue to the Unorganized Elements in the Jewish Community." Participants included Julius Freiberg, chairman of the Department of Synagogue and School Extension of the Union; Lee

Loventhal, temple president from Nashville; Mrs. A. Leo Oberdorfer, Sisterhood president, Temple Emanu-el, Birmingham, Alabama; and Wendell M. Levi, Brotherhood president from Sumter, South Carolina. A symposium on "Factors in the Perpetuation of Judaism in America" featured Leon Schwartz of Mobile, Mrs. Israel Kaplan (the rabbi's wife) of Jacksonville, Dr. Harry Ettelson (rabbi of Memphis) and Professor Josiah Morse of Columbia, South Carolina. The speakers circumscribed the region (Alabama, Georgia, South Carolina, Tennessee, and Florida). For inspiration, Dr. Samuel Goldenson of Rodef Shalom Congregation, Pittsburgh, presented the keynote address. In 1930, the Union of Georgia Hebrew Congregations was still functioning, demonstrating that the Southeast Federation did not supplant it.[194] In 1931 the regional meeting was held in Waycross, and the U.A.H.C. regional rabbi, Gus Falk, was responsible for the "Division Meeting."[195] (Waycross Hebrew Congregation follows a Conservative *minhag* today and does not align with the U.A.H.C., as was the case in 1931.)[196] Rabbi Solomon served the U.A.H.C. by drumming up support for all its endeavors, especially through an annual speaking tour of the region.[197] His camp, Osceola, was a forerunner of the U.A.H.C. Camp Coleman, near Cleveland, Georgia. In 1929, teachers gathered there under the auspices of the Union, for teacher training seminars.[198] In 1939, when the National Federation of Temple Brotherhoods took over the Jewish Chautauqua Society, Mickve Israelites were immediately informed.[199] The temple bulletin was a strong supporter of the J.C.S., lauded its interfaith endeavors, and urged continuing financial support.[200]

Efforts to assist Reform congregations in need were also undertaken by K.K.M.I. In 1921, Temple Beth Or of Raleigh, North Carolina, requested funds for their building campaign, and a response was forthcoming.[201] A tornado in Albany, Georgia, leveled Temple B'nai Israel in 1940.[202] The Emergency Fund campaign of the U.A.H.C., instituted for the purpose of rebuilding it, received the board's support.[203]

The process of introducing liturgical reforms continued through this era. Moderation prevailed at Mickve Israel, so that, as there were advances into new terrain, contrapuntally there were reversions to the old, familiar ways.

In 1920, Rabbi Solomon was urging the congregation to accept the *revised* edition of the *Union Prayer Book*.[204] He acknowledged that differences in "phraseology" existed, but what choice was there, since the old prayerbook would no longer be printed?

Lecture series on Friday nights were instituted in 1925, and pulpit exchanges were arranged with rabbis in the southeast.[205] The celebration of *Succot* (Festival of Tabernacles) in 1930 was marked by the erection of a *sukkah* (booth) in the Reform manner (on the pulpit).[206] *Yom Kippur* Children's Services featured the tots, as readers and listeners.[207]

In the late thirties, open forums and round table discussions were fads.[208] The latter consisted of a public lecture on a contemporary theme during *Shabbat* services, followed by free-wielding debates, conducted by ten leaders, each assigned to a separate table. The Sabbath evening services fluctuated between 6:00 p.m. and 8:00 p.m., a quarter hour added here or there, in an effort to find a formula that would attract the masses.[209]

Rabbi Solomon was eager to experiment. He was prepared to write creative services, if need be, to fill the pews.[210] In addition to Sisterhood, Brotherhood, Council of Jewish Women, and Juniorhood Sabbaths, lay-people were invited as readers on ordinary Friday evenings at the suggestion of the Union of American Hebrew Congregations.[211] Each Sabbath morning two male students of the religious school assisted the rabbi during the Torah service.

While innovations abounded, traditions remained. Unlike some Reform temples, Mickve Israel did not go through an anti-Hebrew turn. President Morton Levy, in his 1929 report, advocated the study of the "Holy Tongue" in religious school

> to enable the sight reading of the traditional Hebrew responses in the prayer book.[212]

A request was put to the rabbi that, when conducting worship, he wear a *tallit* (prayer shawl) and gown.[213] The Reform custom of congregational rising for the mourner's prayer (*Kaddish*) was the last liturgical Reform to be instituted (at the January 11, 1931, annual meeting). It did not hold, for in 1938 the Sisterhood passed a motion that the entire congregation be requested to stand during the *Kaddish*. The *adjunta* responded by informing the ladies,

> that in view of the Ancient Jewish Custom that no one stand during Kadish [*sic*] unless they have lost a parent, that it is the opinion of the Board that it would be better to continue as we are rather than antagonize a minority or majority in the Congregation by changeing [*sic*].[214]

In 1945, during a specially convened meeting following the death of Rabbi Solomon, a member of the congregation made the motion that all should stand to say the mourners' prayer. A tabling motion succeeded, and no *Yitgadal* was sounded in M.I. that night.[215] As late as 1951, *Contact* reported that a poll of members regarding standing for the *Kaddish* (suggested at the annual meeting) proved so equally divided that the board decided to try out the procedure for a few months and then sound out reaction.[216]

The chronology of reforms in Mickve Israel would be incomplete without mentioning the musical program. As early as 1921, Friday night 'Song Services" (a variation of sing-alongs) were popular. So too an occasional organ recital was heard during the *Shabbat* evening worship hour.[217] Mickve Israel had talented people in the choir loft, including Sarah McCandless, choir director and soloist who began in 1923, and Addie May Jackson, organist of the temple from October 29, 1923 on (excepting the depression years). Dwight Bruce served as temporary organist, until re-placed by Mary Louise Key in 1944. Following her departure, Miriam Varnedoe was called upon to perform beginning August 9, 1944. When tight budgets constricted the professional staff, a corps of volunteers ventured into the choir loft and filled the sanctuary with Jewish melody. Dr. Solomon praised the ladies,

> who have so loyally constituted our volunteer choir,

and with them, the man whom he envisioned as the permanent congrega-tional cantor, Fritz Neulander:

> We have in one of our refugees a good musician with an unusually good voice. For a modest monthly stipend we could have him do *cantor* parts, reviving many of the *old rich traditional themes*.[218] (Italics added.)

CONGREGATION AGUDATH ACHIM

Congregation Agudath Achim, Savannah's surviving Conservative congregation, traces its origins to the year 1903. On December 7th, S. L. Lazeron (the Reform rabbi's father) petitioned the Superior Court of Chatham County for incorporation papers. Forty-two male signatories constituted the petitioning corpus. It was not until 1950 that the original spelling "Agoodath Ahhim" was altered to its present form. The charter called for a twenty year life span, with the privilege of renewal. Almost *fifty* years passed before the corporation was renewed. Strangely, in 1916, in the first issue of *The Scroll*, the Jewish Alliance monograph, no mention is made of this congregation. In 1945, it aligned with the United Synagogue of America, the parent body of Conservative synagogues.[219] Yeshurun Congregation had earlier connected to this centrist wing of American Judaism.

The first building of A.A. (as it is cryptically referred to) was con-structed in 1919 on Montgomery and York Streets, in close proximity to B.B. Jacob.[220] Dues increases in 1923 indicated the congregation was still functioning during the post-World War I era, though it had some of the qualities of a fraternal order (fines were imposed on officers for failing to attend weekly Sunday morning meetings).[221] A full time cantor was the first professional staff member (his tenure began in 1927), and in 1933 the first re-ligious school was established for the formal instruction of the children.[222] The early leadership consisted of Joseph Kaminsky, J. Lasky, Sam Kaminsky, and A. J. Fineberg.[223] Later Samuel Tenenbaum, Isaac Feinfeld, Joseph Greenberg, and Joseph Kronstadt entered the circle of synagogue builders—literally, with the proposal to construct a new and architecturally impres-sive building on Drayton and Waldburg Streets, opposite Forsyth Park.[224] By 1936, edifice fever peaked. In announcing the re-election of Nathan Marcus as president, the *Savannah Morning News* hinted that Samuel Tenenbaum, honorary president, was elected vice-president because of important action undertaken.[225] Louis J. Garfunkel was elevated to chairman of the Board of Trustees to strengthen the leadership. Before the Drayton Street site was chosen, the Building Committee, chaired by Sam Kaminsky (with members, Samuel Tenenbaum, Joe Greenberg, Ben Warshaw, and Morris Levine) had two alternatives: one, a lot at Tatnall and Gwinnett Streets, on which an option was held, and the other at 31st and Bull Streets (a block north of Gottlieb's Bakery).[226] To procure the services of the first rabbi, a committee headed by I. Feinfeld was appointed, and the press reported a member was prepared to travel to New York to examine the recent graduates of a "Hebrew seminary," (no hint as to which one).[227] On September 22, 1940, the cornerstone was laid by J. Lasky, A. J. Fineberg, Oscar Levy, and Sam Kaminsky. In the cornerstone box, a letter from President Franklin Roosevelt was included, along with a constitution and bylaws of Congregation B'nai B'rith Jacob.[228] Meyer W. Tenenbaum served as Master of Ceremonies. *Contact* reported the event (because Morton H. Levy was the architect) and described the "Georgian type" building as

handsome and commodious.[229]

(The building, abandoned in 1972, stands and is occupied by one of the Masonic Orders.)

On Sunday, June 22, 1941, nine months after the cornerstone ceremony, the Drayton Street edifice was dedicated. Samuel Kaminsky kindled the eternal light, and the three surviving charter members, Mr. Kaminsky, Louis Kaminsky, and Jacob Lasky were recognized.[230] Two years later, the sanctuary was the scene of a service to mark the "mortgage burning." It was pointed out that, while the Nazis were putting to the torch great Jewish structures in Europe, Savannah Jews had built a magnificent synagogue to the glory of God. Presiding over the service was Rabbi Irving Gordon, the congregation's first spiritual leader, who served from 1941 to 1945.[231] In addition to setting the mortgage aflame, a new Torah, presented by the ladies of the Sisterhood, joined in procession with the older Torahs. Finally all were brought to the pulpit, where Torah scribe, E. Schulman of Atlanta, penned the last letters in the newest Scroll and declared it ritually fit for use. The cantor at the time, Samuel Lieberworth, added traditional *nusachim* (chants) to the ancient ceremonies.[232] Rabbi Gordon was the son of Rabbi E. P. Gordon, then president of the Council of Orthodox Rabbis in Chicago. He had served as his father's assistant, following Ordination at the Hebrew Theological Seminary. His credentials were impressive and wholly *Orthodox*. At his removal in 1945, he returned to Chicago to become a faculty member at the seminary that trained him.[233] Under Gordon's aegis, the congregation prospered and multiplied. By 1946, the first confirmation class was blessed; ten young ladies were in the company.[234] Rabbi Isidore Barnett's ten year tenure is recorded as the longest (the congregation is presently served by Rabbi Raphael Gold).

CONGREGATION B'NAI B'RITH JACOB

The sources are sparse relating to developments in Congregation B'nai B'rith Jacob from the twenties through the forties. In January, 1934, it observed a twenty-fifth anniversary in its new Montgomery Street synagogue. George Solomon announced the milestone in his annual report, noting that he would participate in the Silver Jubilee. He delighted in the fraternity that linked Savannah's four congregations and three rabbis.[235]

Among the rabbis who served B.B.J. in this period, Morris Max received most attention in the *Temple Minute Books*. His Savannah career began in 1932 and lasted until September of 1936. He participated in the bicentennial anniversary ceremonies of the temple in 1933. Gifts and tributes came to him from his people at the farewell reception tendered him in September.[236] His departure was hastened by an offer to serve the largest Orthodox congregation in Albany, New York.

Succeeding him in the pulpit was Rabbi David Shapiro, who functioned as both congregational leader and principal of the Savannah Hebrew School. A native of Denver, he was a graduate of the Hebrew Theological Seminary in Chicago and was ordained only two years before his arrival in Savannah. He had written a book, *Foundation of the Universal Religion According to the Sources of Judaism*.[237] Shapiro's rabbinate lasted three years.

The third in the decade was Rabbi William Drazin of Montreal. *Contact* informed its readers in the March, 1939, issue that on February 19th the new rabbi was formally installed.[238] One of his achievements was the creation of a Brotherhood, numbering two hundred members.[239] (The Temple Brotherhood provided the pattern for the sister synagogue.)

Rev. Hirsch Geffen provided continuity in this period, as cantor and educator. He was the brother of Rabbi Tobias Geffen, perennial leader of the Atlanta Jewish community. (and uncle of the historian-rabbi, Dr. David Geffen of Jerusalem, Israel).

As the period ended, Rabbi Abraham I. Rosenberg, the second Canadian to occupy the office, was elected to the pulpit when Rabbi Drazin relocated. He provided leadership for almost four decades.

Between Rabbi Blumenthal (of last chapter) and Rabbi Max (of this chapter), the following served B.B.J.: Dr. Leonard Palitz, Ben Zion Rosenbloom, Mordecai Hirshsprung, and Nathan Rosen.[240]

YESHURUN CONGREGATION

In his 1932 annual report, President Morton H. Levy announced that during 1931 a new congregation was formed in Savannah. Yeshurun was its name, and its affiliation was with the United Synagogue of America (the parent body of Conservative Judaism). The birth triggered dissention within the Jewish community, which filtered into the non-Jewish community. In response, Levy convened a meeting of all Jewish organizations, resulting in

the formation of the Synagogue Council of Savannah.[241] Patterned after
the Synagogue Council of America, it evolved into the Savannah Jewish
Council (an agency that engages in philanthropic, cultural, and coordinating activities).

Yeshurun's star was ill-fated, a victim of the economic maelstrom of the
1930's. The K.K.M.I. Board, aware that the congregation was without
worshipping space, invited the people to share *Shabbat* prayer in the
temple.[242] By October 9, 1932, the instability of the Conservative community
sparked the creation of a committee of the *adjunta* to see whether individuals
from Yeshurun could be won as members of K.K.M.I.[243] The plan did not
succeed, because on February 3, 1933, the temple lent the "chapel" organ
to Yeshurun. (An organ is not lent, unless there is a physical structure in
which it may be housed.) By 1933, Rabbi Jerome Labowitz was "called" to
serve the new congregation. Interested in the total Jewish community,
Labowitz and Rabbi Solomon instituted the first joint, mid-week Hebrew
School at Mickve Israel since the tenure of Rev. R. D. C. Lewin.[244] The
twice-a-week program, involving Reform and Conservative students,
functioned through the thirties, falling apart after Yeshurun collapsed.[245]
(Not until 1981 was a modern version of the same enterprise established, the
Institute of Jewish Education.) Rabbi Labowitz later became the Executive
Director of the Jewish Educational Alliance. When Rabbi Solomon was
absent from the city, Rabbi Labowitz functioned in his stead. In the late
thirties and early forties, Sisterhood and the Council of Jewish Women
called upon him to offer adult education courses.

By 1934, the experiment in Conservative Judaism was tottering on the
brink, finances being the cause. For the High Holy Days, the request was
made to use the chapel of M.I. Alternative services in the same building
seemed impractical, so while denying the request, the board offered to provide temporary worship quarters for a month or six weeks and to allow the
use of the facility for social purposes.[246] By June, rumors were circulating
that

Yeshurun congregation had disbanded.[247]

A committee was formed to offer Yeshurun members "an opportunity of
worshipping at our synagogue." It was not an exercise in opportunism, as
the July 6, 1934, minutes document. Yeshurun's president, Philip Bodziner
(who later became a member of K.K.M.I.), was invited with his entire
prayer community to connect to the temple,

until they decide to continue their own.[248]

No record exists of the death throes of Yeshurun. Statements that pass
around Savannah suggest that the congregation worshipped for a time at
Lawton Memorial (where St. Paul's Orthodox Church presently prays).

THE JEWISH COMMUNITY

Evidence of harmonious connections among Savannah's Jews have been mentioned in passing. To draw the material together at this point will demonstrate the pattern that prevailed.

Prior to the 1920's, under the leadership of George Solomon, with resources from Colonel Sigo Myers, the Jewish Educational Alliance was formed. It served the non-religious, recreational needs of Savannah Jews. Prior to the J.E.A., a Federated Hebrew Charities was organized by the rabbi and Charles N. Feidelson for purposes of collecting and distributing funds raised, coordinating information affecting Jews, and serving as a defense agency on the local scene. (Many of the features associated with the present Savannah Jewish Council were embodied in the "Federated Hebrew Charities.") Whenever a threat to Jewish status and/or lives was perceived outside these shores, rallies at the synagogues enabled Jews of all affiliations to gather strength and to plot strategies.

In response to the formation of the Yeshurun Congregation, Morton H. Levy initiated the Synagogue Council of Savannah, which sponsored activities to meld the disparate elements.[249] Thanksgiving services were conducted with all synagogues participating. In 1931, the Municipal Auditorium was rented for that purpose, though in later years the synagogues were used.[250] The Synagogue Council assisted the Jews of Brunswick, Georgia. Aid rendered to Beth Tefilloh Congregation resulted in a renewal of Sabbath services and Jewish education for the children.[251]

The Synagogue Council of Savannah was modeled after the Synagogue Council of America, which traced its origin to the 1925 Union of American Hebrew Congregations meeting in St. Louis. There Dr. David Philipson of Cincinnati and Dr. Abram Simon of Washington proposed a

practical cooperation among national Jewish congregational organizations to advance Judaism and Jewish education.

It included the Central Conference of American Rabbis, the Rabbinical Assembly of the United Synagogue of America, the Rabbinical Council of the Union of Orthodox Jewish Congregations of America, and their lay counterparts, the U.A.H.C., the U.O.J.C. (Union of Orthodox Jewish Congregations), and the United Synagogue of America. In 1925, the initial organizational meeting took place at the Harmonie Club in New York, resulting in a permanent coordinating body in 1926.[252] The Synagogue Council of Savannah was an adaptation of the New York experiment (on a reduced scale). In 1935, a local Advisory Committee supplanted it. Under its chairman, Edmund H. Abrahams, it labored for cooperation among all faiths, as well as amity among those of the Jewish faith. It was this committee that initiated the United Jewish Appeal campaign in Savannah. Sam G. Adler was the first general chairman.[253]

The participation of the rabbis of all synagogues in anniversary celebrations has been duly noted, including Rabbis Max and Labowitz at

Temple Mickve Israel's bicentennial in 1933 and Rabbi Solomon at B.B. Jacob's twenty-fifth anniversary. Joint mid-week Hebrew instruction, involving Yeshurun and Mickve Israel, went on for years. In 1934, the rabbi's annual message mentioned the "fine spirit of cooperation" among the three rabbis of the city.[254]

In 1941, *Contact* announced that the Jewish Educational Alliance would mark its twenty-fifth anniversary with a week of festivities. From its beginning in 1911 through its first permanent Barnard Street building, dedicated in 1916, the J.E.A. capitalized on the enthusiasm of its founders to initiate a Boy Scout troop, Hadassah, Hadassah Juniors, the Deborah Circle, the "Don't Worry Club," a ladies auxiliary thereof, the Young Maccabees, and the Progressive Club. World War I removed so many of the young (to fight for the Nation), that the building was rented to the Board of Education as a public school.[255]

By 1920, the Alliance was reopened, due to the saving work of the H.G.H. Society and the Hebrew Women's Aid Society. An executive director, Bill Pinsker, was hired.[257] Through the twenties, a J.E.A. Woman's Club was organized, also a Girl Scout troop, and youth groups galore, everything from the "Wide Awake Girls" and "the Four Square Club" to the "Herman Myers Literary Society." Zionist sentiments generated the "Herzl Club" and the "Flowers of Zion." Concerts, lectures, forum series, and sports competition flourished. An endowment fund, started in 1924, enabled the institution to survive hard times and eventually provided forty thousand dollars for the 1951 building.[258] Bill Pinsker helped organize the local Community Chest, and, as a consequence, fifty percent of the J.E.A.'s budget came from that source.[259] During the depression, the Community Chest went under, and the days of rough sledding returned. The J.E.A. provided leisure services and recreation for those who could not purchase amusements. Matilda Shapiro (later Mrs. H. Sol Clark) replaced Pinsker as executive director, and Rabbi Jerome Labowitz succeeded her. Boxing matches and dramatic presentations featuring local talent pleased the patrons and kept the organization humming. In 1934, the A.Z.A. (a junior B'nai B'rith order) was founded, at a time when Juniorhoods, Junior Sisterhoods, and Junior Brotherhoods were the rage. In response to the Holocaust, the J.E.A. geared up to assist European Jewry. It encouraged the United Palestine Appeal and Youth Aliyah (an organization to settle Jewish young people in Palestine). World War II brought Jewish service men and women to the community, and the J.E.A. served as a U.S.O. center. To meet the needs of the armed forces, *the facilities were opened on Shabbat*. At war's end, Rabbi Labowitz resigned, and that, combined with the death of Jerry Eisenberg, physical education staff member, proved a substantial blow.[260] However, the election of Paul Kulick, a trained professional, as succeeding director, resulted in progress, especially with the formation of the Savannah Jewish Council to replace the defunct Synagogue Council of Savannah. Mr. Kulick served as Savannah Jewish Council's executive director as well.

Another organization that unified Jews was the National Council of Jewish Women, Savannah chapter. Organized in 1895, energized by its first president, Grace D. Mendes (wife of the rabbi) until her death in 1926, it involved Jews of all religious inclinations and elected persons from the various congregations to positions of leadership. Council absorbed both the Young Women's Aid Society and the Orphan Aid Society.[261]

The sole preserve of exclusivity was the Harmonie Club. While some eastern-European Jews were accepted as members, non-Mickve Israelites sought sociability elsewhere. This bastion became a symbol of the divisions among Savannah Jews, even when the modelling of the rabbi of K.K.M.I. was all-embracing. In 1939, the Harmonie Club added to its historically significant Jones Street structure another property, the Withington home on 14th Street at Tybee Island, where members could enjoy ocean breezes in a ten-bedroom facility.[262]

ABOUT PEOPLE

The *Temple Minute Books* and the Brotherhood bulletins (*Contact*) of this period list those whose achievements or philanthropy were deemed worthy to note. They include:

POLITICIANS[263]

1. Arthur B. Levy—the founder of the Temple Brotherhood was successor to Herbert Kayton on the Chatham County Board of Education.[264]
2. Emanuel Lewis—appointed judge of the Municipal Court.[265]
3. Louis J. Roos and B. I. Friedman—Brotherhood members, elected aldermen of the city in 1937.[266]
4. Edgar L. Wortsman—editor of *Contact* and Brotherhood leader, also elected alderman for two terms.[267]
5. Girard Cohen—elected to the state legislature as representative, 1935-38.[268]
6. Hugo I. Frank—served two terms on the Savannah Ports Authority, an elected position at the time.[269]
7. B. H. Levy—served on the Board of Education for the city of Savannah and Chatham County.[270]
8. I. A. Solomons, Jr.—Levy's successor.[271]
9. Herbert Kayton—appointed to the Savannah Housing Authority. In his name, a housing project was dedicated.[272]
10. Julius Morgan—elected mayor of Pembroke, Georgia, in 1938 (a town where barely a handful of Jews reside). Upon his death, a hotel was built and later named the Hotel Julius Morgan.[273]

MEMBERS WHO RECEIVED NATIONAL HONORS

The 1938-39 edition of *Who's Who in America* listed the following Savannah Jews:[274]

Edmund H. Abrahams	Morton H. Levy
Mildred G. Abrahams	Emanuel Lewis
Leopold Adler	Hugo Frank
Sam G. Adler	Morton V. Haas

In 1938, Edmund H. Abrahams served as vice chairman of the Park Service Advisory Board, and in 1940 was elected chairman. The Advisory Board was authorized by the U.S. Department of Interior.[275]

The name Leopold Adler was inscribed in "The Wall of Fame" in the American Common, New York City, as one of six hundred American citizens of foreign birth who made outstanding contributions to American culture.[276]

"Judge" Arthur W. Solomon (a perennial Chatham County Commissioner, after whom a bridge connecting Savannah with the Isle of Hope was named) was featured in *Holland's Magazine* for his estate at Grimball's Point. There bloomed twenty-eight acres of azaleas and camellias. Judge Solomon was remembered as a founder of the American Camellia Society.[277]

An act of generosity that received recognition was the gift by Maria Minis to the Savannah Welfare Society. It enabled that agency to purchase its own facility at 109 West Jones Street.[278]

THE LIGHT IS EXTINGUISHED

The death of George Solomon in 1945 was to the people of Mickve Israel like the demise of Moses. For more than forty years he had led them. The November, 1944, *Contact* announced that the rabbi was back at Mayo Clinic.[279] On February 14, 1945, President Joseph H. Mendes reported to the board that he had visited the rabbi and found him "in very poor health." The *adjunta* authorized that

nothing which would make him more comfortable during his illness

should be lacking.[280] On *Shabbat*, February 24, 1945, his end came in a local hospital.[281] On Monday, the last rites were conducted by Rabbi Youngerman. Active pallbearers included Joseph H. Mendes, Max Guthman, Benjamin K. Victor, Raymond M. Kuhr, David A. Byck, Jr., A. A. Solomons, and B. H. Levy, all members of the board, plus Dr. Henry Scheye and Dr. W. B. Crawford. Among the honoraries were Thomas Oxnard, William Murphey, Father William Brennan, Leopold Adler, Morton H. Levy, Edmund H. Abrahams, I. A. Solomons, T. Mayhew Cunningham, Maxwell Lippitt, Col. Frederick Altstaetter, Merrell Callaway, W. Walter Douglas, Foreman M. Hawes, Judge Alex R. McDonell, Richard M. Charlton, Judge A. B. Lovett, and Dr. A. J. Waring.[282] Prior to the burial, the body lay in state inside the temple. His sister, Mrs. Louis Freund, and brother, Harry

Solomon of New York, were in attendance, along with local kin.[283]

Jacob Gazan and his appointed committee prepared a memorial resolution that appeared in the *Temple Minute Books*. It included these words:

> As one possessing the qualities of a Saint on earth, he caught the inspiration of the seers and Psalmists of Israel. . . .[184]

The April, 1945, issue of *Contact* was devoted to tributes and eulogies. Nina Kulman Weston of St. Louis was inspired to compose a poem, "In Memoriam to our Rabbi":

> His whole life was an immortal symbol
> No man liveth to himself—no man dieth to himself
> And thus he developed the higher consciousness of human
> endeavor, aiding humanity. . . .
> Our beloved teacher labored for the ideals of Judaism—then
> he folded his hands and sank to eternal sleep,
> It has been a long way to go, but in his steps other [sic] will
> walks [sic] and readily and eagerly carry on.[285]

In two ways the congregation perpetuated his memory. First, a marble tablet was affixed to the Wayne Street wall, near the pulpit:

> In this Temple and in the hearts of this Congregation the cherished memory of George Solomon, D.D. our rabbi [for] forty-two years is lovingly enshrined. Died February 24, 1945–5705.

Second, the George Solomon Memorial Endowment was formed and later expanded (upon the death of his wife Julia) to the Rabbi George and Julia Solomon Memorial Fund. (Through this rabbinic discretionary fund, charity is dispensed to aid the poor, to abet Jewish causes, educational and cultural, and to provide resources for the synagogue and its programmatic concerns.)

CHAPTER ELEVEN

THE END OF THE MATTER

$\blacktriangledown$

Two events of the previous half century have determined the destiny of contemporary man—Hiroshima and Holocaust.

Holocaust revolutionized the view of how Jews relate to non-Jews. The historic pattern of dependency on the humanistic impulses of the majority population in one's land of residency was questioned. The existence of the Jewish people was estimated as too precious to risk by relying on the politics of tolerance. Hence the debate in Jewish communities about that tolerance— was it substance or silt? Those who were prepared to repose faith in the benignity of dominant populations rejected any expression of Jewish nationalism as a compromise of loyalty to Mother-Country. On the American continent, a segment of Jewry rejected Zionism over the dual-loyalty issue. Adherents of this Jewish ideology identified formally or informally with the American Council for Judaism. Broader segments of the American Jewish community were concerned that Holocaust could erupt anywhere. A place of refuge was needed for Jews, a haven for the persecuted. The Third Commonwealth of Israel was pursued and, through the instrument of the United Nations, was established in 1948. The people of Israel were again connected to ancient soil. Due to this connection, shifts in Jewish identity took place. Multitudes developed interest in Jewish culture, Jewish communal life, Jewish fund-raising, making pilgrimages to Jerusalem, and learning Hebrew. The term *Zionism* was bantered about.

Debate over Israel was the central issue in the Savannah Jewish community in this era. It is an issue yet, with sides drawn and views strongly held.

Equally divisive in contemporary Savannah Jewish history has been the issue of race. World War II was perceived by Americans as a battle between the forces of good and the minyans of evil. At war's end, the Nation counted its dead, and recounted that for which they perished. The oppression of non-Caucasions in this society, after World War II, represented a compromise of the American dream, especially to Reform Jews reared in a prophetic tradition. However, when one affirms such a tradition and resides in a section of the country where the quality of black/white connections has a history of its own, one may approach social justice concerns with caution.

[296]

During Rabbi Youngerman's term (1944-1948), the issue surfaced and caused trauma.

ISRAEL

The time was just prior to World War I; the country was on the brink of war. President Wilson was urging Americans to think of themselves as separated from any label save American. Rabbi George Solomon was invited to introduce visiting Rabbi Fichman to an audience of Savannah Zionists. Solomon's remarks on that occasion have been preserved.

First, the rabbi stated that he had moved from a formerly anti-Zionist position, and held it no longer:

> In strict honesty, I must admit that there was a time when I too believed that Zionism was a weakening and a dividing of allegiance. I have long since overcome that fear. I wish here and now to emphasize that when the President of the United States appointed Louis Brandeis as Associate Justice of the Supreme Court, . . . it being thoroughly well known at the time that Mr. Brandeis was the leader of Zionism in this country, it must have been quite clear in their minds that Zionism and American patriotism are in no wise antagonistic. When the accredited representatives of the American people are satisfied on this point, I see no reason why we Jews need have any anxiety on the subject.

Second, Solomon affirmed that he no longer regarded Zionism as a passing fancy:

> To begin with I recognize that it is a fundamental error to regard Zionism as a modern movement. As I conceive it, the first Zionist was Abraham and the preamble and fundamental declaration of the principles of the movement were contained in the words of the divine command: "Get thee forth from thy country and thy birthplace and thy father's house, unto the land which I shall show thee. . . ."

Third, about the idea of Jewish separatism from the rest of the world that a Jewish "homeland" would create, Solomon said,

> For well nigh 2000 years the Jew has been forced to live his own life, largely separated from the life of the world about him. . . . Only in the 19th century was the Ghetto wall thrown down, so that up to this time the integrity of Jewish development was kept intact. When several generations of living everywhere as a small minority, gradually losing its distinctiveness, and merging its individuality in the overwhelming waves of assimilation, threatened its life . . . there was driven home the necessity of a center from which might radiate the cultural waves strong and widely enough extended to keep alive the Jewish consciousness everywhere, and wherein, unimpeded and unhampered the Jewish soul might find its expression. . . . So if center there is and must be, it is easy to understand why Palestine, 'the land of our fathers,' the place hallowed by inspiring memories, the spot above all

others which can appeal to and awaken Jewish sentiment, has been chosen as the goal. To me the crowning glory and strength of Zionism lies just in the fact that it is based, not on practical or logical, but on ideal and sentimental grounds.

Finally, about the argument that practical considerations made Israel a necessity (this before Hitler), the rabbi contended:

> ... the present revolution in Russia also lifts the Zionist movement above the mere material or even philanthropic plane. ... I would have small sympathy with the project of setting up another political unit to add to the already over numerous bones of contention between the so-called nations of the world. .. I am heart and soul for anything that will tend to strengthen and preserve, and happily further and develop the distinctive Jewish life and genius . . . to me, Jew AND Judaism are inseparable. One is impossible and unthinkable without the other. To all who hold this view and to any movement that embodies this idea, I am not only blood brother, but companion in the spirit.

Yet underlying his sympathetic view (at the time) toward Zionism was a universalism:

> I deem it the solemn duty . . . [and] the supreme joy of every Jew to be himself, to strive to live up to the traditions of his history and of his people, not for mere race pride, which I disdain and despise, but in the sense that *as member of the human brotherhood, he has something worthwhile to contribute to humanity and civilization.* I glory in Israel, the "chosen people." (Italics added.)

In a concluding comment that echoes down the tunnel of time, Rabbi Solomon declared,

> *Thus as an American Jew would I gladly proclaim myself a Zionist.* On this platform I willingly clasp hands with you.[1] (Italics added.)

(All above from a manuscript in the Temple Archives, in a file entitled "Zionism.")

The events of the thirties weighed heavily upon the rabbi. A believer in the suffering servant concept, he saw Israel's affliction as exceeding any that Jews could endure and survive. In 1938, through the medium of *Contact*, he let his people know that there should be no limit to their giving on behalf of European Jewry.[2] Rabbi Jerome Labowitz, the J.E.A. Executive Director, used the Brotherhood house organ to define the *mitzvah* (commanded act) of *Pidyon Sh'verim* (redeeming those in bondage). He applied it to those Jews who were languishing in concentration camps. Rabbi Solomon taught classes in English for refugees at the J.E.A., encouraged congregants to find employment for the new immigrants, and was behind the effort in 1938 to raise three thousand dollars in just a few days for the aid of Polish Jews being deported to Germany.[3]

In 1936, the U.J.A. campaign in Savannah was initiated by a rally of the Savannah Jewish community. Dr. Joseph Saul Kornfield, a rabbi, educator, and former U. S. Minister to Persia (Iran) was the featured speaker. He and Rabbi Solomon attended seminary together and shared warm and happy associations. The purpose of the campaign was

> to transplant to Palestine afflicted Jews such as those under the Nazi heel in Germany and those hit by dire poverty in Poland.

A ten thousand dollar goal was set. Solomon announced that eleven hundred dollars had been raised by nine subscribers already.[4] Three Mickve Israelites were among those who addressed the assemblage at the J.E.A.: Morris Bernstein, Jacob Gazan and Edmund H. Abrahams. Among the remarks made that night by Dr. Kornfield were these:

> What happened in Germany can happen here. Forget Hitler—but remember your fellow Jews. Help them to get out, to reach their full stature in another land. 100 percent Americanism and 100 percent Zionism are compatible resolves.[5]

By 1940, the prospect of a foreign war that would absorb the best of America's young in battle prompted an ideological turn. *Contact* promoted *Americanism*:

> . . . as American citizens we hold our first allegiance to our Country and our flag, and Judaism as a religious philosophy separate and distinct, marching with and supporting its banner [comments of the president of the synagogue, Edmund H. Abraham].[6]

Here was the seed of an American Council for Judaism ideology. In September, 1942, the Brotherhood newsletter carried sixth page news of a meeting of eighty-seven non-Zionist rabbis in Atlantic City on June 1st. It was described as a conference to

> confirm Judaism's ethical and spiritual values and teachings: and express agreement with a three-point program designed to retard the possible trend of the religious basis of life to a place of secondary importance.

Among those in attendance was Rabbi George Solomon.[7] Note that the meeting occurred in the midst of war, and that *Contact* did not view it as *anti-Zionist*. The purpose of the conference was defined as an effort to safeguard the Jewish religion against replacement by any other ideology on the American scene.[8] By 1944, Rabbi Solomon's views on the subject were clarified:

> As I see it, the cleavage in modern Jewry is more than a difference in ideology. We of the *non-Zionist* group are just as passionately dedicated to the salvation of Israel as the most ardent Zionist. We feel

that the insistence on a sovereign Jewish state—altogether apart from the complicated difficulties of achieving it now—implies and assumes the sympathetic and cooperative aid of the outside world. The story of those luckless ships filled with the helpless victims of Nazi brutality wandering from port to port of the nations (including our own) and denied the privilege of refuge, though these nations were united in their warfare against Nazism, eloquently testifies to the futility of such hopes. Let us realize once and for all that salvation must come from within.[9] (Italics added.)

The virtues of the Zionists were recognized by the rabbi:

Much as we may differ from Zionist views, we could and should learn a lesson from them. They are keenly interested in every phase of Jewish life, studying and living it.[10]

Proclaiming loyalty to one of the foundation stones of Zionism—the peoplehood of Israel—the rabbi called for connection with, not isolation from, fellow Jews of different opinion.

For forty years I nursed a dream and devoted a large part of my activities to the creation of a genuine Keneseth Yisrael, a united Jewish community. The local Jewish scene requires calm enlightening discussion and debate with material evidence of patient, intelligent tolerance. The welfare of Mickve Israel is our immediate concern, *but this is inseparable from the well being of local Jewry.* . . .[11] (Italics added.)

Since 1937 discussions from the pulpit about Jewish nationalism had been routine and gifts to Palestine were recorded in the minutes.[12] In the 1920's, board members were being solicited for overseas aid by the president.[13] In 1929, temple affiliates worked on the U.J.A. drive.[14] *Contact,* in 1940, reported a discussion before the Young Men's League of M.I. by Irving Victor on rebuilding Palestine as a homeland for the Jews.[15] The *lack of clarity in the rabbi's position* allowed for a full airing of the subject. In no wise did it diminish the participation of temple people in fund-raising efforts for the U.J.A.

The establishment of Israel in 1948 resolved the issue of a Jewish homeland. The debate that was to ensue and to vex Reform Jewry gathered around the issue of "hyphenated-Americanism" and an Israel orientation inside the temple. Should the singing of popular Israeli folk-songs, the use of Sephardic Hebrew, the emphasis on Hebrew in worship, the teaching of modern Israel in religious school, Israeli folk-dancing, etc. be expanded or denied? Fundamental to Mickve Israel was a heritage of patriotism, dating back to Mordecai Sheftall, Philip Minis, and Sheftall Sheftall. That tradition was too integral a part of the fabric of temple life to be undone. The question of dual loyalty, resulting from the new state of Israel, was perceived as "threatening."

This was at the heart of a movement in 1945, initiated by two direct descendants of original colonists in Savannah, Edmund H. Abrahams (of the Mordecai Sheftall line) and A. Minis, Jr., to adopt non-Zionist principles at K.K.M.I. Temple Beth Jacob of Pontiac, Michigan, had pursued this course, and Minis urged the board to seek more information.[16] The Lincoln, Nebraska plan, instituted at Congregation B'nai Jeshurun, was a variant thereof, and information about both came to the board secretary on May 9, 1945. A committee to investigate and recommend was chosen (May 22, 1945) with instructions to report back.[17] On October 10th, the report was received with the statement,

> The Committee felt it would be both controversial and undesirable to adopt a Set of Principles at this time.

The issue of Zionism fused with other sensitive issues in Reform Judaism (particularly Reform in the South). The turn to tradition alarmed those who believed the shift represented an appropriation of the movement by newly attached Orthodox elements. In Mickve Israel where such nonclassical Reform traditions as mourners only rising for the *Kaddish* and the option of using head coverings prevailed, the identical form of xenophobia occurred. Further, the involvement of the Reform movement in social justice concerns was interpreted as "political." Zionism, social justice and traditionalism fused to alienate Savannah's Reform congregation from its parent organization, the U.A.H.C. The Union was perceived as purveyor of the new emphasis in progressive Judaism. It became a *symbol* around which hostility gathered.

Back to Zionism. The mounting discontent in some quarters of the congregation over the Israel-centeredness of American Jewry in general, and the Reform movement in particular, was defused temporarily by Sidney B. Levy. His reaction to the 39th Council of the Union of American Hebrew Congregations calmed the leadership (see minutes of March 13, 1946).

Dr. Maurice Eisendrath was then president of the Union. At the beginning of his tenure, he did not exhibit the pro-Israel, pro-social action tendencies of his later years. Levy approved his emphasis on developing Reform's educational, spiritual and synagogue-oriented programs and his dedication to ameliorating the suffering of the displaced persons overseas. Appealing to Levy was the fact that the vital project would be undertaken "without a *political* commitment of any kind."[18] (Italics added.) In Levy's view, a strong pro-Israel posture by the Union would "sabotage" seventy years of bridge-building. This was his conclusion after observing the "explosive" debates at a town meeting that was part of the conference. The subject was how to solve European Jewry's plight. Two sides were drawn—the pro-Zionist and the anti-Zionists. The debate "got to be a bit acrimonious." This display of deep division made it clear to him that to press for either anti- or pro-Zionism might splinter Reform Judaism irrevocably.

Consequently, he made a statement to the Temple Board that restrained action by the anti-Zionist wing:

The anti-Zionists were a pitifully small minority. Not more than one fourth of the delegates, if indeed that many. After a while we called ourselves "His Majesty's Loyal Opposition" and voted consistently but hopelessly on every motion affecting the Palestine policy consideration. *Most of us were from the South.*[19] (Italics added.)

Further,

> ... As the hours went on, the acrimony grew less, and mutual respect and good fellowship were evidenced. Because it suddenly dawned on all of us that neither side was insisting on a declaration of policy as to political Zionism. We all wanted the U.A.H.C. to maintain ... strict neutrality and let the individual members, as individuals be Zionist or anti-Zionist as their consciences dictated.[20]

Finally:

> ... we cannot accuse the Zionists of any lack of generosity ... because *the stark truth is that they could have passed any resolution they wanted to at any time. They had the necessary votes ... and both sides knew it.*[21] (Italics added.)

The choice for the board was either to allow the individual member to follow the dictates of conscience or to press the issue of anti-Zionism and risk divisiveness.

One final matter Sidney Levy brought to the attention of the board. Dr. Greenberger had addressed the assembled delegates on the subject of the displaced persons (DP's). What struck him as fundamentally abhorrent, requiring aggressive action, was Greenberger's statement that, *"it is better to be a conquered German than a liberated Jew,"* (Italics added) so far as receiving the essentials for life in post-war Europe. Many DP's were languishing in concentration camps without hope of work or absorption. They wanted to go to Palestine. In closing, Sidney Levy, an anti-Zionist by his own confession, but open to the pain of his people, pleaded with the *adjunta*:

> ... let me put in an earnest plea for Reform Jewry's enthusiastic and generous support of the United Palestine Appeal this spring. No one who heard the marvelous address of Dr. Greenberger ... could turn a deaf ear to their suffering and despair—to their prayers and aspirations.[22]

There was a response to this plea. The U.J.A. thrived in Savannah because of the assistance it offered to abandoned European Jews.[23] Members of the Junior Sisterhood corresponded with French youngsters who had survived the Holocaust.[24] In 1948, *Contact* announced that forty thousand pounds of food and clothing were donated in a one day S.O.S. drive for them.[25]

Sidney Levy's report provided perspective, but it did not forestall debate. From the pulpit came discussions of Jewish nationalism and the concept of Jewish peoplehood.[26] Brotherhood, reasoning that the debate raging over "political Zionism" was a victim of "too much emotion, to [sic] little fact," scheduled a discussion between Harry Royall, Regional Director of the American Council for Judaism, and Al Freedom, Regional Director of the Zionist Organization of America.[27]

The awareness that on the national scene Reform Jews of anti-Zionist persuasion were numerically overwhelmed by pro-Israel elements triggered an effort to limit temple membership to those who shared an acceptable vision. The board decided to investigate all applicants for membership. This was unanimously adopted as a Thanksgiving gift to the congregation.[28] Against this policy, Rabbi Youngerman lashed out:

> Instead of the encouragement of new members there seemed to be prevalent a policy of watchful waiting for prospective members to apply for membership and then screening them to see whether they are fit to become voting members or not. This is not a healthy situation.[29]

That was part of his final annual message.

Rabbi Youngerman's successor, Solomon Elihu Starrels, was and remains a man of spiritual inclination, a gentle, caring rabbi. Enthralled by prophetic Judaism and its universal message (reflected in his advanced study of world religions), the rabbi had connected to the American Council for Judaism prior to the Holocaust. Philosophically, he was inclined toward this camp more than to the Zionist camp. His love for the land of Israel and his people has since been demonstrated (at a community banquet an award was presented to him by the Israel Bonds Organization).

There is no evidence in either *Contact* or the *Temple Minute Books* that Starrels engaged in discussion, pro or con, of Zionism or Israel. He shifted the focus from *ideology* which could fragment to the task of institution building. A period of tranquility followed in the wake of this new emphasis.

In 1953, a re-evaluation of the religious school curriculum and texts was undertaken. The board preferred that a neutral position on Israel be taught, albeit the books coming out of the U.A.H.C. were anything but neutral.[30] Hence texts recommended by the A.C.J. were ordered in lieu of the Union material. When Rosalyn Hohenstein (Mrs. Wallace) was appointed superintendent, she limited the use of the A.J.C. literature and reinstated the Union publications.[31] A committee made up of ex-Sunday school superintendents was chosen to meet with Mrs. Hohenstein and review the material. On August 25, 1953, it was reported that all the approved texts were being used with one exception.[32] In 1957 the problem was still festering as the congregational board voted to support a resolution on religious education at the Union Biennial which called for

> general agreement to the publication of additional textbooks . . . that will be avowedly oriented to such congregations [classical Reform] and their religious schools.[33]

Attached to the minutes of October 10, 1957, are bills that document that the American Council for Judaism Religious School Department was still providing materials, though the Union's publications bill was almost double.

Concurrent with the replacement of religious school texts, there developed a concern about the philosophic orientation of those who were seeking temple affiliation. The board passed a resolution requiring all applicants to sign on the dotted line that they believed in Reform Judaism.[34] At the same meeting it was pointed out that

> the future of Mickve Israel was primarily dependent upon obtaining new members from the other two congregations.[35]

How these antithetical positions were reconciled is unknowable. A drying up of new members resulted in a policy change by 1956. From then on, a simple signature sufficed. An attempt in 1961 to revive the old policy failed.[36]

An event that may have marked the end of the pendulum swing in the non-Zionist direction occurred in 1954. The B'nai B'rith women had obtained use of the Mordecai Sheftall Memorial for a meeting. A letter of thanks from the B.B.W. sparked a discussion as to what general policy to pursue in dealing with organizations in the community that might seek the use of the temple facility. The board concluded that it

> did not feel that certain organizations which represent viewpoints contrary to those of a majority of the members of this Congregation should be permitted to use the Chapel.[37]

The implication was that a preponderance of members was inclined to anti-Zionism.

It was Rabbi Starrel's annual report in 1963 that began the process of normalization. Claiming ideological difference himself with the United Jewish Appeal, he went on to stress:

> . . . this does not exempt us from the support of the vast range of Jewish charitable endeavor—which deserves the help of the entire Jewish community.[38]

Here was a call for the members of Mickve Israel to pull their weight in support of the campaign.

With the arrival of Rabbi Joseph Buchler, joint United Jewish Appeal services were held involving all three rabbis, rotating among the three synagogues.[39] On an official level, Mickve Israel was beginning to abandon its "neutral" stance, allowing some pro-Israel sentiment to surface.

The momentum was accelerated by people and organizations. Clearly the youth group had a role to play in the process. The teens attended Camp Coleman in Cleveland, Georgia, and received exposure to new ideas.[40] Youth fund-raising activities resulted in donations to such charities as the Leo Baeck School in Haifa. Contacts with young people at conclaves and conventions opened their eyes to what others espoused, resulting in one youth group president signing off his annual report to the congregation with the classic Hebrew signature "shalom."[41]

The Young People's League (the couple's club) also played a role in opening up the congregation. The members came to appreciate their diversity, being a composite of Reform, ex-Conservative, and ex-Orthodox Jews, intermingled with some Gentiles. In his report to the annual meeting of 1959, President Merrill Levy stressed the heterogenous character of the affiliate and the serious study it was giving to the history and traditions of Judaism, including Reform. The message came across: these future leaders were not cast in a Mickve Israel Reform mold, but constituted a diverse collectivity, with differing backgrounds and memories. The future would not be the same as the past.

The administration of Temple President Martin Leffler initiated the greatest change. In his final report, he summarized the meaning of his years of service. The times were changing, and Mickve Israel had to change with them. Modern thinking was the requirement of the age:

> Mickve Israel cannot survive as an independent body in the Jewish community unless we establish and retain communication with our fellow Jews, and work with them for the benefit of the entire community.[42]

His successor, Henry Levy, kept the momentum going. The joint U.J.A. services were first convened in K.K.M.I. during his term.[43] A remarkable action by the board came during the Six Day War in June, 1967. Rabbi Buchler informed the *adjunta* of the developments in the Middle East and announced that on June 4th a community-wide service was scheduled, involving the Christian clergy, as well as Rabbi Rosenberg of B.B.J. and Rabbi Brooks of A.A. The board endorsed the rabbi unanimously in this project. A motion was passed to send a telegram to the President of the United States, Lyndon Baines Johnson, signed by President Levy. It read:

> We wish to express the desire of our congregation, Mickve Israel, whose members first fought for Democracy [*sic*] in 1776, to have our country support the only real democracy in the Middle East in its cause to maintain its freedom.
> We want our country to support and foster democracy wherever it can, whether in Israel or Vietnam, and we pledge to you our support in these efforts.[44]

Copies went to Senators Richard Russell and Herman Talmadge and First District of Georgia Representative, Elliott Hagan. Replies from the President, Representative Hagan, and Senator Talmadge were received and reported to the *adjunta* on July 20, 1967.

From then on the gates were opened. Dr. Meyer Schneider gave a clock from Israel with Hebrew characters on the face to the religious school.[45]

Contact was asked to print a column requesting funds, "for furthering Reform Judaism in Israel."[46]

The Mideast War of 1970 sparked an even stronger commitment to Israel's cause. A special meeting of the *adjunta* was convened on January 7, 1970, to decide

> the position of our Congregation regarding a change in the United States policy regarding Israel and the Mideast.

Urging the United States to supply

> arms and materials to the State of Israel and any and all Democracies in need . . . we strongly declare our undivided loyalty to the United States and its interests, over and above all other nations. . . .[47]

This resolution was forwarded to the Savannah Jewish Council, with the request to pass same. Requesting action, the board sent the resolution to the appropriate congressman and senators.

A. J. Cohen, Jr., in his report to the board on November 18, 1969, summarized the U.A.H.C. Biennial he had attended a few months earlier:

> The single most important item of our young people today is the State of Israel.

Many congregations were providing trips to the Holy Land, and the teens were returning much more dedicatd as Jews. "Expose children to Israel," was his next to concluding remark.[48]

Rabbi Zionts was permitted to go to Washington for a Mideast update and, with Bull Street Baptist Church Pastor Felix Turner, made arrangements for a joint congregation tour of the Land of Promise.[49] Temple Sisterhood furnished funds for the chapel at Beth Shemen Village (a center for orphans in Israel), and Brotherhood was available in 1971 to provide workers for the U.J.A. campaign.[50]

Some limitations remained. The congregational funds were not made available for the purchase of Israel Bonds. A rumor that the Central Conference of American Rabbis had passed a resolution requiring all Reform Jews to make contributions to the United Jewish Appeal as a condition for membership in a Reform synagogue, false though it was, upset some board members and required the rabbi's denial to calm the waters.[52]

In the years since, Mickve Israel has sponsored Holocaust seminars, Israel Independence Day observances, the celebration of *Tu Bishvat* (Jewish Arbor Day), and U.J.A. events including opportunities for the Jewish women of Jacksonville to come to the temple as a part of a U.J.A. fund-raising endeavor.

RACE

The Jew of the South resides in a section of the country with an agonizing history of estrangement between racial groupings. In no area of the Nation is the awareness of racial distinction more powerful, sustained in the past by law and ethos. Because the myth of the Jewish "race" was widespread and generally accepted, the Jewish southerner sought to deny the typology, and assumed the demeanor of southern Caucasians. A suspicion remained in his mind, all the time he enjoyed the acceptance and friendship of his Christian neighbor, that it all could be undone by an unpropitious act. Meddling in racial matters might be one such act.

Albeit Rabbi Solomon provided service to the black community. In his obituary, it was stated that,

> He was foremost among Savannahians in the promotion of better relations among religions and races. . . . *He was chairman for this section of the state of Georgia Interracial Committee, which was formed after the last war.*[53] (Italics added.)

In addition, mention is made of his interest in the Charity Hospital, where he gave

> a great deal of help and counsel to that institution for colored people.[54]

In 1920, he served as the general chairman of the campaign to establish the hospital for the black community.[55] *Contact*, in November, 1938, (vol. 2, no. 11) reminded the congregation of this act of charitable leadership. Illustrative of the interracial activities in which Solomon engaged, or which he encouraged the affiliates to undertake, are *two* specifically mentioned in the Brotherhood bulletin. In 1938, he addressed both the students and faculty at Cuyler School, identified as colored.[56] In 1939, aware of his interest in infirm blacks, Sisterhood used the profits of the Eugenia Coleman Memorial Fund (established by her son, Philip N. Coleman) to treat the patients at Charity Hospital to ice cream and cake.[57] In a previous chapter, it was reported that Savannah blacks found an official way to express support for oppressed Jews in the midst of the Nazi persecutions.

In Rabbi Solomon's time, an outstanding project was undertaken by a northern Jew to assist the non-white population of Georgia. Booker T. Washington had popularized the idea of industrial education as core curriculum for black youth. In this wise, a contingent of skilled laborers could be trained to meet the needs of the "New South."[58] Among the philanthropies that responded was the Julius Rosenwald Foundation which worked with local officials of three hundred Georgia communities. It underwrote the construction of buildings for vocational training.[59] K.K.M.I. took note of Rosenwald's death, not only because of his eminence in Reform Jewish institutional life, but because Georgia benefitted greatly from his beneficent acts.

In 1944, Dr. Gunnar Myrdal published his epic study of race relations, *An American Dilemma*. It directed attention to the dilemma of the white southerner growing up in a milieu where the socialization process sanctioned viewing blacks as different and of lower position. The psychological and sociological effects (on whites) of such attitudes were examined in the book, even as the damage to the psyche of the black was scientifically scrutinized. Further, World War II exposed southerners to other racial norms, and it was understood, at least by some, that if America was what it claimed to be (a bastion of freedom and democracy), then racism was corrosive to its spirit.

Federal action began to alter the southern pattern. The Supreme Court evaluated individual rights under the Constitution. In the late 1940's, President Truman integrated the federal establishment, including the military. The southeast, particularly Georgia, luxuriated in Air Force and Army bases.

In the 1940's, the governor of the state was Eugene Talmadge. His base of power was the white rural vote, a distinctly anti-black contingent at the time. While Talmadge as a *Christian* disavowed religious and social prejudice, as a *politician* he had no problem saying:

> I like the nigger, but I like him in his place, and his place is at the back door with his hat in his hand.[61]

Black soldiers, recently discharged after fighting for their country, were not willing to slip back into the old pattern. Black militancy began in World War II when black and white soldiers challenged the "custom" of blacks sitting in the back of the bus. In Savannah in 1944, Savannah State College students occupied all seats on a city bus and would not relinquish them to the white passengers when they boarded, resulting in two arrests. The NAACP in 1946 had branches in forty areas of the state, along with black political clubs. They succesfully sponsored court cases for the franchise and equal pay for black teachers.[62]

Into this cauldron of contention leaped Rabbi Louis Youngerman, successor to Rabbi Solomon. (On March 25, 1945, he was elected rabbi.) The message of prophetic Reform Judaism resonated in his soul. He believed in the brotherhood of man and emphasized Christian-Jewish dialogue. The March, 1946, issue of *Contact* pictured Dr. Leroy Cleverdon, pastor of the First Baptist Church, in Mickve Israel's pulpit, and in comparable pose, Rabbi Youngerman preaching from the Baptist lecturn. The *Savannah Morning News* responded to the first pulpit exchange of its kind in the city with an editorial,

> It was an inspiring manifestation of brotherhood in America at its best.[63]

The National Conference of Christians and Jews' sponsorship of Brotherhood Week found an enthusiastic supporter in Youngerman. From the heroism of Amos and Jeremiah in the past and their heirs, the "disease ridden remnant" at the Warsaw Ghetto, who fought against overwhelming odds for what they believed in, the rabbi gained courage to espouse the "righteous" cause, come what may.[64] This mindset was operative during the dissension that erupted in the course of his Savannah rabbinate.

The ultimate lesson of Judaism, which Youngerman referred to again and again, was the concept of the oneness of man, corresponding to the oneness of the Diety. He applied it to the introduction of the atomic bomb in the final stage of World War II. He believed the bomb projected man into an era where

> he faced destruction unless he learned once and for all the fundamental lesson of human behavior; that one must live in peace with his fellow man or face inevitable annihilation.[65]

In addition to the teachings of justice, peace and human brotherhood, Youngerman held to a view of Reform Judaism, subtly different from Rabbi Solomon's. Reform to him was progressive, "ever growing and ever-changing" to meet the needs of people.[66] That meant innovation, taking "good traditional rituals" and dressing them up in "modern manner" for "aesthetic appeal."[67] In an effort to revive Chanukkah, a candlelighting ceremony was created. Because of his enthusiasm, his interest in young people (he organized the Young People's League in his own home), and his winning ways, the temple burgeoned with new members—sixty-eight in one year's time.[68] Additionally, he understood the need for the congregation to move toward the mainstream of Reform Jewish life, by adding the warmth of ceremonialism and the richness of tradition:

> The returning veteran has for the first time experienced contacts with all other branches of Judaism and he has [not] remained untouched. He will not be satisfied with a Judaism devoid of ceremonials.[69]

It was he who brought back bar mitzvah and insisted that the *kiddush* (prayer over wine) be read in the temple during the Sabbath worship.[70]

Paine College in Augusta, Georgia, is an established academic institution that serves the black community of northeast Georgia. By invitation of the Jewish Chautauqua Society in 1945, Rabbi Youngerman spoke on campus and met with students and faculty for several days. His visit was so well received that the year following he was back again for a second round of lectures.[71] This led to criticism from members, to which the rabbi took umbrage.[72]

It came to the attention of the Savannah leadership that the rabbi was able to bridge racial differences and was respected for his interfaith endeavors, including service to the local chapter of the National Conference of Christians and Jews. As a consequence, he was solicited to serve on the Interracial Committee.[73] On April 9, 1946, with no explanation given in the minutes, the board advised the president to appoint a committee of two to meet with Rabbi Youngerman and to instruct the rabbi not to engage in any matters of a political and controversial nature.[74]

A month later, the *adjunta* voted to call a special meeting on May 14th, at which the rabbi should explain his conduct.[75] That meeting never occurred. Instead, on August 14th, a petition, dated August 10, 1946, and signed by twenty-six dues-paying members (including former presidents and board members) was put before the board. Article I, Section I of the Constitution required that a special meeting of the congregation must be convened under such circumstances. All temple members were requested to be in attendance on August 19th. Savannah in August is bested only by the temperature in *Gehinnom* (Hades); hence only a matter of extreme urgency would bring members into a non-air-conditioned sanctuary. What deed had the rabbi done?

Included in the August 19, 1946, minutes are two clippings from the local press, undated. The *Savannah Morning News* had initiated a "People's Forum" so that topics of interest and controversy could be brought to the public's attention. Rabbi Youngerman had forwarded an editorial from *The Christian Century* which called for the passage of anti-lynching laws by Congress. Provoked by the recent lynching of four blacks in Georgia (one a veteran of World War II, honorably discharged after serving his country for four years), the *Century* sharply commented:

The administration of justice has broken down in Georgia.

Governor Talmadge was mentioned by name and condemned:

This atrocity occurred as a direct result of the hatred stirred up by Eugene Talmadge in his successful campaign for nomination as governor.

Calling Talmadge

unfitted either by knowledge or by character to administer a democratic system of justice,

the article went on to state that if he became governor, it would be equivalent to giving the

green light to terrorists of the Ku Klux Klan variety.

Conclusion:

Only a federal anti-lynching law can cope with a situation like this. . . .

After quoting the editorial, Rabbi Youngerman added comments, of which the following are examples:

It seems to me that men like Talmadge seek to maintain those so-called traditional institutions which have the unfortunate result of enabling them to secure political power . . .

Intellectually honest people realize that the inevitable result of the preachment of hatred of any kind, whether it be religious, racial, social or economic is violence in its most horrid form . . .

All of us who are bitterly ashamed of what has transpired in our state are not "communists or radicals." We adhere to the fundamental Judaeo-Christian concept of the responsibility of each man for his brother's welfare . . .

The editor of the newspaper reacted with a strong editorial. His points were: (1) Georgia had already "largely" solved the lynching problem. There was no need for federal interference. (2) The argument that Talmadge's election would be a green light to the K.K.K. is "absurd on the face of it." (3) *The Christian Century* article shows a

typical misconception of the South's problems which is so often displayed by northern journalists possessed of admittedly good intentions.

The August 19th congregational meeting followed this course: A motion was made that the rabbi appear before the meeting and that no further action occur until he was present. A substitute was offered: that the matter be discussed, but no decisive action be taken until the rabbi was present. The substitute carried. A resolution was then presented by those opposed to the rabbi's actions.

WHEREAS this Congregation, founded over two hundred years ago by laymen, has continually followed a policy dictated by its laymen and women and has consistently avoided racial and political controversies,

AND WHEREAS it has come to the attention of the members of the Congregation that the Rabbi has lately taken part in political and racial discussions in the public prints,

Now, therefore, be it resolved that the Rabbi be requested to refrain from any public utterances of a political or racial nature so that his policy may conform to that of the Congregation.

Aaron Kravitch, an attorney who had defended black clients, offered a substitute resolution:

The Congregation wishes to express its confidence in the character, conduct and Rabbinical [sic] learning of Rabbi Youngerman and refuses to censure or admonish the rabbi for any alleged acts of impropriety on his part.

The Congregation further recognizes the right of the Rabbi to always speak on any issue that involves the security or well-being of this Nation, State [sic], City [sic] or the good of his people and in no wise wishes to interfere with his discretion in such matters, having full confidence that he will at no time participate in any matter that might be reflective on the Rabbinate [*sic*] or detrimental to the well being of the Synagogue [*sic*].

This motion having been seconded, an alternate resolution was submitted: "Let this meeting be adjourned." It lost. The rabbi then appeared and explained his position.

A motion to table all resolutions was offered and defeated, leading to a proposal that

> this meeting go on record as expressing its confidence in the rabbi by giving him a vote of confidence.

That motion carried.

Aware that a major segment of the congregation no longer reposed confidence in him (even though majority support continued), Rabbi Youngerman began to seek a new setting. In his next-to-last annual message to the congregation, he stated,

> Last October your rabbi informed the Board . . . that, in view of the uncertainty which existed in the relationship of the rabbi to a certain segment of the congregation, he was seeking another position. . . . The basic conflicts have not been resolved. . . . All I have ever desired was an expression of confidence in the ideals for which I stand and which I feel to be a part of the Jewish religious heritage. A rabbi, if he is a real one, must be a leader and not a follower.
> . . . [i]f the price for his security and material well-being is conformity to existing local patterns of thought and deed, then I must in all sincerity, say that the price is too high. Nothing can prevail upon me to compromise with my conscience.[76]

A year later, he delivered his farewell address, concluding with these words:

> Remember, my friends, Mickve Israel is a Temple of Reform Judaism. It is a house of Liberal Judaism. Never allow yourselves to become orthodox in your Reform for that will be a betrayal of the dynamic idealism which fired the founders of our movement.
> May God grant you strength to grow ever greater. May He grant you that vision of purpose which will enable you, together with your rabbi, to create that house of God which shall truly be a "House of prayer for all peoples."[77]

A few months thereafter, Rabbi Youngerman was called to Congregation Rodeph Shalom in Philadelphia, Pennsylvania, as the assistant rabbi. After a few years in that capacity, he moved on to Allentown, Pennsylvania, serving as the honored senior rabbi of Congregation Keneseth Israel until his untimely death in 1960.

REFORM—IN A CLASSICAL MOLD

Documentation offered earlier demonstrated that K.K.M.I. emerged from
Sephardic Orthodoxy of the Portuguese kind to "conservative" Reform. A
congregation that required its rabbi (Solomon) to wear a *tallit* (prayer
shawl) and retained the custom of mourners only rising for the *Kaddish*
until the mid-twentieth century would not qualify as classical "Reform."
Yet that designation was cited by the board with ever-increasing frequency
in the post-World War II era. This turn was accompanied by a contraction of
connections to the Savannah Jewish community and the U.A.H.C. Rabbi
Solomon was the last spiritual leader of the temple to function as a *molder*
of the total Jewish community, with close relations to all constituent elements, including the rabbis. Withdrawal followed his demise.

Determining causation is speculative endeavor at best, when the sources
offer no evidence of a formal decision. The suggestion is advanced that the
two critical issues, Zionism and race, sparked the shift.

On the national level, the institutions of Reform, particularly the Union
(U.A.H.C.), were perceived as proponents of the Jewish homeland, the aforementioned text book controversy providing singular evidence. The sense in
the congregation was that a new constituency was flowing into Reform
congregations, persons of eastern-European background, with pro-Zionist
and pro-ceremony inclinations. Southern Reform synagogue members
viewed the change as threatening to the forms they grew up with, and, in the
instance of Mickve Israel, it prompted a move toward "classical" Reform.

In the 1950's and 1960's, when racial turmoil heated up and freedom
riders (Reform rabbis among them) "invaded" southern cities, a second
layer of hostility to the national institutions of Reform Judaism emerged.
In the early 1960's, the president of K.K.M.I. responded to a request from
the U.A.H.C. for dues with the comment:

> If some of your members would stay in their home territory and
> attend to their business instead of coming down here as freedom
> riders, we would all be better off.[78]

In 1904, the same year that the congregation joined the Union, a resolution was adopted unanimously by the congregation, stating that the character
of Reform in Mickve Israel would be "moderate" or "conservative" Reform.
A half century later, it deemed itself "classical" and somewhat "anti-Union."
The following data is entered into the record to document the transition.

(1) Fear of the new constituency coming into Reform resulted in
attempts to investigate the background of new members.[79] They were asked
to submit applications for membership, including a statement that they
accepted the tenets of "pure" Reform Judaism.[80] Why?

> All of the Board members recognized the danger of having Mickve
> Israel drift toward the tenets of orthodoxy because of the influence of
> these newer members [who were coming from the other two congrega-
> tions in the community].[81]

(2) In 1957, Mickve Israel was represented at the Toronto Biennial
and the local delegates were instructed to vote on several resolutions.[82] One
was to prevent the domination of the rabbis at the conference, by defining
their roles "as spiritual advisors to congregants and to congregations" who
are not "exalted above the laity." Therefore, the laity should lead the debates. At the same convocation, an attack was made on the president of the
Union for public statements and actions on "military, political, economic,
and diplomatic matters," beyond the clear "objects of the Union as set
forth in its constitution." The resolution established the principal that the
Union could

> instill in each congregant's heart and mind an understanding of those
> principles [of social justice] and a firm commitment to advance them
> in daily action

which the laity can then translate into deed. For the leaders of Reform to
speak out in public print on such issues, "giving the impression that all
Jews are of one mind" on any political or military matter, was inappropriate. A second resolution entitled "Code of Practices" was a rejection of an
attempt by the Union to superimpose a code of beliefs or practices upon its
constituent congregations.[83]

(3) In response to the Reform rabbis who joined the freedom marches
and civil rights demonstrations in the South, the president of K.K.M.I., with
the backing of the board (as demonstrated by the resolution following the
minutes of November 15, 1962) led a long, hard fight at the Southeastern
Biennial of the U.A.H.C. Victory was achieved. The resolution which
passed consisted of a request to the Social Action Commission of the Union
to cease from

> taking any action in a Community until that Community's Congrega-
> tion was in agreement.[84]

(4) To protect K.K.M.I. from the erosion of its Reform worship
patterns, a constitutional amendment was proposed on April 26, 1964, which
read,

> No change shall be made in the form of worship as now practiced
> by this Congregation except by a two-thirds vote of the membership
> in meeting assembled,

thirty days written notice preceding the vote.[85]

(5) To discourage bar mitzvahs, all parties who wished their children
to "read from the torah [sic]" were required to petition the board for that
privilege.[86] As late as 1961, when the ceremony began to grow in popularity,
the rabbi was still requesting information about those whom the board approved for the ritual (concerning which the secretary added in the minutes,
"which are not encouraged").[87]

As the interests and convictions of the *adjunta* clashed with the agenda of the Union, the historic goodwill that flowed back and forth in the time of Rabbi Solomon ceased. To demonstrate displeasure, the tact of tightening the purse strings was pursued. When the Union's needs required additional dues, the congregation responded with a closed fist.[88] Debate on the merit of affiliation was not unusual, and, ultimately, the plan emerged to append the Union dues to individual dues statements, allowing those who did not wish to pay the tax, to abstain.[89] On May 21, 1957, a serious effort was made to pull the congregation out of the U.A.H.C., claiming "no useful purpose was served by continuing the congregation's membership."[90] A motion to pay the same amount as the previous year prevented the final breech.

Representatives from the Union made contact with the temple to try to negotiate. Rabbi Israel Gerber, southeastern representative, asked for a M.I. liason, and one was appointed.[91] Rabbi Jacob Rothschild of "The Temple" in Atlanta requested an opportunity to address the board and urge it to pay its fair share.[92] In 1963, in response to the social action stands taken, the threat to resign was again being sounded, and a committee of trustees and past presidents was established to investigate three possibilities: (a) to withdraw, (b) to express to the Union the congregation's displeasure, and (c) to communicate with other congregations who hold similar opinions.[93] Three years later, Rabbi Sanford Seltzer, a Union staff member, visited, and that encounter resolved the money issue (not immediately but in the long run).[94] From that point on, there was an occasional dispute and some difference of opinion. At the present, relations with the Union are at a calm place, and the congregation's support is appropriate.

A further sign of irritation with Union policies was the eagerness with which the board took up the gauntlet whenever other constituent congregations challenged. Temple Emanu-El of New York objected to the Union speaking for all Reform temples in 1948, and a letter proceeded from Savannah to Emanu-El's secretary, expressing approval.[95] In 1967, when Emanu-El again resigned, discussion ensued. Rabbi Buchler's comments, aided by Trustee Meyer Schneider's support, aborted action.[96] In 1957, when the congregation in Norfolk (Temple Ohef Sholom) sent out resolutions to limit rabbinic debate, social action, etc., Mickve Israel voted its support. That triggered a letter from Solomon Elsner, chairman of the Executive Board of the Union, requesting that no delegate to the Biennial be instructed as to how to vote.[97] The action of the temple president at the Southeastern Biennial in 1962—leading an effort to prevent freedom riders from coming into a southern community without the foreknowledge and approval of its leadership—was the apotheosis of anti-Unionism.[98]

The strength of Reform Judaism is the flexibility it allows. One may initiate innovations or restore traditions. In the post-World War II era, an amalgam of practices was instituted at Mickve Israel, some lifted from the past, others fashioned anew. Still others were blendings of the two. Examples: Rabbi Youngerman centered on Chanukkah as *the* festival to revive. A new liturgy was written consisting of a candle-lighting procedure that transformed the darkened sanctuary into a room filled with flickering flames.[99] Rabbi Buchler was another who infused meaning into the "Festival of Lights" by creating a special service (which yet survives). Youngerman also restored the bar mitzvah and instituted the *kiddush* (ceremony over wine) as part of the *Shabbat* evening liturgy.[100]

Judaism historically celebrated the birth or death of no human being in its religious calendar. A break with that long-standing tradition occurred with the introduction of an Isaac M. Wise Sabbath. In Mickve Israel it began in 1947 with a pulpit exchange.

As the Temple Youth Group gained strength, a T.Y.G. Sabbath was instituted which permitted a creative prayer format.[101] Even more innovative, yea revolutionary, was the teens' idea of a "shock the rabbi" Sabbath

on a Friday night when the rabbi expected the same old crowd.[102]

The Temple Youth Group also initiated a ceremony which is nowhere else mentioned in the congregation's records, *Havdallah* (the ritual that marks the conclusion of the Sabbath).[103]

In more recent times, Hebrew has become an integral part of the Sunday school curriculum; Rabbis Buchler and Zionts were arrayed in *tallesim* (prayer shawls) as they led prayer; and the *Gates of Prayer,* the new Union prayerbook, has been accepted for Sabbath evening worship. *Havurah*-style services (informal prayer, emphasizing "community") are customary, and even a dance liturgy has been performed in the main sanctuary on two occasions. Worshippers feel free to don the skull-cap if that is their preferred manner of showing deference to the Almighty, although the majority of the congregation prefers the bare-headed approach. The struggle over issues and ritualism has diminished, as the atmosphere has changed to one of respect for differences and an appreciation of the richness of ancient traditions. The bar/bat mitzvah services have developed into occasions of family reconsecration, as the generations participate in a Torah-transmission rite, and prayers for the fledglings are offered by their parents (in some instances, even by siblings). The introduction of *Havurah* (small group arrangements for friendship and study) has substantially altered prayer modes. Guitar music, Sabbath celebrations (involving families in a Sabbath meal, singing Hebrew songs, and worshipping in the round), and an emphasis on community closeness are as accepted as the standard format. Among the Reform congregations of the Nation, Mickve Israel is at the vanguard of the most contemporary Jewish expressions.

The innovations in forms and rituals have been matched by reformations in synagogue structure. In his annual address to the congregation in 1961, President B. H. Levy recommended that a woman be elected to the *adjunta* in the near future.[104] In 1963 his wife, Marion Abrahams Levy, was honored as the first daughter of the congregation to be elected as a trustee.[105] Mildred Weichselbaum succeeded her two years later.

In 1964, Mrs. Samuel Herman, Sisterhood president, suggested that the presidents of Brotherhood and Sisterhood serve on the temple board.[106] Soon thereafter, her suggestion resulted in the requested structural change. In 1970, Mrs. Maurice Gefen, youth group advisor, recommended the inclusion of the Temple Youth Group president, which was approved.[107] In an effort to democratize and expand the board's operation, a change in the Charter was enacted through the Georgia legislature as a result of a congregational meeting of November 16, 1970. The board was expanded from seven to a maximum of sixteen (seven was acceptable, but no less; sixteen was the outer limit, and anywhere in between was permissible). It received the necessary votes, and eventually the Charter change was signed by the Secretary of State of Georgia.

MICKVE ISRAEL AND THE JEWISH COMMUNITY

It has been suggested that Mickve Israel went through a phase of turning inward during the period when Israel, social justice, and a return to tradition were the principle issues in Reform Jewish life. The effect locally was a reduced level of relating to the total Jewish community. In 1947, when Mr. Chilnick, Director of Activities at the J.E.A., wanted to use one of the rooms of the chapel for a program of recorded music, and a letter was received from a member of the congregation who was head of the Visual Education Committee of the same agency seeking space, a committee to investigate both requests was appointed.[108] Letters from the leadership at the J.E.A. soliciting temple participation in a Jewish lecture series that featured leading figures in American Judaism were rarely acted upon favorably.[109] This policy was in effect from 1954 to 1966.[110] The J.E.A., in 1954, invited a prominent Reform spokesman to address the community, prompting Rabbi Starrels to appear before the board to urge a one time allocation, which it did.[111] Dr. Salo Baron agreed to speak at Agudath Achim on Friday and at K.K.M.I. on Saturday evening, as part of this lecture series. The question was put to the board by the rabbi—would it be acceptable to hold a joint service at A.A. on Friday night so that the eminent historian's speech could be enjoyed by an enlarged congregation? A service would precede Baron's address, involving the rabbis of both institutions. Answer: No; because

> the decades of uninterrupted Friday night services at Mickve Israel would be ended.[112]

As solution, the *adjunta* recommended a brief service at K.K.M.I., allowing participants time to travel from the temple to the Conservative House of Prayer.[113]

In the 1950's, the Bureau of Jewish Education, under the direction of Samuel Rosenberg, was created to serve the needs of all Sunday schools and to provide for the operation of two community schools—the Savannah Hebrew Day School (a parochial school) and the Hebrew Community

School (an afternoon school). It sought ways to involve all of Savannah's congregations. In August of 1954, the minutes mention the Bureau for the first time.[114] An invitation had arrived from the Savannah Jewish Council, requesting participants for the purpose of surveying community needs. Full compliance was at first forthcoming from K.K.M.I. with five representatives chosen to serve on the five committees (Statistics, Program, Administration, Attitudes, and Community Educational Systems).[115] When the representatives reported back, they perceived the ultimate goal as the formation of a consolidated "city-wide" Hebrew school, and, unanimously, the board recommended abstention. The rabbi was consulted to "discuss the most politic method of doing so."[116] To clarify the response to the Community Hebrew School, a central consideration, prompting non-involvement, was the non-Reform orientation that would prevail.

While the board was pulling the congregation away from the larger Jewish community, an opposing tendency was developing among the temple affiliates and individual members. The National Council of Jewish Women attracted ladies from all synagogues. Beginning in 1947, it had been customary for all the Sisterhoods and the N.C.J.W. to gather together once a year for a joint program.[117] Likewise, the Brotherhoods of the city were accustomed to meet annually at the J.E.A.[118] Stephen Traub, Brotherhood president, proudly announced in his annual report of 1958 that Dr. Meyer Schneider, Brotherhood representative on the Savannah Jewish Council, was elected to its Executive Committee. *Contact* regularly included information about *simchot* (happy events) in the lives of members of other synagogues who, it is assumed, were befriended by the people of Mickve Israel.[119]

In 1950, an eleven and one-half acre site in the south side of the city (beyond the incorporated limits) was purchased by the Jewish Educational Alliance Board.[120] By May 30, 1955, the Barnard Street Alliance Building was vacated, and the new Jewish Center and pool were officially opened on June 19, 1955.[121] Seven years later, the fiftieth anniversary of the J.E.A. was marked with ceremonies honoring, among others, Rabbi George Solomon, a founder of the institution. His wife, "Aunt" Julia, was present to respond and to receive recognition. The M.I. Board purchased an ad in the *Anniversary Memorial Booklet* on behalf of the congregation and its subsidiaries. Among the names listed as J.E.A. solicitors, booklet editors and public relations workers were the following Mickve Israelites: Mrs. Betty Platt, Mrs. Julius Edel, Mrs. Lamont Danzig, Mrs. Baldwin Kahn, Stephen Traub, Herman Cranman, Mrs. Alvin Cranman, Philip Cranman, M. J. Becker, Dr. Maurice Fields, Mrs. Henry Kaplan, David Meddin, and Dr. M. M. Schneider.[122] Pictured as former J.E.A. presidents were B. H. Levy, 1914-15 (first president); David Amram Byck, 1916-17; Jacob Gazan, 1918-19, 1925-29, 1932-35; M. H. Bernstein, 1929-31; H. Sol Clark (later a member of the temple), 1935-36; B. B. Eichholz (likewise), 1938-39; Morton H. Levy, 1941-42; and Philip H. Bodziner, 1948-50. This anniversary celebration revived memories of a time when the Jewish community was more unified, and may have prompted efforts at rapproachement.

During Martin Leffler's term as president, the momentum increased. K.K.M.I. participated in a community survey of Jewish youth.[123] At the recommendation of Rabbi Buchler, the *adjunta* contributed generously to a survey initiated by the Savannah Jewish Council in 1966 to review the status of Jewish education in the city.[124] The temple was involved in a study of Savannah's Jewish aged with Julius Oelsner serving as M.I. representative (in the term of Henry Levy).[125] The board sanctioned the closing of religious school one Sunday in 1967 so that the faculty could attend a teachers' institute at the J.E.A.[126]

When Donald Kole, temple member, was elected to the presidency of the Savannah Jewish Council, and former Temple President Martin Leffler became S.J.C. vice-president, President Henry Levy suggested that as many as possible attend the Council's annual meeting.[127] In a previously quoted passage from his annual meeting message of January, 1967, Leffler urged communication and mutual cooperation with all Savannah Jews to benefit the entire community.[128] A year later, President Henry Levy announced,

As a Board and as a Congregation, we participated in more of the organized communal activities of the Jewish community.[129]

Verbalizing the need to be selective, he nonetheless saw benefit in these arrangements. In the years since, the process accelerated. The rabbi of the temple serves as a member of the S.J.C. Board and, in various capacities, on its select committees. Rabbi Starrels was honored by the Jewish community as a recipient of a State of Israel award during an Israel Bonds annual dinner in 1973. In 1981, after extensive deliberation involving the S.J.C., the three synagogues and their spiritual leaders, a new educational institution, the Institute of Jewish Education, was established providing afternoon Hebrew education. It is now a joint venture of Agudath Achim and Congregation Mickve Israel.

THE STARRELS YEARS

In 1948, Rabbi Louis Youngerman resigned. For the first time in seventy years, the congregation lacked spiritual guidance. Without the aid of Rabbi David Marx of "The Temple" in Atlanta, the confirmation class of 1948 would have been denied rabbinic blessing. B. H. Levy provided the weekly confirmation instruction.[130] The search for the new rabbi was commenced by President B. K. Victor, and among those considered were Rabbis Samuel Shillman, Lester Roubey, David Zielonka, and Harry Kaplan. The present Director of Placement for the C.C.A.R., Rabbi Stanley Dryfus, was a candidate as well. The attention of the leaders turned to the only Reform rabbi in New Mexico, Rabbi Solomon Elihu Starrels of Temple Albert in Albuquerque. After his election on July 6, 1948, Sidney Wortsman, secretary, commented,

There were 125 at the meeting, and there was a general feeling of relief and satisfaction of the accomplishments of the Rabbi Procurement Committee and the board and many so expressed themselves at the meeting.[131]

Following the tension of the immediate past, the God-centered man who would be their spiritual leader impressed the congregators as perfect for the task of "calming troubled waters."

Ordained in 1922, Rabbi Starrels had completed his twenty-fifth year in the rabbinate when he came to Savannah. A Brooklyn native, reared and educated in Philadelphia, he attended public schools in the City of Brotherly Love, graduating from a local high school and proceeding to the University of Cincinnati and the Hebrew Union College for a combined program. In 1921, he was graduated from the university and one year later from the seminary. His first pulpit was in New Orleans as assistant rabbi at Temple Sinai. From there he advanced to Congregation B'nai Jeshurun in Lincoln, Nebraska, and later to a new continent for the formative years of his rabbinate. The decade he spent in London on the staff of the Liberal Jewish Synagogue in London and later as rabbi of the newly-organized West London Synagogue (he was instrumental in building its handsome edifice) are years remembered with joy. While in London he furthered his education, earning a Doctor of Philosophy degree in comparative religions at the University of London in 1936. Among those whom he befriended were Lady Montague and Claude G. Montefiore. In the Temple Archives, his written impressions of Claude Montefiore (it appeared in the January, 1961, *C.C.A.R. Journal*) have been preserved.[132]

In 1938, the rumors of war were heard in England, and it was time for the Starrels family to return home. Temple Albert in the growing city of Albuquerque was offered to them. For the next decade, the rabbi served there, functioning in community service as did his wife, Gertrude (the former Gertrude Weil of Evansville, Indiana). There they raised two daughters, Judith and Ruth, who were attending the University of Missouri and Swarthmore College, respectively, when the Savannah rabbinate began.[133]

The major events of the Starrels' years, from 1948 to 1965 (with emeritus status granted on January 9, 1966), punctuated by emergency recalls in 1968 and again in the summer of 1972, are the following (not necessarily in sequence):

He invited to address the congregation some of the ablest spokesmen in the American rabbinate, including Samuel Goldenson, Julian Feibelman, Maurice Davis, Joseph Narot, Joseph Fink, Jerome Malino, Julius Mark, Nathan Perilman, Robert Kahn, and Levi Olan. Each annual meeting was graced by one of these gifted pulpiteers. In 1952, under the auspices of the American Jewish Committee, famed British-Jewish historian, Dr. Cecil Roth, spoke at K.K.M.I.[134]

In 1950, the Lepinsky property was sold. This provided seed money for the building project that was the high point of the Starrels years.[135]

In 1948, Philip N. Coleman announced his intention to provide the funding for a major temple project, later designated as the Charles and Eugenia Coleman Library. At a banquet, arranged through the auspices of the Temple Brotherhood, in the presence of the family as honored guests (wife, Ray Kaufman Coleman; sister, Olivia; and brothers, Leo C. and R. Lester), the gift was given. The Colemans were reared in Savannah and were involved with the temple, making it a place of sacred memories.[136] On January 15, 1950, the Coleman Library was dedicated with an invocation by Dr. Samuel Goldenson of Temple Emanu-El of New York, and a formal address by Rabbi Sidney Lefkowitz, Mr. Coleman's rabbi in Jacksonville, Florida. The door was officially opened by Olivia Coleman. On behalf of the family, P. N. Coleman presented the library to the congregation; Max Guthman, board member, officially accepted it. A memorial tablet, which read, "Erected in Loving Memory of Charles and Eugenia Coleman By Their Children—As An Expression of Everlasting Devotion," was affixed to the fireplace in the handsome room, designed by the architectural firm of Levy and Kiley. In his dedicatory prayer and statement, Rabbi Starrels insisted the library was one of the most beautiful of its kind in the Nation.[137] When the old chapel was replaced, this library was rebuilt panel by panel.

In 1953, a fund-raising effort was undertaken, the largest in the congregation's history, to provide additional space, especially for the religious school. Once again, Benjamin K. Victor was pressed into service.[138] Rabbi Starrels expressed the desire of the congregation to begin the project with all deliberate speed since $80,000 had been raised. An amateur architect (designer of his own beach home at Tybee Island), the rabbi had consulted with Harry Prince on referral by the U.A.H.C. Mr. Prince recommended that the present site be used, that the building be razed, and that new facilities be constructed on the existing foundation.[139] The chairman of the Building Committee, Sylvan Byck, and his associate in the enterprise, Herbert Kayton, were present as the board debated the merits of an in-town versus out-of-town architect. Arnio and Hibner were touted by the Union for this kind of work. The Building Committee and board commissioned temple member Henry Levy, of the firm of Levy and Kiley, as its unanimous choice.[140] It was suggested by Rabbi Starrels and sustained by the board that the new building no longer be called the Mordecai Sheftall Chapel (or more commonly "the Chapel"), but rather be designated as the Mordecai Sheftall Memorial.[141]

On September 12, 1955, the day when the firm of Otto Olaf submitted a bid of $127,000 to construct a two story structure on the eastern portion of Monterey Square, Levy and Kiley were asked to prepare informal cost estimates for the raising of a new Sunday school building on a tract of land on Savannah's south side. (The spirit of Rabbi Solomon must have been hovering low that day!) A special called meeting of the congregation was arranged for October 23rd. The proposal of Sylvan Byck's committee was presented, and a member of the committee, Dr. Semon Eisenberg, rose to express his interest in a south side location which would not cost more than the amount projected. Citing other congregations that had joined the move southward (where most Jews lived), he proposed acquiring sufficient land to accommodate a synagogue as well. The new structure would function as a school, a meeting place for youth, and as a recreational center for the adult congregants.

The objections of Mrs. Wallace Hohenstein, religious school superintendent for many years, were voiced to the assemblage. They boiled down to a concern over the separation of school from sanctuary, and the need for children to be brought into God's house as part of their religious training. This view was sustained by the president of the Sunday school (student council), Nathan Coleman, who represented the children.

When Henry Levy was asked the cost of the undertaking, as proposed by Dr. Eisenberg, his answer was, in essence, this. The Monterey Square Synagogue could be sold for $100,000. With the additional $130,000 the congregation would need to raise in any case, plus $40,000 more, a new complex—temple and school—could be constructed on the south side.

Finally, B. H. Levy moved that the old chapel be torn down and, on the same site, a new structure be built by Levy and Kiley at a total cost of $130,000. The motion was accepted, by a vote of eighty-nine to seven.[142]

On December 20, 1955, the demolition began (a picture of which appeared in a 1955 issue of *Contact*), and while the building project proceeded, the facilities of Wesley Monumental Church were used.[143] The Sabbath services were conducted in the Wesley Chapel. The Sunday school met each Sunday in Gamble Hall on what was the old Armstrong Junior College campus (now the United Way Building). By the time the modern, two-story Sheftall Memorial was completed and dedicated (during the administration of Temple President Stanley Harris) on January 11, 1957, the religious school showed signs of expansion. Four years after the dedication, it served 160 students, a record number.[144] The debt was retired in 1960 through Benjamin K. Victor's heroic effort and the assistance of Dr. William Weichselbaum, Jr. and Sylvan Byck. Alvin Schwab's contribution as record keeper was noted at the time.[145]

In 1955, Rabbi Starrels conceived of a new design for the pulpit of the synagogue. To highlight the ark, the pulpit was to be lowered so that it would more naturally rise from the main auditorium. A sketch by Christopher Murphy, Savannah artist, was reproduced in *Contact*.[146] Opposition developed, and the project was allowed to lapse.

Another capital funds campaign was initiated on October 22, 1961, to raise the funds necessary for repairing, recarpeting, and air-conditioning the temple. Sylvan Byck set in motion the second solicitation of size in a four year span. Milton Eisenberg served as chairman of the Temple Rebuilding Fund. By May of 1962, it was oversubscribed, and the repairs were accomplished on schedule.[147] B. H. Levy in his last presidential message recommended the improvements because B.B. Jacob's new sanctuary was about to be completed (with all the modern conveniences), and A.A. was fully air-conditioned.[148]

In this period, the final effort to construct a new temple and school was initiated when Armstrong Junior College vacated its Monterey Square campus to occupy facilities on the southern edge of town. With the college gone, the area around the temple threatened to deteriorate. Henry Levy called for the investigation of other sites to build on.[149] Herman Edel suggested the purchase of Gamble Hall (part of Armstrong Junior College), which faced the north wall of the temple, across Wayne Street.[150] On February 7, 1966, a committee was chosen to investigate the matter. Milton Kassel and Dr. Meyer Schneider, committee co-chairmen, recommended the submission of a bid to purchase the property as an investment. On March 17, 1966, a bid of $40,000 was offered by unanimous action of the temple board. The bid was rejected.

On April 15, 1962, the official leave-taking service of the B'nai B'rith Congregation (from its Montgomery Street home) took place. It was followed immediately by the dedication ceremonies of the new building on the south side (Abercorn at 74th Street), in proximity to the J.E.A. A dedicatory booklet included all pertinent information about the structure. The elaborate murals adjacent to the ark were painted by Gisbert Palmier; the building itself was designed by Michael M. Hack, A.I.A., and constructed by Worrell Construction Co. Benjamin A. Kantsiper was over-all Building Committee chairman. Louis A. Wexler served as congregation president. The guiding spirit of the enterprise was the rabbi of the congregation for more than a generation, Rabbi Abraham I. Rosenberg.

The new and elaborate B.B. Jacob incorporated into its mortar the lintel stone from the first structure, erected on Montgomery Street before the twentieth century, and also the second cornerstone from the 1909 edifice. Plaques were removed from the old location and affixed to appropriate walls.[151] The synagogue was constructed without classrooms.

ON THE PERSONAL SIDE

In abbreviated form, these are some highlights of Rabbi Starrels' achievements:

In 1952, he celebrated with the congregation his thirtieth year in the rabbinate. An appropriate reception was arranged.

During the Tercentenary of American Jewry (in 1954), he represented K.K.M.I. at a great convocation in Carnegie Hall. A gold medal was given to him, along with a certificate, officially declaring Mickve Israel to be one of the oldest congregations in America.[152]

He spoke, via national radio (ABC), on the "Message of Israel" program on January 14, 1962.[153]

He was appointed by the Central Conference of American Rabbis to the

Liturgy Committee. He also was invited to present the conference sermon in 1961.

In recognition of his long and distinguished service to Jewry, the Hebrew Union College bestowed upon him the Doctor of Divinity degree, *honoris causa* (June 6, 1958).

Because of his temperate manner, he served as a quiet negotiator during the racial crises of the 1960's.[154]

The most popular Brotherhood-Sisterhood show ever was dedicated to him—"Solly's Follies." Alan Gaynor, president of Brotherhood in 1960, recalled that it was the highlight of the year,

Everything [after] was a total anti-climax.[155]

The theme that reverberated through his annual messages was the centrality of worship in synagogue life. The cultivation of meditation, public and private, was his pursuit. In 1959, he mentioned the need for a home manual, a "devotional anthology." At that time he was assembling material with a mind toward publication. In 1981, his collection of aphorisms was finally published. Entitled *Gleanings from a Personal Anthology*, it was, in part, an ethical will to his family and a promise kept with his people.

As this chapter is being concluded, Rabbi Starrels and Gertrude celebrate a sixtieth year in the rabbinate and three and a half decades of ministry to the citizens of Savannah.

Other events that marked Starrels' term include:

Ruth Stern, faithful secretary for thirty-seven years, consultant to three rabbis (Solomon, Youngerman, and Starrels), retired at the end of 1959. She was replaced by Sue Solomon Herman, a daughter of K.K.M.I., and later by Mrs. William Lynch, secretary to four rabbis (Starrels, Buchler, Zionts, and Rubin). A lovely reception and outpouring of affection marked her retirement ceremony in the synagogue on March 31, 1979.[156] For three years, Mrs. Sheila Ferrell, wife of a Southern Baptist minister, Rev. Richard Ferrell, has maintained exceptionally high standards of secretarial and bookkeeping skills.

Cleveland Lewis kept the facilities attended to during the tenure of Rabbis Solomon through Rubin. The Trappios, Walter and Albertha, have been more than sufficient replacements. As visitors have made pilgrimage to K.K.M.I. in an ever increasing stream, the friendliness of the Trappios has sparked praise from many quarters.

The Temple Youth Group flourished in this era. From its inception in September, 1949, it reached its apex in 1962 when forty teens were admitted to membership.[157] In addition to serving the synagogue and the Jewish community, promoting interfaith endeavor and encouraging positive Jewish living, T.Y.G. has been the mechanism for enabling Jewish youth in the southeast to develop Jewish contacts through conclaves, summer camp (at Camp Coleman in Cleveland, Georgia, named after Ray and Philip N. Coleman, K.K.M.I. benefactors), and regional/state conventions. Savannah has been the center to which Reform youth in eastern Georgia and South Carolina have gathered annually for *kallahs* (study sessions), leadership retreats, and the like.

Interest in the history of the congregation was furthered by the work of David Amram Byck, Jr., who was designated the congregation's historian. Described in the minutes as one

who has studied the history of Mickve Israel all the way back to 1733 and is an authority on matters in this connection,

Byck reported the discovery of the original Charter in 1948.[158] The hope was expressed that the original George Washington letter,

either lost or . . . in the possession of some descendant of [an] early congregational leader,

might be located.[159] It was never found. The Charter was lost during the renovation project of 1974 (when the closet in which it was stored was cleaned out by the janitor). The expectation was that David A. Byck, Jr., would one day write a documentary history of K.K.M.I. and such is noted in the minutes of March 24, 1961.

On January 17, 1954, the Southeastern Federation of the U.A.H.C. held its biennial in Savannah, at which time a plaque was dedicated at the site of the first synagogue building in Georgia (Perry Lane and Whitaker Street). The ceremonies included the unveiling by two descendants of first settlers (Joan Levy of the Benjamin Sheftall line and Robert P. Minis of Abraham Minis' seed). The plaque was approved by the Savannah-Chatham County Historic Site and Monument Commission, Thomas H. Gignilliat, secretary.[160] Raymond M. Kuhr served as master of ceremonies, and remarks and Divine petitions were offered by Dr. Starrels.[161]

Through the intercession of H. Sol Clark, the Georgia Historical Commission agreed to place a bronze marker in front of the temple, describing the historic significance of the congregation. Attorney Clark was later appointed by Governor Jimmy Carter to the Court of Appeals of Georgia on January 1, 1972, the first Jew to serve in that capacity. (Judge Clark was subsequently elected to the post the following November and remained on the bench until mandatory retirement.)

Wesley Monumental Church again had need of the temple from August 7, 1953 to July 4, 1954, after having been struck by lightning. A beautiful resolution expressed the gratitude of the church for the hospitality offered.[162] *Contact* reported that the first non-Jewish wedding ever was performed in the K.K.M.I. sanctuary during this period—the marriage of Eileen Christine Cammack and Alvin Robert Gerstenberger with Dr. Albert Trulock officiating. (Lucille and Hadley Cammack, stepmother and father of the bride, retain memory of the occasion and consider it a milestone in Jewish-Christian relations.) Again in 1975, during the tenure of Rev.

Weyman Cleveland, Methodists filled the sanctuary of the temple each Sunday for a year's time, while a restoration effort was undertaken at their Calhoun Square church.

The minutes record unusual individual honors. The Hillyer Award for the "Woman of the Year" in 1952 was presented to Mildred Guckenheimer Abrahams Kuhr. This award was given annually to an individual for service to the community over a protracted period.[163] Henry Levy was chosen one of five Outstanding Young Men of the State of Georgia in 1961 by the Georgia Junior Chamber of Commerce. Since Levy was secretary of the congregation at the time, the president limited him

> to two pages in the minutes with which to praise himself with [sic] this commendation.[164]

The last congregational reception for "Aunt" Julia Solomon, marking her 75th birthday, occurred on August 25, 1955. It attracted a large crowd of well-wishers.[165]

The late fifties were marked by violent acts perpetrated against synagogues. The explosion that violated The Temple in Atlanta on October 12, 1958, was traumatic, though dynamite charges were found in other southern Jewish sanctuaries and centers. (This author served Congregation Beth Israel in Gadsden, Alabama, in 1960 when a Nazi-oriented youth, whipped up by the visit of Admiral Crommelin of Montgomery, then a candidate for governor of Alabama, fire-bombed the sanctuary.) Temple Mickve Israel responded to the rash of bombings and attempted bombings by engaging in precautionary measures. In 1961, in response to the Adolph Eichmann trial in Israel, the exterior lights were left burning all night around the building. The April 14, 1961, minutes added:

> . . . as has been the policy since the bombing of the Synagogue in Atlanta.

In 1965, when efforts were made in the city to integrate churches, and "kneel-ins" were initiated by the black leadership, the board legislated that, if any negroes should present themselves at the temple doors.

> they should be made to feel welcome, given prayer books and shown to seats.[166]

THE BUCHLER TERM

To replace retiring Rabbi Starrels, a search was initiated, resulting in the election of Rabbi Joseph Buchler on August 26, 1965, at a special meeting of the congregation. He was described as having

> a classical Reform background, being reared in Central Synagogue of New York.[167]

A graduate of the University of Cincinnati and the Hebrew Union College, he served neighboring congregation Walton Way Temple in Augusta, Georgia, from 1947 to 1949 and Temple Mizpah in Chicago from 1950 to 1963. That year he returned to the Empire State to officiate at Temple Beth Sholom, New City, New York. His rabbinic thesis in American Jewish history was entitled "The Struggle for Unity: Attempts at Union in American Jewish Life: 1654 to 1868" (submitted on April 28, 1947). His published articles appeared in the *Journal of the C.C.A.R.*, *American Judaism Magazine*, and the *American Jewish Archives Quarterly*. During his tenure in Chicago, his colleagues elected him president of the Chicago Association of Reform Rabbis. History was his field, and he was given the opportunity to teach at the College of Jewish Studies in the Windy City.[168] In a letter dated August 23, 1965, Rabbi Starrels endorsed him wholeheartedly, expressing confidence in his ability and high motivation.

Devastating disease limited his service to Mickve Israel. In his twenty-eight months of ministry, he reorganized a couples club, generated interest in adult education (ten percent of the congregation attended his course in comparative religions), innovated ritually (his Chanukkah service was published), made the religious school the centerpiece of the synagogue operation, and boosted the youth group at every turn. For the first time, at his suggestion, the rabbi attended temple board meetings regularly. Joint services with the sister congregations on U.J.A. Sabbaths became an established routine. It was at Buchler's urging that the congregation participated in a study of the state of Jewish education in Savannah. The teens found him a fascinating teacher and enjoyed his sessions both at youth group and in confirmation class. Outreach to the non-Jewish community was restricted, as the rabbi focused attention on building up the institution internally and establishing himself as its leader. The one controversy that attended his ministry resulted from his 1967 High Holy Day addresses on the morality of the Vietnam war and civil rights concerns. The board discussed the sermons, responding to a member who voiced strong opposition, and defended the rabbi's right to free expression from the pulpit.[169] Then disease struck.

On December 21, 1967, the temple president consulted with physicians about the state of the rabbi's health and the long-term prognosis. Rabbi Starrels volunteered to assist in this time of need. Before the annual meeting on January 4, 1968, the third rabbi in the history of the congregation died in office. Henry Levy, temple president, represented the congregation at the final interment service, which took place in New York City.[170] The resolution passed on the occasion of Buchler's death included the words,

> during his short term as Rabbi of this Congregation, he left a memory that reflected a fine and noble character.[171]

A Rabbi Joseph Buchler Memorial Fund was created which provided campership money for Temple Youth Group members.[172] His widow,

Jeanne, remained with the congregation, serving as religious school principal until her relocation in 1972.

The Search Committee was revived for a second time in less than thirty
months, and by June 24, 1968, a candidate for the pulpit was announced,
Rabbi Joseph B. Messing, Army chaplain. For the full course of his rabbinate, he had been attached to the military. His election on July 9, 1968, as
K.K.M.I. rabbi ended in futility, when a letter was received from him and
shared with the membership.[173] After intensive soul-searching, the decision
was made to continue in the chaplaincy. Instead of civilian life, he went on
to an overseas assignment. From December of 1967 until the summer of
1969, President Henry Levy served as religious officiant in the absence of a
congregational rabbi and during Rabbi Starrels' extended trips abroad.

THE ZIONTS TERM

In his October 10, 1968, letter to the congregation (after Rabbi Messing
withdrew his candidacy), President Levy summed up the frustration of
Mickve Israelites:

> I know this is hard for all of us to take. We can all gain strength by
> leaning on one another . . ."

The cooperation that resulted demonstrated that, when thrown on its
own resources, the temple could survive. Not believing the new found co-
hesiveness a long term solution, the president again reconstituted the Pulpit
Committee. A new rabbi, Richard A. Zionts, arrived for an interview in December of 1968.[174] A *shitach* (contractual arrangement) was made, and at
the annual meeting in January, 1969, the next spiritual leader of K.K.M.I.
was chosen. The election was for an abbreviated term, from the summer of
1969 to the 1970 annual meeting.[175] To ensure stability, the annual election
of the rabbi was altered to a two year term at the special meeting of February 2, 1969. Rabbi Zionts was thereupon elected through January, 1971, in
effect providing him assurance of continuity. At the January, 1971, meeting,
he was re-elected to a second two year term, but he chose to resign in 1972,
relocating to Shreveport, Louisiana, where he serves Congregation B'nai
Zion.

Born and reared in Pittsburgh, Pennsylvania, a Phi Beta Kappa graduate of the University of Pittsburgh, Rabbi Zionts had evinced interest in expanding his knowledge of the Jewish heritage by attending the College of
Jewish Studies during high school and college. This led to an interest in
Jewish community service, prompting enrollment at the Hebrew Union
College following his graduation from "Pitt" in 1960. The five year course of
study was completed in 1965, including a one year leave-of-absence as rabbi-
intern at London's Liberal Jewish Synagogue, St. John's Wood. Following
Ordination, Zionts was called to Temple Emanu-El in San Francisco, where
he rose from assistant to associate during the ensuing four years. Temple

Emanu-El ranks as one of the largest and most prestigious congregations in northern California. In 1969, the opportunity at K.K.M.I. opened to him. Rabbi Zionts was an innovator of sensitivity and imagination. Among the innovations introduced during his tenure are the following:

The Brotherhood recorded worship services for the edification of the infirm and shut-ins.[176]

Sabbath songfests for learning the Hebrew responses and hymns were introduced, as the congregation moved toward incorporating more Hebrew in worship.[177]

A bi-weekly post-confirmation class was begun, and those who attended reported that the rabbi was able to listen as well as to teach. The class prospered to the delight of all. The youth group sessions with the rabbi also "ignited an intellectual awakening."[178]

Luncheons were held following Sabbath services, first for adult worshippers, and later for the children of the religious school who were required to attend a prescribed number of Saturdays.

Rabbi Zionts' tilt toward Israel was reflected in his attendance at a Washington conference on the Mideast, his seeking an arrangement with Rev. Felix Turner for a Bull Street Baptist-Mickve Israel pilgrimage to the Holy Land, and his encouraging interest in the World Union for Progressive Judaism. During his tenure, Sisterhood provided funds for building a chapel in Beth Shemen Village, and Brotherhood worked on the U.J.A. campaign.

As a consequence of attending conferences of the C.C.A.R. and the Union of American Hebrew Congregations, he was made aware of trends and issues in national Jewish life. In his last annual message to the congregation, he spoke of the impact of Dr. Leonard Fein's presentation at the Los Angeles U.A.H.C. Biennial. He called for less of an adaptation to the external world and its emphasis on "church" and more of a turning inward, a concentration on study, on Torah and Hebrew. Emphasizing the role of the rabbi as educator, Zionts asserted (in his annual message of 1972),

> Rabbi means 'My Teacher.' I would personally like to emphasize my true role as a rabbi with adults, not just with children and young people, important as it is to teach them.[179]

The rabbi was also on the threshold of advocating *Havurah* (small group life),

> . . . Why not more small groups meeting in homes or the synagogue . . . studying or discussing what they find interesting in the Jewish heritage? Why not groups meeting around common interests such as creative worship, community service or interfaith?[180]

The racial issue again surfaced during this period (after Zionts' election, but before his installation). Among the demands of some black leaders in the late 1960's were calls for black reparations, payments for abuses wrought in a previous age. Reform synagogues were concerned about efforts to picket and disrupt the worship on the High Holy Days, as well as on *Shabbat*. The U.A.H.C. instructed its member congregations about how best to cope. The *Temple Minutes* of July 17, 1969, reveal that plans were readied to deal with

a demonstration or outburst from minority groups.

At the same meeting, a proposal came from the local Economic Opportunity Administration (E.O.A.) requesting the use of the Mordecai Sheftall Memorial for a Headstart Program (to provide a positive learning experience for pre-school children from culturally disadvantaged homes). A vote was postponed until July 28, 1969, when a split of three for and three against put the matter in President Henry Levy's corner. He cast his vote in the affirmative. A special called meeting of the congregation was scheduled to allow further discussion, and a letter of notification was distributed. It informed the members that an agreement with the E.O.A. was about to be negotiated, offering limited facilities, at a cost to the congregation of no more than $1500 annually.[181] Twenty five-year-olds would participate in the program, which Levy described as

part of our services to humanity as Jews and an important principle of Reform Judaism.[182]

The August 12th special meeting was attended by fifty-seven. A proposal was presented by the directors of E.O.A., followed by questions from the floor. Both Rabbis Zionts and Starrels urged the project. B. H. Levy, Trustee for the Sheftall Endowment Fund (which had certain rights and privileges relative to the building's use), offered no objection. By a vote of thirty to twenty-seven, the motion was defeated.

Finally, in 1970, Rabbi Zionts participated in groundbreaking ceremonies for the new Agudath Achim Synagogue. Under the leadership of Building Fund co-chairman, Murray Galin, a $680,000 edifice was constructed on a site given to the congregation by former Mayor J. Curtis Lewis in honor of member Sam Steinberg.[183] On the High Holy Days, 1971 (September 19th), the last service at the Drayton and Waldburg Streets sanctuary was conducted, and the Torahs were marched in procession to their new White Bluff and Lee Boulevard home. E. Z. Manning, Willie Lasky, Julius Kaminsky, Allen Kooden, Martin Lippman, Ralph Tenenbaum, and Joe Weiner were given the honor of transporting the Scrolls of Law. Samuel Kaminsky lit the *ner tamid* (eternal light) as had his grandfather before him (when the Waldburg Street Synagogue was dedicated).[184] The structure itself seated approximately six hundred in the main sanctuary, with a social hall capable of accommodating a comparable number. The innovative architect was Leon J. Meyer of Savannah. The elongated stained glass windows, representing Jacob's dream and Jacob's wrestling, were the handiwork of Jean-Jacques Duval of Paris and New York, whose reputation was earned by his 135-foot windows at the Episcopal National Cathedral in Washington and his design of the Vatican Pavilion windows at the World's Fair.[185] Of particular interest are the Chanukkah *menorah, ner tamid,* and Holocaust memorial, executed by local artist, Bailey Tenenbaum Kronowitz, exhibited in (and on) the building.

At the time of the dedication, Rabbi William Fertig served as rabbi and Erwin A. Friedman (later chairman of the Board of Regents of the State of Georgia) functioned as synagogue president. Subsequent rabbis have included Rabbi Richard Markowitz who served a brief term and his successor in 1977, Rabbi Richard Fagan of Philadelphia. Rabbi Fagan has helped to establish new patterns of cooperation between A.A. and K.K.M.I., leading to a joint midweek Hebrew school. His five year tenure resulted in a resurgence of interest in the youth group and adult Jewish education.

THE RUBIN ERA

The promise that this history would encompass the full span of two hundred fifty years requires some statement by this writer of his own decade of service as rabbi of K.K.M.I. Here history slides into autobiography and may be self-serving.

The resignation of Rabbi Zionts in 1972 required the convening of a Rabbinic Search Committee. The prospect of finding a successor quickly was assumed impossible, and the congregation was geared up for a return to the post-Buchler period, with Rabbi Starrels covering pulpit responsibilities and teaching confirmation (he could not render other services as he lived at Tybee Island, Georgia). Through a process, unrecorded in the minutes and unremembered by this first hand source, the author (hereafter spoken of in the third person) was elected by the full congregation for two and a half years, the first half year in completion of Rabbi Zionts' term. The High Holy Days of 1972 marked the beginning of the Rubin rabbinate.

Saul Jacob Rubin was born in 1930 in Newark, New Jersey, of a Polish immigrant father, Hyman, and a second generation American mother, Pearl Sawilowsky of Augusta, Georgia. Summer visits to the Peach State by parents and child were commonplace throughout the 1930's and 40's. Savannah was frequented often, as his mother's two younger sisters were married to local physicians, both of whom had residences at Tybee.

Educated in the public schools of Newark, Rabbi Rubin proceeded, after graduation, to Drew University, Madison, New Jersey, where he received his B.A., magna cum laude, with election to both honorary social science and general scholastic fraternities. During the last academic year (1951-2), he attended Columbia University and pursued graduate courses in sociology. At the same time, he studied with Rabbi Arthur Gilbert of B'nai Jeshurun, a U.A.H.C. member congregation in Newark. Acceptance at the Hebrew Union College followed. After six years (a year's internship at Woodsdale Temple, Wheeling, West Virginia, included), he was ordained at the Hebrew Union College in 1958. Illness in the family required accepting a pulpit close to Augusta, where his parents had taken up residency. Congregation Beth Israel, Gadsden, Alabama, was seeking a rabbi and a connection resulted. That opportunity proved fortuitous, as there he met the vivacious Elsie Carolyn Parsons, grandchild of one of the founders and a lay spiritual leader of the congregation, Hugo H. Hecht. Marriage resulted. Congregation Beth Ahabah in Richmond, Virginia, was the rabbi's next post, and for a twelve year span, Rabbi Rubin functioned as assistant, associate and, from 1970 to 1972, as senior rabbi of the congregation. A dispute over whether a temple of such size (estimated from 600 to 850 families) could be served by one rabbi, when it historically had two full-time rabbis, prompted a resignation in 1972. K.K.M.I. was seeking a rabbi at the time of resignation.

To reconstruct the earliest phase of his ministry in Savannah is a task beyond the capacity of any scholar. Reflecting the disarray at the time, the *Temple Minute Book,* vintage 1970-74, was bound backwards, and the materials dealing with the Search Committee's deliberations and the special congregational meetings are not included. (The conditions of the initial contract have been preserved in a letter that proceeded from Temple President David A. Byck, III, with Rabbi Rubin's handwritten emendations and reply.)

In summary, these are the events of the Rubin decade:

The religious school was restored to sound administration and the open classroom format was introduced by the talented administrator, Mrs. Joan Epstein (later Schwartz). An innovative upper religious school program was instituted, involving extensive day-long sessions once a month (later bi-weekly).

Interfaith endeavor interested the rabbi, and, as a consequence, Mickve Israel became a part of an historic downtown Savannah Interfaith Thanksgiving service, involving seven congregations. The rabbi helped initiate the Savannah Professional Clergy Society, served in the chairs of the Chatham County Clergy Association, and participated with Dr. Thomas Austin of the First Baptist Church in a series of television programs.

During the Nation's Bicentennial, the rabbi recalled that in George Washington's administration an effort was made by the six Colonial Jewish congregations to send a single letter to the President. The attempt degenerated into three separate letters. A Bicentennial project was initiated in Savannah to prepare a single instrument for the incumbent President of the United States, Gerald Ford, to be transmitted from the six congregations to the Nation's Chief Executive at the White House. The letter was drafted in Savannah, and comments were offered by the five colleagues. The bar mitzvah of the rabbi's son, Lance Hays, took place on the weekend of July 4, 1976, and while the guests were assembled at the rabbi's home, a call came from the White House, requesting that the rabbi contact his colleagues and make plans to be in the Oval Office on July 12, 1976. The text presented to President Ford read as follows:

The President
The White House
Washington, D.C.

Dear Mr. President:

We, the spiritual leaders of the six Colonial Jewish Congregations, commend to you and our Nation congratulations and divine [*sic*] benediction as the Bicentennial celebration climaxes.

As our forefathers tendered President Washington felicitations on the occasion of his Inauguration, expressing in those documents love of America and dedication on the part of its Jewish citizens to the majestic precepts and freedoms for which it was established, we, in this generation, would affirm their sentiments. May the blessing of liberty, justice and compassion be forthcoming unto our more than two hundred million citizens, to them and their progeny after them. May Washington's promise "to bigotry no sanction, to persecution no assistance" continue to be the bedrock of public policy.

As the founding fathers so clearly understood, love and loyalty to country increase in proportion to the freedoms secured, the privileges extended, and the egalitarian principles promoted. The commitment of the stock of Abraham is ever to vouchsafe these American values for all people, whether descendants of the first settlers, or more recently removed to these shores.

Be assured, Sir, of the steadfast loyalty of the American Jewish community to the American dream and the American territory. We will defend it against its enemies, foreign or domestic. We will give of our energies, wisdom and skill for the common weal. We will promote the cause of other democracies of this world, including the land of Israel, sacred to all generations of our people. We do so on the conviction that democratic governments need the unique strength which sister democracies can provide, especially in a world where many nations are hostile to elemental human freedoms.

May the "wonder-working Diety" Who has revealed to His children their common origin and destiny and has commanded them to be brethren one to the other, excite the will of all American races and stocks to observe this 200th Birthday in benevolent spirit. May we remember that which is most inspiring in the past. May we reclaim the conviction of Presidents Washington, Jefferson and Madison that in this nation [*sic*] men will forever govern themselves.

Your humble and obedient servants,

Rabbi Louis C. Gerstein, The Congregation Shearith Israel, New York, New York

Rabbi Theodore Lewis, Congregation Jeshuat Israel (Touro Synagogue), Newport, Rhode Island

Rabbi Saul J. Rubin, Congregation Mickve Israel, Savannah, Georgia

Rabbi Ezekiel N. Musliah, The Congregation Mikveh Israel, Philadelphia, Pennsylvania

Rabbi Edward L. Cohn, Kahal Kadosh Beth Elohim, Charleston, South Carolina

Rabbi Jack D. Spiro, Congregation Beth Ahabah-Beth Shalome, Richmond, Virginia

In 1973, the 240th anniversary of K.K.M.I. was celebrated with special festivities. In 1976, the Centenary of the laying of the cornerstone of the Monterey Square building was re-enacted. Members of the clergy and representatives of City Council and the County Commission were in attendance. The Supreme Commander of the Georgia Masonic Lodges participated in the service. A new cornerstone box, prepared by David A. Byck, Jr., temple archivist, was buried, containing objects donated by temple members. On April 14, 1978, on the 100th anniversary of the consecration of the Monterey Square Temple, the original ceremonies were reproduced. Rabbi William M. Rosenthall of K.K. Beth Elohim, Charleston, South Carolina, participated, as had his predecessor, Rev. David Levy, a century earlier. Dr. Thomas D. Austin of the First Baptist Church, Dr. A. Jason Shirah of Wesley Monumental United Methodist Church, and Dr. William H. Ralston of St. John's Episcopal Church, brought greetings and salutations.[186] Lay participants included Edwin J. Feiler, Jr., temple president, and Lee J. Kuhr, congregational secretary.

As part of the Cornerstone Centenary, a second service was scheduled. (The pattern evolved that for every ceremony in observance of the past, a comparable service of contemporary orientation would be presented.) A contact initiated by Mrs. Fred Kazlow (Gloria) with Dr. Joanne Tucker of Tallahassee, Florida, relative to a dance liturgy that she and Dr. Irving Fleet prepared for the dedication of their new temple, resulted in the presentation of this creative program at Mickve Israel. For the first time in recent history, the temple doors had to be shut to bar people from entering. (There was insufficient space inside.) Dr. Tucker and her gifted troupe, *Avodah*, have returned to this community for several additional engagements (including the 1978 Southeastern Federation-U.A.H.C. Biennial in Savannah). In 1980, as a memorial to the victims of the Holocaust, Danyse and Julius Edel presented *Avodah* to the general community at the Savannah College of Art and Design. A dance commissioned for the occasion, *Kaddish* (choreographed to Leonard Bernstein's music), was received as an artistic triumph.

The Holocaust Memorial, an annual event underwritten by the Edel family, has brought scholars and artists to Savannah regularly. Armstrong State College has been the scene of two Holocaust seminars, featuring professors from Emory University, including Dr. Jack Boozer, Dr. Fred Crawford, and Dr. David Blumenthal. A travelling art exhibit entitled *Spiritual Resistance* (art rescued from the death camps) was on display in the Mordecai Sheftall Memorial. Savannahians of all creeds, races, and convictions viewed the week-long presentation.

A major renovation of the Mordecai Sheftall Memorial was undertaken in 1974. The stage was removed, and a museum was installed in its stead. Thousands of tourists and students have since visited the temple archives, where repose some of the historic treasures of the congregation, including the 1733 Torah, the 1790 Charter, and letters from Washington, Jefferson, and Madison (even one from Robert E. Lee).

The project had its beginning with a commitment from Sisterhood president, Matiel Leffler.[187] To further the goal, she appointed Joan Gefen (Mrs. Maurice) and Marion A. Levy (Mrs. B. H.).[188] Not until the administration of A. J. Cohen, Jr., was progress realized. He appointed an Archives Committee in 1974 (no record survives as to its membership). Temple historian, D. A. Byck, Jr., played a vital role in this venture, as did Edwin J. Feiler, Jr., and wife, Jane. The Feilers were the driving spirits behind the enterprise. Henry Levy lent his architectural expertise to the reshaping of the assembly room.

The tradition (instituted by Jane and Edwin J. Feiler, Jr., at the bar mitzvah of their son, Andrew Benjamin, in 1974) of presenting to the congregation a token that will serve as a permanent reminder of a significant event in family life has resulted in expanding the synagogue's ritual art collection. Included are new silver ornaments for the Torahs, *kiddish* cups, a *havdallah* set, and art works by Ludwig Volper and Salvadore Dali. Mr. and Mrs. Julius Edel presented a hand-carved portable ark, in memory of their parents, Mr. and Mrs. Herman Edel and Mr. and Mrs. Herbert Greenwald. In honor of the marriage of their children, Roy and Deborah Cranman, a *chuppah* (marriage canopy) of hand-crafted walnut, with white silk covering, was donated by Herman and Helen Cranman. *Contact* has recorded these and other free will offerings.

The emphasis on the history of the congregation has brought K.K.M.I. into leadership of the Southern Jewish Historical Society. Rabbi Rubin attended the Raleigh, North Carolina, conference in 1977 when the society was officially reconstituted, and was elected Chairman of the Board. The following year, the delegates gathered in Savannah. The rabbi has served a two year term as president of the Society (1980-82). This history book is a response to the purpose of the S.J.H.S., which seeks to document the southern Jewish experience.

In 1979, the rabbi, at the urging of Temple Sisterhood, attended the first National *Havurah* Conference at Rutgers University. As a consequence, Mickve Israel has developed one of the model *Havurah* programs in the Nation, written about in such publications as *Moment Magazine*.[189] Mrs. Gloria Kazlow has functioned as a *Havurah* Coordinating Council chairperson and been responsible for the operation of the groups. Nine separate *Havurot* have functioned in this setting of approximately three hundred families. As a consequence of his work, Rabbi Rubin was selected to serve on the National Havurah Committee's executive board and was made chairman of the *Havurah* Committee of the Central Conference of American Rabbis in 1981.

The largest gift in K.K.M.I.'s history was announced at the July 13, 1972, board meeting. Under the terms of Arthur S. Sternshine's will, a major bequest was forthcoming to the temple. The Sternshine Memorial Fund was proposed, and the principle deposited in the safekeeping of the congregational trusts. In 1973, a bronze plaque was dedicated (in the sanctuary) to the memory of Selma and Arthur S. Sternshine.

FINALLY

In 1981, the Two Hundred Fiftieth Anniversary Committee of the congregation was appointed by President Bernard B. Backston. At an early meeting, chairman Julius Edel urged the creation of a sub-committee to meet with Rabbi Rubin to discuss the preparation of a history of Savannah Jewry. In November, sub-committee members, Mrs. Jane A. Feiler, Dr. Martin Greenberg, and Mrs. Gloria S. Kazlow, carried forth the mandate and received assurances that the rabbi would do the research and prepare the text. *Third To None The Saga of Savannah Jewry 1733-1983* is a consequence of that commitment.

FINIS

APPENDIX A

A VIEW OF SAVANNAH, 29 MARCH, 1784, SHOWING LOTS ASSIGNED TO JEWS* by Peter Gordon (Courtesy of Georgia Historical Society)

Key

1. Benjamin Sheftall   Lot 64
2. Jacob Yowel   Lot # not given
3. Abraham Minis   Lot 94
4. Simon Minis   Settled at Hampstead
5. Samuel Nunes Ribeiro   Lot 43

6. Moses Nunes   Lot 49
7. Daniel Nunes   Lot 47
8. Abraham Deleon   Lot 74
   (Delyon)
9. Isaac Nunes Henriques   Lot 57
10. Raphael Nunes Bernal   Settled at Hampstead

11. Jacob Lopez Olivera   Lot 73
12. Benjamin Gideon   Settled at Hampstead
13. Jacob Lopez Decrasto   Lot 122
14. David Lopez DePass   Lot # not given
15. Isaac DeCosta Villareal   Settled at Hampstead
16. Abraham DeMolina   Lot 69
17. David Cohen Delmonte   Lot 63

*Merton Coulter and Albert B. Saye, from *A List of The Early Settlers of Georgia* (Athens: The University of Georgia Press, 1967).

APPENDIX B

LETTER TO PRESIDENT WASHINGTON
FROM LEVI SHEFTALL

Address from the Hebrew Congregation of the City of Savannah to the President of the United States.

Sir,

We have long been anxious of congratulating you on your appointment by unanimous approbation to the Presidential dignity of this country, and of testifying our unbounded confidence in your integrity and unblemished virtue: Yet, however exalted the station you now fill, it is still not equal to the merit of your heroic services through an arduous and dangerous conflict, which has embosomed you in the hearts of her citizens.

Our eccentric situation added to a diffidence founded on the most profound respect has thus long prevented our address, yet the delay has realized anticipation, given us an opportunity of presenting our grateful acknowledgements for the benedictions of Heaven through the energy of federal influence, and the equity of your administration.

Your unexampled liberality and extensive philanthropy have dispelled that cloud of bigotry and superstition which has long, as a veil, shaded religion—unrivetted the fetters of enthusiasm—enfranchised us with all the privileges and immunities of free citizens, and initiated us into the grand mass of legislative mechanism. By example you have taught us to endure the ravages of war with manly fortitude, and to enjoy the blessings of peace with reverence to the Deity, and benignity and love to our fellow-creatures.

May the great Author of worlds grant you all happiness—an uninterrupted series of health—addition of years to the number of your days, and a continuance of guardianship to that freedom, which, under the auspices of Heaven, your magnanimity and wisdom have given these States.

Levi Sheftall, President
in behalf of the Hebrew Congregation

APPENDIX C

PRESIDENT WASHINGTON'S LETTER TO
SAVANNAH'S HEBREW CONGREGATION

To The Hebrew Congregation of the City of Savannah

Gentlemen,

I thank you with great sincerity for your congratulations on my appointment to the office, which I have the honor to hold by the unanimous choice of my fellow-citizens: and especially for the expressions which you are pleased to use in testifying the confidence that is reposed in me by your congregation.

As the delay which has naturally intervened between my election and your address has afforded an opportunity for appreciating the merits of the federal-government, and for communicating your sentiments of its administration—I have rather to express my satisfaction than regret at a circumstance, which demonstrates/upon experience/your attachment to the former as well as approbation of the latter.

I rejoice that a spirit of liberality and philanthropy is much more prevalent than it formerly was among the enlightened nations of the earth; and that your brethren will benefit thereby in proportion as it shall become still more extensive. Happily the people of the United States of America have, in many instances, exhibited examples worthy of imitation—The salutary influence of which will doubtless extend much farther, if gratefully enjoying those blessings of peace which (under favor of Heaven) have been obtained by fortitude in war, they shall conduct themselves with reverence to the Diety, and charity towards their fellow-creatures.

May the same wonder-working Diety, who long since delivering the Hebrews from their Egyptian oppressors planted them in the promised land—Whose providential agency has lately been conspicuous in establishing these United States as an independent nation— still continue to water them with the dews of Heaven and to make the inhabitants of every denomination participate in the temporal and spiritual blessings of that people whose God is Jehovah.

G. Washington

APPENDIX D

PRESIDENTIAL CORRESPONDENCE (Twentieth Century)

January 14, 1954

Dear Dr. Starrels:

I am delighted to learn of the dedication ceremony planned for January seventeenth and of the remarkably long history of your Congregation.

In our young country, so long a record of service to the religious needs of the community is truly remarkable, and I am sure that all of you attending the dedication of the bronze plaque which marks the site of the first synagogue erected in the State of Georgia share a sense of great pride in this record.

May the Congregation Mickve Israel flourish throughout the years to come, bringing to the Jewish citizens of Savannah continued spiritual comfort.

Sincerely,

/s/ Dwight D. Eisenhower

Rabbi Solomon E. Starrels, D.D.
Congregation Mickve Israel
20 Gordon Street, East
Savannah, Georgia

April 4, 1973

TO THE CONGREGATION OF MICKVE ISRAEL

Your two hundred and fortieth anniversary is a source of satisfaction not only to you but also to the nation whose moral fiber you have strengthened by your religious commitment.

It is my hope that the pride you derive from this significant milestone may give you all the confidence you will need to face an even more challenging future with the same high purpose.

By this pride in your past and by the spiritual values of your Faith, may you continue to advance the goals of the true human brotherhood—and may this nation and all mankind benefit from your work.

/s/ Richard Nixon

August 20, 1974

Dear Rabbi Rubin:

Thank you for your very kind and thoughtful message of congratulations. It is encouraging to know I have the goodwill and support of the members of Congregation Mickve Israel. I am especially grateful for the assurance of your continuing prayers for the success of my efforts in the days ahead. Working together, I am confident we can go forward in peace with other nations and in progress here at home. With all good wishes,

Sincerely,

/s/ Gerald R. Ford

Rabbi Saul J. Rubin
Congregation Mickve Israel
20 Gordon Street, East
Savannah, Georgia 31401

APPENDIX E

LIST OF ITEMS IN CORNERSTONE BOX
MARCH 1, 1876
(from *Savannah Morning News*, 3/2/1876)

By Simon Guckenheimer—One Spanish silver dollar, year 1821; one two-franc silver coin, year 1866; one Prussian 18 ckreutzer, year 1823; one Chilean 20 c. silver coin, year 1866; one German 10 kreutzer, year 1733; one Prussian silver Groschen, year 1872; one Hamburg silver coin, year 1758; one Irish half-penny, reign George III, year 1769; one Chinese copper coin, year 1787

By Mrs. A. Friedenberg—One Spanish silver coin, year 1170; one Spanish silver coin, year 1794

By J. Vincent Brown—One Spanish silver coin, 1740

By Mrs. Lewis Lippman—One currency note of the denomination of four shillings issued by the State of Delaware in 1777

By Mrs. Virginia Sheftall—One two-franc piece, 1845; one Dutch silver coin, 1808

By Col. H.H. Eden—One American cent, 1861

By Julius Kaufmann—One American cent, 1789; one English penny (Quebec bank token) 1852; one Nova Scotia half-penny, 1840; one copper coin, 1813; one copper memento [1]860; two English half-pennies, 1769 and 1743; one Spanish real 1860; one ancient Brazilian copper coin

By J. W. Grady—One Confederate note, denomination $20, one of $10, one of $1, one of 50 cents, issued February 17, 1864; one note Bank of Commerce, State of Georgia, $1; one note Bank of the State of Georgia, 25 c.; one note Central Railroad and Banking Company, $2; one note Mechanics Savings and Loan Association, $2; one note Timber Cutter's Bank, 75 c; one note Merchants' and Planter's Bank of Georgia, $5; one English penny, year 1867; one copper coin, 1820; one copper coin (Prince Edward's Island), 1857; one ancient copper coin

By Richard Endelman—Four American pennies, 1817, 1826, 1831, 1847

By Jacob Belsinger—One American penny, 1817

By Simon Gazan—Copy of the first annual report of the Hebrew Hospital and Asylum Association of Baltimore, Md, 1869

By Fannie E. Cohen—One Hamburg silver coin, 1758

By Charles Schwartz—One Roman silver coin, 1836; one copper coin, 2 Kohlhen, 1869; one German 2 pfennig, 1874; one Roman silver coin, 1866

By Mrs. Rebecca B. B. Cohen—Piece of crown moulding from the Ark containing the law, brought to Savannah by the Hebrew emigrants, July 11, 1733

By Joseph Rosenheim—List of members and seat holders of the Congregation Mickva Israel, March 1, 1876; constitution and by-laws of District Grand Lodge No. 5, and of Savannah Lodge No. 217, I.O.B.B.; constitution and by-laws of the Harmonie Club of Savannah, Georgia, 1873

By Mrs. Henry Solomon—One English penny, 1875; one English half penny, 1874; English half penny, reign Georgia II, 1783; one ancient English penny

By J. Rosenband—One Irish copper coin, 1794; one Turkish copper coin, 1700

By Jacob Gutman—Five cent United States fractional currency issued 1863

By E. Kirschbaum—One Brazilian copper coin, 1871

By Edward L. Byck—$10 note Confederate States of America, issued February 17, 1864

By S. Elsinger—One Nova Scotia half penny, 1832; one German Pfenning, 1854; one Brazilian copper coin, 1790; one German kreutzer, 1816; one Canadian half penny, 1844; one Nova Scotia penny, 1854; one Japanese coin

By Theo. Basch—Protection papers to United States vessel, signed by John Adams, President, in 1800; clearance papers to United States ship *Daphne*, signed by Thos. Jefferson, President, in 1804; plan and directory of the House of Representatives, 30th Congress; United States privateer's commission, signed by James Madison, President 1812; four leaves extracted from an English Parliamentary lawbook, AD 1604

By John O. Ferrill—One American half dollar, 1805; one two-franc piece, 1871; one English six-pence, 1814

By Miss Mamie Einstein—One Roman silver coin, 1715

By Wm. H. Scott—One American dime, 1855

By Miss Lena Byck—One Bremen silver coin, 1840

By Lewis Hanff—One Nova Scotia penny, 1840; one English half penny, 1775; one American cent, 1797

By J. G. Davis—One English half penny, 1775

By Simon Hexter—One Spanish silver coin, 1738; one Danish American silver coin, 1767; one Austrian kreutzer, 1851; one American cent, 1798; one American cent, 1829; one French copper coin, 1855

By Mrs. Perla Sheftall Solomons—List of the names of the Israelites that arrived in Savannah, Ga. on the 11th day of July 1733 and who were among the earliest immigrants

By Henry Rich—One Danish silver coin, 1862

By Leah E. Cohen—One Saxon silver coin, 1763

By Lewis E. Cohen—One German silver coin, 1794

By Theo. Basch—Congressional directory, 43rd Congress of United States; one American cent, 1798

By Abraham Mendel—One Roman silver coin, 1658; one Spanish silver coin, 1732

By Henry Rich—Three leaves extracted from English Parliamentary laws, A.D. 1601 and 1604

By Celia E. Cohen—One silver coin, "George Ludwig", 1702

By Sarah E. Byck—One German silver coin, 1790

By Mrs. F. Ball—One Italian silver coin, 1814

By Lehman E. Byck—One Spanish silver coin, 1734

By Elias Cohen—One English penny, 1861

By L. Solomons—*Federal Gazette and Philadelphia Advertiser,* May 9, 1792; *Columbia Museum and Savannah Advertiser,* July 17, 1797

By L. Solomons—Georgia and South Carolina Almanac, 1830

By Richard Brown—One American dime, 1821

By Mrs. Lehman E. Byck—One Prussian silver groschen, 1845

By Jacob Rosenband—One note Brazilian currency, 4000 reis

By C. L. DeLamotta—Picture of Jacob DeLamotta taken at the age of fifty in the year 1852, A.L. 5852

By Joseph M. Solomons—One well preserved Spanish silver coin, 1775; a bill for drugs rendered by Fred Philey to Captain Sheftall, for use of soldiers, September 5, 1781

By Saml. Herman—One Prussian silver thaler, 1831; one German silver coin, 1840

By J. H. Estill—*Daily Morning News,* March 1, 1876; *Weekly News,* March 4, 1876

By Henry Meinhard—One German copper pfenning, 1747; one Spanish silver coin, 1811; one German silver coin, 1824; one German 2½ groschen, 1858; one Mexican silver coin, 1773; one German 3 kreutzer, 1833; one ancient silver coin

By Jos. B. Abrams—One American cent, 1802; one Newfoundland cent, 1873; one Canadian cent, 1859

By Y. H. Wittschen—Two American half dollars, 1861 and 1874

By Samuel Meinhard—One French franc, 1876; one Spanish silver coin, 1798; one Spanish silver coin, 1821

By J. E. Lowenstein—One Russian copper coin, 1798; one ancient copper coin

By E. A. Weil—One German 20 pfenning, 1874; one Mexican silver coin, 1773; one French 50 centimes, 1865; one Bavarian silver coin, 1813; one Prussian silver coin, 1842

By H. J. Reeser—One German silver coin, 1803

By M. J. Solomons—One copper bank token upper Canada, 1854; one coin, Province of New Brunswick, 1864; one Chinese coin

By E. J. Acosta, Jr.—One Russian Reichsthaler, 1791

By Max L. Byck—One Prussian silver coin, 1812

By S. H. Eckman—One copper Brazilian coin, 1831

By Morris S. Meyer—One half cent American coin, 1804; medal, Temple Maximillian, Breggi, France, 1844

By Jacob S. Davidson—Three Confederate postage stamps

By Isaac S. Davidson—One American cent, 1798

By Y. H. Wittschen—Copy of the rules and regulations of the German Volunteers, 1873

By Isaac Epstein—One silver coin, Bamburg four shillings, 1727

By S. Yates Levy—One silver Canadian shilling, 1874

By J. D. Rousseau—One English three-pence; one six centimes piece; one centime piece; one English half penny; one piece copper plate for printing Confederate money; one three-phenning German coin

By Miss C. M. Joseph—Paper printed in Georgetown 1826

APPENDIX F

MEMBERSHIP LIST 1920

	Pew	Seat		Pew	Seat
Abrahams, E. H.	17	3	Falk, W.	59	
Adler, L.	44		Falk, Mrs. I. M.	8	1
Alexander Bros.	48	3 & 4	Fantl, S.	48	1 & 2
Alexander, H. R.	62	4	Ferst, Mrs. A.	42	
Apple, Mrs. B. J.	45	4	Frank, H. I.	21	1 & 2
Apple, Mark	82	3	Frank, Edwin	25	1 & 2
Basch, Theo.	73	2	Frank, I. M.	18	
Bentschner, S.	57	2	Frank, Mrs. Leo	34	5
Bentschner, Miss Essie	57	1	Ferst, M.	81	3
Birnbaum, J.	71	2	Falk, Wash., Jr.	72	3
Brown, Max	4	2	Falk, Abram	72	2
Bentschner, R. L.	39	3	Friedlander, J.	69	1 & 2
Byck, D. A.	23	4 & 5	Fried, Ruben	79	3
Byck, Max L.	82	4	Gabel, L.	37	3
Byck, L. E.	75	1 & 2	Gardner, M. S.	49	1
Byck, Est. M.S.	55		Gazan, Jacob	64	
Boley, H. M.	50	2	Gerst, S. L.	28	3
Beck, Max	78	3	Greenwood, M.	51	3 & 4
Belsinger, Miss	60	1	Grouse, L. E.	36	4
Basch, Evan	73	3	Greenbaum, Dave	66	3
Cohen, A. J.	12	5	Guckenheimer Est.	41	
Cohen, Sam	12	4	Guthman, A.	60	3 & 4
Cohen, S. A.	51	1 & 2	Gross, Paul	39	4 & 5
Coleman, Nathan	71	4	Gutman, J. E.	60	2
Coleman, P. N.	29	4	Goldberg, H.	82	1
Coleman, Leo C.	29	5	Harris, Lester	3	2
Collat, I.	75	3 & 4	Hellman, I.	70	2
Cohen, Mrs. H. M.	3	1	Herman, C. J. & Milton	24	
DeWald, N. J.	46	1 & 2	Herzog, L.	71	3
Dryfus, M.	68	1 & 2	Hirsch, Henry	13	2
Dub, B.	17	1 & 2	Hirsch, J. D.	13	3
Deutsch, A.	66	4	Hirsch, M. D.	13	1
Eckstein, J. P.	17	5	Hirsch, Sol	70	3 & 4
Ehrlich, Albert	57	3 & 4	Hohenstein, Chas.	15	2
Ehrlich, A. & Bro.	22		Herzog, Alva	46	3
Epstein, E. S.	35	1 & 2	Haas, M.	36	1 & 2
Epstein, A. J.	76	1	Iseman, Dr.	25	3
Edel, H. M.	56	4	Joseph, Mrs. F.	50	1
Epstein, Tracy	46	4	Kreis, Carl	69	3 & 4
Eisenberg	35	4 & 5	Kauders, F.	7	2
Eisenberg, N.	28	1	Krapf, N.	40	3

Name	Pew	Seat	Name	Pew	Seat
Kayton, H. L.	14	2	Nussbaum	62	2
Krapf, M.	40	4	Oppenheim, Miss	72	4
Kayton, G. L.	14	3	Orovitz, D.	78	3
Kayton, L.	14	4 & 5	Ortlieb, J. S.	4	4
Kohler, A. S.	40	2	Oppenheim	39	1 & 2
Kuhr, H. J.	9	4 & 5	Orovitz, Nar [?]	72	1
Kraft, Max	78	2	Pinkussohn, J.	49	3 & 4
Kuhr, P. T.	38	3	Putzel, L.	53	1 & 2
Krauss, Max	16	3	Pinkussohn, Sam	29	1 & 2
Kulman, O. S.	38	1 & 2	Prager, Mrs. M.	50	3
Kirschbaum, M. E.	34	3	Rice, Sol C.	28	2
Kuhns, Chas., Jr.	8	5	Roos, L. J.	70	1
Kuhns, A. S.	8	4	Rosenheim, Herman	79	3
Levy, Abram	73	4	Rosenheim, Jos.	19	
Lehwald, A. J. & Bro.	80		Rosenthal, E. W.	31	1 & 2
Levy, A. B.	56	1	Roos, D. J.	62	2
Levy, B. H.	61		Stern, L. W.	74	1 & 2
Levy, Henry	58		Samuels, Mrs. A.	14	1
Levy, S. H.	56	2	Schwab, I. M.	15	4
Levy, Chas.	10	5	Schwab, Jos.	47	3 & 4
Leffler, A. M. & E.	32		Schwab, Leo.	71	1
Lovenstein, Lee Roy	78	4	Shulhafer, A.	54	1 & 2
Lippman, Lawrence	31	4 & 5	Smith, A. E.	33	1 & 2
Lieberls, B.	4	1	Smith, Mrs. B.	13	4
Livingston, H. H.	47	2	Smith, E.	49	2
Lovenstein, J.	10	4	Solomons, A. P.	52	3 & 4
Levy, M. H.	56	3	Solomons, I. A.	11	
Lowenstein, L.	8	2 & 3	Solomons, J. M.	10	1 & 2
Lindauer, L.	7	5	Stern, M. L.	12	1
Lichtenstein, L.	73	1 & 2	Solomons [sic], George	33	3 & 4
Lehwald, Geo.	76	3	Solomon, Abram	33	5
Minis, Mrs. L. F.	65		Schaul, M. S.	62	3
Mohr, Bros.	63		Solomons, I. A., Jr.	54	3
Morrison, Est.	77		Saloshin, L. E.	66	1 & 2
Myers, Sigo	23	1, 2 & 3	Smith, J. G.	40	1
Meinhard, Est.	20		Sheftall, W. R.	82	2
Mendes, Jos.	45	3	Sternshine, Arthur	79	4
Mendes, Mrs.	43		Silver, Mark	73	3
Meyer, M. F.	53	3 & 4	Stern, Mrs. Jonas	9	3
Michels, I. L.	7	1	Solomon, Mrs. A. A.	36	3
Morgan, Julius	37	1 & 2	Simon, Jake	4	3
Morrison, Mrs. S. J.	74	3 & 4	Steinheimer, L. M.	68	3 & 4
Moses, C. F.	35	3	Traub, Est.	30	
Myers, J. D.	47	1	Traub, Herbert	12	2 & 3
Myers, Percy	45	2	Utitz, M.	76	4
Myers, Vivian	45	1	Vaisberg, H.	38	5
Myers, Lee Roy	26		Weichselbaum, Dr. J.	15	1
Marshack, Mortan [sic]	38	4	Weil, Est.	42	
Michels, R. L.	5	1 & 2	Weil, F. A.	27	
Minis, Abram	67		Witcover, H. W.	54	4
Marcus, B.	37	4 & 5	Wolf, L.	78	1
Neuberger, Ferd	25	5	Wolff, Max	10	3
Neuburger, Louis	31	3	Wolff, S. C.	52	1 & 2

	Pew	Seat		Pew	Seat
Wood, H.	7	4	Wachtel, L. M.	16	1
Wortsman, L. W.	34	1	Weil, M. L.	16	2
Wortsman, E. L.	34	2	Wortsman, Sidney	34	3
Wetherhorn, Mrs.	76	2	Wilensky	9	1 & 2

APPENDIX G

RESOLUTION FROM WESLEY MONUMENTAL CHURCH
July 1, 1954

BE IT RESOLVED, That Wesley Monumental Church, its Official Board, its Ministry, and its Congregation publish and present the following formal statement of appreciation to the Congregation and Officials of Mickve Israel Temple for the use of their Synagogue from August 7, 1953 to July 4, 1954:

Struck by lightning, scorched by flame,
Shocked by damage to our home,
Before the smoke had blown away,
You offered us a foster home.

WE THANK YOU!

Looking back along the years
And searching for a sequel,
You did the same for us before,
Gave friendship without equal,

WE THANK YOU!

Many months we've burdened you,
And now we humbly pray
That God will smile on you and us
As leaving you we say,

WE THANK YOU!

BE IT FURTHER RESOLVED, That we include the following human statement of feeling to our God and our Fellowman:

God saw two temples with their backs turned to each other; two congregations with the same religious traditions and heritage, worshipping the same God, their Jehovah; but with their backs turned to each other. In both these temples, the children were taught that sometimes God's people bore great burdens and great sorrows in order to bring about some great good in the end. But still these children grew up to be Jews and Christians with their backs turned to each other. There was never any doubt that they had the same ideals of brotherly love, the same belief in the majesty of God and the nobility of man, the same faith in the final conquest of good over evil, the same confidence in the existence and permanence of the soul, and the same hope that each true worshipper would receive the final blessing of his Jehovah; but they bore the same sin—they turned their backs to each other.

It was time for something to happen—something spectacular—something drastic—time for great burdens and sorrows to bring about great good. God in His wisdom allowed one of the temples to bear great sorrow; it was struck by lightning, caught on fire and would have been destroyed except that God had mercy. The people of the other temple worshipped the same God of mercy who told both people "to do justly, and to love mercy, and to walk humbly with Thy God," so they accepted the great burden of hospitality to their burned-out neighbors and let them use their temple for many months.

These two peoples, thrown together by their God, soon found that they could work together for their God to help Him bring about some great good. Jews and Christians alike have shown their city and their world that they can pray to one God in His Temple. And now the guests have offered their sincere and heartfelt thanks to the hosts and are returning home, they each can show their city and their world that Jews and Christians don't turn their backs to each other but can back each other up and work and pray together to accomplish the great good they both desire with the help of the great God they both worship.

Adopted by unanimous vote of Wesley Monumental Methodist Church in conference assembled, on Sunday, July 4, 1954.

Albert S. Truelock, Minister

1 July 1954
Savannah, Georgia

APPENDIX H

LIST OF PERSONS WHO PLACED ARTICLES IN THE METAL BOX WHICH WAS SEALED IN THE STONE AT THE RE-ENACTMENT OF THE CORNERSTONE LAYING ON MARCH 5, 1976

Ethel Guckenheimer Marks—one 25 Gourdes silver piece, 1974, Republic of Haiti

Eva O. Lipman—one Indianhead penny, 1898

Mr. and Mrs. Ben Schlosser—one U.S. five cent piece, 1869

Stephen Traub—one Bicentennial medal and four Bicentennial stamps

Mrs. Arthur L. Shoenberg—one five Ptas Spanish coin, 1957, Francisco Franco Caudillo; one French two francs coin, 1947; one ten lire Italian coin, 1952; one British new pence, 1971

John Makay Sheftall—one two Pfenning coin; one five Pfenning coin; one ten Pfenning coin

Josephine H. and Phillip Cranman—five coins from Israel

Ellen R. and David A. Byck, III—one Shrine pin, gift from Grandfather, D. A. Byck, Sr.; Russian money; a Kopek

Joan Byck Loeb—one Centennial half dollar, 1776-1976

D. A. Byck, Jr. — 1927 seating plan of Congregation Mickve Israel; short history of Congregation; souvenir booklet of Mickve [sic] Israel Congregation in Curacao, oldest synagogue in the New World

Joseph L. Levington—one Gold Finger ring, with amethyst setting, which was gift from his mother

Charles Udell and Fiancee, Ester Byers—five foreign coins

Samuel Meinhard Ferst—one ancient Portugese [sic] coin, 40 reals

Grand Lodge—Bicentennial coin, Grand Lodge of Georgia, F & AM

Mrs. Lawrence T. Mayer—one 1974 Kennedy half dollar

Elsie Weil Kemper—one Belgian ten centemen piece, 1898; one German fifty Pfenning piece, 1877; one Canadian ten cent piece, 1975

Sylvan M. Byck, Jr.—one two and a half dollar "gold" coin, 1908; one half dime (silver), 1858

Rabbi Saul J. Rubin—Card of acknowledgement from Dr. Alfred Gottschalk for Letter of Endorsement as President of the Hebrew Union College, 8/7/70; one American Jewish Tercentenary medal, 1954

Matiel Roos Leffler, Martin Stuart Leffler, and Martin Stuart Leffler, Jr.—Israeli coins

John Bertram Levy—one 1909 U.S. Indian-head penny

Rabbi and Mrs. S. E. Starrels—one Kennedy half dollar (silver)

Mildred Guckenheimer Abrahams Kuhr—one American Red Cross Volunteer Pin, circa World War II

Alan S. Gaynor—one State of Georgia American Revloution Bicentennial medallion; one Rotary International Emblem; one Boy Scouts of America medallion bearing Scout oath

Mr. and Mrs. Julius Edel, daughter Cathy, son Kenneth—one American Revolution Bicentennial Flag, 1776-1976

Mark Aaron Kahn—one Islands Expressway Toll Fare, worth 25¢

David Guthman Kahn—one U.S. Custom House (Savannah) commemorative coin

Mr. and Mrs. Stanley Harris, Jr., Charles Lee and Carolynne Elizabeth—one Hanukkah medal (Franklin Mint issue)

Mr. and Mrs. Ronald Cohen and children, Rodney, Rebecca and Matthew—Sisterhood calendar and one Kennedy half dollar

Mr. and Mrs. Louis Oppenheim and David and Suzanne—one State of Georgia American Revolution Bicentennial medallion

Calmon P. Mendel, nephew of Abraham Mendel—one Centennial quarter, one half dollar, and one dollar

Juliet Frank Kuhr—one Bicentennial silver dollar

Lee and Diane Kuhr—one silver Bicentennial dollar

Steve Sommers—card from White House bearing signature of Gerald R. Ford

Mr. and Mrs. Alvin F. Kahan—one ten pound Israeli coin

Mr. and Mrs. Benjamin H. Levy—one sheet of Bicentennial stamps

Ruth F. Byck (Mrs. D. A., Jr.)—one Senior Citizens Handbook, one invitation to attend meeting at White House, November, 1971

Murray and Joan Gefen—one Centennial silver dollar, one Centennial half dollar, and one Centennial quarter

Lucile Harris Smith—one copy of Women's American ORT Membership List, 9/75

Leo Blumenthal—list of Mickve Israel Brotherhood, 6/75-5/76

Mildred Kahn Cohen—one Bicentennial fifty cent piece

A. J. Cohen, Jr.—Confirmation prayer book, 1935

Mrs. A. J. Cohen, Jr.—Georgia Day button, 1976, also one Bicentennial quarter and one 1951 nickel

Mary and Joe Gardner—one Bicentennial issue of "Time" magazine

Rabbi and Mrs. Saul J. Rubin—one copy of the Centennial issue of the Hebrew Union College

Mrs. Al Chaskin in Memory of Al Chaskin—one Keepsake religious medal

Dr. Alexander Paderewski, II—American Dental Association Journal, 2/76

Dr. and Mrs. Solomon E. Starrels—one copy of "Contact, Jr.", Vol. 5, No. 1, December 1965, "In Honor of Dr. Starrels' Retirement"

Dr. Jacob R. Marcus—two pamphlets "Jews in American Life" and "The Jew and the American Revolution"

One copy of Mickve Israel Membership list, 2/18/76

One copy of letter sent by Pres. Julius Edel to Congregation, dated 2/4/76, re: cornerstone rededication

Program in Observance of 240th year of Savannah Jewry—1733-1973

Contact Publication, 2/76

One copy of "Highlights of 240th Celebration"

Letter from Gov. George Busbee, State of Georgia

Letter from Major John Rousakis, Savannah, Georgia

Mayor John Rousakis—Key to City of Savannah

Letter from Alexander M. Schindler, President, UAHC

Letter from Dr. Alfred Gottschalk, President, HUC

Copy of *Savannah Morning News,* March 1, 1976

Commemorative issue, *Contact,* March 1955

APPENDIX I

LIST OF PRESIDENTS OF TEMPLE SINCE 1790

Levi Sheftall	1790, 1797, 1801-1802	Isaiah A. Solomons, Jr.	1941-1942
Mordecai Sheftall	1791-1796	Joseph H. Mendes	1942-1946
David Leion	1798-1805	Sidney H. Levy	1947
Sheftall Sheftall	1799-1800	Benjamin K. Victor	1948-1950
Moses Sheftall	1803-1804, 1808-1817, 1823-34	David A. Byck, Jr.	1951-1952
Levy Abrahams [sic]	1806-1807	Raymond M. Kuhr	1953-1955
Abraham D'Lyon [DeLyon]	1818-1822	Stanley Harris	1956-1957
Isaac Cohen	1835-1848	Benjamin H. Levy	1958-1960
Mordecai Sheftall, II	1849-1850	Sylvan M. Byck, Sr.	1961-1962
Jacob De la Motta	1851-1855	Milton F. Eisenberg	1963-1964
Solomon Cohen	1856-1866, 1869-1875	Martin S. Leffler	1965-1966
Abraham Einstein	1867-1868	Henry Levy	1967-1969
Simon Guckenheimer	1876-1879	Lawrence M. Steinheimer, Jr.	1970-1971
Elias A. Weil	1880-1888	David A. Byck, III	1972-1973
Joseph Rosenheim	1889-1918	A. J. Cohen, Jr.	1974-1975
Leopold Adler	1919-1928	Julius Edel	1976-1977
Morton H. Levy	1929-1937	Edwin J. Feiler, Jr.	1978-1980
Edmund H. Abrahams	1938-1940	Bernard B. Backston	1981-1982

APPENDIX J

RABBIS OF MICKVE ISRAEL, 1853 to Present

Jacob Rosenfeld	1853-1862, 1870-1871	Louis M. Youngerman	1944-1948
R. D. C. Lewin	1867-1869	Solomon E. Starrels	1948-1965
A. Harris	1873-1877	Joseph M. Buchler	1966-1967
Isaac P. Mendes	1877-1904	Richard A. Zionts	1968-1972
George Solomon	1903-1945	Saul J. Rubin	1972-

APPENDIX K

1982-1983 BOARD OF ADJUNTA
CONGREGATION MICKVE ISRAEL

Alex Gilmore, President
Dr. Carl Rosengart, Vice President
Ronald Cohen, Treasurer
B. H. Levy, Jr., Secretary
Mrs. Gloria Kazlow
Mrs. Ann Gold
Hyman Winner
Mrs. Simone Fluke
Dr. Ronald Fagin
Dr. Martin Greenberg
Roy Cranman
Philip Solomons, Jr.
Mrs. Virginia Bradley, President of Sisterhood
Robin Schultz, President of Temple Youth Group

APPENDIX L

TRUSTEES FOR THE MEMORIAL ENDOWMENT FUND, 1983

Stanley Harris
Joel Lynch
Philip Solomons

TRUSTEES FOR THE PERMANENT FUND, 1983

Martin S. Leffler
Baldwin Kahn
Albert Mazo

APPENDIX M

INCUMBENT TRUSTEES OF HEBREW CEMETERY TRUST—U/T/I

MORDECAI SHEFTALL, 1773
B. H. Levy
A. Minis, Jr.
Philip Solomons

NOTES TO CHAPTERS

CHAPTER ONE

1. Todd M. Endelman, *The Jews of Georgian England 1714-1830 Tradition and Change in a Liberal Society* (Philadelphia: The Jewish Publication Society of America, 1979), p. 14.
2. Ibid., pp. 16-17 for reasons.
3. Kenneth Coleman, et al., ed. *A History of Georgia* (Athens: University of Georgia Press, 1977), pp. 16-18 (hereafter Coleman, *History of Georgia*).
4. B. H. Levy, *Joseph Solomon Ottolenghi—A Kosher Butcher in Italy—A Christian Missionary in Georgia*, M.I. Archives, pp. 14-16 (typewritten).
5. See Malcolm H. Stern, "New Light on the Jewish Settlement of Savannah," in *The Jewish Experience in America*, Vol. I, (Waltham, Massachusetts: American Jewish Historical Society, 1969) pp. 66-92 as the most definitive examination of the earliest phase of Jewish settlement in Savannah, p. 70 (hereafter Stern, "New Light").
6. Ibid.
7. Letter to David A. Byck, Jr. dated April 17, 1972, K.K.M.I. Archives.
8. Stern, "New Light," p. 75.
9. Ibid., p. 74.
10. Ibid., p. 74.
11. Dr. R. D. Barnett, "Dr. Samuel Nunes Ribeiro and The Settlement of Georgia," in *Migration and Settlement: Papers on Anglo-American Jewish History*, pp. 63-97 (Jewish Historical Society of England, 1971), p. 63. (hereafter Barnett, "Dr. Samuel Nunes")
12. Stern, "New Light," p. 75.
13. Ibid., pp. 72-73.
14. I.e., Torah mantles.
15. Malcolm H. Stern, "The Sheftall Diaries: Vital Records of Savannah Jewry (1733-1808)" (publication of the American Jewish Historical Society, 54), pp. 243-277. (hereafter Stern, *Sheftall Diaries*), p. 247.
16. The Congregation was originally named 'Mickva' Israel." That spelling is found in the sources until the early 20th century. Then the Sephardic *a* gives way to the Askenazic *e*.
17. Stern, "Sheftall Diaries," p. 247.
18. Jacob R. Marcus, *The Colonial American Jew 1492-1776*, 3 volumes (Detroit: Wayne State University Press, 1970), Vol. II, p. 863 (hereafter Marcus, *Colonial American Jew*).
19. Ibid., p. 874.
20. B. H. Levy, "Savannah's Old Jewish Cemeteries", *Georgia Historical Quarterly*, Vol. LXVI (Spring 1982), p. 1 (hereafter Levy, "SOJC").
21. Stern, "Sheftall Diaries, p. 240.
22. Ibid., pp. 254-255.
23. Ibid., see pp. 247, 250 for reference to Rosh Hodash; p. 256 for Succot, and pp. 254, 256 for names of Hebrew months.
24. Ibid., p. 250.
25. Stern, "New Light," p. 70.
26. Solomon Breibart, "The Synagogues of Kahal Kadosh Beth Elohim of Charleston, South Carolina", *South Carolina Historical Magazine*, Vol. 80, No. 3 (July 1979), pp. 215-217.

27. Allen D. Candler, ed. *The Colonial Records of the State of Georgia*, Vol. XX (hereafter Candler, *Colonial Records*).

28. Stern, "New Light," pp. 82-83.

29. Abram Vossen Goodman, *American Overture, Jewish Rights in Colonial Times* (Philadelphia: The Jewish Publication Society of America, 1947), p. 191.

30. Ibid., p. 83.

31. Stern, "Sheftall Diaries," p. 248.

32. Ibid., p. 247.

33. Marcus, *Colonial American Jew*, Vol II, p. 887.

34. Correspondence with my rabbinic colleagues of the other Colonial Jewish congregations has led to this conclusion. Only Shearith Israel in New York did not provide data. To my knowledge, there is no source material to document that any of their Torahs survived from 1730 on.

35. Kenneth Coleman, *Colonial Georgia A History* (New York: Charles Scribner's Sons, 1976), pp. 43, 234. The church at Ebenezer was built in 1767.

36. Rudolf Glanz, *Studies in Judaica Americana* (New York: KTAV Publishing House Inc., 1970), pp. 208-211 (hereafter Glanz, *Studies*).

37. Volumes II, III, IV in particular.

38. Glanz, *Studies*, p. 209.

39. Ibid.

40. Ibid.

41. Ibid., pp. 209-210.

42. Ibid., p. 211.

43. Marcus, *Colonial American Jew*, Vol. III, pp. 1113-1134.

44. Ibid., p. 1119.

45. Ibid.

46. Map of Savannah, prepared by Major Edward White, Custom House Officer, Georgia Historical Society.

47. Marcus, *Colonial American Jew*, Vol. III, p. 1124.

48. Ibid., p. 1126.

49. Ibid., p. 1129.

50. Ibid., p. 1130.

51. Ibid., p. 1133.

52. Ibid., p. 1127.

53. Stern, "New Light," p. 74.

54. Ibid., p. 75.

55. Ibid., p. 76.

56. Ibid., p. 77, see text for exact quote.

57. Ibid.

58. E. Merton Coulter and Albert B. Saye, eds. *A List of the Early Settlers of Georgia* (Athens: The University of Georgia Press, 1967), pp. 88-89.

59. Ibid., p. 71.

60. Stern, "New Light," p. 83.

61. Ibid., p. 87.

62. Ibid.

63. Joseph R. Rosenbloom, *A Biographical Dictionary of Early American Jews Colonial Times through 1800* (University of Kentucky Press, 1960), p. 136 (hereafter Rosenbloom, *Biographical Dictionary*).

64. Ibid.

65. Ibid., p. 105.

66. Malcolm H. Stern, ed. *Americans of Jewish Descent A Compendium of Genealogy* (Cincinnati: Hebrew Union College Press, 1960), p. 40 (hereafter Stern, *Genealogy*).

67. Ibid., p. 141.

68. Ibid., p. 122.

69. Ibid., p. 24.
70. Ibid., p. 174.
71. Rosenbloom, *Biographical Dictionary*, p. 134.
72. Ibid., p. 97.
73. Ibid., p. 134.
74. Harry Simonhoff, *Jewish Participants in the Civil War* (New York: ARCO Publishing Company, 1963), pp. 183-187.

CHAPTER TWO

1. Stern, "New Light", p. 89.
2. Ibid., pp. 88-90, for a record of the migration.
3. Ibid., p. 90.
4. E. Merton Coulter, *Georgia: A Short History* (Chapel Hill, NC: The University of North Carolina Press, 1960) pp. 81-92. (hereafter, Coulter, *Georgia*.)
5. "Autobiography of Levi Sheftall", ms. in Keith Reid Collection, University of Georgia Library, Athens, GA. (photocopy in American Jewish Archives) (hereafter "Autobiography of Levi Sheftall").
6. Peter Gordon, "View of Savannah". Original sketch in Beinecke Library, Yale University, New Haven, CT. (copy as frontispiece in *AJHQ* vol. LIV, March, 1965, No. 3).
7. The schoolmaster appointed by the Trustees was named John Dobell. cf. Leslie F. Church, *Oglethorpe: A Study of Philanthropy in England and Georgia*. (London: The Epworth Press, 1932), p. 231.
8. Coulter, *Georgia*, p. 98f.
9. Ibid., p. 78.
10. Barnett, "Dr. Samuel Nunes", p. 78.
11. Stern, "New Light", p. 183.
12. Coulter, *Georgia*, p. 78f.
13. Stern, "New Light", p. 178f.
14. Coulter, *Georgia*, Ch. IX:
15. John Reynolds, the first royal governor, sought to move the capitol of Georgia to a spot on the Ogeechee River that he named Hardwicke. (Coulter, *Georgia*, p. 85).
16. Candler, *Colonial Records*, xxviii, pt. 1, pp. 351, 527; pt. 2, pp. 594, 671.
17. Ibid., pt. 2, p. 671.
18. For Sarzedas' career, see Jacob R. Marcus, *Early American Jewry* (Philadelphia: The Jewish Publication Society of America, 1953) Vol. 2, p. 328f.
19. Minutes of the Savannah Masonic Lodge, 1756-1757. (original in the Library of Congress; microfilm copy in American Jewish Archives).
20. Marcus, *Col. Am. Jew* Vol. III p. 1170.
21. Indian territory.
22. Candler, *Colonial Records*, xxxi, p. 465.
23. George White, *Historical Collections of Georgia* (New York: Pudney and Russell, 1854) p. 602. (hereafter: White, *Hist. Coll.*).
24. Kenneth Coleman, *The American Revolution in Georgia, 1763-1769* (Athens: University of Georgia Press, 1958) p. 283 (hereafter Coleman, *The American Revolution*).
25. Candler, *Colonial Records*, xxviii, pt. 2, p. 711f.
26. White, *Hist. Coll.*, p. 40.
27. Variant of "cocket", a certified document given to a shipper as a warrant that his goods have been entered and duty has been paid. *Webster's New International Dictionary of the English Language*, 2d ed. (Springfield, MA: G. & C. Merriam Co., 1967), pp. 515, 516n.
28. Candler, *Colonial Records*, xxxviii, pt. 2, p. 401f. This seizure of molasses was one of many instances of rebellion against royal authority that led to the Revolution. (cf. Coleman, *The American Revolution*, p. 50.)

29. Jacob R. Marcus, *American Jewry. Documents: Eighteenth Century* (Cincinnati, OH: The Hebrew Union College Press, 1959) p. 348 (hereafter: Marcus, Documents).

30. Ibid., p. 351f.

31. Malcolm H. Stern, *First American Jewish Families: 600 Genealogies, 1654-1977.* (Cincinnati, OH & Waltham, MA: American Jewish Archives and American Jewish Historical Society, 1978) NUNEZ, p. 234 (hereafter: Stern, *First Families*).

32. This was probably Hannah Minis, who married David Leion, April 17, 1798, and was divorced from him August 22, 1799. (Stern, "Sheftall Diaries", p. 268).

33. "Autobiography of Levi Sheftall".

34. Ibid.

35. Stern, "Sheftall Diaries," p. 250.

36. Levy, "SOJC"

37. Levy, "SOJC", pp. 1-2.

38. Ibid., p. 2

39. Esther Raines Mallard, "The Jews of Savannah 1733-1860," (Masters Thesis, Georgia Southern College, 1972), p. 21 (hereafter Mallard, Thesis).

40. "SOJC", p. 1.

41. Ibid.

42. Stern, "Sheftall Diaries," pp. 250-251.

43. Stern, "Sheftall Diaries," pp. 250-251.

44. Stern, "Sheftall Diaries," p. 251.

45. *Colonial Records of Georgia*, xxxviii, pt. 1, p. 638.

46. Leon Huhner, *The Jews of Georgia From the Outbreak of the American Revolution to the Close of the 18th Century* (Waltham, MA: American Jewish Historical Society, 1909) p. 89 (hereafter Huhner, *Jews of Georgia*)

47. Ibid., p. 92.

48. Ibid.

49. Samuel Rezneck, *Unrecognized Patriots The Jews in the American Revolution,* (Westport, Connecticut: Greenwood Press, 1975), p. 39. (hereafter Rezneck, *Unrecognized Patriots*)

50. Ibid., p. 15.

51. Ibid., p. 17.

52. Ibid., p. 124.

53. Mallard, Thesis, p. 35.

54. Huhner, *Jews of Georgia*, pp. 101-102.

55. Ibid., p. 102.

56. Rezneck, *Unrecognized Patriots*, pp. 46-49.

57. Ibid.

58. Levy, "SOJC," p. 5.

59. Ibid.

60. Marion Abrahams Levy, Collection.

61. Rezneck, *Unrecognized Patriots* pp. 48, 60, 203-204, 221.

62. Ibid., p. 44.

63. Ibid., p. 125.

64. Ibid., pp. 205-206.

65. Stern, "Sheftall Diaries," p. 252.

66. Rosenbloom, *Biographical Dictionary*, pp. 153-4.

67. Rezneck, Unrecognized Patriots, p. 44.

68. Stern, "Sheftall Diaries," p. 265.

69. Bernard Postal and Lionel Koppman, *American Jewish Landmarks A Travel Guide and History*, Vol. II (New York: Fleet Press Corp., 1979), p. 117, (hereafter Postal and Koppman, *Landmarks*).

70. "The Minis Family" *Georgia Historical Quarterly* 1 (1917) p. 45-49

71. Marcus, *Col. Am. Jew*, Vol. III, p. 1318.

72. Ibid.

73. Ibid., pp. 1317-1318.

74. Rezneck, *Unrecognized Patriots*, p. 44.

75. Ibid., p. 49.

76. Huhner, *Jews of Ga.* pp. 105-106.

77. Edwin Wolf II and Maxwell Whiteman, *The History of the Jews of Philadelphia from Colonial Times to the Age of Jackson* (Philadelphia: The Jewish Publication Society of America, 1975), p. 115.

78. Ibid., p. 413, note 4.

79. Ibid., pp. 413, 414, note 10.

80. Stern, "Sheftall Diaries," p. 252.

81. Ibid.

CHAPTER THREE

1. Reznick, *Unrecognized Patriots*, p. 95 and *Congressional Record*, 17 June 1975, E. 3225. The last line was quoted by Congressman Solarz before the House of Representatives. Thanks to Savannah Vice-Mayor Frank Rossiter for this information.

2. Coleman, *History of Georgia*, p. 90.

3. Reznick, *Unrecognized Patriots*, p. 43.

4. Stern, "Sheftall Diaries," p. 254. Notice the attraction of July in early history—this is almost 53 years to the day of the settling of the first Jews in the Georgia colony.

5. Ibid., pp. 254-255.

6. Ibid., p. 255.

7. Ann Morgan is listed in Egmont's records of *Persons Who Went from Europe to Georgia on Their Own Account*, p. 90.

8. Marcus, *Documents*, p. 173.

9. Following are the dates of the Charters of some of Savannah's earliest chartered congregations:

Christ Episcopal Church	December 23, 1789
Evangelical Lutheran Church of the Ascension	March 3, 1790
Mickve Israel	November 30, 1790
First Baptist Church	November 26, 1800
Independent Presbyterian Church	December 6, 1806

from *The Religious Heritage of Historic Savannah, A Bicentennial Monograph.*

10. Marcus, *Documents*, p. 176.

11. Ibid., p. 179.

12. See Marcus, *Documents*, pp. 114-129 for Mikveh Israel, Philadelphia and pp. 148-166 for Shearith Israel, New York.

13. Adelaide Wilson, *Historic and Picturesque Savannah* (Boston: Rockwell and Churchill, 1889), p. 95.

14. See Morris U. Schappes, *Documentary History of the Jews in the United States 1654-1875* (New York: The Citadel Press, 1950), p. 77 and the note on p. 586 (hereafter Schappes, *Documentary History*).

15. Ibid.

16. *Georgia Gazette*, 12 August 1790, p. 3, c. 1.

17. Interestingly, Levi Sheftall was appointed military agent by Thomas Jefferson and was involved in the construction and fortification of Fort Jackson. Thanks to Scott Smith of Fort Jackson for this information.

18. Marcus, *Documents*, p. 167.

19. Ibid., p. 170.

20. Ira Rosenswaike, *An Estimate and Analysis of the Jewish Population of the United States in 1790*, publication of the American Jewish Historical Society, Vol. L (September 1960), p. 34.

21. *Minutes of Mickva Israel Congregation of Savannah Georgia 1790 to 1851*, 9 October 1791 (hereafter *Minutes*).

22. Ibid., 10 April 1792.

23. Stern, "Sheftall Diaries," p. 252.

24. Rosenbloom, *Biographical Dictionary*, p. 28.

25. Charles Reznikoff and Uriah Z. Engelman, *The Jews of Charleston A History of an American Jewish Community* (Philadelphia: The Jewish Publication Society of America, 1950), p. 48 (hereafter Reznikoff, *Jews of Charleston*).

26. New Port, Rhode Island, for example, turned to the Curacao Congregation Mickveh Israel for aid in 1764; Philadelphia's Mikveh Israel requested donations from the Hebrew congregation in Surinam. Marcus, *Documents*, pp. 88, 121.

27. "Snogo" is the common term for synagogue in Colonial texts.

28. Thomas Gamble, Jr., *A History of the City Government of Savannah Georgia from 1790-1901*, p. 478 (hereafter Gamble, *History*).

29. *Minutes*, 14 June 1795.

30. Gamble, *History*, p. 478.

31. *Hatan Torah* and *Hatan Beraysheet*: see under section Congregational Life.

32. *Minutes*, 26 August, 1792.

33. *Minutes*, 8 June, 1794.

34. *Minutes*, 6 August, 1797.

35. *Minutes*, 8 June, 1794.

36. Ibid.

37. *Minutes*, 20 August, 1797.

38. *Minutes*, 24 September, 1797.

39. *Minutes*, 15 October, 1797.

40. Stern, "Sheftall Diaries," pp. 268, 274.

41. *Minutes*, 20 September 1792.

42. See *Minutes*, May, 173 for reference to an hazzan performing weddings. An entry in the Sheftall "diary" June 21, 1807 indicates Emanuel De la Motta performed a circumcision though he was not hazzan at this time. Stern, "Sheftall Diaries," p. 275.

43. *Minutes*, 7 October, 1798.

44. *Minutes*, 20 September, 1792 and 23 September 1792.

45. *Minutes*, 19 August, 1799.

46. *Minutes*, 17, 19 August, 1801.

47. *Minutes*, 4 September, 1803.

48. Stern, "Sheftall Diaries," p. 252.

49. *Minutes*, 11 March, 1792.

50. Postal and Koppman, *Landmarks*, p. 62.

51. *Minutes*, 30 August, 1793.

52. *Minutes*, 9 October, 1796.

53. *Minutes*, 15 August, 1825.

54. Wolf and Whiteman, *Jews of Philadelphia*, p. 127.

55. *Minutes*, 17 September, 1793.

56. *Minutes*, 4 October, 1791.

57. *Minutes*, 20 September, 1795.

58. To conjecture is to violate a taboo of history. However, the author notes that a Rev. Samuel Benedict served as rector of St. John's Episcopal Church in Savannah in 1868. Was this a descendant of the Jewish rebel Samuel Benedix?

59. See William E. Pauley, "John J. Zubley, Samuel Frink and The Savannah Burial Ground Controversy 1769-1770," paper presented at the April 1, 1978, Annual Meeting of the Georgia Historical Society.

60. *Minutes,* 20 September 1795.
61. *Minutes,* 25 September 1803.
62. *Minutes,* 2 October 1791.
63. *Minutes,* 24 September, 1797.
64. *Minutes,* 17 September, 1797.
65. *Minutes,* 2 October, 1791.
66. *Minutes,* 18 June, 1820.
67. Stern, "Sheftall Diaries," p. 251.
68. Ibid., p. 249.
69. Ibid., p. 250.

CHAPTER FOUR

1. *Minutes,* 10 September, 1798.
2. *Minutes,* 19 August, 1799.
3. *Minutes,* 18 August, 1806.
4. *Minutes,* 19 August, 1818.
5. Stern, "Sheftall Diaries," p. 274.
6. See Chapter 4, p. 83 for the incident involving Samuel Mordecai, *Minutes,* 17 August, 1839.
7. *Minutes,* 19 August, 1816.
8. *Minutes,* 7 October, 1804.
9. *Minutes,* 13 April, 1800.
10. *Minutes,* 9 June, 1805.
11. *Minutes,* 5 August, 1804.
12. *Minutes,* 15 August, 1817.
13. Ibid.
14. *Minutes,* 19 August, 1818 and 17 August, 1819.
15. Gamble, *History,* p. 507.
16. Lowry Axley, *Holding Aloft the Torch A History of the Independent Presbyterian Church of Savannah, Georgia* (Savannah: The Pigeonhole Press, 1958), p. 39 (hereafter Axley, *Holding Aloft*).
17. Gamble, *History,* p. 480.
18. *Minutes,* 25 April 1820, letter from A. D'Lyon to E. De la Motta.
19. *Columbian Museum and Savannah Gazette,* 25 October, 1817, p. 2, col. 4.
20. The Masonic Hall was located on President Street, second lot west from the northwest corner of President and Whitaker Streets. The procession had eight half blocks to walk, south on Whitaker. Thanks to Robert Shig Porter, student of local Masonic history for the information.
21. *Minutes,* 23 July, 1820.
22. *Minutes,* 11 April, 1820, letter from E. De la Motta, Charleston.
23. *Minutes,* 25 April, 1820, letter A. D'Lyon to E. De la Motta.
24. *Minutes,* 23 April, 1820.
25. *Minutes,* 18 June, 1820.
26. Frank Deane Lee and James Lawrence Agnew, *Historical Record of the City of Savannah* (Savannah: J. H. Estill, 1869), p. 155 (hereafter Lee & Agnew, *Historical Record*).
27. Text of Dr. De la Motta's speech from Schappes, *Documentary History,* pp. 150-157.
28. Thomas J. Tobias, "The Many-Sided Dr. De La Motta" in *The Jewish Experience in America,* Vol. II, (New York: KTAV Publishing House, Inc., 1969), p. 67.
29. *Minutes,* 23 July, 1820.
30. Axley, *Holding Aloft,* p. 35.
31. Reznikoff, *Jews of Charleston,* pp. 141-144.

32. *Minutes*, 18 August, 1823.

33. At the Annual Meetings 1821 to 1829, no more than six were present; in 1824, only four.

34. *Minutes*, 15 August, 1825.

35. *Minutes*, 17 August, 1829.

36. While the *Minutes* say Mr. Scudder and both Amos and John functioned in Savannah, Amos was the more active in this period.

37. *Minutes*, 25 April, 1820 and 17 August, 1829.

38. *Minutes*, 21 August, 1826.

39. In 1927, the Monterey Square sanctuary was greatly damaged by fire.

40. *Georgian*, 5 December, 1829, p. 2, col. 1.

41. Moses Sheftall created the tradition of a written presidential annual report, a tradition that obtains to this day at Mickve Israel.

42. Coleman, *History of Georgia*, p. 153.

43. *Minutes*, 13 July, 1830.

44. *Minutes*, 13 September, 1831.

45. *Minutes*, 15 August, 1831.

46. *Minutes*, 20 August, 1832.

47. *Minutes*, 19 August, 1833, reporting events August 1832-33.

48. *Minutes*, 17 April, 1833.

49. *Minutes*, 19 August, 1833.

50. Ibid.

51. *Minutes*, 1 July, 1830.

52. *Minutes*, 29 August, 1830, letter to K.K. "Bet" Elohim, Charleston, from Moses Sheftall.

53. *Minutes*, 30 August, 1831, letter to Moses Sheftall from S. Valentine.

54. *Minutes*, 13 September, 1831, letter to S. Valentine from Moses Sheftall.

55. *Minutes*, 20 August, 1832.

56. *Minutes*, 20 August, 1833.

57. *Minutes*, 17 April, 1833.

58. *Minutes*, 14 June, 1834.

59. *Minutes*, 18 August, 1834.

60. *Minutes*, 14 June, 1835.

61. Ibid.

62. *Minutes*, 21 August, 1837.

63. *Minutes*, 20 August, 1838, letter dated 13 July, 1838 from J. De la Motta and Isaac Cohen, Building Committee to congregation.

64. Ibid.

65. Ibid.

66. Mary Savage Anderson, et al., *Georgia A Pageant of Years* (Richmond: Garrett and Massie, Inc., 1933), p. 107.

67. Coleman, *History of Georgia*, p. 154.

68. Lee & Agnew, *Historical Record*, p. 136.

69. The information about Christ Church was communicated through a conversation with Beth Lattimore Reiter, architectural historian, 6 January, 1982.

70. Information about Gilbert Butler is contained in a manuscript prepared by Mrs. Howard Morrison, on file at the Georgia Historical Society.

71. In *The 1860 Census of Chatham County, Georgia* (Easley, SC: Southern Historical Press, 1980), p. 196 (hereafter *Census, 1860*) Edward Sheppard is listed as a 45 year old master brickmason.

72. *Minutes*, 19 August, 1839 and 18 July, 1838.

73. The *Census, 1860* lists D. Ferguson, cabinet maker, p. 126.

74. *Minutes*, 19 August, 1839.

75. Ibid.

76. *Minutes*, 17 August, 1840.

77. Samuel Rezneck, *The Saga of an American Jewish Family Since the Revolution: A History of the Family of Jonas Phillips* (Washington, D.C.: University Press of America, Inc., 1980), pp. 28-30.

78. Ibid., p. 29.

79. Ibid., p. 28.

80. *Minutes,* 21 August, 1838.

81. *Minutes,* 19 August, 1839.

82. The 1840 annual meeting is the first to take place there.

83. *Minutes,* 16 August, 1841.

84. Ibid.

85. *Minutes,* 19 August, 1839.

86. *Minutes,* 16 August, 1841.

87. David T. Morgan, "The Sheftalls of Savannah," in *The American Jewish Historical Quarterly* Vol. LXII, No. 4, (June 1973), p. 350 (hereafter Morgan, "Sheftalls of Savannah").

88. Ibid.

89. Ibid.

90. Ibid.

91. Marcus, *Colonial American Jew,* Vol. II, pp. 534-535.

92. Ibid., p. 623.

93. Ibid.

94. Ibid., pp. 562-563.

95. Ibid., p. 569.

96. Morgan, "Sheftalls of Savannah," pp. 348-349, 360.

97. Ibid., p. 359.

98. See Roland M. Harper, "Some Savannah Vital Statistics," *Georgia Historical Quarterly,* Vol. XV (September 1931), p. 253.

99. *Columbian Museum and Savannah Advertiser,* 24 May, 1796, p. 2, col. 3.

100. *Georgia Gazette,* 3 June, 1790, p. 2, col. 1.

101. *Georgia Gazette,* 3 January, 1793, p. 1, col. 3.

102. *Gazette State of Georgia,* 28 October, 1784, p. 1, col. 1.

103. *Gazette State of Georgia,* 7 July, 1788, p. 3, col. 1.

104. *Gazette State of Georgia,* 12 April, 1787, p. 2, col. 1.

105. *Gazette State of Georgia,* 25 November, 1790, p. 2, col. 2.

106. *Minutes,* 17 August, 1829.

107. *Gazette State of Georgia,* 10 August, 1786, p. 2, col. 2 and *Georgia Gazette,* 25 June, 1789, p. 2, col. 2.

108. See marriage notice, *Columbian Museum and Savannah Advertiser,* 20 May, 1798, p. 3, col. 3, and Stern, *Genealogy,* p. 227.

109. *Georgia Gazette,* 17 October, 1799, p. 2, col. 1.

110. *Georgia Gazette,* 28 January, 1790, p. 2, col. 1.

111. *Georgia, Gazette,* 13 August, 1795, p. 2, col. 1.

112. *Georgia, Gazette,* 8 December, 1797, p. 2, col. 2.

113. *Columbian Museum and Savannah Advertiser,* 6 February 1798, p. 3, col. 3.

114. Ibid., 25 September, 1798, p. 3, col. 4.

115. Ibid., 11 May, 1798, p. 3, col. 4.

116. Ibid., 4 December, 1798, p. 2, col. 5.

117. Ibid., 9 August, 1799, p. 2, col. 2.

118. *Georgia Gazette,* 7 February, 1793, p. 1, col. 3.

119. *Columbian Museum and Savannah Advertiser,* 19 October, 1798, p. 3, col. 5.

120. Ibid., 28 June, 1799, p. 2, col. 2, and 21 December, 1798, p. 2, col. 1.

121. Ibid., 19 May, 1797, p. 3, col. 2.

122. *Columbian Museum and Savannah Advertiser,* 19 September, 1797, p. 4, col. 1, and 9 June, 1797, p. 3, col. 3.

123. Ibid., 5 February, 1799, p. 2, col. 5.

124. *Georgia Gazette*, 5 May, 1791, p. 2, col. 1.

125. Ibid., 24 May, 1792, p. 2, col. 1.

126. *Columbian Museum and Savannah Advertiser*, 6 December, 1796, p. 2, col. 1.

127. Ibid., 9 April, 1799, p. 4, col. 1.

128. Stern, "Sheftall Diaries," p. 267.

129. *Columbian Museum and Savannah Advertiser*, 6 June, 1797, p. 3, col. 3.

130. *Georgia Gazette*, 21 May, 1789, p. 3, col. 1.

131. Ibid., 16 July, 1789, p. 2, col. 3.

132. See *Columbian Museum and Savannah Advertiser*, 15 November, 1796, p. 3, col. 3; 13 January, 1797, p. 3, col. 2; and 30 January, 1798, p. 3, col. 2.

133. *Columbian Museum and Savannah Advertiser*, 17 October, 1797, p. 2, col. 1.

134. Ibid., 1 December, 1797, p. 2, col. 1.

135. See the following for notices of tax defaulters: *Georgia Gazette*, 26 August, 1790, p. 1, col. 1; 28 February, 1793, p. 2, col. 3; 16 July, 1789, p. 2, col. 2; *Columbian Museum and Savannah Advertiser*, 13 March, 1798, p. 3, col. 3; 2 March, 1798, p. 5, col. 2; 6 March, 1798, p. 4, col. 3, 4; *Gazette State of Georgia*, 10 July, 1788, p. 2, col. 2.

136. *Columbian Museum and Savannah Advertiser*, 27 February, 1798, p. 2, col. 1, 2; 13 March, 1798, p. 3, col. 3; 27 September, 1799, p. 2, col. 1.

137. *Columbian Museum and Savannah Daily Gazette*, 3 February, 1817, p. 4, col. 4.

138. See *Columbia Museum and Savannah Daily Gazette*, 21 April, 1817, p. 3, col. 4; 25 May, 1818, p. 3, col. 2; 27 February, 1819, p. 1, col. 1.

139. *Columbian Museum and Savannah Daily Gazette*, 19 June, 1817, p. 3, col. 4.

140. *Georgian*, 11 June, 1821, p. 1, col. 3.

141. *Columbian Museum and Savannah Daily Gazette*, 30 October, 1819, p. 3, col. 1.

142. *Daily Georgian*, 21 January, 1837, p. 2, col. 2; *Georgian*, 25 May, 1837, p. 2, col. 2.

143. *Savannah Daily Morning News*, 8 January, 1851, p. 2, col. 1 and 8 July, 1863, p. 2, col. 5.

144. *Daily Georgian*, 3 May, 1838, p. 2, col. 3.

145. *Savannah Daily Morning News*, 17 January, 1850, p. 2, col. 3.

146. Ibid., 24 February, 1853, p. 1, col. 1.

147. Ibid., 3 December, 1852, p. 2, col. 3.

148. *Savannah Daily Morning News*, 8 October, 1861, p. 2, col. 2; *Savannah Daily Herald*, 10 May, 1865, p. 2, col. 2, 3.

149. William Harden, *A History of Savannah and South Georgia*, Vol. II, (Chicago: The Lewis Publishing Company, 1913), p. 556 (hereafter, Harden, *History*).

150. *Daily Georgian*, 25 November, 1819, p. 2, col. 5; *Columbian Museum and Savannah Daily Gazette*, 2 November, 1818, p. 3, col. 3.

151. *Columbian Museum and Savannah Daily Gazette*, 13 March, 1819, p. 3, col. 2.

152. Ibid., 27 March, 1818, p. 1, col. 1.

153. Stephen Birmingham, *The Grandees America's Sephardic Elite* (New York: Harper & Row Publishers, 1971), p. 195.

154. *Daily Georgian*, 8 December, 1840, p. 3, col. 1 and 6 January, 1838, p. 3, col. 1.

155. *Daily Georgian*, 10 February, 1836, p. 2, col. 5.

156. Ibid., 9 December, 1837, p. 2, col. 3.

157. Ibid., 5 December, 1837, p. 2, col. 7.

158. *Savannah Daily Morning News*, 17 November, 1856, p. 2, col. 2.

159. *Columbian Museum and Savannah Advertiser*, 3 October, 1811, p. 1, col. 4.

160. *Columbian Museum and Savannah Daily Gazette*, 4 September, 1817, p. 3, col. 4.

161. *Georgian*, 1 December, 1832, p. 3, col. 1.

162. *Georgian*, 27 November, 1832, p. 2, col. 3; *Columbian Museum and Savannah Daily Gazette*, 25 July, 1820, p. 3, col. 2; 12 August, 1820, p. 3, col. 1.

163. *Daily Georgian*, 30 October, 1837, p. 3, col. 1.

164. *Georgian*, 5 January, 1833, p. 2, col. 1; *Daily Georgian*, 28 May, 1838, p. 2, col. 3-5.

165. *Georgian*, 5 April, 1833, p. 2, col. 3.

166. Harden, *History*, pp. 554-555.

167. *Daily Georgian,* 7 November, 1820, p. 3, col. 1.

168. *Georgian,* 27 May, 1836, p. 2, col. 6; 25 June, 1836, p. 2, col. 3; *Daily Georgian,* 19 January, 1837, p. 2, col. 1.

169. *Daily Georgian,* 1 May, 1839, p. 3, col. 2.

170. *Daily Morning News,* 24 October, 1856, p. 2, col. 1; 10 July, 1855, p. 2, col. 7; *Georgian,* 31 May, 1837, p. 2, col. 2; *Daily Georgian,* 10 May, 1839, p. 2, col. 3.

171. *Georgian,* 6 April, 1837, p. 2, col. 6.

172. *Daily Morning News,* 21 January, 1850, p. 2, col. 3.

173. *Savannah Daily Republican,* 18 December, 1840, p. 3, col. 1.

174. Reznikoff, *Jews of Charleston,* p. 84.

175. Lee & Agnew, *Historical Record,* p. 190.

176. Stern, *Genealogy,* p. 39; Lee & Agnew, *Historical Record,* p. 195.

177. Lee & Agnew, *Historical Record,* p. 196.

178. Gamble, *History,* pp. 11-22.

179. *Savannah Daily Morning News,* 19 June, 1860, p. 2, col. 1.

180. Gamble, *History,* p. 492.

181. Ibid., p. 450.

182. Ibid., p. 451.

183. Ibid., pp. 500-504.

184. Ibid., p. 495.

185. Ibid., p. 491.

186. Ibid., pp. 488-490.

187. Ibid., pp. 495, 497-499, 504.

188. *Daily Georgian,* 28 July, 1840, p. 2, col. 2.

189. Ibid., 5 April, 1838, p. 2, col. 2.

190. *Daily Morning News,* 16 February, 1852, p. 2, col. 1.

191. *Daily Morning News,* 30 May, 1851, p. 2, col. 2; *Daily Georgian,* 29 April, 1837, p. 2, col. 2.

192. *Daily Georgian,* 30 October, 1840, p. 2, col. 3.

193. Ibid., 8 September, 1840, p. 2, col. 4 and 28 October, 1840, p. 2, col. 2.

194. Ibid., 12 July, 1840, p. 2, col. 2, 3. See also Isaac DeLyon in 1854. *Daily Morning News,* 21 November, 1854, p. 2, col. 1.

195. *Daily Georgian,* 30 July, 1840, p. 2, col. 2 and 5 December, 1839, p. 2, col. 7.

196. *Daily Georgian,* 10 February, 1838, p. 2, col. 3; *Georgian,* 11 September, 1832, p. 3, col. 2, 3.

197. *Daily Morning News,* 21 June, 1858, p. 2, col. 1.

198. *Gazette State of Georgia,* 12 February, 1784, p. 2, col. 3.

199. *Georgia Gazette,* 17 October, 1799, p. 2, col. 1.

200. Ibid., 20 December, 1792, p. 4, col. 3.

201. Coulter, *Georgia,* p. 178.

202. *Georgian,* 2 July, 1836, p. 2, col. 2, 60th Anniversary of the Declaration of Independence; *Daily Georgian,* 3 July, 1840, p. 2, col. 2.

203. Levi S. Hart served in the Republican Blues, *Daily Georgian,* 8 July, 1839, p. 2, col. 2.

204. Lee & Agnew, *Historical Record,* p. 187.

205. *Daily Georgian,* 19 March, 1836, p. 2, col. 4.

206. *Daily Georgian,* 17 October, 1836, p. 2, col. 2; *Daily Morning* News, 26 May, 1853, p. 2, col. 1; 8 January, 1861, p. 3, col. 2.

207. *Daily Georgian,* 26 February, 1836, p. 2, col. 6.

208. *Daily Morning News,* 17 December, 1857, p. 2, col. 2.

209. Ibid., 23 December, 1862, p. 2, col. 1.

210. *Savannah Daily Republican,* 11 December, 1840, p. 2, col. 7; *Daily Georgian,* 6 January, 1837, p. 2, col. 2.

211. *Georgian,* 4 May, 1830, p. 2, col. 3 and 17 May, 1831, p. 2, col. 4.

212. *Georgian*, 12 August, 1834, p. 2, col. 5.

213. *Savannah Daily Herald*, 27 October, 1865, p. 2, col. 5.

214. *Columbian Museum and Savannah Daily Gazette*, 4 February, 1820, p. 3, col. 2, and 16 December, 1820, p. 2, col. 5.

215. *Georgian*, 6 July, 1820, p. 3, col. 1.

216. Ibid., 12 April, 1836, p. 3, col. 1.

217. Ibid., 13 September, 1832, p. 3, col. 4.

218. Wilson, *Historic and Picturesque Savannah*, p. 239.

219. *Columbian Museum and Savannah Daily Gazette*, 30 October, 1819, p. 2, col. 3.

220. *Columbian Museum and Savannah Daily Gazette*, 30 December, 1819, p. 2, col. 2, and 1 January, 1820, p. 3, col. 1.

221. Ibid., 1 December, 1820, p. 2, col. 3.

222. Gamble, Thomas Jr., *Bethesda, An Historical Sketch of Whitfield's House of Mercy in Georgia and of The Union Society, His Associate and Successor in Philanthropy* (Savannah: Morning News Print, 1902), pp. 93-96 (hereafter Gamble, *Bethesda*).

223. Ibid., pp. 98-99.

224. Ibid., p. 100.

225. Lee & Agnew, *Historical Record*, p. 185.

226. Gamble, *Bethesda*, pp. 101-103.

227. *Daily Morning News*, 25 April, 1854, p. 2, col. 1; Lee & Agnew, *Historical Record* p. 185.

228. Rezneck, *Unrecognized Patriots*, pp. 4-5.

229. "Solomon's Lodge No. 1 Free & Accepted Masons, Savannah Georgia 1734."

230. Lee & Agnew, *Historical Record*, pp. 182-183.

231. Reznikoff, *Jews in Charleston*, p. 95.

232. Ibid., p. 97.

233. Mary L. Morrison, ed., *Historic Savannah*, 2nd. ed. (Savannah: Historic Savannah Foundation, 1979), p. 124.

234. Lee & Agnew, *Historical Record*, pp. 163-164.

235. See Chapter 2, pp. 23-24.

236. *Columbian Museum and Savannah Advertiser*, 21 March, 1800, p. 4, col. 1.

237. *Republican and Savannah Evening Ledger*, 16 July, 1812, p. 3, col. 4.

238. Ibid., 26 December, 1807, p. 4, col. 2. The first and last incidences were brought to my attention by Karen King and Julia Taylor, whom I assisted in researching a paper for Dr. Roger Warlick, Department of History Chairman, Armstrong State College. The paper was entitled "The Congregation Mickve Israel from 1790 to 1820."

239. See Joseph Jacobs, "The Damascus Affair of 1840 and The Jews of America" in *The Jewish Experience in America*, Vol. II, (New York: KTAV Publishing House, Inc., 1969), pp. 271-280.

240. Ibid., pp. 271-272.

241. Ibid., p. 273.

242. Ibid., pp. 274-275.

243. *Daily Georgian*, 4 September, 1840, p. 2, col. 3.

244. Ibid., 11 April, 1841, p. 2, col. 5.

245. *Columbian Museum and Savannah Advertiser*, 6 December, 1806, p. 3, col. 3.

246. *Minutes*, 4 December, 1806.

247. Lee & Agnew, *Historical Record*, p. 134.

248. Wilson, *Historic and Picturesque Savannah*, p. 108.

249. Gamble, *History*, p. 76.

250. *Minutes*, 15 February, 1795.

251. Ibid., 6 May, 1798.

252. See Chapter 5, pp. 130-131.

253. Reznikoff, *Jews of Charleston*, pp. 46-47, 291, note 143.

254. Stern, *Genealogy*, p. 41.

255. *Minutes*, 3 January, 1816.

CHAPTER FIVE

1. Coleman, *History of Georgia*, p. 172.
2. Ibid., p. 170.
3. Ibid., p. 155.
4. *Minutes*, 17 March, 1843.
5. Ibid.
6. Ibid.
7. *Minutes*, 21 August, 1843.
8. Ibid.
9. *The Occident*, Vol. 3, 1845, p. 358.
10. 17 West Bay Street.
11. *Minutes*, 17 November, 1849.
12. Ibid., 23 November, 1849.
13. Ibid., 17 November, 1849.
14. Ibid., 16 January, 1844.
15. Ibid., 21 August, 1848.
16. Ibid., 19 August, 1850.
17. Grinstein, Hyman B., *The Rise of the Jewish Community of New York 1654-1860* (Philadelphia: Press of the Jewish Publication Society, 1947), pp. 5, 56 (hereafter Grinstein, *New York*).
18. Ibid., p. 92.
19. *Minutes of the Congregation Mickva Israel of Savannah*, Vol. II, 1852-1888, 6 November, 1851, p. 1 (hereafter *Minutes*, Vol. II).
20. *Minutes*, Vol. II, 4 January, 1852, p. 5.
21. *Minutes*, Vol. II, 25 January, 1852, p. 9.
22. Stern, *Genealogy*, p. 44.
23. *Minutes*, Vol. II, 26 February, 1852, pp. 10-12.
24. *Minutes*, Vol. II, March, 1852, p. 15.
25. Stern, *Genealogy*, p. 44.
26. *Minutes*, Vol. II, 13 June, 1852, pp. 19-20.
27. Stern, *Genealogy*, pp. 44 and 135.
28. *The Occident*, Vol. III, 1845, p. 142 and Vol. IX, 1851, p. 106.
29. Stern, *Genealogy*, p. 149.
30. Ibid.
31. *Minutes*, Vol. II, 5 November, 1852, p. 23.
32. *The Occident*, Vol. IV, 1846, p. 210.
33. *The Occident*, Vol. X, 1852, pp. 220-221 and 48.
34. *The Occident*, Vol. III, 1845, p. 142.
35. *The Occident*, Vol. XIV, 1856, pp. 137-139.
36. *Minutes*, Vol. II, 19 June, 1853, p. 38.
37. *The Occident*, Vol. X, 1853, p. 490.
38. "Shebungot" in the *Minutes*, Vol. II, 19 June, 1853, p. 38.
39. Ibid.
40. *The Occident*, Vol. X, pp. 278-280.
41. Ibid., p. 280.
42. *Minutes*, Vol. II, 19 June, 1853, p. 38.
43. Ibid., 6 November, 1853, p. 42.
44. Ibid., 4 April, 1854, p. 47.
45. Ibid., p. 48-49.
46. Ibid., 23 April, 1854, p. 50.
47. Ibid.
48. *The Occident*, Vol. XIII, 1855, pp. 238-244.
49. *The Occident*, Vol. XII, 1854, p. 422.
50. *The Occident*, Vol. XVII, 1859, p. 126.

51. *Savannah Morning News*, 30 October, 1872, p. 3, col. 3.
52. *The Occident*, Vol. XVII, 1859, p. 210.
53. Ibid., p. 48.
54. *Savannah Morning News*, 15 May, 1856, p. 2, col. 5.
55. Ibid., 14 March, 1861, p. 2, col. 1, 2.
56. *Minutes*, Vol. II, 12 January, 1862, p. 113.
57. Ibid., 11 May, 1862, p. 115.
58. Ibid.
59. Ibid.
60. Ibid., 10 September, 1862, p. 116.
61. Ibid., 14 September, 1862, pp. 117-18.
62. Ibid., 25 October, 1863, p. 120.
63. Stern, *Genealogy*, p. 149.
64. *Minutes*, Vol. II, 18 January, 1870, p. 178.
65. *Savannah Morning News*, 25 November, 1874, p. 3, col. 2.
66. *Minutes*, Vol. II, 5 January, 1852, p. 8.
67. Ibid., 25 June, 1855, p. 74.
68. Ibid., 6 November, 1853, pp. 42-43.
69. *Minutes*, 19 August, 1850.
70. *Minutes*, Vol. II, 2 September, 1853, pp. 40-41.
71. Ibid., 25 June, 1855, p. 75.
72. Ibid., 27 May, 1857, p. 90.
73. See all account records from 1857 on. *Minutes*, Vol. II.
74. Ibid., 21 June, 1857, p. 90.
75. I. Zachariah may have more prominent status than the *Minute Books* account unto him. It is conjecture that it is he who bears relationship to Dr. Isachar Zacharie, President Lincoln's chiropodist, confidant, agent, and spy. The Zacharie-Banks Peace Plan is well attested to in the documents [see Bertram Wallace Korn, *American Jewry and The Civil War* (Philadelphia: The Jewish Publication Society of America, 1951), pp. 194-200 (hereafter Korn, *Civil War*)]. It offered promise of a solution to the war in 1863, two years before its conclusion. After the fall of Savannah, Lincoln promised his friend that he could visit his family who lived here during the war. On January 25, 1865, Zacharie received a pass that enabled him to proceed to this city. No record of Zacharie exists in the community. Is it possible that I. Zacharie (Zachariah), the *shochet*, was a family member? Surgical skills are required in both professions and one cannot rely on the accuracy of spelling in the *Minute Books*.
76. *Minutes*, Vol. II, 10 September, 1862, p. 117.
77. *Minutes*, 16 January, 1844.
78. *Minutes*, Vol. II, 6 November, 1851, pp. 1-3.
79. Ibid., 2 March, 1852, p. 16.
80. Ibid.
81. Ibid., 28 June, 1852, p. 20.
82. Ibid., pp. 16-17.
83. Ibid., 13 June, 1852, pp. 17-18.
84. Ibid., 10 December, 1852, pp. 24-25.
85. Ibid., Accounts for 1852, p. 28.
86. *The Occident*, Vol. X, 1852, p. 171.
87. Ibid.
88. Other minor repairs wrought during this period include: replacing lamps, *tabah* cloth, and new oil cloth or matting for the floor as well as carpeting the *tabah* (27 August, 1850). The roof repair was wrought by famed Savannah builder Amos Scudder (see cash accounts, 8 July, 1842). The ceiling was plastered by this same gentleman and payment was dispersed to him on 20 May, 1844.
89. *Minutes*, Vol. II, 2 March, 1852, p. 17.
90. Grinstein, *New York*, pp. 168-169, and p. 126.

91. Indicating Jacob De la Motta ranked as a Hebrew scholar.

92. *Minutes*, Vol. II, 22 May, 1853, p. 36.

93. Ibid., Cash Accounts, 27 February, 1854, p. 68.

94. *Minutes*, 17 August, 1846.

95. Note that Scudder also did work on the Market Square property, probably on Lot 23 Franklin Square which adjoins the market area. *Minutes*, Accounts, 28 May, 1847.

96. *Minutes*, Vol. II, 2 January, 1853, p. 26.

97. Ibid., 4 April, 1854, p. 47.

98. Ibid., 14 May, 1854, p. 53.

99. Ibid., 11 June, 1854, p. 54.

100. Ibid.

101. Ibid. Cash Accounts, 11 December, 1855, p. 82. The 43rd item in Touro's will reads: "I give and bequeath to the Hebrew Congregation Mikve [*sic*] Israel of Savannah, Georgia, five thousand dollars." (See Max J. Kohler, "Judah Touro, Merchant and Philanthropist" in *The Jewish Experience in America*, Vol. II, p. 173). This mistaken spelling, clearly a confusion with Philadelphia's congregation may be the first inclusion of the "e" for "a" on record.

102. Among the officiants at Newport were Dr. M. J. Raphall and Rev. S. M. Isaacs of New York. Both rabbis had connection to K.K.M.I., the latter as a fund-raiser for Palestinian Jews. Jacob De la Motta was one of his friends by virtue of generous support.

103. Grinstein, *New York*, p. 552, note 24.

104. *Minutes*, Vol. II, 21 November, 1858, p. 98.

105. Ira Rosenwaike, "The Jews of Baltimore: 1820-1830" (*American Jewish Historical Quarterly*, Vol. LXVII, No. 3), March, 1978, p. 259.

106. *Minutes*, Vol. II, 20 January, 1856, p. 84.

107. Ibid.

108. Ibid., 3 January, 1859, p. 98.

109. These names appear throughout the *Minute Book* from 1840-1870. See in particular the membership list in the beginning of *Minutes* (*1790 to 1851*) and *Minutes*, Vol. II, Treasurer's accounts for 1858-1859, pp. 100-108, and 9 August, 1864, p. 126.

110. *The Occident*, Vol. XII, 1854, p. 325.

111. *Minutes*, Vol. II, 27 May, 1857, p. 90.

112. *Minutes*, 16 August, 1841.

113. Korn, *Civil War*, p. 9. The answer of K.K.M.I. was unknown to Rabbi Korn when his book was published.

114. *Minutes*, 15 February, 1850.

115. Stern, *Genealogy*, p. 138.

116. *Minutes*, Vol. II, 12 August, 1852, p. 22.

117. Ibid., 28 June, 1852, p. 21.

118. Grinstein, *New York*, p. 83.

119. *The Occident*, Vol. X, 1852, p. 360.

120. *Minutes*, Vol. II, 17 August, 1854, p. 64.

121. Ibid., 20 May, 1855, p. 74.

122. *The Occident*, Vol. XII, 1854, pp. 324-325.

123. *Minutes*, Vol. II, 29 July, 1855, p. 77.

124. Bertram Wallace Korn, *The American Reaction to the Mortara Case: 1858-1859* (Cincinnati: The American Jewish Archives, 1957) pp. 3-11 and pp. 156-161.

125. Ibid., pp. 36-37.

CHAPTER SIX

1. Coulter, *Georgia*, p. 345.
2. Ibid., p. 348.
3. Ibid.
4. *Savannah Morning News*, 12 April, 1878.
5. Bertram W. Korn, "The Jews of the Confederacy." *American Jewish Archives*, Vol. XIII, No. 1 (April, 1961) p. 4 (hereafter Korn, "Jews of the Confederacy").
6. Spencer Bidwell King Jr., *Ebb Tide as Seen Through the Diary of Josephine Clay Habersham 1863* (Athens: University of Georgia Press, 1958) pp. 35, 39, 44, 47.
7. Harry Simonhoff, *Jewish Participants in the Civil War* (New York: ARCO Publishing, Inc., 1963), p. 203 (hereafter Simonhoff, *Jewish Participants*) and Korn, "Jews of the Confederacy," pp. 53-54.
8. "Diary of Philip Phillips" (Chapel Hill: University of North Carolina Library, Southern Historical Collection) (Typewritten copy), pp. 22-32.
9. Ibid., pp. 58-59.
10. Much has been written about Phillips. See work of David T. Morgan of Montevallo College "Philip Phillips and Internal Improvements in Mid-Nineteenth Century Alabama," *The Alabama Review*, April, 1981, pp. 83-93. Also the same author's paper delivered before the Southern Jewish Historical Society in Savannah, Nov. 17-19, 1978, "Philip Phillips, Jurist and Statesman: The South Carolina and Alabama Years." Note the extensive bibliography at the conclusion of this unpublished document.
11. *Daily Georgian*, 25 May, 1837, p. 2, col. 3; *Daily Morning News*, 19 June, 1862, p. 2, col. 3; *Daily Morning News*, 4 May, 1853, p. 2, col. 1.
12. *Savannah Daily Herald*, 1 August, 1865, p. 3, col. 1; Lee & Agnew, *Historical Record*, p. 150; *Daily Morning News*, 25 January, 1860, p. 2, col. 2.
13. Ishbel Ross, *First Lady of the South: The Life of Mrs. Jefferson Davis* (New York: Harper & Brothers Publishers, 1958), p. 266.
14. Debra Sparkman: "Solomon Cohen: Nineteenth Century Savannah Lawyer." (Research Paper, Armstrong State College, 1979), pp. 2-4.
15. Ibid., p. 5. Cohen was an opponent of secession who spoke out against it at the 1860 Democratic Convention.
16. Ibid.
17. Ibid.
18. Ibid., p. 4.
19. Korn, *Jews of the Confederacy*, p. 56.
20. *Historic Savannah*, p. 132. The house is located at 330 Abercorn Street and faces the home built for Andrew Low, where Juliette Gordon Low founded the Girl Scouts of America.
21. Agnew & Lee, *Historical Record*, p. 3.
22. *Savannah Morning News*, 19 May, 1877, p. 3, col. 5.
23. Agnew & Lee, *Historical Record*, p. 119.
24. Ibid., p. 196.
25. See Simonhoff, *Jewish Participants*, pp. 148, 179, 192, 198-203, 315-17; Korn, "Jews of the Confederacy," pp. 42-44. Dr. David Morgan of Montevallo State College presented a definitive paper on Eugenia Levy Phillips before the Southern Jewish Historical Society Conference, Charleston, South Carolina, 1979.
26. Agnew & Lee, *Historical Record*, pp. 119-128. These names have counterparts in the temple minutes from the 1790's on. Whether these are specifically Jews cannot be determined from the Agnew & Lee material.
27. Leonard Dinnerstein and Mary Dale Pallson, eds., *Jews in the South* (Baton Rouge: Louisiana State University Press, 1973), p. 73 (hereafter Dinnerstein, *Jews in the South*).
28. *Minutes*, Vol. II, 25 October, 1862, p. 120.
29. Ibid., 11 May, 1862, p. 115 and 27 November, 1866, p. 127.

30. Korn, *Civil War*, p. 112.
31. Ibid.
32. Simonhoff, *Jewish Participants*, p. 190.
33. Korn, *Civil War*, pp. 178-9.
34. Simonhoff, *Jewish Participants*, pp. 190-192.
35. Korn, *Civil War*, p. 293, note 143.
36. Korn, "Jews of the Confederacy," pp. 58-59.
37. Ibid., 1961, p. 59.
38. See Chapter 4, p. 68.
39. See Chapter 5, p. 130.
40. *Minutes*, Vol. II, 21 June, 1857, p. 90.
41. Ibid., 15 March, 1868, p. 144.
42. Ibid.
43. See for example *The Occident*, Vol. XIV, 1856, p. 478.
44. See section on Savannah Hebrew Collegiate Institute.
45. *Minutes*, Vol. II, 17 November, 1868, pp. 146-48.
46. Ibid., p. 147.
47. *The Occident*, Vol. XXV, September, 1867, p. 19.
48. *Minutes*, Vol. II, 26 November, 1868, p. 150.
49. Ibid., 27 November, 1868, p. 154. Letter from R.D.C. Lewin to B. Phillips, Esq.
50. Ibid., 27 November, 1868, pp. 154-155, from E. Fisher to the "President and Adjuncta, Congregation Mickva Israel."
51. Ibid., 10 January, 1869, p. 157.
52. Ibid., pp. 157-59.
53. Ibid., p. 159.
54. *Index To Chatham County Marriages*, 1806-1837, p. 37.
55. Stern, *Genealogy*, p. 29.
56. *Minutes*, Vol. II, 17 January, 1869, p. 160.
57. Ibid., 16 February, 1869, pp. 161-62.
58. Ibid., 8 April, 1869, p. 167.
59. Sylvan D. Schwartzman, *Reform Judaism in the Making* (New York: Union of American Hebrew Congregations, 1966), pp. 92-95.
60. *Minutes*, Vol. II, 8 April, 1869, p. 167.
61. See section on S. Yates Levy.
62. *Minutes*, Vol. II, 13 April, 1869, pp. 170-71.
63. Ibid., p. 171.
64. Ibid., 10 March, 1870, p. 181.
65. Agnew & Lee, *Historical Record*, p. 173.
66. Ibid.
67. *Minutes*, Vol. II, 10 September, 1862, p. 116.
68. Agnew & Lee, *Historical Record*, p. 173.
69. A direct descendant, Dr. Jerome L. Haym of Canandaigua, New York, having visited Mickve Israel in the late 1970's and knowing of his family connection to Savannah, provided me with a copy.
70. G. Brown is Gotchalk Brown, identified as a clerk of a dry goods store in the *Census, 1860*, p. 173. H. Haym is incorrectly identified as Harry Hayan, a dry goods merchant from Prussia, Germany. Harry and his wife Emlia (Amelia?) and Gotchalk Brown and his wife Pauline lived in the same residence.
71. *Savannah Daily Herald*, 25 March, 1865, p. 4, col. 4.
72. This family tree is contained in the family Bible of Harry Haym, now in the possession of his descendant, Gordon Haym of New Jersey.
73. Agnew & Lee, *Historical Record*, p. 173. Rev. Rosenfeld had entered the business world following his resignation as *hazzan* of K.K.M.I. When is unknown, but definitely by 1864 when an account appears in the *Daily Morning News* of an attempted robbery at his establishment in Gibson's Range, July 11, p. 2, col. 2.

74. See Agnew & Lee, *Historical Record*, pp. 173-174 and letter from H. Haym to President and Board of Trustees, B'nai B'rith Jacob, 9 January, 1877, K.K.M.I. Archives.

75. Agnew & Lee, *Historical Record*, pp. 173-74.

76. Bruyn was one of Savannah's leading designers of the late Victorian townhouse according to Beth Lattimore Reiter, art historian. This style was dominated by an Italianate influence with curved windows, lintels of cast iron and ornamental brackets under wide projecting eaves.

77. *Savannah Daily News Herald*, 16 July, 1876, p. 3, col. 2.

78. Mills Lane, *Savannah Revisited: A Pictorial History* (Savannah: The Beehive Press, 1969), pp. 26-27.

79. Gamble, *History*, p. 484.

80. *The Daily News and Herald*, 17 July, 1867, p. 3, col. 1, 2.

81. Ibid., 18 July 1867, p. 1, col. 1-3.

82. Agnew & Lee, *Historical Record*, p. 174.

83. See Louis Schmier, ed., *Reflections of Southern Jewry: The Letters of Charles Wessolowsky 1878-1879* (Macon GA: Mercer University Press, 1982) for more about this family (hereafter Schmier, *Reflections*).

84. Letter from H. Haym to President and Board of Trustees of Congregation B'nai B'rith Jacob, 9 January, 1877, K.K.M.I. Archives.

85. Both W. Barnett and Levy S. Hart had been officers of K.K.M.I. elected in the administration of Mordecai Sheftall, Sr. That administration had been turned out of office by the De la Motta—Solomon Cohen faction. *Daily Morning News*, 20 August, 1850, p. 2, col. 5.

86. *Minutes*, Vol. II, 25 October, 1862, p. 120.

87. Ibid., 11 October, 1863, p. 124.

88. Ibid., 9 August, 1864, pp. 125-26.

89. Ibid., 27 December, 1866, pp. 127-28.

90. Ibid., 13 January, 1867, p. 130.

91. Ibid., 5 February, 1867, p. 131.

92. Ibid., 16 February, 1869, p. 162.

93. Ibid., 4 December, 1869, p. 175.

94. *Savannah Morning News*, 4 September, 1869, p. 2, col. 3.

95. *Minutes*, Vol. II, 9 May, 1869, pp. 171-72.

96. Ibid., 13 January, 1870, p. 177.

97. Ibid., 18 January, 1870, p. 178.

98. Ibid., 17 July, 1870, p. 183.

99. Ibid.

100. Letter from Solomon Cohen to Rev. N. Baar, 25 November, 1870, K.K.M.I. Archives.

101. Letter from Solomon Cohen to Rev. H. S. Jacobs, 7 January, 1871, K.K.M.I. Archives.

102. Stern, *Genealogy*, p. 97.

103. George Jacobs served as the rabbi in Richmond, Virginia, succeeding his brother, Henry, who also served Beth Shalome Congregation until 1869. He then assumed the pulpit occupied by Isaac Leeser in Philadelphia, where he remained throughout his long and illustrious career. Myron Berman, *Richmond's Jewry, Shabbat in Shockoe 1769-1976* (Charlottesville: University Press of Virginia, 1979), p. 60 (hereafter Berman, *Richmond's Jewry*).

Incredibly, when Richmond's Beth Shalome was searching for a rabbi in 1873, it consulted its former spiritual leader, Henry Jacobs of New Orleans, and received as recommendation Isaac P. Mendes, (like Jacobs a native of Jamaica). I. P. Mendes distinguished himself at a later period as beloved rabbi of K.K.M.I. in Savannah.

104. Letter from Solomon Cohen to Rev. H. S. Jacobs, 7 January, 1871, K.K.M.I. Archives.

105. Ibid.

106. Letter from Solomon Cohen to Rev. M. N. Nathan, 25 November, 1870, K.K.M.I. Archives.

107. *Minutes*, Vol. II, 7 February, 1875, pp. 186-87.

108. Ibid., 9 February, 1875, pp. 187-88.

109. Ibid., 19 March, 1871, pp. 188-89.

110. Letter from Solomon Cohen to Rev. R. D. C. Lewin, 21 June, 1871, *Minutes*, Vol. II, pp. 190-91.

111. Letter from Solomon Cohen to Rev. R. D. C. Lewin, 5 July, 1871, K.K.M.I. Archives.

112. Letter from Solomon Cohen to Rev. R. D. C Lewin, 14 July, 1871, K.K.M.I. Archives.

113. *Savannah Morning News*, 12 April, 1872, p. 2, col. 5. Mr. Lewin is identified as living in Brooklyn.

114. *Minutes*, Vol. II, 25 April, 1872, pp. 198-99.

115. *Encyclopedia Judaica*, 1972 Ed., Vol. 14, S. V. "Schneeberger, Henry William" p. 982.

116. Abraham J. Karp, "Simon Tuska Becomes a Rabbi," *Publication of the American Jewish Historical Society*, Vol. L, no. 2 (December, 1960), p. 96. This information is contained in a family record given by Miss Ruth Stern to the Temple Mickve Israel Archives.

117. Letter from Solomon Cohen to Rev. Henry W. Schneeberger, 20 February, 1871, K.K.M.I. Archives.

118. Letter from Solomon Cohen to Rev. Henry W. Schneeberger, 6 March, 1871, K.K.M.I. Archives.

119. Letter from Solomon Cohen to Rev. Joseph H. M. Chumaceiro, 20 June, 1870, K.K.M.I. Archives.

120. Reznikoff, *Jews of Charleston*, p. 166.

121. This is Rabbi James Gutheim, prominent Reform rabbi who served Temple Emanu-El in New York from 1868 to 1872, returning to serve the new Reform congregation, Temple Sinai, New Orleans, and ultimately attaining a position of foremost Jewish leader of that Gulf port city. *Encyclopedia Judaica*, 1972 ed., Vol. 14, p. 986.

122. Letter from Solomon Cohen to Rev. J. K. Gertheim (Gutheim), 6 March, 1872, K.K.M.I. Archives.

123. In the archives is a copy of *Hymns Written for the Use of Hebrew Congregation, 1866*, given by Phillip Wineman to his close friend.

124. *Savannah Morning News*, 16 January, 1869, p. 3, col. 4.

125. *Savannah Daily News & Herald*, 3 March, 1868, p. 2, col. 5.

126. *Savannah Daily News & Herald*, 4 April, 1868, p. 2, col. 5. It was also put on sale at Estill's News Depot three months later, *Savannah Daily News & Herald*, 9 July, 1868, p. 2, col. 6. Also "What is Judaism," Herman L. Schreiner offering for sale, *Savannah Morning News*, 25 March, 1869, p. 2, col. 6.

127. *Savannah Morning News*, 28 December, 1868, p. 3, col. 4.

128. *Savannah Daily News & Herald*, 24 December, 1868, p. 3, col. 1.

129. Ibid., 15 September, 1868, p. 3, col. 2.

130. Agnew & Lee, *Historical Record*, p. 173.

131. Ibid., p. 156.

132. Henry Roots Jackson had served as Commander of Georgia forces in the Mexican War, was Brigadier General during the War Between the States, was active in the secession movement and served as Minister to Austria from 1853 to 1858 and to Mexico from 1885 to 1887 as appointee of President Cleveland. Mary Savage Anderson, et al., *Georgia: A Pageant of Years*, pp. 117, 128, 165.

133. Lee & Agnew, *Historical Record*, pp. 156-158.

134. Steven Hertzberg, *Strangers within the Gate City: The Jews of Atlanta 1845-1915* (Philadelphia: The Jewish Publication Society of America, 1978), pp. 62-65.

135. *The Occident*, Vol. V, 1847, p. 475. For a full description of the efforts to found institutions of higher Jewish and general learning operated by Jews see Bertram

Korn's essay "The First American Jewish Theological Seminary: Maimonides College, 1867-73," in *Eventful Years and Experiences* (Cincinnati: The American Jewish Archives, 1954), pp. 151-213.

136. Letter from Solomon Cohen to Rev. A. Harris, 5 November, 1872, K.K.M.I. Archives.

137. *Richmond Times Dispatch*, 25 January, 1891, p. 2, col. 1-2.

138. Berman, *Richmond's Jewry*, p. 218.

139. See copy of funeral service in archives, Congregation Beth Ahabah, Richmond Virginia.

140. *Minutes*, Vol. II, 3 November, 1872, pp. 200-201.

141. In a letter dated 27 November, 1872 accepting "with great pleasure" the call, Harris explains, "I shall, if possible, take the steamer from Liverpool direct for Charleston, SC where I intend to spend a few days with my friend Mr. Wineman." He also informed President Solomon Cohen that he would "avail" himself of "your kind invitation that I become your guest until I can make permanent arrangements for a home." K.K.M.I. Archives.

142. *Minutes*, Vol. II, 16 February, 1873, pp. 203-204.

143. *Savannah Daily News & Herald*, 15 September, 1868, p. 3, col. 2 describes the congregational choirs of both M.I. and B.B.J., adding "Mickve Israel has in addition a fine melodian which with the choir is under the management of the well known Professor Lessing."

144. *Savannah Daily News & Herald*, 22 September, 1866, p. 3, col. 1 describes a "grand concert" to be given by him at St. Andrews School.

145. *Savannah Daily News & Herald*, 19 April, 1866, p. 2, col. 5.

146. See *Minutes*, Vol. II, 15 January, 1871, p. 185 and 7 February, 1871, pp. 186-87.

147. *Minutes*, Vol. II, 30 January, 1870, p. 179.

148. Ibid., 11 March, 1873, p. 204.

149. *Minutes*, Vol. II, 31 August, 1874, p. 219. Letters from Solomon Cohen to Mr. Hexter and letters from Hexter to the board have been preserved and are in the Temple Archives.

150. *Minutes*, Vol. II, 3 May, 1874, p. 213.

151. Ibid.

152. *Savannah Morning News*, 18 May, 1872, p. 3, col. 1.

153. *Minutes*, Vol. II, 28 June, 1874, p. 216. The original letter from Harris to Cohen survives. Not reported to the board is a claim that the state of the congregation precluded such an extensive vacation. The letter contains a request to go to England where his aged mother lived, and while there to "get a good theological library as the expense of which if bought in New York would be enormous." Another letter survives dated 15 June, 1873, requesting a salary of $3000 to cover passage of his mother and an attendant to the United States. K.K.M.I. Archives.

154. *Minutes*, Vol. II, 12 May, 1875.

155. Ibid., 6 December, 1874.

156. See Gamble, *History*, pp. 114-115, 232-233, 301-304.

157. *Minutes*, Vol. II, 14 December, 1876. Falk's letter read as follows:
As a member of your Congregation, I desire herewith to enter my protest, against Mr. A. Harris, who has been our minister, but, contrary to his office, deserted his congregation in the greatest need and when his services were most needed by all of our co-religionists, and laymen had to perform his office. I protest against his again entering the pulpit and ask the action of the board.

158. *Minutes*, Vol. II, 14 December, 1878.

159. Ibid., 26 March, 1877.

160. Where is harmony?

161. *Minutes*, Vol. II, 8 April, 1877.

162. Ibid.

163. Ibid., 8 April, 1877.

164. See aforementioned obituaries.

165. *Richmond Times Dispatch*, 25 January, 1891, p. 2, col. 1-2.

166. "A Minister's Tribute to Dr. Harris," *Richmond Times Dispatch* by J. Cleveland Hall, 21 January, 1891.

CHAPTER SEVEN

1. Dinnerstein, *Jews in the South*, pp. 160-163.

2. Agnew & Lee, *Historical Record*, pp. 139-140.

3. Gamble, *History*, p. 301.

4. Ibid., p. 304.

5. John D. Hicks, *The American Nation: A History of the United States from 1865 to the Present* (Boston: Houghton Mifflin Company, 1949), pp. 74-81 (hereafter Hicks, *American Nation*).

6. *Minutes*, Vol. II, 2 May, 1867, p. 133.

7. Ibid., 23 October, 1868, p. 145.

8. Ritual slaughterer who provides kosher meat.

9. *Minutes*, Vol. II, 7 April, 1863, p. 122.

10. Ibid., 27 January, 1867, p. 130.

11. Ibid., February, 1872, pp. 195-196. Original in K.K.M.I. Archives.

12. Ibid., 3 March, 1872, p. 196.

13. *Historic Savannah*, pp. 164-71.

14. See deeds in the Mickve Israel Archives.

15. *Census, 1860*, p. 345.

16. Ibid., p. 350.

17. *Historic Savannah*, pp. 170-71.

18. *Census, 1860*, p. 158 where he is erroneously identified as Claude Gros.

19. Letter from Solomon Cohen to William Hunter, Esq., 11 March, 1872, K.K.M.I. Archives.

20. The cathedral was constructed from 1872 to 1876. *Historic Savannah*, p. 130.

21. First cousin of Thomas Cooper DeLeon and David Camden DeLeon, famed author and surgeon general of the Confederacy, respectively.

22. Letter from Harmon Hendricks DeLeon to S. Cohen, 2 July, 1874, K.K.M.I. Archives.

23. Letter from Solomon Cohen to Rev. R. D. C. Lewin, 5 July, 1871, K.K.M.I. Archives.

24. *Minutes*, Vol. II, 28 March, 1875, p. 224.

25. Ibid., 12 April, 1875, p. 225.

26. Ibid., 27 April, 1875.

27. *Savannah Morning News*, 8 December, 1875, p. 3, col. 3.

28. *Minutes*, Vol. II, 6 December, 1874, p. 221. Harrison's plan was 60' x 130' costing $35,000, a plan Foley at first favored until new specs. were drawn.

29. *Minutes*, Vol. II, 2 July, 1875.

30. Ibid., 11 October, 1875.

31. Ibid., 24 October, 1875.

32. See *Savannah Morning News*, 8 December, 1875, p. 3, col. 3.

33. *The American Architect and Building News*, Vol. 49, 1895, pp. 97-98.

34. Ibid.

35. Garden City was founded by Mr. Stewart and was intended to be developed as an elaborately planned community. Mr. Harrison was architect-in-charge of all public buildings. The scheme ended with Stewart's demise.

36. The information about Harrison's cathedral is to be found in the brochure, "A Short History and Guide to the Cathedral of the Incarnation, Garden City, New York."

37. See Stephen Birmingham, *Our Crowd: The Great Jewish Families of New York*

(New York: Harper and Row, 1967), pp. 158-167.

38. *Minutes*, Vol. II, 23 February, 1867 and 1 March, 1867.

39. Ibid., 2 February, 1873, p. 202.

40. Letter of L. Lillienthal to Solomon Cohen, 4 June, 1873, K.K.M.I. Archives.

41. *Minutes*, Vol. II, 12 May, 1875.

42. Ibid., 28 June, 1874, p. 217.

43. Ibid., 9 January, 1876.

44. See eulogy, *Minutes*, Vol. II, 16 September, 1875.

45. See *Minutes*, Vol. II, 9 January, 1876. It took one year before his eulogy was prepared and included in the minutes. See eulogy preceding annual meeting, 7 January, 1877.

46. *Minutes*, Vol. II, 11 December, 1876.

47. Ibid., 9 January, 1876.

48. Ibid., 15 May, 1876.

49. Ibid., 19 June, 1876.

50. Ibid., 7 January, 1877.

51. Ibid.

52. Ibid., 29 January, 1877.

53. Ibid., 9 April, 1877.

54. Ibid., 29 April, 1877.

55. Ibid., 7 March, 1876, p. 242.

56. Ibid., 26 February, 1878. A letter accompanied the check, addressed to S. Yates Levy, who was given responsibility for "transmitting it to its destination." The purpose was declared thusly "it is an unsolicited contribution to the building fund of the new synagogue on Drayton Street, a testimony of respect for the people, who worship God after the ancient fashion of their fathers, who care for their own poor, as they have learned of him to do, and who always lend a willing helping hand to every public project of benevolence."

57. *Minutes*, Vol. II, 10 January, 1876.

58. *Savannah Morning News*, 22 August, 1898, p. 8, col. 2.

59. Ibid., 29 June, 1880, p. 3, col. 4.

60. *Historic Savannah*, pp. 182, 186.

61. *Savannah Morning News*, 8 January, 1880, p. 3, col. 5-6; 28 November, 1878, p. 3, col. 4; 19 December, 1878, p. 3, col. 4.

62. *Minutes*, Vol. II, 16 April, 1877.

63. Ibid., 15 May, 1877, and 29 May, 1877.

64. Conversation in 1981 with Herbert Brito, architectural historian associated with the Savannah Battlefield Park.

65. At a cost of $50.00, *Minutes*, Vol. II, May 29 May, 1877.

66. *Minutes*, Vol. II, 25 September, 1877, and 1 July, 1877.

67. Ibid., 26 February, 1878.

68. Ibid., 25 September, 1877.

69. Ibid.

70. Ibid., 26 February, 1878.

71. Ibid., 20 March, 1878.

72. Ibid.

73. Ibid., 31 March, 1878.

74. Ibid., 28 April, 1878.

75. Ibid., 25 September, 1877.

76. Ibid., 26 February, 1878.

77. Ibid., 25 September, 1877.

78. Ibid., 30 December, 1879.

79. Ibid., 1 July, 1877.

80. Ibid., 25 September, 1877.

81. Ibid., 9 June, 1878; *Savannah Morning News*, 30 May, 1878, p. 3, col. 2 and 7 February, 1878, p. 3, col. 2.

82. *Savannah Morning News*, 30 May, 1878, p. 3, col. 2.
83. *Minutes*, Vol. II, 23 November, 1875.
84. Ibid., 22 May, 1877.
85. *Savannah Morning News*, 6 February, 1879, p. 3, col. 2.
86. See *Minutes*, Vol. II, 11 April, 1878, Joseph Rosenheim, secretary; and *Savannah Morning News*, 12 April, 1878, p. 3, col. 4-6.
87. *Minutes*, Vol. II, 5 June, 1877.
88. *Mendes Scrapbook*, Vol. I, p. 6, from the *New Orleans Times*, September, 1876, K.K.M.I. Archives.
89. Ibid., p. 9, from *Savannah Recorder*, 12 April, 1878, K.K.M.I. Archives.
90. Ibid., p. 12, from the *Hebrew Leader*, 5 May, 1878, K.K.M.I. Archives.
91. *Savannah Morning News*, 12 April, 1878, p. 3, col. 4-6.
92. *Minutes*, Vol. II, 7 January, 1879.
93. Ibid., 4 April, 1879.
94. Ibid., 28 April, 1878.
95. *Savannah Morning News*, 7 February, 1878, p. 3, col. 2, and *Jewish South*, 1 March, 1878.
96. *Minutes*, Vol. II, 1 December, 1878.
97. Ibid., 7 January, 1879.
98. Ibid., Torah to New Orleans.
99. Ibid., 14 September, 1879 and 26 August, 1881.
100. Ibid., 19 February, 1880.
101. Ibid., 20 April, 1879.
102. Letter from S. Mayer and Glauber to S. Guckenheimer, 3 March, 1879, K.K.M.I. Archives.
103. See *Census, 1860*, p. 312, for Augustus Reich; Agnew & Lee, *Historical Record*, p. 188, and *Harmonie Club Minute Books*, Georgia Historical Society.
104. Grinstein, *New York*, p. 205; *Savannah Morning News*, 14 March, 1873, p. 3, col. 2.
105. *Harmonie Club Minutes*, 22 October, 1865, pp. 6-7, Georgia Historical Society.
106. *Minutes*, Vol. II, 31 March, 1878.
107. *Savannah Morning News*, 29 July, 1874, p. 3, col. 3.
108. Ibid., 4 May, 1875, p. 3, col. 2.
109. Ibid., 21 May, 1879, p. 3, col. 6.
110. Ibid., 4 May, 1875, p. 3, col. 2.
111. Ibid., 28 June, 1877, p. 3, col. 2, and 18 March, 1880, p. 3, col. 2.
112. Ibid., 10 September, 1878, p. 3, col. 3.
113. Ibid., 21 May, 1880, p. 3, col. 4-5.
114. Ibid., 28 January, 1876, p. 3, col. 4.
115. Ibid., 26 December, 1876, p. 3, col. 3.
116. Ibid., 28 January, 1876, p. 3, col. 4.
117. Ibid., 31 January, 1876, p. 3, col. 7.
118. Ibid.
119. Ibid.
120. Ibid., 28 June, 1880, p. 3, col. 2.
121. Grinstein, *New York*, p. 145.
122. *Savannah Morning News*, 17 December, 1880, p. 2, col. 3, announcement of a charity ball; *Savannah Morning News*, 14 January, 1879, p. 3, col. 2, account of "dime-reading" entertainment; *Savannah Morning News*, 8 June, 1875, p. 3, col. 1, tribute of respect to Abraham Einstein.
123. *Savannah Morning News*, 18 December, 1873, p. 3, col. 1, where such leaders as Joseph Lippman, S. E. Byck, S. H. Eckman, H. Haym, S. Herman, M. Ferst, and S. Meinhard constitute the officers and directors.
124. See cornerstone dedication of B'nai B'rith Jacob Synagogue.
125. Schmier, *Reflections*, p. 19, note 47.

126. *Savannah Morning News*, 29 December, 1876, p. 3, col. 2, and 30 May, 1874, p. 2, col. 5.

127. Ibid., 13 June, 1877, p. 3, col. 3.

128. For details see Hertzberg, *Strangers Within the Gate City*, pp. 120-121.

129. *Savannah Morning News*, 10 July, 1876, p. 3, col. 1.

CHAPTER EIGHT

1. *Mendes Scrapbook*, Vol. II, p. 77, K.K.M.I. Archives.

2. Ibid., pp. 73-74 and Stern, *Genealogy*, p. 135.

3. Stern, *Genealogy*, p. 135.

4. *Mendes Scrapbook*, Vol. II, pp. 73-74, K.K.M.I. Archives.

5. Herbert T. Ezekiel and Gaston Lichtenstein, *The History of The Jews of Richmond 1769-1917* (Richmond, Virginia: Herbert T. Ezekiel, 1917), p. 199 (hereafter Ezekiel, *Jews of Richmond*).

6. *Mendes Scrapbook*, Vol. I, p. 1 (from *The Jewish Messenger*), K.K.M.I. Archives; and Berman, *Richmond's Jewry*, p. 61.

7. Stern, *Genealogy*, p. 45.

8. Ibid., p. 43.

9. Ibid., pp. 43-45.

10. Ibid. p. 45.

11. *Mendes Scrapbook*, Vol. I, pp. 1-6, K.K.M.I. Archives.

12. Ibid., p. 1, from the *Richmond Times Dispatch*, 12 January, 1874.

13. Ibid., p. 6, from *The Jewish Messenger*, 10 November, 1876; 15 April, 1877.

14. Ibid., p. 4, from the *New Orleans Times*.

15. Ibid., p. 5, from the Richmond, Virginia, *Enquirer*, 16 January, 1876 and Ezekiel, *Jews of Richmond*, p. 254.

16. Berman, *Richmond's Jewry*, p. 61.

17. *Minutes*, Vol. II, 27 May, 1877.

18. *Mendes Scrapbook*, Vol. I, p. 7 from *The Jewish Messenger*, K.K.M.I. Archives.

19. Ibid., p. 6 from the *Richmond Times Dispatch*, 7 June, 1879.

20. *Minutes*, Vol. II, 18 February, 1877.

21. Ibid.

22. Ibid.

23. Ibid.

24. *Minutes*, Vol. II, 26 March, 1877.

25. Ibid., 27 May, 1877.

26. Ibid., 18 February, 1877.

27. Ibid., 9 April, 1877.

28. Ibid., 10 April, 1877.

29. Ibid., 29 April, 1877.

30. Ibid.

31. Ibid., 27 May, 1877.

32. Anne Nathan Cohen, *The Centenary History—Congregation Beth Israel of Houston, Texas 1854-1954*, p. 27 (hereafter Cohen, *Congregation Beth Israel*).

33. *Mendes Scrapbook*, Vol. I, p. 12, from *Hebrew Leader*, 5 May, 1878, K.K.M.I. Archives.

34. Ibid., p. 13, from *Hebrew Leader*, 11 August, 1878.

35. Ibid.

36. *Minutes*, Vol. II, 15 September, 1878.

37. Ibid., 30 September, 1878.

38. Ibid., 8 October, 1878.

39. *Mendes Scrapbook*, Vol. I, from *Hebrew Leader*, 17 February, 1879, K.K.M.I. Archives.

40. Ibid., from *Hebrew Leader*, 13 March, 1879.

41. *Minutes*, Vol. II, 30 December, 1879 and 12 January, 1880.

42. Ibid., 15 February, 1880.

43. Ibid., 19 February, 1880.

44. Ibid., 11 March, 1880.

45. *Mendes Scrapbook*, Vol. I, pp. 20-21 from *The Savannah Recorder*, 2 June, 1879, K.K.M.I. Archives.

46. Ibid., pp. 21-22.

47. Ibid., p. 21 from *Hebrew Leader*, 9 June, 1879.

48. Ibid., p. 22 from *Jewish South*, letter to the editor from *Veritas*, 2 June, 1879.

49. Ibid., p. 54 from *The Savannah Recorder*, 17 May, 1880.

50. Ibid., p. 55.

51. Ibid., p. 37 from *The Savannah Recorder*, 24 May, 1881.

52. See *Mendes Scrapbook*, Vol. I, pp. 58, 63, 84, 94, and 96.

53. Ibid., p. 78, from a letter to *American Hebrew*, "From Time to Time."

54. Ibid., p. 67, from a letter to *American Hebrew*, "From Time to Time," 17 September, 1882.

55. *Minutes Mickva Israel 1889-1912*, Vol. III, 19 May, 1889, p. 3. (hereafter *Minutes*, Vol. III).

56. *Minutes*, Vol. III, 21 November, 1889, p. 6 and 2 May, 1980, p. 15.

57. Ibid., 14 April, 1891, p. 20.

58. Ibid., 31 May, 1893.

59. Ibid., 22 November, 1894, p. 39.

60. Ibid., 8 January, 1899, p. 69.

61. Ibid., 2 April, 1902, p. 97.

62. *Mendes Scrapbook*, Vol. I, p. 20 from *The Savannah Recorder*, 2 June, 1879, K.K.M.I. Archives.

63. *Minutes*, Vol. III, 3 June, 1901, pp. 86-87.

64. Ibid., 7 June, 1901, pp. 87-88.

65. *Savannah Morning News*, 12 April, 1878, p. 3, col. 4-6.

66. See *Minutes*, Vol. II, 30 December, 1879, 16 January, 1881, and *Minutes*, Vol. III, 1 October, 1893, 19 February, 1896, and 28 December, 1896.

67. *Minutes*, Vol. III, 8 October, 1878.

68. *Mendes Scrapbook*, Vol. I, p. 14, from letter to the editor of *Hebrew Leader*, from *ILA*, 10 October, 1878, K.K.M.I. Archives.

69. *Minutes*, Vol. II, 8 October, 1878.

70. See *Daily News & Herald*, 17 June, 1868, p. 3, col. 2 for example.

71. *Minutes*, Vol. II, 14 November, 1880.

72. N. E. Solomons, Jr., for example. See *Minutes*, Vol. II, 14 November, 1880.

73. *Minutes*, Vol. II, 1 March, 1876.

74. *Savannah Morning News*, 10 October, 1875, p. 2, col.2.

75. Rebarer wielded political power, serving as Clerk of City Council. *Savannah Morning News*, 15 January, 1885, p. 4, col. 2.

76. *Minutes*, Vol. II, 23 December, 1885.

77. Ibid., 10 January, 1886.

78. Ibid., 9 February, 1888.

79. *Minutes*, Vol. III, 5 April, 1893, p. 30.

80. Ibid., 18 April, 1893, p. 31.

81. Ibid., 24 February, 1897, p. 58.

82. Hicks, *American Nation*, pp. 255-256.

83. Coulter, *Georgia*, p. 394.

84. *Minutes*, Vol. III, 24 February, 1897, p. 59.

85. Ibid., 13 February, 1898, p. 66.
86. *Minutes*, Vol. II, 13 January, 1886.
87. *Minutes*, Vol. III. 29 May, 1902, p. 101.
88. See photo of Confirmation Class of 1885, K.K.M.I. Archives.
89. *Mendes Scrapbook*, Vol. II, p. 68, from the obituary of Eliza Mendes, K.K.M.I. Archives.
90. Ibid.
91. *Minutes*, Vol. II, 10 May, 1874, pp. 215-216.
92. Ibid., 12 May, 1875.
93. Ibid., 2 June, 1879.
94. *Minutes*, Vol. II, 10 January, 1892.
95. See *Minutes*, Vol. III, 7 February, 1892, for full details.
96. *Mendes Scrapbook*, Vol. I, p. 34, from *Jewish South*, K.K.M.I. Archives.
97. *Minutes*, Vol. II, 18 September, 1879.
98. *Mendes Scrapbook*, Vol. I, p. 34, from *Jewish South*, K.K.M.I. Archives.
99. Ibid., from letter to the editor of *Jewish South*, from *Veritas*, 21 September, 1879.
100. Ibid., p. 35, from letter to the editor of *Jewish South*, 6 October, 1879.
101. Ibid., from letter to the editor of *Jewish South*, 28 September, 1879.
102. Ibid., p. 39, letter to the editor of *Jewish South* from *Adonis*, 21 December, 1879.
103. Ibid.
104. Ibid., letter to the editor of *Jewish South* from *Adonis*, 1 January, 1879.
105. *Minutes*, Vol. III, 17 November, 1892, pp. 27-28.
106. Ibid., 13 February, 1898, p. 66.
107. *Mendes Scrapbook*, Vol. I, p. 13, K.K.M.I. Archives.
108. *Mendes Scrapbook*, Vol. II, p. 63, *American Israelite*, 5 June, 1902, K.K.M.I. Archives.
109. *Minutes*, Vol. III, 22 August, 1902, p. 108.
110. See *Minutes*, Vol. III, 24 June, 1890, p. 16 and a host of others.
111. *Mendes Scrapbook*, Vol. I, p. 14, letter to the editor of *Hebrew Leader* from *ILA*, 10 October, 1878, K.K.M.I. Archives. The service is described as "an entirely new feature in the ritual of the congregation."
112. Ibid., p. 45, from *Savannah Morning News*, 28 November, 1899.
113. Ibid., p. 45, from *Savannah Morning News*, 10 November, 1899, where he reviewed Voynick's novel, *The Gadfly*.
114. *Minutes*, Vol. III, 17 November, 1892, p. 28.
115. *Mendes Scrapbook*, Vol. II, pp. 48-50, K.K.M.I. Archives.
116. *Mendes Scrapbook*, Vol. I, p. 14, letter to the editor of *Hebrew Leader* from *ILA*, 10 October, 1878, K.K.M.I. Archives.
117. Ibid., p. 15, letter to editor of *Hebrew Leader* from *ILA*, 17 April, 1879, K.K.M.I. Archives.
118. See *Mendes Scrapbook*, Vol. I, inside front cover letter from Thomas F. Thomson of the United States Fidelity and Guaranty Company, 10 December, 1897, complimenting him on the "impressive manner in which he approached Diety . . ." on behalf of the Savannah Lodge of Elks, K.K.M.I. Archives.
119. See *Mendes Scrapbook*, Vol. I, inside front cover letter from John L. Hardee, treasurer of the Board of the Savannah Female Orphan Asylum, 22 February, 1879, K.K.M.I. Archives.
120. *Mendes Scrapbook*, Vol. II, p. 60, from *Savannah Morning News*, 28 May, 1902, K.K.M.I. Archives.
121. *Minutes*, Vol. II, 3 March, 1880.
122. Ibid., 9 January, 1887.
123. Ibid., 13 January, 1889.
124. *Minutes*, Vol. III, 5 December, 1889, p. 7.
125. Ibid., 12 January, 1890, pp. 8-9.

126. Ibid., 11 January, 1891, p. 18.

127. Ibid., 10 January, 1892, pp. 22-23.

128. Ibid., 13 January, 1895, pp. 41-42.

129. Ibid., 12 January, 1896, p. 49.

130. Ibid., 13 February, 1898, p. 66.

131. *Order of Prayers for the New Year and Day of Atonement,* adopted by the Congregation Mickva Israel, Savannah, Georgia, 1891, Vol. II, preface.

132. *Minutes,* Vol. III, 13 January, 1895, pp. 41-42.

133. Ibid., 14 January, 1900, p. 75.

134. Ibid., 28 January, 1902, p. 95.

135. See *Minutes,* Vol. II, 2 June, 1887.

136. *Mendes Scrapbook,* Vol. I, p. 31, K.K.M.I. Archives.

137. *Minutes,* Vol. III, 21 November, 1889, p. 6.

138. *Mendes Scrapbook,* Vol. I, p. 91, from the *Savannah Daily Times,* 27 October, 1884, and *Savannah Morning News,* 27 October, 1884, K.K.M.I. Archives.

139. Ibid., p. 95 from *Savannah Morning News,* 2 November, 1885.

140. *Minutes,* Vol. II, 3 March, 1880, and *Mendes Scrapbook,* Vol. I, p. 39 from *The Savannah Recorder,* 9 March, 1880, K.K.M.I. Archives.

141. See David J. Goldberg, "The Administration of Herman Myers as Mayor of Savannah, Georgia, 1895-1897 and 1899-1907." Masters Thesis, University of North Carolina, 1978, p. 84 (hereafter Goldberg, Thesis) for information on Peter W. Meldrim. Meldrim's telegram is contained in the *Mendes Scrapbook,* Vol. I, p. 38.

142. *Mendes Scrapbook,* Vol. II, p. 41, from *Savannah Evening Press,* 21 June, 1899, and *Atlanta Journal, Jewish Sentiment, Morning News, Jewish South,* K.K.M.I. Archives.

143. *Mendes Scrapbook,* Vol. I, p. 87, from the *Savannah Daily Times,* 29 June, 1884, K.K.M.I. Archives.

144. Ibid., p. 90 from *American Hebrew,* 29 September, 1884.

145. See Berman, *Richmond's Jewry,* p. 61. Note that the footnote is inaccurate, providing no proper citation for statement.

146. *Mendes Scrapbook,* Vol. II, pp. 58-63, from the *Savannah Evening Press,* 24 May, 1902, *Savannah Morning News,* 25 May, 1902, and *Savannah Morning News,* 29 May, 1902, K.K.M.I. Archives.

147. *Minutes,* Vol. II, 27 April, 1881, for example.

148. Ibid., 10 January, 1886, 3 January, 1887, 30 January, 1887.

149. See *Historic Savannah,* pp. 10, 20, 90.

150. *Minutes,* Vol. II, 12 May, 1887.

151. *Mendes Scrapbook,* Vol. II, p. 46, *Savannah Evening Press,* 1 November, 1899, K.K.M.I. Archives.

152. *Minutes,* Vol. II, 9 September, 1887, letter from S. B. Adams, C. H. Carson and W. F. Beals dated 7 September.

153. *Minutes,* Vol. III, 5 December, 1899, p. 73.

154. A non-Jewish gentleman, Dr. J. Lawton Hiers offered a generous contribution for the new building program, and it was returned to him as were all other donations, *Minutes,* Vol. III, 12 August, 1902, p. 107.

155. *Minutes,* Vol. III, 2 November, 1893, p. 34.

156. Ibid., 19 February, 1896, pp. 50-51.

157. See Levy, "SOJC," p. 13.

158. *Minutes,* Vol. III, 3 June, and 7 June, 1901, pp. 86-87.

159. *Minutes,* Vol. III, 27 October, 1892, p. 27.

160. Ibid., 8 July, 1902, p. 106, and 12 August, 1902, p. 107.

161. Ibid., 6 November, 1902, p. 110.

162. According to family tradition.

163. *Mendes Scrapbook,* Vol. II, pp. 44-45, from *Savannah Evening Press,* 5 October, 1899, K.K.M.I. Archives.

164. *Minutes,* Vol. III, 9 January, 1898, p. 63.

165. Ibid., 29 May, 1898, p. 67.
166. Ibid., 3 February, 1896, p. 50.
167. Ibid., Accounts 9 January, 1897, p. 56.
168. Ibid., 4 December, 1896, p. 52.
169. Ibid., see David J. Rosenheim's report, 5 January, 1897, p. 54.
170. Ibid., 10 January, 1897, p. 53.
171. *Minutes*, Vol. II, 1 December, 1878, and 14 February, 1881.
172. *Minutes*, Vol. III, 19 November, 1890, p. 17.
173. Ibid., 11 October, 1893, p. 33.
174. Ibid., 22 November, 1894, p. 39.
175. Ibid., 29 October, 1896, p. 52.
176. Ibid., 24 February, 1897, p. 59.
177. Ibid., 10 November, 1898, p. 68.
178. Ibid., 9 December, 1897, p. 62.
179. Wilson, *Historic and Picturesque Savannah*, p. 225.
180. *Minutes*, Vol. II, 12 September, 1881.
181. Ibid., 2 June, 1887.
182. Ibid., 8 January, 1888.
183. *Minutes*, Vol. III, 19 May, 1889, p. 3.
184. Lee & Agnew, *Historical Record*, p. 199.
185. Wilson, *Historic and Picturesque Savannah*, pp. 173-176.
186. *Minutes*, Vol. II, 13 January, 1889 and *Minutes*, Vol. III, 10 February, 1889, p. 1.
187. *Minutes*, Vol. III, 21 November, 1889, p. 6.
188. *Mendes Scrapbook*, Vol. I, p. 28, from *The Reformer and Jewish Times*, 25 July, 1879, K.K.M.I. Archives.
189. Ibid.
190. *Mendes Scrapbook*, Vol. II, p. 41, from *Atlanta Journal*, 15 September, 1899, K.K.M.I. Archives.
191. Ibid., p. 41, from *Savannah Evening Press*, 15 September, 1899.
192. Ibid., p. 44, from *Savannah Evening Press*, 25 September, 1899.
193. *Mendes Scrapbook*, Vol. I, pp. 40-41, K.K.M.I. Archives.
194. Gamble, *History*, pp. 11-22.
195. Goldberg, Thesis, p. iii.
196. Ibid., p. iv.
197. Ibid., pp. 3-4.
198. Ibid., pp. 109-148.
199. *Minutes*, Vol. II, 13 January, 1889. He headed the committee to draw up resolutions for deceased members S. E. Byck, A. Lehman and J. H. Eckman.
200. *Savannah Morning News*, 20 September, 1871, p. 3, col. 3.
201. *Savannah Morning News*, 31 July, 1877, p. 2, col. 7; 2 November, 1887, p. 8, col. 1; 5 April, 1890, p. 8, col. 1; and 13 January, 1888, p. 8, col. 3.
202. *Savannah Morning News*, 1 January, 1880, p. 3, col. 4.
203. Wilson, *Historic and Picturesque Savannah*, p. 214.
204. *Mendes Scrapbook*, Vol. I, p. 35, letter to editor of *Jewish South* from *Adonis*, 28 September, 1879, K.K.M.I. Archives.
205. *Historic Savannah*, pp. 20, 22, 24, 34.
206. Goldberg, Thesis, pp. 17-18.
207. See Abraham J. Karp, "The Era of Immigration," pp. VII-XXI (hereafter Karp, "Era of Immigration"); Esther L. Panitz, "The Polarity of American Jewish Attitudes towards Immigration (1870-1891)," pp. 31-62 (hereafter Panitz, "Polarity"); and George M. Price, "The Russian Jews in America," pp. 265-355; all in *The Jewish Experience in America*, Vol. IV (New York: KTAV Publishing House, Inc., 1969). See also Irving Aaron Mandel, "Attitude of the American Jewish Community Toward East European Immigration as Reflected in the Anglo-Jewish Press 1880-1890," in *Critical Studies in American Jewish History*, Vol. I (Cincinnati: American Jewish Archives, 1971) (hereafter Mandel,

"Attitudes of the American Jewish Community").

208. Mandel, "Attitudes of the American Jewish Community," p. 266

209. Ibid., for southern colonies see "Hebrew Emigrants Aid Society of the United States (1881-1883)," *American Jewish Experience*, Vol. IV, p. 79.

210. Karp, "Era of Immigration," p. VIII.

211. Ibid.

212. Mandel, "Attitudes of the American Jewish Community." pp 264-286.

213. *Mendes Scrapbook*, Vol. I, p. 63, letter to *The American Hebrew* from *From Time to Time* 13 April, [1882, assumed by context], K.K.M.I. Archives.

214. Ibid., p. 66, letter to *American Hebrew*, from *From Time to Time*, 6 August [1883 assumed by context].

215. *Minutes*, Vol. III, 2 January, 1890, p. 7.

216. Panitz, "Polarity," pp. 56-57.

217. *Minutes*, Vol. III, 3 February, 1892, p. 24.

218. Ibid., 10 March, 1892, p. 25.

219. Ibid., 27 October, 1892, p. 27.

220. Ibid., 17 November, 1892, p. 28.

221. Panitz, "Polarity," p. 32.

222. Coulter, *Georgia*, pp. 406-407.

223. Goldberg, Thesis, pp. 24, 75-76.

224. Ibid., p. 19.

225. Ibid., p. 177.

226. Ibid., p. 179.

227. *Mendes Scrapbook*, Vol. II, pp. 66-67, from *Savannah Morning News*, 31 December, 1903, K.K.M.I. Archives.

228. *Mendes Scrapbook*, Vol. I, pp. 66-67, from letter to *Hebrew Leader* from *From Time to Time*, 27 August, 1882, K.K.M.I. Archives.

229. *Savannah Morning News*, 26 January, 1891, p. 8, col. 3.

230. Ibid., 16 July, 1889, p. 8, col. 3.

231. Ibid., 17 August, 1891, p. 8, col. 5.

232. Ibid., 5 March, 1886, p. 8, col. 1-2.

233. Ibid., 9 March, 1887, p. 8, col. 3-4.

234. Ibid., 14 January, 1889, p 8, col. 2 and 20 January, 1889, p. 8, col. 2.

235. Ibid., 16 May, 1889, p. 8, col. 2.

236. Ibid., 10 April, 1890, p. 8, col. 2.

237. Ibid., 15 January, 1891, p. 3, col. 3.

238. Ibid., 27 February, 1891, p. 8, col. 5.

239. Ibid., 28 November, 1889, p. 8, col. 2.

240. Ibid., 29 March, 1887, p. 8, col. 2.

241. Ibid., 6 February, 1890, p. 8, col. 3.

242. Ibid., 18 March, 1891, p. 8, col. 3.

243. See *Little Helpers Minute Books*, Vol. I, p. 1, K.K.M.I. Archives.

244. Ibid., p. 2.

245. *Savannah Morning News*, 17 March, 1889, p. 8, col. 4.

246. Constitution of The Hebrah Gemiluth Hesed Society of Savannah, Georgia, 20 June, 1888, revised 24 December, 1916, p. 14, K.K.M.I. Archives.

247. Ibid., p. 15.

248. Ibid., p. 16.

249. Ibid., pp. 17-19.

250. Ibid., p. 19.

251. Ibid., pp. 20-22.

252. Ibid., p. 22.

253. Ibid., see list of members, pp. 31-35.

254. Ibid., p. 6.

255. See Secretary's Report, 1903, included in *Teacher's Union Minute Book*, 1900-

1903, K.K.M.I. Archives.

256. *Teacher's Union Minute Book,* 10 June, 1901, p. 29, requesting that Rabbi Mendes be on the building committee for the new annex and 12 May, 1900, pp. 19-20, a petition to the board requesting children's worship on the Sabbath which the board had officially opposed.

257. Ibid., 6 January, 1901, p. 11.

258. Ibid., 3 March, 1901, p. 13.

259. Ibid., 2 December, 1900, p. 5.

260. Ibid., 3 March, 1901, p. 13.

261. Ibid., 1 December, 1901, p. 41, and 29 December, 1901, p. 43.

262. Ibid., 2 February, 1902, p. 53.

CHAPTER NINE

1. Acknowledgement is made of the helpfulness of A. J. Cohen, Jr., whose mother, Mildred, was Rabbi Solomon's niece by marriage.

2. Oral tradition, A. J. Cohen, Jr. source.

3. *Minutes 1929-1933,* p. 223, from the *Savannah Morning News,* 8 November, 1933.

4. *Minutes 1940-1944,* p. 168, rabbi's annual report 1943.

5. *Contact,* November, 1938, Vol. II, no. 11, p. 1.

6. *Minutes,* Vol. III, 25 December, 1902, p. 115.

7. *Mendes Scrapbook,* Vol. II, p. 70 from *Savannah Morning News,* 25 December, 1902, K.K.M.I. Archives.

8. Ibid., p. 71 from *Savannah Morning News,* 28 December, 1902.

9. Ibid., from a New Orleans newspaper and *Jewish Spectator,* 2 January, 1903.

10. Ibid., pp. 71-72, from *Savannah Morning News,* 2 February, 1903, and *Savannah Evening Press,* 2 February, 1903.

11. *Minutes,* Vol. III, 11 January, 1903, p. 116.

12. Ibid., pp. 118-119.

13. Ibid., p. 119.

14. Ibid., 25 January, 1903, p. 121.

15. Ibid., pp. 121-122.

16. Ibid., 1 February, 1903, pp. 123-124.

17. Ibid., 8 February, 1903, pp. 125-126.

18. Ibid., 10 February, 1903, pp. 127-129.

19. Ibid., pp. 129-132.

20. Ibid., 19 February, 1903, p. 133.

21. Ibid., and 1 March, 1903, p. 134.

22. Ibid., 8 March, 1903, pp. 136-139.

23. Ibid., p. 137.

24. Mendes' letter in response to his election as Rabbi Emeritus reflects the gracious manner of one who realized that the inevitable had to be accepted with dignity:

Your favor under date March 16th informing me of my unanimous election as Minister Emeritus, for life, has been duly received.

I would request you to convey to the members of the Congregation my thanks and appreciation of the further proof of their feelings towards me. I desire to assure them, that, with God's help I shall in the future, as I have endeavored to do in the past, labor unceasingly for their welfare and advancement, and I ask a continuance of the support they have accorded me during the past quarter of a century. *Minutes,* Vol. III, 10 January, 1904, p. 149.

25. *Minutes,* Vol. III, 10 January, 1904, p. 150.

26. Ibid., 28 June, 1904, p. 163.

27. Ibid., 3 July, 1904, p. 168 and 31 October, 1904, p. 172.

28. *Mendes Scrapbook,* Vol. II, p. 75, from *Savannah Morning News,* 1 July, 1904, K.K.M.I. Archives.

29. Ibid., from *Savannah Evening Press,* 30 June, 1904.

30. Ibid., from *Savannah Morning News,* 30 June, 1904.

31. Ibid.

32. Ibid., p. 74, from *Savannah Evening Press,* 29 June, 1904.

33. Ibid., pp. 76-77.

34. *Minutes,* Vol. III, 3 July, 1904, p. 166.

35. See pages 174-177, *Minutes,* Vol. III.

36. *Mendes Scrapbook,* Vol. II, p. 76, from *Savannah Morning News,* 19 July, 1904, K.K.M.I. Archives.

37. *Minutes,* Vol. III, 24 February, 1906, p. 193.

38. In 1907, the matter of Union dues was an issue, as the congregation felt the obligation to alter an accurate report of 88 members to include the new congregants. The question was, is a member defined solely as a pew owner, or are renters to be included as well. (*Minutes,* Vol. III, 10 December, 1907, p. 210.) Then as now the instinct of UAHC members is to come down on the side of literalism resulting in the original dues of $88, one dollar per constituent seat owner. (*Minutes,* Vol. III, 12 January, 1908, p. 211.) A budgetary item regularly reported at K.K.M.I.'s annual meetings was payment to Lippman Levy, treasurer of the UAHC. (See *Minutes,* Vol. III, 9 January, 1910, p. 237, and others.)

39. *Minutes 1912-1924,* George Solomon's Annual Report to the Officers and Members, Congregation Mickve Israel, 12 January, 1913.

40. *Minutes 1912-1924,* 11 December, 1913.

41. Ibid., Solomon's Annual Report, 12 January, 1913.

42. *Minutes,* Vol. III, 24 April, 1904, p. 157.

43. Ibid., 12 January, 1908, p. 213.

44. *Minutes 1912-1924,* 12 October, 1915.

45. Ibid., see also letter from George Solomon to Jos. Rosenheim, 6 October, 1915 and *Minutes 1912-1924,* 9 January, 1916.

46. Ibid., 9 May, 1916, letter from choir committee to the board.

47. Ibid., 9 May, 1916.

48. Ibid., letter from choir committee to the board.

49. Ibid., 3 July, 1916.

50. *Minutes,* Vol. III, 7 January, 1906, p. 191.

51. Ibid., 13 January, 1907, p. 203.

52. Ibid., 10 January, 1909, pp. 223-224.

53. Ibid., 8 January, 1911, p. 252.

54. See letter from George Solomon, Temp. Chairman and C. N. Feidelson, Temp. Secretary, Federated Hebrew Charities, 11 January, 1912, K.K.M.I. Archives.

55. *Minutes 1912-1924,* 14 January, 1912.

56. Ibid., Annual Report of Rabbi George Solomon to Mickve Israel Congregation, 8 January, 1912.

57. Ibid.

58. Ibid. A year later, Edwin and Hugo Frank presented a silver breastplate and crowns and a set of Torah covers in honor of their father's 80th birthday. *Minutes 1912-1924,* 12 January, 1913.

59. Ibid., Annual Report of Rabbi George Solomon to Congregation Mickve Israel, 12 January, 1913.

60. Ibid., 23 January, 1913.

61. Ibid., Solomon's Annual Report, 12 January, 1913.

62. Ibid.

63. *Minutes 1912-1924,* letter from George Solomon to A. Shulhafer, 20 October, 1913.

64. Ibid., financial statement, 31 December, 1914.

65. D. A. Byck, Jr., of blessed memory, the official archivist of the congregation, was aware of the lacuna and requested information of this writer, if any should ever turn up.

66. Hicks, *American Nation*, pp. 474-482.

67. Coulter, *Georgia*, p. 430.

68. Hicks, *American Nation*, p. 488.

69. *Minutes 1912-1924*, report of Julia F. Solomon, President of the Temple Sisterhood, 13 January, 1918 and Minutes of the Annual Meeting, 13 January, 1918.

70. *Minutes 1912-1924*, Annual Report of Rabbi George Solomon to Congregation Mickve Israel, 9 January, 1916.

71. Ibid. Annual Report of Rabbi George Solomon, 13 January, 1918, and Minutes of the Annual Meeting, 13 January, 1918.

72. Ibid., Rabbi's report, 1919.

73. Hicks, *American Nation*, p. 493.

74. *Minutes 1912-1924*, Report of Julia F. Solomon, President of Temple Sisterhood, 13 January, 1918.

75. Ibid., 6 August, 1917.

76. Ibid., 19 December, 1917.

77. See undated newspaper clipping in the K.K.M.I. Archives.

78. Ibid. The letter bears the heading, "Jewish Welfare Board, Camp Wadsworth, Spartanburg, South Carolina."

79. *Minutes 1912-1924*, 12 January, 1919.

80. Ibid., Rabbi's report, 1919.

81. The fighting men of Mickve Israel included:

Joseph Solomons	Samuel Adler
Joseph Lax	Carol Minis
Sam Eisenberg	Mark Cohen
Bertram Birnbaum	Lewis Pinkussohn
Harold Ferst	Sylvan Weil
Isaac Minis	Arthur Rosenthal
Peirne Prager	Max Guthman
Clarence Lehwald	Harold Basch
Leonard Unger	Edward Weil
Moses Ferst	David Hirsch
Walter Falk	Joseph Falk
David Falk	Arthur Marks
Herman Edel	Joseph Dreyer
Joseph Oppenheim	Melvin Adler
Lawrence Steinheimer	Irving Meinhard
Arthur Dillon	Sylvan Byck
Alvin Ferst	Leon Ferst
Seina Collat	Washington Falk, Jr.
Leon Schwab	Mark Silver
Comer Hughs	Everett Iseman
Jerome T. Cohen	Edgar Weil

82. The trial lasted from 24 July, 1913 to 26 August, 1913. See Dinnerstein, *Jews in the South*, p. 192. The lynching occurred in August, 1915, and was reported in the *New York Times*, 18 August, 1915. Ibid., p. 194, footnote 78. For reports of anti-Semitism from pulpits and economic dislocation, see Ibid., pp. 183 and 185. For information on the shift to an urban economy, see Hertzberg, *Strangers Within the Gate City*, pp. 202-203.

83. Coulter, *Georgia*, p. 400 and Hertzberg, *Strangers Within the Gate City*, pp. 208-209.

84. Hicks, *American Nation*, pp. 188-189.

85. Ibid., p. 457.

86. *Minutes 1912-1924*, see letter of Simon Wolf, 27 January, 1915, and the full text of the Union resolution accompanying it.

87. Ibid., 30 January, 1915.

88. Hicks, *American Nation*, p. 497.

89. *Minutes 1912-1924*, Rabbi's report 1919.

90. Ibid., 9 April, 1918.

91. George Solomon, Conference Sermon, Birmingham, Alabama, 12 March, 1904, p. 4, K.K.M.I. Archives.

92. A year later a sermon entitled "The Jews of the Past and the Present" was reproduced in the *Savannah Morning News* (Sunday, November 19, 1905, p. 10), containing a further expansion of his view; "Having eloquently and valiently fought against the injustice of the world placing all Jews in one class, and condemning and praising all alike, we have the modern Zionist, reviving the worn out fiction that we are a separate race, bound by one tie, having one common interest, looking forward to an eventual separation from the world and a return to our ancestral land of Palestine, which alone we can regard as our home, viewing our present countries but tarrying places in which we can have but a passing interest."

93. Solomon, Conference Sermon, 12 March, 1904, p. 4.

94. Ibid., p. 7.

95. George Solomon, sermon outline, undated, K.K.M.I. Archives.

96. George Solomon, "Woman Suffrage" (sermon), 17 May, 1893, p. 3, K.K.M.I. Archives.

97. Ibid., p. 11.

98. Ibid., p. 14.

99. George Solomon, "Religion and Evolution" (sermon), p. 8, K.K.M.I. Archives.

100. Ibid., p. 9.

101. Ibid., p. 11.

102. Ibid., p. 12.

103. Letter from George Solomon to the Members of the Board of Education, Chatham County, 30 October, 1917, K.K.M.I. Archives.

104. Letter from George Solomon to Editor, *Savannah Press*, 26 November, 1907, K.K.M.I. Archives.

105. Ibid.

106. Rabbi Solomon, "Equal Justice Asked for All," newspaper clipping, undated, K.K.M.I. Archives.

107. Conversation with George Solomon Cohen, 26 May, 1982, great-grandnephew, reporting an understanding he was given by his grandmother, Mrs. A. J. Cohen, Sr., George Solomon's niece.

108. George Solomon, sermon, undated (title page missing), K.K.M.I. Archives.

109. Samples of Bar Mitzvah prayers are to be found in the K.K.M.I. Archives. One *Rosh Chodesh* prayer (for the new moon) is preserved, dated 16 November, 1917. Solomon created his own beautiful ceremony for circumcision that surpasses (in tender prose) any in common use today. It begins "Blessed be thy coming, little one. With prayerful benediction we welcome thee into the covenant hallowed by Father Abraham in the long ago." It also includes this felicitous line, "May the sign with which we now mark thy slender body be ever more and more a symbol of the sublime teachings of the glorious faith it is intended to represent."

110. See conversion ceremony of Emma Rosenfeld of Savannah, 4 October, 1905, and Jessie Gibson of Dorchester, Georgia, 4 November, 1906, K.K.M.I. Archives.

111. Rabbi George Solomon, "Confirmation," *The Jewish Conservator*, Vol. 3, No. 4, 27 January, 1905, p. 5.

112. Ibid.

113. Solomon's article on confirmation is a thoroughgoing analysis, authored in a period when Reform was considering standards and goals. It commends itself to all in positions of influence in synagogue life because of its logic.

114. Letter from George Solomon to Mr. V. H. Kriegshaber, Atlanta, Georgia, 12 September, 1919, K.K.M.I. Archives.

115. Letter from Madison C. Peters, Brooklyn, New York, to George Solomon, 10 February, 1910, K.K.M.I. Archives.

116. Letter from George Solomon to Madison C. Peters, 15 February, 1910, K.K.M.I. Archives.

117. *Savannah Evening Press*, 26 November, 1906, clipping in K.K.M.I. Archives.

118. Letter from George Solomon to Editor, *Savannah Evening Press*, 27 October, 1906, K.K.M.I. Archives.

119. Letter from George Solomon to Honorable George T. Cann, Judge, Superior Court of Chatham County, Georgia, 21 December, 1906, K.K.M.I. Archives.

120. "A Merited Rebuke," undated newspaper clipping in K.K.M.I. Archives.

121. "Hebrew Democratic Club May Change Its Name," undated newspaper clipping in K.K.M.I. Archives.

122. *Savannah Morning News*, 6 December, 1905, clipping in K.K.M.I. Archives.

123. A program copy has been preserved.

124. Date unknown, clipping in K.K.M.I. Archives.

125. The 10 May, 1908, coverage in a North Carolina newspaper (which one is unknown) is entitled "America is Called The Promised Land."

126. Letterhead dated 12 September, 1919, K.K.M.I. Archives.

127. Date unknown, text preserved in K.K.M.I. Archives.

128. George Solomon obituary, *Savannah Morning News*, 25 February, 1945, p. 24, col. 6.

129. 4 December, 1910, text preserved in K.K.M.I. Archives.

130. George Solomon obituary, *Savannah Morning News*, 25 February, 1945, p. 24, col. 6.

131. *Raleigh News and Observer*, 29 June, 1913, clipping in K.K.M.I. Archives.

132. *Minutes 1912-1924*, Annual Report, George Solomon to Mickve Israel Congregation, January 1916.

133. The *Scroll*, January 1916, Vol. I, no. 1, p. 3.

134. See preceding chapter. It met in the K.K.M.I. Chapel on Sunday nights during the period when the Alliance was being constructed. *Minutes 1912-1924*, 4 May, 1913.

135. Letter from George Solomon and C. N. Feidelson, 11 January, 1912, K.K.M.I. Archives.

136. *The Scroll*, January 1916, Vol. I, no. 1, p. 7.

137. *Historic Savannah*, p. 116.

138. *The Scroll*, January 1916, Vol. I, no. I, p. 8.

139. *Minutes 1912-1924*, Annual Report, George Solomon to Mickve Israel Congregation, January, 1916.

140. *Minutes 1912-1924*, 23 April, 1912.

141. Ibid., financial statement of Lawrence Lippman, 12 January, 1913.

142. See *Minutes*, Vol. III, Annual Report of George Solomon, 9 January, 1910, p. 242.

143. *Minutes*, Vol. III, 23 June, 1904, p. 162.

144. *Minutes 1912-1924*, 14 March, 1916, and 9 May, 1916.

145. Ibid., 28 November, 1916.

146. Ibid., 9 June, 1916.

147. Ibid., 9 January, 1916.

148. Ibid., 9 June, 1916.

149. Ibid., 7 January, 1917.

150. Ibid., 30 April, 1918.

151. See *Minutes 1912-1924*, annual meeting, 11 January, 1920.

152. *Minutes*, Vol. III, 13 August, 1908, p. 220.

153. *Minutes 1912-1924*, 12 October, 1913.

154. Ibid., 4 May, 1913.

155. Ibid., 23 November, 1913.

156. *Minutes*, Vol. III, 22 January, 1911, p. 258.

157. *Minutes 1912-1924*, annual meeting, 9 January, 1916.

158. *Minutes*, Vol. III, 14 January, 1909, p. 227; 13 January, 1907, p. 203; *Minutes 1912-1924*, 28 November, 1916.

159. *Minutes*, Vol. III, 21 May, 1906, p. 196.

160. Ibid., 8 July, 1910, p. 249.

161. *Minutes 1912-1924*, 12 October, 1915, and 9 January, 1916.

162. *Minutes*, Vol. III, 11 April, 1907, p. 205.

163. Ibid., 12 July, 1905, p. 183.

164. Ibid., 14 October, 1909, p. 233.

165. Ibid., p. 246.

166. Ibid., 11 April, 1907, p. 205.

167. Ibid., 23 May, 1907, p. 206. Notice the synagogue is called *Berith* Jacob.

168. Ibid., 1 April, 1909, p. 231.

169. Ibid., 13 August, 1908, p. 220.

170. Ibid., 19 November, 1908, p. 221.

171. *Minutes 1912-1924*, 22 June, 1917, and letter of 3 May, 1917, Mrs. A. J. Garfunkel to Jos. Rosenheim appended to same.

172. In researching this book, the author did request from the synagogue leadership records and documents. Little was forthcoming, less through lack of effort as through lack of awareness of where the sources might be located.

173. *Historic Savannah*, p. 56.

174. *The Scroll*, January 1916, Vol. I, no. I, pp. 33-35.

175. *Minutes*, Vol. III, 26 March, 1908, p. 215.

176. Ibid., George Solomon Annual Report, 8 January, 1911, p. 255.

177. Ibid., *Minutes 1912-1924*, 4 August, 1913.

178. *The Scroll*, January 1916, Vol. I, no. 1, pp. 40-41.

179. *Minutes 1912-1924*, 16 November, 1916.

180. Ibid., 7 January, 1917.

181. Ibid., 20 February, 1917.

182. Ibid., Sisterhood Report, 13 January, 1918.

183. *Minutes*, Vol. III, 10 December, 1907, p. 210, and annual meeting, 8 January, 1911, report of Carl Herman, secretary, p. 252.

CHAPTER TEN

1. Hicks, *American Nation*, p. 527.

2. Ibid., p. 531.

3. Ibid., pp. 532-534.

4. Ibid., pp. 537-539, 407-408.

5. Ibid., pp. 544-548.

6. Ibid., pp. 548-556.

7. Coleman, *History of Georgia*, p. 257.

8. Ibid., p. 259.

9. Ibid., p. 263.

10. Ibid., pp. 264-267.

11. Ibid., p. 264.

12. Ibid., p. 269.

13. Ibid., p. 270.

14. Stern, *Genealogy*, p. 138.

15. Coleman, *History of Georgia*, pp. 270, 272.

16. Hertzberg, *Strangers Within The Gate City*, p. 103.

17. Coleman, *History of Georgia*, p. 276.

18. *Minutes of Congregation Mickve Israel 1925-1928*, 18 January, 1925, p. 7.

19. Ibid., p. 8.

20. *Minutes of Congregation Mickve Israel 1929-1933*, 2 August, 1929, p. 38; 6 September, 1929, p. 39; 2 October, 1929, p. 41; 1 January, 1930, p. 64.

21. Ibid., 11 January, 1930, p. 67.

22. *Minutes 1925-1928*, 5 March, 1926, p. 66.

23. Ibid., 20 April, 1927, p. 105.

24. Ibid., (no date), pp. 129-132. From the comprehensive report authored by historian-architect and later temple president, Morton H. Levy.

25. Ibid., p. 135, from the *Savannah Press*, 19 April, 1927.

26. Ibid., p. 138, newspaper clipping.

27. Ibid., p. 135, from the *Savannah Press*, 19 April, 1927.

28. Ibid.

29. Ibid., p. 138.

30. Ibid.

31. Ibid.

32. See Rabbi Solomon's sermon entitled, "Exposition of the Needs of a New Synagogue," dated 1911 from internal evidence, K.K.M.I. Archives and *Minutes 1925-1928*, p. 138.

33. *Minutes 1925-1928*, from report of Morton H. Levy, p. 130.

34. Ibid., p. 131.

35. Ibid., p. 132.

36. Ibid., p. 142.

37. Ibid.

38. Ibid., p. 138.

39. Ibid., p. 136, from the *Savannah Press*, 21 September, 1927.

40. Ibid., Report of Public Worship Committee 1927, p. 145.

41. Letter from Harvey Granger to Rabbi George Solomon, 21 April, 1927, K.K.M.I. Archives.

42. *Minutes 1925-1928*, p. 146, from the *Savannah Press*, 20 December, 1927.

43. Ibid.

44. Hicks, *American Nation*, p. 585.

45. Ibid., p. 586.

46. Coleman, *History of Georgia*, p. 263.

47. *Minutes 1912-1924*, 9 January, 1921, p. 28.

48. *Minutes 1925-1928*, 3 July, 1925, p. 37.

49. Ibid., 7 January, 1926, Delinquent list, p. 58.

50. *Minutes 1912-1924*, 11 May, 1921, p. 35, and 22 September, 1921, p. 39.

51. Ibid., 11 September, 1920, p. 21. Freely translated, "without resources, Judaism cannot endure."

52. *Minutes of Congregation Mickve Israel 1940-1944*, 18 January, 1942, p. 113. In 1940 they had fallen to $7800 and in 1941 to less than $7600.

53. *Minutes 1929-1933*, 10 January, 1932, p. 156, and *Minutes 1934-1939*, 22 June, 1934, p. 36.

54. *Minutes 1929-1933*, 6 November, 1931, p. 147.

55. Ibid., 31 December, 1932 and *Minutes 1934-1939*, 14 January, 1934, p. 20.

56. *Minutes 1929-1933*, Report of the President 1930, p. 107, and Sabbath School Report, p. 193.

57. Ibid., p. 111.

58. Ibid., Report of the President 1930, p. 107.

59. *Minutes 1934-1939*, Report of the President and Board 1934, p. 85.

60. Ibid., 14 June, 1934, p. 35.

61. *Minutes 1929-1933*, Report of the President 1930, p. 106.

62. *Minutes 1934-1939*, p. 85.

63. Ibid., p. 81, and letter from George Solomon to Adjunta, Congregation Mickve Israel, 14 February, 1906, K.K.M.I. Archives.

64. *Minutes 1934-1939*, 18 January, 1934, p. 26.

65. *Minutes 1929-1933*, 7 November, 1930, p. 97 and Report of the President 1930, p. 105.

66. Ibid., 8 January, 1933, p. 201, and 15 January, 1931, p. 101.

67. Ibid., 13 October, 1933, p. 220, and 3 November, 1933, p. 221.

68. Ibid., 5 October, 1934, p. 40.

69. Ibid., 7 January, 1937, pp. 107, 166.

70. Ibid., 15 January, 1939, p. 205, and *Contact*, Vol. 3, no. 6, June, 1939, p. 2.

71. Ibid., p. 190.

72. Ibid., 6 March, 1936, p. 97.

73. *Minutes 1929-1933*, letter from Girard Cohen, Chairman, Membership Committee, 8 January, 1932, p. 152, and *Minutes 1934-1939*, 4 May, 1934, p. 33.

74. *Minutes 1929-1933*, 28 October, 1931, p. 145, Questionaire and Analysis.

75. Ibid., 3 April, 1931, p. 129.

76. *Minutes 1934-1939*, 3 September, 1937, p. 139; 2 July, 1937, p. 138; 10 January, 1937, pp. 108-109.

77. Ibid., 12 July, 1935, p. 73.

78. *Minutes 1929-1933*, 8 May, 1931, p. 131, and 5 June, 1931, p. 133.

79. *Minutes of Congregation Mickve Israel 1940-1944*, 5 April, 1940, p. 29.

80. *Contact*, Vol. 7, no. 1, January, 1943, pp. 1, 7, K.K.M.I. Archives.

81. Ibid., p. 1.

82. *Contact*, Vol. 2, no. 1, January, 1938, p. 4.

83. *Minutes 1929-1933*, Sisterhood Report, 11 January, 1932, p. 166.

84. *Contact*, Vol. 1, no. 2, May, 1937, pp. 1, 4.

85. *Contact*, Vol. 2, no. 5, May, 1938, p. 3.

86. *Contact*, Vol. 6, no. 3, May, 1942, pp. 2-3.

87. *Minutes 1940-1944*, 8 January, 1940, p. 11.

88. *Contact*, Vol. 4, no. 5, May, 1940, p. 5.

89. *Contact*, Vol. 2, no. 5, May, 1938, p. 2.

90. *Contact*, Vol. 4, no. 1, January, 1940, p. 3 and Vol. 4, no. 2, February, 1940, p. 4.

91. A conversation with one escapee revealed that the resources available were so abundant that he was told not to worry about gainful employment, "just to take life easy for a while." The gentleman's hunger was to find a job and make his own way in the world.

92. *Contact*, Vol. 3, no. 2, February, 1939, p. 2.

93. *Contact*, Vol. 1, no. 3, June, 1937, p. 3.

94. *Minutes 1940-1944*, Sisterhood Report, 1940, p. 67.

95. *Contact*, Vol. 3, no. 3, March, 1939, p. 4.

96. *Contact*, Vol. 2, no. 12, December, 1938, p. 4.

97. Ibid.

98. *Contact*, Vol. 3, no. 2, February, 1939, p. 3.

99. *Contact*, Vol. 3, no. 4, April, 1939, p. 1.

100. *Contact*, Vol. 3, no. 2, February, 1939, p. 3.

101. *Minutes 1934-1939*, 13 October, 1938, p. 185.

102. Ibid., Rabbi's Message, January, 1935, p. 54.

103. *Contact*, Vol. 4, nos. 3, 4, March and April, 1940, pp. 4-5.

104. *Contact*, Vol. 4, no. 8, December, 1940, p. 3.

105. *Contact*, Vol. 9, no. 2, February, 1945, p. 1.

106. *Contact*, Vol. 4, nos. 3, 4, March and April, 1940, p. 3.

107. *Contact*, Vol. 3, no. 6, June, 1939, p. 1.

108. *Contact*, Vol. 3, no. 3, March, 1939, p. 2.

109. See *Minutes 1940-1944*, p. 54, newspaper clipping from *Savannah Evening Press*,

29 November, 1940.
110. Ibid.
111. Ibid., 18 January 1942, p. 103.
112. *Contact*, Vol. 6, no. 3, May, 1942, p. 6.
113. *Minutes 1940-1944*, 27 May, 1942, p. 125.
114. *Minutes 1934-1939*, 12 January, 1935, p. 59.
115. *Contact*, Vol. 4, no. 5, May, 1940, p. 5.
116. *Contact*, Vol. 8, no. 8, November, 1944, p. 9.
117. *Contact*, Vol. 18, no. 3, September, 1954, p. 2.
118. *Minutes 1940-1944*, 11 October, 1944, p. 256.
119. Ibid., Report of Sisterhood, 9 January, 1944, p. 214.
120. Ibid.
121. *Contact*, Vol. 5, no. 4, September, 1941, p. 1.
122. Ibid.
123. *Minutes 1940-1944*, Sisterhood Report, 1941, pp. 105-108.
124. Ibid., Sisterhood Report, 10 January, 1943, p. 166.
125. Ibid., Brotherhood Report, 1941, p. 104.
126. Ibid., Brotherhood Report, 7 January, 1945, p. 278.
127. Ibid., Sisterhood Report, 1941, p. 105.
128. *Minutes 1934-1939*, 2 January, 1935, p. 74.
129. *Minutes 1940-1944*, 13 March, 1942, p. 116.
130. Ibid., Brotherhood Report, 10 January, 1943, p. 164.
131. Ibid., 18 January, 1942, p. 103.
132. *Contact*, Vol. 6, no. 3, May, 1942, p. 1.
133. *Contact*, Vol. 6, no. 1, February, 1942, p. 4.
134. *Contact*, Vol. 7, no. 1, January, 1943, p. 5.
135. *Minutes 1940-1944*, 12 November, 1941, p. 93.
136. *Contact*, Vol. 6, no. 3, May, 1942, p. 5.
137. *Contact*, Vol. 3, no. 5, May, 1939, p. 2.
138. *Contact*, Vol. 7, no. 1, January, 1943, p. 7.
139. Ibid., p. 8.
140. *Minutes 1940-1944*, Brotherhood Report, 10 January, 1943, p. 164.
141. *Contact*, Vol. 8, no. 7, September, 1944, p. 4.
142. *Contact*, Vol. 9, no. 3, April, 1945, p. 3.
143. *Contact*, Vol. 8, no. 8, November, 1944, p. 8.
144. *Contact*, Vol. 9, no. 2, February, 1945, p. 1.
145. *Minutes 1912-1924*, See resolution appended to minutes of 9 April, 1923, p. 95.
146. Ibid., 5 December, 1924, p. 122.
147. *Minutes 1929-1933*, Annual Report of the President and Board of Trustees, 10 January, 1932, p. 162.
148. Ibid., Report of the President, 8 January, 1933, p. 194.
149. Ibid., 11 March, 1939, p. 171.
150. Ibid., Report of the President, 8 January, 1933, p. 194.
151. Ibid.
152. Ibid., 6 April, 1933.
153. Ibid., p. 223 from *Savannah Morning News*, 8 November, 1933.
154. Ibid.
155. *Minutes 1934-1939*, President's Report, 1938, p. 200.
156. Ibid., Rabbi's Report, 15 January, 1939, p. 203.
157. Ibid., 13 October, 1938, p. 185, and 4 November, 1938, p. 186.
158. *Contact*, Vol. 7, no. 4, September, 1943, pp. 2-3.
159. *Minutes 1940-1944*, President's Report, 9 January 1944, p. 217.
160. Ibid., 8 October, 1942, p. 148, and 7 December, 1944, p. 264.
161. Ibid., Sisterhood Report, 10 January, 1943, p. 166.
162. Ibid., 1 July, 1943, p. 187.

163. Ibid.

164. Ibid., 22 April, 1943, p. 181.

165. See also *Minutes 1925-1928*, 18 January, 1925, p. 8 where he is described as "Supply Rabbi."

166. *Minutes 1940-1944*, 31 October, 1940, p. 46.

167. Ibid., see items labelled "H"—"L", pp. 51-56.

168. Ibid., from *Savannah Morning News*, 30 November, 1940, p. 57.

169. Ibid., and 30 November, 1940, p. 43.

170. *Contact*, Vol. 2, no. 3, March, 1938, p. 1.

171. *Contact*, Vol. 2, no. 8, August, 1938, p. 4.

172. *Contact*, Vol. 2, nos. 9, 10, September/October, 1938, p. 6.

173. *Contact*, Vol. 3, no. 1, January, 1939, p. 2.

174. *Contact*, Vol. 3, no. 2, February, 1939, p. 2.

175. *Contact*, Vol. 13, no. 4, December, 1949, p. 2.

176. Ibid., letter from B. H. Levy to David Byck, 10 January, 1937, pp. 118-119.

177. Ibid., 19 December, 1941, p. 94.

178. *Minutes 1934-1939*, Report of President and Board of Trustees 1934, p. 64.

179. *Contact*, Vol. 4, no. 6, October, 1940, p. 4.

180. *Minutes 1934-1939*, 6 March, 1938, p. 97.

181. *Minutes 1912-1924*, letter from Sol Hirsch to Jacob Schwartz, p. 24 and 2 March, 1924, p. 111.

182. *Minutes 1934-1939*, 5 November, 1937, p. 143.

183. *Minutes 1929-1933*, Report of the President, 1930, p. 107.

184. *Minutes 1940-1944*, 6 June, 1941, p. 85.

185. Ibid., 10 February, 1943, p. 176.

186. *Minutes 1925-1928*, 8 May, 1925, p. 34.

187. *Minutes 1912-1924*, Sisterhood Report, 6 January, 1923, p. 85.

188. Ibid.

189. *Minutes 1940-1944*, 2 February, 1944, p. 221.

190. *Minutes 1912-1924*, 6 February, 1924, p. 107.

191. Ibid., see Report of the Meeting of the Representatives of the Hebrew Reformed [sic] Congregations of Georgia, 16 March, 1924, p. 114.

192. *Minutes 1929-1933*, 7 February, 1930, p. 74.

193. Ibid., p. 82.

194. Ibid., Report of the President, 1930, p. 105.

195. Ibid., 3 December, 1931, p. 147.

196. Note the Temple Sisterhood in Waycross was a co-sponsor of this event with the Daughters of Abraham.

197. Ibid., 3 November, 1933, p. 221.

198. Ibid., Report of the President, 1930, p. 105.

199. *Contact*, Vol. 3, nos. 8, 9, October/November, 1939, p. 1.

200. Ibid., p. 1 is dedicated to a full exposition of the NFTB and its wonderful work.

201. *Minutes 1912-1924*, 11 May, 1921, p. 36.

202. *Contact*, Vol. 4, nos. 3, 4, March/April, 1940, p. 3.

203. *Minutes 1940-1944*, 15 October, 1940, p. 38.

204. *Minutes 1912-1924*, Rabbi's Report, January, 1920, p. 17.

205. *Minutes 1925-1928*, Auxiliary Committee Report, 10 January, 1925, p. 12.

206. *Minutes 1929-1933*, Sisterhood Report, 12 January, 1930, p. 69.

207. Ibid., Sabbath School Report, 1933, p. 192.

208. *Minutes 1934-1939*, 5 April, 1935, p. 69, and 3 November, 1939, p. 27.

209. Ibid., President's Report, 1937, p. 168.

210. Ibid., Rabbi's Report, 14 January, 1934, p. 17.

211. *Minutes 1940-1944*, 7 January, 1940, p. 2.

212. *Minutes 1929-1933*, President's Report, 1929, p. 58.

213. Ibid., 20 March, 1930, p. 84. Rabbi Solomon's *tallit* survives in the Temple

Museum.

214. *Minutes 1934-1939*, 8 June, 1934, p. 34.

215. *Minutes 1945-1949*, 25 March, 1945, p. 8.

216. *Contact*, Vol. 15, no. 2, May, 1951, p. 3.

217. *Minutes 1912-1924*, 24 January, 1922, p. 53.

218. *Minutes 1940-1944*, Rabbi's Annual Message, 12 January, 1941, p. 70.

219. All information from a dedication monograph prepared in 1972 as the third A.A. synagogue was consecrated, (hereafter "Agudath Achim Dedication Booklet").

220. Ibid., p. 11.

221. Ibid.

222. Ibid., p. 12.

223. Ibid., p. 14.

224. Ibid. According to *Contact*, Vol. 4, no. 5, May, 1940, p. 4, this site was formerly occupied by the Park View Sanitarium.

225. *Savannah Morning News*, 12 October, 1936, p. 10, col. 3.

226. Ibid.

227. Ibid.

228. "Agudath Achim Dedication Booklet," p. 14.

229. *Contact*, Vol. 4, no. 6, October, 1940, p. 5.

230. "Agudath Achim Dedication Booklet," p. 15.

231. *Savannah Morning News*, 26 February, 1945, p. 8, col. 6.

232. "Agudath Achim Dedication Booklet," p. 16.

233. *Savannah Morning News*, 26 February, 1945, p. 8, col. 6.

234. "Agudath Achim Dedication Booklet," p. 20.

235. *Minutes 1934-1939*, Rabbi's Report, 14 January, 1934, p. 17.

236. *Savannah Morning News*, 14 September, 1936, p. 10, col. 5.

237. *Savannah Morning News*, 12 October, 1936, p. 10, col. 2.

238. *Contact*, Vol. 3, no. 3, March, 1939, p. 3.

239. *Contact*, Vol. 3, nos. 8, 9, October/November, 1939, p. 3.

240. "Congregation B'nai B'rith Jacob Leave-taking Services of the Old Synagogue Building and the Dedication Services and Ceremonies of the New Synagogue Building," Savannah, Georgia, 15 April, 1962, p. 12.

241. *Minutes 1929-1933*, President's Report, 10 January, 1932, p. 165.

242. Ibid., 1 July, 1932, p. 178.

243. Ibid., 14 October, 1932, p. 185.

244. Ibid., Sabbath School Report, 1933, p. 192.

245. Ibid., President's Report, 8 January, 1933, p. 194.

246. *Minutes 1934-1939*, 25 April, 1934, p. 32.

247. Ibid., 8 June, 1934, p. 34.

248. Ibid., 6 July, 1934, p. 37.

249. *Minutes 1929-1933*, President's Report, 10 January, 1932, p. 165.

250. Ibid. and *Minutes 1934-1939*, President's Report, January, 1935, p. 86.

251. *Minutes 1929-1933*, President's Report, 10 January, 1932, p. 165.

252. See booklet, "The Synagogue Council of America Its Origin and Activities," (New York: 1931), pp. 1-3, K.K.M.I. Archives.

253. *Minutes 1934-1939*, Report of the President, 13 January, 1935, p. 64.

254. Ibid., Rabbi's Report, 14 January, 1934, p. 17.

255. *Contact*, Vol. 5, no. 1, February, 1941, p. 4.

256. "Jewish Educational Alliance, Fiftieth Anniversary Booklet," 1962, p. 10.

257. Ibid.

258. Ibid., p. 15.

259. Ibid.

260. Ibid., pp. 19, 27.

261. *Contact*, Vol. 6, no. 1, February, 1942, p. 2.

262. *Contact*, Vol. 3, no. 4, April, 1939, p. 3.

263. The following list is from *Contact*, supplemented by information provided by Mrs. Sophie Gottlieb, Clerk of Council:

Aldermen of Jewish origins who have served since 1903:

A. J. Garfunkel, 1903-1905, 1920-1929

Abe Guckenheimer, 1907-1911

Girard M. Cohen, 1919-1923

Dr. Herman W. Hesse, 1923-1925

Edgar L. Wortsman, 1925-1937

Albert Blumberg, 1929-1933

Sam Hornstein, 1933-1938

Louis J. Roos, 1937-1947

B. I. Friedman, 1938-1946

Henry F. Meyer, 1939-1941 (Jewish origins uncertain)

Dr. William A. Wexler, 1947-1949

A. L. Karp, 1949-1955

Kayton Smith, 1955-1957

Jay Shoob, 1957-1966

Benjamin M. Garfunkel, Mayor Pro Tem, 1966-1970

Leo E. Center, 1970-present

In addition to Judge Emanuel Lewis, Judge Charles N. Feidelson should be included. He served in the early 1920's as Judge of Juvenile Court.

264. *Contact*, Vol. 1, no. 10, December, 1937, p. 3.

265. *Contact*, Vol. 3, no. 1, January, 1939, p. 3.

266. Ibid.

267. *Minutes 1934-1939*, Report of the President, 13 January, 1935, p. 64.

268. Ibid.

269. *Contact*, Vol. 6, no. 3, May, 1942, p. 5.

270. *Contact*, Vol. 6, no. 1, February, 1944, p. 6.

271. Ibid.

272. *Contact*, Vol. 7, no. 2, March, 1943, p. 3.

273. *Contact*, Vol. 2, no. 4, April, 1938, p. 4.

274. *Contact*, Vol. 2, no. 3, March, 1938, p. 2.

275. *Contact*, Vol. 2, no. 5, May, 1938, p. 3, and Vol. 4, no. 7, November, 1940, p. 5

276. *Contact*, Vol. 4, no. 7, November, 1940, p. 4.

277. *Contact*, Vol. 6, no. 2, March, 1942, p. 2.

278. *Contact*, Vol. 7, no. 1, January, 1943, p. 3.

279. *Contact*, Vol. 8, no. 8, November, 1944, p. 4.

280. *Minutes 1945-1949*, 14 February, 1945, p. 3.

281. *Savannah Morning News*, 26 February, 1945, p. 2, col. 3.

282. Ibid., also *Savannah Morning News*, 25 February, 1945, p. 24, col. 6.

283. Ibid.

284. *Minutes 1945-1949*, 25 March, 1945, p. 10.

285. *Contact*, Vol. 9, no. 3, April, 1945, p. 3.

CHAPTER ELEVEN

1. All of the above from an undated manuscript in the Temple Archives entitled "Introductory Remarks Made by Rabbi Solomon in introducing Rabbi Fichman concerning Zionism."

2. *Contact*, Vol. 2, no. 12, December, 1938, p. 1.

3. Ibid., pp. 1-4.

4. *Savannah Morning News*, 13 May, 1936, p. 14, col. 6.

5. Ibid.

6. *Contact*, Vol. 4, no. 6, October, 1940, p. 4.

7. *Contact*, Vol. 6, no. 4, September, 1942, p. 6.

8. Ibid.

9. *Contact*, Vol. 8, no. 1, February, 1944, p. 2.

10. Ibid., p. 3.

11. Ibid.

12. See *Contact*, Vol. 1, no. 1, April, 1937, p. 4 for example.

13. *Minutes 1929-1933*, 6 September, 1929, p. 39.

14. *Minutes 1940-1945*, Sisterhood Report, 7 January, 1945, p. 277.

15. *Contact*, Vol. 4, no. 1, January, 1940, p. 3.

16. *Minutes 1945-1949*, 18 April, 1945, p. 16.

17. Ibid., 22 May, 1945, p. 19.

18. Ibid., Report on 39th Council of the Union of American Hebrew Congregations, 12 March, 1946, p. 55.

19. Ibid., p. 56.

20. Ibid.

21. Ibid.

22. Ibid., p. 59.

23. *Contact*, Vol. 10, no. 4, April, 1946, p. 3.

24. *Contact*, Vol. 10, no. 7, January, 1947, p. 4.

25. *Contact*, Vol. 12, no. 2, March, 1948, p. 8.

26. *Contact*, Vol. 10, no. 7, January, 1947, p. 2.

27. *Contact*, Vol. 12, no. 1, January, 1948, p. 6.

28. *Minutes 1945-1949*, 26 November, 1946, p. 69.

29. Ibid., Rabbi's Annual Message, 1947, p. 87.

30. *Minutes 1950-1954*, 28 April, 1953, p. 131.

31. *Minutes 1955-1959*, 18 May, 1955, p. 13.

32. Ibid., 25 August, 1955, p. 20.

33. Ibid., p. 87.

34. *Minutes 1950-1954*, 28 April, 1953, p. 131.

35. Ibid.

36. *Minutes 1960-1964*, 16 February, 1961, p. 57.

37. Ibid., 28 January, 1954, p. 176.

38. *Minutes 1960-1964*, Rabbi's Annual Message, 1963, p. 170.

39. *Minutes 1965-1969*, 20 January, 1966, p. 103, and President's Report, 8 January, 1967, p. 221.

40. Ibid., letter from Allan Solomon, Camp Director to Rabbi Joseph Buchler, 26 January, 1967, p. 239, relative to the exposure of campers to Modern Jewish history, including Holocaust and the State of Israel.

41. *Minutes 1970-1974*, 10 January 1971, p. 232.

42. *Minutes 1965-1969*, President's Report, 8 January, 1967, p. 223.

43. Ibid., 19 January, 1967, p. 237. The vote against was cast by the president.

44. Ibid., 2 June, 1967, p. 257.

45. Ibid., 21 September, 1967, p. 289.

46. Ibid., 20 February, 1969, p. 405.

47. *Minutes 1970-1974*, 7 January, 1970, pp. 298-299.

48. Ibid., UAHC Biennial Convention Report, A. J. Cohen, Jr., 18 November, 1969, p. 338.

49. Ibid., 22 January, 1970, p. 293, and 18 March, 1971, p. 211.

50. Ibid., 18 March, 1971, p. 210, and Sisterhood Report, 1970, p. 245.

51. Ibid., 10 December, 1970, p. 263.

52. Ibid., 12 August, 1971, p. 199.

53. *Savannah Morning News*, 25 February, 1945, p. 24, col. 6.

54. Ibid.

55. *Contact*, Vol. 2, no. 11, November, 1938, p. 4.

56. *Contact*, Vol. 2, no. 5, May, 1938, p. 3.

57. *Contact*, Vol. 3, no. 6, June, 1939, p. 3.

58. Coleman, *History of Georgia*, p. 326.

59. Ibid., p. 327.

60. Ibid., pp. 363-364.

61. Ibid., p. 362.

62. Ibid., p. 363.

63. *Contact*, Vol. 10, no. 3, March, 1946, pp. 1, 3, and *Contact*, Vol. 10, no. 2, February, 1946, p. 1.

64. *Contact*, Vol. 8, no. 4, May, 1944, p. 4.

65. *Minutes 1945-1949*, Rabbi's Annual Message, 13 January, 1945, p. 50.

66. *Minutes 1940-1944*, Rabbi's Report and Message, 1944, p. 281.

67. Ibid.

68. *Minutes 1945-1949*, President's Report, 1945, p. 53.

69. Ibid., Rabbi's Annual Message, 13 January, 1945, p. 51.

70. Ibid., Rabbi's Annual Message, 12 January, 1947, p. 85.

71. *Contact*, Vol. 10, no. 2, February, 1946, p. 3.

72. *Minutes 1945-1949*, Rabbi's Annual Message, 12 January, 1947, p. 84.

73. Ibid., p. 83.

74. Ibid., 9 April, 1946, p. 60.

75. Ibid., 7 May, 1946, p. 61.

76. Ibid., Rabbi's Annual Message, 12 January, 1947, pp. 87-88.

77. Ibid., Rabbi's Message, 11 January, 1948, p. 111.

78. *Minutes 1960-1964*, 16 October, 1962, p. 137.

79. *Minutes 1945-1949*, 26 November, 1946, p. 69.

80. *Minutes 1950-1954*, 28 April, 1953, p. 131.

81. Ibid.

82. *Minutes 1955-1959*, 19 March, 1957, pp. 88-90.

83. Ibid., p. 90.

84. *Minutes 1960-1964*, 15 November, 1962, p. 141.

85. Ibid., 26 April, 1964, p. 266.

86. *Minutes 1950-1954*, 27 August, 1954, pp. 195-196.

87. *Minutes 1960-1964*, 17 August, 1961, p. 75.

88. *Minutes 1950-1954*, 22 September, 1953, pp. 147-148.

89. Ibid., 28 January, 1954, p. 174.

90. *Minutes 1955-1959*, 19 January, 1959, p. 177.

91. Ibid., 21 May, 1957, p. 95.

92. Ibid., 5 May, 1959, p. 179.

93. *Minutes 1960-1964*, 22 August, 1963, pp. 205-206.

94. *Minutes 1965-1969*, 7 July, 1966, pp. 139-140, and letter from Rabbi Seltzer to Martin Leffler, 1 September, 1966, p. 160.

95. *Minutes 1945-1949*, 13 January, 1948, p. 113.

96. *Minutes 1965-1969*, 18 May, 1967, p. 259.

97. *Minutes 1955-1959*, letter from Solomon Elsner, UAHC, 4 April, 1957, p. 94.

98. *Minutes 1960-1964*, 15 November, 1962, p. 141.

99. *Contact*, Vol. 9, no. 1, January, 1945, p. 3.

100. *Minutes 1945-1949*, Rabbi's Annual Message, 12 January, 1947, p. 85.

101. *Minutes 1965-1969*, Temple Youth Group Report, 8 January, 1967, p. 196.

102. Ibid.

103. *Minutes 1970-1974*, 8 October, 1970, p. 272.

104. *Minutes 1960-1964*, Annual Report of the President, 15 January, 1961, p. 43.

105. Ibid., 13 January, 1963, p. 173.

106. Ibid., 26 April, 1964, p. 268.

107. *Minutes 1970-1974*, 11 January, 1970, p. 326.

108. *Minutes 1945-1949*, 7 October, 1947, p. 98.

109. See for example, *Minutes 1965-1969*, letter from Dr. Leonard Rabhan to Martin

Leffler, 12 January, 1966, p. 114, and letter from Lawrence M. Steinheimer, Jr., to Dr. Leonard Rabhan, 24 January, 1966, p. 113.

110. *Minutes 1950-1954*, 28 January, 1954, p. 176.

111. Ibid., 11 March, 1954, p. 184.

112. Ibid., 11 April, 1954, p. 187.

113. Ibid.

114. Ibid., 27 August, 1954, p. 195.

115. Ibid., 18 December, 1952, p. 114.

116. Ibid., 10 February, 1953, p. 124.

117. *Minutes 1945-1949*, Sisterhood Annual Report, 8 January, 1949, p. 142, which states that this is the second year of the program.

118. *Minutes 1955-1959*, Brotherhood Annual Report, 1959, p. 168.

119. For example, *Contact*, Vol. 17, no. 2, June, 1953, p. 3. Congratulations were extended to Isadore Movsovitz on his election as president of B.B.J. In many places one finds expressions of cordiality to persons firmly identified with the other congregations, including the Tenenbaums (A.A.) and the Garfunkels (B.B.J.).

120. "JEA 50th Anniversary Booklet," 1962, p. 27.

121. Ibid., p. 30.

122. Ibid., p. 47.

123. *Minutes 1965-1969*, 21 January, 1965, p. 6.

124. Ibid., 8 December, 1966, p. 182.

125. Ibid., 18 May, 1967, p. 260.

126. Ibid., 16 February, 1967, p. 242.

127. Ibid., 21 September, 1967, p. 291.

128. Ibid., Report of the President, 8 January, 1967, p. 223.

129. Ibid., President's Annual Report, 14 January, 1968, p. 316.

130. *Minutes 1945-1949*, President's Annual Report, 1948, p. 141.

131. Ibid., 6 July, 1948, p. 123.

132. It appeared in the *CCAR Journal*, January, 1961, pp. 29-31.

133. *Minutes 1945-1949*, p. 126, clipping from *Savannah Morning News*, 10 July, 1948.

134. *Minutes 1950-1954*, 16 April, 1952, p. 103.

135. *Minutes 1950-1954*, 28 June, 1950.

136. *Contact*, Vol. 12, no. 4, December, 1948, p. 1.

137. *Contact*, Vol. 14, no. 1, March, 1950, p. 2.

138. *Minutes 1950-1954*, 21 January, 1953, p. 120.

139. Ibid., 11 April, 1954, p. 187.

140. Ibid., 14 April, 1954, pp. 188-189, and 18 June, 1954, p. 192.

141. Ibid., 27 August, 1954, p. 195.

142. *Minutes 1955-1959*, 23 October, 1955, pp. 27-31.

143. Ibid., 20 December, 1955, p. 48.

144. *Minutes 1960-1964*, 15 January, 1961, p. 36.

145. Ibid., 10 January, 1960, p. 5.

146. *Contact*, Vol. 19, no. 2, September, 1955, p. 3.

147. *Minutes 1960-1964*, 11 May, 1962, p. 122.

148. Ibid., President's Annual Report, 15 January, 1961, p. 41.

149. *Minutes 1965-1969*, 16 December, 1965, p. 68.

150. Ibid., 20 January, 1966, p. 102.

151. See "Congregation B'nai B'rith Jacob Leave-taking Services of the Old Synagogue Building and the Dedication Services and Ceremonies of the New Synagogue Building," 15 April, 1962.

152. *Minutes 1950-1954*, President's Annual Report, 9 January, 1955, p. 221.

153. *Minutes 1960-1964*, President's Annual Report, 7 January, 1962, pp. 99-100.

154. Ibid., 18 July, 1963, p. 201.

155. Ibid., Brotherhood Report 1960, p. 30.

156. *Contact*, March, 1979, p. 1.

157. *Minutes 1960-1964*, Temple Youth Group Report, 7 January, 1962, p. 104.

158. *Minutes 1950-1954*, President's Report, 10 January, 1954, p. 165.

159. *Minutes 1945-1949*, 23 September, 1948, p. 132.

160. See *Minutes 1950-1954*, Letter from Thomas H. Gignilliat, Secretary, Historic Site and Monument Commission, Savannah, Georgia, 4 January, 1951, pp. 179-180.

161. *Contact*, Vol. 18, no. 1, January, 1954, p. 1.

162. A copy of the resolution is found in the appendix. See also *Minutes 1950-1954*, 16 December, 1954, pp. 203, 205-207, and *Contact*, Vol. 17, no. 3, September, 1953, p. 3.

163. *Minutes 1950-1954*, Rabbi's Annual Report, 1954, p. 167.

164. *Minutes 1960-1964*, 23 February, 1962, p. 116.

165. *Minutes 1955-1959*, 25 August, 1955, p. 20.

166. *Minutes 1965-1969*, 15 April, 1965, p. 26.

167. Ibid., 26 August, 1965, p. 46.

168. Ibid., pp. 46-47.

169. Ibid., 19 October, 1967, pp. 296-297.

170. Ibid., 18 January, 1968, p. 339.

171. Ibid., 14 January, 1968, p. 314.

172. Ibid., p. 309.

173. Ibid., 10 October, 1968, pp. 383-384.

174. Ibid., 12 December, 1968, p. 391.

175. Ibid., 23 December, 1968, p. 394 and 19 January, 1969, pp. 395-396.

176. Ibid., 17 April, 1969, p. 410.

177. Ibid., 17 July, 1969, p. 416.

178. *Minutes 1970-1974*, Rabbi's Annual Report, 11 January, 1970, p. 302, and Temple Youth Group Report, 11 January, 1970, p. 309.

179. Ibid., Rabbi's Report, 9 January, 1972, p. 165.

180. Ibid.

181. *Minutes 1965-1969*, 30 July, 1969, p. 420.

182. Ibid.

183. "Agudath Achim Dedication Booklet," pp. 25-26.

184. Ibid., p. 29.

185. Ibid., pp. 27, 30.

186. See "Centenary of the Consecration of Mickve Israel Synagogue," Savannah, Georgia, 14 April, 1978, p. 1, K.K.M.I. Archives.

187. *Minutes 1970-1974*, Sisterhood Annual Report, 9 January, 1972, p. 173, and 14 October, 1971, p. 195.

188. Ibid., 17 February, 1972, p. 149.

189. See *Moment Magazine*, Vol. 6, No. 2, January/February, 1981, p. 17.

SELECTED BIBLIOGRAPHY

K.K. Mickve Israel Archives

Centenary of the Consecration of Mickve Israel Synagogue. Savannah, Georgia. April 1978.
Congregation Agudath Achim. Savannah, Georgia. (Dedication Booklet). 1972.
Congregation B'nai B'rith Jacob Leave-taking Services of the Old Synagogue Building and the Dedication Services and Ceremonies of the New Synagogue Building. Savannah, Georgia. April 15, 1962.
Constitution of the Hebrah Gemiluth Hesed Society of Savannah, Georgia, organized June 20, 1888, revised December 24, 1916. K.K. Mickve Israel Archives.
Harmony Club Minutes. Georgia Historical Society.
Jewish Educational Alliance. Fiftieth Anniversary 1912-1962.
Mendes, Isaac P. Scrapbook, 2 Vols. K.K. Mickve Israel Archives.
Minutes of the Mikva Israel Congregation of Savannah, Georgia 1790 to 1851.
Minutes of The Congregation Mickva Israel of Savannah 1852-1888.
Minutes Mickva Israel A.M. 5649 (1889-1912). K.K. Mickve Israel Archives.
Minutes of Congregation Mickve Israel 1912-1924. K.K. Mickve Israel Archives.
Minutes of Congregation Mickve Israel 1925-1928. K.K. Mickve Israel Archives.
Minutes of Congregation Mickve Israel 1929-1933. K.K. Mickve Israel Archives.
Minutes of Congregation Mickve Israel 1934-1939. K.K. Mickve Israel Archives.
Minutes of Congregation Mickve Israel 1940-1944. K.K. Mickve Israel Archives.
Minutes of Congregation Mickve Israel 1945-1949. K.K. Mickve Israel Archives.
Minutes of Congregation Mickve Israel 1950-1954. K.K. Mickve Israel Archives.
Mniutes of Congregation Mickve Israel 1955-1959. K.K. Mickve Israel Archives.
Minutes of Congregation Mickve Israel 1960-1964. K.K. Mickve Israel Archives.
Minutes of Congregation Mickve Israel 1965-1969. K.K. Mickve Israel Archives.
Minutes of Congregation Mickve Israel 1970 thru 1974. K.K. Mickve Israel Archives.
Order of Prayers for the New Year and Day of Atonement, adopted by the Congregation Mickva Israel. Savannah, Georgia. 1891, Vol. I.
Teacher's Union Minute Book 1900-1903. K.K. Mickve Israel Archives.

Newspapers

Columbian Museum and Savannah Advertiser, 1796-1800, 1806, 1811.
Columbian Museum and Savannah Daily Gazette, 1817-1820.
Columbian Museum and Savannah Gazette, 1817.
Contact, Vols. 1-19, 1937-1955.
Daily Georgian, 1819-1820, 1836-1841.
Gazette State of Georgia, 1784, 1786-1788, 1790.
Georgia Gazette, 1789-1792, 1795, 1797, 1799.
Georgian, 1820-1821, 1829-1830, 1832-1834, 1836-1838.
Raleigh News and Observer, 1913.
Richmond Time Dispatch, 1891.
Republican and Savannah Evening Ledger, 1807, 1812.
Savannah Daily Herald, 1865.
Savannah Daily Morning News, 1850-1853, 1855-1856, 1860-1861.
Savannah Daily News and Herald, 1866-1868, 1876.
Savannah Morning News, 1856, 1861 1868-1869, 1872, 1874, 1877.
Savannah Daily Republican, 1840.
The Scroll, Vol. I, No. 1 (January 1916).
The Occident, Vols. III-XXV, 1845-1867.

Government Records and Documents

Candler, Alan D., ed. The Colonial Records of the State of Georgia. XXXVIII, Part L. Chapel Hill, North Carolina. University of North Carolina Library, Southern Historical

Collection, "Diary of Phillip Phillips" (typewritten copy).
Chatham County Index to Marriages, 1806-1837.
The 1860 Census of Chatham County, Georgia. Compiled by the Genealogical Committee of the Georgia Historical Society. Southern Historical Press, 1979.
State of Georgia, Georgia Official and Statistical Register 1971-72. Ben W. Fortson, Jr., Secretary of State; Caroll Hart, Director Archives and History.
The Congressional Record, E 3225, 17 June, 1975.

Interviews

Brito, Herbert. Savannah, Georgia. Interview, 1981.
Reiter, Beth Lattimore. Savannah, Georgia. Interview, 6 January, 1982.

Unpublished Materials

Goldberg, David J. "The Administration of Herman Myers As Mayor of Savannah, Georgia 1895-1897 and 1899-1907." Masters Thesis, University of North Carolina, 1978.
Levy, B. H. "Joseph Solomon Ottolenghi—A Kosher Butcher in Italy—A Christian Missionary in Georgia." K.K. Mickve Israel Archives (typewritten).
Mallard, Esther Raines. "The Jews of Savannah 1733-1860." Masters Thesis, Georgia Southern College, 1972.
Pauley, William E. "John J. Zubley, Samuel Frink and The Savannah Burial Ground Controversy 1769-1770." Presented to Annual Meeting of the Georgia Historical Society. April 1, 1978.
Sparkman, Debra. "Solomon Cohen: Nineteenth Century Savannah Lawyer." Research Paper, Armstrong State College, 1979.
"Autobiography of Levi Sheftall" ms in Keith Reid Collection, University of Georgia Library, Athens, Georgia (Photocopy in American Jewish Archives).
Minutes of the Savannah Masonic Lodge, 1756-1757. (Original in the Library of Congress; microfilm copy in American Jewish Archives).

Books and Articles

Adler, Cyrus, ed. *The American Jewish Year Book 5660 September 5, 1899 to September 23, 1900.* Philadelphia: The Jewish Publication Society of America, 1899.
_____. *The American Jewish Year Book September 24, 1900 to September 13, 1901.* Philadelphia: The Jewish Publication Society of America, 1900.
Alexander, Henry Aaron. *Notes On The Alexander Family of South Carolina And Georgia And Connections.* Atlanta: Henry A. Alexander, 1954.
Anderson, Mary Savage; Barrow, Elfrida DeRenne; Screven, Elizabeth Mackay; Waring, Martha Gallaudet. *Georgia A Pageant of Years.* Richmond: Garret and Massie, Inc., 1933.
Axley, Lowry. *Holding Aloft The Torch A History of the Independent Presbyterian Church of Savannah, Georgia.* Savannah: The Pigeonhole Press, 1958.
Barnett, Dr. R. D. "Dr. Samuel Nunes Ribeiro And The Settlement of Georgia." In *Migration and Settlement: Papers on Anglo-American Jewish History.* Jewish Historical Society of England, 1971.
Berman, Myron. *Richmond's Jewry 1769-1976 Shabbat in Shockroe.* Charlottesville: University Press of Virginia, 1979.
Birmingham, Stephen. *"Our Crowd" The Great Jewish Families of New York.* New York: Harper and Row, 1967.
_____. *The Grandees America's Sephardic Elite.* New York: Harper & Row, Publishers, 1971.
Breibart, Solomon. "The Synagogues of Kahal Kadosh Beth Elohim of Charleston, South Carolina." *South Carolina Historical Magazine,* Vol. 80, No. 3 (July 1979).

Church, Leslie F., *Oglethorpe: A Study of Philanthropy in England and Georgia.* London: The Epworth Press, 1932.

Cohen, Anne Nathan. *The Centenary History Congregation Beth Israel of Houston, Texas 1854-1954.*

Coleman, Kenneth, *The American Revolution in Georgia, 1763-1789.* Athens: University of Georgia Press, 1958.

—————————. *Colonial Georgia A History.* New York: Charles Scribner's Sons, 1976.

Coleman, Kenneth, Bartley, Numan V., Holmes, William F., Boney, F. N., Spalding, Phinizy, and Wynes, Charles E., *A History of Georgia.* Athens: University of Georgia Press, 1977.

Coulter, E. Merton. *Georgia A Short History.* Chapel Hill: The University of North Carolina Press, 1960.

Coulter, E. Merton and Saye, Albert B., eds. *A List of the Early Settlers of Georgia.* Athens: The University of Georgia Press, 1967.

Dinnerstein, Leonard and Palsson, Mary Dale, eds. *Jews in the South,* Baton Rouge: Louisiana State University Press, 1973.

Encyclopedia Judaica, 1972 ed.

Endelman, Todd M. *The Jews of Georgian England 1714-1830 Tradition and Change in a Liberal Society.* Philadelphia: The Jewish Publication Society of America, 1979.

Ezekiel, Herbert T. and Lichtenstein, Gaston. *The History of the Jews of Richmond 1769-1917.* Richmond, Virginia: Herbert T. Ezekiel, 1917.

Gamble, Thomas, Jr. *Annual Report of Herman Myers Mayor of the City of Savannah 1900 And a History of the City Government of Savannah From 1790 to 1901.*

—————————. *Bethesda, An Historical Sketch of Whitfield's House of Mercy in Georgia and of The Union Society, His Associate and Successors in Philanthropy.* Savannah: Morning News Print, 1902.

Glanz, Rudolf. *Studies in Judaica Americana.* New York: KTAV Publishing House, Inc., 1970.

Goodman, Abram Vossen. *American Overature, Jewish Rights in Colonial Times.* Philadelphia: The Jewish Publication Society of America, 1947.

Grinstein, Hyman B. *The Rise of The Jewish Community of New York 1654-1840.* Philadelphia: The Jewish Publication Society of America, 1947.

Grollman, Jerome W. "The Emergence of Reform Judaism in the United States." *American Jewish Archives,* Vol. II, No. 2 (January 1950): 3-14.

Harden, William. *A History of Savannah and South Georgia.* Chicago: The Lewis Publishing Company, 1913.

Harper, Roland M. "Some Savannah Vital Statistics." *Georgia Historical Quarterly,* Vol. XV (1931).

Hertzberg, Steven. *Strangers Within the Gate City The Jews of Atlanta 1845-1915.* Philadelphia: The Jewish Publication Society of America, 1978.

Hicks, John D. *The American Nation A History of the United States From 1865 to the Present.* Boston: Houghton Mifflin Company, 1949.

Huhner, Leon. *The Jews of Georgia from the Outbreak of the American Revolution to the Close of the Eighteenth Century.* American Jewish Historical Society, 1909.

Jacobs, Joseph. "The Damascus Affair of 1840 and The Jews of America." In *The Jewish Experience in America,* Vol. II. New York: KTAV Publishing House, Inc., 1969.

Karp, Abraham Jr. "Simon Tuska Becomes a Rabbi." Publication of the American Jewish Historical Society, Vol. L, No. 2 (December 1960).

—————————. "The Era of Immigration." In *The Jewish Experience in America,* Vol. IV. New York: KTAV Publishing House, Inc., 1969.

King, Spencer Bidwell, Jr. *Ebb Tide As Seen Through the Diary of Josephine Clay Habersham 1863.* Athens: University of Georgia Press, 1958.

Kohler, Max J. "Judah Touro, Merchant and Philanthropist." *The Jewish Experience in America,* Vol. II. New York: KTAV Publishing House, Inc., 1969.

Korn, Bertram Wallace. *American Jewry and The Civil War.* Philadelphia: The Jewish

Publication Society of America, 1951.

—————————————. *The American Reaction to the Mortara Case: 1858-1859*. Cincinnati: The American Jewish Archives, 1957.

—————————————. "The Jews of the Confederacy." *American Jewish Archives*, Vol. XIII, No. 1 (April 1961).

Lane, Mills. *Savannah Revisited A Pictoral History*. Savannah: The Beehive Press, 1973.

Lee, Frank Deane and Agnew, James Laurence. *Historical Record of the City of Savannah*. Savannah: J. H. Estill, 1869.

Levy, B. H. "Savannah's Old Jewish Cemeteries." *Georgia Historical Quarterly*, Vol. LXVI (Spring 1982).

Levy, Marion Abrahams. "Savannah's Old Jewish Burial Ground." *Georgia Historical Quarterly*, Vol. XXXIV (1950).

Mandel, Irving Aaron. "Attitude of the American Jewish Community Toward East European Immigration as Reflected in the Anglo-Jewish Press 1880-1890." In *Critical Studies in American Jewish History*, Vol. I. Cincinnati: American Jewish Archives, 1971.

Marcus, Jacob Rader. *American Jewry Documents Eighteenth Century*. Cincinnati: The Hebrew Union College Press, 1959.

——————————. *Early American Jewry The Jews of Pennsylvania and the South 1655-1790*, Vol. II., Philadelphia: The Jewish Publication Society of America, 1953.

—————————————. *The Colonial American Jew 1492-1776*. 3 vols. Detroit: Wayne State University Press, 1970.

Morgan, David T. "The Sheftalls of Savannah." *American Jewish Historical Quarterly*, Vol. LXII, No. 4 (June 1973): 348-361.

Morrison, Mary L., ed. *Historic Savannah Survey of Significant Buildings in the Historic and Victorian Districts of Savannah, Georgia*. Savannah: Historic Savannah Foundation, 1979.

One Hundred Years A Narrative of The Founding And The Growth of Solomons Company And Other Items, and of General Interest From The Year 1845 Up To And Including The Year 1945. Savannah.

Panitz, Esther L. "The Polarity of American Jewish Attitudes towards Immigration (1870-1891)." In *The Jewish Experience in America*. New York: KTAV Publishing House, Inc., 1969.

Postal, Bernard and Koppman, Lionel. *American Jewish Landmarks A Travel Guide and History*, Vol. II. New York: Fleet Press Corporation, 1979.

Rezneck, Samuel. *Unrecognized Patriots The Jews in the American Revolution*. Westport, Conn.: Greenwood Press, 1975.

—————————————. *The Saga of an American Jewish Family Since the Revolution: A History of the Family of Jonas Phillips*. Washington, D.C.: University Press of America, 1980.

Reznikoff, Charles and Engelman, Uriah Z. *The Jews of Charleston A History of an American Jewish Community*. Philadelphia: The Jewish Publication Society of America, 1950.

Rosenbloom, Joseph R. *A Biographical Dictionary of American Jews Colonial Times through 1800*. University of Kentucky Press, 1960.

Rosenwaike, Ira. "An Estimate and Analysis of the Jewish Population of the United States in 1790." *Publication of the American Jewish Historical Society*, Vol. L (September 1960).

—————————————. "The Jews of Baltimore: 1820-1830." *American Jewish Historical Quarterly*, LXVII, No. 3 (March 1978).

Ross, Ishbel. *First Lady of the South The Life of Mrs. Jefferson Davis*. New York: Harper & Brothers, Publishers, 1958.

Schappes, Morris U. *A Documentary History of the Jews in the United States 1654-1875*. New York: The Citadel Press, 1950.

Schmier, Louis. *Reflections of Southern Jewry.* Macon, Ga.: Mercer University Press, 1982.

Schwartzman, Sylvan D. *Reform Judaism in the Making.* New York: Union of American Hebrew Congregations, 1966.

Simonhoff, Harry. *Jewish Participants in The Civil War.* New York: ARCO Publishing Company, Inc., 1963.

Stern, Malcolm H. *First American Jewish Families: 600 Genealogies, 1654-1977.* Cincinnati, Oh. & Waltham Ma.; American Jewish Archives and America Jewish Historical Society, 1978.

_____. "New Light on the Jewish Settlement of Savannah." In *The Jewish Experience in America*, Vol. I. New York: KTAV Publishing House, Inc., 1969.

_____., ed. *Americans of Jewish Descent A Compendium of Genealogy.* Cincinnati: Hebrew Union College Press, 1960.

_____. "The Sheftall Diaries: Vital Records of Savannah Jewry (1733-1808)." Publication of The American Jewish Historical Society, Vol. 54.

The American Architect and Building News, Vol. 49, 1895.

Tobias, Thomas J. "The Many-Sided Dr. DeLaMotta." In *The Jewish Experience in America*, Vol. II. New York: KTAV Publishing House, Inc., 1969.

Wilson, Adelaide. *Historic and Picturesque Savannah.* Boston: Rockwell and Churchill, 1889.

Wolf, Edwin, II and Whiteman, Maxwell. *The History of the Jews of Philadelphia from Colonial Times to the Age of Jackson.* Philadelphia: The Jewish Publication Society of American, 1975.

Maps

Gordon, Peter "View of Savannah." Original sketch in Beinecke Library, Yale University, New Haven, Ct.

Made in United States
Orlando, FL
04 December 2021